The Power of
Love

by Floyd R. Oliver

DORRANCE
PUBLISHING CO
EST. 1920
PITTSBURGH, PENNSYLVANIA 15238

This is a work of fiction. Names, characters, places, and incidents are either the product of the author's imagination or are used fictitiously, and any resemblance to actual persons, living or dead; events; or locales is entirely coincidental.

All Rights Reserved
Copyright © 2024 by Floyd R. Oliver
No part of this book may be reproduced or transmitted, downloaded, distributed, reverse engineered, or stored in or introduced into any information storage and retrieval system, in any form or by any means, including photocopying and recording, whether electronic or mechanical, now known or hereinafter invented without permission in writing from the publisher.

Dorrance Publishing Co
585 Alpha Drive
Suite 103
Pittsburgh, PA 15238
Visit our website at *www.dorrancebookstore.com*
ISBN: 979-8-89341-252-9
eISBN: 979-8-89341-751-7

Dedication

To Abigail P. Cason
The Ali'i Nui of Bali Hai

Chapters of The Power of Love

	Chapters	Page
1.	Prisoner in Paradise	1
2.	Home Sweet Home	81
3.	United States Army	130
4.	The Ice Princess	141
5.	Supreme Headquarters	173
6.	OCS	215
7.	Hell	235
8.	The Leper Colony	248
9.	Into the Valley	293
10.	You Know Who	327
11.	The President of the United States	362
12.	Hope Farm	395
13.	The Third Miracle	408
14.	Speed Kills	442
15.	Tar Baby	458
16.	The Foaling	483
17.	The Schuylerville	495
19.	The Revelation	516
20.	The Mithra Society	533
21.	The Bottomless Pit	563

Prisoner in Paradise

"Fate is the hunter", and although you may not be aware of its presence it stalks you, as we speak.

We all have a destiny waiting to be fulfilled, and a young boy in Brooklyn was about to embark on a world-changing journey, the end of which couldn't be foreseen or imagined. As the sun rose on August 15th, 1948, everything was in place in the young boy's small world which was not unlike a small piece of heaven; by day's end, he would be in Hell. That's how life unravels; you never know what's right around the corner.

Six-year-old Raphael Hawkins woke with a start! He didn't know it at the time but this would be the only day of his life he would remember from beginning to end. Not some flashback to childhood where you remember some significant event and forget the rest. This day would become embedded in his consciousness like a tape that can be replayed over and over. It was not unlike opening Pandora's Box of Life, and what jumped out would prove to be an overwhelming shock.But, at that waking moment, a sense of excitement stirred within his six-year-old mind. Today he was taking a trip on a train with his mother the purpose of which was to visit his brother, who for some unknown reason, was at a summer school or camp. He'd never been on a real train just the New York City Subway. A real train meant adventure and even as a six-year-old, adventure was the lure he couldn't resist. With that in mind, Raphael (Rafe to his family) leaped out of bed and began to get dressed. He listened to the tapping of his mother's feet as she moved with her unusual rapid movements at the other end of the railroad apartment. His Mother moved with an unusual quickness so much so that it was hard to keep up with her even when she was only walking. Rafe didn't know it, but he would inherit his mother's speed and quickness. Like most six-year-old children Rafe didn't know much about anything, but today the learning process would swing into high gear. He dressed quickly and joined his mother in the kitchen. She smiled when she saw him dressed and ready to go. His four-year-old sister was sleeping upstairs in his grandparent's apartment so she wouldn't have to wake up when they left. It was going to be a rather long trip and she wasn't going along. None of this bothered little Rafe because he lived in a child's small world completely trusting his mother whom he dearly loved. If he had known the truth, he would never have gotten up that day, and there is no way he would have left 887 St. John's Place. Wild horses couldn't have dragged him out of his home. But what do children know?

Rafe and his mother left and walked the 2 ½ blocks up to Eastern Parkway where they caught a yellow cab in front of the Cameo Theater at the corner of Nostrand Avenue and Eastern Parkway. Soon the cab was speeding down Eastern Parkway, past the Brooklyn Museum, through Grand Armee Plaza, and down Flatbush Avenue towards the Manhattan Bridge. From the middle of the bridge, the panoramic view of the city lay before them in the early morning sunlight. Wall Street was to the left, and midtown was to the right.

Rafe looked down to his extreme right and saw, to his amazement an Aircraft Carrier. "Look Mom", he excitedly exclaimed, "it's an Aircraft Carrier!"

His mother smiled at him and said, "That's the Brooklyn Navy Yard where Uncle Ernie used to work".

"Uncle Ernie told me he built the battleship Missouri, isn't that right Mom?"

"Well, he didn't build the whole ship, but he helped". The cab pulled off the Manhattan Bridge onto the Bowery a very oddly named street to a little boy. His mother pointed out to him that the Bowery was the street where all of the drunks lived and he could see them sleeping on the sidewalk and in doorways. It was August 15th, 1948, and in those days homeless people sleeping in the street was very unusual. The Bowery led to Park Avenue and within ten minutes they were pulling up to Grand Central Station. Once inside Rafe was awestruck by this cavernous monument to a fading era. Trains were slowly becoming obsolete, but Rafe always loved them and Grand Central Station would always be one of his favorite buildings in New York City. His mother bought tickets and they hurried down to the track where their train was waiting. On the track next to their train was a platform with a red carpet leading from the terminal all the way down the length of the platform. His mother told him that the train on that track was the 20th Century Limited, a special train that went to Chicago. Trains were exciting and romantic and from the moment he discovered it the 20th Century Limited would always be his favorite train. They boarded their train and about 10 minutes later the train slowly pulled away from the platform and eased its way slowly through the dark underground network of tracks under Park Avenue. The train was speeding up as it suddenly emerged into the morning sunlight around 96th Street. A short stop at 125th Street, and then over the Harlem River into the Bronx. A few minutes later the train had sped up to 50 miles per hour branched off the main line to the West and continued until it began to run parallel to the Hudson River.

His mother took Rafe to the dining car where they sat on the left side and watched the early morning sun glistening off the river like a sheet of silver. As Rafe ate his pancakes he was thinking, "What a beautiful day". So far so good Rafe might have been thinking as the worst day of his life was unfolding, he had no way of knowing how this day could take a turn for the worse, but he was a child and completely unaware. The ride continued uneventfully and after about 2 hours the train stopped at a strange-sounding place named Poughkeepsie. He remembered his mother telling him it was an Indian name. Like everything else that day, he remembered that the platform the train arrived on was below street level and they had to go upstairs to get off the platform. Parked at the curb was a yellow school bus that he and his mother boarded. They were only on the bus for a few minutes and the bus pulled away from the station and made its way through the city of Poughkeepsie. Poughkeepsie wasn't as big as New York City and it didn't look the same either. It certainly wasn't as grand and impressive but, it only took about 15 minutes before they left Poughkeepsie behind and found themselves speeding through the rural countryside. Maybe 30 minutes after leaving the train station the bus pulled off the main highway onto a blacktopped country road and continued past a huge farm called Maple Valley Farm. All along its road frontage was a stand of huge Maple trees lining both sides of the road for about 200 yards. It formed a shady tunnel that was breathtakingly beautiful. Five minutes later the bus slowed and came to a place with a big triangle of grass in front of what, in the distant past, had been a stone gate. What should have been a gate were two stone pillars on either side of the road where the gate once stood. On the grassy triangle in front of the pillars was a sign that said, "Greer School, A Children's Community.

The bus slowed to about 15 miles per hour and slowly made its way up the main road beneath the majestic maple trees which lined it. The bus climbed a hill through one of the most beautiful properties Rafe would ever see. The place had a quiet almost serene atmosphere that immediately appealed to him. A couple of minutes later the bus pulled up and stopped in front of a huge red brick building called Main House. Everyone made their way off the bus into a crowd of children who had been waiting. There among the children was his brother Tom who rushed to greet them with big hugs and kisses. After greeting his brother his mother said, "Rafe we're going over to a place called Plum Cottage where you're going to stay and play while I go down to Marcy Cottage and take care of some things for Tommy".

Plum cottage was about 200 yards from Main House at the end of a wide gravel path. If Rafe had known what was going on he never would have walked down that path, but in their innocence children, just don't get it. They have complete almost dog-like faith in their parents. So, Rafe and his mother and Brother walked down the path to Plum Cottage where he was introduced to a nice woman called Miss Sutton. About 18 children ages 6 to 7 lived at Plum and Rafe was introduced to them also. All of the kids seemed very nice and Plum itself was a beautiful place. It was just off the dirt county road which passed through Greer School from West to East. A big lawn extended from the entrance of Plum out to the county road which was lined with huge maple and pine trees. On the Western side of Plum was a field about 200 yards in length which was filled with a herd of dairy cattle. More stately trees lined the field and gave the cattle shade from the August sun.

After they had lunch at Plum Cottage his mother left with Tom while Rafe was given the grand tour by the other kids. They showed him the Sand Box, the See-Saw, and the Monkey Bars. However, the children called the Monkey Bars the Jungle Jim. Since Rafe had never heard the expression, Jungle Jim, he mistakenly thought that a huge Forsythia bush next to the Monkey Bars was the Jungle Jim. It looked like a jungle to him and he was anxious to get into it and explore. The Forsythia bush was about 100 feet long and maybe the largest Forsythia bush Rafe would ever see. He didn't go right into it because of the clothing he was wearing, but it definitely intrigued him.

Rafe enjoyed the afternoon playing in such a beautiful place but before long it was time for dinner. Rafe began to get worried, where was his mother? It was getting late, time for the return trip to Brooklyn. As the shadows lengthened, he went to Miss Sutton and asked, "Where is my mother? It's time for me to go home"

Miss Sutton took him into her private apartment away from the other children and gave him the profoundly shocking news. "You're not going home today, Rafe, maybe not for a long time, you're going to live here with the other children and become a Greer Schoolboy.

The horror of those words overwhelmed him. "What! That was too crazy to believe. His mother wouldn't do that to him. She loved him. He was a good boy. He wanted to jump up and run; until another awful thought struck him. He didn't know where he was. He didn't even know the direction to follow to find his way home. He was lost and abandoned. He didn't cry. He was struck dumb. His lack of reaction led Miss Sutton to believe that Rafe was accepting of his situation, but that couldn't have been further from the truth. The impact on him was so great that he didn't know how to react. He left the room went out on the porch and sat silently by himself. He kept hoping his mother would come back for him, but by bedtime, he knew all hope was lost.

Upstairs in Plum Cottage were two dormitories one for girls and one for boys. In between, them was the bathroom with its tubs and toilets. Miss

Sutton sat in the bathroom between the two dorms and read a story to the children. When she finished reading the story, she turned out the lights. Rafe who had been lying on a cot; got up, and standing on the end of the cot looked out the window. The sight that greeted him was one of true splendor. There was a full moon that lit up the landscape with a gentle glow. It was incredibly beautiful, but he thought "I have to get out of here". He was panic-stricken because he didn't know where he was. If he knew which way to go, he'd run for it. 'I have to find the way back" he thought. "I don't care how long it takes; I'll find my way home. But at that point in time things looked pretty hopeless.

He stared out the window for about 20 minutes feeling despair wash over him. He finally lay down on his cot and considered his situation. Years later he would come across a World War II rhyme emanating from the dark days of early 1942 with the Japanese running amok in the Pacific. It went, "We're the battling bastards of Bataan, no Mama, no Papa, no Uncle Sam. No aunts, no uncles, no cousins, no nieces, and nobody gives a damn. Back then he didn't know that little rhyme, but it summed up how he felt.

He thought things were as bad as they could get, His Father had abandoned the family, and now his mother had abandoned him. Things couldn't get any worse, but if he knew what lay ahead, he would have run off into the night even if he didn't know where to go. His last thought that day was, "I have to find the way back to Brooklyn. I have to find my way home".

When morning came the next day Raef awoke feeling like a newly arrived prison inmate. He didn't know the routine so he just followed along and did what the other kids were doing. He wasn't afraid because he was already determined to find the direction to Brooklyn and then make a run for it. In the meantime, he would just go along with the program. After breakfast, the children were allowed to go out and play as long as they stayed in the immediate area around Plum Cottage. Later that morning Miss Sutton gathered the children together to take them on a walk. The purpose of the walk was to show Raef and the other new kids the boundaries of Greer School. The school encompassed two square miles and it was necessary for the children to know which part of the surrounding countryside belonged to the school and which belonged to the neighbors. On this particular day, she led them to Ledge Cottage on the Northern side of the school property. It wasn't more than 500 yards from Plum, but between Plum and Ledge Cottage was the Cannery. The Cannery was just a big shed with machinery to can vegetables. They stopped there and Miss Sutton explained that all of the older boys and girls helped grow and can part of the school's food. The field around the cannery must have been 40 acres with row upon row of vegetables growing; Carrots, string beans, tomatoes, potatoes, corn, and you name it, were growing to help support the school.

It turns out that Greer School was one for single parents in need of a place for their children to stay while they worked. It was supported by the Episcopal Church and by wealthy private benefactors. The children were the primary workforce that ran the school. From the time they were 10 or 12 years old, they began to work as dishwashers, stewards, trash collectors, and farmhands. They worked in the laundry, central kitchen, and forestry crew. Every year the students planted 40,000 pine trees which when grown would supply a timber crop to help support the school. In the meantime, the students would learn to become independent and develop work habits that would be to their advantage later in life. The school was huge, and a virtual Garden of Eden.

Of course, at this time Rafe was unaware of the inner workings of the school. He saw it as an extremely beautiful and tranquil place, but when given the opportunity he would make his run for Brooklyn. The siren call of home was the strongest emotion in him.

The walk continued as Miss Sutton led the children past the cannery then past the small cemetery and into the shade of the forest which surrounded the huge vegetable field. About 200 yards into the forest, they came upon Ledge Cottage where the older girls ages 14-18 lived. Just past Ledge Cottage was a knoll surrounded by towering pine trees that looked down into a small valley which to Rafe's surprise held the school camp. Rafe was fascinated by the physical beauty of the forest and the overall tranquility of the school. One would think that with 200 students from ages 6 to 18 inhabiting the place there would be constant noise. To his surprise, the school was incredibly silent. If there was any consolation to being there it was the physical beauty of the place for it certainly beat the streets of New York City hands down. Of course, it was no substitute for home. That was the sticking point and the beginning of Rafe's problems with Greer School. It had a perfect atmosphere, but Rafe didn't want to be there. Home is a powerful lure for all humans. Even criminals on the run almost always want to run for home. It is a primeval desire deeply rooted in the human physique. A place of safety, where you can go to ground.

Rafe felt trapped. In many ways, his situation was that which had bedeviled man from the beginning of time. He was trapped in the Garden of Eden yet he wasn't happy. Man's ultimate dilemma is the fact that he can never be satisfied.

Rafe settled in as best he could, making the best of a bad situation. He felt like a prisoner in a beautiful prison, but a prison nonetheless.

A few days later Miss Sutton took the Plum children on another walk. This time they went to the farm which occupied the Western boundary of the school. Again, for a city boy, the farm was a place of great fascination. He was exposed to the herd of dairy cows and the big bull named Willie. The pigs were very interesting to a boy who was totally unfamiliar with them. One of the sows had a litter of piglets that were unbelievably cute. Grunting and running around their mother, all pink with little curly tails. For some reason, Rafe and the other children were most intrigued by Willie the Bull. He didn't know it at the time but Willie was going to lead to his first confrontation with the Greer School staff. It was a confrontation that would lead to his being classified as having a resistive personality. The children at Greer School were classified one of two ways either amiable or resistive. Almost all of the Greer children were amiable meaning they were indifferent to being imposed upon. Rafe was amiable in most ways meaning he wasn't difficult to get along with. He was very polite and friendly, but where he differed from the other children was that if he didn't agree with something important, he would resist. It was not unlike being a bee in a hive. The only thing a bee has to do is follow the rules of the hive. Then everything is relatively easy. The hive provides the bees with all that a bee needs, a social structure of queens, workers, and drones all organized for the common good. Fighting the structure of the hive is very dangerous. For a bee, life without the protection of the hive is fraught with danger.

Back at Plum Cottage Rafe plunged right into the giant forsythia bush where he hollowed out the center to make a fort. Since Rafe was one of those children that always seemed to find fun and adventure, the other children who had never paid attention to the Forsythia bush were soon joining Rafe in his jungle adventure. They would venture out from their fort and raid the field where the vegetables were grown, bringing back tomatoes and carrots which they washed and consumed. Raef was amazed at the size of the carrots which were about a foot long and 6 inches in diameter.

Three weeks passed and the day after Labor Day school started. Rafe was in the 2nd grade and his teacher was Mrs. Fisher the wife of the football coach Joe Fisher. Coach Fisher was 6'6" tall and a former Marine. Both he and his wife had the same lanky body type, tall and slender. Actually, Mrs. Fisher was about 5"10" tall and seemed the perfect mate for her husband. Whereas Coach Fisher always wore a sort of grim facial expression, Mrs. Fisher was always smiling and friendly. That's not to say that Coach Fisher wasn't a great person for he certainly was. It is hard to imagine how many young boys he served as a male role model. If you want to talk about a straight shooter and a person of great character it was Joe Fisher.

So far nothing about Greer School was anything to be concerned about except to Rafe just being there was a problem. His first major problem arose when after school one day he and his new friend Cassius Tandy decided to cross the two-hundred-yard-long pasture that separated Plum Cottage from the Farm. Rafe wanted to see if they could find Willie the Bull. It wasn't for any particular reason, just for something exciting to do. So, the two boys crossed the pasture and found the herd of cows grazing in the fields around the cattle barn. After some time of moving among the cows, they finally came upon Willie. As Willie began to approach, they decided that maybe getting into a field with a bull wasn't such a good idea and they took off running for their lives. After ducking under the electric fence, they sat down and rolled on the ground laughing. To them, it was a great adventure. Unfortunately for the boys, they had forgotten about time. Since they didn't wear wristwatches, they could only judge time inaccurately. When they got back to Plum Cottage, they realized they were going to be a few minutes late for dinner. This was not a good thing in the very structured environment of Greer

School. They knew they were in trouble and would be punished. "Well Rafe, what do we do, we're late for dinner. Rafe answered, "Idon't know about you, but I'm out of here!"

Cassius made his way towards the rear door of Plum to take his punishment like a man. while Rafe headed for the vegetable field over the ridge line behind Plum. He was headed towards Ledge Cottage and the forest behind it, but he was heading north when if he wanted to get to New York City he should have been heading south. Upon approaching Ledge, he stopped next to a huge outcropping of rock that was off the side of the dirt road leading up to the cottage. The girls were inside eating dinner and Rafe had just stopped to decide where to go. He was standing there looking at the house when someone grabbed him from behind. It was Miss Jones the girl's gym teacher who resided at Ledge and was on her way home. She came walking up the road from the cannery and had found Rafe crouching behind the rock obviously up to no good. "What are you doing here Rafe, why aren't you back at Plum having dinner? 'What could he say, he was caught.

With a downcast look, he admitted, "I ran away". "Well, this is serious I'm going to take you back to Plum and call Mrs. Fink."

"Uh Oh!" Rafe thought. Mrs. Fink was the assistant director of Greer School and was the person running the day-to-day operation. She handled any problems concerning difficult children. It was her job to straighten them out.

Rafe awaited his fate sitting on a small chair in the Plum Cottage living room. About 45 minutes later a very severe-looking Mrs. Fink showed up. Rafe wasn't the only new kid who had the delusion of making his way back to New York City 85 miles away. Mrs. Fink had a way of dealing with that, and Rafe was about to find out what her method was.

Taking Rafe by the hand she led him back down the gravel path towards Main House, then down the blacktop road at the bottom of which were the boy's dormitories of Marcy, Daisy, Gate House, and Rapello. By the time they reached the gate and the sign Greer School a Children's Community, it was dark. Mrs. Fink led him about 100 yards down the road towards the village of Verbank; then stopped. "Ok Rafe, you want to run, go ahead!" Rafe couldn't believe his ears, but it took only a split second for him to respond. He ran across the road, jumped the ditch on the far side, and began to scramble up the embankment leading to a large meadow. He never expected a 55-year-old woman like Mrs. Fink to move as fast as she did. She caught him before he was halfway up the embankment and dragged him back onto the road. She then knelt, bent him over her knee, and began to spank him. Rafe was shocked! The spanking didn't bother him so much as the confusion created by her telling him he could go and then spanking him when he did.

When she thought she had made an impression on him Mrs. Fink pulled him upright and said, "Rafe you and I are going to have a serious discussion." "Don't you know how dangerous it is out there? I have never had a child your age willing to run off into the night".

She took him by the wrist and began to lead him back to the gate. As they walked Mrs. Fink said, "Rafe you are not at Greer School because your mother doesn't love you or because she has abandoned you. You are here with your brother because your father has abandoned your family and your mother is working three jobs in order to provide for you. By running away, you only make your mother's position more difficult. She's doing the best she can. But there is one more thing you must understand. If you were to run away and by some miracle, and it would be a miracle, you could get home to Brooklyn, you would be brought back. Think about that Rafe."

He did think about that, and as terrible as that first day was, to relive it would be 10 times worse. To risk everything and make it home, only to be brought back was his ultimate horror. So, then he knew that Greer School was a prison without walls. He knew he couldn't run away from it. The remarkable thing was that from that moment on he loved Mrs. Fink. She was the only one who had told him the truth.

That settled that. He was led back to Plum Cottage and as it turned out Mrs. Fink had worked her magic yet again; a potentially difficult child had been pacified. At least for the time being! Rafe didn't realize that this one incident would have far-reaching effects on future events. That is how he got classified as resistive. The other staff members were advised to watch Rafe because he might run away at any time. If he chose to do so, he would do it. He wasn't afraid like most kids and was very strong-willed. They would have to keep an eye on him and hope for the best. His strong character was the reason his mother hadn't revealed the truth to him that first day.

On the other hand, Rafe was moved by the incident and what Mrs. Fink had told him. He loved his mother dearly and didn't want to add to her troubles, he would just have to endure, so he did.

The next problem for Rafe would be at school, and it would be a problem of his own making. Rafe wasn't resistive because he wanted to be. He was resistive because that is what he was. He felt he didn't belong at Greer and he felt the need to express his displeasure. Actually, he was protesting his situation. He didn't really understand this need to make a statement and neither did anyone else. If he misbehaved in school, it was because deep in his heart, he was hoping they would kick him out.

His major way to protest was, that if things didn't go his way, he would go into the coat closet and sit on the floor and not come out. He would sit in there for hours driving Mrs. Fisher to distraction. This was Bea Fisher's first teaching job and she wasn't sure how to handle a difficult child. It wasn't that Rafe disliked her because he thought she was very nice, but he had this need to rebel.

First, Mrs. Fisher sent him to see the principal. Rafe didn't like that one little bit, and sat outside Mr. O'Brien's office for 45 minutes before he summoned up the courage to knock on his door. What scared him most was that he knew he was on his own and had no safe haven to run to if things got really bad. If he had been living at home the trip to the principal's office would have been nothing.

When that didn't work Mrs. Fisher called for her husband to intervene. One day, midway through the school morning, Coach Fisher showed up and took Rafe for a walk down to Daisy Cottage, where the Fishers were the house parents to 25 ten to twelve-year-old boys. During the walk, Coach Fisher asked Rafe, "Don't you like Mrs. Fisher?" Rafe answered truthfully, "I like her a lot". "Then why are you giving her a hard time by hiding in the coat closet?" The truth was, back then, Rafe had no idea why he was doing what he was doing. It was more of an emotional response to being at Greer, but he wasn't aware of the reason. He answered, "I don't know why I'm doing it". "Well, Rafe it has got to stop. So, I'm asking you to be nicer to

Mrs. Fisher and do what she says. Stop giving her a hard time. Ok?" Rafe was scared to death. Coach Fisher was a giant with a very stern demeanor. Besides, he actually liked Mrs. Fisher. Rafe agreed to try harder to be a more obedient child. The walk ended with Rafe being delivered back to his second-grade classroom having been given a needed attitude adjustment. This lasted for a couple of weeks until the children began to tease Rafe about his pronunciation of the word Monticello, the home of Thomas Jefferson. Rafe was outraged that his classmates would make fun of his pronunciation when they had never even heard the word before and had no idea of what or where Monticello was. Mrs. Fisher didn't intervene so Rafe headed into the refuge of the coat closet.

He would learn years later that Mrs. Fisher was a believer in group punishment. Meaning if someone misbehaved punish the whole group and make the group show the problem child the error of his ways.

With that in mind, she kept the class after school for 45 minutes. On a beautiful Indian Summer Day, this was serious punishment. The kids wanted to be out playing in the two hours between getting out of school at 3 P.M. and dinner at 5 P.M. When finally released the 2nd-grade kids went running out the door. Rafe stayed behind and apologized to Mrs. Fisher for his bad behavior. After all, he had promised Coach Fisher to do better. When he raced out the door after the other children, he found them standing in a group about halfway between the school and Main House. As he approached, they began yelling and charged him knocking him down by the sheer force of numbers. They then beat him up. They kicked, punched, and threw dirt in his face. Then they ran off toward Plum. Rafe lay on the path more outraged than hurt and then got up and dusted himself off.

Rafe thought of a course of action. His classmates had attacked in a group like the cowards that they were. Rafe immediately knew how to respond. Instead of following the path around Main House and down to Plum Cottage, he branched off the path and took the road that led to the Cannery and Ledge Cottage. He used the gentle ridge line leading down to the vegetable field as cover and made his way around to the back of Plum. Out in the woods in another of his forts, he kept a garbage can top he thought of as his shield. He was about to become Prince Valiant like the character in the funny papers. He filled his pockets with rocks and searched the woods for a sword. He soon found a big stick that was just the right size. Now he was ready!

He came out of the woods from the back of Plum. His classmates were playing by the Jungle Jim and raised a shout when they saw him. Unfortunately for them, they didn't realize their jeopardy. Trying to repeat their successful assault outside the schoolhouse, the group of 12 boys and girls rushed to attack Rafe. The first one to reach him was the ring leader, Mathew Coleman. With one blow from the big stick, Rafe laid him out flat on his back. Seeing what had just taken place the rest stopped dead in their tracks then turned and ran screaming in all directions. Rafe was on them like a wolf among a flock of sheep. They never had a chance. Had Rafe wanted to hurt them he could have done some serious damage however it was the terror that he wanted to inflict, and that he did with measured efficiency. Some of the children went screaming into the cottage to find Miss Sutton so Rafe only had a couple of minutes to make his point. By the time Miss Sutton came running out to stop the mayhem Rafe had run down the ring leaders and gave them a dose of their own medicine. Rafe was called over by Miss Sutton and forced to give up his shield and sword, then told to go into the cottage and sit by himself until she restored order. Rafe sat in a corner and knew that some sort of serious punishment would be inflicted on him later, but deep inside he was satisfied. He had made his point which was; Attack me and I'll inflict 10 times more pain on you.

That night he received his punishment which was 15 stokes with a ping pong paddle on his bare butt. This was done in the bathroom, between the two dorms, for all to witness. Rafe bore the pain stoically knowing that it was unlikely that anyone would ever attack him again. No one ever did.

That pretty much sums up Rafe Hawkin's initiation to Greer School. Although he thought of himself as being just like the other children nothing was further from the truth. He wasn't afraid to run away, he wasn't afraid of the dark, he would resist when he wanted to, and if attacked he would fight. That is how he became to be classified as a resistive personality by the school staff. The classification itself wasn't the problem because it was basically true on the merits. The problem would come later.

Aside from these incidents Rafe slowly adapted to life at Greer School. These early incidents would come back to plague him later, but at the time they were just minor incidents to him.

On the positive side, Rafe quickly learned that he would get to go home for two weeks at Christmas, two weeks at Easter, and two weeks sometime during the summer. All was not lost as he would get to see home again. In a way his attitude towards Greer School was peculiar. Think of it like being a prisoner held in the Garden of Eden. For in many ways, Greer School was like the Garden of Eden. It was very beautiful and it was staffed by some very good people. If Rafe had not had this thing about getting home, he would have loved the place. Most of the other children thought it was a Godsend.

Within a couple of months, Rafe began to adjust to being at Greer School. His mother would come to see the boys every other week or once a month. Visiting Sunday was every other week and it was something Rafe always looked forward to. His mother didn't come to visit every visiting Sunday, but she made the trip frequently. His four-year-old sister Angela was still living at home so that complicated things. By the time October came to an end, Rafe was beginning to look forward to Christmas vacation. He was going to pay close attention to the route the school buses took from the school to New York. He'd learn the route and he wouldn't forget it.

On the Saturday before Christmas two, yellow school buses showed up on the road in front of Main House. These buses were picking up the children from Plum, Greer, Crest, and Ledge Cottages while two more were down the hill picking up the boys from Marcy, Daisy, Gate House, and Rapallo. The girls and the little kids lived up the hill while the boys lived down the hill. Rafe could not have been more excited. Not only was he getting to go home for two weeks, but more importantly he was going to learn the way home. Ever since that first day, he had been obsessed with learning the way back to 887 St. Johns Place. Until he learned where home was, he considered himself lost.

This time Rafe would be paying very close attention to the route the buses took. The way to New York was quite simple. Once the buses passed through the gate, they continued down Camby Road for three miles to the village of Verbank. After a left turn on Route 82 it was about 20 miles to Fishkill where another left turn put Rafe's bus on Route 9 also called the Albany Post Road. Route 9 went straight south paralleling the Hudson River and terminated in New York. At a rest stop along Route 9, Rafe picked up another piece of very valuable information. Many of the trucks traveling down Route 9 had the name and address of the Company they belonged to stenciled on the driver's door. Rafe noted some of these trucks were from Brooklyn or one of the other boroughs of New York. He quickly developed a plan. If he could get to route 9, he would hide in the woods next to one of the rest stops until he saw a truck from Brooklyn. He'd look for a truck from Brooklyn, heading south and sneak into the back of one that was open, and hide. With luck, within a few hours, he would be in Brooklyn. He only needed a dime for the subway and once he got to Brooklyn, he would soon be home.

Once he knew the way home; and had a plan to get there, he adjusted his attitude toward being at Greer School. He would tolerate it in order to help his mother. She was working two jobs to keep him in school so the least he could do was to try not to cause trouble.

Rafe had some sort of emotional attachment to 887 St. Johns Place. Not only was it his immigrant grandparent's American dream come true, but to Rafe it was the family fortress where his people were. That first Christmas vacation was the best thing Rafe had experienced in his short life. He could actually say that he enjoyed every second of the two weeks he was home. Since his father had abandoned the family and took off for parts unknown Rafe would grow up only knowing the Italian side of the family which was alright as far as he was concerned. He considered himself an Italian from Brooklyn. He never knew how the other side of the family lived but being Italian was a very good thing. His grandmother could be described as a matriarch in the true sense of the word. It seemed like the whole extended family revolved around her. Even more than that, through her Italian grocery store on Atlantic Avenue in Brooklyn she was the center of the entire Italian community. She and her children made 400 pounds of Italian Sausage every week and people came from all over New York to purchase it. It would be a long time before Rafe would understand what made his grandmother such an important figure. In the end, after she was gone, he realized that it was because she took care of everyone. When families fell on hard times, she gave them credit so they wouldn't go hungry. Although she spoke only broken English

Rafe and his siblings were able to communicate with her fairly easily. Among her immediate family, she was reputed to be a genius being able to calculate a check-out bill in the store as fast as a cash register. She would just pass the items across the counter in front of her and come up with the correct total. Her brother Peter Cardone, Rafe's great Uncle, hung out in the back room of the store using it as the headquarters for his somewhat nefarious business dealings. Later as a teenager, Rafe would find out that Uncle Pete had killed three men that had tried to hold up a high-stakes poker game he was involved in. When they came in and pulled their guns Uncle Pete thought they were friends of his playing a joke; or police officers. That is until one of them shot him in the left wrist. It was too bad for them because when they walked in the door with guns in their hands Uncle Pete had pulled out his gun and had it positioned under the table. When one of the holdup men shot him Uncle Pete brought up his pistol and bang, bang, bang, shot three of them dead right on the spot. Bedlam ensued! One of the card players struggled with one of the gunmen and was shot down dead. Another player dived out a kitchen window attempting to grab the fire escape, but he missed and plunged to his death. Uncle Pete shot the fourth gunman in the neck, but he escaped down the fire escape. Rafe hadn't learned of this incident concerning Uncle Pete until he was a teenager. In fact, it was at his grandmother's funeral, that Uncle Pete had told this story to Rafe and his cousins. Since Uncle Pete was in his middle eighties at the time Rafe thought it was just a wild story made up by an old man. Of course, Rafe had not been brought up among his family so he was unaware of the actual character of Uncle Pete. The only part of the story that gave him pause was why Uncle Pete was carrying a gun and why did he at first think the holdup men were friends of his. The first thing Rafe did after hearing this seemingly outrageous story was to go ask his mother about it. "Mom, Uncle Pete just told us that he shot and killed three men in a shootout years ago. Is it true? "Yes Rafe it's true, you can go to the New York Times micro files in the Library on December 23, 1928, and the story is on the front page." Needless to say, the next day Rafe was at the library reading the story. It was on the front page of the New York Times and it had a diagram showing how the holdup unfolded. There were eight men playing cards on the 3rd floor of an apartment at 293 Prospect Park West when four gunmen broke in and yelled "Stick 'em Up." The card players were so surprised that they thought it was a joke being played by some friends or a police raid. Nevertheless, Uncle Pete pulled his licensed .25 pistol out of his hip pocket. When the gunman inexplicably began to fire hitting Uncle Pete in the left wrist, he returned fire killing three men with three shots. Chaos ensued and the fourth gunman shot and killed one of the card players who was grappling with him. Another card player dived out of the kitchen window trying to grab hold of the fire escape. Unfortunately, he missed and plunged to his death. The fourth gunman did make it to the fire escape and got away although Uncle Pete fired hitting him in the neck as he dove out the window. In a one-minute gun battle, three gunmen and two card players were killed. The New York Times reported that Peter Cardone was not the timid type, describing him as stalwart, sharp-eyed, and grizzled.

Rafe's mother told him that Uncle Pete was a big-time gambler who hung out with some very dangerous people. She also told Rafe that Uncle Ernie, her brother worshiped Uncle Pete and was his protégé. Uncle Pete was his grandmother's brother and Rafe's great-uncle. Uncle Pete and Uncle Ernie were essentially cut out of the same genetic material. Learning this when he was 18 years old impressed Rafe once again as to the importance of family. Being sent to Greer School at an early age never allowed him to know that some resourceful and dangerous men were his close relatives. If he had known this he would have acted differently. Back in those early years at Greer, he felt defenseless. He was unaware that the men in his family would have defended him to the death. That is a consequence of being sent away from home. Under those circumstances, you really don't know who you are and who your people are. In all likelihood, Rafe was in Greer School as much to keep in away from his Italian family's influence as for financial hardship. When an incident at school put Rafe in dire circumstances, had he truly known the character of some of his family members he would have acted differently.

Rafe loved his grandmother, but could never quite understand the exact reason why. She was like the sun with the planets revolving in orbit around her. His grandfather had left her in Italy for two years with their first two sons while he came to America to get established. She had an extreme dislike for her mother-in-law who one night came around in the woods behind her house to howl like a wolf. That turned out to be a big mistake because his grandmother took up a shotgun and went out into the woods to shoot her. She took two shots at her and missed but ended up getting arrested and placed in jail for two nights. It turned out that Uncle Pete and Grandmother definitely had some of the same genes.

Tragedy struck shortly after her arrival in New York. Her oldest son Raphael was run over and killed by a Trolley car right in front of her. In order to find relief from the depression caused by this traumatic event Grandmother started the Italian Grocery store on Atlantic Avenue. From the profits from the Grocery store, she saved enough money to purchase the brownstone house on St. Johns Place. To get an idea of how ridiculous human beings can be, Rafe's Grandfather berated his wife for holding out on him where the profits from the store were concerned even though it ended up giving him his American Dream. His Grandfather retired from working in Uncle Pete's Peroxide Factory and took over caring for his building which included six apartments. He did a good job at maintaining it as it was immaculate. The floors and banisters were waxed. The runners that ran through the halls and up the stairs were vacuumed and spotless. Even the cellar was spotlessly cleaned. The backyard was a big garden with rows of Asparagus, Tomatoes, and Corn, not to mention the Rose bushes and Fig trees that lined the walkway around the vegetable garden. It may not have been as great a place as Rafe remembered it to be, but this is where he was secure and loved. This was where his people were and he would love it more than any other place he would ever know.

So, whenever he got home to St. John's Place, he was happy. He loved to go upstairs to Grandmother's apartment and just hang out there. It seemed like everyone wanted to hang out with his grandmother. He wanted to hang out with her the same way her brother Pete wanted to make the back room of her grocery store the center of his activities. So, whenever Rafe was home on vacation he tended to hang with his grandmother. He just liked to go to her apartment to watch the Friday night fights with Uncle Ernie and Grandfather or the million-dollar movie. It really didn't matter what they were doing or what they were watching on television as long as he could sit with them and just be part of his family. Of course, every Sunday would be a big

Italian dinner when all of his aunts; and Uncles would come over. His cousin Salvatore was only a month younger than Rafe and he always loved seeing him. It was a very good thing. He never spent a day at St. Johns Place when he wasn't happy.

The first Christmas vacation home from Greer School was the best. But you know what they say, "Time flies when you're having fun." Just before Christmas Vacation ended, Rafe went to his grandmother and asked her for two dimes. When she asked why he wanted them he said, "In case I need to get home." He already had a plan to get to New York City from Greer School but once he got to the city, he would need a dime to get on the subway. He had learned how to read the subway map so if he could get to the subway, he could get home. So, he needed a dime to put in the turnstile, and one in reserve in case he made a mistake and took the wrong train. It was unlikely that he would make such a mistake, but he needed the second dime as a backup. His Grandmother looked at him and could see the gravity on his face. She turned walked over to her purse took out two dimes and handed them to him. No further questions were asked. His beaming smile told her all she needed to know. That's why Rafe loved his grandmother. Those two dimes were his lifeline!

The Greer School children had come home on December 18th and were returning Jan 2nd. As far as Rafe was concerned things had taken a turn for the better. He had gotten home for two weeks and had loved every second of Christmas Vacation. He had learned the way home and now had a plan if he ever had to make a run for home. Now he knew he could get home in an emergency, and because he knew he would get home at least three times a year, he decided in his mind to just tolerate Greer School. It was beautiful and could hardly be considered all bad. It just wasn't home.

So, Rafe settled in and began to become a Greer Schoolboy. Everything was fine until June of 1949 ten months into his stay at Greer. During the summer the Greer School children went to Camp. It was called Camp Barbay and it was nestled in a small valley on the North Western side of the 1,500-acre campus. A dirt road led to the camp starting at the farm and winding steeply down through the forest before crossing a small wooden bridge over a crystal-clear stream. Once across the bridge the road leveled off and ran through the middle of a pine forest planted many years before by the students to give the school revenue from lumber. It was about 150 yards from the bridge to the opening in the forest where the camp was situated. The children thought the camp was a special place. It was a break from the routine almost like a vacation except you were living in the forest. It wasn't much to look at but the way it was laid out captured its character.

The camp comprised a 500 by-200-yard clearing in the forest. It sloped gently downhill from the White House where the camp director lived, leveled off for about 50 yards, and then fell off more steeply eventually ending up at the swimming pool. When first entering the camp one would see the White House up a gentle hill to the left and a big redwood building about 100 yards directly ahead. This large building was called the Rec. Hall, short for Recreation Hall. The Rec. Hall contained the Dining Room, Kitchen, and the Rec. Hall was a huge room for the children to play in on rainy days. The road that led into the camp continued straight ahead and ended up in the rear of the Rec. Hall where the Kitchen was located. Along the sides of the open area leading down from the White House to the road were eight cabins made of redwood which were screened in on all four sides. The cabins were named after birds such as Chickadee, Robin, Lark, Owl, Oriole, Bobolink, Chewink, and Bluebird. Sitting back in the woods not far from the Kitchen was the cook's cabin called Blackbird. Another cabin for the counselors was about 100 feet to the right of the White House and it was named Wren. Most of the cabins could sleep about 8 campers while Wren was smaller and only had room for two.

The Camp was different and it was fun. Mrs. McMaster ran the camp and she and her husband Albert had been members of the Greer School staff since near its beginning. Mrs. McMaster was beloved by the students. The camp had a special atmosphere and it can be attributed to the character of Mrs. McMaster.

Every evening around dusk all of the campers and the staff would gather around the flag pole which was situated close to the area where the dirt road entered the camp. Everyone would form a circle and then the American Flag would be lowered from the flag pole and folded. Then with joined hands, they would recite this prayer.

> Now the day is over
> Night is drawing nigh,
> Shadows of the evening
> Steal across the sky
> Jesus give the weary
> Calm and sweet repose;
> With thy tenderest blessing
> May our eyelids close.
> Grant to little children
> Visions bright of thee;
> Guard the sailors tossing
> On the deep blue sea.
> Comfort every sufferer
> Watching late in pain;
> Those who plan some evil
> From their sin restrain.
> Through the long night watches
> May thine angels spread;
> Their white wings above me
> Watching round my bed.
> When the morning wakens,
> Then may I arise
> Pure and fresh and sinless
> In thy holy eyes. Amen

After the little service, the children would go to their cabins to get ready for bed. Hanging on a nail outside each cabin was a kerosene lantern to be used if the children had to visit the Trees (Latrine) at night. Every night Rafe would lie on his cot and listen to the mournful song of the whippoorwills singing from the woods behind the flagpole. It was a beautiful, peaceful, and tranquil place as one could imagine, at least it was; until the serpent entered.

Yes, the serpent, is the representation of evil. Did it not get into the Garden of Eden? And just as Greer School was a representation of the Garden of Eden, the serpent had to make its malignant presence felt.

It started out quite innocently just another day in the beautiful setting of Camp Barbey. The school had acquired six army surplus Pup Tents and a couple of Mountain Tents the counselors had set up on a wooded hill behind the White House. On top of the hill was a large clearing that was used for the young campers to have a place to sleep out in the forest using sleeping bags. A blazing fire would be built in the center of the circle and the young boys and girls would gather around it to roast marshmallows and tell scary stories. To Rafe, the tents were interesting but not unusually so. He thought the Mountain Tents were more interesting because they had a cord you could pull to close the front so cold breezes couldn't penetrate the interior. Of course, since it was summer, once the tent was closed off the interior got hot very quickly. So, Rafe crawled in with one of his playmates and checked it out, but when it began to heat up, he decided he'd rather be outside. The two counselors Lynn McMaster, and Judy Freeman, the daughter of the school math teacher, were home from college and were helping out at the camp. Before they left the hill campsite Lynn McMaster whose mother ran the camp, gathered the children around her and said, "I can see that a lot of you are fascinated by the tents, However, you are not to come up here and play in the tents until after you take your nap. After Lunch you will take your nap, then we'll go swimming in the pool, and then after that, you can play in the tents. Under no circumstances are you to come up here until after swimming, is that clear?" The children answered yes and then they raced back down the hill screaming with the exuberance of youth.

After lunch, Rafe was sprawled out on his cot taking his one-hour mandatory nap when the thought popped into his head. "Why don't they want us to go near the tents until after swimming?" It made no sense to him; after all, they were only tents and there was nothing unusual about them. The thought crept into his youthful mind, 'I'm going to go up there and see what's so unusual about the tents that we've been warned to stay away from them." It was probably his sense of adventure that led to this life-changing mistake. "After all, I'll only be up there 5 minutes, what can happen in that amount of time?" It was almost as if some unseen force was drawing him up that hill. Rafe slipped off his cot and walked out the door as if he were heading for the East Trees. Once he was a few yards out of the clearing in which the cabins were located he branched off into the woods and began to walk up the hill. Sunlight was streaming through the trees and the forest had an almost magical glow. It was silent except for the sound of a light breeze rustling the leaves and the songbirds calling to each other from high above. It was very beautiful in the forest and Rafe was quite happy.

He reached the clearing and saw the tents standing in silent rows, with not a soul in sight. There was no noise just the gentle sounds of the forest. When he didn't see anything unusual, he stepped into the clearing and began to walk down the line of pup tents. As he passed each tent, he peered into each to see if they contained anything of interest. When he reached the end of the tent line and was about to turn back, all hell broke loose. Stretched out in the last tent were two almost naked women. He recognized them as being the counselors Lynn and Judy. When Lynn McMaster saw him standing there with an astonished look on his face, she crawled out of the tent leaped to her feet, and then pounced on the Rafe like a wild beast. She knocked him down and straddled his lower body keeping him pinned. She was yelling and screaming, "You filthy little bastard, I told you not to come up here." She slapped him across the face and then backhanded him making his lip bleed. "You disobedient little Son-of-a Bitch I'm going to kill you." Then she started to do just that. She placed her hands around his throat and began to strangle him. Rafe struggled but she was a big woman 5'9" and 150 pounds. She outweighed him by 100 pounds and easily kept him pinned. Rafe would never forget that moment for he was looking into the mad eyes of a savage beast, and it was killing him. She would have killed him then and there except suddenly she was jerked backward off his body by Judy Freeman, who had grabbed Lynn McMaster by the hair and was now screaming also. "Are you out of your mind, are you out of your mind?" "You're killing him, Stop for God's sake, Stop Lynn!" The two young women were wrestling standing up, grappling, and pushing each other trying to get control. Finally, Lynn who was the bigger of the two came to her senses, "Ok, ok, just get your hands off me." Rafe was getting to his feet shaking like a leaf. He had no idea what was going on. What could he have done to bring about such a savage response? He had no idea what he had just seen. He knew nothing about sex. He thought that he had just seen two half-dressed women in a tent.

Lynn McMaster knew better, she was thinking "I should have known better, we were so stupid to think we could get away with it. We couldn't do anything in Wren, someone could have easily come up and looked through the screen door and seen us together, and it could even be my mother. We should have just taken a blanket and gone into the pine forest. Now we have a really big problem. I can't kill the little shit, not with Judy as a witness. I'll just terrify him into silence. They warned us that he was wild and might run away; that gives me an opportunity. I can kill him later and bury him in the woods and everyone will think he just ran away never to be seen again. I'll just have to wait until things die down."

She grabbed Rage by the front of his shirt and yanked him towards her. "I hate little bastards like you. Can't you obey the simplest instructions? You're going back to Chickadee and you're not to tell anyone about what just happened. I'll deal with you tomorrow. If you think what just happened was bad, then tomorrow will prove to be the sorriest day of your life." She was thinking "Yeah, tomorrow without Judy around to intercede, I'll put the fear of God into this little shit." Rafe stood there trembling thinking this would be as scared as he would ever be in life, he waswrong, tomorrow would be worse.

"Now go back to your cabin and keep your stupid mouth shut."

She released her hold on him and Rafe quickly made his way back to Chickadee and lay down on his cot. The whole incident had taken less than 20 minutes but things would never be the same again. Before this Greer School just represented being separated from home and his people, now it was exceedingly dangerous. Rafe who wasn't afraid of much

He kept a low profile for the rest of the day playing by himself in the woods trying to decide if he should make the run for home. He had a plan and he had his two dimes. "Maybe I should wait and see what happens tomorrow, maybe she'll change her mind and forget about the whole thing, and after all, I haven't done anything really bad". He decided to take a wait-and-see attitude. He could always run away tomorrow.

That evening at supper Lynn and Judy were nowhere to be seen and he realized they had something planned, that's why she said she would get him tomorrow. He didn't sleep much that night much too worried about what was coming in the morning.

When morning came Rafe was irrational with fear. He knew he couldn't go down to the Rec Hall for breakfast, not with her waiting for him. The only thing he could think of doing was to hide. Of course, being a child, he picked exactly the wrong hiding place to hide. He picked the East Trees to hide in. The trees were big latrines, screened in with a door at one end and seven stalls in a row. He hid in the seventh stall at the end. It took about 15 minutes after breakfast started before, he heard her coming. She was cackling like a witch. "He! He! He!" Followed by maniacal laughter. "I told you this would be the worst day of your life. I'm going to get you! You little bastard". Then more cackling laughter. Cold ice ran through Rafe's veins. Death was approaching and he was trapped. "I should have hidden in the woods", he thought. Now it's too late I'm trapped."

He heard the screeching of the springs as the screen door opened. Heard her laughing as if someone possessed. The footsteps were coming down the line of stalls. His last thought before her head popped around the side of the stall was, "Please God Save me!"

Her eyes were something out of hell! He could see the madness in them or was it just pure evil? She reached in grabbed him by the arm and yanked him out of the stall. She pulled him out of the Trees and when he resisted like a mule being pulled into the slaughterhouse, she slapped him upside his head. He was so terrified he hardly felt the blow.

She led him to the North; down a trail that led into the forest. She was berating him every step of the way. "You are so stupid! Did you really think you're a match for me? Hiding in the Trees, when it's the first place I was going to look. But at least you remembered what I told you yesterday, that this is going be the worst day of your life; that is if it's not your last."

Rafe felt as if he was going to pee in his pants. Three hundred yards down the trail they came to another campsite. It was just a clearing next to the trail with a circle of stones in the center for a campfire. At this point, Lynn McMaster reached under her blouse a pulled out a huge knife from its sheath tucked into her jeans. It was a razor-sharp Bowie Knife made to do harm. With a slashing movement, she cut down a small sapling and placed it on a tree stump, and cut off the top. Now she had a nice little switch to use on Rafe. There was a fallen tree lying near the edge of the clearing. She forced Rafe down on it and then administered 10 lashes with the switch across his butt. The pain was awful but Rafe wasn't worried about the switch, he was worried about the knife and what she intended to do with it.

She yanked him to his feet and then standing behind him pulled back his head and brought the razor-sharp edge of the knife up against his throat. Rafe was praying to God, "Please God save me, you're the only one who can."

Her voice sounded far away but he could hear her saying, "If you ever disobey me again, I'm going to cut your throat and bury you in the forest. Do you understand?" He was too scared to speak. "Do you understand", she repeated. "Yes, I understand," he stammered.

"And I'll get away with it too, they'll just think you ran away again and no one will ever find you. Not that anyone cares." "And don't think if you tell, anyone will ever believe you. Who are you going to tell? My Mother, what a joke, she runs the camp. Mrs. Fink, that's a Joke too. She knows you're a screwed-up kid. Remember I was born here I'm part of Greer School and you're just a castoff whose parents dumped. Not even your mother would believe you, and where is your father? You don't even have one. and if you did, he's worthless. He doesn't give a shit about you."

The words were worse than the knife because it was mostly true. She held all the cards and he was completely helpless. After that, she led him back to the camp. He went to his bunk in Chickadee and lay down to consider his plight. He had already made up his mind on the trail back to camp that he was going to run for home. He knew the way, he had a plan, and he had his two dimes. Tonight, he would make the break for home.

Ever put yourself in the place of a mouse with a cat terrorizing it. The cat is having a wonderful time but the mouse is suspended in abject terror. No place to run, and no place to hide. That's how Rafe was feeling that night. That's why he ran.

After lights out Rafe just waited for the other kids to fall asleep then around 9 P.M. he left the cabin and made his way quietly around the back of the White House, up the trail to the West Trees then up the road leading to the main campus. It's a good thing he wasn't afraid of the dark because the only light was that from a half-moon. As he made his way through the main campus and down towards Gate House, he was laughing to himself that Mrs. Fink was surprised that he wasn't afraid of the dark. The dark could hide him and make him almost invisible. In its ability to hide him the night was his friend. What really scared him was the beast he was leaving behind.

Once outside the gate and heading down the road to Verbank, he became acutely aware that he must not be seen by passing cars. He would see the lights coming from a long way off, but he had to be sure that he wasn't caught in their headlights in some open area, without cover. When he had plenty of cover he moved fast, when he came to open areas, he planned ahead usually resorting to speed to get through any open area in which he could be seen. What might have taken two hours took four before he came to Verbank and the bigger challenge of Route 82. During those four hours only 10 cars had passed him and he had easily found cover from their searching headlights. Route 82 was a much bigger problem. It had considerably more traffic and more areas with little or no cover. It was his inexperience that would get him caught. He would have been better off just hiding in Verbank until dawn. During daylight, a seven-year-old walking alongside Route 82 would not have attracted any attention whereas a young boy walking alone at three or four in the morning would set off red flags. Rafe went sneaking down Route 82 heading for its intersection with Route 9. By 4 A.M he was coming up on the intersection of routes 82 and 55. There was a wide-open area there, occupied by a country store on one side and a gas station on the other. Rafe decided to make a run for it and raced across the junction of the highways as fast as his legs would carry him. If he had made it across, he may well have made it to Fishkill and Route 9. If he made Route 9, he might have gotten home, but unfortunately, he never saw the state police cruiser parked alongside the gas station until he was halfway across. And as luck would have it both of the Highway Patrolmen were in the cruiser while they watched the intersection for red-light runners or speeders. Needless to say, Rafe got about 50 yards before the cruiser was after him. The police yelled for him to stop but Rafe kept going. One of the officers jumped out of the Cruiser and ran him down grabbing him by the collar of his shirt. Rafe was so distraught that he screamed in frustration. "What are you doing out here running around in the middle of the night, one officer asked? Rafe refused to answer. "Look young man we're going to find out anyway so you might as well tell us."

It was then that Rafe knew the officer was telling the truth and they would eventually find out so he said, "I ran away." The other officer asked, where did you run away from, where do you live?"

"Greer School, Hope Farm,"

"One of the officers said, "Do you know how dangerous it is out here in the middle of the night for someone your age? Anything could happen. You could be run over by a car, Kidnapped, or, even murdered."

"Rafe was thinking, "Yeah, murder! What do you think you're taking me back to."

Regardless, before he knew it, Rafe was sitting in Mrs. Fink's office in Main House. To say that Mrs. Fink was somewhat perturbed with him would be an understatement. He didn't know what to tell her when she asked why he had run away. He wanted to tell her the truth. He didn't want to lie and cover for the bestial Lynn McMaster. If he didn't tell the truth he would have to lie to cover up, and if he lied, he would just come out looking like a screwed-up defiant child. The bottom line was he didn't trust anyone, not even his mother. She had left him in this place without even saying goodbye, so if he couldn't trust his own mother how could he trust Mrs. Fink or anyone else. He was alone as he would ever be. So, his answer to Mrs. Fink was that he just wanted to go home. If he had been older and worldlier, he would have known that by telling the truth he would have put Lynn McMaster in an impossible situation. She couldn't kill him without having the finger of suspicion pointed right at her. And, if his Italian family even suspected the danger he was in, all hell would have broken loose. The truth was Rafe was a child and didn't know shit. He felt abandoned and helpless. As Mrs. Fink drove him back to Camp, he began to think maybe God will save me again.

He was turned over to Mrs. Mac and she and Mrs. Fink had a long talk. Rafe didn't know what was said, but he was acutely aware of Lynn McMaster standing in the background with a malevolent smile on her face. He felt like a rabbit with a hawk circling, just waiting to swoop down. Somewhere deep inside him, Rafe was beginning to realize that he was going to have to fight for his life.

Nothing happened that day, he just returned to the everyday routine of Camp Barbey, but he didn't have to wait long. The following day Lynn McMaster caught him coming out of the trees and began to lead him back down the same trail. Unfortunately, no one was around. He was right back to where he started. He was alone, outgunned, with no help in sight. So, he reverted back to the only help there could be; God! He prayed, "Help me God she's going to kill me, only you can save me." Within a millisecond his prayer was answered. As he was being hauled down the trail in the forest and they came to a tree that had fallen across the trail during the winter. As he looked down to step over the tree. he noticed that she was wearing sandals while he was wearing shoes. He then had the answer. A strategy instantly popped into his mind. He walked down the trail with his wrist firmly grasped in her hand. He knew she had her big knife in its sheath under her shirt. He was expecting a repeat of the other day and knew what he had to do. When they arrived at the campsite and stopped; Rafe reacted instantly. He stomped down on her instep, as hard as he could, with the heel of his shoe. As the pain hit her, he yanked his wrist out of her opening hand and bolted to his right, and in a second was in full flight, back down the trail. He would never run so fast in the remainder of his life. When you're running for your life and every once, of adrenalin is pumping into your bloodstream it is amazing how fast you can move. He ran like he was in a nightmare and the devil was two feet behind. He never knew that he wasn't being pursued because he wasn't about to look back. Lynn McMaster was hopping around the clearing on one foot protecting her injured foot. Rafe flew down the trail and entered the Camp at full speed. He didn't stop once in the Camp, but ran right through it, up the trail leading to the West Trees, and then right by them into the pine forest on the other side. Even then he didn't stop until he came to the stream that led to the wooden bridge near the camp entrance. He spotted a huge fallen tree lying not far from the stream and leaped over it and collapsed on the other side. He was out of breath and panting. Rafe sat there and slowly caught his breath. At this point Rafe realized that no one was going to save him from this monster; he would have to save himself. This meant that he had to have a plan. First, he must never allow her to get him out in the woods alone. If she tried, he would fight to the death right there. He would make sure everyone knew what was going on. Second, if he couldn't fight and he couldn't run what was the alternative? He could make himself scarce, he could hide. Just like the night was his friend, so would the forest become his friend. Looking back, he found the situation almost laughable, he was 7 years old and he was at war. You could say he matured 10 years in 30 minutes.

Even with a plan, he was still scared, but at least he wasn't terrified. He just became extremely aware of his surroundings. He noted who was around, where they were, and what was happening. Now he knew what it was like to be the prey and he didn't like it one little bit. He had two more weeks of camp before returning to the sanctuary of Plum Cottage. If he could make it through the next two weeks, he'd be ok.

The next day while the other kids played in the open areas of the camp Rafe took to the forest. In the quiet sanctuary of the pine forest, Rafe felt safe. Out of sight and out of mind wasn't such a bad idea. They say that children are resilient and they are. All children want to play, so if Rafe couldn't play out in the open, he would play in the woods. So began Rafe's love affair with the forest. It wasn't that much different than his appreciation of the night. Darkness could offer protection and so could the forest.

As he lay on the carpet of pine needles and looked around, Rafe felt almost like he was in church. The sun streamed down through breaks in the pine branches and gave a soft glow to the forest floor, not unlike light filtering into the dark recesses of a cathedral through a stained-glass window. It gave him a feeling of security even if it was only an illusion. One thing that delighted him was the profusion of birds flying and hopping from branch to branch. Since he wanted to get as close to the birds and animals as he could to better observe them, he first had to learn their ways. He quickly learned that movement and noise would quickly attract their attention and most likely frighten them off. The noise would alert a bird, and make it turn its head in the direction of the sound. Once it was looking in your direction any movement would allow its eyes to quickly pick you out from the natural camouflage provided by the surrounding vegetation. If you were to remain perfectly still the chances, are it wouldn't be able to discern your presence. He also learned that while it is easy to see from darkness into light, it is almost impossible to see from light into darkness.

Learning from the wildlife he began to make himself almost invisible in the forest a defense mechanism that gave him confidence. You'd almost think that spending two weeks alone in the woods would be an unhappy experience for a young person however this couldn't be further from the truth. First, he wasn't going to be out in the woods alone for long. While he was moving around observing the birds, he became fascinated by the stream that bordered the South side of the camp. He didn't know it at the time but the stream originated at a dam about two miles north of the camp. The stream had been dammed and formed a big lake and the overflow from the lake gave the stream a steady flow. With not too much to do, Rafe began to explore the banks of the stream. He was delighted to find the banks were the habitat of numerous frogs of all shapes and sizes. He quickly pulled off his shoes and went right into the stream attempting to catch them. He came upon a large pool where a tree had fallen across the stream causing the water to back up. The water was crystal clear and Rafe soon picked out darting flashes of silver. Lo and behold the silver streaks were fish. It didn't take long before Rafe was in the pond pursuing the fish in a fruitless attempt to capture one.

That night when the kids were back in Chickadee getting ready for bed his friend Cassius asked, "Rafe where are you all day? I never see you playing. What do you do all day?"

Rafe answered, 'I've been playing out in the woods."

"Playing out in the woods," said Cassius, "what's there to do out in the woods, it can't be much fun playing out in the woods all day."

"Oh yes, it can!" Answered Rafe. "For one thing I found a pond with fish in it and I go into the pond and try to catch them."

So, in effect "Rafe lured the other kids out into the woods to share his adventures. It wasn't like he spent a lonely two weeks cowering in the forest. He just had the other kids join him. He was just very careful not to be caught out there alone by the evil one.

He only had one more serious encounter with Lynn McMaster during the remaining two weeks at camp. She cornered him one morning in the Rec.

Hall. When he saw her approaching, he began to plan which way to bolt if he had to run. She sat down across from him looking like an angry cat. If she had been a cat her ears would be laid flat back on her head. Her smile was pure evil.

"I've missed you Rafe where have you been keeping yourself? You're not hiding from me, are you?" Rafe was thinking, "If I were a dragon, I'd breath fire on you and burn you to a crisp", but he dared not express his hatred so he looked right into her evil blue eyes and said, "If you ever try to drag me into the woods again, I'll scream and yell, bite and kick so if you kill me everyone will know who did it, I'll be screaming about what I saw, I'll tell everyone.

She sneered at him knowing she should have killed him when she had the chance, but there was always Judy to contend with. Judy would know the truth if anything happened to Rafe, and you could never tell, about a person's conscience. Rafe stood coiled like a spring ready to run or fight.

Lynn McMaster was evil, but not stupid. She began to think, "He's smarter than I thought considering he's only seven. "If I try to get him into the forest again, he's going to resist and put me into a very serious situation. If he runs up to Main House and spills his guts to Mrs. Fink the shit will hit the fan."

Rafe blurted out, "I said I wouldn't tell, but if you won't leave me alone, and keep coming after me, I will."

She wasn't sure what to do. He certainly wasn't your normal kid. If he'd been normal, none of this would have happened. He never would have caught her in the first place. She decided, "If I can't kill him or terrify him into submission, I'll have to marginalize him. I'll make him look so bad that no one will ever believe a word he says."

She got up and said, "Just watch your step Rafe you're not as smart as you think you are." Much to his relief, she stalked off, and a minute·later He was headed for the woods.

Rafe survived the next two weeks at camp with just the minor inconvenience of being accused of minor infractions he actually never committed. Sitting on the Mosquito Bench at night and having the mosquitoes chew you up didn't compare to having a person hold a razor-sharp knife at your throat.

It boiled down to everything being relative. Finally, the day came when the three-week camp period ended and the children were set to return to the main campus. Rafe waited by the Flag Pole and when the word came that they could leave, Rafe took off running and didn't stop until he breathlessly reached Plum Cottage. What he had just experienced was the worst experience of his young life. It was even worse than the first day at Greer School. However, children really are resilient, and Rafe thought this terrible experience was behind him. And it was, for a few years, before it returned with a vengeance.

Rafe was slowly accepting the fact that he would be at Greer School for a long time possibly until he graduated from High School. Although the idea was depressing there was little or nothing, he could do about it.

He went to camp, the following year, and sure enough, Lynn McMaster was home from college and helping her mother. This time there were no terrifying incidents just harassment. She had finally realized that Rafe would keep her secret but she still hated his guts. The hours spent on the Mosquito Bench were a joke compared to what she could be doing. He'd also heard that this would be Lynn McMaster's last year as a counselor at the camp. She was due to graduate from nursing school and would soon have a full-time job preventing her from having the summer off. Rafe thought that at the end of this camp period, he would put this whole thing of Jean McMaster behind him. All he wanted was peaceful coexistence. It's a good thing we don't know what destiny has in store for us, if we did, it could ruin the present.

When Rafe left the camp that summer of 1950 he was headed for Marcy Cottage where boys 8 and 9 years old resided. For the next two years, he would come under the guidance of one of the truly great women he would ever know, Mom Morton. Mom was a great person because she molded the character of her boys and in the process made them good citizens and later fine young men. The way she did it was amazingly simple. She let them know what her concept of acceptable behavior was. She then expected the boys to live up to what they had been taught. Every night without exception they gathered around her in the living room while she read to them from the Bible. Most of what Rafe knew about the Bible he learned at the feet of this beloved housemother. Mom would sit in her easy chair and smoke a cigarette while she read from the Bible. He would always remember with affection watching the smoke from Mom's cigarette drift around the room in the air currents. After the bible reading, Mom would take out a Léger book and call each boy by name. When your name was called you had to get up in front of the group raise your right hand in the Cub Scout salute and state, "On my honor as a Cub Scout I think I tried to do my best." Or you might say that you didn't try to do your best. If you had done your best, you got a checkmark in the Léger book, not having done your best and you got an X. Since there are 7 days in the week you had to get 4 checks to go to the movie on Friday night. Since there was no television at that time the Friday night movie shown in the school auditorium was a big deal. Of course, most people hearing about Mom's method would be convinced that everyone would simply lie about their behavior, but they would be wrong. You could say that Mom had a series of checks and balances. If you had called one of your housemates a bastard or a son-of-a bitch or had treated someone in a mean manner, or had done anything else that was considered unacceptable behavior you had to answer for it. The check preventing anyone from lying was that when you stated. "I think I tried to do my best", anyone who knew differently could get up and say "I challenge you." Then the boy making the challenge would state his case with Mom being the arbiter of who was telling the truth. A person not involved in the process would think that this method would lead to descension in the group where the one making the challenge would be considered a squealer or a rat for turning on his friend however, this was not the case. Mom expected us to do the right thing and being a mean inconsiderate boy was not acceptable. In effect, Mom taught the boys to be their own policemen where we would have no trouble if we just did the right thing. Since she had also educated us as to what the right behavior was, getting to the movie on Friday nights was relatively easy; just be a good person.

 Rafe who could be disobedient was one who might have run aground on the shoals of Mom's policy but that never happened. He had too much respect for Mom to disobey her. In fact, he grew to love her although he never hugged her or told her that he loved her. He felt lucky to be in her care for he knew she was a very good person.

 Rafe only had one run-in with Mom Morton and it was really a test of will rather than Rafe trying to be disobedient. The food at Greer left something to be desired. Rafe's Mother and Grandmother were Italian and were wonderful cooks so the fare at Greer was good enough to keep you alive but not very palatable. Mom's rule was that anything you put on your plate you had to eat. It was Cole Slaw that led to the confrontation. At Greer, Cole Slaw was just chopped-up cabbage. Rafe for some unknown reason decided to eat some even though he knew he didn't like it. He tried to eat it but it made him gag. There was no way he was going to eat it even though he had put it on his plate. Sure enough, when he wouldn't eat it, Mom said, "Well you can't have anything else to eat until you eat the Cole Slaw." That meant that he couldn't eat the next meal or the one after that until he complied with Mom's directive. So, Rafe wouldn't eat. He had the uneaten Cole slaw for every meal. This went on for two days by which time Rafe was very hungry. Since it was a battle, he couldn't win by following the rules Rafe decided to cheat. At the end of lunch on the second day after all of the boys and mom had left the dining room, Rafe put the Cole Slaw in a paper napkin and ran out of the house and dumped it in the woods. That accomplished Rafe went to Mom and proudly announced that he had eaten it. He knew he was breaking one of her cardinal rules by lying but there was just no way he was eating that stuff. Mom accepted his explanation for she had wanted the whole episode to end. However, that evening was Friday, and Rafe had to get up and state whether or not he had done his best. He was aware that for the week he had 3 checks and 3 x's and whatever he said that day would determine if he would go to the movie. When it came to his turn to get up and swear on his honor as a Cub Scout that he had either tried or didn't try to do his best he could have lied again. No one but he knew the truth. He got up and said, "On my honor as a cub scout, I didn't try to do my best." Mom looked at him over the top of her bifocals and said, "What did you do that made you not do your best Rafe." He responded, "I told a lie." 'Who did you lie to Rafe?" He stammered, "I lied to you Mom." She didn't ask what he had lied about but he felt she knew.

That night Rafe was the only Marcy boy not going to the movie. He was in bed in 1st dorm only a few feet from the door to Mom's apartment. Her door was open and she was in bed reading a book. He had only just gotten into bed when Mom called him, "Rafe come here."

He walked into her room and said, "Yes Mom?" She asked, "What did you lie to me about". Although he was a little concerned as to what a truthful answer would bring, he answered, "I said I ate the Cole Slaw but I really dumped it." Mom looked at him over the top of her bifocals and said, "You could have lied tonight and said you tried to do your best, no one would have known. So why did you tell the truth and admit you didn't try to do your best knowing when you told the truth you would miss the movie?" "I knew that dumping the Cole Slaw was wrong, but since I got away with not eating it by lying to you, I decided to take my punishment and miss the movie. I really don't like lying to you, Mom. Lying to you once was bad, but I couldn't do it twice."

Mom looked at Rafe standing next to her bed in his pajamas and said, "I'm proud of you Rafe. Telling the truth when you could have avoided punishment by lying is very commendable. It seems like you're learning the lessons I've been trying to teach you. Since punishment is administered in order to teach you a lesson, and since the lesson has already been learned then there is no reason for you to miss the movie. Get dressed and run up to the school before you miss too much. You'll probably only miss the Newsreel and the Cartoon. It's driving rain out there so be sure to dress for it." Rafe raced back into the dorm and practically jumped into his clothes. As he ran down the stairs past Mom's open door she called after him, "Be careful on the path up the hill they'll be torrents of water coming down; hold onto the handrail. Remember, you don't have your 24 brothers to look after you."

Rafe put on his goulashes and raincoat and then ran to the path leading up the hill. It was a steep hill but the river of water pouring down it didn't make a dent in his enthusiasm. Having Mom approve of his behavior was far more rewarding than going to the movie. As he grew up Rafe would always remember Mom and that particular night. In fact, he had many fond memories of the time he spent at Marcy Cottage. He would always recall her 25 charges spread out on the lawn on a warm summer day while Mom read to us from the children's classic Tal by Paul Fennimore Cooper. Or Mom taking the boys on a hike with her leading the way, like a mother duck with 25 ducklings in tow. These were happy times for Rafe coming on the heels of his ordeal at camp. Things were not so bad at Greer School with Lynn McMaster out of the picture.

During this time Rafe began to run the mile block. Rafe could never get over being run down by the state police officer when he ran away from camp. He was determined never to be run down again, by anybody. In order to accomplish this, he would have to become a very fast runner and not only fast over a short distance but one who could carry that speed over a distance of ground. The mile block, as the students called it was actually 1 ¾ miles. Starting on the blacktop road at Gatehouse it ran up the hill to Main House. From there one made a 90-degree turn to the right and followed the dirt county road, also known as Flint Road that ran past Crest Cottage and then the Gymnasium and the towering stone schoolhouse. Following this road for ½ miles brought you to Camby Road which was the road that started in Verbank and ran past the school on its southwestern side. Gatehouse was situated on Canby Road so after making a right turn at the intersection of Flint and Canby Roads it was a straight shot to the school entrance at Gatehouse. Rafe ran this 1 ¾ mile block every day that he could. He also ran wind sprints on the boy's athletic field to build up his speed. Rafe was obsessed with running because he thought one day it might be his only defense.

One other major event took place during this time period when Rafe was reaching the age of 10 and was about to move from Mom's Marcy Cottage to Daisy Cottage where Coach Joe Fisher and Mrs. Fisher were the house parents. Rafe had no problems with the Fishers even though his defiant behavior had given Mrs. Fisher fits when he was in the 2nd grade. By now Rafe was a good boy in the Mom Morton mold and he readily did whatever the Fisher's asked of him.

After he moved to the 3rd grade, he got a new teacher Mrs. Van Tassel the wife of a nearby dairy farmer. She was in her 50's a lot older than Mrs. Fisher. Aside from his refusal to do well in school, he was actually the favorite of his new teacher. Mrs. Van Tassel had a wonderful dog named Victoria which she sometimes brought to school for the children to play with. Victoria was an English Shepard and when Rafe learned that she could "bring in the cows' on command he became absolutely fascinated by her.

Every June, Mrs. Van Tassel, took her class out for a picnic at her farm. Aside from the food, the kids had a ball playing in the hayloft jumping from the stacks of hay bales into a pile of hay at the bottom. Rafe wanted to see Victoria bring in the cows and when it was time for milking so Mrs. Van Tassel said to Victoria, "Vicki, bring in the cows". Victoria bounded off into the pasture and disappeared. 15 minutes later Victoria reappeared herding the cows ahead of her. Rafe was amazed and thought that Vicki had to be the smartest dog in the world.

Two years later when Rafe was in the 5th grade and making his final visit to the Van Tassel Farm, he discovered that Victoria had a litter of puppies. Apparently, she had been impregnated by a dog from a nearby farm and her puppies were as cute as could be, but not purebred, English Shepherds. None of this mattered to Rafe who had never seen anything as cute as her litter of mongrels. One, in particular, captured Rafe's attention. He was all white with black and brown ears and was the cutest and friendliest creature Rafe and ever encountered during his short life. While the other children played in the hayloft Rafe played with his newfound friend. The ever-observant, Mrs. Van Tassel saw the connection between the boy and dog and walked over and asked, "Do you like this puppy, Rafe?"

His answer was immediate, "I think he's the coolest thing I've ever seen."

Mrs. Van Tassel thought for a few minutes then said, "Would you like to have him as a pet?"

The answer was obvious but Rafe was thinking they'll never let me have a dog at the school. Rafe looked crestfallen when he answered, "I'd love to have him more than anything, but they'll never let me have a dog at Greer."

Mrs. Van Tassel thought for a minute before responding, "You know Rafe you never know until you ask. Would you like me to call Mrs. Fink and see if some arrangement can be made?"

Rafe was thrilled at the idea but didn't think that such a thing was possible, but maybe he was wrong. "Would you really ask her?" "I will for you Rafe because I don't think the puppy could have a better companion." With that said Mrs. Van Tassel walked over to her house to make the call. It took about 30 minutes before she reappeared walking across the lawn towards where Rafe was playing with the puppies. From the smile on her face, Rafe knew that she had been successful and his spirits soared. Could something this good really be happening to him? Mrs. Van Tassel delivered the good news, "Mrs. Fink agrees that you can have the puppy once he's old enough to be weaned from his mother. Rafe jumped up and down with joy, "Wow my own dog how could I be this lucky". That is how this life-changing event unfolded. When Rafe moved from Marcy to Daisy, he was not alone he now had this fantastic animal with him. Now Rafe had someone to run the mile block with and a constant companion. At this point, Rafe was beginning to think that being a Greer School boy wasn't so bad. The dog, soon to be named Max, was as friendly and loveable as any dog that ever lived. Now on his constant excursions into the forest, Rafe had someone to share his enthusiasm. Max always waited outside the school for Rafe to appear and followed him around like a shadow.

The only problem Rafe had was schoolwork. It was a problem because Rafe just wouldn't do it. It wasn't as if Rafe couldn't do it as he was later to learn he had the highest IQ of any student that had ever attended Greer School. The problem was one between Rafe and his mother. He didn't want to please her because he felt she and his father had put him into a very difficult situation. Because they couldn't get along with each other Rafe had lost his home. It wasn't that Rafe didn't learn the material in school. He knew it. He just wouldn't show how much he knew. He was protesting although the method he chose was just plain stupid. In the end, the only one he was hurting was himself, but at that early age, Rafe was not well-adjusted. The reason Mrs. Fink had gone along with Mrs. Van Tassel's suggestion that Rafe be allowed to have the dog was that she felt it might make Rafe more compliant.

Neither the school nor Rafe himself knew just how intelligent he was. This changed when a graduate student from Vassar College in nearby Poughkeepsie, asked if she could test some student volunteers for her master's thesis. When Rafe learned that he could get a morning off from school by taking a few tests he was the first to volunteer.

The test consisted of 500 words repeated 5 times during which the subject would respond with a color that the word brought to mind. It was basically a simple test to see if people associated certain words with certain colors. By the time Rafe had gone through the first 100 words he had figured out the purpose of the test and, then making a game of the process, thought of a way to give the questioner the exact outcome she was looking for. When finished Rafe watched the young woman named Ruth score the test. She ended up with an amazed look on her face. She looked at Rafe and said, "Rafe did you figure out the purpose of the test and then found a way to give me the results I wanted." Rafe was thinking "What's this all about" then answered, "Yes I understood what you wanted to prove." Ruth asked, "How long did it take to figure out the test. Rafe thought about it and then answered, "Maybe 30 seconds." Then she asked, "And how long did it take you to determine how to make it come out as you wanted it to." He thought for a few seconds and responded, "Maybe a minute." With that Ruth arose and said, "Do you mind waiting here for a few minutes." He answered, "Sure, no problem."

Since the test was being given in the dining room of Main House it was only about 50 feet from Dr. Elliott's office. Ruth hurried over to his office and when entering said, "Dr. Elliott could I talk to you for a few minutes." He answered, "Sure, pull up a chair. Ruth sat down and asked Dr. Elliott, "What can you tell me about Rafe Hawkins" Dr. Elliott smiled at her and responded, "What has he done now?" Ruth answered, "Well to make a long story short he just did something rather amazing for a child his age. "What I'd like to know is how he does scholastically. Is he at the top of his class or maybe the best in the school?" Shaking his head Dr. Elliott answered, "No he only does well enough to get by. We know he can do better but he just will not apply himself to schoolwork. Other than that. he is a very nice boy. Why do you ask?" "I'm convinced that he may have an extraordinary intelligence of the creative kind, and if you and he will agree, I'd like to come back and test him with a battery of intelligence tests." Dr. Elliott rubbed his chin as he thought about her proposal. Then asked, "What gives you the idea that he may be unusually intelligent?" Ruth explained that he had figured out the purpose of the test and in seconds had devised a method of giving her the results she had hoped to find. Furthermore, the speed at which he had accomplished this was amazing. Ruth went on to say that she had the opinion that Rafe may have an unusual thought process called directed intelligence. Dr. Elliott knew that Rafe was an unusual child and thought that the testing could lead to a better understanding of his behavior. Dr. Elliott answered, "I'm sure Rafe wouldn't mind taking the test and I have no objections as it might actually be helpful. Just let me know when you want to schedule the tests."

The next week Rafe was given an afternoon off from school and took a battery of 6 intelligence tests. About a week later Ruth called Dr. Elliott and gave him the test results. "Just as I thought Rafe has what is called a directed intelligence. This means that he can perform at a genius level in whatever he directs his mind. The downside of this is that he will not do well in things that do not interest him. In those areas, he will actually test below average. This doesn't mean he could not do well in all areas of the test it just means he won't. One might almost confuse his intelligence with savant syndrome. The difference is that Rafe can apparently direct his intelligence onto anything that interests him and be as good at it as a savant. In the process, he ignores that which does not interest him. I also believe that he knows a lot more about certain subjects than you could even imagine. He has a rare intelligence and I would keep that in mind when dealing with him." Dr. Elliott thought about what Ruth had just told him. He finally said, "We've known for some time that Rafe has a deeply seated emotional problem. One could say that he is a massive underachiever. However, he has made great strides in the last couple of years ever since he became a charge of Mom Morton. We can only hope that he will continue to move forward. Overall, he is a very nice young boy and a leader in his age group. I'd like to thank you for taking an interest in him as knowing something about how he thinks should prove very helpful."

It might have proven helpful if Dr. Elliott had called Rafe in and told him about the test results as Rafe didn't think he was any more intelligent than any of the other children. Dr. Elliott did tell Rafe's Mother but that only led to her yelling at him when he got bad report cards. Later his mother began to say things to Rafe like, "You have a one-track mind." In response Rafe laughed and said, you're wrong Mom, I have 10 tracks but only one engine." Years later his mother would tell him that he had the highest IQ of anyone who had ever attended Greer School.

After two years with Mom Morton Rafe was as well-adjusted to Greer School as he was ever going to get. He was beginning to accept the idea that he would be at Greer until he graduated from High School. The summer of 1952, when he was 10 years old, was when he made the move from Marcy Cottage to Daisy. It was an easy transition as the house parents at Daisy were the Fishers whom Rafe thought the world of.

During the next two years, under the tutelage of Coach and Bea Fisher, Rafe completed the transition from a defiant child to a model Greer School-boy. He was happy running the mile block and exploring the forests with Max. The 10, 11, and 12-year-old boys were developing an interest in sports and that was where most of their energy was focused. Rafe was developing another problem. It was about this time he stopped growing. He was 5' tall when he left Daisy for Gate House and didn't grow another inch until after he left Greer School.

The Fishers were wonderful role models for boys at that impressionable age. Joe Fisher was a former Marine and straight as an arrow. He taught the boys that it was not winning that counts but how you play the game. In a very succinct way that summed up the philosophy of Greer School. Do what is right even if you have to pay a price.

The five years Rafe spent at Marcy and Daisy were happy ones. Once he accepted the idea that he wasn't going to escape to home, he adjusted. In many ways, Greer School was better than home. Living year-round with 25 other children allowed him to develop interpersonal skills usually not acquired in a normal home. Rafe sensed that his own mother could not have given him the guidance of Mom Morton. The following is a quote from the beloved Mom Morton. "So, day by day, by living a good life these children are taught to build a character that will withstand the storms of life. From a child, thoroughly spoiled emerges a generous, unselfish personality. From a boy inclined toward bullying emerges a kind boy, and from a headstrong boy comes a boy able to reason within himself and choose the right. How wonderful to take young lives and mold them into citizens such as we Americans are proud to have our people be."

Rafe under the loving care of Mom Morton and the Fishers had become a model citizen. He was a leader and had come to appreciate the wonderful environment Greer provided. About the time Rafe moved to Daisy the Fishers became the proud parents of a baby boy christened Joe Fisher Jr. When Joe Jr. was a two-year-old whenever the Fishers had to leave the cottage for a short period the boy chosen to babysit the toddler was Rafe. Rafe, considering his initial conflict with Mrs. Fisher when first arriving at Greer was deeply honored by their expression of approval. Rafe would never let them down.

When Rafe reached 13 years old, he had to leave the wonderful home he had at Daisy cottage and moved to Gate House. He would stay there for the remainder of the time he had left at Greer. His brother had always been two years ahead of Rafe and now Rafe had finally caught up with him. This was 1955 and Tom would graduate in 1957 so the boys would have two years living in the same house. At this point, Rafe was a happy boy. The line from the old spiritual comes to mind. "Summertime and the living is easy." These were good times for Rafe he was finally becoming a happy teenager. He was well-adjusted and popular. He had many friends and he had Max. He and Max ran the mile block every day and while Rafe ran down the road Max would bound into the fields and undergrowth only to reappear to leap up on Rafe. The Gate House boys built a dam on Fairyland Stream caught fish in the reservoir and stocked the pond formed by the dam. It occurred to Rafe that life at Greer was better than what he would be experiencing on the streets of Brooklyn. Mr. and Mrs. Snelling were the house parents at Gate House and they were easygoing and created a happy atmosphere for the boys. If things had stayed that way Rafe would have graduated from Greer and would have considered himself lucky to have ever been part of such a great place. If you recall, Adam and Eve were perfectly happy in Eden until the serpent got in. Rafe had long since forgotten the terror of his first year at camp and considered it an unlikely twist of fate that he had unwisely ventured upon the hill behind the white house. But if he had known what lay just over the horizon his blood would have run like ice water through his veins.

Gate House was easy living as the Snelling's were a very nice easy-going couple. Rafe and his friends found a fawn stuck in a wire fence and brought it back to the house. The Snellings adopted it and often brought it up to their apartment to feed and play with it. We all thought the Snelling's were great because the atmosphere they created was one of peace and harmony. Unfortunately, at the end of Rafe's first year at Gate House, just before Christmas Vacation in 1955, the Snelling's announced that they were leaving Greer to return to Vermont. We were saddened to see them go but weren't too concerned because all of the house parents at Greer were the best of people. We were sure that whoever replaced the Snellings would be equally as nice. So, a week before Christmas we climbed aboard the school buses for our two-week holiday in New York.

On returning to Greer shortly after the New Year, the boys came charging through the front door of Gate House with all the exuberance of youth. They weren't very far inside when they heard a female voice scream, "Who just came in the front door?" A chill ran down Rafe's spine. He thought he recognized the voice. But it couldn't be! That would be madness! When he rounded the corner into the hallway his worst fears were realized. He couldn't have been more shocked if someone had thrown a bucket of freezing cold water in his face. There she stood the devil's handmaiden none other than Jean McKinley herself. "Oh, Dear God", Rafe thought." I can't make it for three years with this monster in charge. My life has just turned to shit." She quickly announced that she was Lynn McMaster and that she and her new husband were our new house parents. She also made it crystal clear that none of us boys could use the front door; we would now enter the house through the basement door. She went on to say that at dinner she would give us a new set of rules we would live by.

Rafe made his way up to Little Dorm and stood there while his friends came in. George said, "What's the matter with you Rafe you're as white as a sheet; like you just saw a ghost or something".

"Hey guys gather round we need to talk," Rafe replied. They stood in the aisle, between the cubicles where the boys slept. "George, you say I look like I just saw a ghost well it's worse than that. Our new housemother is as evil as Satan himself. You have no idea how bad she is, but you're about to find out. You will soon see that I will never be able to do anything right again. She'll come after me with a vengeance and when she's finished with me, she'll go after you".

"Come on Rafe, no one is that bad, how do you know", asked Ingo?

"Rafe responded, "Let's just say I do know, and leave it at that. Once I'm proven right, we'll talk again." Rafe went into his cubicle and lay down on his cot. He lay down and prayed to God. "Please God help me again. Your hand shielded me before, and only you can save me now. I'll be your little warrior, I'll stand against evil, but I need your strength. Without your help I'm powerless."

That night at dinner they met Mr. Brinkman her new husband, and her enforcer. He was a big former marine about 6'1" and 230 pounds. Then they lay down the law of the new regime. Rafe felt as though they had just been condemned to a concentration camp and here was the new commandant. The only thing she didn't have was a swastika around her arm. None of the other boys realized what was coming, only Rafe.

Within a few weeks, her method became apparent. She came up with a new policy where you were given demerits for any infraction of her rules. The only problem was she was the sole arbiter of who did what and there was no appeal. Not only that, but she believed in the concept of divide and conquer. Within a short period of time, she began to turn the older boys against the younger ones. She went so far as to turn brother against brother. When you have total power it's easy to accomplish. The older boys could do no wrong. If they committed an infraction, it was overlooked and before long, they began to think they were as good as the distorted illusion she was creating. They were near perfect and the younger guys were screwed up. .

The system worked like this. If one of the boys ran up the stairs, he would get one demerit. If one of the older boys ran up the stairs, she wouldn't see him. If Rafe ran up the stairs, he would get 1 demerit for running on the stairs, 4 more for disobeying her rule not to run on the stairs, and if he protested, he would get 4 more for talking back.

She had a nasty habit of sitting in her apartment with the door open. She had a little two-person table where she could sit looking out the door. From her chair, she could see the upper 10 feet of the staircase which ended in a hallway landing. From the top of the stairs, you would turn left to get to the Kingdom (one of the dorms) and straight ahead to go into Big Dorm; but to get to Little Dorm you had to make a right turn and walk past her open apartment door. One Saturday afternoon Rafe came walking up the stairs and turned to walk into Little Dorm. As he passed her open door she called out, "Rafe come in here!" He walked over and stood in the doorway. She grinned at him with her usually evil countenance. "Why did you run up the stairs, Rafe?" He responded, "I didn't run up the stairs, I walked up." If I said you ran up the stairs you ran up; So, I'm giving you 5 demerits, 1 for running on the stairs, and 4 for disobeying."

"But you know I didn't run up the stairs, you were watching me."

"You have to learn that my word is law so for talking back, you get 4 more."

"So, what you're saying is that if you say I did something it doesn't matter if I did it or not, I'll still get the demerits anyway."

"That's about the size of it Rafe, you will have to learn that I have total control. I'm going to break your defiant attitude Rafe, and make you wish you'd never been born." Rafe couldn't do anything but glare at her but a thought came to him that gave him comfort.

"If you have God on your side and you stand against evil, you can win." Just like years ago, he was in God's hands. "May I go?"

"Get out of here, the sight of you makes me sick".

The bad part of the demerit system was that you could only get 10 demerits in a week then you would miss the movie, and worse, any dance held at one of the Cottages. The boys at Gate House were just getting into girls, and a dance was the big attraction of the week.

None of this mattered too much to Rafe because he was always in detention for not doing his homework. Detention was held in the 7th-grade classroom in the school building so at least he could get away for a few hours from Brinkman. Rafe was still defiant about schoolwork and that would never change while he remained at Greer. He knew everything that was taught in the classroom and could always pass the state regents examination so he wouldn't be left behind, but he refused to do homework. While in detention, often sitting in the room by himself, he became self-educated. He snuck in his favorite library books and read Dickens, Kipling, Aristotle, Plato, Tacitus, Herodotus, Dante, Shakespeare, Milton, and more. Of all the literature he read in detention his favorite was *Paradise Lost by Milton*. He came upon a verse in that beautiful epic that would give him the resolve he need going forward. He memorized it and would forever keep that sheet of paper on which he originally wrote it down. It goes like this:

So spake the Seraph Abdial, faithful found
Among the faithless, faithful only he;
Among innumerable False, Unmoved, Unshaken, Unseduced, Unterrified,
His loyalty he kept, his love, his zeal,
Nor number, nor example, with him wrought
To swerve from truth or change his constant mind, though single.
From amidst them forth he passed a long way through hostile scorn,
Which he sustained. Superior, nor of violence feared aught; and with
Retorted scorn, his back he turned on those proud towers to swift
Destruction doomed.

Somewhere at the beginning of the Brinkman regime, Rafe decided to stay and fight rather than run away. By now he could easily make it to New York but that was no longer on his mind. Mom Morton had taught him to be a good citizen and to resist evil, and that he intended to do.

The imposition of the demerit policy began the downward spiral of the former pleasant atmosphere at Gate House. The newly created hostile environment began to cause bitter resentment among the residents, especially among the younger boys. The problem the Brinkmans were having was brought on by the natural human thought process of comparison. If the boys hadn't had house parents like Mom Morton and the Fishers, they might have thought the Brinkman way was normal. That was not the case as the boys knew they were being harassed for no reason other than meanness. While the older boys enjoyed the special privilege granted to them, the younger boys banded together to resist. Because of her enmity towards him, the natural leader of such resistance was Rafe!

By summer, Brinkman had decided that her policy of punishment for minor offenses was casting her in a bad light. To try to counteract this resentment she devised what she thought was a clever device, it was called the tribunal. If you were to receive over 10 demerits in one week the tribunal would decide the punishment taking the onus off Brinkman, and on to the tribunal members. It is here that she made a tactical mistake. It began when Rafe's classmates moved to Big Dorm while Rafe was left behind in Little

Dorm as punishment. This was justified as Rafe was not growing normally and had the physical stature of the younger boys. This proved to be a major mistake on her part. Since Rafe was older than the other residents of Little Dorm, and the leader of the resistance, he was elected to represent the dorm on the tribunal. His classmates in Big Dorm elected George Sievers as their representative. Rafe and George were best friends and key members in resisting the new regime. Since the tribunal had only three members, the resistance controlled the vote. As a result, the punishments handed down were just slaps on the wrist so to speak. It didn't take Brinkman long to find out what was going on in the tribunal. She called in Russell Holder the representative from the Kingdom and asked him why the punishments meted out were so trivial. When she found out that Rafe was behind it, she began to make his life a living hell.

The first thing she did was abolish the tribunal. If it wasn't going to work to her advantage, why have it? At the time Rafe was going home to Brooklyn for the weekend every 6 weeks to have the braces on his teeth adjusted. One particular week Rafe left for Brooklyn with only four demerits, but when he returned, he had 24. He had been given 20 demerits without even being there. In retaliation, Rafe let the air out of one of the tires of the Brinkman's car. It was a minor inconvenience but Brinkman couldn't stand the fact that someone was resisting. She had no doubt who the culprit was.

Brinkman had a problem in that at least half of the boys at Gate House were Mom Morton raised. Many good people wonder why they are attacked by evil ones without an apparent reason. There is a hidden reason that good people fail to consider. Evil can do its thing as long as there isn't any good present to be compared to. Once good shows up, evil begins to look like what it is. Just the presence of a good person in their midst begins to reveal evil in its true light. With good present, evil begins to look like the dark side of the force. Mom Morton and Brinkman were polar opposites and Brinkman suffered badly in the comparison. The boys had experienced how a cottage could be run in perfect harmony and now they were learning the opposite.

The noose was tightening on Rafe. He could do no right. The pressure of living under the Brinkman regime was depressing. His only joy was running the mile block with Max and taking him on excursions through the forest and meadows of the 1500 acres comprising Greer which in earlier times was known as Hope Farm. If Max liked anything it was chasing Woodchucks. He never caught them but after chasing them into their holes he would try to dig himself in. His head would be down the hole and dirt would be flying back through his hind legs as he dug like he was possessed. It always put a smile on Rafe's face watching his beloved companion having such a wonderful time.

In reality. Max was everyone's dog. He had a wonderful disposition and freely gave his love. If any of the boys at Gate House felt he was unloved Max put an end to that, he loved everyone. When the boys were gathered in the living room to watch TV, they were spread all over the room. Since there wasn't enough room on the chairs or couches on which to sit, many of the boys spread out on the floor. Max had a habit that endeared him to the boys. He would come in, look for a target, then lay down next to the boy and take his wrist in his mouth. Holding the boy's arm gently between his teeth he would run his tongue back and forth under his wrist. Invariably the boy in question felt honored to be chosen for this ritual by the loving Max. If the boys could have agreed on anything it was, that they all loved Max.

Rafe had no life, and the vise was tightening. Things finally came to a head when he was assigned as the dishwasher at Gate House. It was a little over a year into the Brinkman regime and Rafe was coming to the end of his rope. How could a simple job like washing dishes lead to a confrontation that would eventually blow the whole place apart? It was easy because having that job placed Rafe in the position of having Brinkman in total control over whether or not he did the job satisfactorily. Of course, it proved to be an impossible task as it didn't matter if he did the job well or not. She was the sole judge and if she said the silverware was greasy it was greasy. To try to get her off his back, Rafe went to extraordinary lengths to comply. After school, he would return to Gate House and rewash all of the silverware to make sure it was absolutely clean. Then that night she would accuse him of not doing his job to her satisfaction. This led to demerits and being confined to the cottage for the weekend. Rafe didn't know where all the harassment was leading, but he was sure it wouldn't have a good outcome. The cat was again enjoying tormenting the mouse. Things soon came to loggerheads when

Rafe realized that he was in an impossible situation. The showdown came when Brinkman advised him that he was going to learn to do things her way or else and that night he would be punished in front of the whole group. That evening after supper, while the boys were still in the dining room, Rafe then learned what that punishment would be. She announced that he would stand and stretch himself out across a dining room table and her husband would administer 20 strokes with a ping-pong paddle. She went on to say, "We don't tolerate rebellion or defiant attitudes in this house". She then turned to Rafe and said, I'm going to make you do things my way or else!" At that point, Rafe crossed the Rubicon. Before he could bite his tongue, he snapped back, "You'll eat Shit first!"

With that said, he bolted out of the dining room and headed for the front door. On the way, he shouted for Max to follow. The two of them came out of the front door like they were shot from a gun, like, faster than a speeding bullet. Once outside there was no one in Greer School who had a chance of catching them. Rafe headed up Main Road towards Main House like an athlete running 200 meters in the Olympics. He never slowed down until he topped the hill and reached the girl's athletic field. He was hardly out of breath, but he needed to think. Off to his right was a thicket of Birch Trees so he headed in that direction. Nearby was a thicket of sumac trees and some thick undergrowth. Rafe and Max lay down in the thicket while Rafe considered his situation. He knew her harassment was meant to curtail opposition to her authority. She wanted to humiliate him in front of his friends. In one of his many hours in detention, he had come across a quote from the political philosopher Edmond Burke. It had made an impression on his young mind since it seemed to fit with the values of Mom Morton. The line stated, "The only thing necessary for evil to triumph is for good men to do nothing."

Rafe realized the die had been cast and there was now only one course of action; he had to talk to Dr. Elliott. It would serve as a declaration of war and if Dr. Elliott did not act the consequences would be dire. This is what had always been Rafe's primary concern. He would tell those in authority the truth and might not be believed. After all, Brinkman had been born at Greer School, she had been part of the place since birth. Her mother was one of the most beloved staff members, and she was now one of the staff herself.

On the other hand, Rafe was a somewhat difficult child, defiantly refusing to do school work, running away, and could be disobedient. With no other options except to take Max and run away again, Rafe left the thicket and walked the 200 yards to Bittersweet where Dr. and Mrs. Elliott resided.

Dr. Elliott called out from the dining room where the Elliotts were just finishing dinner, "Who is it, Gwen?"

She answered, "It's Rafe and he wants to talk to you". Mrs. Elliott ushered him in and asked him to pull up a chair at the dining room table. Dr. Elliott a man who commanded an enormous amount of respect in Rafe's mind took a chair opposite him. Dr. Elliott was one of the best men Rafe would ever know. He didn't have to be where he was, running a school for parentless children. He had the ability and credentials to be the president of a university and Mrs. Elliott was equally well educated and qualified. Mrs. Elliott was Rafe faculty advisor and his tutor in mathematics. Of all of the subjects in school, Rafe disliked math the most. With his unusual type of intelligence, if Rafe didn't like a subject, he couldn't do it. The amazing thing was that under Mrs. Elliott's tutelage, he could even learn math. It wasn't that the Elliott's didn't know Rafe, as ever since the visit by Ruth Henderson and the intelligence testing they had taken a special interest in Rafe's academic progress. Or in a certain way, they were interested in his lack of progress and why.

Dr. Elliott simply asked, "What's wrong Rafe?"

With all the emotion Rafe could muster he said, "Gate House is run like a concentration camp with Lynn McMaster as the commandant! The only difference between her and a Nazi is that she doesn't wear a swastika on her arm. She's an evil monster. Where Gate House used to be a happy home it's now a prison where the younger boys live in fear."

Dr. Elliott was shocked. If Rafe's allegations were true, he had a major problem. "Explain how Gate House is run like a concentration camp Rafe." For the next half hour, Rafe explained how the younger boys lived in a state of constant fear. Punishment could be meted out arbitrarily and there was no recourse if one was unjustly accused. What had once been a happy place was now a place of fear and hostility where the boys were being turned one against the other." He added that unless something was done the situation would eventually lead to revolution, and a revolt against Brinkman's authority. Under such a situation something terrible could happen.

These very serious accusations forced Dr. Elliott to act. He told Rafe to return to Gate House that no harm would come to him and that he would send Mrs. Fink down to Gate House the next day to meet with the boys and hear their concerns. In front of Rafe, Dr. Elliott called Brinkman and told her that Rafe was coming back to the cottage and that nothing was to happen to him or else. He advised her that Mrs. Fink would be having a meeting with the boys the next day to get to the bottom of Rafe accusations.

Rafe slowly walked back to Gate House passing across the green expanse of the girl's athletic field and down the hill called Daisy Suicide. He was thinking that the cat was out of the bag and that now progress could be made. Hopefully, this would lead to the sacking of the Brinkmans and the end of their tyrannical regime. One could hope!

When arriving back at Gate House Rafe was confronted by the furious Brinkman's but they were smart enough not to take action obeying the dictate of Dr. Elliott. But if looks could kill Rafe would have been dead right then and there. Rafe was fearful but hopeful at the same time. He knew that of the 25 boys at Gate House, he had at least 12 in his corner. The problem was that the 12 were the youngest while those opposed were the older boys. It was an unfair fight right from the beginning, but Rafe thought good would prevail over evil even in an unfair fight. He entered the meeting confident his side would win.

The meeting was a close thing. Rafe and his friends presented their case against the Brinkman's while the older boys took the other side. In the end, it was a close vote, 13 to 12. The younger boys lost by one vote. Her strategy of divide and conquer had worked. The older boys had said, they were not that bad and the younger boys were exaggerating!

Rafe went up to his cubicle and lay down on his cot feeling defeated he couldn't even begin to imagine what terrible consequences their aborted revolt would bring. If his life had been shit before, he had a distinct feeling he was about to descend into hell. How could the authorities that ran such a wonderful place as Greer School act in favor of such a degenerate person as Brinkman? Of course, as a teenager, he didn't understand the primacy of the institution. If Greer School was home to disadvantaged children, it would be natural to think that the welfare of the children would be the primary consideration above all other things. But that idea came from a child's mind. In reality, the primary consideration was the survival of the school itself. If Brinkman had been an ordinary employee, she would have been fired that day. But seeing that she was the daughter of a beloved member of the staff created a difficult obstacle. No one wanted to believe that a founder's daughter was some sort of monster abusing the boys in her care. Just as the older boys had stated, it was all some sort of exaggeration made by a boy of questionable stability. After all, the staff knew they were never sure of what Rafe was capable of, and what he might do in any given situation. Protecting the school was what was important, after all, think of what good it did for so many children. No matter what the truth, this would hopefully be a minor blip in the history of the school. Rafe would graduate and things would get back to normal. One must protect one's turf, right? Otherwise, the whole façade could crumble taking everything with it.

From that point on things only got worse. The reign of terror intensified week by week. Brinkman continued to play the sweet loving housemother on visiting Sunday's completely snowing the parents. The boys were too fearful to complain to their parents now realizing if their parents didn't take action, they would be left completely vulnerable.

It is hard to put into words as to why the boys called it the reign of terror. No one was beaten to a pulp, hung, or dismembered. There were a few bloody noses and a few cases of being slapped silly but, the bad part was the boys lived in an almost completely hostile environment. They were conditioned to expect the worse and no one knew who would be the object of Brinkman's wrath. It didn't matter if it was you or your best friends that were being punished, the mental strain was equal. They were being abused and had no recourse. Things were bad, but they were about to take a quantum leap for the worse. What was coming would shake the house to its foundations.

It happened on a quiet summer afternoon a couple of months after the aborted revolution. The previous month Rafe's brother, Tom, and his classmates had graduated and left the school. Rafe's class was now entering its junior year. As usual, Rafe was avoiding the house and was spending the day down at the dam on Fairy Land stream which he and his buddies were constantly enlarging. By now it had a big pond ehind it and the boys had caught carp in the reservoir with which to stock it. You could say it was the meeting place for members of the resistance which would soon grow to include almost everyone.

Rafe was clearing brush and cutting down saplings to make the clearing around the pond larger. Max had gone back to the cottage with Fenton who wanted to take him woodchuck hunting. Rafe startled when he heard what had to be a rifle shot coming from the direction of Gate House. It didn't particularly faze him as it was Saturday and one of the older boys might be out hunting. One of the rights of passage at Greer was reaching 16 years old and being allowed to have a rifle. After taking the hunter safety course from the State Police the boys were allowed to hunt in various specially designated areas of the school.

Five minutes after hearing the shot, here came Raoul LaValle, one of Rafe's best friends, running like a bat out of hell. He plunged through the bush separating the stream from the huge field that lay beyond the tree line. He stopped in front of Rafe panting from his exertions. Between gasping for breath, he managed to say, "Come quick, back to the house, something's happened to Max." Immediately alarmed because of the speed at which Raoul had arrived, Rafe yelled over his shoulder as he took off running, "What! What's happened to Max?" He didn't bother to wait for a reply as he called for every once, of speed, his body could generate. He reached Gate House in about a minute and a half. As he approached, he saw a group of about 8 boys standing in a circle on the front lawn. Someone must have seen him coming and alerted the others because as he reached them the group parted revealing the shattered body of the beloved Max. As though struck by a giant fist Rafe dropped to his knees next to the body of his dog. He stared out with horrified eyes realizing something had torn Max apart. He began to yell with a cry that came from deep within his soul. "No! No! No! What happened? Who could have done this?" Blonde-haired Fenton Keenan with tears streaming down his cheeks said, "That fucking bitch Brinkman shot him. Rafe looked at Fenton, incredulous at what he had just heard. "Brinkman did this! Why would she do something so horrible?" Fenton turned away still crying, "She said he attacked her son." Rafe jumped to his feet exclaiming, "I'm going to kill that son-of-a-bitch". Before he could launch himself into the house the eight boys jumped him, knocked him down, and piled on. It looked like a rugby scrum with Rafe struggling and screaming at the bottom. Adrenalin poured into his blood steam giving him super strength, but the boy's total weight held him captive. George was whispering in his ear. "Think Rafe, Think! She's in there waiting for you to get a butcher knife or some other weapon and go charging in on her. She'll shoot you too, and claim self-defense. Think it out, and then act!" Rafe was struggling and snarling as he fought his friends. Some unholy thing was scratching and clawing to get out from deep within him. It was blind rage, and it lusted for Brinkman's blood. Soon the adrenalin high began to pass. He felt weak and drained. George was right; there would be time for revenge. You have to wait! George whispered again, "We'll let you up Rafe if you promise not to blow up and do something stupid. Just think it out is all we ask, OK?" Rafe stopped fighting the weight of bodies pressing him down into the grass and said, 'Ok George, let me up I promise I'll think it out."

In those few short minutes while pinned to the ground by his friends Rafe amazingly changed from the hunted to the hunter. All fear of Brinkman vanished as if it had never existed. The latent fear was replaced by a blood lust Rafe had never known existed. If it was the last thing he ever did, he would bring down this evil beast. When the boys released him, Rafe stood up and turned his mind to the task at hand. He asked Raoul to go up to his cubicle and bring down his extra blanket. The boys stayed gathered around cursing the miserable bitch of a house mother who in their eyes had just murdered one of them. To them, Max was better than they were; and beloved by all. Brinkman never realized it but at that moment the seeds of revolt were planted. From that point on there was never a question that she was the epitome of evil. One way or another she would pay. When Raoul showed up Rafe wrapped the bloody shattered body of his beloved pet in the blanket and picked him up. "Raoul, will you get a shovel and pickaxe from the garage and meet me at the dam." Raoul nodded in the affirmative and the boys formed a sad funeral procession as they carried Max down to Fairy Land stream.

Rafe spoke to George and told him he was staying down at the dam to think things out. If Brinkman asked where he was to tell her he would be back. He didn't say when he would be back only that he would return to Gate House.

Rafe sat on a log next to Max' grave trying to control his overwhelming grief. How could he be so stupid? He should have seen it coming. Unbeknownst to him, he couldn't have seen it coming. Decent people's minds never descend into the dark recesses where evil resides. It would never occur to a teenager that anyone could be that sick. That is the advantage they have over normal people they are capable of things that your mind can't even conceive of. Rafe had just read about the scumbag Joseph Stalin. This man was so despicable even fellow members of the Communist Party despised him. He once called his mother who had struggled to raise him; and get him educated after his Father had died early of alcoholism, an old whore. Another time while his daughter served his fellow Bolsheviks dinner, he asked aloud, "I wonder who's fucking her now?" Nice person, right? Then the Russians allowed him to take over their country where he proceeded to murder tens of millions of people. How about another modern scumbag; Adolph Hitler. He hated Jews and wanted to eradicate them from the face of the earth. When his army invaded Russia he had special operations units following behind his advancing army. Their job was to round up the Jews in the rear, and execute them by the thousands. They would dig trenches march the Jews into them, and then mow them down with machine guns. There was just one problem with this method, the troops doing the killing could only last for a week or two before going stark raving mad. So, rather than destroy his army murdering innocent Jews he came up with the idea of the gas chambers. In this way, he wouldn't be destroying his own men by having them shoot innocent civilians. The gas chambers were much more efficient in that they could kill millions of people without destroying the morale of their own troops. It wasn't as if people weren't aware of their lack of character, they just wouldn't stand up to evil. The same thing was going on at Gate House, just on a smaller scale.

Rafe sat on the log and considered his situation. As the shadows lengthened, he decided he needed to go to the chapel and pray. He needed God's help because frankly there wasn't any alternative. He believed that God's hand had shielded him from Brinkman during the terrible time at camp, and he believed God would protect him now.

The Chapel of the Child, as it was called, sat on the top of the ridgeline with the best view in the school of the surrounding countryside. It was a beautiful building situated on a perfect site. It was made of stone with a roof of slate and had a majestic bell tower shading the entrance. It even had a stained-glass window behind the alter giving the interior an atmosphere of peace. It was the only building in Greer School in which Rafe felt secure. At this point in time, he was very religious, because he believed only God could save him from this evil, certainly, there wasn't anyone else about to intercede. The front door of the chapel was usually locked but it had a side door called the choir entrance which was often left unlocked. As luck would have it the choir door was unlocked and Rafe carefully made his way into the darkened chapel. He didn't turn on any lights just felt his way into the chapel. There was a ¾ moon and its light showed through the stained-glass window, illuminating the chapel with a soft glow. Rafe sat down in his usual place and began to talk to God. Maybe this was only a delusion on his part, but he believed God would show him the way.

He prayed to God. She simply told him that she was near to winning and he needed help. It only took seconds for the answer to come. From outside the stained-glass window came a clear strong voice, it said, "Fear not I am with you" and a few seconds later came. "You are my Drawn Sword." No matter what the cost the evil one would have to be brought down. Of course, by being brought down Rafe meant BreMiller had to be killed. After all, she had tried to kill him down at camp and had now killed Max. There was no telling what evil was next on her agenda. Rafe felt he had the right to a preemptive strike. His dilemma was how to carry it out. He didn't have much going for him except an extraordinary intelligence that tended to focus on one thing at a time. Unfortunately for Brinkman, it was now focusing on her demise.

He knew if he made a big scene over her killing of Max the solution would probably be moving him from Gate House to Rapello. Not that he didn't want to get out of her clutches, but now he needed to be close to her to find the chink in her armor. She had to have a vulnerability and if he was nearby, he would find it. The other thing was that he had to give an academy award-winning acting performance to convince her that she had won and he was now beaten and subservient. That would take a herculean effort, as the truth was, he wanted to rip her throat out. How do you suppress your rage and act beaten?

If he didn't care about spending the rest of his life in prison, he could have easily blown Mrs. BreMiller to hell. The problem was, he could commit the act, but he couldn't get away with it. If he had wanted to, he could have taken her shotgun out of the unlocked gun locker and blown her to hell right in front of everyone. Sometimes as he lay in bed he would think, "If she only knew what was bearing down on her." You couldn't have something like the shooting of Max take place in a small insulated community without everyone hearing about it. When Mrs. Fink made her inquiries to Rafe he acted like he accepted Brinkman's story that the dog had attacked her year-old son even if there were no marks left on him. The administration of the school wanted the story to go away so when Rafe seemed to show little hostility over the shooting of his dog the matter was quickly shuffled to the backburner. Let's just say the matter was quickly dropped.

Rafe remained depressed but that only allowed him to play his part better; that being one of a defeated and subservient boy. Brinkman in her arrogance never guessed the truth; She finally thought she was gaining the upper hand. For his part, Rafe was searching for a way to send the evil bitch straight to hell. The best part was no one suspected what he had in mind.

It took him about a month to find her weakness. One of her requirements was that for every demerit you received over 10 per week, you had to work one hour in the house during the week. Of course, if you received 30 demerits which Rafe often did it would be impossible to work an extra 20 hours in the house. You just became a permanent slave. So, Rafe went to school, went to detention, and did his regular vocational job. The rest of the time he worked for Brinkman in Gate House doing whatever dirty jobs she could think up. It was while cleaning her living room that he discovered what could prove to be her fatal error. Brinkman's had their own separate living room located off the hallway between the dining room and the very large boy's living room. While the boys watched television in their living room the

Bremiller's had their little room where they could be alone. While cleaning her living room Rafe made the discovery. On achieving their sixteenth birthday the boys of Greer School were allowed to own a rifle. It was a rite of passage at Greer to get a rifle and be able to hunt on weekends. The rifles were kept in an army barracks-type locker, tall with a shelf at the top where ammunition was stored. It was supposed to be kept locked at all times with a padlock. On this particular day, Rafe found the gun locker unlocked. He really couldn't believe his eyes for he was thinking "How stupid can she be". Even after the shooting of Max, she thought she was invulnerably, Rafe's acting performance had worked and she didn't realize the grave danger that such a lack of deliberation produced.

Seeing the unlocked gun locker was a light going off in his head. Now the question was how often does she make this mistake? From that point whenever no one was around Rafe would poke his head around the door of her living room to see if the gun locker was indeed locked. He found over a few months that it was unlocked more than half the time. A plan began to materialize. He needed to catch her alone in the house on a day on which the gun locker had been left unlocked. The Brinkman's were using the job of house parents at Greer as a way to get started in life. Although Mrs. Brinkman didn't receive a large salary part of her compensation was free room and board. Mr. Brinkman worked for a large corporation in Poughkeepsie and the setup allowed them to bank most of his salary. Rafe had been watching the Brinkman's like a hawk ever since the killing of Max. He learned that maybe twice a month Mr. Brinkman would go to work overtime on Saturdays and be gone all afternoon. Rafe didn't want to kill Mr. Brinkman whom he considered just an enforcer for his evil wife. He simply wanted to cut off the head of the serpent.

The plan was very simple. On weekends the house parents were given a break as the students spent Saturday and Sunday afternoons on different activities. In the winter they could be sleigh riding or ice skating. The summer usually provided swimming or hiking or organized sports. You had the option of spending the afternoon in the library if that suited you better.

Rafe knew the lay of the land at Greer as well as anyone but he checked the Rapello pond very closely. The pool at Rapello had been originally built for swimming but the runoff from the farm had caused pollution. Now the pond, which remained frozen most of the winter, was only used for ice skating. After checking closely Rafe determined that one could not see the front driveway of Rapello from the pond area. This was critical for Rafe's ability to leave the Rapello area without being seen. He would go ice skating and sign in. During the first 20 minutes of skating, he would make sure to skate with one of his old friends and engage them in a conversation he could easily remember. This was to reinforce his alibi that he was indeed at the pool skating when inevitably the detectives began checking. He did not doubt that in the end if anything were to happen to Brinkman he would end up as a prime suspect. Of course, it's one thing to suspect someone and it's quite another to put them on the scene of the crime. The hit would take approximately 30 minutes and it was unlikely that anyone would miss him from skating for that amount of time. He would leave the pool to use the restroom about 20 minutes into the 1 ½ hour skating session. He would sit off by himself and take off his skates then make his way up the hill to Rapello. Instead of going into Rapello, he would sneak across the driveway where he would be invisible to anyone down at the pond and use the wood line leading down to Fairy Land stream as cover. Once he reached the stream which originated from the runoff from Rapello Pond, he would be off to the races. The plan was to follow Fairy Land stream for about 300 yards until it passed 200 yards behind Gate House. Then still using the forest for cover he would make his way up to the rear of the cottage. There were 200 feet of open space between the edge of the forest and the rear door of Gate House. This wasn't a big problem as the big garage behind the house would give cover. If he saw anyone the mission would be aborted. Upon reaching Gate House he would enter through the rear door into the kitchen. There he would take off his coat and leave it in the kitchen (no reason to risk blood splatter), and go up the fire escape to check the upper floors. The fire escape had access to four upstairs rooms, the Bathroom, Little Dorm, Big Dorm, and the Kingdom. He'd check all three and make sure no one was there. Then he would sneak through the bathroom and make his way to Big Dorm through the hallway. This was the only sticky part of his plan. If Brinkman had the door to her apartment open he would be exposed for a few short seconds as he made his way to Big

Dorm. However, if she wasn't sitting at her little table by the door, she wouldn't see him. He had to make sure the cottage was empty except for his intended victim. If her door was closed, which it usually wasn't, that created another problem. He had to be able to get to her. He had a solution for that too, just in case. After checking the upper floors, he would check the rest of the house. If by some chance Brinkman was downstairs in her living room and saw him that would just be a reason to abort. He'd make the excuse that he had forgotten a book he needed to return to the library later. If the house was clear he would quickly proceed to the gun locker, take out her shotgun and load it with two shells of double ought buck. Yes, he would kill her with the same gun she had used on Max. Poetic Justice!

With her apartment door opened he would simply walk in and without hesitation blast her to hell. If her door was closed, he had placed an empty bucket in the bathroom which he would proceed to roll down the stairs. The noise would bring Brinkman out to see what had made the crash, and when she opened her door she would be as good as dead.

Once the deed was done, he'd proceed back down the stairs, remove the spent shells, replace the shotgun in the gun locker, and then lock it with the padlock. He would leave by the rear door picking up his coat, and within seconds he would be in the tree line heading back to Rapello Pool. Along the way, he would have a paper bag cached, with a clean set of shirts, pants, socks, and gloves. He would change his clothes and bury the ones he had been wearing in a previously dug hole. He expected the whole operation to take 30 minutes. He would then go to the bathroom at Rapello and return to ice skating. In order to catch him, they would have to put him on the scene or have physical evidence and he doubted they'd have either.

The day finally came when all the pieces came together. Mr. Brinkman went to work on Saturday, the gun locker was unlocked, and the Rapello Pool was frozen over for ice skating. Rafe had even done a dress rehearsal to time the run from Rapello to Gate House using the route he planned.

Rafe went to Rapello and put the plan into action. He skated around the pool talking to Pat Monza a girl he had known since Plum and had witnessed the incident when he had run into the hornet's nest and been stung about 30 times. They skated and talked about other things for about 20 minutes. Then Rafe skated off by himself for a few minutes before he took off his skates and headed for Rapello. No one was paying any attention to him meaning so far all was well. He went into Rapello and went to the restroom downstairs. He only checked it to see if there was anything unusual, he might be asked about later. Within a minute Rafe walked out the front door and began to walk slowly towards the tree line that would shield him from the skaters and staff at the pool. Once he was behind the tree line, he set off running at his best speed. It only took about 1 minute to reach the trail to Fairy Land Stream. In another minute he was walking alongside the stream to a position where it passed a few hundred yards behind Gate House. He cautiously approached the house and quietly entered through the rear door into the kitchen. Took off his coat and laid it on a table. It took another minute to check the lower house to make sure it was empty. He checked to see if the gun locker was still unlocked. Then he made his way up the fire escape to check the dorms. He observed that BreMiller's apartment door was closed which meant he would have to roll the bucket down the stairs to lure her out. He very cautiously made his way back down the fire escape and into the Brinkman's private living room. He opened the gun locker, took out the Brinkman's shotgun, and loaded it with double-ought buck. He stood there ready to kill, feeling fully justified. It was then that the awful realization hit him. He couldn't kill her like this. For one thing, her little toddler would come walking out and probably walk around in the pool of blood surrounding his mother. It would also be the end of Greer School. He could imagine the headlines. "House Mother Gunned down at Greer School!" Even if he could get away with the crime, the school would be destroyed. He stood there like a deer in the headlights, frozen in place. Finally, reality set in and he knew that if he wasn't going through with his plan, he had better put the shotgun back in the gun closet. He opened the shotgun, took out the two shells, and replaced the shotgun and shells in the locker. He quickly and quietly left Gate House and followed the plan just like heally gone through with it. On the way out he picked up his coat from the kitchen and instead of changing his clothes and burying the ones he was wearing he simply picked up the paper bag with his change of clothes. There was no need to hurry but he did anyway. If he changed his mind this could serve as a dress rehearsal.

Rafe spent the rest of the day in the library deeply depressed. He now understood why evil has an advantage. Those who are evil have no rules by which they abide. They don't think they answer to a higher authority. In effect, they think on this earth they are God. The rest of us find ourselves playing an unfair game. Not too much different than playing with a Card Shark. With you playing by the rules while they cheat, who do you expect to win? The answer is obvious, you lose.

As he sat there Rafe was thinking, so, "What's the answer? I can't just let her get away with killing Max. I can't go around acting like I'm her new lap dog." Coincidently he had just read a book on Sir Francis Drake. When England was facing the Spanish Armada, Drake had led a squadron of ships into the Harbor of Cadiz and burned 1/3 of the Armada ships. Drake commented that he had, "Singed the beard of the King of Spain." Well in a manner of speech, Brinkman's beard could be singed also. Keep in mind that Rafe was 16 years old and still thought like a teenager. He thought, "What is the best way to embarrass Brinkman behind her back. How can I make her a laughing stock to the resistance? What is the worst offense you could commit at Greer?" It didn't take him long to figure that out, Raid the girl's dormitory in the middle of the night. In the very religious atmosphere under which the students lived this would be a very serious event. Of course, that depended on whether or not you were caught. Brinkman thought of herself as an absolute monarch and no one would dare to carry out such a raid in view of the consequences if caught. A lot of the blame would fall on her since after all she was responsible for her charges, and their behavior. He would have to be careful and only involve those he could absolutely trust.

The raid would be fairly simple to carry off. Rafe already knew that Brinkman never did bed checks after midnight. That was most likely the hour she retired for the night and she wouldn't want to get up at 2 or 3 A.M. and venture into the freezing cold dorms just to see if everyone was where they were supposed to be. Actually, it was just laziness on her part, not unlike leaving the gun locker unlocked.

Ledge Cottage was the target because the girls at Ledge lived in individual rooms with two girls in a room. Crest, the other Cottage for older girls was set up like Gate House with the dorms divided into cubicles that led to a central corridor. Ledge also had a central corridor but it had individual rooms on either side and the rooms had doors. Rafe's sister Angela lived at Ledge and she provided the information Rafe required.

His plan was simple; He would leave Gate House at 2:30 A.M. and be back in his bed no later than 3:30 A.M. One hour was ample time considering he was only going to be in Ledge Cottage about 30 seconds. Rafe's mother had given him a medallion that resembled the Blue Max which was a German metal for bravery. Rafe's mother was in the costume jewelry business and Rafe had seen one of these Blue Max look-alikes at her office. Everyone identified Rafe with his metal which he always wore. He was going to leave his Blue Max hanging on the doorknob of one of the girl's rooms at Ledge. When the girls woke up in the morning, they would find his Blue Max and know he had been there in the middle of the night. He chose the room occupied by Darby Sievers and Karen Townsend on which to leave the medallion. Darby was his best friend George's sister, and Karen and Rafe were good friends. He had to be careful that the girls on whose door he would leave the Blue Max could be trusted and not go spreading what he had done to the general population. "Loose lips sink ships" was what he was thinking. He didn't want to carry out the raid, and then be caught because someone couldn't keep their mouth shut. Something like this would spread like wildfire in the insular environment of Greer. After all, there is nothing like a good rumor to liven things up. Unfortunately, the rumor would eventually reach Brinkman's ear.

Late one night Rafe got up and left Gate House via the fire escape and made the run to Ledge in about 20 minutes. He could have done it in 5 minutes but stealth was a major consideration. He entered Ledge via the fire escape and proceeded four doors down the corridor and placed the Blue Max on Darby and Karen's door. Seconds later he was down the fire escape and heading back to Gate House. It had gone off perfectly and couldn't have been easier.

There was just one problem. When Darby and Karen discovered the Blue Max they didn't believe Rafe had actually placed it on their doorknob. When Darcy returned the medallion the next day at school she said, "We don't believe you left it on our door. Karen, and I think you had your sister Angela put it there so you could impress us." Rafe was undeterred. He knew that often, the best-laid plans backfire. He knew what he had to do. He would wait two weeks and repeat the raid only this time he'd go into their room and wake them. There would be no doubt after that!

Two weeks later Rafe repeated the operation only this time instead of leaving the Blue Max on the doorknob he stealthily made his way into Darcy and Karen's room and with great trepidation woke Darby. He was afraid she might scream when he awakened her but she didn't. She simply sat up, looked at him, and said, "Oh my god it's you!" He put his finger to his lips indicating the need for quiet and answered, "Yup, it's me and there can be no question about it this time." Darby looked at him, her eyes wide open, and said, "I can't believe you did it. Do you know how much trouble you'll be in if you get caught?" Rafe laughed and replied, "Darby I'm in so much trouble that one more infraction, no matter how egregious, won't make any difference." When Darby asked Rafe why he was doing it he told her he was making Brinkman look like a fool. He asked Darby to wake Karen since he didn't want to risk startling her. When both girls were awake, they chatted for a few minutes with the girls being more than a little excited about the situation. Rafe told them if he were somehow to be caught, he would say they knew nothing about his plan. In a whisper, Rafe explained to the two girls not to tell anyone about what was happening unless they were members of the group that hung out at the Beaver Dam. If Brinkman found out she would make his life even more difficult even if she couldn't prove he'd been sneaking out at night. He didn't want to get caught, because of what someone did, or said. He explained that he was going to reignite resistance by defying Brinkman even if she was unaware of what he had done.

It worked very well as Darby told George the next day and George told everyone else. Soon the boys would walk around Gate House and whenever they passed another member of the resistance, they would laugh out loud. It was juvenile but they had to do something. Although Brinkman didn't find out exactly what happened she began to hear rumors. Someone was sneaking out at night. One evening after study hall Brinkman came into the dining room where the boys were studying and Mrs. Brinkman said, "I know one of you has been sneaking out at night! I know who you are and if I catch you, you'll wish you were never born. She stood there staring at the boys while Rafe was thinking, "Damn, how could she have found out?" She then went on to say, "Right now the perpetrator is sitting here with a smirk on his face. Well, boy; you better wipe it off your face if you know what's good for you." Rafe looked around and couldn't believe his eyes. She was talking about Larry Von Radics one of the youngest of the resisters, and one who thought of Rafe as a big brother. "Shit, Larry is trying to copycat me and has blabbed to the wrong person," thought Rafe. Even though Brinkman had no proof, Larry was put on bounds for a full month. This meant no movies, no dances, or any other kind of activity.

It was at this point that Rafe decided that the boat needed to be rocked again. By this time, he had lost all fear of Brinkman and only wanted her removed at all costs. He didn't need to be pushed any further but the final confrontation was imminent. After study hall, she called him into her private living room. As he entered, she said, "Close the door and stand here in front of me." Rafe did as he was told wondering what the bitch had on her mind. She got directly to the point. "Rafe I know you're the leader of the opposition to my authority. Larry would never be sneaking out at night without you being involved somehow. Therefore, you are being put on bounds for a month along with your protégé. Now, what do you think of that?"

"Are you telling me that you can put me on bounds for just the suspicion that I'm somehow involved?" She glared at him and answered, 'That's about the size of it Rafe, I told you before that I have complete control of you and that I was going to bend you to my will." Rafe smiled at his tormentor and said, "Yes, and I said, "You'll eat shit first!" The evil smile never left her face as she responded, "Yes you did and it cost you didn't it" Rafe knew what she meant and he felt the rage rising from deep within him. Now he stared into her eyes like an enraged lion about to charge. He finally said, "By that, you mean the killing of Max, right?" The tension between them was extreme. If Rafe had the shotgun in his hands now, he'd blast her to hell. She continued her cat-and-mouse game as she added, "I warned you not to cause me trouble but you never listen, do you?" Throwing caution to the winds, as the only emotion he was feeling was rage, Rafe said, "Killing Max was a big mistake on your part because now I have nothing left to lose. I now know you're the lowest form of life ever to crawl upon the surface of the earth. You have to answer for Max, and you will, if it's the last thing I ever do."

"I'd think about that Rafe because it may indeed be, the last thing you ever do."

Rafe in a very low menacing voice said, 'Your days are numbered, as far as I'm concerned you can put me on bounds permanently, but if I was you, I'd watch my ass." With that Rafe turned and walked out.

War had been declared and now Rafe needed a strategy. The next afternoon Rafe walked down to the Beaver Dam and sat watching the Beavers at work. This was a place Rafe and Max had loved. Max loved to chase the beavers but he also hated water so his great fun was chasing them off dry land into their lake. Now Max was gone, and nothing could bring him back. Rafe contemplated the situation. He had already decided he couldn't kill her, but now he was determined to rock the boat even if it capsized. He at last had the upper hand although Brinkman hadn't realized it yet. When he had told her he had nothing to lose he was correct. He didn't have anything to lose, but she did. She could kill him but that was it. Rafe had learned about terror the first year at camp. He realized that two could play the same terror game. He may not be able to kill Brinkman, but he was going to terrorize her. He had been pushed over the edge and now like a cornered animal, he would fight.

The plan he devised was simple. The next time the stupid bitch left the gun locker unlocked he would take his rifle and run away. On his 16th birthday, Rafe had received as his birthday present a Marlin 17-shot semi-automatic .22 Rifle. It was sitting relatively unused in the gun locker. Yes, he had been terrorized at camp, but now he had the ultimate equalizer. He would run away from Gate House but he wouldn't leave the campus. Once she realized he had his rifle with him she would reflect back on their last conversation and realize that Rafe wanted revenge for Max. She would then know he was stalking her. Then she'd know fear! She had a lot to lose, namely a husband, a child, as well as her reputation. Let the authorities try to deal with this mess especially when his mother showed up demanding to know what happened to her son. Rafe had never wanted to involve his mother since she already had bought into the idea that Rafe was undisciplined and defiant. He had never wanted to be a burden to his mother, but this was war and he needed to finally call upon his family. His mother could be very nice, but she could also be hell on wheels if provoked. Rafe's mom was the most ferocious person he knew, and if Rafe told her the truth about Brinkman His mother would kill her in 15 minutes. Then his mother would end up in prison, and he'd be parentless. One of Rafe's first childhood memories was his mother taking a big butcher knife and placing it against his Father's chest and saying, "If you ever lay a hand on me again, I'll stick this right through you, and she had meant it. If the school didn't have an acceptable explanation as to what was going on, he knew his mother would call in the State Police. After all, her troubled son was running around in the woods with a rifle and no one knew what he had in mind.

Consider poor Brinkman knowing he was out there stalking her and how much he hated her. His rifle could fire 17 shots as fast as he could pull the trigger. If he wanted to, he could walk right into Gate House and wreak havoc at any minute of the day or night. She also knew he could run like the wind and was as stealthy as a Fox. If he was unconcerned about the consequences, it was because he held all of the cards.

It was the perfect time of the year for such an activity. It was early May and the leaves were coming out adding much cover to anyone hiding in the forest. It wouldn't be very cold at night either since Rafe would be sleeping in a tent. At the time Rafe was working in the school commissary and had access to the storeroom where all of the canned goods were kept. He would leave the window in the back of the storeroom unlocked so he could enter in the dead of night, and take whatever food he needed.

He didn't have long to wait. A week after devising his plan the gun locker was left unlocked. Rafe could never get over Brinkman's arrogance in not realizing her danger. She eventually would, but by then it would be too late.

He had packed a tent in his duffle bag along with some spare clothing and was just waiting for opportunity to knock. He wasn't planning to be gone for weeks only 3 or 4 days. He didn't want to upset his mother more than he had to, but long enough for her to raise hell.

The afternoon he found the gun locker open he took his rifle and his supplies and left. Keeping to the woods he made his way to camp and then followed the stream to the far northern corner of the school property. He pitched his tent while it was still light and when darkness fell, he returned to the campus. He knew the rifle was going to be a big problem once it was discovered missing so he took it with him. About midnight he made his way to Gate House and hid the rifle behind a loose board in the garage. He didn't really need the rifle since he didn't intend to use it, he only wanted Brinkman to know he had it.

When Rafe didn't show up for work at the commissary later that afternoon the search for him began. No one had any idea what was actually transpiring. When Rafe was still missing at 5 P.M. when he should be delivering food from the central kitchen to the cottages people began to get concerned. When he wasn't home for study hall Brinkman was forced to call Dr. Elliott to report him missing. or one could say absent without leave. At this point, no one had any idea as to what was going on. By 8 P.M. Dr. Elliott was forced to call Rafe's Mother to ask if by some chance he was home in New York. When his mother found out that he was missing she immediately picked up her sister Mary and drove the 85 miles to the school.

By this time Brinkman had begun to think about the implications of Rafe running away. She remembered their conversation the previous week and how Rafe had said, "You have to answer for Max." She immediately checked the gun locker and to her chagrin found his rifle missing. She then began to get the picture. She was being hunted! At first, she held out hope that by now Rafe was 100 miles away and would never be seen again, but that only lasted until the next day. Rafe had left on a Thursday and he only intended to be gone till Sunday and that was only because he knew how worried his mother would be. If it wasn't for that he would have stayed out in the woods for a month or two. In the end, the only way they would ever capture him would be with bloodhounds. There was nothing to say that he had to stay on the school property either. He could camp 5 miles away and come back each day.

The next afternoon after having spent a pleasant afternoon in the woods he intercepted Karen and Darcy on the way home from the school. He came walking out of the woods on the path that led from Crest to Ledge Cottages. Needless to say, they were shocked by his sudden and unexpected appearance. "Rafe what are you doing here?" asked Darcy. "Everyone is looking all over for you." Rafe smiled at his friends and said, "Girls I have an agenda and I'm not coming back until I carry it out. I'd like for you to do me a favor, tell my sister that I'm still here and to let my mother know I'm all right. Then tell your housemother that you've seen me."

With that said Rafe walked off into the forest. The word quickly spread that Rafe was still on the school property. It didn't take long for the word to reach Brinkman either. She now realized she had a very big problem. When her husband returned home from work that night, she took him up to their apartment and told him of her concerns. "Charles, that little bastard Rafe Hawkins has been seen on the campus. He's still here and he's armed. I think he's going to try to kill us." Mr. BreMiller stared at his wife in disbelief the said, "Try to kill us! Why would you ever think that he'd want to do that." Becoming somewhat agitated she said, "Because he hates my guts. He blames me for shooting his damn mongrel. He told me just last week that I had to answer for Max. He's always hated me, look at all the trouble he's caused since we got here. He went to Dr. Elliott to get us fired and he almost succeeded. He can come walking into Gate House anytime he desires and gun us down. What am I supposed to do? Carry a shotgun around with me all day? His fellow insurgents would make me a laughing stock. We can't leave, we can't hide, and we can't catch him. So would you mind telling me what we're supposed to do?" Charles BreMiller had never seen his wife that agitated before. He put his arm around her shoulder and quietly said, "We'll; just have to be careful, keep to the apartment, keep the shotgun handy, he's probably only bluffing." Jean BreMiller practically spat, back her response, "Jesus Christ! Charles, you just don't get it. He's coming for me!"

Now the cat knew terror. The mouse was coming for her, except it was an armed mouse!

Of course, other events of consequence were taking place When Rafe's mother learned that he was still at Greer instead of heading for New York and that he was armed she called the State Police. Dr. Elliott had not wanted the police involved because of the school's reputation. However, Mrs. Hawkins knew her son's temperament, primarily because it was just like her own, and knew that if he was out in the woods with a rifle someone was in trouble. She wanted the State Police to find him before he did something very bad.

That was Friday so Rafe figured he'd let the pot boil until Sunday afternoon. That night he snuck into Main House and had a dinner of leftovers in the kitchen. Instead of finding his way back to his campsite in the middle of the night, he slept in the cab of the dump truck which was parked behind the cannery.

On Saturday morning Rafe made his way through the field of tall grass between Marcy Cottage and Gate House. He lay in the grass behind the stone gate where he could observe the front door of Gate House about 150 feet away. He watched the comings and goings and even saw a State Police car pull into the driveway. Two troopers exited their patrol car and entered Gate House. About 45 minutes later they reemerged and drove away. Rafe watched for about three hours. Then when by luck someone came down the Main Road, none other than his friend Larry. When he got close enough, Rafe whistled and got up and waved to him. Larry recognized Rafe and scaled the fence and ran over to his location.

Rafe waved him down saying, "Get down Larry, I don't want anyone to see us." Larry dropped down in the tall grass next to Rafe. "Rafe smiled and asked, "So, what's going on Larry?" It was obvious that Larry was excited to see Rafe as he could hardly contain himself.

Larry asked, "Rafe, what in the hell are you doing? Everything is in an uproar. Brinkman is hiding in her apartment with the shades drawn, your mother is here and so are the State Police. Everyone knows you're here but no one knows where. Then there is the rumor that you have your rifle with you, is that true?"

Rafe chuckled trying to suppress a laugh and said, "Yes, I have my rifle and I don't intend to go anywhere."

"What's this all about?"

"It's a declaration of war Larry. I want Brinkman to think that her days are numbered.

"Well, she's in hiding so that's working.",

"Look Larry I need your help, and it is vitally important that you don't tell another living soul what I'm about to tell you

"Ok?"

"You know I'd never let you down Rafe. What is it you want me to do?"

"First do not tell anyone what I'm telling you because I don't want Brinkman to get wind of it and then use it against me when I come back in."

"Ok, Rafe I won't tell anyone." Not even George or any of the other resisters, understood?

"I get it Rafe absolutely no one."

"Good here's the deal and you are going to be the only one that knows. Last week she put you on bounds for a month because she got the word you were sneaking out at night. Where you made your mistake was that you told someone and the word got back to her. You may not have told the person who turned you in but unfortunately, the word gets around. Minutes later she called me into her office and accused me of somehow inspiring you and then put me on bounds for a month also. She had no proof against either you or me, but that never stopped her. During my meeting with her, I dropped all pretenses and told her that she was going to answer for Max. The reason I'm out here is to scare the shit out of her. I'll let myself be caught tomorrow only because of my mother, but when I come back it will be all-out warfare. Now here is what I need you to do. Go into Gate House and knock on her apartment door. If she answers tell her that you saw me a couple of minutes ago out by the gate. If she asks you if I had my rifle with me tell her that you didn't see it but that I said it was nearby. Hopefully, she will ask why I had run away and if she does. tell her I said, "someone has to answer for Max. That's all I want you to tell her. Don't elaborate; the primary reason I want you to talk to her is so that she knows I'm nearby and that I want to collect on a debt."

"Ok Rafe I get it; you just want to scare the shit out of her, right?"

"That's right Larry my running away is just an exercise in counter-terrorism. Let's see how she handles it when the hunter becomes the hunted!"

"I knew you were up to something when you disappeared on Thursday, I can't believe that you're the one after her, and not the reverse."

"She's had her way long enough Larry and now it's our turn. Keep in mind that if something happens to me that you now hold the upper hand with 20 of the 25 Gate House boys firmly in the resistance. Next month when the seniors graduate the count is invariably going to become 25 to 0. We failed the last time because the older boys couldn't see her for what she is. There is safety in numbers and now the numbers are on our side. The administration can't continue to turn a blind eye toward the situation at Gate House with all of these incidents cropping up. I'm out here rocking the boat and when I come in tomorrow, I'll rock it some more."

"Ok Rafe I'm off, I'll tell her exactly what you told me to say and no more."

"Good, then if you get a chance, meet me where the trail from Daisy intersects Fairy Land Stream in about an hour. Make sure you're not followed. Take your time and watch your back trail."

"Will do Rafe, and good luck."

Larry ran off towards Gate House and disappeared into the basement door. Rafe stealthily made his way around Gate House and followed Fairy Land Stream to the rendezvous point. About an hour later Larry showed up grinning from ear to ear. Rafe asked, "Well how did it go?"

"When I knocked on the door to her apartment, she answered holding her shotgun. When I told her I had seen you out by the gate she turned white as a sheet and rushed to the front window and peeked out at the gate to see if she could see you. She didn't ask why you had run away but she did ask if you said anything about what you were doing out by the gate. I told her you said someone had to answer for Max."

"What did she do then?"

"She was so upset she slammed the door in my face."

Rafe laughed and told Larry he had carried out his mission perfectly. Rafe bid Larry farewell and headed for the far side of the Beaver Dam which was actually off the school property. He spent the rest of that Saturday afternoon watching the beavers doing their thing. Tomorrow would be Sunday and he would let himself be caught and then face the music. If it hadn't been for his mother and the stress, he had put her under he would have stayed out in the forest for another two weeks. In reality, he had made his case. This was the 2nd time he had created an uproar over conditions at Gate House.

The staff could avoid taking action but, in the end, the paper trail remains. Each such act of defiance added up until eventually, the dam would burst. Rafe didn't know how long the administration would protect Brinkman but he knew if the rebellion continued, she would fall. If she hadn't been the daughter of one of the school's founders, she would have been fired two years ago. He made up his mind that tomorrow he would face the music.

That evening he moved his tent into the pine forest outside of camp. The camp was one of the places where the search for him was concentrated. For a couple of days he had heard voices calling his name in the area around the camp. The next afternoon he would allow himself to be caught.

Sunday afternoon he observed Mike and Bernie searching the camp and calling his name. As they walked back up the dirt road leading from the camp to the main campus Rafe came walking out of the forest as if unaware of their presence. They quickly took off in pursuit and Rafe pretended he had injured his ankle and they quickly overtook him. He didn't resist when they grabbed him and he made it look like he was defeated. After all, they were almost twice his size and resistance was futile. As they led him back up the road, he was laughing to himself that if he had wanted to get away, he would already be 500 yards ahead of them. There was no way anyone at Greer School could run him down. On the way to Main House, he was contemplating what he was going to say about his outrageous behavior. He had one story for the State Police, another for his mother, and a third for Dr. Elliott.

He was turned over to Dr. Elliott in his office at Main House. His Mother and the State Police were found and advised that Rafe had been caught. Rafe sat in a chair in Dr. Elliott's office waiting, and acting subdued. The state police arrived first and asked what he was doing running around in the woods with a rifle. Rafe explained that he wanted to run away but knew if he made it to New York, he would be brought back. So, he decided to live in the woods for a couple of weeks to show his contempt for the school. When they asked about the rifle he told them he brought it along to shoot rabbits and squirrels to eat. He was surprised that they believed his bullshit explanation but they were unaware of the history of what had gone on previously. When his mother arrived, she exclaimed, Rafe, How could you do this to me?" She kept repeating it over and over and Rafe was getting a little annoyed. He was thinking, "Right Mom, you marry my Father who you can't get along with. When you throw him out you put me in this school and leave me without even saying goodbye. Trying to make things easier for you I put up with years of torment and then when I finally take action it comes down to "How could you do this to me." Rafe sat there thinking, "This world is sort of a twisted joke."

When his mother asked him why he had run away he told her that he didn't think he would be able to pass the state regents examination at the end of the year ensuring he would pass from the 11th to the 12th grade. If left-back he would have to spend another year at Greer which he refused to do. Then the most miraculous words came out of his mother's mouth, "Rafe, do you want to come home?" At first, he thought he had heard her wrong so he didn't answer. So, she repeated her question, "Well do you want to come home?"

After being prompted a second time his answer was swift. "Do you mean like right now, in the next hour when you leave for New York I can come with you?"

"Yes, however, you'll have to go to summer school to make up for the year you're not going to complete. You may even graduate in January of 1960 instead of the spring of 1959, but if you're willing to do that you can come home today."

His answer was instantaneous, "Yes, I'll do it. I'll go to summer school or whatever else I have to." Talking about being overjoyed, Rafe couldn't believe his good luck. How could fortune turn so quickly? One moment he's faced with fighting for his life, and the next comes the reprieve. More than that, he was going home.

With that settled the State Police were satisfied. If there had been a problem at Greer School it had just been solved. They said goodbye to Dr. Elliott and Rafe's Mother and Aunt and left. Rafe's Mother said she had to go to Ledge Cottage and tell Rafe's sister Angela that she was taking Rafe home. She told Rafe she would be back for him in about half an hour.

This left Rafe alone with Dr. Elliott. As soon as his mother left the office Dr. Elliott still seated behind his large Oak desk asked, "Why did you do it Rafe. What were you really up to?"

Dr. Elliott was a very moral man who commanded a great deal of respect. He was another person at the school beloved by the children. However, like most people, he couldn't deal with evil. Most people when confronted by evil will shy away from it. If they can, they'll just push it out of their lives, or they'll rationalize and pretend it's not that bad. Throughout history, evil has been allowed to run its course and triumph. There is an old saying from the Englishman, Edmond Burke that goes. "The only thing it takes for evil to triumph is for good men to do nothing." In effect, history was repeating itself. A year earlier Rafe had told Dr. Elliott what was going on at Gate House. Since that time Max had been killed and things had gotten much worse. Yet here was Dr. Elliott asking him why he was doing what he was doing when it was so obvious.

Rafe knew the urgency of the current crisis was caused not by his running away, but by his running away with his rifle. The rifle was an equalizer and was a weapon of death. It wasn't a toy and whoever wielded it had to be taken seriously. No one knew what was on Rafe's mind when he ran away with the rifle. They only knew that if they guessed wrong mayhem might be the result. That is why he was getting out of Greer School. His mother realized that her son might be about to get himself into big trouble and was simply removing him from the situation.

Rafe looked at Dr. Elliott and replied, "A year ago I told you what was going on at Gate House and I wasn't believed. What I told you was the truth and it has since gotten much worse. Look what she did in retaliation, she killed Max.

Dr. Elliott responded to this by saying, "Rafe we thought that you were accepting of her story that Max had attacked her son!"

"Well, I was just acting because I wanted to stay at Gate House to get retribution. My running away with my rifle was part of that. Do you want to know what I was doing for the last 4 days? I was stalking her, making her believe I was going to show up at any second and send her to hell." And, if you think it's over, with all due respect, let me give you some advice. It's not over. Gate House is like a volcano with the pressure building internally; when it blows it's likely to take the whole school with it. Your choice is to remove the evil or face the consequences. I'm a Mom Morton Boy, I've been raised to stand for what is right, and now I'm done.

Rafe didn't wait for an answer he simply said, "Goodbye Dr. Elliott, then he turned and walked out. A minute later he was standing out front of Main House waiting for his mother to pick him up. He was elated and felt like jumping up and down and screaming with joy. He felt as though a huge weight had been lifted off his shoulders and he was finally free.

Years later a great film would be made called The *Shawshank Redemption*. Near the end, the central character escapes from prison by crawling through what is described as ¾ of a mile of unimaginable filth. Emerging from the sewer pipe he stands in a stream while a driving rain washes him clean. With lightning flashing in the stormy sky, he raises his arms towards heaven like one beseeching God. That's how Rafe felt while standing out in front of Main House. Rafe stood there for about 20 minutes, grinning like an idiot until he saw his mother's 1954 red and black Studebaker slowly coming up the circular drive.

When the car stopped next to him, he got in saying, "We need to stop at Gate House and pick up my clothes and stuff." A couple of minutes later they were parked in the Gate House driveway and the boys came running out to greet him. Everyone but Larry had been kept in the dark as to what his original motivation was. Now he told his friends what had happened. First, he told them in a few minutes he would be leaving Greer never to return. This caused an "Oh No, this is shit" reaction. He told his friends he had run away to rock the boat and scare the shit out of Brinkman. Furthermore, he had again told Dr. Elliott that Brinkman was a tyrant and had to be fired. He added that he doubted that Dr. Elliott would fire her, but that the paper trail had been created which would eventually lead to her downfall. The solution was simple just continue what had been done up to this point; stick together and resist. He told his dear friends that the way to win was when the next inevitable incident occurred, to simply walk out of Gate House and refuse to return until she's fired. If the school refuses, tell them you're going to the press to tell them you're being abused at Greer School. That will leave them with a simple choice, save Brinkman, or save the school!"

That being said, he retrieved his Rifle from the garage and placed it in the trunk of his mother's car. He asked Fenton to go up and get the key to the clothing room from Brinkman so he could pick up his stuff. He went to his cubicle and took his duffle bag and proceeded to the clothing room and emptied his locker. His friends gathered around trying to be of assistance. In a way, it was quite sad. He had grown up with these boys and they were like brothers to him, but as they all knew, things were spinning out of control.

Rafe said goodbye to his friends on the front lawn hugging them and shaking their hands, then without further ado, he climbed into the rear seat of the Studebaker and awaited the moment that had been almost 10 years in coming. The car was put into gear and slowly made its way down the driveway to Main Road, then turned right. In seconds they were through the Gate and Rafe glanced to his left at the grassy triangle which was his first memory of the school. The sign was still there; Greer School a Children's Community! The car picked up speed and although he was sad to lose his friends, he couldn't help but think, "Free at last." The nightmare was now in the rearview mirror!

It's been said that the best trip is the one that leads to home and for 16-year-old Rafe that 2 ½ half hour ride was the best he would ever take. He knew his mother was very unhappy with him as she hardly spoke a word to him the whole way home. She had fallen for Brinkman's propaganda that he was just a defiant teen who could not take discipline. So, in effect, he left Greer School in disgrace and his mother now thought of him as a Black Sheep. This hardly brought him down from the high he was on. He thanked God for interceding on his behalf. He knew there was no other explanation for his surviving that ten-year ordeal. He recalled Paradise Lost and the part that ended, "To those proud towers, too swift destruction doomed". It was too bad, that he wouldn't be around to see the towers tumbling down but he had left the cauldron boiling and George and the boys had rebellion on their minds.

It wasn't as though Rafe despised Greer School for he envisioned it as a worldly "Garden of Eden" It was certainly the most beautiful place he would ever live. It had a certain physical splendor and tranquility that surrounded one's soul. Sometime later Rafe would ask his brother Tom if there was a song that seemed to capture the essence of Hope Farm. Tom immediately answered Summertime. The old song that goes,

Summertime and the livin' is easy

Fish are jumpin' and the cotton is high

Your daddy's rich and your momma's good lookin'

So, hush little baby, don't you cry.

It was a beautiful spring evening and the ride to Brooklyn was memorable. His mother was talking to his Aunt Mary about what a difficult child he was who probably was cut out of the same material as his great Uncle Pete and his Uncle Ernie. Rafe had no idea what all of that was about, but he did not doubt that his mother couldn't be more displeased with him. As he watched the scenic Taconic State Parkway slip by, he was thanking God fervently for his deliverance. He felt there was no one, anywhere, happier than he.

Suddenly his mind was focused on the future and not on what lay behind. He didn't know it but he was about to move from an underprivileged existence to a privileged one with one mighty leap.

Home Sweet Home

Rafe sat in the Studebaker and gazed at the white Cape Cod that was his new home. He had seen it for the first time during Easter Vacation not many weeks before. It had four bedrooms and one of the two on the upper floor was all his. It might not be a palace but that didn't matter to Rafe, it was home. It was on a wide tree-lined street with a huge maple tree providing shade out front. Rafe jumped out of the Studebaker, waited for his mother to unlock the trunk then took out his duffle bag and rifle. At that moment Rafe had no idea he was about to cross a very distinct line between being disadvantaged and privileged. Things seemed to happen to him that way, swiftly, suddenly, and without any prelude or warning. The day he was dropped off at Greer School had happened without warning, and his leaving was just as unexpected. Still, not quite believing his good fortune, he bounded into the house and ran up the stairs to his room. As he stopped at the door to his room, he looked across the alcove into his older brother's room.

There, sat Tom, working at his desk on one of his electronic gadgets. Rafe called out, 'Hey there big brother, look who finally broke out!"

Tom looked over at his grinning brother and said, "Well seeing is believing, would you mind telling me how you managed it?"

Almost, laughing Rafe answered, "I guess you could say I used a little bit of counter-terrorism."

Tom gave him a somewhat disapproving look and replied, "What is it between you and Lynn Brinkman? You act as if she were the worst person to ever walk the planet."

Rafe knew that his brother had gotten on well with Brinkman and that he had no idea as to what sort of person she really was. His reply was direct. "Although I wouldn't expect you to know why; I consider Lynn Brinkman to be among the lowest forms of life ever to crawl upon the surface of the earth. What happened between us to bring about such visceral hatred is now water under the bridge and I'll never talk about it again. I only know one thing, after 9 years 8 months, and 26 days I'm free."

Tom smiled at his younger brother and said, "Ok, whatever makes you happy, welcome home."

Rafe just wanted to put the whole Greer School mess behind him. Today was the start of a new life. "So, Tom", Rafe asked, "How are things, living at home, in the big city, and all that?"

Tom Replied, "Actually they couldn't be any better. Ever since Mom dumped her old boyfriend Joe Navarra and took up with Everett again, things have become very easy. You may not know this but Everett bought Mom this house, and this place is so warm in winter you won't believe it, nothing like the frigid dorms of Gatehouse when the temperature outside dropped down to near zero. And the food! There is no comparison between Mom's cooking versus the Greer School fare. Mom may not be the world's best cook because Grandma is, but she's a close second. Maybe you'll even grow now that you'll be eating mom's great cooking all the time."

At sixteen years of age, Rafe was five feet tall and weighed 100 pounds. He had recently reconciled himself with being of small stature forever. This led to his obsession with horse racing. He had always thought he had something in common with a great racehorse considering his desire to run and his closing burst of speed. If he stayed small and light, he would become a jockey and win the Kentucky Derby along with all the other classic races numerous times. However, Tom was right, and within a few months, Rafe sprouted like a weed. He had always wanted to be exactly six feet tall, and within 14 months of his return home, Rafe reached that height exactly.

Rafe's thoughts returned to Everett, his mother's on-again-off-again boyfriend. "You know I think Everett Massoletti is one cool dude! Don't you remember the Mink Coat?"

"No, what Mink Coat are you talking about."

"It must have been Christmas Eve 1949 we were sitting in the room we used as both a dining room and living room at St. John's Place. We were begging Mom to take us out of Greer School and let us live at home. For Mom, trying to raise us without any help from our father, was a heavy burden. It wasn't enough that she was working three jobs to pay the bills, but now we were letting her know that we were desperately unhappy. Mom who could easily be compared to a lioness in disposition was really down. I don't see how you don't remember this. Mom was so depressed she said she wanted to kill all of us children and then kill herself. For a person like her, that was an incredible revelation. Then the doorbell rang. Mom buzzed the visitor in through the vestibule and he was soon knocking at the apartment door. The visitor turned out to be a courier with a large box. She opened the box and took out a very beautiful fur coat. It was a mink coat of such quality that the dark fur seemed to shimmer. Immediately a wide smile swept across her face. She tried on the coat and it fit her perfectly. She walked around the room in it, admired how she looked in the mirror, and just stood there looking like she just won a great prize. Finally, she took off the coat, put it back in the box, and told the courier that she couldn't accept it and to take it back to the furrier.

I remember piping up and saying, "You can keep it, Mom it's a Christmas Present."

"Don't you remember any of this Tom", Rafe asked

Tom shook his head and said, "vaguely, but I don't remember the details like you."

Rafe couldn't understand why his brother couldn't remember this incident when he could remember it like it happened yesterday. "So, you hardly remember the Mink Coat showing up on Christmas Eve? Then, I suppose you've forgotten Mom's explanation as to how it arrived that night?"

"You're right there I don't remember anything about how it happened."

'Well, this is the story as I remember it. Everett was sitting in Mom's office at Coro Inc. waiting for her to finish work one evening. If you recall she always worked late and Everett was going to take her out to dinner. While he was sitting there one of the women who worked as a buyer for Mom's firm came in wearing the Mink Coat. Mom tried it on and it fit her perfectly. Everett is sitting there taking this in and when the buyer leaves and walks down the corridor to her own office Everett gets up and follows her. He asks the woman if she's going to purchase the coat and she says no that it was far beyond her price range. Everett then obtains the furrier's contact information and when Christmas Eve arrives, a great surprise shows up. Now, don't you think that was a super cool thing to do?"

"Yeah, I guess", Tom answered. It was obvious to Rafe that his brother didn't see the incident in the same light he did.

"That's not the only cool thing he's ever done for Mom either! Remember the story of the Limo and Mom's friends from work?"

Tom shook his head and said, "Can't say that I do."

"Well let me refresh your memory, Everett always wanted to take Mom out to dinner after work and she often went as he would take her to the best restaurants so she wouldn't have to fix dinner for herself after the subway commute from Manhattan to Brooklyn. On one particular evening, Mom had made a date to go out to dinner with three of the girls from the office. They were going to have dinner at the McAlpin Hotel right across the street. Everett wanted to see Mom, as he usually did; asked if he could join the ladies for coffee when they had finished their meal. Mom knowing that Everett would pick up the check agreed. Mom watched as Everett waited by the matrie'd stand for about 30 minutes until dessert was ordered. At this point, Everett came over and presented to each of the ladies, including Mom, a $75 bottle of perfume. This was not a small amount in 1953 dollars. As Mom expected he picked up the tab and then walked Mom and her friends out to the street. Here they were treated to another surprise when they found a limo waiting to drive them home. Everett and Mom drove the ladies home, in luxury, and then Everett drove Mom home to Brooklyn before having the limo drop him off at this apartment in midtown Manhattan. So how cool is that?"

Tom shook his head and said, "That's not such a big deal for someone as rich as Everett."

Rafe was not deterred by Tom's reply and continued, "Tom that's not the point! Everett did it to make Mom happy. He's not like Joe Navarra or some of Mom's other boyfriends, or our own Father for that matter. Just because he's rich doesn't mean he has to be interested in her happiness."

"Well, maybe you're right."

"I am right Tom, think about it. This house we're standing in right now; We wouldn't be here without Everett, and I wouldn't be standing in front of you right now. I'd still be at Greer School contemplating my fate. Anyway, Everett is super cool as far as I'm concerned."

Rafe turned and walked into his room, threw his duffle bag on the floor near his bed, and put his rife in the closet. Lying down on the bed Rafe put his hands behind his head and thought. "I'm home, finally! This is the best thing that's ever happened to me." Then, "Thank you God for bringing me home in one piece." It was at this point that Rafe, who believed that God had it in for him, thought, maybe I'm wrong. If he knew what lay right over the horizon, he'd have no doubt, God Loved him!

An event took place before summer school began in New York City which would have life-changing implications. One day his mother called from work and told Rafe that Everett Massoletti wanted to meet him for dinner at Trader Vic's at the Plaza Hotel. She wasn't going to be joining them it would just be Rafe and Everett. His Mom explained that Everett had a proposal to make to Rafe, and that he should take it very seriously.

Rafe liked the idea of having dinner with Everett whom he held in high regard. Everett met him in the lobby of the Plaza Hotel and they walked downstairs to Trader Vic's. It had an exotic Polynesian décor that appealed to both of them. During dinner, Everett related to Rafe that he too had spent years in a boarding school although the one Everett had attended had been for boys from upper-class families. What Rafe found interesting was that Everett didn't like being away from home any more than he did. Their conversation started over the tropical décor. Everett remarked that from time to time he went to Hong Kong and along the route stopped in Hawaii and stayed at the Royal Hawaiian Hotel. Rafe enquired, 'Is that where the navy submariners stayed when given R&R between war patrols?"

Everett was surprised that Rafe was aware of this piece of World War II trivia. He smiled and said, "I didn't know you were into naval history." The truth was that Everett and Rafe knew very little about each other except in a very general sense.

Rafe was quick to reply, "I'm really into it. At one time I was even thinking about going to Annapolis and pursuing a naval career."

"I take it you've since changed your mind?" Everett asked.

"I have. I've always been very interested in submarines, but there is not a chance that I would ever go down in one. They're fine to read about, but I'm afraid of depths. I also figured I could walk a thousand miles, but I couldn't swim that far". Everett laughed and responded, "Well we have something in common. I was in the Navy during the war." Rafe was impressed as he had never heard his mother refer to Everett's military service.

"Did you serve at sea?"

"Yes, I did, on the light cruiser Helena".

"Wow, are you serious? Rafe replied. "Then were you at the Naval Battle of Guadalcanal?" Again, Everett laughed because he was beginning to realize that Rafe was indeed a student of naval history.

"Yes, I was there. The Helena was number 8 in the line of battle."

"I can't believe were you there, and were on the Helena no less. Didn't Tokyo Rose call her the Machine Gun Cruiser?" Without the two of them knowing it a bond was forming. Everett Massoletti, a man without children, but the same age as Rafe's Father was talking to a young man who knew all about Helena and her battle record just as if Rafe were his own son. Everett went on to say that Helena was called the Machine Gun Cruiser because her main battery of 15 six-inch guns, mounted on five triple turrets, could fire at such a rate that the tracers took on the appearance of machine-gun tracer fire. The Helena also mounted 8 five-inch guns giving her quite an arsenal for such a lightship.

Rafe couldn't get enough of the story of the battle at Guadalcanal. "Didn't you go up against the Japanese battleship Hiei at point-blank range?"

"Yes, that's true, we were only about 3,000 yards away. We poured a fusillade of 6" shells into her superstructure and took only a few glancing hits in return."

"Could you actually see her?"

"She seemed to tower over us like a huge building. She was on fire from stem to stern. Remember we weren't the only ones firing on her. There was also the Atlanta, San Francisco, Portland, and Juneau not counting the destroyers which were also firing at point-blank range." They talked for a long time about the battle and its aftermath including when the Juneau had blown up as the victorious American task force was retiring to the safety of Espiritu Santo. A Japanese submarine had torpedoed the Juneau and the torpedo must have hit a magazine as the Juneau simply blew up and disappeared in a cloud of vapor. Captain Hoover of the Helena, who had taken command of the task force after the death in the battle of Admirals Scott and Callaghan, was later unjustifiably relieved of his command for not searching for survivors of the Juneau. This was the cataclysmic event that killed the famous five Sullivan brothers who all perished in the sinking of the Juneau.

Everett related the sinking of the Helena at the Battle of Kula Gulf and how he and 160 other survivors were in the water for 2 days before drifting to the Island of Vella Lavella where they were finally rescued. By the time their discussion of the exploits of the U.S.S. Helena ended, Rafe was firmly in the confines of hero-worship where Henry Everett Massoletti was concerned. He had always thought Everett was one cool man, but now he had no doubt.

As they neared the end of dinner Everett switched to the reason for their meeting. He asked Rafe a question and told him that his answer would be kept strictly between the two of them. By this time Rafe had begun to trust Everett and saw him as a person of character. Everett told him that his answer would just be between the two of them, not even his mother would ever know.

Everett then asked Rafe, "Was something going on at Greer School that you've been keeping a secret, something bad?"

"So, you want to know the truth about Greer School?"

"Yes."

"Ok here it is, Mom put me into Greer School without even telling me why. She didn't even say goodbye. I thought I had been abandoned." He related the story of how Brinkman tried to murder him three times and that he only escaped by the hand of God. He explained that his defiant behavior was not really directed at the school but at his mother for never having believed in him. If he had told his mother the truth, he probably would have ended up dead because she would have believed Brinkman, over him. But, to make matters worse, if his mother had believed him, Brinkman would have ended up dead in less than fifteen minutes, and he and his siblings wouldn't have a mother who would end up in prison. So, he had to handle it himself. When this evil person came back to the school as his house mother it was like a declaration of war. It was a fight for survival, and if his mother had not taken him out of the school when she did, all hell would have broken loose. He reiterated that he didn't care if his mother thought of him as the Black Sheep of the family, or for that matter, as a bad seed, because he was home. He had escaped and now life would be as it should.

Everett nodded and said, "I thought so. It had to be something like that."

"Why do you say that?" Rafe asked.

Everett looked directly into his eyes and said, "Because you're too smart to have been doing that badly in school. You were waving a red warning flag and no one was paying any attention. I've told your mother that in the past, But, you're right; what happened at Greer School is now over and it's time to get back on the right track and begin to prepare for the future. That's why I asked you to have dinner with me tonight. I have a proposition for you. I'll send you to Rhodes School, the best prep school in New York City if you promise me one thing."

Rafe asked, "What's that."

"You devote 100% of your time to your studies. Show the world what you can do when you apply yourself. Give it your very best". He looked seriously at Rafe and said, "What do you say, do we have a deal?"

Rafe smiled a most genuine smile a little overwhelmed that someone would have such faith in him, and said, "Deal!" Everett reached across the table and offered his hand and they shook on it.

As they walked out of the Plaza Hotel that warm May evening Rafe knew he had just crossed a bridge into a new world, one he was determined to make the most of. But, by far, the best thing about that evening was that Rafe had finally found someone who believed in him. Come hell or high water, he would never let his benefactor down.

Everett offered to send Rafe home to Flushing by cab but Rafe thanked him and told him he'd rather take the subway. Everett climbed into a yellow cab in front of the Plaza Hotel and Rafe walked the few blocks to the subway at Lexington Avenue and 59th Street. He caught the Lexington Avenue line down to Grand Central where he transferred to the line to Main Street, Flushing. A block from the subway at Main Street, Flushing was the bus stop where he boarded the bus which would drop him off three blocks from home. For some strange reason, Rafe liked the commute from midtown Manhattan to home. That turned out to be a good thing too, as he would be spending the next couple of years taking that ride 5 days a week. At that time there was a television program called The Naked City. At the end of the program, the announcer would say, "There are 8 million stories in the Naked City and you have just seen one". Since the rail line from Main Street Flushing to Midtown was elevated, Rafe would often wonder what was going on in the apartments and businesses the train sped past. The city was vibrant and full of energy and excitement. It couldn't be more different than the pastoral setting of Greer School.

Most important to Rafe was that he didn't have to constantly watch his back. The sick and vengeful character of Brinkman was quickly put aside. You know what they say? The only revenge is living well, and Rafe starts to live very well. Rafe quickly turned his attention to Schoolwork. When Summer School opened at Rhodes School in June, he decided to devote himself to subjects he would ordinarily not like. That included Mathematics and Science. It wasn't as if he ignored the other subjects but he didn't have to devote as much attention to them as they were easy for him to master. Because of his directed intelligence, anything he focused his mind on he could do as well as anyone. As he progressed through Rhodes his final scores in math were always 99 or 100. He rarely made mistakes to the point if he did make one the instructor had to check the problem to see if he was the one who had made an error. In Chemistry the instructor told the class that never in the history of Rhodes School had anyone ever scored above 95 on the state regent's examination. Rafe took it as a challenge and scored 99.

His mother couldn't believe the dramatic turnaround in her son, but still considered him to be a ticking time bomb that could go off at any time. This is the likely outcome when you believe the enemy's propaganda. For years Brinkman had been telling her what an awful son she had. In truth, once Rafe was home, he became an ideal teenager. He never did anything that in any way caused his mother any concern. His grades at Rhodes were nothing short of remarkable and Rafe went out of his way to make his mother's life easier. After he got his driver's license, he would call his mother to see when she would be finishing work. He would then take the car and drive down the Long Island Expressway, through the midtown tunnel, and across town on 35th street to 6th Avenue where his mother's office was located. He'd pick her up and turn back down 36th street to the Midtown Tunnel. Since his mother's commute was 1 hour and 20 minutes Rafe would save her 50 minutes by picking her up this way. Since his mother almost always worked late, they would miss the outbound rush hour traffic and she'd be home in 30 minutes.

Life had become ridiculously good for Rafe and his siblings. Whenever Rafe wanted to go see a movie at the Fresh Meadow's shopping center, which was only four blocks away, he'd just tell his Mother, 'Hey Mom I want to go to the movies tonight". The answer was always the same, "Do you need money?" "Nope, I have plenty" Rafe was given a generous allowance to commute to the city and he never spent it all. No more detention for him. He was living the life of Riley. When Everett found out he liked Broadway show music he began to give him tickets to all of the Broadway shows.

It seemed a little bit ridiculous the way things had changed for Rafe. He simply had no worries. He no longer had to watch his back, or for that matter be punished for offenses he didn't commit. Rafe even liked the commute to Manhattan on the Subway. He took the IRT Subway line which was elevated for most of the trip from Main Street, Flushing. For some unknown reason, Rafe particularly liked the feeling he got when the IRT train emerged from underground after passing under the East River; from there it would remain above ground until reaching the end of the line at Main Street, Flushing. Not long after coming above ground, it would make a sweeping, almost 90-degree turn to the left, and off to its right side would be the famous Pepsi Cola sign atop the Pepsi Bottling Plant. Rafe loved seeing the Pepsi Sign. For years he couldn't figure out why the Pepsi Sign had such a positive effect on his thinking. Years later he realized the sign represented home; his return to New York. Even though he had been raised in a place, not unlike the Garden of Eden, there's still no place like home. Even the commute on the IRT to Manhattan made Rafe happy.

Rafe had become one very happy teen, yet he didn't know, what lay just ahead, was something so extraordinary that there was no way to anticipate its arrival. Lightening comes without warning, a bolt from the blue. Rafe had already experienced a couple of life-changing events. The first was when his mother dropped him off at Greer and left him there without a word. The second was walking up on Brinkman when she was engaged in a little Lesbian liaison. Another bolt from the blue was on its way, and it happened quite unexpectedly. In September of 1960, at the beginning of Rafe's senior year, he was asked to report to the principal's office. He didn't like the idea since up until that point in time visits to the principal's office usually ended up being very unpleasant, to say the least. On arriving he knocked and entered and was greeted by a smiling Dr. Moskowitz. No problem here Rafe was thinking, not like Greer, this time it was different. After Rafe was seated Dr. Moskowitz got right to the point. "You've done remarkably well since you came to Rhodes, Rafe. I don't know what was going on at Greer School but you were a massive underachiever. Now you're the best student we've had in years. Because of this, we'd like you to do us a favor.

"Sure Dr. Moskowitz I'm willing to do anything to help."

"Dr. Moskowitz went on to say, "We have a young lady coming to Rhodes from Great Britain that's missed a year and a half of school and she's way behind in math and science. She's asked for a student tutor and we'd like to know if you'd be willing to tutor her. Keep in mind it would be on your own time."

Rafe was thinking, "Well I don't mind; I don't do anything but study, so nothing would be that much different. I'll probably like it. This way I'll have someone to talk to every day. Then he asked, "Why has she missed a year and a half of school? Did she have an illness or an accident?"

Dr. Moskowitz only smiled and said, "No, she's been making a motion picture."

Rafe couldn't believe what he was hearing; "What! You've got to be kidding." So, his response was, "What motion picture?"

Dr. Moskowitz was smiling, obviously enjoying himself, as he asked Rafe, "Have you seen the film, Exodus?"

"Yes, Rafe replied, I sure have I liked it so much I saw it twice."

"Do you remember the girl that played Karen?"

"Do you mean Jill Haworth?"

She's the one. How would you like to tutor her in math and science?"

Rafe just sat there in a state of shock. He was thinking, I'd have to be crazy to say no. She was, very appealing. Lovely is the word. In fact, incredibly beautiful. He was wondering if she was as nice a person as she was beautiful. Then he realized he would soon find out if he accepted. He had another good reason to accept. Since starting at Rhodes, he had completely devoted himself to schoolwork. He took his promise to Everett Massoletti very seriously. Everett was the first person to ever believe in him and he was never going to let him down. Consequently, Rafe did nothing but study and take his exercise runs. He had no time for friends and his interaction with others was confined to his family. Here was the opportunity to make a new friend, and what a friend.

"Ok, Dr. Moskowitz I'll do it, on one condition".

"What's the condition, Rafe?"

"That you call us into your office and formally introduce us."

"Well, that seems easy enough, how does 2:30 P.M. on Monday sound for the introduction".

"Ok, that sounds great, I'll see you then."

Riding home on the subway Rafe was in another world. He was thinking, "Can this be happening to me? I've never had a date with a girl, and now I'll be tutoring this beautiful young lady. God must love me, or something, because this is unbelievable."

When Monday rolled around, and Rafe had been introduced to Jill by Dr. Moskowitz the two teenagers stood outside the entrance to Rhodes School and took a few minutes to get acquainted. The first thing Rafe noticed about Jill was that she was much more beautiful in real life than in the film. Her eyes had a deep blue color and were the most beautiful eyes Rafe had ever seen. He was to learn later that the movie producer Otto Preminger had signed Jill to a movie contract just from seeing her photograph,

Jill was the first to speak when she said, "Rafe, how did you get to be my tutor?"

"Actually, it happened because I have a benefactor".

"A benefactor, what do you mean by that?"

"In the school, I attended previously I was considered a rebel and a troublemaker. They considered me a resistant personality. Then when I came home to New York my mother's boyfriend Everett took an interest in me. He believed in me and told me he would send me to the best school in New York if I would show the world what I could do by becoming the top student. So, to reward Everett for the confidence he placed in me I became the top student. That's what led me to become your tutor."

"So, I have a rebel as a tutor?"

"You might say that, but if you knew the whole story, I think you'd agree that I had no choice".

Jill smiled a big genuine smile and said, "I'm just teasing you, Rafe. Actually, I'm a little bit of a rebel myself".

He responded, "You a rebel, you seem like the sweetest girl in the world".

"I am, but don't let looks deceive you, I'm probably just as much a rebel as you".

"Well, that's very interesting. Looks like we have something in common, and you know what they say?".

"No, what do they say?"

Smiling Rafe answered, "Birds of a feather flock together".

Jill looked at Rafe a little more seriously and asked, "Do you think we'll be friends?"

Rafe said, "I certainly hope so because I could use a good friend".

Then Jill in a playful way said, "You know what they say?"

"No what do they say".

"You can't have enough good friends".

Rafe now smiling at her same play-on-words said, "Ain't that the truth".

Jill went on to say, "I have to admit I asked Dr. Moskowitz to find me a tutor close to my own age, meaning a teenager. I've been living in an all-adult world for too long and I wanted to interact with someone my own age".

"I'll admit the same thing Jill, ever since I came back to New York City from Greer School I haven't made a single friend. I just study night and day."

"Do you think we're off to a good start"? she asked

"What do you think"?

"I asked you first", she said with a big smile. Rafe was finding out that she could be very playful.

"To tell you the truth I think we're going to get along very well, but can I ask you a question"?

"Ok, go ahead"

"What are you going to tell your mother about me when you go home"?

She gave him a cute look and said, "I'm going to tell her you are tall, dark, and handsome, and a very nice young man, someone I'll enjoy studying with. How about you, what will you tell your mother about me, since we're getting personal"?

"I'll tell her you're a real sweetheart and have the most beautiful eyes I've ever seen, And, you know what they say? The eyes mirror the soul".

That got him a big smile and as they left the school both had the feeling that things would go well between them. For his part, Rafe couldn't believe that things had taken such a positive turn since he had left Greer School for New York. Instead of being a pariah, he was an honor student and this tutoring of Jill was something beyond his wildest imagination. Later as the subway train emerged from the tunnel under the East River and the Pepsi Sign was illuminated off to the right side, Rafe was thinking, "There's no doubt, God loves me!"

The two teens got along famously and Rafe proved very astute at teaching math and science. They were into the tutoring for about three weeks when Jill suggested the two of them go for a walk after completing their session at 4:00 P.M.

"How about walking up to the Central Park Zoo which is only about six blocks from here"? Rafe said.

"Oh, I'd love that", said Jill. So, they walked up to the Zoo and slowly began what was to develop into a daily routine. They'd study for one and a half hours and then walk up to the Zoo. They didn't always look at the animals, but would often sit on a park bench and talk about the things that interested them, and all sorts of other normal teen topics like American Bandstand, Rock and Roll, and Elvis. They had no idea that they were becoming friends because they never really thought much about it. They just knew because of each other, they weren't lonely and enjoyed each other's company.

As the weeks went by Rafe learned that Jill wasn't primarily interested in Hollywood, but had a very strong interest in Broadway. He also became aware that Jill's idol was another British actress, Julie Andrews. Since Rafe was interested in Broadway musicals and since My Fair Lady, in which Julie Andrews starred, was his favorite, the two had plenty to talk about.

Jill Learned to her amazement that when Rafe had left Greer School a little over a year ago, he was 5' tall and weighed 100 pounds. This led to his great interest in thoroughbred horse racing because he wanted to become a Jockey. He figured it was a good choice for a male who would probably be 5' tall for life. He had grand ideas of winning the Kentucky Derby and every other classic race.

On her part, Jill could not believe that Rafe had grown one foot in fourteen months. She asked Rafe, "How could that possibly happen?" He explained that he was under great stress for most of his life at Greer School and he considered it may have stunted his growth. He started growing at an accelerated rate as soon as he came home. Of course, it might have been his mother's great Italian cooking. The Greer School fare was edible, but just barely, while his mother was a super great cook.

Then of course the subject came up of what sort of stress Rafe was under while attending Greer School. This subject was one Rafe was very reluctant to discuss. However, since it was a key to Rafe's personality, Jill insisted. Since she was, who she was, and since Rafe absolutely adored her, he finally began to unravel the tale. Neither Jill nor Rafe realized it, but there was a growing intimacy between them. The truth was they liked and trusted each other, and as such, they were beginning to confide in one another.

"Before I tell you the story, I want to say that I'm concerned that by the time I finish, you will think less of me than you do now. I left Greer School in disgrace, at least according to my mother and the school authorities, however, the boys saw me as a hero. The only person outside of the boys at Gate House, to believe in me, is Everett Massoletti. He's the reason I attend Rhodes School and the reason I'm sitting here talking to you. I also want you to know, that I believe in you, and I feel you won't turn against me because of what I'm about to tell you. If I didn't believe in you, I wouldn't tell you the story."

"You have no idea how much I admire you Rafe so don't worry that I'll think any less of you after you tell me your story".

Rafe started telling Jill of his first day at Greer; how his mother tricked him and left him at the school without even saying goodbye. He didn't completely understand the effect that had on him, but one key outcome was that he never trusted his mother again. This would lead to serious complications later.

He told her about running away the first time, and his confrontation with Mrs. Fink, which would lead to his being classified as a resistive personality.

Next came that awful discovery at the camp of the two young women having a lesbian liaison at the campsite. The attempts at murder, his failed attempt at running for home. He related that it was like playing the part of a mouse with the cat hunting it. Knowing what it's like to be on the run, and terrorized. How his tormentor graduated from college and leaves the Greer School scene. This is followed by his receiving the greatest gift of a lifetime, his dog Max. Then followed a five-year period of happiness, except he showed his resistive personality by refusing to do school work. This led to his spending every Friday night in detention while the rest of the school watched the Friday night movie in the school auditorium. Rafe spent his Friday nights in the seventh-grade classroom supposedly making up his missed homework. Actually, he was studying everything but what he was supposed to. Instead, he read Plato, Aristotle, Julius Caesar, Polybius, Shakespeare, Milton, Dante, Hobbs, Wordsworth, Sir Walter Scott, Cervantes, etc.

This didn't do any good for his reputation, where he was considered defiant and rebellious, even though he was very popular and was a perfect citizen. Where Rafe was concerned nothing added up. He was considered an enigma.

Things went well for 5 years until the fateful day when Lynn McQueen, now married and Mrs. Lynn Brinkman, returned to Greer as his house mother.

Then the war began. Rafe was no longer a seven-year-old, he was now thirteen and was quite capable of resistance. It became like the French Resistance against the Nazi occupiers.

Over a time period of a year and a half, things began to swing out of control until he revolted and went to see the director of the school in direct defiance of Brinkman. Then it all hit the fan. There was a meeting between Mrs. Fink and the Gate House boys. Brinkman wins the confrontation and the Reign of Terror begins.

Then Max is murdered!

Jill starts crying. Rafe gives her his handkerchief and asks her to stop crying or he'll probably start crying too.

He tells her of going to the chapel that night and crying his heart out. He was defeated, one could even say, utterly destroyed. Still breathing, but crushed. So, like the other times when he was cornered, he prayed to God. Only God could help him now.

As he sat in the dark church with the only light coming through the stained-glass window, he heard the voice of God. It said, "Fear not, I am with you." And then 15 seconds later, "You are my drawn sword."

Instantly, all fear left him and was never to return. He then set out on the mission to destroy Brinkman. He plots her murder right down to the final seconds. When he gets right down to committing the act, he can't. It's contrary to God's will, he just misunderstood the command. Then he realizes how to even the score; Counter-Terrorism!

He tells Jill how he runs away with his rifle but doesn't head for New York, instead, he stays on the school grounds and lets Brinkman know he's stalking her. For four days she lives in terror. She knows he wants retribution regarding Max.

When he comes in and gives the State Police a half-baked story of why he had his rifle, they just want to return the responsibility back to the Greer

Staff. He never made any threats that were reported to anyone in authority, so the State Police accepted his explanation and left. It was his mother who knew he was up to something very serious and asked him if he wanted to leave the school. Rafe told Jill that if he had gone back to Gate House that evening, the outcome would have been violence, so he decided to leave.

When his mother went to Ledge Cottage to tell his sister, Angela, that he was leaving Greer School that evening, he was left with the school's director, Dr. Elliott. He told him what was happening and said, "If you don't act immediately the revolution is imminent. If I don't leave in the next hour, it will start tonight, and I would be leading it. If you don't act, the coming revolt will bring down the school."

Within the hour he was on the way home after 9 years, 8 months, and 26 days. He prayed halfway back to New York and thanked God for his salvation.

Then his life changed overnight. Everett Massoletti arrived on the scene and decided to send him to Rhodes School. He repaid Everett's faith in him by becoming the top student at Rhodes. And the rest is history.

Jill didn't say anything after hearing the story she just stared at Rafe before saying, "My God! How did you get through that? Losing Max must have been horrible beyond belief."

"I had no choice, Jill, my mother would never have believed me, and if she did, she would have killed Brinkman. Then I would end up with no mother. It's called, being caught between a rock and a hard place. I just had to make the best of a bad situation.However, things have a habit of turning for the better as you can see by looking at me now."

Jill smiled at him and said, "What do you mean?"

With a big smile on his face, Rafe replied, "Well 16 months ago I was 5" tall and was being constantly harassed, and now I'm six feet tall and I'm sitting on a bench in Central Park with the most beautiful girl in the world."

Staring at him with her big beautiful blue eyes Jill said, "Does sitting here with me make you happy."

Rafe nodded affirmatively and said, "Jill you can't even imagine how happy it makes me just being here with you."

"Well, I guess we're both lucky to have someone who makes us happy. Maybe God was smiling at us by having the school assign you as my tutor," she said.

Rafe answered, "I call it a miracle!"

They got up and slowly began to walk out of the park and down fifth avenue toward the school. She slid her arm through Rafe's and pressed up against him. Rafe didn't realize he was in love with her because he didn't know much about love, he only knew she was the brightest star in the firmament. He would have been completely shocked if he knew what thoughts were germinating in her beautiful head, but he wouldn't have to wait too long to find out.

The next Monday as they were concluding their study session in the school library, Jill leaned toward Rafe with a very different and beautiful look in her eyes. Rafe hadn't figured out what a come-hither-look was yet, but he was looking at one without even realizing it. Jill whispered to him, "Rafe, tell me the most beautiful thing you have ever heard."

Rafe was thinking, "What has gotten into Jill? Why does she want to know that?" Rafe said, "Do you mean beautiful in a romantic way."

Jill nodded, "Yes, that's exactly what I mean, something romantic."

Rafe knew the answer immediately because he only knew one really beautiful thing. So, he began;

True love's the gift that God has given

To man alone beneath the heaven:

It is not fantasy's hot fire,

Whose wishes, soon as granted, fly;

It liveth not in fierce desire,

With dead desire it doth not die;

It is the secret sympathy,

The silver link, the silken tie,

Which heart-to-heart and mind to mind

In body and in soul can bind.

Jill just stared at him in astonishment. She was thinking to herself, "That's a pretty good description of what's going on between us, we share the secret sympathy. What does that mean? Is it? My god, is it true love? I'll bet he wrote that himself. It sounds just like him."

She asked, "Rafe did you write that?"

He smiled at her and replied, "No I wish I had, but I'm not that smart."

Now she had to know so she asked, "If you didn't write it, who did?"

He knew he had her interest so he said, "It was Sir Walter Scott."

She gave him a quizzical look and asked, "Who is Sir Walter Scott? I've heard the name before."

Rafe answered, "He wrote Ivanhoe."

Jill more interested than ever, said, "I've seen the film with Robert Taylor, Elizabeth Taylor, and Joan Fontaine.It's a story of knights and ladies, right? That's how I see us Rafe, a Knight, and a Lady. How did you come across the poem about true love? Did you seek out everything else Sir Walter Scott wrote after reading Ivanhoe?"

Rafe was enjoying the conversation because he knew that his recitation of Sir Walter Scott's poem was perfect. It didn't matter that it was the only thing he knew about love. He just replied, "More or less, that's what happened. I came across his poem about true love and was so taken with it that I committed it to memory knowing that someday some beautiful young lady would want to hear something beautiful. I'm going to write it down for you so you can memorize it too."

Sitting across from him, Jill, with her elbow on the table, and with her chin in the palm of her hand, turned her intense blue eyes on him causing the thought to pass through his head, "What is she up to now"?

If he knew what she was thinking he would have been in shock, but she had decided to save her thought to the end of the week, then she would spring it on him

That Friday afternoon they were in their usual place in the library finishing the tutoring session when Jill fixed Rafe with another of her come hither looks. Rafe recognized it as the same look, she had on Wednesday, before asking for the most beautiful thing he knew. He didn't know what it meant, but he knew something was coming.

Again, Jill leaned across the table so her lips were about a foot from Rafe's and whispered, "Rafe, I think you should take me out!" Rafe was so shocked that he thought he had misheard what she said.

He said, 'What?"

She repeated, "I think you should take me out,"

Trying to recover from the shock and to buy some time he said, "Do you mean on a date?"

"Of course, silly, what else", she answered.

Rafe responded, "Jill, I can't take you out."

"Why not?" she wanted to know, with concern beginning to show on her pretty face.

"Because you're a movie star."

Beginning to get a little bit anxious, she said, "Well movie stars like to go out too, and I want you to take me."

Rafe was at a complete loss for words. How could this be happening? After a long pause, Rafe finally said, "Jill until a year ago I was 5' tall and weighed 100 pounds, girls wouldn't even look at me. The truth is I've never had a date with a girl, and certainly not one like you.

With that explanation, Jill was a little more encouraged. She said, "Then think of what an opportunity taking me out becomes. You will always be able to say that your first date was with a movie star!"

Rafe started thinking, "Yeah it would be great if I knew where to take you. This is New York, I've never been out on a date and you're a beautiful movie star".

Jill was aware of his indecision so she played her ace card, she exclaimed, "You're not turning me down, are you?"

That comment placed Rafe in a quandary. In his mind her asking him out was ridiculous, but on the other hand, his refusal would be even more ridiculous.

So, since he wasn't crazy, he said what any sane young man would say to the most beautiful girl he had ever met. "Ok, I'll take you out, but you need to give me this weekend to think things over."

Jill, just gave him a beautiful genuine smile and said, 'Ok Rafe, I'll give you this weekend to think it over, then on Monday you can tell me what we're going to do. Maybe next weekend? Do you think we can go out then?"

"That will be good, I just need time to think it over."

Jill then said she needed to run to the hairdresser to get her haircut, and said goodbye leaving Rafe in the library.

On his part, Rafe could not believe this incredible turn of events. Nothing could have surprised him more than what had just transpired. He knew he would have to ask his mother for advice. After all, she had attracted a man like Everett so she had to know about these things. As it turned out he hardly remembered the trip home he was so lost in thought.

After dinner, as he was washing the dishes, he turned to his mother and said, "Mom I need your advice on something." His mother looked at him with a surprised expression and asked, "What do you need advice about Rafe? You've never asked for advice once in your life you are the most decisive young person I know, always very sure of yourself."

He replied, "Well in this area I'm quite ignorant."

"Well, what is it about Rafe."

He said," Jill wants me to take her out on a date."

His mother looked shocked, then replied, "Oh my God, you do have a problem. How did you arrange this?"

"Well, she leaned over and whispered to me in the library that I should take her out. I tried to say no, but she then asked if I was turning her down. So, what could I do", Rafe, explained.

His mother answered, "We'll have to think about this over the weekend."

"That's what I told Jill. That I would think about it over the weekend. After all, I've never been on a date, this is New York, and she's a movie star."

His mom trying to make him feel better said, "Don't worry we'll find a solution."

His mother was thinking to herself," How did he manage to accomplish this? I'll have to call Everett."

As soon as Rafe went up to his room, she immediately called Everett, and when he answered she said, "You'll never believe what your son has gotten himself into now". She always referred to Rafe, when talking to Everett, as your son.

Of course, Everett had no idea what was brewing, he said, "Well I hope it's nothing serious. What is it?"

"Well, his little movie star has asked him to take her out on a date, and he doesn't know what to do."

Everett laughed and responded, "I should have known this would happen. I think that's the greatest thing I've ever heard."

"Let's be serious, he's never been out on a date, if you recall about 14 months ago, he was 5'tall. I don't know why she ever asked him out, you know a girl like that, a movie star", replied his mother.

Everett said, "I think you underestimate your son. He's not only 6' tall now, but he's very good-looking. Not only that, but he's super intelligent, and has a very engaging personality. I think his movie star pupil is developing a crush on him and figured he'd never ask her out, so she asked him."

Rafe's mother who had swallowed most of the Greer School propaganda concerning her son just couldn't resist adding, "Well I still think he's a ticking time bomb that could explode any second."

"El (which Everett used as short for Elvira) why not cut your son some slack? Since he's been home, he's been a perfect teenager. He's the top student in the top school in the city and never has to be asked to help around the house. Regardless of how you view your son, I'm going to fix this problem with his first date. Tell him to meet me in the lobby of the Waldorf Astoria at 11:30 tomorrow morning. I'll ensure that his first date is something very special. Just leave it all to me."

"Everett, what are you planning?"

"Let Rafe tell you tomorrow afternoon. You'll agree that I have the perfect idea."

Saturday morning Rafe met Everett at the Waldorf and they immediately headed for Rogers Peet the top men's clothier in Manhattan. On the way, Everett told Rafe, "If you're going to date a starlet you have to look the part which means being impeccably dressed." Rafe couldn't argue with that, remembering the old adage "Clothes make the man".

Later at lunch, Everett revealed his bombshell plan. "This is how your date is going to play out Rafe," Everett said with a broad smile. First, you're going to take Jill to Trader Vic's for dinner. I think she'll like its exotic South Seas decor.

Rafe responded with. "Wow, Pop! That's a great date, she will love Trader Vic's."

Everett shook his head and said, "Rafe that's not the date, that's just dinner before the date." Rafe sort of frowned and asked, then what's the date?" Everett added, "After dinner, you take a cab down to 44th Street to the Majestic Theatre to the opening of Camelot with Julie Andrews, and Richard Burton." For the second time in as many days, Rafe was struck dumb. He felt the same way when Jill leaned over and whispered, "Rafe I think you should take me out." Now Everett had just told him he had somehow gotten tickets to the opening of Camelot on just a few hour's notice.

He also remembered that in one of their conversations, he had told Everett that Jill didn't want to be a star in Hollywood, but a star on Broadway, and her idol was none other than Julie Andrews. This was nothing short of fantastic. When he finally recovered, he said, "How did you arrange this on such short notice? The tickets must have cost a small fortune!" Again, Everett smiled and said to Rafe, "Son one of the things you'll learn about life is that it's not all about money. I'm going to get more enjoyment out of seeing you kids have the date of a lifetime than in any other way I could spend the money.

At this point, Rafe couldn't wait to tell Jill where, and what, they would do on their date. Everett had only one thing to say about the upcoming date. He said, "Just promise me one thing. When you take her home don't be a chicken, be sure to kiss her goodnight. First, because she'll be expecting it, and second because for the rest of your life you'll know that your first date was with a movie star, and the first girl you kissed was a movie star." Rafe just laughed and said, "Ok pop I promise I will kiss her goodnight."

When Monday rolled around Rafe was as high as a kite. He couldn't wait to tell Jill what they would be doing on their date. This would sort of even the tables as to the look on his face when she asked him to take her out. He couldn't wait to see the look on her face when he told her they were going to the opening night of Camelot.

It was an exciting moment when they met in the library. It didn't take Jill longer than thirty seconds to ask the question, "Where are we going on our date?" Rafe thought he'd tease her a little so he said, "We're going to Trader Vic's for dinner." This brought a big smile from Jill who responded with, "That's great, I've heard about Trader Vic's and its Polynesian decor. I think we'll have a great time, and we can talk the night away." Then Rafe replied, "Well not exactly, after dinner we're going to take a cab down the Majestic Theatre on 44th Street to see Camelot with Julie Andrews and Richard Burton."

Then it came the perplexed look, then one of shock. Rafe knew how he had looked when Jill asked him to take her out. He almost laughed but he managed to restrain himself. Jill looked directly into his eyes and said, "I can't believe it. How did you arrange it?" Rafe just sort of chuckled, and said, "I guess I have friends in high places."

Jill exclaimed excitedly, "It was your dad Everett, wasn't it?" Rafe nodded and said, "Yes it was Everett and I have no idea how he managed to do it overnight; because he didn't find out about our date until Friday night. Then by noon Saturday, he had it all arranged. He thinks it's very cool that my first date is with you."

"It is cool Rafe, and I'm beginning to think asking you out was the best idea I've ever had. And, think of it, things haven't even started yet. I'm so excited."

On the evening of their big date, Rafe drove into the city and parked near the Gotham Hotel in which Jill and her mother had a suite. When he rang the doorbell, her mother answered and smiled at him and said, "You must be Rafe."

He replied, "Yes, Mrs. Haworth I am."

She then said, "Well come in, Jill will be ready in a few minutes." Mrs. Haworth took Rafe's coat and they then sat across from each other in the living room to get acquainted. Rafe was well aware that he facing the guardian at the gate. This was going to prove a critical conversation no matter how short. The mother of a starlet carries a lot of weight. It began when Mrs. Haworth said, "What did you think when Jill asked you to take her out?"

Rafe wasn't surprised that Jill had told her mother about how their date had come about. He smiled at her and said, 'I thought I didn't hear what she was saying correctly. So, I just said, "What!" When she repeated it, my initial reaction was that I couldn't take her out because I thought it was inappropriate. I didn't say that, but that's what I thought."

Her mother raised an eyebrow indicating she was interested and said, "Inappropriate in what way?"

Rafe explained, "Jill's a movie star and I'm nobody. There's a huge gap in status."

Mrs. Haworth asked, "Do you think status is important?

"It's not so much what I think as it is what the rest of the world thinks," Rafe said.

Jill's mother then asked, "So you never would have asked Jill out if she hadn't asked you."

Rafe looked at her for a minute before saying, "Not in a million years Mrs. Haworth. I never would have done anything that would have risked my friendship with Jill. What if I asked her out and she felt I was being pushy? It could have changed our relationship. Then out of the clear blue, he said, "You know what they say?"

Mrs. Haworth took the bait and answered, "No Rafe, what do they say?"

Rafe simply repeated one of the first things Jill had said at their first meeting, "You can never have enough good friends." Jill is my best friend and I place the highest value on that, above all other things, I would never risk that for a date."

At this point, Mrs. Haworth saw something behind Rafe that drew her attention and Rafe turned to look behind him. He was greeted by what he could only describe as a vision of loveliness. Rafe had been accustomed to seeing Jill dressed like any other teen schoolgirl, not dressed to attend the opening of a major Broadway show. With her hair done up, with makeup, and wearing a beautiful evening gown Rafe knew he had never seen a more beautiful woman. She may have been only sixteen years old, but she was stunning. She was so stunning in fact that Rafe was speechless for a few moments. He finally exclaimed, "Jill you're the most beautiful girl I've ever seen."

He was rewarded with a devastating smile, and a response from Jill, "You're looking pretty good yourself Sir Rafe." He smiled at that. Ever since he had recited Sir Walter Scott's poem, she had begun calling him Sir Knight in a playful manner.

It wasn't long after Jill made her appearance that she and Rafe were on their way to Trader Vic's. Rafe knew the Maitre d' having spent many evenings at Trader Vic's which was his and Everett's favorite restaurant. Dinner was perfect and before they knew it, they were in a cab heading for the theater on 44th Street. They were having so much fun on their incredible date and were unaware that the biggest surprise had not yet been revealed.

Upon arriving at the theater, they made their way through the sizable crowd to the box office. When the ticket agent handed Rafe the tickets she said, "I have a note for you." As she handed it to Rafe she continued, "Stay in your seats after the performance and you'll be ushered backstage to meet Julie Andrews." If you had been watching them it would have been hard to tell which of the two had the more shocked expression. Jill was so excited her fingernails were digging into Rafe's arm with great intensity. She exclaimed, "My God Rafe, how did your dad arrange this." Rafe said, 'I have no idea, but this is the most fantastic thing." "Jill was almost giddy with excitement and she looked up at Rafe and said, "I'm so happy I could kiss you!" Rafe looked into those beautiful sparkling blue eyes and said, "You mean later I get a reward for this?" She had that look again, the same as when she asked him to take her out. He didn't know what it meant to that point, but she just looked at him and smiled and nodded her head, and said, "Yes!" Rafe couldn't believe how lucky he was. This was turning out to be the night of all nights.

You could say that Jill was in her glory as they took their seats. Rafe had always thought she was the most beautiful girl in the world. To Rafe, she was like a beautiful golden daffodil among lesser blooms. As the audience took their seats many had their attention drawn to the beauty seated next to Rafe. I wasn't long before some began to recognize Jill as being Karen from Exodus. This led to some of the ladies asking Jill to autograph their playbill to which Jill gladly acquiesced. Rafe could tell that Jill was enjoying her newly found celebrity.

Then the orchestra began the overture and they became lost in the music. To say their date was magical would be a major understatement. The musical

Camelot was beyond good, especially for two young teens who were just beginning to look for that place, for happily ever aftering. It wasn't long before Richard Burton was singing, I wonder what the King is doing tonight. It's said that time flies when you're having fun and this special evening sped by although Rafe and Jill wished it could last forever.

When the final curtain fell the next step in their great adventure was about to begin. They were ushered backstage and duly introduced to Julie Andrews in her dressing room. Even for Rafe, this was something extraordinary, but for Jill who idolized Julie, this was the ultimate. Rafe, when introduced, simply said that he thought Julie was the greatest and was a great fan of hers. With Jill, it was a much greater experience. For one thing, both Julie and Jill were British, and Julie had seen Jill's film debut in Exodus. Julie complimented Jill on her film debut whereupon Jill told Julie that although she had a contract to make four more films her real desire was to be the next Julie Andrews and follow Julie onto the Broadway Stage. Unfortunately, there wasn't much time for Julie and Jill to carry on much of a conversation due to the chaos of the opening night, but then just meeting her was unbelievable.

Jill snuggled up to Rafe during the taxi ride back to her hotel. She was looking up at him like he was indeed her knight in shining armor. Rafe couldn't be happier considering he thought Jill was the most beautiful woman on earth. Jill, had him fixed with those beautiful eyes when she suddenly said, "How would you describe our date?"

Rafe responded, "To tell the truth it's been like taking a magic carpet ride." Jill giggled and said, 'I think you are exactly right. It's been a magical evening. I keep thinking that asking you out was the greatest idea I've ever had."

The date ended in front of the door to Jill's hotel suite. They were facing each other and Rafe had his hands on her hips. Jill slid her hands up to his shoulders and Rafe knew the moment of truth had arrived. He had no doubt that she was receptive to being kissed so he leaned down and kissed her. The truth is although it was sweet, it was on the platonic side. When Rafe broke the kiss, Jill looked up and said, "Since you just took me out on the best date, I'll ever have, you're entitled to another kiss." Rafe didn't need further encouragement and leaned down and their lips met for the second time. Unlike their first kiss, this one was passionate; and intoxicating, longer-lasting too.

When they broke apart the second time, they were breathless. Jill smiled up and him and said, "Thank you so much for the most wonderful night of my life." Still smiling, she added as she began to turn towards her apartment door, "The question is, what do we do for an encore?"

Rafe quickly responded, "Does that mean I get another date?" As she turned away Jill looked back at him over her shoulder, and while giving him the cutest look he had ever seen said, "You'll get one if you ask for one." Then added, "Then you'll get to kiss me goodnight again."

What they were unaware of was that for a couple of minutes, after Jill entered her suite, Rafe just stood outside the door, staring at it. While inside the door, Jill was standing with her back to it, not moving. Both realized at the same time, they were in love. Their kiss was absolute, pure beauty.

That's how it ended. Rafe could not believe his good fortune. Two years ago, he was fighting a bitter fight at Greer School and tonight he was at the top of the world. For about two minutes he stood frozen in place Then as he turned and walked down the corridor towards the elevator he was thinking, "This whole thing was an act of God." With that in mind, he said a short prayer of thanksgiving. God definitely loved him.

He reached the elevator and pressed the button for service. When the elevator arrived, he stepped into it and turned, and faced the door next to the rather elderly man that was the operator. He must have had a silly grin on his face because the operator looked at him and said, "Young man you look like the cat that just swallowed the canary."

Rafe looked at him and replied, "You know that's just about how I feel."

When he walked out onto the street the cold December air hit him, not that anything was going to bother him on this night. He walked towards the parking garage where he had parked his mother's car and was thinking, "I had better drive very carefully on the way home because my mind is going to be off in space. I don't want to wrap the car around a telephone pole. In fact, Rafe didn't even remember driving home.

After parking the car in the garage Rafe entered his home through the side door. He knew his mother would be waiting up for him to find out how the date had gone. His mom was already in bed reading when he entered the house and called him into her room. She immediately asked, "Well how did your date go." Rafe found it easy to describe, 'Mom it was like taking a magic carpet ride. Everything was perfect. Everett even found some way to get us introduced to Julie Andrews. Jill thought it was the greatest day of her life, and to top it off Julie invited Jill to lunch to discuss how to make it on Broadway. Just simply unbelievable is all I can say. I'll never be able to sleep tonight just thinking about it."

"Well, I'm glad it turned out so well and I have to admit it was an extraordinary turn of events. Even now I can't understand how you managed to get Jill to ask you to take her out." His mother replied.

Rafe just smiled and said, "Actually it was easy Mom, I just got her to trust me." That happened to be the truth. Where Jill was concerned Rafe was as straight as an arrow. This was primarily because he was in love with her, although he didn't even understand what that meant, it would be the last thing in the world, for Rafe, to do anything that would hurt Jill, and she was well aware of that.

The next day was another first when Jill called Rafe at home to tell him how much she enjoyed their date. Rafe had never been this happy in his short life, and if he knew where things were headed, he would have been even happier.

When they met in the library on Monday things were not quite the same as they had been the previous Friday. They were beginning to act like boyfriend and girlfriend although Rafe never noticed the difference. Jill told Rafe that she was having lunch with Julie Andrews on Wednesday so she would not be at school that day. She was very excited about talking to Julie because she admired her so much and she could tell Jill many things that would help her succeed on Broadway.

The luncheon went off wonderfully and on Thursday Jill could talk of nothing else. Then came Friday, one week after Jill had proposed that he take her out. Jill wanted to go for a walk, but Rafe said, "It's pretty cold, not the best day to sit on a park bench." Jill was insistent and said, Let's go anyway, I have something to ask you I don't want anyone to overhear. If it's too cold we can walk over to the Plaza Hotel and find a place to sit and talk."

Rafe was agreeable and said, "Ok let's go." Off they went walking down Fifth Avenue toward Central Park. Things were different between them as was demonstrated by her leaning into him as they walked and his putting his arm around her. When they were seated on their regular park bench, they turned towards each other and Rafe immediately noticed her blue eyes had that same come hither look he had seen just before she asked him to take her out.

Jill asked, "you don't have a girlfriend do you, Rafe." Rafe was thinking, "What's this about? She knows I don't have a girlfriend." So, he answered, "Jill you know I don't have a girlfriend, you're the only girl I've ever been out with, and that was six days ago."

Then she said, "You know Rafe, I don't have a boyfriend either."

Rafe began thinking, "Where is this leading? What is she up to?" Then he responded, "You may not have a boyfriend but you could have a thousand if you wanted to."

Then it came. It's been said it's like being struck by a thunderbolt. Jill looked into Rafe's eyes and said, "But the only one I want is you! I think we should go steady, you know, be high school sweethearts."

The effect on Rafe was overwhelming. He was thinking, "This can't work. She's a movie star, she's the most beautiful girl I've ever seen. I'm nobody." Unfortunately, he said what he was thinking, "Jill this can't work, I'm nobody, why do you want to go steady with me." Then she said the most beautiful six words he would ever hear. She said, "Because I'm in love with you." This was beyond his comprehension it didn't register immediately. He just sat staring at her unable to put it all together and respond. Then it happened. Jill started crying. Not just a few tears, but a stream running down her cheeks accompanied by sobs.

Rafe thought, "My god! What have I done? I'm breaking her heart. She's got to stop." He reached into his pocket fumbled for his handkerchief and handed it to her and said, "Please don't cry Jill, I'm just having trouble taking this in."

Then she asked, "How do you feel about me, Rafe?" This time his response was immediate. "I love you more than life itself, Jill. I absolutely adore you and I have for a long time."

Jill looked up and tried to smile as she dabbed at her eyes with the handkerchief, "Then I don't understand what the problem is with us going steady."

Rafe reached down lifted her to her feet and kissed her. The kiss said everything.

Rafe asked, "Is that what you wanted? Jill smiled and nodded yes. Then said, "Kiss me again." Rafe didn't need further encouragement, so he kissed her again. Jill then said, "If we're going together, we can do this all the time!"

Rafe then responded with, "And that would be a good thing because I would never be able to put into words how I feel about you. I can say it with a kiss, but what I feel for you can't be expressed with words."

Jill had stopped crying and was now smiling. Then she said, "I know what you mean. When you kiss me, I can feel your love for me, and you're right, it's a feeling too strong and beautiful to be expressed with words, even if you are someone like Sir Walter Scott, whom you have to admit made an admirable attempt." Jill then gave Rafe her cutest look and said, "Well are we now going steady? Are we now high school sweethearts?"

Rafe said, "Almost, but let's do it formally." He continued, Jill, I'm in love with you, and I'd like you to be my steady girlfriend. Jill threw her arms around his neck gave him a super passionate kiss and said, "Yes Rafe, I'm your girl."

Now they were beaming at each other. Jill said, "I guess that's all it takes, we agree, and we're going steady, right?" Rafe nodded and answered, "That's all it takes, we make an agreement between the two of us, and as long as we both want it to continue, it will. Let's go over to the Plaza Hotel and sit in the lobby where it's warm and talk."

Off they went, happy as two teens could be. After walking the two blocks to the Plaza Hotel they found an out of- the way place to sit, down a corridor that led from the grand entrance to Trader Vic's restaurant.

Then Rafe began the conversation that would enable them to continue their little romance. Although unworldly in many ways Rafe was also super intelligent. He understood what the repercussions would be once the rest of the world found out about their intentions. In order for it to work, Jill had to understand the ways of the world. With this in mind, Rafe said, "Jill the reason I didn't immediately say I wanted to go steady with you is that any romantic relationship between us presents certain problems. To put it mildly, it's going to be frowned upon."

Jill looked at Rafe a little confused and said, "What do you mean Rafe?"

Then he said, "What I mean Jill is if we're going to go steady and love each other, it must be a secret between the two of us. Once others find out they will do anything to keep us from being, linked romantically. Let me give you a scenario. You'll go home in a little while. When you arrive, your mother is home. You naturally want to tell her the exciting news so you tell her that you have a boyfriend. When she asks who, you tell her it's Rafe. So, my dear little dancer (his nickname for her) what do you think she'll do?"

Jill was a bit nonplussed by the direction the conversation was taking, but answered truthfully, "I think she'd be fine with us going together. She told me she thinks you're a person of great character."

Then Rafe countered with, "That was because we weren't romantically involved. What is likely to happen once your mother realizes you are serious about me, is you're likely to be in Hollywood next week."

Jill then said, "Why would she do that Rafe. I just said she likes you. What are you driving at?" Then he said, Jill, there is a huge gap in status between the two of us. You are a movie star even if that hasn't sunk into your consciousness yet. You're a movie star and I'm no one. It may make no difference to you, but why do you think I at first tried to get out of taking you out? Why do you think your mother likes me?

Jill then curious said, "Why?" He answered, "Because I told her I would never ask you out because I thought it would be inappropriate. Because of the gap in status. I thought if I asked you out and you weren't receptive, I'd lose your friendship and I couldn't risk that. I didn't tell her that your company had turned my life from a dull humdrum into the most exciting adventure one could imagine. If you weren't Jill Haworth the movie star, and instead were just another girl attending Rhodes School, I would have asked you out long ago. So, my darling little dancer, if no one knows the truth about our relationship they won't have a reason to break us up."

Jill looked at Rafe with a skeptical expression and replied, 'Rafe I think you're blowing things out of proportion. My mother wouldn't fly me off to Hollywood just because we're going steady."

Rafe then said, "Ok, what do you think my mother is going to say tonight when I break the exciting news to her?"

Jill replied, "Well I have no idea. I don't know your mom and don't know her attitude."

Then Rafe said, to Jill, "Her most likely response will be to turn and wave her index finger at me and say something like, "Are you crazy, that girl will break your heart."

Up to this point, Jill wasn't buying into Rafe's argument. So, he took another tack. He said, "Suppose we're living in Great Britain. Let's say that you are the daughter of the Duke of Norfolk. You live on a 10,000-acre estate in one of those early 19th-century manors with 100 rooms. You are also an equestrian and live to ride your mare Skyrocket. I'm a stable lad who grooms your mare and we interact quite a bit since a big part of your life is riding. I'm always there to saddle your horse, put the bridle on, and even give you a leg up. Over a long period of time, against all the odds, we fall in love. Once we decide to be a romantic couple you rush up to the manor house to tell your father. You find him in his study and rush to deliver the good news. You tell your father that you have a new boyfriend and it's Rafe, one of the Stable lads. What do you think your father would do?"

Jill gave Rafe a wry smile and nodded her head. Rafe then said, "You know what would happen. Your father would immediately gather his retainers, and proceed to the stable where I would be summarily fired. I would then be kicked off the estate and told never to come back. Is that what would happen?" Jill had to admit that would indeed be the outcome.

Rafe then carried his argument to the next level. He said, "Jill it's not about two people being in love. It goes to the very foundation of human identity. The idea is called the duality of man. One could say that man is half beast and half divine and struggles to have his divine side rule. One could also say that is God's grace entering the world. In other words, God's presence, Love is the most powerful force on earth. It's even above sex or money because, in fact, it wouldn't be worth living on this earth if love didn't exist. Then one might say that nature represents man's more animal side. What does nature desire first and foremost from not only man; but from all species? Reproduction! The creation of the next generation. This is where the problem arises with us going together. Normally I wouldn't speak to you like this Jill, but this is much too important to avoid. Rafe leaned over and kissed Jill. He then looked her in the eye and said, "Did you like that?" Jill just nodded yes, and then said, "I like it very much." Then Rafe said, "So now that we're going steady, we can do that whenever we want, right?" Jill responded, 'Oh yes, that's one of the reasons I want us to go steady." "Ok let's be honest. Now that we've started communicating non-verbally by kissing, the next likely step will be to find a quiet secluded place to make out. Am I right?" Jill just nodded yes. Rafe continued, Then, after many months or even years the inevitable will happen, we'll want to do it! You know what I mean Jill; sooner or later we'll want to mate. That's nature's way. That's how the next generation comes into being. It also happens to be what everyone fears when we become romantically involved. They're afraid we'll reproduce. Now that wouldn't be so bad in their minds if we had the same status in society. It would even be acceptable. Think of it like this. Suppose I wasn't Rafael Hawkins but was Rafael Massoletti. If Everett was my real father, I would have greatly enhanced status. Then your mother and, the rest of society, for that matter, would look kindly on a romantic relationship between the two of us. However, as matters stand now, the reaction of those in charge will be very negative.

Are you with me so far Jill?" Jill didn't say much just nodded and said, 'I'm beginning to see where you're coming from."

Rafe then said, 'Ok, I have only one more point to make. Have you seen the film Wuthering Heights with Sir Lawrence Olivier and Merle Oberon?" Jill nodded yes so Rafe continued, "The story starts when Mr. Earnshaw the master of Wuthering Heights returns from Liverpool with an orphan named Heathcliff. He has decided to raise Heathcliff as one of his own along with his two children, fourteen-year-old Hindley, and six-year-old Cathy. Heathcliff and Hindley grow up to hate each other while Cathy and Heathcliff grow up as close as two people can be. When Heathcliff and Cathy are young teens, Mr. Earnshaw dies and Hindley becomes Master of Wuthering Heights. With no love lost between Hindley and Heathcliff, Hindley relegates Heathcliff to the status of a servant, in fact, a stable boy. This doesn't change anything between Cathy and Heathcliff who remain as close as could be. Everything is fine as long as the love birds stay on the Wuthering Heights estate. However, one summer evening Cathy and Heathcliff venture down to the Grange where a big party is in progress in one of the manor houses. Since they rarely see anything exciting, the two teens climb over a stone wall and sneak up on the house to peer through a window. While they're observing the merriment the dogs get out and they are forced to run for safety. They need to scale a wall to escape, which Heathcliff manages, but Cathy fails when a dog grabs her by the ankle. She is rescued by the Lintons, the family giving the party. They keep Cathy at their home for several weeks while she recuperates. During the following months, Cathy is invited to all of the parties given by the upper-class residents of the Grange. Of course, Heathcliff is not invited since he is now a servant.

After six months or so go by, we find Cathy and the housekeeper of Wuthering Heights sitting in the manor house having a discussion. The housekeeper has known Cathy since she was born and has a close relationship with the young woman. During this particular discussion, Cathy says that Edgar Linton has fallen in love with her and has proposed marriage; and that she is thinking of accepting. The housekeeper aware of the relationship between Cathy and Heathcliff says to Cathy, "What about Heathcliff?" Not knowing that Heathcliff is in the house and standing around the corner Cathy says the fateful words, "I could never marry Heathcliff, I would find it degrading."

Heathcliff hears those words and to him, they're a dagger in his heart. He flees the house, runs to the stable, saddles a horse, and flees for parts unknown. A few minutes later Cathy comes to her senses and admits, "I am Heathcliff." Unfortunately, Heathcliff doesn't hear her retraction as he's gone. Cathy searches for Heathcliff in vain and after realizing he's gone forever, finally marries Edgar Linton.

An unspecified period of time goes by maybe five or ten years and one day a visitor arrives at the Linton home. The visitor is none other than the missing Heathcliff returning to the Grange after becoming a rich and powerful man. Now he has the status to court his beloved Cathy but it's too late. The story has a very tragic ending."

Then Rafe says, "So my beautiful Little Dancer why am I telling you all this? It's because in our relationship I'm Heathcliff and you're Cathy. I don't have the status to be your boyfriend. So, if we're going to go steady, we must keep it a secret. What do you think?"

By now Jill could easily understand Rafe's concerns. She said, "I think you're right, maybe nothing would happen, but there is a good chance it would." Rafe then said, "Jill the way I've reacted towards you is a reflection of not having status. In about five months when the school term ends, you'll be heading to Hollywood to make your next movie. After all, you told me that Otto Preminger who signed you to a five-movie contract; didn't want you in Hollywood because the atmosphere would be detrimental to your career. If it wasn't for that, you would have never come to New York and we never would have met. I don't want anything to ruin our budding romance. I want to experience the next five months with you as my girlfriend. We'll just have to cross, that you're leaving for Hollywood Bridge when we get to it."

Jill had bought into his arguments and said, "I think you're right. I don't want anything to upset the next five months. I've never been this happy before and I want it to continue." Then she said, "Well Sir Knight (her Pet name for him whereas he referred her to as Little Dancer) do you like having a girlfriend?" Rafe responded by pulling her close to him and giving her a long passionate kiss. He said, "Does that answer the question." Jill was beaming and just nodded yes, then said. "I've never been this happy. Now I feel that I have everything." Rafe felt the same and said, "I feel just like you do. I'm still on the magic carpet ride that started last Saturday. I never thought I would know happiness like this."

Jill then said, "Well Sir Knight, you better walk me home before our secret is discovered. Rafe took her hand and they left the Plaza Hotel and walked south down 5th Avenue toward her residence in the Hotel Gotham.

So began the great subterfuge where Jill and Rafe allowed everyone to believe that their relationship was simply a platonic one, that is, between tutor and pupil. It wasn't that hard when you consider what teenagers do anyway. They didn't go out on dates, instead, they would visit the Museum of Natural History and spend the day looking at the exhibits that they found very interesting. It didn't take them long to realize that a great part of the experience of loving another person comes from the pleasure of their company. In order to cover their secret romance, they did the usual things a visiting tourist might do. Rafe took Jill to the Statue of Liberty, the Empire State Building, Coney Island, Grant's Tomb, and the Metropolitan Museum of Art.

During the last five months of the school term, one event of consequence would occur that raised Jill's awareness that she was dealing with a much more powerful entity than the young man she viewed as her boyfriend. It started out in a most normal sort of way, and then quickly escalated into something frightening. Rafe believed, since the night after the killing of Max, that the hand of God protected him. God had said to him, "Fear not, I am with you." Now one of two things had happened, Rafe had imagined it and was, in fact, being delusional, or he actually had heard the voice of God and he was backed by the Almighty.

The incident started in a very innocent way. Rafe and Jill were sitting on their favorite bench in Central Park. It was April and the trees were just beginning to bud. Against all the odds Rafe and Jill were very much in love. They had a great affection for one another, very close to adoration. Jill had a cute way of teasing Rafe and he loved playing with her. They had been sitting on the bench for about 20 minutes when Rafe glimpsed a disturbing trio walking down the path toward them. Three young black males in their late teens approached. Just the fact that they were black males wasn't anything in itself, but their demeanor and their way of carrying themselves were. Jill's eyes followed the direction Rafe's were looking and when she turned back and looked up at Rafe she was shocked to see that his eyes had suddenly, and remarkably, taken on the look that was fierce, and focused, almost like an eagle or hawk

The three young thugs sashayed up and came to a halt in front of the young couple. The leader boldly gave Jill the once over and then said, "Well lookee, lookee, what have we here, if it's not a prime piece of honky ass." Not realizing he was about to step into the mouth of hell, he continued, "Hey honky she as good a piece of ass as she look?"

Rafe smiled a smile devoid of mirth and said, "You punks ever heard of the expression Barking up the Wrong Tree?" Thug number one said, 'No whitey what do that mean?" Rafe answered, "It means that I don't approve of your thuggish manner of speaking, and if you don't take off running for your life in the next twenty seconds, I'm going to tear you new assholes."

With that, thug number one reached into his pocket and pulled out a switchblade, and snapped it open. Thugs two and three followed their leader and drew their knives in unison. Thug one waved his blade back and forth in front of Rafe and said, "How you, gonna, tear us a new asshole honky?" Rafe glanced down the pathway to his right and said, "I'm not, but he is."

Barreling down the path at high speed came a huge black and white pit bull. When it was about ten feet from the group it leaped through the air with its powerful jaws gaping open and seized thug number one by his knife-wielding arm and clamped down with its powerful jaws. The knife went flying as the beast knocked the stunned thug to the ground. The young man began to scream bloody murder while the dog worried his right forearm shaking his head back and forth and growling in a frightening manner. At first, the other two were too shocked to move, but, finally, thug two advanced with his knife to help his beleaguered friend. As he advanced, Rafe called to the dog and it spun around to face its new adversary. It just took one look at thug number two then crouched and leaped straight at his throat. Seeing the bulldog coming thug two raised his right arm to shield his throat and the bulldog latched on to his knife-wielding right arm and bore him down to the ground and began mauling him too. This took about fifteen seconds, and as the second of the two fell, thug number three took off running for his life. Again, Rafe called to the dog which immediately stopped the attack, and looked questioningly at Rafe. He pointed down the path in the direction of the fleeing thug three, and the dog took off in pursuit. It was no contest and the hound from hell caught the third unfortunate before he had gone thirty yards. The dog grabbed him by the buttocks and dragged him down. Then began the same savage mauling the other two had been subjected to. When Rafe felt the third thug had absorbed enough, he called to the hound which stopped his attack and looked questioningly at Rafe. Rafe simply pointed down the path in the opposite direction from which the dog had first appeared and it took off running until it disappeared from sight.

Jill was standing a few feet away in a state of shock. It had all happened so fast that she didn't know what to think. Rafe walked over to thug number one, who was wreathing on the ground, and calmly said, "The next time you try something like this the hound will reappear and rip out your throat. So, you have a choice. From now on, be a good little thug, or a dead one."

Rafe turned to Jill and took her by the hand and simply said, "I think we should go." Jill said, "What about them?" Rafe said we'll walk over to the Plaza Hotel and call the incident to the police, they'll help them."

As they walked out of the park Rafe looked over at Jill and said, "Are you all right?" She gave him a wan smile and said, 'I think so, but what just happened? Where did that monster dog come from?" Rafe could only say, "We'll talk about it in a minute."

In front of the Plaza Hotel they found a mounted policeman and they reported that a huge dog had just attacked three men on a pathway near the Zoo. Rafe then escorted Jill into the hotel where they found a place to sit and talk. Jill was obviously shaken although she was trying to put on a brave face. As soon as they were seated, she said, "Ok Rafe what just happened? Where did that dog come from? He seemed to materialize out of thin air." Rafe then responded, "Jill do you remember when I told you what happened when Max was killed." She just nodded yes. Rafe continued, "Remember I told you I went to the school chapel and prayed? I was beaten. I cried like a baby. Then the voice of God came from up above, through the stained-glass window, and said, "Fear not, I am with you." this was followed by, "Fear not, you are my drawn sword. The truth is Jill, since that moment I've lived without fear. I fear nothing."

He went on, "When I saw that trio approaching, I knew what was coming. Remember I stood up and faced them. When they began their stupid crap, I warned them by telling them that they were barking up the wrong tree. Then I told them if they didn't take off running, I was going to tear them a new asshole. Then when they drew their knives, the hound appeared. What did he do? He tore them up. This is an example of God watching out for me. Now, I could be delusional, or in fact crazy, or on the other hand, I could be protected by the hand of God, it's one or the other. The question is do you believe your own eyes? Do you believe what you yourself witnessed?"

Jill said, "I don't know Rafe, what I witnessed was so extraordinary that I don't know what to think. It was simply unbelievable. That dog, or should I call him the Hound from Hell, simply disappeared. He appeared out of nowhere and when you waved him off from the third guy, he began to run down the path towards the hill, but he didn't run over the hill, he simply disappeared into thin air.I know because I was watching him. So, what am I to think?"

"I don't know what to tell you, Jill," Rafe said. "No matter how much we think about what happened we're not going to come up with a definitive answer to what we saw. I just think God loves us and has us under his protective wing. Jill nodded in agreement and said, "I think you may be right we'll never figure it out so what is the use worrying about it.". Finally, Rafe said, "If you think about it, I think God has been involved in our relationship right from the start. When you think about it, what are the chances of us ever getting together? Without the intercession of God, it could never have happened." Rafe then leaned over and kissed her. He then said, "How did that feel?" "Wonderful." She answered.Rafe then said, "That feeling of love we get when we kiss is God's presence. That's how he shows himself on Earth. He brought us together, and I think he feels the love we share, and it pleases him."

Jill kissed Rafe and said, "I think you're right God loves us. That's what protected us." The young teens walked over to the Gotham Hotel, arm in arm, as happy as any two people could be.

Another event took place as the school term approached its end. Rafe set it up; because Jill was a very playful girl and he decided to engage her in something he was sure she'd like. It was the beginning of May on a warm spring afternoon. Jill and Rafe were walking down a path in Central Park. Rafe waited until they reached a quiet, out-of-the-way place, and stopped and turned Jill around so she was facing him. He then said, "You're a good singer aren't you little dancer?"

"I'm pretty good otherwise I wouldn't have ambitions to be on Broadway."

Rafe smiled at her and said, "How come you never sing to me?"

"Would you like me to?"

Rafe answered, "You Know I would."

"Do you have any special song you'd like to hear?

Rafe answered, "Do you know the music from Oklahoma?"

Jill gave Rafe a knowing look and then a big smile before she said, 'I know what song you want to hear me sing."

Rafe said, 'Oh yeah, what song do I want to hear?"

Jill had a big smile on her face when she answered, "People Will Say We're In Love"

Rafe then said, "How did you know?"

"Maybe because it explains our situation

"Do you know the words?"

"Yes, but it's a duet. Can you sing?"

"I can try. I know I'll be able to sing to you." Rafe reached into his pocket and pulled out a sheet of paper. He handed it to Jill and Said, "Here are the words if you've forgotten. Jill looked over the sheet of paper and then said, "Are you ready?" Rafe nodded and Jill began,

Jill sings;

"Why do they think up stories that link my name to yours?"

Rafe sings;

"Why do the neighbors gossip all day, behind their doors?"

Jill sings;

I know a way to prove what they say is quite untrue.

Here is the gist, a practical list of "don'ts for you.

Don't throw bouquets at me

Don't please my folks too much

Don't laugh at my Jokes too much

People will say we're in love!

Don't sigh and gaze at me

Your sighs are so like mine

Your eyes mustn't glow like mine

People will say we're in love!

Don't start collecting things

Give me my rose and my glove

Sweetheart they're suspecting things

People will say we're in love.

Rafe sings

Some people say that you are to blame as much as I.

Why do ya take the trouble to bake my favorite pie?

Grantin' your wish, I carved our initials on that tree.

Just keep a slice of all the advice you give so free.
Don't praise my charm too much
Don't look so vain with me
Don't stand in the rain with me
People will say we're in love
Don't take my arm too much
Don't keep your hand in mine
Your hand feels so grand in mine
People will say we're in love
Don't dance all night with me
Till the stars fade from above.
They'll see it's all right with me
People will say we're in love.

They finished their song gazing lovingly into each other's eyes, and then kissed tenderly. Jill said, "You can sing Rafe, now we can sing duets together. He replied, "I'm not really that good, I usually only sing to myself in the shower." Jill then said, "Come on Sir Knight, you know you can sing, maybe we'll be on stage together someday.

"I don't mind singing a duet with you because you're so playful and I love playing with you. However, I don't think I'll ever be on stage. It's just not my thing." Jill wrinkled up her nose and gave him one of her cutest looks and then said, "Maybe I'll change your mind." Rafe smiled and replied, "If anyone can change my mind it's you." Then, hand in hand, they headed towards Jill's residence on 5th Ave.

Both Rafe and Jill were well aware that their idyllic romance was coming to an end. In another month the school term would end and Jill would be heading for Hollywood. When the day came for their final goodbye Rafe and Jill stood on the steps leading to the entrance to the Gotham Hotel. They stood facing each other with Jill's head pressed against Rafe's chest. It was a warm late spring day with the Maples in full foliage and a gentle breeze flowing down 5th Avenue. Jill was near sobbing and asked Rafe, "What's going to happen to us? Will we ever see each other again? Is this a final goodbye?"

Rafe lifted up her chin so he could look into her deep blue eyes and said, "In the end, it's going to be up to us to determine our destiny. I can't believe that our meeting and the love we feel for each other happened by chance. As far as I'm concerned it was a miracle. It only proves God loves us."

Jill Asked, "How do you mean that our relationship is a miracle?"

Refe replied, "Think about it, Little Dancer, You are only in New York, because Otto Preminger thought the Hollywood culture would corrupt you. So, you end up at Rhodes School. Then you ask for a student tutor. That's your side of the equation. On my side, I'm at Greer School leading an insurrection when my mother pulls me out of Greer because she senses I'm about to get involved in real trouble. She didn't know that I'd been in real trouble for years. When I get home, Everett says he will send me to the best school in the city, if I agree to become the top student. Becoming the top student in math and science sets in motion the events that lead to our relationship. I believe it's God's will that brought us together, and it will be his will that keeps us together."

Jill looked up at Rafe and said, "If that's true, then why is he separating us now?" Rafe wanted to reassure her and answered, "It's only temporary, he'll reunite us again in his own time. Remember wedding vows say, "What God has joined together let no man put asunder."

That brought a slight smile to Jill's face, but she needed more reassurance so she asked the same question that had ignited their relationship at the beginning. She said, "Rafe, tell me something beautiful." Rafe knew this was a critical moment and responded with, "Do you mean something romantically beautiful that relates to our current situation." Jill nodded yes and said, "Yes, that's exactly what I mean."

Rafe thought about it for a minute and then said, "This is from the Bible 1st John chapter 4."

'Beloved, let us love one another because love is from God; Everyone who loves is born of God and knows God. Whoever does not love does not know God, for God is love. God's love was revealed among us in this way: God sent his only son into the world so that we might live through him. In this is love, not that we loved God, but that he loved us, and sent his son to be the atoning sacrifice for our sins. Beloved, since God loved us so much, we also ought to love one another. No one has ever seen God; but, if we love one another, God lives in us, and his love is perfected in us."

After reciting the passage Rafe said to Jill, "God loves us Jill that's why he allowed us to experience this incredible love. He loves how we are together, and he won't tear us apart."

Jill looked up into Rafe's eyes and said, "Are you sure? I'll die if I lose you."

Rafe smiled at her and said, I'm very sure Jill, in fact, I'm so sure I'll make a prophecy about our future. Would you like me to do that?"

Jill nodded yes and then said, "Please do, I need to hear something that gives me hope"

"It could unfold like this; You're heading for Hollywood where you will fulfill your contract and make four more films. Following this, you will come back to New York and audition for a smash Broadway musical. You'll get the lead role by beating out 200 other actresses. On the other hand, I'll venture forth from New York to seek the status I need to be a serious suitor for your hand. The musical will be well into its long Broadway run when one night one of the ushers will bring you this." Rafe then reached into his pocket and brought out a small envelope which he handed to Jill. He said, "Open it." Jill quickly opened the envelope which was not sealed and brought out a plain card. On the card were a row and seat number, Row 14 Seat A. It also had a name in the center of the card, Heathcliff. Then Rafe smiled and said, "The card will be from me and it means I'll be in the audience. Then if you still have that secret sympathy for me, just send the usher back to say I'll be escorted to you after the performance. We'll be back together then, forever!"

Jill lit up and gave Rafe one of her dazzling smiles and said, "You were planning this all along, how did you know what I'd ask you?"

Rafe answered, "The same way I could make the prophecy about our future. Believe me my darling there is more to our romance than meets the eye. If you believe in the prophecy, it will happen. It's in the hands of God, and he'll make sure we're reunited, he'll provide another miracle. Even if through our years of separation, it looks as though our being reunited seems impossible, don't give up hope. Always remember our meeting was a miracle and so will our reunion.

They hugged each other and kissed goodbye. Jill turned and walked into the entrance to the Gotham Hotel. She turned with tears in her eyes and waved goodbye then disappeared from sight.

Rafe stood there for about ten minutes then slowly made his way down Fifth Avenue to the subway station. He didn't remember the ride home as he was lost in thought. Was he delusional? Was God really looking out for them? Rafe was convinced he was, as he thought his relationship with Jill as being a miracle. Where did this prophecy idea come from? It was pretty far-fetched. Jill was heading to Hollywood a place teaming with temptation. Jill was beautiful in a very sweet innocent way. The Hollywood land sharks would be on her like she was "the only prey in town." That evening as the IRT train exited the tunnel under the East River and made the left turn near Jackson Avenue, Rafe looked up and saw the Pepsi Sign that always gave him an emotional lift. His heart was heavy; he knew there was a good chance he'd never see Jill again, yet he wasn't completely down. Yes, having her leave for Hollywood was a real downer, but just as the Pepsi sign always made him happy that he had finally made it home, he realized how lucky he had been ever to be involved in the sort of relationship he had with Jill. How many people go through life hoping they would find true love and never experience it?

Everett was a married man who lived a separate life from his wife who had been his Navy Nurse while he recovered from the ordeal of the sinking of the Helena. She had discovered his father operated the largest restaurant in New York, and that is about all it took. Everett would probably have found a way to get a divorce from his wife if it had not been for one thing; he was deeply involved with the Catholic Church. In fact, he was a Knight of Saint Gregory the highest position a layperson could attain. Of course, Everett could never have foreseen meeting Rafe's Mother who was quite a remarkable personality. Everett found himself in quite the quandary, he was married, deeply involved with the church, and then meets the love of his life. Bummer!

On the other hand, Rafe's mom wasn't that much different than his wife. Her real interest in Everett was that he was rich. In fact, her interest in Rafe's biological Father had been because he was from a wealthy English family. His mother wanted the prestige and power that went with being the wife of a wealthy man. Rafe was aware that Everett loved his Mother, but he was also aware that his mother was only using Everett. That should have made a big impression on the young Rafe, but he continued to see the world as he wanted it to be. It was delusional thinking and this same type of delusional thinking would lead to terrible consequences in the future.

The storm clouds came in the form of his mother becoming tired of waiting for Everett to divorce his wife. She often told Everett that he might as well divorce his wife now because she was only waiting for his father to die and for him to inherit everything. Everett was an only child and would inherit a big estate. Rafe's mother, thinking, like a gold digger, would do the same thing, under similar circumstances. That would be, wait and divorce Everett after he had inherited and gotten twice as much. Knowing that she would never marry Everett in the foreseeable future she dropped him for another man.

To make a long story short his Mom started dating the top salesman in the company she worked for. The problem was he was Jewish and she hated Jews. It wasn't that she just hated Jews but she had an equal amount of contempt for Negro's, Puerto Rican's the Irish, Poles, and Germans. In other words, she disliked anyone who wasn't Italian and you had to be from the central part of Italy at that. She couldn't stand Northern Italians and thought Sicilians were especially bad. Her attitude reminded me of a rhyme from Greer School. "People are funny, people are a sight, everybody's crazy, but I'm all right!"

All of this happened within a short six-month period and the way his mother handled herself revealed to Rafe how he ended up spending 10 years in Greer School. It ended with Rafe telling his mother that if she married this guy, Jerry Rosen, he was joining the Army and getting out of town. Nothing was going to deter his mother from the course she was on so Rafe had dinner with his surrogate father Everett and let him know what he planned. By now the relationship between the two had strengthened to the point that Rafe called Everett Pop, and Everett called Rafe Son.

When Rafe told Everett his plans to join the army if his mother married Jerry Rosen, Everett Responded, "Son, it would be better if you go to Harvard or Yale or some other elite University and further your education." Rafe knew where Everett was coming from and knew that in most ways it was the right advice so he let him know exactly why he was going to join the Army. "Mom has a way of unsettling our home life. I don't like her dumping you for someone she doesn't even like. I know if she marries this guy, it won't last six months, and I don't want to be around to watch it unravel. I know I could go to an Ivy League school, and you would pay for it as we've often talked about that, but I wouldn't do well in college at this time in my life. I don't want to do it, and I'm not ready for it. The truth is I'm backward; or put in other words, unworldly. I just don't know how the game is played. You know how I am about schoolwork. If I want to do it, I'm among the best, But, if I'm not engaged, I'm among the worst. At this time, I think I'd flunk out of Yale. I'll join the Army, gain some experience and when I get out, I'll go to college and graduate at the top of my class."

Rafe knew nothing was going to sway his mother from the course she was on, so when she married Jerry Rosen, Rafe joined the United States Army. Two days before he was scheduled for induction Rafe had dinner with Everett at Trader Vic's. Trader Vic's always gave the diners fortune cookies and when Rafe opened his that evening it said, "It is not flesh and blood, but the heart, which makes us father and son".

He showed it to Everett who exclaimed, "You know it's true, in fact, I wish I had sired you myself."

Rafe responded. "I wish you had too; it would have made a big difference in my life. But I'm glad we finally met and I want to thank you for all that you've done for me, but most of all for having faith in me. You're the only one that has ever believed I could accomplish great things".

Everett responded saying, "Since there's no doubt about my belief in you, I have a proposal for you. When you get back from your three years of service, you go back to school and get your degree, and then join me in starting a new business. I was thinking about an air freight business to ship perishable air cargo. Massoletti's serves only the finest Vegetables and Fruits but during the winter it's in short supply, so the logical solution is to ship them by air freight from the Southern Hemisphere. Since I want to do it for my own restaurant we might as well make a business of it, and do it for everyone. What do you think Rafe? Would such a venture interest you?" "It sure would Pop and I'd love to be in business with you, I think we'd be an unbeatable combination."

After dinner, Rafe drove Everett home to his apartment at 48th Street and Lexington Avenue. As they we saying goodbye, Rafe asked Everett if he had any last-minute advice, and Everett told him, that in basic training keep a low profile. It would be to your advantage if the drill instructors never know you by name." Having given Rafe that last bit of advice Everett walked across 48th Street into his apartment building. Rafe drove to the East Side Highway and headed for the George Washington Bridge and up the Palisades to Alpine, New Jersey. Two days later he left home for the big adventure. If he had only known what that would entail.

United States Army

If Rafe had thought it out, he would never have joined the army to be inducted in February. The truth is he hadn't thought it out and was inducted on the 5th of February primarily because of his family circumstances more than anything else. The 5th dawned cold and dreary with a low-lying overcast and a temperature in the 30's. On the way from his home in Alpine, New Jersey to the induction center in downtown Newark, Rafe patiently listened to a litany of warnings and advice from his mother whose primary concern was that he would never be able to stand Army discipline. She had never gotten over his rebellious conduct at Greer School and had somehow gotten the idea that he would repeat himself in the Army. While his mother was reading him the riot act Rafe was thinking, 'Mom, you left me at Greer School without even saying goodbye. Anyone would know the traumatic effect such action would have on a six-year-old, but that didn't stop you from taking that step. Then when I developed an attitude about being at Greer, what did you do? You blamed me." In spite of his mother's ranting and negative attitude towards him, Rafe still loved her. She had a hard time raising three children without any support from his father, plus she was the toughest woman he would ever know.

Their parting at the Federal Building in Newark was short and sweet. His mother kissed him goodbye and told him to stay out of trouble. Rafe knew his mother was well aware that he was joining the army because of her marriage, and she was happy to see him go. After all, he was the black sheep of the family, even if Everett Massoletti held him in the highest regard. It could be she saw her son, and Everett as birds of a feather, which in most cases seemed to be true, almost as if Everett was Rafe's biological father.

Rafe entered the Federal building and reported to an army sergeant and was told to take a seat in a large hall to await swearing-in. Just after 9:00 A.M. the three hundred recruits gathered in front of a stage and were told to raise their right hand and repeat after the officer in charge, "I Raphael Hawkins due solemnly swear that I will support and defend the Constitution of the United States against all enemies foreign and domestic; that I will bear true faith and allegiance to the same; and that I will obey the orders of the President of the United States and the officers appointed over me, according to regulations and the Uniform Code of Military Justice. So, Help me, God!"

With that being sworn the great adventure began. It took all day for the buses that would take them to Fort Dix to show up. This was an example of one of the Army's key axioms, hurry up and wait.

The drive to Fort Dix was uneventful. The only thing Rafe remembered was the wide diversity among the inductees. One could tell quite a bit about them from their manner of dress to their individual hairstyles. This would all change the next day when the Army would shave their hair and replace civilian clothing with uniforms. Then everyone looked the same and you had to judge individuals on their character rather than their appearance.

After a ride of about 1 1/2 hours, the buses arrived at the Fort Dix training center. The inductees piled off and gathered around an officer who was standing on a PT stand. It was about 11:00 P.M. by this time, and the temperature had dropped below freezing. The young troopers were about to learn a valuable lesson. After about 30 minutes into his indoctrination speech, the Capt. asked the assembled group, who were all wishing they were inside somewhere warm, "Who can type?" About five suckers raised their hands whereupon the Capt. said, "Follow Sergeant Jackson down to the Mess Hall. Report to the chief cook, you're on KP. So, while they may have escaped from the cold, they were now subject to hours of washing endless mountains of pots and pans. It is not fun. The moral to the assembled troops was simple, never volunteer. Not everyone immediately got that the Army would use asking for volunteers as a trick. Those who were most unworldly, like Rafe, took till the end of the week to get it, after that, it would be too late.

The next day the young troops were given a series of tests that included intelligence and aptitude after which the Army began to issue uniforms and gave each recruit the famous Army hair cut which was basically to shave your head. On the second day, Rafe was ordered to report to a Lt. Colonel in a small office. After reporting, the Colonel told Rafe that he had scored exceptionally high on the intelligence test and he wanted to know if Rafe would like to volunteer for a special assignment. Of course, Rafe was interested in what the special assignment was. The officer would only tell him that it was very top secret and that he would have a Top Secret, Security Clearance and would always carry a side arm. Rafe being the naive teen that he was, thought of himself as becoming a "secret agent man". The Colonel went on to say that the organization he would be joining was called DASA and that if he failed to receive his Top Secret, Security Clearance the Army could assign him to anything they thought him suited for. He had enlisted for Airborne so he would have to sign his commitment to Airborne away in order to volunteer for DASA. The idea was so appealing that Rafe signed away his commitment and volunteered.

Rafe found basic training a piece of cake. If there was anything that particularly bothered him it was the cold. Going through basic training at Fort Dix, New Jersey starting in February was not the smartest idea Rafe ever had. He hated cold weather and that first month was bitterly cold. When this was combined with the slow rate of learning of some of the recruits this led to misery. The army was amazingly good at taking a totally diverse group of trainees and in eight weeks turning them into a synchronized group that can march in formation without stepping all over one another, and actually fire and maneuver in the field. However, during the first week, this seemed an impossible task.

One thing Rafe found particularly frustrating was when on a day when the temperature was about 7 degrees the platoon was out in a parking lot learning the basics of military movements. Which included things such as learning to stand at attention, right face left face, and about-face. To his dismay, he discovered that it took some recruits over half an hour to learn to stand at attention. This didn't take into consideration how much longer it took them to learn right face, left face, and about-face. Since the process was like a naval convoy that moved at the speed of its slowest member, everyone had to freeze for hours while these morons were taught the simplest movements. Rafe was quickly learning that everyone was not alike. Not only were some people mentally challenged, but others were totally lacking in morality. Rafe was learning that character counts and unfortunately, some men didn't have any, to the point, that a cat or a dog was on a much higher level.

Other than the cold weather, basic training was somewhat enjoyable to Rafe. He actually loved learning to fire the M1 Grand rifle even to the point that he loved the sound of the ka-ching noise it made when it ejected an empty clip. He was a little disappointed that he didn't fire expert when he qualified with the M1 but he did fire sharpshooter.

As it turned out Rafe occupied the top bunk in the squad bay and the recruit in the lower bunk was a New Jersey boy named Bert Mueller. Bert and Rafe hit it off and became good friends. They also had something else in common. Both Rafe and Bert were the only volunteers for DASA in their company. They were also the only ones the Army had asked to volunteer. When the end of basic training arrived, the entire company went on a two-week leave and then on to their next assignment. That is all except the two volunteers Bert and Rafe. Instead, they were kept at Fort Dix for 5 more days during which they were put on KP washing mountains of pots and pans from dawn till dusk. By this time, they had learned the Army axiom, Never Volunteer, in spades.

 Five days into their KP ordeal they finally received orders which were to go on leave for two weeks and then report to Military Police School in Augusta, Georgia.

Their arrival at Fort Gordon was interesting when compared to their arrival at Fort Dix. For one thing, Fort Dix was freezing cold whereas Fort Gordon was hot and humid. In the case of Fort Dix, there was a Captain up on a PT stand trying to trick the inductees into KP, whereas at Fort Gordon there was a pair of NCOs warning the soon-to-be MPs about the danger of snakes on the post. They then held up a couple of dead six-foot-long cotton mouth rattlers to prove their point. Their warning didn't fall on deaf ears because for the remainder of their time at Fort Gordon all of the troopers were constantly on alert for the presence of snakes. They didn't see any, but that was beside the point.

Rafe joined the Army because he was very unworldly despite having gone out with a movie star on his first date. When they met Sergeant First Class Gates, their new Platoon Sergeant, he gathered the troops together for their first briefing during which he told them that he could make their journey through Military Police School a breeze. That is if they were all to chip in $20 each, to sort of grease the path. In a way, it was a sort of protection money. Or it was another way of saying "One hand washes the other." The troops agreed and as a result, a lot of the chickenshit which would have accompanied their class was eliminated. It was all sort of you-go-along-to-get-along philosophy. It was a good lesson that proved helpful.

Other than constantly fighting off chiggers and having to endure torrential thunderstorms from which the lightning could be dangerous, the only other thing that happened to Rafe during Military Police School, was his prowess in firing the .45 pistol. The M1911 .45 caliber was the standard sidearm for the United States Army from 1911-1986. Rafe had a natural, and phenomenal ability to fire a .45. When he fired it the first time, he fired a perfect score. The master sergeant instructor asked Rafe if he had been trained in civilian life and when he said he had never fired a pistol before the Captain, in charge, was called and he asked Rafe to fire again. The result was the same, a perfect score. None of this meant anything to Rafe except that he would be able to wear an expert badge for the pistol. However, the Army noted this ability and it would come back to haunt him later.

History repeated itself at the end of Military Police School. Everyone received orders and left for their next assignments except the six DASA volunteers. This time Rafe and his comrades were relegated to painting the outside of wooden barracks in the hot humid Georgia heat. This lasted for a week during which the six volunteers were given inoculations, almost daily, because no one knew where they would be going once their orders arrived.

Finally, on June 29th their orders arrived. They were to take a train across the United States from Augusta, Georgia to Albuquerque, New Mexico. Upon arrival in Albuquerque, they were to call a telephone number and wait to be picked up. Well, if they had volunteered because of the hush-hush aspect of DASA they weren't being disappointed. The train ride across the United States was an adventure in itself.

It started at the Railroad Station in Augusta where they boarded an Atlantic Coast train bound for St. Louis. Rafe remembered the following morning, watching as the train crept through Evansville, Indiana at about three miles per hour. It was the morning of June 30th and Rafe was amazed at how high the corn was standing in rows next to the tracks. Later that day they crossed the Mississippi and stopped in St. Louis. They changed trains to the Wabash and continued onto Kansas City, Missouri. At this point, they had to change railroad terminals to catch the Atchison, Topeka, and Santa Fe from a different terminal. It was about a five-block walk and the six troopers headed over to the Santa Fe carrying their duffel bags over their shoulders. Along the way cars filled with young ladies were slowing down, honking and waving. By the time they arrived at the Santa Fe Railroad Terminal, they were feeling pretty good.

The train called the Grand Canyon Special was the local that stopped at each and every station along the route to Albuquerque. That didn't mean anything to the six young men as they weren't in any hurry and really had no idea where they would eventually end up. None of them had been anywhere so traveling West was new and exciting. They would also be sleeping in Pullman berths which were a first for all of them. They left Kansas City about 9 P.M. and early morning found them stopped on a siding in Dodge City, Kansas. Rafe was up early and was standing at one of the Dutch doors of the rail car with the top half open, and the bottom closed. Off in the distance was the legendary city of Wyatt Earp, Doc Holliday, and Bat Masterson. While Rafe stood there gazing out at the sleeping city, he had a distinct feeling that somewhere ahead of him lay a great adventure. He was hoping it would lead him to something that would increase his status as he still had the intention of pursuing Jill, if Hollywood didn't make that impossible. Nevertheless, Rafe was excited about the future, he knew something big lay ahead.

The run from Dodge City to Albuquerque was interesting to the young men from the East. For one thing, they traveled miles without seeing even one human being. There were plenty of cattle, but hardly a soul. When they passed through Raton Pass from Colorado into New Mexico the cattle disappeared also. Then it was just miles and miles of sagebrush and tumbleweeds. Rafe remembers stopping in the town of Wagon Mound which was about five blocks wide and ten blocks long. From there he sent his mother a postcard which she kept for years. He was just keeping her informed of his progress as they moved southwest.

At about seven in the evening, the train finally pulled into Albuquerque and the group got off on the platform which led right into the Hotel Alverado. The Hotel Alvarado was an Albuquerque landmark, but the citizens allowed it to be torn down in 1970. Rafe was impressed with the architecture of the Alvarado which was distinctly representative of the southwest. He knew he was in a different world once he stepped off the train. What he didn't know was that living 300 yards from the place he alighted, lived a person who would have a major impact on his life.

They called DASA and were told to wait at the station and a truck would be sent to pick them up. They checked out the Hotel Alverado while waiting, and then settled down not knowing if the Army would send the truck in one hour like promised, or three or four hours. They had no idea where they were headed so they had no idea how long it would take the truck to arrive. When the truck showed up right on time, they were surprised that it was not an Army vehicle but one from the Department of Defense.

They piled aboard and the truck took off, headed East through Albuquerque. It took about 30 minutes to reach the outskirts of town and there they came upon a huge sign that said, Sandia Base, Home of Sandia Laboratories. The sign went on to say Your entry upon this base gives permission for your person to be searched, and your vehicle to be searched, and a list of other security regulations.

They were checked through the security checkpoint and drove about a half mile before pulling up in front of a very substantial two-story building.

Anywhere else it would have been headquarters, and they assumed it was. They got out and asked the driver if this was headquarters and if they should go in and report to someone. The driver said, 'No this is your barracks, go in and report to the First Sergeant."

That's when they found out what DASA was. The First Sergeant told them that DASA stood for the Defense Atomic Support Agency and that Sandia Laboratories manufactured and assembled nuclear weapons. They learned that they were detached from the Army to the Department of Defense, and would serve in the security force that protected this very sensitive base. He also told them that they were lucky to have been chosen for this assignment because it was one of the best they could have been assigned to. They would be treated much like civilians and as long as they did their jobs exactly as ordered they would have no trouble. However, he made it crystal clear that screwing up on the job was a good way to get into some very serious shit.

Just being curious, Rafe asked why they had been held back at Basic Training and Military Police School. The Sergeant said they were waiting for your Secret and then your Top Secret security clearances to be approved because if they weren't, you would have been reassigned.

The work wasn't hard; you just had to be careful not to become complacent and to strictly follow orders. For the most part, Rafe was patrolling in a pickup truck, at night, around the desert perimeter of Sandia Base. His group also controlled access to the secure technical areas where assembly or training was taking place.

The group of young men Rafe served with were exceptional for the most part. Since the Army didn't want a bunch of yahoos around the nuclear facility most of the security guards were draftees from elite universities such asHarvard, Yale, and Stanford. Rafe's roommate Dick Simpson was a Yale graduate and was about three years older than Rafe.If Rafe had a problem in his new company, it was that he was a few years younger, and not as well educated. One problem he had was that he wasn't 21 years old which meant he couldn't go out drinking with the boys as 21 was the drinking age in New Mexico. Upon his arrival at Sandia Rafe had about six more months to go before reaching the established drinking age. This didn't particularly bother Rafe except it brought down on his head a little bit of harassment. Most of the young men were all right, but in every group, you've got a few assholes. It wasn't much different from high school, but Rafe had never experienced any because, at Greer and Rhodes School, it wasn't tolerated. However, here he was out in the real world where every kind of human behavior existed.

An incident occurred one night that would begin to change the perception his older comrades held of Rafe. Several times during the night, the roving patrols would come into the base to take a thirty-minute coffee break. The break room was a large guard shack at the entrance to one of the secure tech areas. This is where the Sergeant of the Guard could usually be found and on this particular evening, there were about 15 guards present along with the sergeant.

As usual, the conversation centered around drinking and women and their number one hangout the Grand Canyon Saloon. Even in the short time, he had been at Sandia, Rafe had heard dozens and dozens of outrageous tales concerning the sexual prowess of his buddies. Of course, since he couldn't accompany them, this led to a certain amount of derision directed at the unworldly Rafe. Although most of the M.P.s were good guys and treated Rafe like a younger brother, this wasn't universal. One of the men named Brannigan was a big uncouth braggart from Boston who would always get on Rafe's case, but not in a playful manner. He was a typical bully and Rafe sort of held him in contempt.

One night during the break Brannigan turned his attention to Rafe and was ridiculing his lack of knowledge of the opposite sex. Of course, this came in the form of Rafe having no sexual knowledge of women; and having to be a virgin. Finally, Brannigan blurted out, "You've not only never been laid, but you've never even had a date." Rafe laughed and replied, "Actually I have had a date." This only encouraged Brannigan to go on, Yeah, so you've had one date and probably with the ugliest girl in the school." Rafe laughing said, "No Brannigan, but she'd make every woman you've ever dated look like a pack animal, and that would be all fitting and proper looking at you."

Trying to get the last word Brannigan blurted, "Don't tell me you dated the Prom Queen." Then Rafe dropped the bomb, "No actually she's a movie star!"

Rafe thought Brannigan was going to fall down and roll around on the floor in a fit of laughter. Then Brannigan came right back with, "That's the biggest crock of shit I've ever heard. All right wise-ass, I'll call your bluff, what movie star did you go out with?"

The room was suddenly deathly silent as everyone thought they were about to hear the biggest tall tale ever told. Rafe answered, "Jill Haworth."

Not to be turned aside Brannigan asked, "You mean that beautiful blond that was Sal Mineo's girlfriend in Exodus?"

Rafe was laughing to himself as he answered, "The very same one." Brannigan was like a dog with a bone, he was not going to let the matter go. He came back with "OK smart ass, how did you get up the nerve to ask her out?"

Now Rafe delivered the coup de grace, He simply said, "I didn't ask her out, she asked me."

Now Brannigan did fall down and began to roll around kicking his feet in the air and making sounds like a braying jackass. He was yelling, "Of all the bullshit stories I've ever heard that takes the cake."

Rafe headed out of the break room and said in parting, "Frankly I don't care whether you believe it or not."

Of course, by the next day, the story was the talk of Company A. The kid Rafe said he had taken out the movie starlet Jill Haworth and not only that but she had asked him out.

The following night when Rafe and his roommate Dick had turned out the lights and were ready to doze off Dick said, "Hey Rafe, that story about having dated a movie star. If I was you, I'd drop it. You'll become an object of ridicule if you're not already."

Rafe responded with, "It happens to be the truth, Dick."

So, his unconvinced Roommate said, "Well how did you ever come to know her?"

Rafe told him the truth, 'I was her tutor at Rhodes School in New York."

Dick then said, "It may be true, but no one will ever believe it."

So, Rafe said, "I really don't care whether they believe it or not."

A few weeks later Dick was passing the mail room in the barracks when the mail clerk yelled out, "Hey Dick come over here I've got to show you something." When Dick walked over the mail clerk showed him a letter addressed to Rafe Hawkins, but in the upper left-hand corner, the return address was Jill Haworth with a Beverly Hills address. Dick smiled and shook his head and exclaimed, "Well I'll be damned, he was telling the truth." The word spread like wildfire in an atmosphere rife with rumors.

While that letter caused an uproar in the Company it began to give Rafe the impression that the Hollywood lifestyle was beginning to change Jill. The tone of that letter was different, being less intimate, and not as playful and teasing. Rafe had been expecting the change, although he still had hopes that his playmate, the Hollywood starlet, wouldn't fall victim to all of the temptations she'd encounter out there. As her letters became less frequent Rafe thought maybe I should find a girlfriend here in Albuquerque just in case my prophecy is a delusion. Rafe was thinking, "I joined the Army to gain worldly experience so I had better gain some with women, who to me represent a real mystery."

The Ice Princess

It was the 12th of October 1962 and Company A was out in the desert at the range practicing with their .45 caliber 1911 pistols. Rafe fired first as it was a given that he would fire a perfect score and the rest would try to match him. Although it was only 11:30 A.M. it was already scorching hot and Rafe was sitting, leaning up against the front of the gray Dept. Of Defense bus that was waiting to take them back to the base. At least it offered a bit of shade. It was Friday and as the men completed their firing, they were congregating at the rear of the bus talking about the subject that was always on their minds; getting laid. Of course, most of them couldn't get laid if their life depended on it, but let's put it this way, they had high hopes.

Rafe wanted to go along, but he was still under the legal drinking age so he'd have to wait a few more months until he could drink legally. Rafe was sitting in the sand listening to his buddy's conversation most of which involved money. It was the 12th of the month and the men had already spent their entire month's wages drinking and chasing women. Finally, John Elliott said, "Well someone must have some money" to which Rafe's roommate Dick replied, "No one I know." Then John came back with, "How about your roommate, the kid? He's loaded he hasn't spent a cent since he was inducted. Tell him we'll take him down to the Grand Canyon if he buys the drinks."

Rafe was down near the front of the bus listening so he knew what Dick was going to ask him as he walked down the length of the bus. Dick said, "Hey Rafe, how would you like to out with us tonight, down to the Grand Canyon Saloon, drinking, picking up girls, and all that." Rafe already knew what he was going to say so he responded, "I'd love to, but I'm underage, they won't let me in." Dick had an answer to that, He said, "Don't worry about that, we spend all of our time off at the Grand Canyon, we know the guy at the door, he'll let you in. However, you'll have to buy the drinks. We're all broke." Rafe said, "Ok I'll buy the drinks if you take me along."

So, it was all set, Rafe was going out with the boys for the first time since he arrived at Sandia Base on July 1st. He was well aware that they were only taking him along to buy the drinks, and if they knew the guy at the door as they said they did, then they could have taken him along back in July or August just as easily. After they were driven back from the desert to the main base Rafe went to the bank and withdrew some money and waited for the big event.

After dinner eight of the members of Company A piled into two cars and headed downtown. Rafe felt this is what he had joined the Army for, going out with his buddies and gaining real-world experience. He didn't know it, but fate was stalking him. If he only knew what was about to happen!

What Dick had said would happen at the door to the Grand Canyon was accurate. The eight young men walked in a single file with their military IDs out for inspection. Rafe was in the middle of the eight and the man at the door hardly glanced at this identification. Just like that, they were in. They took a table about 20 feet from the entrance with three guys on each side with one at the head of the table and another at the other end. Rafe looked around and took the place in. There wasn't anything fancy about it. It was a large room with booths down the outer walls next to the windows. It had a very long bar at least 75 feet long and a fairly large dance floor behind which was a stage occupied by a live band. The center of the Grand Canyon was filled with numerous tables like the one Rafe was seated at. It was still early, yet the place had a big crowd with more young people coming in every minute.

Rafe couldn't get enough of the Grand Canyon. He had heard literally hundreds of tales about the goings on in this one particular place. Rafe just sat there sipping a beer, the first one he had ever had in a bar, and he surveyed the scene. He was thinking, "This is great."

At the head of the table, John Elliott said to Dick, "I wonder if she'll come in tonight?" Dick responded with, "Well you never know, but I've seen her in here quite a few times on Friday nights." Rafe being curious asked, "Who are you talking about?" Dick answered, "The Ice Princess! Rafe wanted to know who this Ice Princess was. John said, "She's got to be the hottest girl in Albuquerque, she's drop-dead gorgeous. She walks through that door you'll know it's her." Now Rafe was really curious so he said, "Why is she called the Ice Princess?" Dick piped in and said, "Because she's untouchable. You can dance with her but no one ever gets a date. She's gorgeous but cold as Ice, hence the name. If she walks through that door, you'll know what we mean."

Wow! Rafe was thinking this girl must really be something. I wonder how she compares to Jill. About 30 minutes later he found out. He was looking over towards the door, which was the type of double swinging door found in an old western saloon when two girls entered together. One was short and unattractive and the other was the Ice Princess. Rafe had no doubt mainly because his heart started pounding in his chest. It was an adrenalin rush. Dick grabbed his arm and squeezed it and whispered, "The Ice Princess."

Rafe said, 'I know, you said I'd know her when I saw her."

John said, "Don't get your hopes up, you who date movie stars, this one's way out of your class.

The Ice Princess and her friend took a booth about fifteen feet away, and the Princess was right in Rafe's line of sight. This saved him the embarrassment of constantly turning around to look at her. Rafe had never had such a powerful initial reaction to a woman, not even Jill. It's called being struck by the thunderbolt. It wasn't long before John Elliott got up from the head of the table and said, "I must be a glutton for punishment, but I've got to give it another try." He proceeded to walk over to the Princess and asked her to dance. She accepted and he led her out to the dance floor. Rafe watched them dancing and realized that he was jealous already and that he had never even met the girl. The truth was he didn't want anyone else near her. After about three minutes the dance ended and John walked the Princess back to her booth and stood there, talking to her for a minute, and then returned to their table, shot down in flames. Rafe almost wanted to cheer. Next to try his luck was Dick. Dick was a Yale graduate and a pretty cool guy, but he received the same treatment as John, which meant, being shot down in flames. The young men were going around the table like it was a peck order, with the perceived coolest guy first, and then down the order. After the first three struck out Rafe realized that in the end, it was going to get down to him. He was last and least, and he was going to have to go over and dance with the Ice Princess and try to score. At least that is how the other guys would have put it. He knew what they were thinking, If, you can date a movie star, let's see what you've got.

Sure enough, about 30 minutes later it was his turn. All of the others had struck out. This made Rafe feel pretty good because at least he couldn't do any worse than they had.

Finally, John said, "Ok kid show us what a swordsman you are. Show us how you did the movie star."

Rafe thought he'd make a joke out of it and said, "Ok guys, you've been waiting for this all night, and now I'm going to show you how a really cool guy puts the moves on a chick."

With that, Rafe got up and walked over, and approached the Ice Princess. Was Rafe a little intimated? You bet he was. With Jill, he had developed a friendship with her over three months before they went out. In this case, he had three minutes to make an impression, and the truth was he had no idea how to do it. Rafe walked up and politely said to the Princess, "I'd be honored if I could have the next dance." He was rewarded with a dazzling smile and she got up and they walked out onto the dance floor.

She was wearing a brown dress that accentuated her body. Large breasts, small waist, and the most perfect legs. She was 5'9" tall and seemed to fit perfectly into Rafe's arms. With only three inches difference in height, she was practically looking into his eyes. She had dark eyes, almost black, and shoulder-length wavy black hair. Rafe was thinking she is nothing like Jill who was 5"2" tall with deep blue eyes and a very fair complexion. Rafe knew he only had three minutes, but he had no pickup line. So, he just acted like a normal human being.

The first thing he said was, "Hi I'm Rafe Hawkins."

The Ice Princess answered, "Glad to make your acquaintance Rafe, I'm Pilar Trujillo, but everyone calls me Ella."

Rafe just asked her the next logical question as he guided her across the dance floor, very much aware of the fact his arm was around her waist. "Are you from Albuquerque?"

She shook her head slightly and said, "No I'm from a small mountain town up near the Colorado border called Cimarron. Where are you from Rafe?"

Rafe answered I'm from Brooklyn, New York."

Ella answered, "Wow, the big city, that's exciting."

Rafe smiled and said, "I guess you could say that. Then he asked, "What do you do here in Albuquerque?"

To which Ella said, "I work for the Dept. Of the Interior in Sport Fisheries and Wildlife."

Rafe came back with I'm at Sandia Base in security."

Ella said, "I figured as much since all of your friends that asked me to dance are from Sandia also, and you have the military look."

Rafe was running out of things to say to this gorgeous creature so he commented on her very slight accent. The Hispanic population from the Southwest sort of drag out the last syllable of a word, so Rafe said, "I love the way you speak English, your slight accent, it's almost melodic, I could listen to you all day." Rafe wasn't lying, but it wasn't only her accent that made him want to listen to her all day."

She countered with, "I like your accent too." Of course, Rafe knew that wasn't exactly true as New York accents don't exactly have a nice sound.

At this point Rafe didn't know what else to say, so like a drowning man grasping at straws, he said the first thing that came into his mind. Talk about divine guidance! It turned out to be just the right thing. Rafe asked, "Do you have a large family, any brothers or sisters?" Ella answered, "Actually I do, I have four sisters and a brother and two of my sisters are living with me here in Albuquerque. I'm helping them get through Secretarial and Nursing school so that they can get a good job." The two then got into discussing Ella's family and how they were doing, when the dance suddenly ended. Rafe then knew he had about one more minute before his chance with Ella would slip away.

They walked back to her booth and when they arrived Rafe figured he had nothing to lose since he and Ella were having a nice conversation about her siblings Rafe said, "Do you mind if I sit down and talk to you for a while?"

Ella looked at Rafe gave him another big genuine smile and said," Sure I'd like that." She sat down and Rafe slid into the booth next to her, this brought to mind the start of a popular TV program that went like this. "You're traveling through another dimension, a dimension not only of sight and sound but of mind. A journey into a wondrous land whose boundaries are that of imagination. That's the signpost up ahead-your next stop, the Twilight Zone. What was happening was like stepping into the Twilight Zone. From the moment he sat down it was as if Rafe could do no wrong. Every word he said, was the right word.

Pilar introduced him to her companion who happened to be her cousin Elena. The conversation began with what is it like to live in New York and drifted into living in Cimarron and Albuquerque. After a few minutes, Elena said to Ella, "Ella, remember, I have to be in Santa Fe early tomorrow so I have to cut out and leave you two, much as I'd like to stay."

Ella replied, "That's right Elena I almost forgot, but I'm sure Rafe can entertain me with tales of New York."

With that, Elena excused herself and left Ella and Rafe sitting side by side in the booth. Rafe loved sitting next to her, but he wanted to sit across from her while they talked so he could be looking at her lovely face. When he moved over across from her, she asked why he was shifting over to the other side. He gave a truthful answer and said, "So I can look into your lovely eyes while we're talking." while he was shifting over, he glanced over at his buddies sitting not far away and the look on their faces was that of pure consternation. They couldn't believe their eyes. Rafe couldn't be bothered with them as he turned his attention back to the object of his desire.

Rafe then said to Ella, "I have to admit that I didn't really grow up on the streets of New York City, but went to a boarding school in the Hudson Valley about 85 miles north of the city."

"Really, then you must be from a rich family?"

Rafe replied, "Actually, although my father is from a wealthy family he abandoned my mother, and us kids, and I was raised in a school supported by the church."

Ella then asked, "Can I ask you something Rafe?"

Rafe answered, "Sure, go, ahead." Then she said, "Why are your friends sitting over there with such surprised looks on their faces?"

Rafe laughed and replied, "Because they can't believe I'm sitting over here talking to you."

"Why?"

"Because they think I'm unworldly and that I've lied about the only date I've ever had in my life."

"You've only had one date"

"Yes, but it was extraordinary"

"Why did you have only one date"

"Because when I finished my junior year in High School, I was only 5' tall and weighed 100 pounds."

'I don't believe it." Ella was smiling by this time having a good time.

Then she said, "You're tall now. How tall are you Rafe?"

He answered. "6' tall and 160 pounds. I grew a foot in 14 months"

Ella was almost giggling when she said, "Guess what Rafe?"

He said, "What"

Then she said, "Two years ago I was as skinny as a rail and men wouldn't give me a second glance."

Then Rafe asked, "Do you think you have a beautiful body now?"

Ella replied, "Well I attracted you, as well as all of your friends, didn't I."

"Then you'd like to know what they were saying about you before you even arrived tonight."

"What were they saying."

"Basically, that you were so drop-dead gorgeous that I would know it was you, as soon as you walked through the door. And they were telling the truth because that's what happened"

"Getting back to your only date, what do they think you lied about?"

"That my first and only date was with a movie star"

"Are you kidding?"

"No, it's true, my first date was with a movie star."

"Who was it"

"Jill Haworth"

"You don't mean that beautiful blond who was in Exodus do you?"

"Yes, that's who it was."

"I can't believe it! How did it happen?"

"Well now you know why my buddies don't believe me, it's pretty unbelievable."

"How did it happen?"

"I'll tell you if you want to hear the story. It's very interesting. It may take a while. Are you up for it?"

"Oh yes, you have to tell me."

So, Rafe told Ella the story which took about 30 minutes, at the end of which She said, "That's incredible. You mean to say you had a movie star as your high school sweetheart and no one knew?"

Rafe said, "Yes that's how it happened.

"So, your friends still think you're lying; and made up the whole story?" Rafe Said, "No, they believe it now because I received a letter from her from Hollywood and the mail clerk spread the word to the whole company."

"Rafe, this is so exciting! Tell me something she told you about Hollywood that no one else knows."

Rafe thought a minute and then said, "She hates John Wayne and thinks he's the meanest nastiest man in Hollywood."

"I can't believe this. This is the craziest story."

"Imagine how I felt when she asked me out."

Ella said, "Can I ask you something?"

Rafe said, Sure go ahead."

"How do I compare to your movie star." Rafe asked in return, "Do you mean in looks?"

"Ella answered "Yes, am as good-looking. You said I was drop-dead gorgeous, but how do I compare to a movie star?"

"You are as beautiful as Jill, but in a different way."

"How do you mean."

"Well, you're both beautiful, but Jill is 5 foot two, eyes of blue, while you are 5 foot nine eyes of brown."

"Is that all?"

"No, there's a pretty big difference between you."

'I still don't get it."

"Well, Jill was discovered by the producer, director Otto Preminger, because he saw a picture of Jill when she was 15 years old and was so taken by her beautiful face that he went and found her and signed her to a five-movie contract"

"So, I'm not as beautiful."

'Yes, you are, you're just as beautiful, but in a different way."

"Are you going to tell which way?"

"Ok, but don't get angry with me. Remember when I said that the guys were talking about you and I asked them whom they were talking about and they said, The Ice Princess."

"Is that what they call me?"

"Yes, they do, and you were so gorgeous that I would know it was you, as soon as you walked through the door. Have you ever heard the expression 'built like a brick shithouse?" 'I'm sorry for the crudeness of the expression, but it gets the idea across

"Yes"

"Well Ella that's you, God made you far out of the ordinary." Is that what you wanted to hear?"

"Yes, now I understand."

"How about another turn, around the dance floor, I should add you're very graceful too."

Rafe took Ella out for another dance and this time they danced very close together with Ella's head on his shoulder. He was thinking, "I definitely stepped over the line into the twilight zone, God must really love me."

That's the way the evening went. Rafe was convinced that he was going to get a date and may have even found a new girlfriend.

A few hours into their budding relationship Ella asked a seemingly innocuous question which Rafe answered truthfully like the innocent young man that he was. The question was "What do you plan to do when you get out of the service?" It is a very simple question yet Rafe failed to realize that his answer would seal his fate. It would take a couple of years for the implications of his answer to play out, but if he could see into the future he would have answered in another way. As it was, he said, Everett Massoletti wants me to go to one of the top business schools like Wharton or Harvard and then join him in a new business venture as his partner. He's thinking of starting an Air Freight company possibly named Air Fresh Perishables. Anyway, that's the plan."

Rafe and Ella had a great evening dancing and talking about what they had experienced in life which wasn't that much since they were young. Life was just starting. You could say they were in the springtime of their youth, and all things were possible. One thing Rafe learned was that Ella was two years older than he. It should have set off alarm bells, but it didn't. Rafe was actually beginning to believe that he was charming enough to attract Jill and now Ella. He hadn't learned about delusional thinking yet.

Time flies when you're having fun and before they knew it the evening was coming to an end. The last call was given. and Rafe asked Ella if she needed a ride home. She indicated she only lived about 8 blocks away and could easily walk. Rafe seeing this as a golden opportunity to find out where she lived said, "Would you like me to walk you home?" This isn't the best part of town and it's almost 1:30 A.M. Ella accepted Rafe's proposal and said she's like him to walk her home.

Rafe walked over to the table where his buddies were still shaking their heads in wonder and paid the bar bill. He told them he wouldn't be riding back to the base with them and instead would walk Ella home. John Elliott said, "If I hadn't witnessed it with my own eyes, I'd never believe it. How the hell did you pull it off? Jesus! It's the Ice Princess"

Rafe answered jokingly, 'I told you guys I was going to show you how a cool dude picks up a girl. Someday I'll clue you in."

It wasn't ten minutes later that Rafe and Ella walked out through the swinging western doors, made a right turn, and headed down 2nd Street towards Central Avenue. Rafe was as high as a kite. He couldn't figure out how this had come about, and he really didn't care. If it worked, it worked. Along the route, Ella and Rafe chatted about New Mexico and Albuquerque.

When they reached Central Avenue, the main street of Albuquerque, they broke into an area of bright Neon lights coming from the Kimo Theater, Alverado Hotel, and many stores along the street. They turned North on Central and walked under the Santa Fe Railroad tracks using the underpass that Central Avenue had under the tracks. Rafe had no idea where they would end up, but he didn't care much either.

When they were halfway up the rising slope that led from the Santa Fe tracks to the old Albuquerque High School Ella stopped and said, "What are you smiling about Rafe?"

Rafe who wasn't aware that he had been smiling, Said, "Have I been smiling?"

Ella answered, "Yes you have, like the cat that just swallowed the canary." Rafe almost started laughing because the last time someone had said that to him it was the elevator operator just after he had kissed Jill goodnight.

Rafe didn't want to tell Ella what had brought the smile to his lips so he said, "I can't tell you, it's too embarrassing."

Ella pleaded, "Oh Rafe, please tell me."

Rafe again said, "No I can't."

Ella then said, "If you tell me I'll give you a reward!"

Rafe took the bait and exclaimed, "What reward will I get?"

Then Ella played her ace card, she gave him her most dazzling smile and said, "Will you settle for a kiss?"

As she well knew, there was no way he was going to refuse, so he said, "I was thinking that there must have been over 200 men in the Grand Canyon tonight, considering all those that were coming and going, so how did I end up with the Ice Princess?"

Ella was really enjoying their interaction and looked at him rather seriously, although only acting, and said, "It was always you Rafe. When Elena and I first walked in and sat down in the booth, the first thing we did is look around the room. We both saw the eight good-looking young men sitting together, and Edna asked me, "Which one do you like?" I answered, "The young one in the boat-necked sweater." She continued, "You kept me waiting for almost 45 minutes before you asked me to dance." After hearing that, Rafe couldn't contain himself and took her into his arms and kissed her. The kiss was more than intoxicating. When it ended Rafe kissed her again. So, there they were standing on the sidewalk in the middle of the night making out.

When they finally stopped kissing Rafe said, "I think this is the start of a beautiful friendship."

Ella said, "I agree." Then they continued walking up Central Avenue.

A right turn on Broadway S.E. and another couple of blocks brought them to the large adobe house in which Ella occupied the basement apartment. There was a driveway paved with concrete stretching to an open area behind the house which had a few more apartments with a staircase leading up to a balcony, not unlike what you would see in a motel with stairs leading to the upper floor.

The couple made their way down to Ella's basement apartment entering from the backyard. Ella whispered to Rafe to be very quiet so as not to wake her two sisters who were sleeping in a back room. The apartment was a little on the chilly side since it was the 12th of October and the Albuquerque evenings were getting a little cool. After walking through the dining room, the couple came to the largest room in the apartment which was the living room which was about 25' long and 16' wide. Near the front of the living room next to an easy chair was a fairly large gas space heater. Ella whispered I'd like to start the heater since It's so cold in here, but I think it's broken.

Rafe said I'll look at it and see if I can get it started." It took about fifteen minutes at which time Rafe said, "I hope we don't blow ourselves up when I strike a match to light it." Luckily it started right up and soon the room was warm. Ella and Rafe sat on the sofa and Ella snuggled right up to him. Rafe; was thinking, "Calling her The Ice Princess was a miss characterization as she was more smoldering hot than ice cold." Rafe and Ella then took up where they left off when they were making out on Central Avenue. It was the most erotic experience in Rafe's short life. Soon the two were stretched out on the couch and practically wrapped around each other. Rafe wanted to take things further and let his hands explore her fantastic body, but he didn't want to ruin what could be their budding romance. He didn't know what Ella was thinking, but he wasn't looking for a one-night stand. He wanted a girlfriend. He wanted to see this beautiful girl over and over. If the physical part had to wait that was fine with him. He knew in the back of his mind that if he didn't screw this up, Ella would be the first girl he would ever make love to.

To say they had a good time that evening would be a massive understatement. As it turned out Ella fell asleep in his arms with the lights out and a faint glow coming in through the windows. Rafe looked down at the sleeping beauty and couldn't get over his good luck. First, it was Jill, and now Ella. He was thinking to himself, 'Maybe there's more to me than meets the eye." After watching Ella sleeping for about 30 minutes Rafe gently lifted Ella's sleeping form from his lap, lay her down on the couch, went into her bedroom, and returned with a blanket. He covered her with the blanket and made himself comfortable in the easy chair. Early the next morning Rafe awoke when he heard some faint giggling. He opened his eyes to find two young ladies staring at him and quietly laughing. He smiled, got up, and said, "Hi Girls, you must be Lorie and, Delcy I'm Rafe." They smiled and introduced themselves. Rafe then said, "This isn't as bad as it looks in fact It's quite innocent. We got home so late that I couldn't get back to the base."

Emily the eldest said, "don't worry Rafe we don't think anything of it." The four of them chatted for a while and then Rafe said, "I think now that the buses are running, I'd better be getting back to the base."

Ella walked Rafe to the door where she handed him a slip of paper. When he looked down at it, she whispered, "It's my telephone number."

Rafe said, "Does this mean I get a date?"

Ella kissed him and said, "Yes, I had a wonderful time last night and I want to go out on a date with you. I'll be your second date."

Rafe laughed and answered, "Looks like we're off to a good start, it might turn out to be a beautiful friendship." With that, he turned and left her apartment. As he walked down the driveway from the rear of Ella's apartment building, he was as high as a kite. To Rafe everything that happened was unbelievable. As he turned down Broadway, he felt like he was the king of the world and the luckiest man alive. As he stood on the corner of Central Ave. and Broadway, waiting for the bus, he could have been singing the Eagles song that went "Standing on the corner in Winslow, Arizona, such a fine sight to see." He was also thinking "God definitely loves me."

Once on the bus headed up Central towards Sandia Base Rafe began to think about the reception that was sure to greet him. His buddies would want to know the details of the seduction of the Ice Princess. It would be ridiculous to tell them the truth that basically nothing happened. He was gone all night and to them, that meant only one thing, Rafe had scored! Since nothing he said would be believed, Rafe decided to say nothing, just let them think whatever they wanted.

When he walked into his room there was Dick who was a witness to the previous night's unbelievable events. The first words out of his mouth were, "Hawkins, you son of a bitch. How did you manage to pull that off?" If I hadn't witnessed it with my own eyes, I'd never believe it. Imagine seducing the Ice Princess." Rafe simply lay down on his cot and smiled. Then he said, "I told you guys you were about to witness how a real smooth operator puts the moves on a chick." Dick was sitting on his bunk across from Rafe's shaking his head, then chimed in, 'Maybe we're all wrong about you because we didn't believe a word you said about Jill Haworth either; until we saw you in action last night. What the hell did you say to her anyway. I mean she seemed to fall into your hands right from the beginning?"

Rafe was really smiling now as he answered, "I just have a different approach to women than the rest of you guys, and apparently women like it. Remember She's only the 2nd girl I ever tried to date. Also, I'll be taking her out later this week and I think I may have a new girlfriend."

Dick said, "Well you must be doing something right because we never saw anything like it. When the word gets around. you'll probably even get Brannigan to shut his big mouth."

Rafe came back with, "If he doesn't shut his mouth, I'll shut it for him."

Dick responded with, 'Don't get too far up on your high horse, Brannigan outweighs you by 40 or 50 pounds."

That didn't deter Rafe who countered with, "Brannigan doesn't scare me. What he doesn't know is that my dad arranged for me to take boxing lessons at the New York Athletic Club from a private trainer for two years. The trainer never told me, but told my dad, that I had the speed of a striking cobra, and although the size of a middleweight, I punched like a heavyweight.

So, It Brannigan decides to go after Ella the way he did with Jill, I'm going to tear him a new asshole, Figuratively, speaking, of course."

Dick said, "Well I'm not going to argue with you since everything you say seems to come true."

And the word did get around the company, for soon Rafe was treated with more respect and admiration, and the teasing about lack of knowledge about women stopped. Of course, it stopped everyone except Brannigan, who just happened to be a big-course bully. In fact, nothing was going to stop him until he got knocked on his ass.

Later that week Rafe called Ella and asked her out to dinner. She accepted and he took her to the Cole Hotel just off Central Avenue which had a very nice atmosphere and was highly recommended by the officers and NCOs. Ella was wearing the same dress she'd been wearing the night he'd met her. She was a lovely girl, but obviously didn't have much money to devote to nice clothing. It didn't matter to Rafe as he would have thought she was the most beautiful girl in Albuquerque if she had been dressed in rags.

On the way home, walking down Central Avenue, they stopped at the same spot they had stopped the previous Friday and did the same thing, kissed. There was no question anymore Rafe and Ella were girlfriend and boyfriend. It was the start of a beautiful friendship and both were as happy as they could possibly be.

The only downside was Brannigan's desire to turn something beautiful into something ugly. One night when the MPs were gathered in the break room alongside the Military Tech Area the trouble started. Addressing Rafe, Brannigan began, "First you tell, that tall tale of dating that little whore who's now blowing everyone in Hollywood, and then you expect us to believe you're banging that whore the Ice Princess whom we all know has fucked every GI at Sandia Base and Kirtland. Man, that is one well-used pussy." That was the last straw as far as Rafe was concerned, and he countered it with.

"Brannigan a hog like you couldn't get a date with a decent girl if your life depended on it, but those of us who can, aren't going to listen to any more of your filthy sewer mouth.Brannigan countered with, 'Oh yeah! What's a little piss ant like you going to do about it?

Rafe looked straight into his eyes and said, "Introduce you to the arsenal of democracy, and then tear you a new asshole."

Brannigan wasn't about to take that from someone he outweighed by fifty pounds and said, "You want, to step outside right now and settle this?"

Rafe countered, "I don't think getting a court-martial for fighting on duty is the way to go, but how about we meet at the gym after chow tomorrow night and go a few rounds?"

Brannigan couldn't wait and said, "I'll be there you little blowhard, and I'll teach you a lesson you'll never forget."

Rafe came back with, "Talk is cheap Brannigan, and you know what they say? The bigger they are, the harder they fall."

Brannigan was under the assumption that he had won a great victory, so wanting to have the last word as he left the room he said, "Spread the word that if anyone wants to see the little asshole get put in his place, be in the gym tomorrow after chow.

Rafe turned to the sergeant of the guard, Sergeant Ellis, and asked, "Will you ask Lt. Connolly if he'll act as referee, for the big event? He'll be the officer of the guard when we go out for tomorrow night's patrols and I think he'll be interested in seeing this settled."

Sergeant Ellis asked, "Why do you think that he'll be interested in seeing this resolved?"

Then Rafe told him what he was thinking, and why he challenged Brannigan to a fight in the gym, "Because if a fight breaks out on duty everyone will be in trouble. That includes you, me, and the Lieutenant. This way the Army will approve."

Sergeant Ellis replied, "I like the way you think kid. You're right, the Army would have a shit fit if we had a fight break out while on duty, especially here at Sandia. In some places you might get away with it, but not here. We'd all end up in a shit storm and that includes the Lieutenant."

So, the big event was on, and the word spread like wildfire. By the time 1900 hours arrived the next day just about everyone from Company's A and B, that weren't on duty, gathered at the base gym for the big fight. After his seduction of the Ice Princess, Rafe's reputation had been enhanced immeasurably. His fellow troopers knew he was the best pistol shot at Sandia Base, then he takes down the Ice Princess, and now he was showing he had a big pair by taking on the big bully of the base. They were all thinking the same thing. Hawkins isn't that big! It was a big deal, even the officers and NCOs came in from off-base, to witness the showdown.

Most of Company A was firmly in Rafe's camp, but they were concerned about the outcome. Brannigan was big and nasty and would like nothing better than to knock Rafe's head off. On the other hand, Rafe was developing a certain mystique. The only question remaining was whether he could hold his own against someone so much heavier.

The two adversaries met at the center of the ring dressed in Army-issued shorts and gloves, with Lt. Connolly acting as referee. He gave them a few short instructions then they returned to their respective corners and waited for the bell. The commanding officer of Company A had advised Lt. Connolly not to let Rafe take too much of a beating before stopping the three-round fight.

When the bell rang Brannigan charged across the ring and swung a couple of roundhouse rights and lefts that hit only thin air as Rafe showed his natural speed and easily dodged away. Brannigan began to stalk Rafe around the ring as Rafe moved to his right away from his opponent's, dominant hand. A couple of more big swings had the same results, the only thing they met was thin air. Then, Rafe stepped in front of Brannigan and hit him with a left jab strong enough to snap his heavier opponent's head back. Brannigan didn't see the straight right coming down the pike with tremendous speed. It hit him on the point of the jaw and he went down like a ton of bricks.

Brannigan found himself sitting on the canvas shaking his head and muttering, "Son of a bitch"." He wasn't hurt so much as unbalanced. His coordination was missing. He staggered to his feet and the Lt. Looked into his eyes to ensure he could continue. He had hardly moved a foot when he was stunned by a left, right combination to the head, delivered with blinding speed. He never saw the second straight right. The next thing he knew he was sitting on his ass again with the crowd roaring.

This time his reaction was, "What the fuck!" Again the Lt. brushed his gloves and gave the signal to continue. This time Brannigan backed up against the ropes and raised his hands to cover his head. It didn't do much good as he was then hit with a couple of murderous combinations to the midsection which really hurt. Brannigan was getting desperate and lunged around the ring trying to catch his smaller speedier rival with a lucky punch. Rafe simply stood off and peppered his face with jarring left jabs. Finally, Brannigan was able to get hold of Rafe in a clinch, and holding him with one arm hit him repeatedly behind the head with the other. Definitely against the rules. When the Lieutenant broke the clinch Rafe unleashed the arsenal of democracy which consisted of six lightning-fast left, right combinations. Brannigan crumbled to the floor while the crowd roared its approval. Whatever he may have been thinking before the fight started, Brannigan now knew he was in big trouble. When he staggered to his feet, he charged Rafe who used his momentum to swing him into the ropes. At this point, Rafe decided to deliver the coup de grace. With his larger opponent pinned to the ropes he delivered a hard left-right combination and as Brannigan turned away to the side he fired his hardest punch of the fight hitting him next to his kidney on the left side. Down he went again, this time curling up in agony. The Lieutenant waved off Rafe signaling the fight was over. Rafe walked back to his corner to the cheers of both military police companies. Brannigan was still rolling around on the canvas in agony from the body shot.

Rafe waved to his cheering comrades, took a look at poor Brannigan, then walked over and knelt beside him. "Are you Ok, Brannigan?"

With agony still painted on his face, he answered, "Yeah, I'll be Ok, but damn, where did you ever learn to fight like that?"

Rafe knowing Brannigan was still trying to recover said, "We'll talk about it later, I'll ask the sergeant of the guard to assign us to patrol together tonight."

Brannigan had a perplexed expression on his face as he responded, "You mean you'd do that?"

Rafe said, "Sure why not, you know what one of the first things my girl Jill said to me when we met?" "No what did she say." She said, "You can never have enough good friends." Then Rafe said, "See you later."

Fifteen minutes later as the officers of Company A left the gym the Company Commander said to Lieutenant Connolly "That kid Hawkins is something else isn't he."

The Lt. answered, "You only know the half of it, Sir. Of course, you know he's one of the best pistol shots in the Army, but he'd been telling this story that his first date was with a movie star. Everyone thought he was telling the greatest bullshit story of all time, then low and behold he gets a letter from her.

Captain Kline asked, how did they find out he got a letter from her?" "The mail clerk Sir saw a letter addressed to Hawkins from Jill Haworth with a Beverly Hills address.

Capt. Kline asked, Is that the beautiful blonde from Exodus?"

"That's the one sir."

The Capt. went on, "Well that's impressive, how did he manage that?"

"No one knows sir, but that's what led to the fight with Brannigan. He was shooting off his mouth about Jill, and Hawkins, as one could well expect, took offense. Brannigan wanted to step outside and duke it out right then and there, but Hawkins as much as he'd like to have punched Brannigan's lights out knew what that could lead to, in a place like Sandia. So, Hawkins suggested they meet in the gym."

Captain Kline went on to say, "You know Lt. I just received an inquiry from Washington concerning a replacement for the Body Guard to the Supreme Allied Commander in Paris. They wanted someone with a Top Secret security clearance, to be Regular Army, and not a draftee. They're looking for Regular Army so that the person selected will have at least a couple of years left to go in their enlistment. This kid Hawkins is one of the best pistol shots in the Army, and now we found out he can more than handle himself in a fight. His IQ is off the charts although he's not an Ivy Leaguer like most of the members of the Sandia Base security force. His decision to have the fight in the gym instead of on duty shows his good judgment. I think I'm going to call Washington and let them know I think we have the perfect candidate.

Little did Rafe know that the fight would seal his fate. At the time he was as happy as a pig in mud with the way things were shaping up in his life. Jill may be falling victim to the Hollywood culture, but Ella was just something else.

That night Rafe asked Sergeant Ellis to assign himself and Brannigan to a pickup truck making a two-man desert patrol. Sergeant Ellis inquired, "You sure you want to do that Hawkins, in view of what happened?"

Rafe smiled, and said, "Yeah I'm sure Sarge, we'll smooth things over."

Later that night, after picking up their weapons, Rafe and Brannigan climbed into their Dept of Defense pickup truck and headed into the remote areas of Sandia Base to patrol. Rafe was driving and Brannigan was riding shotgun. Brannigan started the conversation with, "How the hell did you learn to fight like that."

Rafe answered with, "My adoptive father got me a private trainer at the New York Athletic Club. The trainer was very good, a real pro. As strange as it may seem I'm a naturally hard puncher. You might say I'm a middleweight with a heavyweight punch."

Brannigan agreed, "I'll say you are. In fact, that's the hardest I've ever been hit." Brannigan went on to ask, "Are you a rich kid from New York? How did you get a date with Jill Haworth?"

Rafe chuckled and said, "You'd never believe it, but if you're interested, I'll tell you the story. We might as well talk since we'll be driving around all night. By the way, my first name is Rafe, short for Raphael." Brannigan reached across and said, "You can call me Bill." They shook hands and began the process of becoming friends.

As they navigated the rutted desert trails, they continued their conversation. Rafe told Bill the story behind his getting a date with Jill. When he had heard the story as it actually happened it made sense. Of course, this led Bill Brannigan to ask the sixty-four-thousand-dollar question. He said, "Ok I get the Jill Haworth deal. You formed a relationship with her as her tutor. It wasn't like you just met her and asked her out, but how about the Ice Princess? How did you manage to pull that off? I mean it was cold turkey. You just walked up and within a few minutes, you had her eating out of your hand. The guys said it was the most amazing thing they ever witnessed. How did you pull that off?"

Rafe thought about it for a minute then answered, "Ok Bill, but this is strictly between you and me, right?"

Bill said, "Ok I won't tell a soul, I just have to know how it happened."

Then Rafe said, "Actually, luck played a part in it. The truth is I had no idea what I was doing and was somewhat intimidated. So, while I was watching the other guys get shot down, I was thinking about what had to happen to even stand a chance. I realized that I only had about three or four minutes to make an impression which is the length of the dance and a minute to walk her back to her booth. The problem was I had no idea how to do it. So, I didn't try anything special, no smart pickup line or any such thing. I just acted normal. I introduced myself, we talked about where we were from and what we were doing as far as work went. Then I told her I thought the way she spoke English sounded very nice, almost melodic. That went over well and got me a big genuine smile. However, that was it, I had no idea what else to say. So, the first thing I thought of was her family. I asked if she had a big family, any brothers or sisters. It just so happens I hit on the right subject as she had two of her sisters living with her and she was helping them get through school. While we were talking about her sisters the dance ended, and I knew I only had a minute left. When we got to her booth I asked if I could sit down and talk to her for a while and she said, yes, and the rest is history. We liked each other."

Bill was silent for a minute then said, "It was just that easy?" Rafe answered, "It was all in the approach. I wasn't interested in a one-night stand. Even if I was, I wouldn't know how to go about it. I was interested in getting to know the girl and somehow getting a date. I just let her know I was very interested in her and the rest took care of itself. You might say I was very nice to her to get my foot in the door. Now I have a beautiful girlfriend."

Bill said, "Do you think the same approach would work for me?"

Rafe replied, "I do if you really like the girl and show sincere interest in her. And, Bill there's a reason for that. I know most guys are interested in one thing more than any other and that's getting laid, right?"

Bill nodded his head and said, "You got that right."

Then Rafe added, "Well that potentially creates huge problems. This is because nature's intent is for us to reproduce. I'm sure you can remember when you were ten years old and had no interest in the opposite sex. Then around twelve or thirteen the girls start to look really good. Now, you don't think it was some sort of intellectual renaissance that led you to desire women, do you? No, it was hormonal. Your body started to produce testosterone and male hormones and then you developed an instant desire for women. Nature wanted the next generation to be produced. All of this is great for nature, but to us humans, it presents a huge challenge. This is primarily because we're social animals. We want our offspring to have every chance to succeed. I'm sure there are some who could care less about what happens to their children, but most of us would look upon the failure of our children as a disaster. I look upon it this way, and it's not the same as everyone else in Company A, I'm not going to try to go to bed with anyone I can't take seriously as a lifelong mate. Or more precisely, as the mother of my children. Would you want some dingbat as your mother? It's the same as being born behind the eight ball, or with a ball and chain around your leg.

Bill then says, "Well how about the Ice Princess? Granted she's drop-dead gorgeous; but is that enough? We've all gone right after her, including you, so aren't you breaking your own rules?"

"Well not really," Rafe replied. "Sure, when I approached her to ask for a dance it was strictly based on her looks, but after I talked to her for five hours, I was beginning to get a good sense of her character. Imagine if she had turned out to be the bitch from hell, do you think I would have asked to walk her home. And imagine if I had walked her home, gone to bed with her, and gotten her pregnant. Think of the awful consequences; My child would have a bitch for a mother and I'd be tied to the bitch for the rest of my life, and all for a little short time pleasure."

Bill looked at Rafe, shook his head, and said, "Easier said than done!"

So, Rafe added, "We're young Bill and we can easily screw up our lives just when we're getting started. I know you have a high IQ or you wouldn't be in this unit, but it's really incumbent on us to use our intellect to steer clear of some of the pitfalls that can ruin our lives. If I'm successful with women it's only because I only go after the ones I can really like, and they know that."

Bill said to Rafe, "Maybe you're right. Maybe I can learn something from you."

Rafe answered, "Maybe we can learn something from each other because the truth is I joined the army because I'm very unworldly; no street smarts."

From that point onward Rafe Hawkins and Bill Brannigan developed a friendship which was a relief to Sergeant Ellis because the two liked to be assigned on patrol together and this alleviated trying to pair Brannigan with others who didn't exactly appreciate his company.

Things were going great for Rafe although he and Ella had to accept the interference that the Cuban Missile Crisis caused just as their budding romance was getting started. Sandia Base was shut down for a week during which the 5th Mechanized Infantry Division, En route from Fort Carson, Colorado to Florida arrived. The 5th was moving to Florida in case an invasion of Cuba was necessary. When they showed up, and we learned about their destination, we knew it was a serious situation. The Army went to Defcon 3 while the Strategic Air Command went to Defcon 2 one step away from nuclear war.

Thankfully, the crisis was of short duration and Rafe was soon spending most of his free time at Ella's apartment on Broadway. Since her sisters, we always about, Rafe and Ella used to spend hours sitting on a bench in Highland Park about four blocks North. It used to make Rafe feel guilty as he seemed to be repeating the same pattern he had when he was with Jill. In the first few weeks of their relationship, the two simply told each other about their upbringing, and Rafe who thought he had problems at Greer School soon realized it was all relative. At least he had enough to eat. Ella told him of doing stoop labor in fields picking vegetables and never knowing if she would get to eat every day. He then began to realize how Ella could have been skinny and hardly noticeable when she first arrived in Albuquerque. She certainly must have changed dramatically for she now had the loveliest body he had ever laid eyes on. He still couldn't believe he had such a beautiful girlfriend. It took him about three weeks to realize he was hopelessly in love. He even remembered where he was when the realization hit him. He was riding the bus from Sandia Base, down Central Avenue toward downtown. As the bus pulled over in front of Albuquerque High School the thought hit him. I'm in love with her. He came to that conclusion because he was thinking about what life would be like if he had to go back and live without her. When he realized it would be an unmitigated disaster, he knew he was, in love. So, while they were sitting on their bench in Highland Park, he decided to tell her.

It is not a hard thing to say I love you when you really mean it, so while they were talking about nothing special Rafe said, "I have something to tell you."

Ella detected the serious look and said, "What is it?"

Rafe looked into her eyes and said, 'I'm in love with you."

Ella smiled and said, "That's pretty serious, are you sure." Rafe smiled back and said, "I've never been as sure of anything."

For a moment, Ella didn't say anything then her face lit up and she said, "That's great; because I'm in love with you too. I just wanted you to say it first."

Rafe kissed her and said, "I've never been this happy." Ella looked at him and said, "What happens now?" Rafe answered, "We live happily ever after of course."

A week later Ella said that Dolores and Emily were going up to spend the weekend in Cimmaron and when they returned Ella's mother and her two other sisters Maryann and Elsie were returning with them to live in Albuquerque. All of this was perfectly all right with Rafe because he felt he was meeting future family members, and he already thought the world of Dolores and Emily. The girls left on Friday afternoon so Rafe had Ella all alone for most of the weekend.

That Friday night Ella was stretched out on the couch and Rafe was sitting next to her just talking. Rafe was thinking, 'My girlfriend has the most beautiful legs I've ever seen. So, he decided to run his hands from her ankles to her knees. Sort of feeling her calves. Ella allowed him to do it for a minute then pulled her legs up towards her midsection and said, "Stop it, that tickles." Rafe was aware that your calves aren't a particular ticklish part of your body so he assumed that Ella probably thought he was just starting with her legs and had plans to move further up. Rafe wasn't really thinking that, but now the idea was firmly in his mind. He would have loved to run his hands all over her. At this point, Ella got up and said, 'I'm going to take a bath, be back in about twenty minutes."

Rafe just said, "OK"

About twenty minutes later Rafe looked up and there was Ella walking into the living room wearing nothing but a towel. She smiled, walked along the far wall where a mirror was placed about shoulder high, turned away from Rafe and then pulled up the towel waist-high and said, "Is this what you want?" Rafe found himself staring at the most beautiful ass he'd ever imagined. He was so stunned he couldn't speak. Then Ella turned around facing him and dropped the towel while holding her arms out about six inches from her body. Her palms were turned towards him and she Said, "If you want me, I'm all yours."

Rafe stared at the most beautiful vision he would ever see, Ella naked. She was half Hispanic and half Native American, but whatever the gene combination, it had produced perfection. Rafe couldn't speak, he walked over and took his beloved Ella in his arms, and kissed her passionately. His hands slid down her bare skin and he realized he was now in possession of all he had ever desired. Ella took his hand and led him towards her bedroom and said two simple words, "Take me."

Rafe could not have imagined what getting into his beloved would have been like, but later as he held her in his arms, both of them completely spent, and having reached someplace called nirvana, or a place of complete happiness, he realized how much he loved her.

He couldn't believe how she had responded to him, and the feeling her response had engendered deep inside him. If he hadn't been in love with her before he definitely was now. As she lay in his arms pressed together like a pair of spoons, she turned her head towards him and whispered, "Do you love me?" She already knew the answer but wanted the security of hearing him say it. "Rafe whispered in her ear as he held her body tightly against him, "I wish I could put it into words, but it's far beyond that, I love you more than I thought I could ever love anything. I could never have believed that making love to someone could be this beautiful and perfect. Ella said, "I love you just as much," then added, "Want to do it again?" So, they did, over and over again until they fell asleep exhausted, in each other's arms.

They spent the weekend making love and by the time Rafe returned to Sandia Base he was so completely in love that he knew if Ella felt the same way as he did, nothing would ever break them apart. Rafe had found complete happiness, but he was unaware of the forces bearing down upon them. Life went on and Ella's mother and youngest sisters arrived in Albuquerque on Sunday. When Rafe met the girls, he found them as charming as Dolores and Emily. He especially liked her mother who was about 5' tall and reminded Rafe of his grandmother whom he dearly loved.

The next month could be described as nice and easy. Rafe interacted with the newly arrived family members and they all seemed to get along just fine. Although Ella's apartment was crowded it didn't present a problem for Rafe who had spent almost ten years in the dorms of Greer School. It wasn't long before Rafe was lying on the living room floor helping Maryann and Elena with their homework. Of course, this type of family scene endeared him to Ella's mother, who was a full-blooded Native American. If Rafe had any problem with the new living arrangements it was that having time alone with Ella was nearly impossible.

Rafe wasn't particularly disturbed by the lack of privacy because he really had it in his mind, that he had all the time in the world. He was convinced that this was the girl he would eventually marry and everything would happen in its own good time. Getting to know Ella's family was very important because they would all eventually become members of the same family. The truth was he loved helping Ella's sisters with their schoolwork because he wanted them to succeed. Ella and Rafe started dating like any normal couple, double dating with Ella's coworkers, going to the Kimo Theater on Central Ave, to take in a movie, and of course, sitting on their park bench in Highland Park watching the squirrels and dreaming about the future.

The axe fell without warning on Rafe's 21st birthday December 12th. He was going down to the mail room to see if he had any mail when the 1st Sergeant saw him and called him over and said,

"I've been looking for you Hawkins. Report to the Commanding Officer."

Rafe said, "Do you mean immediately?"

"Yes, he wants to see you right away."

Rafe asked, "Do you have any idea what he wants to see me about" Sergeant just shook his head and said, "I have no idea."

The 1st Sergeant accompanied Rafe to the orderly room, knocked on the Captain's door, told him Hawkins had arrived then told Rafe to go in and report. Rafe was a little concerned because the one thing you didn't want to be involved in at Sandia Base was a security violation concerning anything nuclear. With that on his mind, Rafe walked in stood at attention in front of the Commanding Officer, saluted, and said, "Private First Class Hawkins, reporting as ordered."

The Captain looked at him, smiled, and said, "Congratulations Hawkins, pack your bags, you're going to Paris, France. With those ten words, Rafe's world came crashing down.

He looked at the Captain like he was out of his mind. He didn't know what to say so he simply said, "Paris, France?"

The Captain nodded his head, and said, "You've been selected to be the Body Guard to the new Supreme Allied Commander Europe, General Lyman L. Lemnitzer."

Rafe answered questioningly, "Why me?"

The Captain looked at Rafe and said, "Washington has been inquiring about this for a while, and when you dismantled a man who outweighed you by about 50 pounds in your little grudge match, that sealed the deal. You have the right MOS (Military Occupational Specialty), a Cosmic Top Secret Security Clearance, you are one of the best pistol shots in the Army, and you've shown yourself to exhibit excellent judgment.

Rafe looked at him and thought to himself, "And you're destroying my life." Rafe interjected, "Sir you can't send me to France."

The Captain looked at him a little perturbed, and asked, 'Why not?"

Rafe answered, "Because when I arrived at Sandia I wanted to transfer because I didn't like the desert. The clerks at personnel said I could never transfer because I have a Permanent Assignment, then they showed me my 201 file, and down in the lower right-hand corner it showed Permanent Assignment."

The Captain shook his head, and said, 'Hawkins, for your information the Army has one order that supersedes all other orders!"

Rafe asked, "What's that sir?

The answer was surprising, "It's called, for the good of the service. So, you're going to Paris for the good of the service."

Rafe couldn't get past this sudden debacle so he exclaimed, "What if I refuse to go?"

The captain, Retorted, "What's wrong with you Hawkins? This is a great assignment and a great honor, most men would jump at a chance like this."

Rafe said, 'Let's just say I have a good reason and leave it at that. When am I supposed to go?"

"You have about six more weeks here at Sandia and then two weeks' leave before you have to report. So about eight weeks."

Rafe asked, "How long will I be there?"

Captain answers, "Till you get out of the service."

"Do you mean I have another permanent assignment?"

The captain getting a little displeased said, "Don't be a smart ass, Hawkins."

Rafe now knowing he was screwed said, "Will that be all Sir?" Captain said, "Yes, the first sergeant will keep you informed, you're dismissed."

Rafe saluted, Said, "Yes Sir." and left.

Rafe walked upstairs towards his room thinking, "I am so fucked! This is the end of the world; how will I tell Ella? This is the end of everything. What are the chances Ella will still be unattached two years from now? I'm so screwed, I can't believe how bad this is."

Rafe walked into his room and glanced over at his roommate Dick who was lying on his bunk reading. He looked up and said, "What's the matter, Rafe? You look like you just lost your best friend."

Rafe sat on his bunk with his head down and said, "It's worse than that."

Now Dick was curious, "What could be worse than that?"

Rafe answered, "I'm being transferred to Paris, France."

"Christ! Rafe, what's wrong with that?

Rafe said, "What's wrong with that? Ella is what's wrong with that. Do you think she'll still be here when I get back, with every male in Albuquerque pursuing her for the next two years?"

Dick thought for a second and said, "Yeah, I know what you mean. Shit, what bad luck."

Rafe said, "If I hadn't just met her, it would be a dream assignment."

Dick answered, "I know what you mean."

Then Rafe added, "I'm going to be the bodyguard to the Supreme Allied Commander Europe, and do you know what brought this about? My fight with Brannigan convinced the officers that I could not only shoot better than anyone else, but I could fight too. It just so happens Washington was canvassing all the stations with MPs with top-secret clearances for someone with the right credentials. When the inquiry first came, they couldn't think of anyone. Then the commanding officer came out and witnessed the fight. That's how my name made it to Washington as the perfect candidate."

Rafe went on, "How I have to figure a way back, or I'll lose Ella."

Dick sat there thinking for a minute and then said, "I have an idea that might work."

Rafe was all ears and said, "What is it."

Dick went on, "What do you think of becoming an officer?"

Rafe said, "Never considered it."

Dick said, "Maybe you should think about it. Here's why. There are only two Officer Candidate Schools. Both are in the United States, one at Fort Benning, Georgia and the other at Fort Sill, Oklahoma. If you're overseas and are accepted they have to send you back. Just go up to personnel right now and check the Army Regulations on OSC. It might be your salvation."

Rafe jumped up and as he headed for the door he said, "Thanks Dick, you're a lifesaver."

Rafe raced over to Personnel and asked to see the Army Regulations concerning Officer Candidate School. The specialist handed him the correct volume of Army Regulations, and Rafe began to read those concerning OCS. It took him about 1/2 hour to find what he was looking for because, without this little piece of information, the attempt would prove futile. Officer Candidate School was six months long and divided into three eight-week periods. A successful candidate had to stay in OCS for the first period of eight weeks after which he could resign for cause, meaning for any reason he desired. If he resigned after eight weeks, he would be promoted to sergeant E5 and reassigned to the Army Area of his choice in the United States. Rafe figured with his record, and top-secret clearance, if he were to get his new boss General Lemnitzer to recommend him, he would be in, and on his way back to Ella; After all, with a top-secret clearance where else would the Army reassign him other than Sandia Base. After this discovery, Rafe felt much better. It would be bad for a while, but he'd get back.

That night he had to tell Ella the terrible news, but before he did, he and Ella went out for his first legal drink at a bar called the Inferno, on Central Avenue across from the Fair Grounds. The interior of the bar was constructed to look like the caverns of hell, with lighting that made it look like flames were licking up the walls. As they walked in, they saw a placard sign, over the door, on which was a quote from Dante, "Abandon all hope, Ye who enter here." Rafe had no idea of the significance of that sign, and what it would come to mean, at a later date.

While having his first legal drink Rafe said to Ella," I have some very bad news." Considering it was his birthday Ella could tell he was not too happy about something. She said, "What is it, Rafe?" Taking a deep breath Rafe delivered the bad news. "The Army has decided to send me to Paris, France to be the Body Guard to the Supreme Allied Commander Europe." A shocked look came over Ella's face and she said, "No! How can they do that to us." Rafe went on to explain that, as he had just learned, the Army could do whatever it wanted. Then the tears followed. Ella was crying, and Rafe felt like this was the worst of all things. When she began to come to her senses Rafe told her about OSC and how he intended to get back. He added that if he was so highly qualified to be the Body Guard to the Supreme Allied Commander he'd also be qualified for OCS. The only thing he had to avoid was letting the Army become aware of his true intentions, that being, he wasn't interested in becoming an officer, but only in getting back to New Mexico. If they ever figured out his true intentions, they'd crush him like a bug. He explained that there was nothing else to do. If they loved each other, they'd survive whatever curve balls life threw at them.

Rafe and Ella made love only a few more times, but in Rafe's mind, she was the loveliest thing on earth and possessed the most perfect body. When the awful day finally arrived Ella and her mother and sisters accompanied him to the airport to see him off to France. Rafe kissed his lovely girlfriend goodbye and would always remember walking across the tarmac towards the TWA 707 feeling he was walking away from everything he held dear. He turned and looked back over his shoulder and watched Ella and her family waving. He boarded the jet and took his seat at a window on the right side. Twenty minutes later as his flight roared down the runway Rafe was wondering if he'd ever see Ella again. Shortly after liftoff Rafe looked down and could make out the building where Ella lived next to the Coal Avenue bridge over the Santa Fe Railroad tracks. The plane banked right and began its climb parallel to Sandia Crest as Albuquerque drifted behind.

By evening the flight was landing at Kennedy Airfield which back in those days was called Idlewild. Rafe was surprised when Everett and his mother met him in a Limo. His mother had gotten an annulment for her two months, marriage and Everett was back on the scene which pleased Rafe no end. Rafe loved Everett as a real father and nothing could please him more than seeing Everett and his mother back together. Of course, Rafe thought Everett was getting the short end of the stick.

Rafe spent his leave in New York visiting his Aunts and Uncles in preparation for his overseas assignment. One evening he had dinner with Everett at the Bull & Bear at the Waldorf Astoria. Everett knew Rafe was wildly in love with Ella and tried to give him a little Fatherly advice. He told Rafe, "Where women are concerned be careful about putting all of your eggs in one basket. What I'm trying to say is that where women are concerned you are very inexperienced.

Rafe answered, "I know I'm inexperienced, but so far I'm doing all right with the opposite sex." Everett told Rafe, "So far you seem to be doing all right, but that may prove to be delusional."

Rafe said, "What are you driving at Pop?"

"Well, you seem to have no trouble attracting beautiful women, however, how would you be feeling if Ella hadn't come along when she did? How did you feel when Jill started being seen with her co-star Sal Mineo? I expect not too well, but then along came Ella, and Jill was quickly forgotten. Just remember I saw you and Jill together. It seemed like real love to me, and then she's gone for a year and that's the end. What I'm trying to say is the same thing could happen with Ella. You two are about to experience a long estrangement. Look, Rafe, what I'm trying to say is that you need to play the field. I've heard those French girls are something else."

Rafe knew Everett made a lot of sense and was just trying to give him good advice, however, he was too committed to Ella. He would never risk falling for some French girl and breaking her heart. Everett also did not know about his plan to beat the Army at its own game.

Everett wasn't finished yet. He asked Rafe, "Ever heard of a Gold Digger?" Of course, he had heard of women called that, in fact, he wondered about his own mother. So, he answered, "Sure I know about them." Then Everett said something that, had Rafe been more sophisticated, he would have taken to heart. "Rafe we are actors and actresses on the stage. Some are better at it than others, but all men can be delusional. It's very important that you understand this because when you are being delusional you are experiencing a goal that is unattainable because it exists only in dreams or hopes. Rafe shook his head, Yes, and said, "I understand that Pop." Then Everett went on to explain, "What you don't yet realize is that women can be the major source of delusional thinking in a man's mind. Always keep that in mind. Ella may be very beautiful, but be sure you test her for character." Rafe Said, "Ok I got it Pop, I'll be careful. Thanks for the good advice." There was just one problem. He really didn't get it. Not yet, at least.

Rafe's mother drove him down to McGuire Air Force Base to be transported to Le Bourget Airport in Paris. She kissed him goodbye and shed the only tears he would ever see her shed on his behalf. Considering what a tiger his mother was it sort of surprised him. His Mother left and he waited for another four hours, the typical hurry up and wait always exhibited by the Army. When it came time to board, The CL44 aircraft was a converted cargo plane with a swing tail designed to accommodate cargo. It had been remodeled to carry passengers and was carrying 160 passengers mostly military personnel and military dependents. Rafe was thankful he had a flight to Paris and wasn't making his first trip across the Atlantic in a troopship that took ten days. It would be a miserable ten days with half the troops seasick during a winter crossing. It was a ten-hour flight and that beat ten days at sea by a mile.

Supreme Headquarters Allied

The CL44 was flying over a solid overcast when it began its descent into Le Bourget airport. Rafe didn't know it, but once the aircraft descended into the overcast, he wouldn't see the sun again for six weeks. One could say, welcome to the beautiful French climate in winter.

He was met by an MP patrol car which drove him through the suburbs of Paris to the home of the 591st MP company in Versailles. In fact, the barracks were part of what used to be the Palace of Versailles which was only two blocks away.

Rafe's first impression of France was its miserable weather and beautiful architecture. Beautiful buildings and foggy, cold, wet weather. Rafe was thinking, "What do I care, I'll only be here for a year, or maybe less, then back to the USA and Ella. Of course, he was young and ignorant, although he wasn't aware of that quite yet. If Rafe had a shortcoming, it stemmed from the fact that he hadn't yet figured out what it meant to be Delusional. Unfortunately, for him by the time he learned this valuable lesson, it would be too late. One of the key traits of delusion as explained in the dictionary, is that it exists in a goal, that is unattainable because the goal exists only in hopes and dreams.

Rafe thought he had it all figured out. He was the bodyguard to the Supreme Allied Commander; and one way or another he was going to get the General's recommendation to attend OCS. He would also get the same recommendation from his company commander, then he'd be on his way back to Albuquerque with a detour through either Fort Benning or Fort Sill. At least in his own mind that was the plan. Of course, we all know what often happens to the best-laid plans.

As soon as he arrived Rafe reported to Captain F. Scott Haldane the Company Commander of the 591st MP Company. The meeting was to set the stage for future events. Rafe had already decided that his two major goals were to get the recommendations of Capt. Haldane and General Lemnitzer. This would ensure his acceptance into OCS. His initial meeting with Captain Haldane gave him a clear insight into how to win over the Company Commander. Capt. Haldane started with, "Welcome to France Hawkins, we've been waiting for your arrival. After looking at your record and being briefed by Counter-intelligence it looks like you're the ideal candidate. Let me explain why. You may be the best pistol shot in the Army, and apparently, it's a natural gift. If we're going to have someone as the last line of defense between the Supreme Commander and some terrorist, we want it to be someone who can be relied on to take them down. You may not realize it but before you got this far, our intelligence agency has been taking a hard look at you. It's obvious from your record that you can shoot, however, there was no mention anywhere that you can box, and do that so well that you could knock out a man forty or fifty pounds heavier."

Rafe responded with, "Well I didn't actually knock him out, Sir."

"We know you didn't knock him out, but the consensus is you could have if you wanted to. Then we have the good judgment you exhibited by not getting involved in a fight while on duty. Had you, the fallout would have been, how should I put it, far-reaching. As it was, the way you handled it was perfect. In fact, you handled it like you were an officer."

Rafe then interjected, "Sir, while we're on the subject I was thinking once I've been here a while, I might apply to OCS and become an officer."

Captain Haldane took a harder look at Rafe and then said, I'm glad to hear that. It shows you're serious and determined to get ahead."

Rafe then asked, "Is there anything you would suggest I do in order to positively advance my application?"

Captain Haldane shook his head in the affirmative and answered, "Actually there is. First, go back to school. You can apply to the University of Maryland Overseas Division which has classes in the evening. Second, purchase Tropical Worsted Uniforms which will make you a standout among all other enlisted men at SHAPE. Believe me, in the area of SHAPE to which you'll be assigned, looking like the sharpest soldier around will make a very positive impression. Remember, your boss is a four-star General and so is his deputy. Your post is right between their respective offices. Everyone, who is anyone, at SHAPE, passes your post and all visiting dignitaries will come through there as well. We're talking about people like Charles de Gaulle, as well as Kings, Queens and Prime Ministers. You look the part, and that's half the battle." Captain Haldane had one further suggestion which was the most important to Rafe, "I'm into martial arts. You might say I'm a little obsessed with it. I'm a sixth-degree black belt holder and one of my problems is I can't find willing partners to train with. I was wondering; since you seem to be a fighter, if you, might want to learn a new discipline. In that way, I get someone to spar with, and you enhance your ability to protect the Supreme Commander. What do you think?"

Rafe immediately recognized the opportunity this presented. If he became the sparring partner of Captain Haldane it would insure his recommendation to OCS. He would just have to throw himself into it even if that meant he took a beating. With that in mind, Rafe said, "That sounds like a good idea to me Sir. I'm always interested in learning new methods of self-defense." Captain Haldane replied, "Good! I'm glad to have you aboard Hawkins, check with the First Sergeant and he'll get you squared away. Tomorrow, we'll take you up to SHAPE.

The next day was as rainy and miserable as the day he arrived. SHAPE itself was a major disappointment. Talk about Ugly! It consisted of about a hundred offices connected together by long metal fingers. Of course, it was military so what could you expect? Hell, the rooms in the barracks were heated by pot-bellied stoves like one would expect to find in World War II. At least he wasn't sleeping in a tent out in the field freezing to death. After visiting SHAPE, the next stop was the Supreme Commanders Chateau near Saint-Germain-en-Laye. While SHAPE was not very impressive the General's Chateau was the exact opposite. Rafe wasn't sure of when it was built or by whom, but it certainly was impressive and was surrounded by the most beautiful grounds and gardens. Rafe was told that he would be spending every third month at the SACEUR'S quarters. SACEUR was the acronym for Supreme Allied Commander Europe. If he had to be standing around someplace pulling guard duty the chateau was as good a place as any.

His 2nd full day in France was spent being briefed by the counter-intelligence people and you might say it was a wake-up call for someone as inexperienced and unworldly as Rafe. Among other things, he learned that there were Russian agents in Paris and how they went about gathering intelligence. In effect. it was the gathering of small pieces of information to put together the larger mosaic. If he were in France long enough, he would inevitably run into such an agent and it would likely be in the form of a beautiful female. He was also told that he would be working closely with members of the Serete, which was not the French version of the American Secret Service; but was more like a cross between the FBI and the KGB. Their power over the population was much greater than any American agency had over US citizens. Furthermore, He would have a very high, Top Secret Security Clearance called a Cosmic Top Secret, and although he didn't have the "need to know" anything, he was authorized to overhear almost anything. It was explained in very plain terms that in security, one was required to have both the clearance and the need to know. Because of his position, he had an exception, as he was likely to overhear things that he did not have the need to know. They also explained that he would have a counter-intelligence handler who would speak to him every few weeks to gather intelligence even if was just fragmentary. They were also interested in knowing anything he considered to be a security threat. The final piece of information given to him was that he would be working with a Serete agent that was considered to be a very dangerous person, possibly the most dangerous person in France. His nickname was The Killer! Rafe was wondering, what have I gotten myself into? One thing Rafe found intriguing was that everything was taken so seriously. After his briefing, Rafe was under no illusions that he had to perform at the highest level.

Day three was the big day. He was told to dress in his Class A uniform as today he would be introduced to his new boss, General Lymon L. Lemnitzer, the SACEUR.

Rafe was somewhat nervous when he walked in stood at attention and saluted General Lemnitzer, and said, Private First Class, Rafael Hawkins, reporting to the Supreme Allied Commander, as ordered. The general looked him over and said, "Stand at ease, Hawkins." Rafe had no idea what to expect and the truth was he had never been in contact with a General. The commander of Sandia Base had been a full colonel and here he was standing in front of the highest-ranking general in Europe.

The General told Rafe that he had been specially selected because he was a crack shot with a pistol and had shown exceptionally good judgment in his short term of service. The General went on to say that judgment was the essential trait they were looking for because of the environment that would be surrounding them. He also explained that the enemy of good security was complacency and in order to perform at the level that was expected of him, he would have to always be alert. The General went on to say that although there was a very carefully defined chain of command in the Army, Rafe would have his ear; and if he saw or felt that security was being compromised in any way, he was to bring it to the General's attention and he would decide if any corrective action was necessary.

After talking for a few minutes, the General said, "See that little dog lying on his bed over in the corner." Rafe had noticed him lying quietly. "Well, his name is Brady and he's very dear to me. I found him in a village in North Korea after it had just been subjected to a severe artillery bombardment. I saw Brady trembling beside the road and he looked so pitifully that I picked him up. He's been with me ever since. I'd like to try an experiment. Kneel down and call him to you. I want to see what he does."

Rafe knelt down and called Brady, "Brady, come here little guy. Come over here and let me pet you. Come on over and be friends." Brady looked at Rafe, made a little growling noise, and then took a few tentative steps toward Rafe. Then he stopped and stared at Rafe who said, "Come on over here Brady, you can't fool me. I know you want to." Brady took another couple of steps and then his rear end started to wriggle and his tail began to wag. He walked right up to Rafe, put his paws on Rafe's shoulder, and began to lick his face. Rafe said, "Good Boy!", and picked up the squirming K9

.General Lemnitzer was smiling when he said, "This is just great. You wouldn't know this, but Brady might like one in every fifty people, and he rarely takes to people as he did to you. This is the problem I have where you can be a big help. I often bring Brady to work especially when I know I won't be having any visiting dignitaries. Since he's a little on the rambunctious side and likes to go out for a run halfway through the day, it wouldn't seem proper to see the SACEUR running around the SHAPE grounds chasing his little dog. However, if you would take him out on one of your breaks that would all seem to be in good order. So, what do you think?"

Rafe immediately answered, "Sir I'd consider it a privilege to take Brady out for his walks. I'd actually enjoy it very much. It's been a long time since I've had a dog to walk."

That settled the matter and Rafe and the General were off to a good start, and Rafe wasn't lying about taking Brady for a walk. Since the demise of Max, Rafe had missed the companionship of a dog. Brady was obviously part Jack Russell Terrier, and Rafe liked the idea of taking him out for his exercise.

The first three days at Supreme Headquarters set the tone for everything which would follow. Somewhere along the line, Rafe had learned, "If you don't know where you're going, you'll probably end up somewhere else." At least Rafe now knew where he was going and how to get there. Rafe quickly settled into the routine of guarding the Supreme Allied Commander and felt fortunate that most of his work was indoors and not out in what seemed to be perpetual rainfall. It rained so much that the MPs carried their raincoats with them at all times as it would rain off and on all day.

About midway through his first week on duty while he was standing outside the entrance to the Supreme Allied Commander's office, he noticed a short bald man in civilian clothes walking down the narrow concourse towards his post. As he got closer Rafe noticed he had very unusual eyes. You might say he had eyes like a shark, flat with no emotion, actually, Rafe was thinking, "This is one scary dude!"

He instinctively knew who it was. There was a certain boldness in his stride, and when he reached Rafe he stuck out his hand and introduced himself saying, "Jacque Lemaire, Surete!"

Rafe took his hand and replied, "Rafe Hawkin's, glad to meet you, Jacque; I've heard a lot about you."

"Jock tilted his head a little to one side and inquired, "Who did you hear about me from, and what did they say?"

.Rafe answered, "Counter-intelligence, and they said you were a dangerous man. In fact, they call you "the killer."

Jock laughed and responded with, "That's very funny, looks like we may be peas from the same tree."

Rafe chuckled, and shot back, "You mean we're peas from the same pod."

Jacque shook his head from side to side and said, "You know what I mean," my people say you're dangerous too, and that you are known as The Shooter."

Carrying on the conversation Rafe added, "Well I can shoot straight, but I've never killed anybody."

Back came Jacque's response, "That may be true, but if some threat suddenly materialized out in front of the door, someone would end up dead, in short order, that is, if you had time to draw your weapon."

"But, so far I haven't killed anyone."

Then Jock added, "That's probably because you're too young and haven't had a chance yet."

"What makes you think so?"

"You know the old American expression "It takes one to know one." You can't fool me Monsieur Rafe, your eye is like the Eagle, the bird of prey, no?"

"Right Jacque, just like you have the look of a shark!"

Jacque laughed and said, "Very funny Monsieur Rafe, I think you and I will work very well together."

That was his introduction to "The Killer." Later Jock would relate his recruitment by the Surete during World War II. Rafe could hardly believe what Jock had to say when he asked him if he had been involved with the resistance during the war tracking down and eliminating the Gestapo and the SS. Jacque asked if Rafe was crazy, even thinking such a thing. He went on to tell Rafe that the resistance was nothing more than a bunch of Communists and Jews and he had been tracking down members of the resistance for the Vichy Government.

Rafe later learned that Jacque became known as the killer because while serving in Algeria, the first seven men the Surete sent him out to arrest, he brought back dead. Rafe was slowly beginning to gain worldly experience. Who would think that the Government of France would hire men who were fighting the resistance during World War II to work in the Surete after the war, that is, instead of giving them the guillotine for collaboration, or for that matter treason? If you could believe that, then it wouldn't be a stretch to believe that the OSS the forerunner to the CIA would take Nazis and give them new Identities and hide them in South America.

Right from the first week of his assignment to Supreme Headquarters Rafe was certain that he had the answer to getting reassigned back to the USA. There was only one problem. In his mind, it was not exactly an honorable thing to do. He was going to have to con the General, as well as Capt. Haldane, and convince them he really wanted to be an officer, and that couldn't be further from the truth. However, Rafe had to learn about life and this was to prove to be one of his greatest learning experiences.

Garrison life in the Army can only be described as routine. Rafe did what his position required, but he also followed the course Capt. Haldane had suggested. He signed up with the University of Maryland overseas division to further his education. That in itself would look good on his application for OCS. His big hurdle would be in becoming the sparring partner for Capt. Haldane being the Captain was obsessed with martial arts such as Karate. This was his problem. Captain Haldane was 6'3" tall and weighed about 225 pounds. Rafe was 6' tall and weighed in at about 170 which added up to a 55-pound weight differential. Nonetheless, Rafe knew that if he impressed Capt. Haldane in the ring with his fearlessness; he would win his approval. None of the other MPs wanted to have anything to do with the Captain's obsession with Karate. He was big and tough and one could easily get injured playing that game. They were quite willing to watch some sucker like Rafe getting thrown all over, rather than have to do it themselves. So, while the others watched, Rafe participated. It wasn't fun because in order to avoid getting hurt Rafe had to throw himself into the whole martial arts scene.

The Captain, realizing he had finally found what he was looking for, made sure Rafe was well-trained in taking care of himself before they got into any serious sparring. For a few weeks, Rafe was taught by the Captain how to fall and land without serious injury. After that initial training, Rafe began to learn moves like the Arm Bar, The Scissor Take Down, Double Leg Take Down, Spinning Back leg Kick, Hip Throw, Body Slam, and others too many to name. Of course, Rafe got the shit beat out of him. Rafe was extremely fit, and very fast, but this was trumped by size and weight. The important thing was that Rafe could give the Captain a tremendous workout. Keeping in mind, his directed intelligence, it didn't take him too long to create a strategy to deal with the Captain's superior weight; He'd wear him down. On his part, Captain Haldane realized the great character Rafe displayed by continually fighting a losing battle.

One day after the contest the Captain took Rafe aside and said, "Look Hawkins, if you want to beat someone who outweighs you as much as I do, you have to attack them as if your life depends on it.

"Rafe Rafe thought to himself, "My life does depend on it, so I'll take your advice." During this conversation, Rafe brought up something that he had heard from others in the company that didn't make any sense to him. So, he said, "Captain Haldane I've heard that if I stay at SHAPE for the next two years, or basically until I'm discharged from the Army, I'll still be a PFC. In other words, I'll never receive a promotion. And this considering that I'm the bodyguard to the Supreme Allied Commander. I was told when I was reassigned to SHAPE that it was a special assignment, yet how special can it be if you are never promoted? I've also been told that no one in the 591st MP Company can be promoted as long as they're at SHAPE. Now it might not be too bad for someone like me, but some of the NCOs are career soldiers with families. Is what I'm hearing correct?"

Captain Haldane said, "It's true Hawkin's, that none of the enlisted personnel at SHAPE can be promoted, while they're here."

Rafe asked, "Could you tell me why?"

The Captain said, "It's some sort of glitch in the way SHAPE and NATO was set up; Because SHAPE isn't in any Army Command and therefore doesn't get allocation for rank."

Rafe said, "Captain, that doesn't seem fair. It's something that should be fixed. Capt. Haldane came back with. "It's easier said than done. Remember, the Army is a big bureaucracy, maybe if you could get the attention of the right person, you might get it fixed."

Rafe, was thinking to himself, "That's exactly what I'm going to do."

General Lemnitzer and Rafe would chat informally whenever Rafe brought Mr. Brady in from his walk. One day Rafe said, "General I know about the chain of command and military protocols, but there's something I'd like to bring to your attention that you probably know nothing about."

The General being in a good mood said, "What's that?" Rafe told the General about the enlisted men at SHAPE not being eligible for promotion. Rafe went on to say that if by serving at SHAPE you were in an elite group, then you shouldn't be deprived of rank because of your assignment. The General said that he was unaware of such regulations and would look into it.

About three weeks later after having an evening sparring match with Capt. Haldane the Captain said, "Hawkins I was informed through the chain of command that the men of the 591st will no longer be penalized where rank is concerned. It's interesting that this should come about shortly after your inquiry on the same subject. Do you know anything about this?"

Rafe looked at the Captain nodded in the affirmative, and said, "Well I did mention it to General Lemnitzer seeing that it's so unfair to some of our NCOs who are career soldiers raising families. Think of this sir, Corporal Preese is a Korean War Combat Veteran and He's still a Corporal and that's after spending a couple of years in a Chinese Prisoner of War Camp. I think he's a hell of a good NCO."

The captain looked at Rafe and said, "It's not always a good thing to go outside the chain of command, but this happens to be an exception as it's a big morale booster. I think I'll let the word out as to how it all came about."

Rafe had a serious dislike for being in France. It wasn't the people or the climate it was the loneliness. Everyone has heard of being lonely in a crowd and for all practical purposes, this was Rafe's condition. It wasn't that he didn't have good friends and companions, for he did. It stemmed from the fact that he was madly in love and missed his Ice Princess. Ella wrote him two or three times a week, but he felt if he didn't get back to her soon it might prove to be too late. He was aware of the saying, Absence makes the heart grow fonder, but he was thinking, "Yeah, for somebody else." Ella was just too beautiful and he knew every GI and Airmen at Sandia Base or Kirtland Airforce Base would give anything to steal her affections.

He wasn't like his roommates, Fred Johnson, Norn West, and John McGruder, all great guys but interested in only one thing, getting laid. If it hadn't been for Ella, he would probably have had the same attitude. One of their biggest problems was they couldn't find girls who could speak English. Since half their time was spent around the pot-bellied stove in their room, shooting the bull, eventually Rafe was pulled into their discussions. They had seen Ella's picture which was taped to the inside of his locker and knew Rafe had a drop-dead, gorgeous girlfriend. So, they reasoned if he had such a girl, he must know a lot about women. The truth was, none of them, including Rafe, knew jack shit about the opposite sex. That didn't stop them from drawing their own assumptions. One day while sitting around, on their foot-lockers, spit-shinning their boots Fearless Fred said, "Rafe how do we find some women to hit on?"

Rafe smiled and said, "Why ask me? I'm the only one who never goes out trying to pick up women."

"Fearless, who had earned that sobriquet because where members of the opposite sex were concerned, Fred was fearless, and by that, it meant that Fred had no standards, if it was female, Fred was after it, and neither age looks, or size would deter him. Fred felt that Rafe had the answer and persisted, 'Come on Rafe, give us a break, we know you know more than you're saying. If you were going out with us, where would you suggest we look?"

Rafe laughed and said, 'Look if I were to tell you what I think you'd just dismiss it out of hand."

Then Norm chimed in and said, 'Hey we couldn't be doing any worse than we are, and hell we're in France and we're striking out right and left, so come on Rafe tell us where you'd look.

This was a typical GI bull shit session so Rafe thought what the hell, they want to know, so I'll tell them. Rafe said, "Ok you want to meet girls you can hit on, go to church!"

Imagine the uproar this caused. John jumped up and said, "Damn it, Rafe quit fucking around with us, this is serious business. You say go to Church; Are you fucking crazy?"

Rafe shook his head and said, "I told you that I'd never convince you, but if you follow my advice, you'll meet some very nice girls that speak English. They speak English because they're real American girls."

Fearless Fred got back into the conversation and said, "Rafe, do you really believe if we go to church this Sunday, we'll meet some girls?"

So, Rafe told him, "Fred you can lead a horse to water, but you can't make him drink. I can find you the water, but that doesn't mean you won't screw the whole thing up."

Then John piped in with, "Well how about you come along with us and show us how to pick up, girls?" Rafe shook his head in the negative and said, "Look guys, you know I'm in love with Ella who to me is the most beautiful girl on earth. I can't go out running around with you lechers. I'm engaged to be married."

Now they were all getting into the idea so Norn said, "You don't need to get involved with any girls, just show us how to do it."

Rafe knew they were lonely, and what else did he have to do anyway, so he said, "OK, I'll show you how to succeed with girls, but you must do what I tell you, I don't want to waste my time.

So, what do you say, next Sunday we all go to church at the American Cathedral with the idea of meeting some enchanting young women." They all agreed and began to talk excitedly about their prospects. Rafe finished spit-shining his boots and hit the sack.

Now his friends had something to look forward to and the topic of conversation was women. Rafe was thinking to himself, "Why ask me, hell I don't know the first thing about girls. I don't have any secret method, I'm just nice to them and try to get to know them. If anything works, that's what it is. Oh well, we'll see what happens, at least it will give us something to do."

The next Sunday they took the bus that ran from SHAPE every hour to its destination next to the Arc de Triomphe where Ave. Des Champs-Elysees meets Avenue de Wagram. They were familiar with this area as their favorite bar, known as the Sun Club, was only two blocks away, and they were continually taking the bus from SHAPE into the center of Paris when they didn't take the train. The American Cathedral was about a six or seven-block walk from the Arc de Triomphe on Avenue George V. The group of young men filed in and took part in the service singing hymns and praying with the rest of the parishioners all the while checking out any young ladies who might be available. It didn't take them long to zero in on four young ladies sitting together a few rows in front of theirs. Rafe noticed his friends whispering about their obvious quarry.

   When the service came to an end the young men followed the very well-dressed, young women out onto the street while Rafe being the most confident approached the girl who in his opinion, was obviously the leader. He knew he didn't know any pickup lines so he acted his usual self and said to the tall very pretty platinum blonde, "Hello, It's, nice to finally see some good weather, actually, some sunlight for a change. The young woman turned to Rafe with a surprised and somewhat annoyed look, but before she could say anything he gave her his best smile and stuck out his hand, and said, "Hi, I'm Rafe Hawkins,"

    She took a harder look wondering, who is this guy, then said, "Hi, there Rafe, "I'm Elizabeth Ryan, pleased to make your acquaintance." It was obvious to Rafe that she was sizing him up, because she quickly added, "What are you and your friends doing here at church, we haven't seen you here before."

   Rafe looked over at his buddies trying to hit on Elizabeth's friends and said, "I'm a little embarrassed to say, but we're looking to meet some American Girls."

   Now Elizabeth put on a somewhat perplexed expression and said, "You mean you came to church to try to pick up girls?"

   Rafe Responded with, "Well, not exactly. We're in the Army based at Supreme Headquarters in Versailles, and we'd like to find some American girls to talk to, maybe someone to see the sights with. We don't speak French and it gets kind of lonely hanging around the barracks in this lousy weather, never getting to even talk to a pretty girl. The truth is we get tired of talking about the same subjects over and over."

Then Elizabeth said, "Who came up with the idea to find girls in church?"

Rafe gave an embarrassed look and said, "I guess that was me."

Now Elizabeth was beginning to get more interested. She said, "By the way, my friends call me Liz." She added, "What made you think church was the right place?"

Rafe knew if he could get this lovely girl into an interesting conversation, he might win her over so he went on to say, "Well I thought if a person is well-bred and properly raised, they're going to be going to church on Sunday, after all, it's the proper thing to do."

This time he was rewarded with a genuine laugh, and a big smile. Liz was getting interested and asked, "What do you do at SHAPE?"

Rafe said, "We're sort of in security work."

She said, "What do you specifically do?"

Rafe had no reason to hide the truth so he told Liz, "I'm the bodyguard to General Lemnitzer, The Supreme Allied Commander Europe."

Liz took another hard look at Rafe, waited a few seconds, and then said, "So you must be a real tough guy."

Rafe was wondering where this was leading, but answered truthfully, "Some people think so, however, I'm not one of them."

Liz was getting interested and asked. "Then how did you become the bodyguard to the Supreme Allied Commander?

"Well, at my previous assignment in New Mexico I met the girl I thought was the world's most beautiful woman, and a few days later the company bully decided to make some very, how should I put it, very uncomplimentary comments about her. I mean very uncomplimentary. So, after taking as much as I could, I told him to shut his mouth, or I'd shut it for him. He never thought it would happen because he outweighed me by 40 pounds or so. Not only that, but we were on duty, and fighting on duty at Sandia Base would never be tolerated. So, I told him to meet me in the Gym the next day and go three rounds with me."

Now Liz had to hear the rest of the story, and said, "So what happened?"

Rafe shook his head from side to side and said, "Well the whole thing got out of hand, and when we finally faced off the next day everyone from both MP Companies A and B showed up to witness the big event, including all of the officers. To make a long story short, he didn't last three rounds. However, if I thought I was doing the right thing, it all backfired in my face. About this time the Army was looking for a bodyguard for the new Supreme Allied Commander. The ideal candidate would have a Top-Secret Clearance, would be a crack shot, and be one who exhibited good judgment. The Company Commander at Sandia Base thought my avoiding fighting on duty was a sign of good judgment, and I was also an expert shot with a .45, and had a Top-Secret Clearance. So here I am 5,000 miles from where I most want to be."

Liz asked, "Is she really that beautiful? You said she was the most beautiful woman in the world?" Rafe wasn't exactly sure how to answer so he simply said, "Well, beauty is in the eye of the beholder, but she's a real knockout, in my opinion, the most beautiful girl in Albuquerque. I would call her a real exotic beauty. She was known around Sandia Base as the Ice Princess."

Curiosity was getting the best of Liz so she asked, "How did you end up with this beautiful girl?" Rafe smiled and said, "It's a long story, Liz. I could tell you, but it will take at least half an hour."

Liz frowned and said, "We don't have time right now, we have to be back at Madame Clemenceau's Finishing School in less than an hour, she's very strict about punctuality. However, I have an idea. Do you still want to take us out to see the sights of Paris?"

Rafe nodded yes, and said, "Of Course."

Liz giving Rafe a sweet smile said, "Ok, how about this, next Sunday after church we'll meet you guys right here, and we'll go sightseeing together, OK?"

Rafe quickly said, "You got a deal, we'll be right here next Sunday."

With that said, Liz called to the others and said, "Come on girls, we'll be late and Madame Clemenceau will have a fit."

The girls headed off down Avenue George V towards the Etoile while Rafe walked over towards his disappointed friends. Fearless said, "Shit Rafe, in a few more minutes we might have gotten a date."

"Don't worry about that, I fixed everything for next Sunday."

"Like what for instance?" said Fearless

"Like, I've arranged for us to meet them here after church next Sunday, and take them sightseeing."

John exclaimed, "No shit, how did you arrange that, Rafe."

"Well, it wasn't that hard, I just told Liz that we were looking for some American Girls to take out sightseeing, girls who spoke English. Then I was in the middle of telling her a very interesting story when she realized they had to get back to their school. Since she wanted to hear the end of this interesting story, she said they'd meet us next week and go out with us."

Norm inquired, "You mean it was that easy? Why do you think she agreed to go out with us next week?"

"I think the explanation is fairly simple. They really aren't that much different than us, except they're rich and we're not. Maybe they're just as lonely for home as we are. Let's head back to the barracks and sit down and make plans for next week."

"Yeah!", John said, this is heady stuff. Imagine us going out with a bunch of heiresses."

Then Fred chimed in, "This is unbelievable."

As they walked back to the Etoile to catch the bus back to SHAPE Rafe added, "This just goes to show you what happens when you go to church. If you want to meet some fine young ladies, the place to look is in church. The church is what is known as a target-rich environment."

"Amen to that!" stated Norn. So, the foursome headed back to the barracks to make plans.

The 591st MP Company had its barracks in Versailles while the rest of the SHAPE enlisted men were quartered in a French compound called Camp Veluceau which was only about a mile from SHAPE. Because the MPs were segregated from the rest of the American contingent and didn't have the use of the enlisted men's club they were allowed to have their own club in the Versailles barracks. It wasn't much of a place but a beer was only 20 cents, and a dime on Friday nights. Once Rafe and his roommates got back to Versailles, they settled down to have a few beers and plan for the next Sunday. The club was sort of dark and run down, with a bar and 8 tables scattered around the room. In one corner was a jukebox with such songs on it as the country and western classic **I want to go Home**. The song was by far the most popular song. Invariably, when one of the guys would walk in, he'd pick up a beer at the bar, then walk to the far corner and put a coin in the jukebox, and soon everyone would hear the lyrics that went like this:

I want to go home
I want to go home
Oh how I want to go home
Last night I went to sleep in Detroit City
I dreamed about those cotton fields back home
I dreamed about my mother, my dear Papa, sister, and brother.
I dreamed about that girl that's been waiting for so long.
I wanna go home
I wanna go home
Oh how I wanna go home.
Home folks think I'm big in Detroit City
From the letters that I write, they think I'm fine
But by day I make the cars
By night I make the bars
If only they could read between the lines.
I wanna go home
I wanna go home
Oh how I wanna go home.

If you'd ever wondered how GI's feel when serving overseas that song sums it up. It was so popular that Captain Haldane had it removed for destroying morale.

It didn't take long for their favorite topic of conversation to rise to the fore, and that was getting laid. One might wonder how young GI's act when living together in the barracks, and the answer to that is simple, pretty much like a bunch of dogs, or one might say animals. So, it started immediately when Fearless Fred said, "We're finally going to get laid, and we've found some high-class pussy at that." Norm and John were quick to agree, while Rafe, still being a Mom Morton-raised boy, was appalled. Even though he was a little bit younger, in many ways he was years ahead in maturity. He knew if they were going to have a good time with the girls next Sunday, he'd have to stop them in their tracks and give them a tutorial on women. Not that he was any kind of expert, but then, everything is relative. He may not know much, but they were virtually idiotic. With that in mind, he began his little lecture.

"Guys, if you approach next Sunday's date with the girls we've just met at church, with the attitude you're exhibiting now you're wasting your time. The truth is you aren't going to get laid, but if you play your cards right you might have the best time you'll ever have while in Paris. Now don't get, all up in arms, or get to protesting until you hear me out. You know how we sit around in the barracks and bullshit constantly. Most of what we say is made up and equates to simply posturing. So, without our usual bullshit, let's discuss getting laid in a serious manner." Rafe continued,

"After all, what is getting laid anyway? I'll tell you what it's all about, one simple thing, Reproduction. Nature wants the next generation produced. In order to do that it made sex pleasurable. I'm sure all of you remember back when you were eight or nine years old, that you had no interest in girls other than to throw snowballs or spitballs at them. Then around the time we reached twelve or thirteen, they suddenly started to become very appealing." Then Rafe said, "Fearless, do you remember when their budding breasts, poking out from under their sweaters began to attract you like nothing else." Fred nodded and said, "Hell yes I remember." Then Rafe went on to say, "Do you think that was an intellectual renaissance that suddenly came over you? No, it was hormonal. When your Y chromosome started to emit testosterone, you suddenly developed an interest in the opposite sex. Not just a small interest either but an overwhelming one. That's how it all happens, our hormones tell us to pursue women, so we do. It should also be on our mind that once we impregnate a female, nature is satisfied because the next generation is on its way. That may be fine for nature but for us, it's far more serious. Here is the crux of the argument. We, humans, are theoretically half-animal and half-divine. When we sit around the barracks and talk about getting laid or getting some pussy, we are succumbing to the animal side of our nature."

Norm then asked, "What do you mean, sex is a natural act."

Rafe went on to say, "Yes, it is, but we are a higher form of animal. You know when a bitch is in heat every dog in the neighborhood will try to jump and breed her. Then if he manages to impregnate her, does he stick around and try to help with the pups, or does he run off to find another female in heat? We should be above all that. Let me ask you guys this question. How many of you were raised by a mother with a father to support you?"

All three of his buddies agreed they had been raised by a mother and a father. Then Rafe told them that he only had his mother, and that, as a result, he encountered very serious problems. Then he continued. "Let's say, that we were the ones who could get pregnant and deliver babies, and not women. In other words, what would be your attitude if by screwing a woman it would be you that ended up pregnant. How careful would you be about who or how many you screwed?

When Rafe finished his rant about sex, Norm chimed in with, "Come on Rafe, don't you think that's carrying things a little too far? Deep down you think just like us, and want to get laid as much as we do, right!"

Rafe just shrugged and added, "Look I've had my say. That's how I look at things, I'll just add this, If, you want to have a good time this coming Sunday, behave like a gentleman. These are girls from good families sent here by their families to become real ladies, if you want to get along with them, act like gentlemen. It's that simple. Besides, I have a way for all of us to have the time of our lives."

John asked, "And what might that be, you who know everything?"

Then Rafe asked, "Did you guys happen to see the movie **On The Town** with Frank Sinatra and Gene Kelley?" They all nodded in the affirmative so Rafe continued, "It's a fun-filled film about three sailors who spend a couple of nights in New York looking for girls and the great time had by all. Life is about experience, and so far, we've had very little, but think if we can carry this off, what a great movie it would make. Four GIs, stationed in Paris, meet four girls in the church and go out the next Sunday to see the town. In the process, they have the time of their lives and paint in their memories a day they will never forget. You guys up for it?"

Again, they all nodded yes, so Rafe went on. "In our case, we're just average GIs"s and the girls are rich oil heiresses from Texas. Don't you think it would be outrageously funny to take the rich girls sightseeing, and in the process see how little we can spend on them, and still show them the time of their lives? How does that sound?" One after the other they all agreed that that sounded like a great plan.

They developed a plan for which sites to see and they included the Sacre-Coeur in Montmartre, the Cathedral of Notre Dame and the West Bank of the Seine River, the Tuileries Gardens, the Eiffel Tower, and of course, a ride on the Bateaux Mouches also known as the fly boats. The Bateaux Mouches cruise up and down the Seine with views of the Left Bank, Eiffel Tower, Notre Dame, Alexander III Bridge, Pont Neuf, and the Louvre Museum. Norm who loved photography promised to bring his camera to record whatever happened.

The next Sunday the young men were ready to paint the town with their newly found friends. Aside from being from very wealthy Texas families whose money came from oil, the girls couldn't have been more different. The one trait they had in common was they all comported themselves as classy young women.

Liz Ryan was a striking 5'6" platinum blonde, very self-assured, and a little reserved. She was also the leader of the group. Grace Richardson was a 5'3" brunette, with an easy grace and was very good-natured. Victoria Cullen was very much like Grace and because they looked alike and acted the same way one could easily mistake them for sisters. The wild card was Priscilla McCarthy who was about 5' and a little chubby, however, she was a live wire, and was fascinated by things too numerous to count. One of the things to strike her fancy happened to be Fearless Fred who despite his seeming lack of taste where women were concerned was quite good-looking. Fred wasn't only good-looking, but like Priscilla he was a live wire. The two of them took to each other like bees take to honey, sort of made for each other. The rest of the group had such a good time watching the two of them that it added to their sense of merriment. After Church, they took the metro to Montmartre to see the Basilique du Sacre-Coeur. Next was the Eiffel Tower followed by the Left Bank of the Seine. Although they were from completely different backgrounds the eight young Americans were beginning to have a great time.

Liz was clearly interested in Rafe and while standing on the first stage of the Eiffel Tower gazing over the River Seine at the magnificent city she said, "Rafe, remember you were going to tell me about how you got a date with the Ice Princess."

Rafe looked at Liz, whom many would think was even more attractive than Ella, and answered, "Are you sure you want to know?"

She gave him one of what he now knew as a come hither look, the one that women give you when they seriously want something and nodded, "Yes, I want to know,"

"Ok this is how it happened," Rafe began the story with his initial skirmish with Brannigan about his never having had a date. Of course, the next bit of information revealed was that his first date was with the starlet Jill Haworth. When he related this fact to Liz she couldn't believe what she was hearing. She gave him a disbelieving look and said, "Do you mean to say that your first date was with a movie star?

Rafe blushed and replied, "Yes, she was my first date."

Now Liz was really interested so she asked, "How did it happen? How did you meet her and get to know her well enough to ask her out?" When he told her that he didn't ask Jill out and that she asked him, Liz had to hear the whole story in detail.

He finished the story as they cruised the Seine in the Bateaux Mouches, and by this time he had her completely enthralled. Liz finally said, "Rafe you're a real ladies' man, aren't you?"

Rafe blushed and responded, "I'm hardly that, but I seem to get along with beautiful girls."

Liz was now very interested in Rafe and wanted to know what his ambition in life was, she asked, did he have a dream he wanted to fulfill?

He thought for a while and then said, "If I could do anything I would breed the fastest racehorse to ever live, a legendary horse, one of the ones."

Since they were talking about their dreams Rafe asked Liz, "What would you do, if you could do anything?"

She answered right away seeing that she knew exactly what she wanted to accomplish in life, "I want to paint a masterpiece.!"

"You mean you're an artist?"

"Yes, I am, and I'm very good."

"How do you know" It's pretty easy to be delusional about your own work."

"Well, I can paint a complete painting in one hour."

Rafe laughed, and playfully said, "So can I but it wouldn't be worth ten cents."

Liz knew Rafe was teasing her and added, "I also paint with my hands a on the blank canvas. I think I'm somewhat psychic as I can see the images on canvas."

Rafe thought all she was telling him was extremely fascinating so he asked, "If you can paint a complete painting in one hour will you let me watch?"

"I'll go one step further if you'll agree."

"Ok, what do you have in mind?"

"Ever since you showed up last week at church, I've had this very strong feeling that if I were to paint you, I'd have my masterpiece. Like a painting that would propel me to the top of the class as an emerging artist. So, I was thinking, if you would be my subject and sit for me for an afternoon you would get to see if I can indeed paint a painting in one hour. However, with this one, I might take a tad bit longer. What do you say?"

"Why would this one take, a bit longer than usual?"

"Because it's going to be my masterpiece. You know, like the Mona Lisa."

"What makes you think I'd be such a great subject for a painting?"

"I get these feelings about things, like psychic feelings and I'm getting one about you. So, Can I paint your portrait?"

Rafe was quite flattered that Liz wanted to paint him so he said, "Ok, when would you like to do it?"

"Maybe next Saturday or the one after that. Do you think you can do it then?"

"Sure, anytime is all right with me. It should be fun. Will I be able to talk while I'm posing? There's nothing like sitting around talking to a beautiful woman."

"Yes, you can talk to me while I'm painting. Do you really think I'm beautiful?"

"I think you're very beautiful, and I think you know it."

"Why do you say that?"

"You must notice the men who gawk at you as you walk by, or those that stop and try to look nonchalant when they stop and take a surreptitious look back at you."

Rafe was grinning when he said it, and Liz smiled back and said, "Ok, I know men find me attractive. But I'm more interested in what you think of me. Like how do I compare with the other two girls you've dated, meaning Jill and Ella?"

"It's hard to say because beautiful is beautiful and it's in the eyes of the beholder. Like in a beauty contest, all of the girls are beautiful, yet one still wins. You, Ella, and Jill are all beautiful and yet different. It's also interesting that Ella asked me the same question. She wanted to know how she compared to Jill. So, I guess what you're really interested in is how I perceive you. Is that what you want to know?"

Liz nodded yes and added, "That's exactly right. I want to know how you see me. In truth, that's how I paint. I'm an impressionist and when I paint you it will be my impression of you."

"This is not going to be easy, but I'll try. First, you are very beautiful. Your platinum blonde hair and facial structure are stunning. However, there is more. Let me go off on a tangent as to how horses are sold. When a horse is well-bred and beautiful it will bring a very high price. If the horse is well-bred and ugly the price will drop dramatically. Much about selling horses is based on what they look like. Humans assume that if it looks good, it is good. This is delusional thinking. Many great horses are plug-ugly. However, after they achieve greatness people begin to think they're better looking than they appeared as yearlings. In other words, in the beholder's eye, they begin to look like what they really are. There are a few horsemen that are able to see the essence of the horses, character, it's referred to as **the look of eagles.** This doesn't mean that the horse has the look of an eagle. It means that its character is reflected through its eyes. It's intangible. To most horsemen, it's invisible and can't be seen. So, Liz, while you're strikingly beautiful, you have that look. Do you understand what I'm saying?"

"I think I'm beginning to."

Rafe was thinking, "How lucky can a person be? I'm engaged to a beautiful sexy girl, and here I am in Paris talking to a girl who is equally beautiful, possibly even more beautiful. The amusing part of it all is that Liz can't be objective about herself where beauty is concerned. If he joined the Army to gain experience what could be better than this? This was as good a way to learn about women as anything he could think of. How do you explain to a beautiful woman, the essence of her beauty?"

Liz asked, "What are you thinking Rafe?"

He said, "I'm thinking about beauty and how different beautiful women actually are."

"Well go on and tell me how the three of us differ!"

"Ok, you asked for it. Jill is a beautiful young woman, she has startlingly beautiful blue eyes, but aside from being beautiful, she is cute and playful. Sort of like a cute kitten. When I was around Jill, I wanted to play with her. I wanted to hold her, and yes, I wanted to do more than just hold her, if you get my drift. Ella is very sexy, a perfectly made woman. With her, you see her, and you start to imagine what she's like sans clothing. Put another way, you want to get your hands on her. Finally, there is you, you're the classic beauty but with an intangible quality. It's what is called the **look of eagles** in racehorses. What is it? It's the character, confidence, or more to the point, fortitude. You combine that, with beauty, and you have a very alluring combination, and that's you."

Liz looked over at Rafe and said, "You are definitely a lady's man. Is that really how you see me?"

"If I was an artist like you, I would try to capture that special quality on canvas. Maybe I'd be the one to paint a masterpiece?"

They both laughed at that and Liz playfully said, "Wait till you see how I capture you on canvas.

"I can't wait!"

As the Bateaux Mouches cruised up the Seine, Rafe and Liz turned to check out what the other three couples were up to. Fearless and Priscilla were chattering away like a pair of magpies while Norm and Victoria, and John and Grace were lost in conversation. Liz said, "Will you look at Fred and Priscilla? Priscilla seems to be having a wonderful time." Then Liz went on to say, "Priscilla seems to be having such a good time. She usually doesn't get this much attention from men."

Do you think Fred really likes her?" Rafe nodded Yes. "If you knew Fred, you'd realize he likes Priscilla very much indeed. I think it's wonderful that they're having such a great time."

They say time flies when you're having fun and before they knew it, it was almost time for the Girl's curfew at 2200. The young couples were running late and it would not be a good thing to break curfew by being late. They came running out of the metro near the Opera and sprinted down Boulevard de la Madeleine to Madame Clemenceau's school. They arrived with two minutes to spare, out of breath, and yet laughing uncontrollably. There was just enough time for a quick and sweet goodnight kiss and saying thanks for a wonderful day. Liz handed Rafe a slip with the school's telephone number and quickly said, "Call me this week and we'll arrange for you to sit for a portrait. The Bois de Boulogne might be a good spot. I'll bring the girls and they can run around with your roommates while I sketch you." She gave him an affectionate kiss and ran inside.

The four young men stood in front of the school's entrance and laughed and grinned like idiots pleased with how the day turned out. Norm was the first to speak and he said, "I can't believe we had such a good time and spent so little money. And to think we met these girls in church."

John added, "You're some kind of genius Rafe, how did you know that church was the place to meet girls?"

Rafe told them, "It's really kind of logical. We wanted American girls. Where do they go? On Sundays, church. We go there and the rest is history. Oh, and there's something else. Are you guys up for another date next Saturday?" They all responded in the affirmative so Rafe said, "Liz says we should meet them in the Bois de Boulogne next Saturday and she's going to paint my portrait, so while she's doing that you can see the Park with Liz's friends."

Fearless asked, "Do you mean Liz's an artist?"

Rafe answered, "yes, and apparently a good one. She thinks if I act as her subject she can paint her masterpiece, so how was I to say no? So, while we're doing that, the rest of you can have some fun." It was obvious from their demeanor that Rafe's friends had had a wonderful day.

Norm Said, "This was the best day I've had since arriving in France." He thought about it a minute then changed his mind to, "No this is the best day I've ever had. I can't remember when I've had so much fun." They all agreed that they had had a great time.

Rafe finally said, "This just goes to show how much fun you can have when acting like a gentleman instead of like a bunch of assholes. I'm telling you right now, good behavior pays dividends."

The next Saturday found Rafe sitting at a table in the Bois de Boulogne with Liz sitting across from him busy at her sketch pad. Rafe was sitting there smiling at Liz when she looked up and said, "What?"

"I don't know. What do you mean?"

"Why are you looking at me like that?"

"I don't know. How am I looking at you?"

"I don't know either, but I think you're unaware of the affect you have on people."

"Am I having an affect on you now?"

"Yes, but I'm not sure what it is. That's what it's all about. I'm trying to turn my thoughts into artistic expression. Remember, I'm an impressionist artist. I'm going to put on canvas my interpretation of the essence of your character. If I can capture that I'll have my masterpiece."

"How are you doing?"

"So far I'm stymied"

Liz was thinking. "He's not the greatest-looking guy yet there's something about his look. What is it that makes him so appealing?" Then it suddenly came to her. "It's the look of love in his eyes. It's irresistible. It encompasses you, yet not in a threatening manner, it's something you want to experience." She thought about it and felt she was getting close to what she was seeking. Then it suddenly hit her; It's a combination of two powerful and different themes of character. The first is love and the second is power. Floating just below the surface lies a pool of overwhelming power. It doesn't show, but I sense it. I'll have to do something to get him to reveal this to me. I'll say something that will really get him angry. With that in mind, Liz said, "Can I ask you a question, Rafe?"

He said, "Sure go ahead," Not expecting anything unusual until she said, "How did you attract that Mexican slut they call the Ice Princess?"

It was like throwing a switch and in a split second, she was looking into the eyes of an Eagle, a Bird of Prey. She remembered that Rafe had told her that his Serete partner, Jacque had said he looked like a bird of prey. Then she had his essence. Love and Power. If she could combine the two, she'd have her masterpiece.

Rafe responded, "What did you say?"

"Don't take what I said seriously Rafe, I just wanted to make you angry so I could see another side of your nature. I was just testing you, and I saw what I needed to see. Now I'm done. Let me make a sketch of what I saw, and then we can track down the others and go to the Louvre and see the Mona Lisa or do something else that's fun. Fifteen minutes is all I'll need."

"I thought this was going to take hours."

"It could have, but in this case, it only took forty-five minutes."

"Why such a short time?"

"It only took that short period of time for me to see the essence of what you are."

"Are you going to tell me what that is?"

"Nope, you'll just have to wait for the finished painting. I think it's going to take much longer than one hour. In fact, it may take a month or possibly more. However, in the end. I think the painting will speak to you. If I can capture your character on canvas, it will be a great painting."

"And you think you have that in your head now."

"Oh yes, I see it. Now I have to use every ounce of my talent to express it. I even have a name for it."

"Can you tell me what you're going to call it?"

"Sorry Rafe, you will have to wait to see when It's finished. Then I'll tell you what I think, OK?"

"Sure, that's Ok, but don't take too long as I'll be dying of curiosity."

Liz finished her sketch then they Headed off through the Bois searching for their missing companions. They knew where they were headed yet it still took them about thirty minutes to locate their wayward friends. On a roundabout way to the Louvre, they stopped at a bistro on the left bank and had lunch while discussing the upcoming masterpiece Liz was about to create.

The Louvre was special even if you're not a connoisseur of the masterpieces therein. Works of art like the Mona Lisa, The Venus De Milo, Liberty Leading the People, The Winged Victory of Samothrace, Raft of the Medusa, and The Winged Bulls. These are just a sample of the major works of art, they saw, with Liz giving a tutorial about their significance.

Later walking up the boulevard to Madame Clemenceau's school Rafe told Liz, "I hope it doesn't take too long for inspiration to hit you. I can't wait to see what you create."

Liz told him, "Once I get it straight in my head it will only take a short time to produce the image. Remember, it's supposed to speak to you. Send you a message."

"Let me know when it's ready. By the way, thank you for a wonderful day." Liz smiled and said, "No I should be the one to thank you. Looks like we belong to a mutual admiration society."

"It sure looks that way."

That's the way things went for the next month. The young American's got together whenever possible and took in the sights of La Ville-Lumiere, or The City of Light. The name seems to have come from Paris, the birthplace of the Age of Enlightenment. The girls even came out to visit Versailles to see the famous Palace. When the four roommates brought them into the 591st MP Company bar for a quick beer it caused an unending sensation. For weeks the rest of the men wanted to know where Rafe and company had met such high-class, American girls. When they told them it was in church no one believed them.

Just after the July 14^{th,} Bastille Day celebration Rafe got word from Liz, the painting was finished. Madame Clemenceau had arranged for a Tea Party to be given, and the guests of honor would be Liz's four American Army friends. When Rafe told Liz that the Tea Party idea might not be the best of ideas seeing that Rafe and his friends did not have clothing fit for such an auspicious event held at a place like Madame Clemenceau's Finishing School, it was suggested they come in uniform. Since Rafe and his friends were a little on the good-looking side, Liz figured they would cause a small sensation representing the United States Army.

Rafe told his buddies that while they were at the school they absolutely had to be on their best behavior as if they were visiting the White House or having an audience with the Queen of England. After all, their friends were in Paris to learn to become the epitome of refined young ladies, and if they didn't want to make complete fools of themselves, they had to act more like gentlemen than they had ever in their lives. He told them that Madame Clemenceau would be watching them like a hawk just waiting for them to slip up. This meant no smart-assed remarks, about anything. No clowning around, no loud talking. Where decorum was concerned, they had to be perfect. They could either make the girls look smart or like those with bad judgment.

On the next Sunday the 21st of July, the guys met the girls at church and escorted them back to their school. Their arrival caused somewhat of a sensation as the entire student body of young ladies was aware of what was going on concerning Liz's painting. Although no one had actually seen it the unveiling was only about an hour away and nobody wanted to miss the big event. The young men were under close scrutiny from Madame Clemenceau, but they were on their best behavior and passed with flying colors.

The painting was sitting on an easel in the middle of the courtyard in which the tea party was taking place. With great fanfare, with the entire student body in attendance, Liz and Priscilla approached the easel and from either side lifted the covering and revealed 's masterpiece. There was a murmur from the assembled group while Rafe simply stared in amazement. He had never seen a painting like this. It actually seemed to be talking to him, in a non-verbal way. It was moving yet enigmatic. There was a powerful message being transmitted, but at first, Rafe couldn't figure out what that was. There seemed to be a dichotomy between two competing but powerful visions. Liz was watching Rafe to see what his expression would reveal. At first, it was more one of consternation. Then it began to sink in. The first emotion expressed was one of great power, but the countenance of the subject was also one of great love. Rafe was wondering how the two went together and at the same time how did Liz capture it. Rafe continued to stare at the portrait thinking to himself that this was indeed a masterpiece. While he was absorbed in the painting Liz walked over to him and said, "What do you think?"

Rafe took Liz by the hand and led her over to the other end of the courtyard. They turned and faced each other and Rafe said, "Liz that's the most amazing thing I've ever seen. It's so deep that I could stand there and stare at it for hours in order to understand its meaning. The painting almost speaks to you, in a non-verbal way of course, but it has a message. I'm not sure I completely understand what the message is, but I have an idea.

Liz asked, "What do you think the message is?"

Rafe responded, "I feel an underlying sense of great power, but it lies beneath the surface. On the surface, Its love that is projected. Not a simple form of love, but pure love. It's said that God shows himself in the world through love. Pure, unadulterated love, that's what you've captured. It's your masterpiece. If you can paint anything else approaching this, you'll be famous."

Rafe could see how happy this made Liz and she asked, "Do you really think it's that good?"

"Liz, it's the best thing I've ever seen in my life. Beats the Mona Lisa in my opinion. I just have one question. What is the meaning, of the chain in one hand, and the key in the other?"

"You know I'm not exactly sure. I waited for the image to form in my head and this is how I saw you. Remember this is my impression of you."

Rafe added, "Well, it's a hell of an impression."

"I know it's special, and so are you, even if you're unaware of it."

"This is too much Liz, I never expected anything like this. You are a true genius."

Liz and Rafe slowly walked back across the courtyard to where her masterpiece was sitting on its easel. The student body was gathered around it making a murmuring sound as they quietly discussed the amazing work of art. Liz made her way into the crowd of mesmerized students while Rafe stood off to the side with a big smile on his face.

He knew Liz had hit a home run when Madame Clemenceau walked up and said, "Well monsieur Rafe, what do you think of Liz's work considering you are the subject?"

"Madame I think it's so extraordinary that I can't put it into words. She said she wanted to paint a masterpiece and I think she's done it. The painting sends a powerful message." The headmistress agreed and told Rafe that Liz was undoubtedly the most talented young woman ever to attend her academy.

The next Sunday Liz gave Rafe some news that was not totally unexpected. At the end of the summer, Liz and her friends were leaving for Switzerland to attend another school. It reminded Rafe of the saying from Alfred Lord Tennyson, "Tis better to have loved and lost than never to have loved at all." Rafe wasn't referring to romantic love as neither was Tennyson, but the loss of friendship. Who's to say that love for a friend is not the purest expression of love?

The girls were moving on, following the script laid out by their parents. Norm, John, and Fearless Fred were due to rotate back to the States in October as their discharge dates loomed. As for Rafe he was going to get admitted to Officer Candidate School, by the end of the year, come hell or high water. Each of the eight was secretly satisfied, after all, they were young, and they had just spent a wonderful summer in Paris, in a way, having the time of their lives.

Liz had her masterpiece crated and shipped back to Houston to the care of her Dad whom she knew would keep it ultra-safe. There's a saying that, "All good things must come to an end." The end of their romantic sojourn came at Gare Lyon the railroad station right off Rue Van Gogh. Rafe thought its location was quite appropriate considering he thought Liz was the modern version of Van Gogh. They said goodbye standing on the platform next to the train about to depart for Geneva. Rafe and Liz knew they were forever bound together in her wonderful work of art, but this didn't help Rafe feel an overwhelming sense of loss. It was the feeling of what if. What might have been if he hadn't met Ella first? If he wanted to learn about life and become more worldly this was a perfect learning experience. If Rafe left Ella, and took up with Liz what would that say about his character? It might say that he didn't have that much. Ella was from a dirt-poor background, not knowing whether she would get to eat every day or not. Now she had a chance to turn her life around and reach for the brass ring. If Rafe left Ella for Liz what would prevent him from leaving Liz for some other woman if the opportunity presented itself? One thing Rafe was not, and that was an ally cat. That didn't stop him from having regrets. Liz was a hell of a woman in more ways than being beautiful. She had a genius for painting, was ultra-smart, and Rafe believed she was psychic.

Rafe and Liz stood on the platform next to the departing train. Rafe was at a loss for words, but Liz Said, "You won't forget me, will you?" Looking into her beautiful blue eyes Rafe answered, "You know that's impossible Liz. We're bound together forever. We've just spent a perfect summer in Paris. How could I ever forget you?"

"Do you have any regrets?"

"Just one very big one."

"Kiss me goodbye. Let me know what could have been."

They kissed and the kiss said it all. Rafe had one final question, "Will you write to me?" Liz said, "You know I will." Then she said quietly, "I think I'm going to cry, and she turned away and stepped aboard the waiting train."

Rafe watched as she appeared in the window of her compartment soon to be joined by Victoria, Grace, and Priscilla. Liz's three companions waved and smiled cheerfully at their friends, but Liz stared straight ahead and didn't turn and look at Rafe until the train lurched forward and began to leave the station. She then turned and blew him a kiss. He thought he detected a tear on the cheek of her very sad face.

Rafe stood and watched the train slowly depart. He watched it until he could only see the two red lights on the rear of the last car. Finally, Norm said, "Let's go, Rafe, no sense crying over spilt milk.

When Rafe thought back over his short three-year relationship with women, he realized he had loved Jill, but had always realized she was far out of his reach. Despite his optimistic prophecy, that they would be returned to each other. Ella was the sexy one who was actually below him in social class and probably saw him as a good prospect. Then finally, there was Liz, Beautiful, classy, from an extremely wealthy family, and talented beyond words. He had no doubt he could easily fall in love with her. However, the problem was he was already committed. Liz was just as far out of his reach as Jill had been, and Rafe was committed to Ella. He was engaged to her. What sort of man would he be if he abandoned his poor fiancée, for a rich heiress? He also realized after all, who was he. In reality a kid from a school for disadvantaged children. who never would have come in contact with Jill if it hadn't been for Everett Massoletti.

As he followed his friends out of the Gare Lyon he thought, "At least I'm gaining some worldly knowledge, It has got to serve some good purpose, after all, who else has encountered three such lovely creatures, and all within three years?

Having had enough of introspection Rafe Said, "Hey guys let's head up to the Sun Club and drown our sorrows." They all agreed that was a plan, and they headed for the Metro. Like Norm had said, "No sense crying over spilt milk, especially when you're 21 years old and in Paris, France.

After the girls left for Switzerland Rafe turned his attention towards his returning to the United States. He put in his application for Officer Candidate School and as expected he was able to obtain the recommendation of General Lemnitzer, and Captain Haldane, which was all he really needed, but he was also able to get the recommendation of the first commandant of Artillery OCS to whom he was introduced by General Lemnitzer. The whole process was a mere formality after which he only had to pass a physical training test and go before a board of officers. The physical training test was a breeze since he was still running miles per day and could do so at a very rapid pace. After his questioning by the board of officers the lieutenant who had acted as the board secretary told Rafe that his board had been the easiest, the lieutenant had ever witnessed. Rafe was thinking well what do you expect? One only had to look at who had recommended me to know the outcome. Army officers aren't going to buck the Supreme Allied Commander. In fact, the only question asked by the board that Rafe had any difficulty answering was "What's more important to a soldier, his food, or his pay?" Since Rafe had only been a garrison soldier up to this point, he answered, "his pay."

The officers quickly pointed out that Pay was the wrong answer, but added they wouldn't expect Rafe to know the correct answer. They then suggested that Rafe find someone in his company who had experienced prolonged combat; to ask the same question. The next day Rafe was having lunch with Corporal Preese who has served on the front lines in Korea for an extended period and had been captured by the Chinese communists. Out of the clear blue, Rafe asked, Corporal Preese, what is more, important to a soldier, his food, or his pay?" In a flash, Corporal Preese answered, "His food," Rafe asked, "Why?" The corporal said that combat is so dehumanizing that after an extended time in those conditions, a person regressed and began to exhibit animal-like behavior. The longer one stayed in combat without relief the longer the animal-like behavior remained. In the end, a soldier begins to believe that he will never be able to return and become a normal human being. A hot meal was one of the things the Army could do to alleviate these dehumanizing conditions. If anything could accomplish that end it was worth its weight in gold.

With the board behind him, nothing stood in Rafe's way on his path to an appointment to a class at OCS. During the interim, his roommates reached the end of their deployment to Supreme Headquarters and were being rotated back to the States for discharge. In October Rafe made another trip to Gare Lyon this time to bid farewell to Norm, Fred, and John. It was almost a repeat of the girls leaving in September. A lot of good wishes, oaths of undying friendship, promises to write, and then a sad farewell. Again, Rafe watched the train's lights as they disappeared down the track. As he walked out of the station he was thinking, "Well I'm the only one left. The next time I come to this place I'll be the one boarding. The only difference is this time I'll have no one to see me off."

Only one other significant event took place before Rafe received his acceptance to attend Artillery Officer Candidate School at Fort Sill, Oklahoma. Rafe had just come off duty about 1900 hours and had turned in his .45 and returned to the barracks where a GI party was in full swing. It was Friday and there would be an inspection on Saturday. The General had worked late and Rafe had a long day. He had just stretched out on his bunk and turned on the radio when the program was interrupted by a news bulletin announcing that someone had taken a shot at President Kennedy as his motorcade passed through Dallas, Texas. The Bulletin didn't originally say whether anyone had been injured. Rafe quickly passed the word to the rest of the men and they gathered around the radio for more news. The next bulletin said that the president had been hit, but there was no word as to his condition. Maybe forty-five minutes later the terrible news was broadcast that the president was dead. This caused great shock among the troops who were not at all sure that this wasn't a prelude to an attack on the United States. At any minute they expected an alert to be sounded where the entire company would head for the armory and then hightail it to the underground war headquarters. That didn't happen, but the assassination of the very popular John F Kennedy brought the morale of the 591st M.P. Company to an all-time low. Kennedy was unusual in that he was almost universally admired even if not everyone agreed with him politically. Most who had heard the PT 109 story considered John Kennedy to be a true war hero.

By the time December rolled around Rafe received the news that he had been accepted to Artillery OCS at Fort Sill, Oklahoma, and now only needed to wait for a class assignment which might take a month or two. Rafe placed his only overseas phone call to Ella to give her the good news and she seemed to be as excited about the prospect as he was. He wouldn't make it home for Christmas, but he was sure to make it by January or February. It looked like Rafe's plan to return to the States was going to work.

At this point, Rafe was feeling a little bit guilty having conned Captain Haldane and General Lemnitzer into recommending his appointment to OCS. At the time he was thinking something along the lines of All's Fair in Love and War. He felt, if it was all right for the Army to send him to France even though he had a permanent assignment, then he would take advantage of their own regulations and have them send him back. At the time any thought of Duty, Honor, and Country was not on his radar screen. He would later regret his delusional train of thought, however, at the time it seemed like a great idea.

By the time Rafe left the 591st MP Company Captain Haldane had schooled him into being a lightning fast, and tenacious practitioner of Martial Arts. The Captain had been amazed at the hidden strength Rafe possessed. Considering that the Captain outweighed Rafe by about 50 pounds he was amazed that when he had Rafe pinned and wanted to twist one of his arms behind his back that it proved to be impossible. Although the Captain fought against reality, he finally had to admit that Rafe was not only stronger than he was, but he was much stronger. It was impossible, yet it couldn't be denied. Rafe had been right when he surmised that becoming

Captain Haldane's sparring partner would be the surest way to get his recommendation to attend OCS.

The last day that Rafe stood guard for General Lemnitzer he was called into the General's office to bid farewell to his little charge Brady whom he would dearly miss. Rafe hadn't had any interaction with a dog since the untimely loss of Max. The General told Rafe he thought he'd make an excellent officer and asked if there was anything he could do for Rafe before he left for the States. Rafe asked if he could have an autographed photograph of the general and also asked if the general could arrange for him to get a flight home rather than take the troopship from Hamburg. The troopship took ten days and that wouldn't allow Rafe anytime for leave before reporting to OCS. The general told Rafe not to worry and that he'd fix it so Rafe would fly home with plenty of time for leave.

With that decided Rafe only had to wait for the big day. When it arrived Rafe found he departed in a similar way to that of his arrival. He was driven in an MP car exactly like the one which had picked him up on his arrival, to the train station, where he boarded the train to Frankfort, Germany. He couldn't say that he wasn't riding in style as he had his own private compartment making him think he was James Bond in From Russia with Love. It was obvious that General Lemnitzer saw to it that he had a good farewell trip. As the train slowly pulled out of Gare Lyon Rafe had a flashback of watching Liz's train leaving the same platform and wondered if he hadn't made a mistake where she was concerned. She was truly amazing and not just where beauty was concerned as he had no doubt about her physic genius. If he hadn't already been committed! Well, that was water under the bridge, so to speak. She was way out of his class anyway being an heiress, but this departure from Paris brought her memory back into sharp focus. It was one of those great what-ifs in his life.

It wasn't long before the train fled the confines of urban Paris and was racing through the French countryside. Rafe was supremely happy. He had made it. Heading back to Albuquerque and Ella. The first part of his master plan had worked and the second and final part lay just ahead. As he finally fell asleep visions of his beautiful girlfriend danced in his head. He was thinking, "I won; I beat the odds, now Ella and I will be happy forever.

Rafe had joined the Army to gain worldly experience. He was slowly gaining some, however, he still hadn't learned much regarding delusional thinking. In fact, he hadn't learned anything about how a human can believe any absurd concept no matter how ridiculous, to the point they will lay down their life for it. Rafe was aware, of the phrase "Fate is the Hunter" the title of a book by Earnest K. Gann, and although he was unaware of it at the time he was being hunted by fate. He had a destiny, and a force powerful beyond his imagining was directing it. Although completely unaware of it at the time, the next day would bring about a trivial error that would change the direction of his life in a very significant way. But, at the time he slept happily, rocked by the rhythm of the rails.

Morning dawned on a sunny, cold, blustery day. Rafe emerged from the Rail station in Frankfort and easily found a bus heading to Rhein-Main airbase outside of the city. Rhein-Main was a huge sprawling facility but the bus driver dropped him off right in front of the military terminal. Rafe found the right ticket counter, checked his duffle, and started the long wait for his flight. He wouldn't be flying into New York, but rather into Charleston, South Carolina. From there Rafe would make his way first to New York and then on to Albuquerque. It wasn't direct, but it beat the hell out of a troop ship plowing through the surging North Atlantic in mid-winter. Rafe was only carrying two things after checking his duffle bag, that being his overcoat and the manila envelope containing his orders.

He checked in at 0900 and had to wait until 1500 for his departing flight. Rafe purchased a paperback called Pastoral by Nevil Shute and settled down to while away the day. As it turned out Pastoral would turn out to be the best book he would ever read. He spent the day reading the novel about a British bomber pilot in World War II and his romance with a Section Officer. Rafe found the book inspiring. When he wasn't reading, he spent the time people-watching and daydreaming about his Ice Princess.

Finally, at about 1430 his flight was called. Rafe put on his overcoat and walked over to the gate where boarding was in progress. Like all things military the flight was boarded by rank and that's when Rafe found out that he was the lowest-ranking person boarding. Then, come to think of it, what could he expect? By rights, he shouldn't even be on the flight. When the aircraft lifted off his spirits soared. He was on his way. He sat in his window seat and watched the setting sun for what seemed like an hour when a very troubling thought hit him. Where were his orders? Had he put the envelope in the overhead with his overcoat? He got up and looked. Not There. There could only be one explanation when he got up from his seat in the terminal prior to boarding and put on his overcoat, he had forgotten to turn around and pick up the manila envelope from the chair next to his. This was a very bad development.

In truth, Rafe had no idea how serious this small oversight was going to prove to be. He did remember Everett telling him to maintain a low profile and not to bring attention to himself, but at this stage, his mind was focused on one thing, Ella. He had no idea that this one little slip-up could upset his big plan.

The chartered flight arrived in Charleston in the late evening. Just as the boarding of the flight was done by order of rank so was the clearing through customs. By the time Rafe cleared customs, it was close to midnight and the airlines didn't have any flights scheduled toward the Northeast at that time. Rather than wait until the next day Rafe took a cab to the Railroad Station and caught a midnight train to Washington, D.C. He had read in the Stars and Stripes that Eastern Airlines had inaugurated a new service between Washington, New York, and Boston. The flights didn't require a reservation and you paid your fare inflight. Therefore, when the train arrived at Union Station in Washington, Rafe got off, hailed a cab, and took the short ride over to National Airport which was only about five miles away. The flights left every hour on the hour. While waiting for the next departure Rafe called his mother and let her know where he was and when he would be landing at La Guardia. Things were going well and Rafe couldn't be happier, that was until he arrived in New York.

As he walked across the tarmac, he saw his mother waving to him at the entrance to the finger area into which the shuttle flights deplaned. He gave her a big hug and a kiss. His mother actually seemed glad to see him which was surprising since she had only written to him twice in the thirteen months he had been in France. However, Rafe loved his mother and was glad that he had such a tigress as a mom. If it wasn't for her, he was sure he would have ended up on the dung heap of life. After all, she had attracted Everett Massoletti who would always be in Rafe's estimation the greatest man he would ever know. Unfortunately, he was about to learn something about his mother which he found to be really appalling. It didn't take long either. Once they were in his mother's car and were cruising down the Van Wyck Expressway his mother laid it on him. Once he began asking about Everett his mother said, "Rafe something has happened between Everett and myself which could have an effect on your relationship."

Rafe was thinking to himself, "Now what could that be? You've already dumped him for another man whom you married for a few months before getting an annulment, then while I was in France you took up with Everett again."

She then said, "I blackmailed Everett for $100,000 and he paid me."

Rafe just looked at her as if she'd gone mad. At first, he couldn't speak at all. Finally, he responded, "Mom how could you do such a despicable thing, and how did you get away with it? Everett is an honorable member of the International Association of Chiefs of Police. He knows every major law enforcement officer in the United States. For God's sake Mom, he's a good friend of J. Edgar Hoover."

She answered, "Rafe you don't know everything that goes on between Everett and me. I know you worship him and think of him as a father, but he has his flaws, like all of us."

Rafe was thinking, "Yeah, he may have his flaws, but he set up that dream date for Jill and me, and he said it would be the best date two young people ever had, and it was." He went on thinking, 'If Everett didn't love you as much as he does, he could have you locked up in a heartbeat."

His Mother went on to say, "I just told you this in the event that you notice a change in his attitude when you see him. I know you two are close, but you never know about these things."

Rafe didn't say it but he was thinking, "Great Mom, you may have screwed up a relationship that meant everything to me. You may not realize it, but Everett is the only person that ever believed in me, and that includes you. Just Great!"

H didn't have much else to say to his mother as they continued down the Van Wyck to the Tri-borough Bridge and then to the George Washington

Bridge into New Jersey. A great homecoming was ruined in ten minutes. Rafe just made the best of a bad situation and enjoyed his six-day stay in New York. His mother had a big Italian dinner with the whole family in attendance. All of Rafe's aunts, Uncles, and Cousins were there, as well as Everett who came to his mother's new home in Fort Lee, New Jersey in a limo. As Everett was leaving Rafe walked him out to the limo so they could have a chat in private. Rafe said, "Look Pop I know what mom did to you and I'm absolutely appalled by her actions. I hope you know where I stand when it comes to such behavior."

Everett put his arm around Rafe's shoulder and said, 'Don't worry about it, Son. I knew where you stood when you said if your mom were to marry Jerry Rosen you would join the Army in protest. She did, so you showed your loyalty to me and joined the Army. So don't worry, we're solid. Rafe said, thanks Pop, I was hoping you'd see things that way.

The five days he spent in New York were great. He enjoyed seeing the family, especially His Mom, his sister Angela, and of course Everett. Time flew by, and on a cold overcast day, his mom drove him to the Idlewild Airport, as JFK was known in those days, for his flight to Albuquerque. His mother kissed him goodbye at the entrance to the TWA terminal and he went in to check in for his flight to Albuquerque with a stop in Chicago.

About six hours later the TWA 707 skirted the North end of the Sandia Mountains, descended over the Western suburbs of Albuquerque, and flew the base leg headed East over the Manzano Mountains before turning over Sandia Base for final approach. Rafe couldn't be happier; he had made it, and soon Ella would be in his arms.

When he walked across the tarmac towards the terminal, he was thinking of the day thirteen months before as he walked out to board another TWA 707, but that one was heading for New York and then Paris. As he approached the gate there, she was; and she took off running right into his waiting arms. Nothing had ever felt as good as his beautiful girlfriend's body wrapped in his arms. He'd done it. He promised he would return to her and as they kissed passionately the promise was fulfilled. Thirteen long months, but it was over. Lorie, Delsey, Mary Ann, and Evelyn, Ella's four lovely sisters all gave him a hug and a kiss as well as Ella's mother. This began a joyful week of just hanging out and getting reacquainted. Of course, Rafe wanted to get Ella away from her family and alone. He had rented a car for the week so on the second day after his arrival, he checked into the Land of Enchantment motel on Central Avenue, across from the fairgrounds and next to the Inferno, his favorite bar. Later that evening as Rafe ran his hands all over his beautiful naked girlfriend, Ella asked, "You love to touch me, don't you?" Rafe looked at her perfect, naked body and said, "More than you could ever know."

Ella was sort of playing with him so she continued with, "Why do you like it so much?"

Rafe had to think about it for a minute before answering, "I guess it's because I've never touched anything that feels so good. Almost like you're a work of art that was made to touch. I don't think I can put it into words, but I really like it."

Ella was teasing him so she then asked, "Which part of my body do you like best?"

Rafe really didn't like this sort of questioning. it was something similar to when she asked him how she compared to Jill. So, he simply said, "I don't know, I like all of you."

However, Ella was insistent, "Come on Rafe, I really want to know. If you tell me I'll give you a reward."

Rafe knew she was referring to, the night they met, were walking home, and stopped on Central Avenue where she asked what he was smiling about. His reward was a very intoxicating kiss. She knew she had him, and he couldn't resist. She said, "Well, my darling, think of the reward!"

He couldn't resist, "Ok against my better judgment it's your ass!"

Ella pulled back, and then with a mocked look of shock, said "Why my ass?"

"Because it's perfect that's why, in fact, it's the most beautiful thing I've ever seen."

Ella smiled one of her most genuine smiles and said, "Really!"

Rafe smiling said, 'Ok, now you know, so what's my reward?"

Ella knelt in the middle of the bed, and while her giving him a dazzling smile said, "Anything you want, I'm all yours!"

They fell into each other's arms, and that began a lovemaking session that lasted till they were both utterly exhausted. You know what they say, time flies when you're having fun. Before he knew it Rafe was kissing Ella goodbye at the Greyhound Bus Terminal in downtown Albuquerque not far from the Grand Canyon Saloon. As the bus pulled out onto the street Rafe waved goodbye to his lovely girlfriend thinking it should only be about eight or ten weeks until he'd be heading back for good. Even if he didn't get reassigned back to Sandia Base anywhere in the Fourth Army would be a lot closer than France. One other factor he was considering was that by the time he exited OCS, he would have about nine months left in the service. During those nine months, he would have forty-five days of leave to use. That would mean every three months he'd have two weeks leave to spend with Ella. Now everything depended on going to OCS and resigning after the first eight weeks as allowed in Army Regulations.

As the bus sped East down Route 40 toward Amarillo, Texas Rafe was confident things were going to work out as he planned. His brother Tom who was an Electronics Warfare Officer in SAC and was based at Amarillo Air Force Base was going to meet him in Amarillo and drive him to Fort Sill in Lawton, Oklahoma, the home of Artillery OCS. This was good as it allowed Rafe to visit with the only member of his family that he had missed seeing in New York. Rafe was confident he had the world by the tail and OCS would present just a small bump in the road to fulfilling his dreams.

There were just two little problems standing between him and his goals. The first, and by far the greatest, was that he hadn't yet learned about delusional thinking. Half the world's population never learns about delusions even though they have the power to destroy your dreams. The other seemingly trivial mistake was leaving his orders in the departure lounge at Rhein-Mein Airbase in Frankfort. None of these were on Rafe's radar screen as he sped toward Lawton.

Officer Candidate School

Rafe's first impression of OCS was that it was a circus. Tom dropped him off and wished him good luck and Rafe made his way into the OCS compound called Robinson Barracks. The first thing that caught his attention was seeing cadets walking around bent over from the waist with their knees locked in place picking up items off the ground. Later he would find out that this was the OCS version of Police Call. You couldn't find anything on the ground more than 1/4 inch long. Rafe was soon going to learn what it was like walking around like an idiot searching for infinitesimally small pieces of anything that would bring down an upper-class man's ire.

The worst was yet to come and it didn't take long for the future to rear its ugly head. When he walked into the barracks to register for his class the shit hit the fan. When the upperclassmen asked for his orders, Rafe stated that he had inadvertently left them in Frankfort, Germany. That's all it took. He was told to drop down and do twenty-five pushups while those members of the upper class who were present began to berate him like he was some sort of lower form of life.

It went something like, "Why you stupid shit bird. Did you really think you could report to OCS without orders? How the hell did you expect to come in here with such a cock and bull story. Get on your feet and stand at attention." When Rafe was standing at attention the upperclassman got right in his face and began, 'I've seen some stupid pukes come in here, but you take the cake, and you expect to be an officer."

Rafe was thinking, "Well actually I don't expect to become an officer, however, if I did, I'd make a hell of a lot better officer than you."

That's how it started, a lot of profanity, jerks getting in your face, then ordering you to drop down and give them push-ups. It wasn't much different than what he expected; something like marine boot camp, but it was going to get a lot worse, and all because he left his orders in Germany. Sure, as hell, as one thing follows another, his reporting without orders required the sergeant major at OCS to call Supreme Headquarters to get a copy of his orders. In the process the Supreme Headquarters Sgt. Major tells the Sgt. Major at OCS that Hawkins was the bodyguard to the Supreme Allied Commander, was very well thought of, and that it wouldn't be a good idea to give him too much trouble, in that, he was closely connected to the highest-ranking general officers in the Army. Of course, gossip being what it is in the Army, this small unverified piece of information somehow made its way into the general population of upperclassmen which led them to the assumption that Hawkins, the worthless scumbag who showed up without orders was going, to skate through the OCS program because he had a political appointment.

That's how it began. The one thing Everett had warned Rafe about when he was leaving for basic training was to maintain a low profile and not to bring attention to himself. Well, that idea was shot. With one unintended mistake, Rafe had made himself a noted candidate, and it wasn't the sort of notoriety one would wish to acquire.

It was amazing how quickly this notoriety spread, and it extended through all classes. OCS was organized into three classes. For the first eight weeks, the candidates were lower class and played the part of privates. During the second eight weeks called middle class, the candidates played the role of Non-commissioned officers. Finally, for the final eight weeks of the upper class, the candidates acted as officers.

Normal harassment would be bad enough if carried to the extreme, however, one of the more creative members of the upper class devised a special sort of torment for Rafe. The way OCS was organized the upperclassmen who were weeks away from becoming commissioned officers controlled the daily activities. The tactical officers who were actually commissioned officers in the Army monitored the activities of the upper class. As long as the upper class didn't get totally out of control, they pretty much had carte blanche as to how they handled things.

The special torment consisted of a little choreographed dance that Rafe had to perform anytime an upperclassman yelled out "Candidate Hawkins, Hit It!" At this point, Rafe had to act like he was vaulting out the door of a C47 like a paratrooper, hit the ground then throw his arms skyward like he was holding on to the parachute risers, then go into a dance routine for about ten seconds. Now ten seconds may not seem like a long time, but it's longer than you think, in that men can run 100 yards in ten seconds. Rafe was required to close this little dance by snapping to attention and growling as loud as he could before yelling at the top of his voice, "Airborne Sir."

It was actually quite funny if you were one of the audience, however; if you were the subject of this charade it had the exact opposite effect. It was meant to humiliate and it would probably have had that effect if it hadn't been overdone. If the upper class had inflicted this on Rafe three or four times a day, he might have found it humiliating. But, that's not what happened. They made him do it twenty-five times a day, in other words, they got completely carried away. If you were to multiply 25 times 7 days a week, Rafe was doing this little charade 175 times a week or 1400 times in the first eight weeks. Now if you are one of the group-thinking types you might think you were casting Rafe Hawkins in a very bad light, but this didn't take into account that the tactical officers who had no skin in this game were watching a large group, ganging up on one candidate. They also were, observing that the candidate took the punishment like water off a duck's feathers. They came away with the opinion that Rafe Hawkins was one tough dude.

It appeared that Rafe's introduction to OCS was not exactly what one could call a pleasant experience. The whole place was a three-ring circus, and the next unpleasant experience for most of the candidates was punishment marches. To understand punishment marches, one first had to understand how OCS was organized. If you were to look at it from the outside, the place seemed to be nothing short of lunacy, but from the Army's point of view, it all made sense.

To begin when you slipped into your cot at night you tried to do it in a way that disrupted the way the bed was made as little as possible. This meant that you usually slept on top of the sheets and blankets instead of sliding under them. There was a very good reason for this unusual way of sleeping. There were some other things you did in the half hour before lights out. They were to take a shower, spit shine their boots, polish their brass, which included, things like your belt buckle, and finally break the starch in their uniforms. What does breaking the starch in your uniform mean? The uniforms were so full of starch that in order to put on a pair of trousers one had to force his leg down the pants leg to break the starch to make it easy to get into the uniform. Why would you break the starch in your uniform pants before going to bed? Because of the insanity of OCS, Sleep came instantly; you were so exhausted that once you lay down on your cot and closed your eyes you were instantly asleep. You lay down, close your eyes, and you instantly heard a bugle playing reveille. When the lower class heard reveille being played, they sat up, and in unison yell. "The Horn." From that moment the entire battalion had two minutes to get up, get dressed, make their beds; and lay out all of their equipment in a line between the front two legs of their cot on an invisible straight line. Since one could not wear footwear in the barracks there was a mad rush to get out onto the front porch of the barracks, there to put on your boots and lace them up. From the time the bugle blew the entire battalion had to be out in the street fully dressed and in formation. If you were an outsider watching this take place, you'd think you were in a nut house. First, the bugle would sound, and then a hundred voices would scream, "The Horn." Following which, for the next minute and one half, you would hear a cacophony of sound followed by a flood of near panic-stricken cadets disgorging onto the poach there to lace up their boots as if their life depended on how fast this could be accomplished. Once everyone was in formation the tactical officers would inspect the companies to make sure everything was exactly perfect. Any discrepancies were awarded demerits. Collect enough demerits and you were subjected to a punishment march which took place on both Saturdays and Sundays. The dreaded punishment marches, called Jark marches after the commander of the Fourth Army, were 4.2-mile marches that had to be completed in forty minutes. Any march completed in less than forty minutes didn't count. Those marches that didn't count had to be repeated after a ten-minute rest.

The uniform for a Jark March consisted of Combat Boots, Army-issued red shorts, a tee-shirt, a baseball cap, an ammunition belt with a canteen of salt water, and an M1 Rifle. The march was done in formation and stayed that way until the halfway point from which the formation broke up and the candidates ran up a steep hill about 300 yards up and 300 yards back down. Those down first got to rest until the last of the runners rejoined the formation.

The column moved at one of two speeds which were at a rout step, or double time, when moving at a rout step, which was a very fast walking march, the candidates had to lean forward because they had rifles on their shoulders. To try to walk fast with a rifle on one's shoulder would be virtually impossible. After completing about 300 yards at route step the NCO leading the formation would give the command of port arms, which is to hold the rifle diagonally in front of the body with the muzzle pointing upward to the left. Once at port arms the formation would be commanded to double time. In this manner, the formation would alternately proceed at route step for a few hundred yards and then go to double time for another few hundred, then back to route step. This continued for approximately two miles when they would reach the halfway point which was the hill with the bunker on top.

Following the formation would be a truck that would pick up the bodies of those who fell out, passed out, or cramped up. The purpose of the saltwater in the canteens was to keep the candidates from cramping up when they became dehydrated in the ninety-plus-degree heat. Rafe had always been a runner ever since the State Police caught him during his first attempt to run away from Greer School. So, while everyone hated Jark Marches, Rafe loved them. First, because he loved to run, but second because it gave him the opportunity to show up all of his contemporaries. It's one thing to think you're superior to someone and it's another when you actually have to prove it. Since Rafe was at the bottom of the totem pole, he picked up more than his fair share of demerits and therefore made every one of the punishment marches. Another advantage to punishment marches that pleased Rafe was that no one could harass him while on a march.

It became quite clear to the tactical officers that if Rafe had to, he could run the entire battalion into the ground with commensurate ease. Just as they watched everything else, the tactical officers observed the punishment marches. While watching they were amazed to see the candidate who was the butt of an unprecedented amount of harassment was physically fit beyond belief. They thought that if they were to turn the battalion loose at the halfway point and have them run back to the OCS area free of formation, Number 41 would beat the next closest competitor by a country mile. So, although he didn't know it the Jark Marches were working in his favor as the tactical officers were beginning to believe that there was more to Number 41 than met the eye.

Then the question arises how did he get to be called number 41? It came about the second week Rafe was attending OCS. The Commandant received a call from the Supreme Allied Commander in Versailles, France. He inquired as to how his previous bodyguard was doing. The Commandant hated to give him bad news but related that Candidate Hawkins had become the object of derision among the candidates. The General asked how he managed to get himself into such a predicament and the Commandant told him it had to do with showing up without his orders. General Lemnitzer said he didn't see how that would get him in such hot water, but that he thought over time Hawkins would figure a way out of his problems. Colonel Gattis, the commandant related to the General that Hawkins had been saddled with the sobriquet Number 41 because he was number 41 out of 41 candidates in his barracks. In other words, the bottom of the barrel. The General thanked Colonel Gattis for the info and said he'd check back in a few weeks to see if anything changed.

Of course, nothing changed. If anything, the situation for Rafe Hawkins got worse. In an all-male environment where no one wants to be number 41 especially if it could affect your chances of becoming a commissioned officer, everyone piled on. They all were thinking, at least that maggot Hawkins is below me.

During the third week of OCS General Lemnitzer called again and asked Colonel Gattis if there had been any improvement in Rafe Hawkins's status. The answer was, "Sorry sir, but he's still number 41. At this, the General laughed and said, "Do you know what famous character in Hollywood films was also known as number 41." The Colonel replied, "No can't say that I do."

General Lemnitzer went on to say, "Do you recall in a famous scene in which the Roman Consul is walking down the catwalk on the fighting galley looking over the galley slaves chained to their oars? He stops and hits one on the back with a whip. The slave turns on the consul and wants to attack him, but restrains himself. The Consul says "You have spirit number 41, but the good sense to control it." The Colonel responded with, "Yes, I remember it now. The slave was Ben Hur." General Lemnitzer laughed and said, "Don't count Hawkins out yet Colonel, he's as tough as they come, and smart as a whip. Let's just see how things play out."

Rafe didn't like what was being done to him and he probably would have been even angrier if he had wanted to be a commissioned officer and these fools were denying him the opportunity. But, so far everything was going according to plan; that is until they hit week four. When week four rolled around the lower class was told that they would be required to write a one-paragraph critique of everyone in their barracks and everyone in the Barracks that was in the class above them.. This was only done for those in your own barracks which meant since there were eight lower classmen in Rafe's barracks, he would write seven evaluations on his own classmates since he wouldn't be writing one on himself, and eight on the middle classmen, one class ahead. This was done every two weeks starting in the fourth week. No one liked doing it, however, it was mandatory. It was a good way for the tactical officers to see how each candidate was viewed by his peers.

One might think this was no big deal, that is unless you were Rafe Hawkins, or should it be said unless you were number 41. This is how one of his typical evaluations would read. Keeping in mind that they were all practically the same because the battalion suffered from group thinking and wanted to believe at least they were superior to one person. Keeping in mind there was no validity in any of the evaluations, they read as follows: "This candidate must be one of the worst ever admitted to OCS. He has no common sense, can't do anything right, picks up demerits like a magnet, has made every punishment march since arriving, looks bad in his uniform, and is totally deficient in leadership ability."

This would have been bad if the only person having knowledge of what was written was the tactical officer, however, this was not the case. The day after these evaluations were turned in to the tactical officer, he called in each candidate and read him the evaluations written about him by his peers.

The evaluations were the beginning of the end for Rafe's carefully laid plans to get back to Ella.

Rafe was hard to anger and up to this point he had taken all of the harassment in his stride, but this was over the top and personal. "Who did these clowns think they were? None of them was capable of independent thought, plus they were insecure assholes."

Rafe was thinking, "Imagine if these jerks had to go a few rounds in the ring with me. Or a few minutes wrestling, or try to beat me in a race. And God forbid, they try to match me in academics." On the other hand; he thought, "Only four more weeks and I'll have Ella back in my arms."

Although no one was aware of it, Rafe was sliding into confrontational mode. He was getting angry and he was beginning to want to kick ass.

Actually, it was almost a joke when he considered some of the dimwits that considered themselves officer material, the same ones who would trash him in the evaluations. One of the exercises the candidates were first taught was to do a survey of the positions in which a battery of guns would be placed. The survey is important in making artillery one of the most devastating weapons of modern warfare. The survey enables field artillery to destroy, neutralize, or suppress the enemy with quick, accurate deadly fire. In addition, the survey was the process of determining with sufficient exactness, the relative horizontal and vertical location of the guns and the targets so that they could be plotted on a firing chart, and for providing accurate data for the guns. The survey done by two men, was fairly simple, measuring distances, measuring horizontal and/or vertical angles, and recording all pertinent data.

The survey team consisted of a front tape man, and a rear tape man, with a thirty-foot steel tape. They also had a few other pieces of equipment, but the survey was a fairly simple process. On this particular day, Rafe was assigned to do a survey with one of his classmates from his barracks. Rafe knew he was one of those who had given him a bad review because the one thing the reviews had in common was that they were all bad, some just worse than others.

Before venturing out on the wide grassy fields of that area of Fort Sill the tactical officer warned them of one thing. He said, "This area has been used recently for live artillery fire. You may come across some unexploded duds. If you see one give it a wide berth, and when I say wide, I mean wide. An eight-inch artillery shell has a kill radius of about thirty meters. I think you get my drift."

About an hour later as Rafe and his teammate crossed the open terrain they had been ordered to survey, low and behold, what do they come across, you guessed it; an unexploded eight-inch artillery shell. Now Rafe was the rear tape man holding the tail end of the thirty-meter-long steel tape. His partner was the lead tape man and was thirty meters ahead of Rafe. When he comes upon the dud eight-inch shell sticking out of the ground instead of making tracks away from it as rapidly as possible, he walks over and starts kicking it. Rafe hits the ground and begins calling the moron every name he could think of, and can only get him to desist when he threatens to turn him into the tactical officer.

Rafe was well aware that this was one of those that wrote the critically bad evaluations of him. You could say that it was the final straw and it was at that point Rafe decided to put the whole bunch in their rightful place. Their rightful place is vis-a-vis compared to him. Was this a good decision? Hardly, in fact, it was one of the worst decisions Rafe would ever make, but his blood was up, and he wanted to fight. What he had no way of knowing was, that it was destiny calling.

When they reached the six-week point of the twenty-four-week course the cadets were again required to write a one-paragraph evaluation of their fellow cadets. If anything, the fifteen evaluations read to Rafe were worse than those done two weeks before. You could say they were unbelievably bad.

After reading the fifteen evaluations to Rafe his tactical officer, asked Rafe, "What do you think about these appraisals?"

Rafe looked at the Lieutenant and said, "Can I speak directly?"

Lt. Muscato replied, "Yes I'd like to know what you really think."

Rafe considered his answer for a minute then responded, "Sir I know that I'm referred to as number forty-one by the tactical officers. But let's say for argument that I'm not number forty-one, but I'm actually number one, and I don't mean number one in a close race, but I'm actually number one by a mile. Do you know what that would mean?"

Lt. Muscato, answered, "No, you tell me, what does that mean?"

Rafe gave the Lieutenant a sardonic smile and then said, "It means they all suffer from bad judgment, and to make matters worse they also suffer from groupthink. They seem to be incapable of thinking for themselves or how else do you explain, they're all wrong, and wrong, in exactly the same way."

Then Lt. Muscato asked, "So what do you plan to do?

Rafe gave the Lieutenant one of his piercing looks, and told him, "As they say in the old army, I'm going to show them where the bear shit in the buckwheat!

Lt. Muscato asked, "Do you really think you can do it?" Rafe simply said, "We'll soon know."

During the eighth week. the lower class was tested in academics and leadership. The academics consisted of five tests given in one day in various disciplines the most important of which was math. Much of the laying down and firing of artillery has to do with math. If one subject was going to disqualify a candidate from becoming an artillery officer it was invariably math. Since Rafe had made up his mind to make his contemporaries look ridiculous, he scored a perfect one hundred on all five tests. He completed the math test in fifteen minutes although the allotted time to complete it was one hour. When he went to turn in his test after fifteen minutes the instructor made him keep it for the entire hour thinking it was impossible to complete it satisfactorily in so short a time, and that he should review it in case he wanted to make corrections.

Since Lieutenant Blackman knew Colonel Gattis was interested in the performance of "number 41" he reported his test results the next morning. The Colonel said to the Lt., "Do you know that no cadet has scored 100% on all five tests since we opened Artillery OCS?

The Lt. Answered, "No sir I had no idea, but I think Hawkins is on a mission. I showed you the last series of evaluations his classmates had written about him, and I think in spite of all the harassment he's taken in lower-class, these evaluations really pissed him off. Frankly, sir, I think he's laid an ambush for them with the intent to kick their collective asses. I also think the culmination will take place tomorrow during the leadership course."

The colonel smiled at that and said, "The Supreme Allied Commander has been calling to check up on Hawkins' progress every couple of weeks, and when I let him know, his status as being number 41 he didn't seem that bothered. He more or less told me that Ben Hur in the famous film was the number 41 galley slave and look what happened there. He could almost foresee something like this happening." Lt. Blackman added, "I think number 41 is going to put in a superhuman effort in the leadership course tomorrow to complete his mission." The Colonel said, "I want to be there to observe his group when they go through the course. Be sure and tell me when they're scheduled to begin."

The leadership Course was dreaded by all Officer Candidates. If anything could deny their hopes of becoming commissioned officers it was the big obstacle in their path. As it turned out it was exactly appropriate in that it consisted of an obstacle course with five major parts. The candidates began the course by entering the area of the first obstacle in a group of eight. Their mission in which they were graded both individually and as a group was to first find the path through, then communicate it to the group, and then finally get your group through the obstacle. It wasn't easy and it was timed. You had fifteen minutes for each obstacle. Adding to the difficulty were areas that were marked radioactive and couldn't be entered, or be in fields of fire which would disqualify anyone entering into it. The object of the exercise was to get through in the shortest time possible, with your group intact, losing members' cost points, and sometimes carrying a box of ammunition or blood plasma. The object was to complete the mission with as little loss of life and as quickly as possible.

The tactical officers would be watching to see which candidate could find the way through and then could communicate it to the others, and then lead them through. Some candidates wouldn't see the way through if they were looking at it for an hour, and others wouldn't be cooperative even though it was in the group's interest. The tactical officers watched and took notes on all of the dynamics of the group's efforts.

The seven candidates going through the course with Rafe were those from his own barracks, the same ambitious men that had written those awful evaluations. Colonel Gattis had arrived to watch the group ahead of Rafe's go through the course and stood beside Lt. Blackman when Rafe's group entered the area of the first obstacle. To the cadets. it was more like a gladiatorial area than an obstacle course. Everything hung in the balance. Not unlike the gladiators of old, their futures were at stake.

Rafe walked into the area and looked around, and turned his directed intelligence towards one goal, find the way through. It took him all of twenty seconds to see it. He then walked over to his seven comrades and explained to them how to get through. He pointed out where to climb and turn without having to backtrack. Half the group couldn't see it even when explained to them in simple terms. So, Rafe who could climb like a monkey, having all those years of experience climbing trees at Greer School, ran through the course in about two minutes showing those who were unimaginative the way through. When he returned to the group, he said, "Let's go, this exercise is timed." So off they went, and they got through in record time without losing any men. They all got through together. With Rafe's guidance, they breezed through all five obstacles in record time. When they had completed obstacle five, there was a wild celebration. Rafe's classmates knew they had just taken a giant step toward realizing their dreams. On the other hand, although happy at the moment Rafe had no idea, he had just placed himself in the path of a huge shitstorm. But, as the saying goes, enjoy it while you can.

There was only one step left to make Rafe a true hero to his contemporaries and that revolved around the OCS tradition of amnesty. On graduation day the upper class had a graduation luncheon during which the lower class, now moving up to the middle class, was required to put on a skit to entertain the luncheon guests. If the skit was considered overwhelmingly entertaining the upper class could grant amnesty. Amnesty meant that the entire battalion at OCS got a three-day pass in beautiful Lawton, Oklahoma. It was a welcome break from the stress of the 6-month course. Men with wives and girlfriends could have them fly into Lawton for this rare break, and even those unattached men would have time for a great party in town. No inspections, no punishment marches, just rest and relaxation. However, amnesty was rarely granted. Maybe once every five years. It was something more hoped for than ever realized.

Once the skit began to be considered by his class, Rafe began to think, "If we get amnesty, I get to see Ella for a weekend. A weekend, half of which would be spent in bed making love." Once that idea got into his head Rafe was determined that he was going to participate in the skit and win amnesty. He knew exactly how to do it. The upperclassmen would be in a very good mood celebrating after just having gold bars pinned on their shoulders. They were aware of the unprecedented amount of shit they had piled on Rafe during the last eight weeks. They were now well aware that number 41 had emerged as an extraordinary candidate and that their harassment had been unfair and unwarranted. They also knew that number 41 was one tough dude and had taken the worst they could meet out without turning a hair.

At the end of the skit, Rafe went into an elaborated version of the Candidate Hawkins humiliation dance. He was throwing it back in the face of the upper class and ended his performance with a smile on his face. The upper class and their guests went wild, and before Rafe trotted out of the mess hall, he knew amnesty would be granted. He went back in and took a bow which brought even greater applause. As he walked out of the mess hall Rafe was a very happy cadet. He was at the top of his game, and he had earned his place among his peers. Not only that, but Ella would be visiting Lawton to spend a weekend.

The next Friday Ella came flying in on Continental Airlines and Rafe was waiting at the Lawton Airport to meet her. As she walked across the tarmac Rafe was thinking, "How did I ever attract such a beautiful woman." They took a bus into town, and registered at the Hotel Lawton, right in the middle of town. Everyone said that the best restaurant was called the Bullseye right on the edge of town. The entire lower class, now middle-classmen, had decided to meet there for a celebration. By now Rafe was universally recognized as a hero. Amnesty was no small event. Even if you didn't have a wife or sweetheart to fly in to visit. Just the break after eight weeks of hell couldn't be more welcome. Everyone knew how it had come about, and now the consensus was that Rafe Hawkins was one cool dude. Everyone was coming up to introduce their wives and sweethearts to Rafe and Ella. Three of the single cadets approached together and were completely taken by Ella's beauty. The bravest of the trio, and maybe the one having consumed the most alcohol, when introduced blurted, "It's such a pleasure to meet you, you're even more beautiful in real life than in your photograph. Ella looked at him with a surprised look and said, "What Photograph?" Rafe quickly explained, "When moving from class to class all cadets carry a clipboard, on the back of which we were allowed to tape a picture of our wives or girlfriends, to keep our spirits up, or to motivate us. The slightly inebriated cadet said, "That picture was probably the reason you took so much harassment; everyone was jealous. He then ended by being very courteous and said, "Anyway miss, you're very lovely and we're so happy to make your acquaintance."

After the threesome had staggered off Ella asked Rafe, "Which picture of me did you have taped to your clipboard?" Rafe smiled and answered, "The one you took in your dining room, you know the same one I had hanging in my locker at Supreme Headquarters."

Ella looked shocked, "Not the one of me in my bathing suit?"

Rafe was laughing when he told her, "Yep, that's the very same one." With a mock look of shock, Ella added, "You mean you let everyone gawk at me in my swimsuit?" "You bet I did. If there is anyone that should be walking around in a swimsuit it's you. Besides the picture wasn't there for them, it was for my morale. Just one look at that picture reminded what I was doing at OCS and how important it was, and it worked. Ella gave Rafe her most sexy, come-hither look and said, "Do you like how I'm made?" Rafe looked into her dark almost black eyes and said, "I think you're perfectly made, so much so that I feel like a king just walking down the street with you. I can't explain how beautiful I think you are in words, so when we get back to our hotel room, I'll give it another try." Ella rewarded Rafe with a radiant smile and added, "I can hardly wait!"

When they returned to their room at the hotel Rafe spent the rest of the night telling Ella that she was the most beautiful woman on earth without saying a word. They fell asleep early in the morning, exhausted, but in each other's arms.

Rafe woke with Ella's head on his shoulder. He gazed down at her and felt that God truly loved him. To Rafe, Ella was like a living work of art. Every part of her was perfect, even her hands and feet. As he stared at her face she awoke and snuggled up closer to him. He whispered to her, "Looks like we made it. Nine more months and I'll be getting out of the Army. Then we can get married and live happily ever after, we're almost there."

They say when you're standing on the edge of a cliff, you're fine, just as long as you don't take another step. Rafe was about to take it. Everything seemed to be perfect. He was back from France. He had completed eight weeks of OCS, and could now resign for cause and be reassigned to the Army Area of his choice in the United States. He would also be promoted to Sergeant E5. That's what he was thinking when Ella asked, "Where will we live when we get married?" That was a real question. Rafe hadn't told Ella about his mom's blackmailing Everett for $100,000. This had changed all of Rafe's plans. Although he and Everett were like Father and Son, who would have thought his mother would act in such a despicable manner? Because of this, Rafe had his doubts that Everett would still want to start an Air Cargo business with himself as his partner. In truth, it didn't matter much to Rafe. They could stay in New Mexico, and Rafe could get a job in the Albuquerque Police Force and go to the University of New Mexico at night. They'd get Ella's sisters through school and then live happily ever after. Rafe knew if he had Ella, he'd be happy anywhere. So, that's what he told Ella. Maybe at some later date, they could move to New York, but the plan would be to start out in New Mexico and get the girls settled. Rafe thought that is what Ella wanted, as it was that conversation, during their first dance that had started their romance. From Rafe's point of view, things were perfect. Yeah, as perfect as things could be when you've just taken the final step off the edge of the cliff.

With Ella by his side, Rafe felt he had achieved his goal. Even if he wasn't reassigned to Sandia Base and instead was sent to Killeen, Texas where DASA had another base, he would only be 700 miles from Albuquerque. This was a damn sight better than the 8,300 miles distance from Paris, France to Albuquerque. In addition, Rafe would only have about nine months left in his three-year enlistment, and he had forty-five days of unused leave accrued. This would mean he could take two weeks of leave every three months and before you knew it, he'd be home for good. No more extended separations. To Rafe, this meant they were home free. There was just one big problem standing in the way, now that Rafe had left no doubts in the eyes of the officers running OCS that he was indeed a very superior candidate, how was he going to resign?

He wasn't thinking ahead when he decided to leave his status as number 41 behind and move up to number 1. His mind wasn't focused on resigning at that point in time. He had just wanted to show his classmates who needed to have their eyes opened. He accomplished that goal easily, but in doing so he had created another. When he began to consider this after Ella had gone back to Albuquerque, he realized he needed to be very careful about how he would go about his resignation.

With that in mind, he waited another eight weeks until the end of Middle class before he asked to see the commandant, Colonel Gattis. When he told Colonel Gattis that he had a change of heart and no longer wanted to be an officer he thought the Colonel was going to have a stroke. Rafe was standing in front of the Colonel's desk when Col. Gattis slammed his fist down on his desk and yelled, "Are you out of your mind Hawkins? That's the most outrageous, and stupid thing I've ever heard."

Rafe was thinking to himself, "Damn, I've really stepped into it this time."

Colonel Gattis went to on say, "Hawkins you're not aware of this but General Lemnitzer has been calling every few weeks to check on your progress. At first, I had to say that you were number 41 in a in your barracks of 41 cadets, and he responded that Ben Hur, was also the number 41 galley slave in the film, and look what happened in that case. We had a laugh over that and this was the beginning of you picking up the nickname number 41. We then witnessed your incredible run from last to first at the end of your first eight weeks. Then to top it off, you use the very merciless harassment inflicted on you, to gain amnesty for the entire battalion. In less than a week you went from last to first and gained what will someday prove to be legendary status in this school. For you to resign now would create the greatest crash in morale this place has ever seen. If you wanted out, why in the hell didn't you stay down at number 41, and resign at the end of lower class? But It's worse than that! It was 399 to 1, and you defeated them all."

Rafe just shook his head and answered, "I don't know." Although the truth was, he knew exactly why he did it, and he was never going to relate the truth to the Colonel. The colonel wasn't through yet, "I'll tell you something Hawkin's, I've never seen anyone take the amount of punishment meted out to you during your first eight weeks. That's why I told General Lemnitzer you'd never make it through the course. Then low and behold you come through the last week like a fox coming through a flock of chickens, like the leadership course was a walk in the park. It was the most outstanding performance in the history of Artillery OCS. Then to top it off you do your little harassment dance for the upper-class luncheon daring them not to grant you amnesty. They knew what they had put you through, and you could tell by the applause that they were glad to reward your guts. Shit Hawkins, you've done the impossible. I'll tell you something else. There is something not right about this whole idea of you resigning. So, I have only one thing to say. Go back to your company and continue because the only way you're getting out of here, is with gold bars on your shoulders. Go back and continue, you are dismissed."

Rafe saluted and walked out of the Colonel's office. On the way, he was thinking "Shit! I'm fucked, and I did it to myself. I did this just to show them up. It was arrogance. Now I have to pay the price, or think of another tack."

In the end, there was no other tack. He knew the Army couldn't force him to become an officer even if they were acting in his best interests. Being young and naive he couldn't imagine that Colonel Gattis could actually have figured out what he was doing, so when he had only three weeks to go until graduation, he had his final confrontation with the Colonel.

Standing at attention in front of the Colonel's desk Rafe told the Colonel that he was going to resign or he was going to see the Inspector General. In his ignorance, Rafe didn't understand that it was the worst thing he could have said. If he thought he had seen the Colonel's temper before, this eruption was like Mount Vesuvius. Imagine, the Colonel was trying to save Rafe from making the mistake of a lifetime, and in return, Rafe was threatening to go to the Inspector General. Talk about being an ingrate, well there stood Rafe playing that role in spades.

At first, the Colonel sat and stared at Rafe while he gathered his thoughts. Finally, he said, "Hawkins I'm going to give you a bit of advice. I'm going to tell you the facts of life because no matter how smart you think you are, you are, amazingly ignorant. The Colonel stood up and put both of his fists on his desk and leaned forward, glaring at Rafe who was standing at rigid attention. The Colonel continued, "You have no idea what you're doing. Grown men stand where you're standing and break down and cry like babies when I tell them they don't have what it takes to complete this course. But You! You are number one in everything, and on the way to graduating number one in your class, and what do you want to do, Resign! Well, let me tell you something that we all know, mister, there is only one thing in the world that would make you do what you intend to do, **It's a woman!**"

Rafe was standing there thunderstruck, thinking, how could he possibly know? Rafe wasn't worldly enough to understand that the colonel was a man of the world. He was a decorated combat veteran who had been around the block a few times. The Colonel went on, "It's a woman behind your entire cockeyed plan, so let me tell you the facts of life where women are concerned. Obviously, you're dumb as a tree stump where women are concerned. So, here are the facts. You, Hawkins, are nothing right now. You're just raw material. Think of yourself as a bushel of corn on the commodities exchange and right now corn is selling for fifty cents a bushel, and frankly, that ain't Jack Shit." While he was saying this, he had picked up a riding crop, and he was using it to point at the baseboard where the wall met the floor. He was tapping that spot with the riding crop, and telling Rafe he was at the bottom of the barrel. Then he turned back to Rafe, glared at him, and said, "But, in three weeks, when you pin gold bars on your shoulders and graduate number one in your class; He was tapping the point of the crop where the wall met the ceiling, your bushel of corn is going to rise from fifty cents a bushel to fifty dollars a bushel, and if you want the woman, you'll become fifty dollars a bushel corn, or you'll get fucked!"

Rafe couldn't believe the Colonel had figured it out, and this just went to show how unsophisticated he actually was. There wasn't anything to say he just stood there in silence and stared back at the angry officer. After a minute of silence that seemed like an hour, the Colonel said, "All right Hawkins now that you've been told the facts of life you can make your decision. If you want to ruin your life, go ahead and make your decision."

Rafe stood there stunned. He knew a lot of what the Colonel said was true. He was aware of the power of status. He had even lectured Jill on this very subject when she wanted to go steady, but the Colonel had no idea about the relationship he had with Ella. It was worth dying for. In fact, nothing came before it. He thought, "What about Duty, Honor, and Country? Then he quickly rationalized that the country wasn't at war, and if the Army could ship him to France for 'the good of the service" then he could use their own regulations, to have them ship him back.

He stood for a few minutes thinking, until Colonel Gattis interrupted his thoughts with the question, "What will it be Hawkins? Will you act as a pussy whipped loser, or will you accept a commission in the United States Army?" Rafe knew there was only one way to go. He had worked and planned and suffered through a tidal wave of harassment to get back to his beloved girlfriend.

While still convinced that love conquered all, Rafe answered the Commandant, "Sir, I'm not going to become an officer, I'm going to DOR (Drop on Request)."

With contempt written all over his face, Colonel Gattis said, "Very well, you're out of here. Go back to your barracks and gather your stuff. I want you out of Robinson Barracks in thirty minutes. You are a disgrace to everything Officer Candidate School stands for. One last thing. Do you know what Dereliction of Duty means? If I was in your shoes, I'd brush up on it! You are dismissed."

Rafe saluted and left the Colonel's office. He should have been elated, but that wasn't the case. Actually, he was very downhearted. He had let down a lot of men who believed in him and wanted the best for him. He had to hope that all would turn out for the best and that his return to Ella would make it all worthwhile.

Rafe cleared out of OCS and reported to personnel. He asked if he could go on leave while awaiting orders since he had over fifty days of leave coming and only 270 days left in the service. One week of leave was authorized and. he would be allowed to pick up his orders at Sandia Base in Albuquerque.

Late the following afternoon Rafe boarded a Trailways Bus to Albuquerque with stops in Amarillo, Texas, and Tucumcari, New Mexico. He took the seat behind the front door on the right side just a few feet back from the driver. He wanted a good view of the highway and wanted a front-row view of Tijeras Canyon as the bus descended through the Sandia Mountains into Albuquerque the following morning. Rafe was elated; he had made it. His plan was working and soon he and Ella would be together forever. He watched the Sun disappear behind the horizon, like a red rubber ball. It was a beautiful sunset and Rafe felt as if he had just won the World Series of Life. Too bad he wasn't aware of the effects of delusional thinking.

Hell!

> Regions of sorrow, doleful shades,
> Where peace and rest can never dwell,
> Hope never comes, that comes to all;
> But torture without end
>
> *Milton*
> *Paradise Lost*

The Trailways bus coasted down the steep incline where Tijeras Canyon breached the Sandia Mountains. This was the day; the day Rafe had anticipated for so long. Albuquerque was stretched out across the valley glistening in the early morning sunlight. Rafe remembered the mornings when he had been patrolling Sandia Base, watching the sunrise from the East. The Sandia Mountains would block the rays of the sun as it was rising. The first rays would shoot out across the valley lighting the far western side, then as the sun rose higher, and was no longer screened by Sandia Crest, the valley was lit by a moving wave of light that sped across the valley and Albuquerque. *It was a scene of great beauty that was only seen if you were awake at sunrise and positioned near the base of the Sandia's*

Rafe was anticipating his homecoming with great excitement. Once off the bus at the Trailways Terminal downtown, Rafe checked his Duffel Bag in a locker, then headed down 2nd Street towards Central Avenue taking the same route past the Grand Canyon Saloon he had taken on that first night. He was thinking since it was the time when Ella would be walking to work and since he knew the route she would take, he thought it would be exciting if he walked right into her. However, that wasn't to be. As he approached the Federal Building at the corner of Gold Avenue SW and 5th Street SW, he saw Ella Enter the side entrance to the building. He wasn't more than thirty seconds behind her so he decided to follow her up to her office a greet her there. He would always remember walking up and standing at the door to the Dept. Of Sport Fisheries and Wildlife. Ella's desk wasn't more than 10 feet away. Ella who had just sat down at her desk turned to see Rafe and smiled at him. This was the moment he had dreamed of for the past 18 months, but instead of a feeling of euphoria flooding over him, it was one of dread. Not pronounced or strong, but he sensed something wasn't right. It was subconscious so he didn't understand what was happening, but he was receiving a warning. Months later he would figure it out. Ella didn't smile like a woman in love welcoming her lover back home. Her smile was a worried smile, somewhat forced. Because of what was at stake Rafe simply brushed it off. No sense in being paranoid! After all, what could be wrong?

Ella quickly got up and walked over into Rafe's embrace. They kissed and Rafe began to think, "Everything is going to be just fine." Rafe waved to Ella's coworkers most of whom they had double-dated with and then stepped out into the hallway with Ella. Rafe was kind of effervescent and said, "We've done it. The deal is done, I'm back, and everything is going to work out." Rafe said he wouldn't hang around and get Ella in trouble with her boss, so he would go back to the bus station retrieve his Duffel Bag, and take a cab over to Ella's apartment. Rafe asked Ella to call him when she was about to get off so he could come back and walk her home. Then he kissed her goodbye and headed back to the Trailways Bus Terminal.

Rafe spent the afternoon at Ella's apartment hanging out with her mother. Rafe thought of Ella's mother in the same way as he thought of his own grandmother. She looked 15 years older than her chronological age due to hard stoop labor in vegetable fields in order to feed six children. Still, Rafe thought she was the greatest, and always let her know he thought of her that way. Just before 5 o'clock. Rafe headed over to meet Ella. He was still sky-high because he thought he had won against insurmountable odds.

Ella was a little quiet on the walk home, but Rafe was too high to pay much attention. Whenever he walked down the street with her, he felt like he was a king. Everything was fine until they turned into the driveway between Ella's apartment building and the Auto parts store next door. Although he had noticed it before he hadn't asked Ella's mother who owned the 1955 Pontiac Star Chief Catalina which was parked at the end of the driveway. So out of curiosity, he asked Ella, "Who owns the Pontiac?" When she answered, "We do!" He stopped in his tracks. He was standing on the edge of the precipice, or you could say he was standing in the mouth of hell, but he wasn't yet aware of his peril. Rafe said, "We do, what do you mean?" Ella gave him a nonchalant look and replied, "I took $550 out of our savings account and bought it." Rafe asked, "Don't you think you should have discussed purchasing a car with me first? That amount represents 2/3 of all the money we saved as a nest egg for when we get married. You should have asked me"

Then the hammer fell. Ella looked at him, this time kind of contemptuously, and said, "There was no sense in asking you, after all, I can wrap you around my little finger." Rafe was profoundly shocked! The statement could mean she thought she could make him do whatever she wanted, or it could mean that she thinks she owns you, has you whipped? You're the puppet and she's the puppet master pulling your strings.

Up until this point, Rafe thought he was just being a little paranoid, but now he knew he was in deep trouble. A woman in love does not speak to her lover in such a derogatory manner. Rafe asked, "Are you telling me that you've been manipulating me?" Ella shook her head and looked at him as if he was being ridiculous and said, "Don't be silly, I'm doing no such thing."

Rafe knew it was a lie. He well understood that it's not hard to manipulate someone who is in love with you, the question is why would you want to do such a thing? It's as easy as taking candy from a baby. However, the Salient point is this, if you love someone, and are not just using them, why on earth would you manipulate them? It's the easiest thing to do, but why do it? Rafe now knew what was coming, although he was hoping against hope that he was wrong, he knew deep in his heart that it was over.

He didn't have to wait long for the ax to fall. The next afternoon he and Ella stopped in the middle of the Lead Avenue Bridge, as was their habit on the walk home, to look at the Santa Fe Railway Station and the Alverado Hotel. Ella was not her usual self, and, was acting very distant and hardly talking. Rafe knew something was wrong, so he asked her, "What's wrong Ella? You've been acting strange ever since I arrived home. I think we should talk about whatever's bothering you." Ella responded, "Ok let's get the car and drive up to Robinson Park where we can be alone."

Rafe drove the Pontiac the six blocks to the park and pulled over under the shade of a big tree. Once parked he turned to Ella and said, "Ok, do you want to tell me what's going on?" Ella looked at him and said the most terrible words he would ever hear. "I don't love you anymore. I've met someone else and I want to break up!" That statement was like an atomic bomb exploding 500 meters overhead. In a millisecond Rafe's world was turned to dust. Or you could say it was vaporized. There was just one problem for Rafe. He was still alive. His world had vanished, but not him. What was the problem with that? When you're dead you can't suffer; that remains to be experienced by the living. Rafe was so stunned. He was struck speechless. He couldn't respond.

He just sat and looked at his beloved girlfriend unable to speak. After all, what was there to say? Ella then said, "Don't look at me like that, these things happen all the time."

Rafe finally answered with one word, "Why?"

Ella seemed almost as if she were angry when she replied, "Why? Well to start, you're so backward where women are concerned. When I said I could wrap you around my little finger I wasn't kidding. You and all that talk about your movie star girlfriend, she was probably leading you on just like I was."

Rafe said, "You mean it was all bullshit, right from the start?"

She went on to say, "Well you did tell me that you and Everett were going to start a business together when you were discharged, and the thought of living in New York was an exciting prospect. Then when I came to visit you in Lawton, you tell me that your mother blackmailed Everett and your plans had changed. So, look at it from my point of view, without money you're nothing!"

"Rafe couldn't believe what he was hearing, it was the verbal dagger being driven into his heart. But he had to know, so he asked, "Why didn't you tell me to stay in OCS and become a commissioned officer if you were planning this back then? I was number one in my class. I was at the top of my game. I was a leader among men. Why have me give that up, for this?"

Ella came right back with, "If you really want to know, maybe it's a form of payback from when your Anglo friends, you know your Ivy League buddies, used to use and abuse this little Spanish girl when she first came to Albuquerque. Do you have any idea how they used me? Rafe was beyond shocked so he added, "So it was revenge to make me pay for past offenses, committed by others?" Ella was glaring at him when she made her final comments. "You were so pathetically easy. I guess you just needed to be loved!"

Rafe sat behind the steering wheel feeling mortally wounded. What else could be said? He took the keys from the ignition dropped them in Ella's lap opened the door and stepped out of the car. He said, "The car belongs to me. Give it to your mother and sisters. Keep the rest of the money that remains in our account." Then he gave Ella a terrible look and said the last words he would ever say to her. "There is only one thing to learn from this."

She said, "What?"

As he turned to walk away, he said, "All that glitters is not gold!" He turned and walked down Elm Street N.E. towards Central Avenue. He would never see her again.

Rafe slowly made his way to Central Avenue turned left and walked down Central, towards downtown. He wasn't paying attention to where he was going, he just wanted to be alone. If he were an animal, he'd find a cave *and go to ground. He'd pull back, and lick his wounds. However, he wasn't an animal and he couldn't rid his mind of Ella's terrible words. When He came to Union Square Street, a block north of the Santa Fe tracks, the place close to where he had stopped and kissed Ella for the first time, he made a left turn and walked down the deserted street. There wasn't much on Union Square Street just some old buildings dating back to around 1890. One had three concrete stairs leading from the back door to the street. Rafe sat on the stairs with his elbows on his knees and his head in his hands. Now he knew what it was like to be Humpty Dumpty sitting on a wall 10,000 feet high when along comes his true love and gives him the big push, knowing with certainty what the result would be. When he hit bottom, he would be shattered into a million pieces, and all the king's horses; and all the king's men couldn't put him back together again.*

His thoughts were torturing him and he couldn't turn them off. He remembered the lyrics of a song that went, "In the corner of mind stands a Juke Box, it's playing all my favorite memories, and one by one they take me back to the days when you were mine, and I can't stop the Juke Box in my mind." His thoughts were tortuous and they were driving him into the depths of hell. From his perspective, it would have been more merciful if Ella had just drawn a gun and shot him in the head. At least the horror would only have lasted a second or two when he realized what was coming, but now, torture without end, real hell.

So, what do you do when you find yourself in such a situation? One of two things, you get a gun and blow your brains out, or you anesthetize yourself. After sitting on the stairs for about an hour and a half, Rafe decided on the latter course. He got up walked about a half-block down to Gold Ave and made a left turn and walked across Broadway Blvd to a little liquor store on the corner of Broadway and Gold. He walked in and continued down an aisle knowing exactly what he was looking for. When he came to the shelf with Bourbon, he picked up a fifth of Old Grand-Dad and walked up to the front counter to purchase it. He was thinking, "This should do the trick." He paid for the bourbon, picked up a couple of packs of Marlboro's and some matches, and then headed down Broadway towards Ella's place. He was glad to see the Pontiac wasn't in the driveway because the last person he wanted to see was her. Rafe walked into the backyard and sat on the cinder block wall which served as a divider between Ella's apartment building and the vacant lot next door.

He took the bottle out of the brown paper bag, opened it, and took a long swig. He was thinking if I drink it fast enough, I'll either die of alcohol poisoning or pass out. Either outcome was fine with him as long as he could blot out the thoughts that had driven him into despair.

Of course, he didn't pass out immediately. The first thing that happened was that Ella's sisters and mother came out and tried to talk him into stopping, but that wasn't going to happen. After a while, they gave up and left him in his misery. As Rafe sat on the wall smoking and drinking his mind slowly turned to, "How the hell did I get myself into this awful predicament?" Since he was super intelligent it didn't take him long to come up with the answer. He had joined the Army to gain worldly experience and inadvertently he had just learned one of life's greatest lessons, that is, that all humans can be delusional. That's right, humans are often delusional thinkers. When they're in a delusional mindset, they're not aware they're in it. They actually believe the delusion is the truth, to the extent that they will die for their delusional thought. Rafe realized he would have died for Ella even though, she was, in fact, playing him for a fool. He had gamboled everything he had, on one throw of the dice, in order to get back to her and preserve their great love, never considering that it had no basis in fact. The fact was he had been played, and screwed to the wall.

It happens all the time. Consider the Japanese Kamikaze pilots of World War II, they crashed their planes into Allied ships because they believed the emperor was God. However, the Emperor was far from being a God, and in fact, they had died of for a delusion. It didn't matter how much they believed in that ridiculous fantasy. They died for nothing. The same could be said for modern Jihadis Right! Kill yourself while killing innocent civilians, and you go to heaven and get sixty virgins. Talk about delusional thinking, but it doesn't stop hundreds of Jihadis from killing themselves.

If you think delusional thinking is easily mastered, guess again. A perfect example is a great artist, Vincent Van Gogh. While alive he was considered an abject failure. His brother told him to give up painting and get a real job.

He gave away his paintings for food and lodging and never sold a single one. Eventually, he cut off his ear and later committed suicide. On the surface one could say that Van Gogh was living a life based on delusion, however now, 100 years later, his paintings sell in the fifty to one hundred-million-dollar range. He never lived to see this great success. There is even a question of whether or not they're worth a fortune. Are they worth one hundred million on the merits or were they promoted into being worth a fortune? If they are worth a fortune, why wasn't their worth realized when he was still alive?

But that's art, and Rafe was thinking about human relationships. It was too bad that he was so young and inexperienced because as he matured, he would learn things that would explain his current circumstances. One story he learned has many versions, but it is usually called The Farmer and the Snake. It goes like this; A Farmer walked through his field one cold winter morning. On the ground lay a Snake, stiff and frozen with the cold. The farmer knew how deadly the Snake could be, and yet he picked it up and put it in his coat to warm it back to life. The snake soon revived, and when it had enough strength, bit the man who had been so kind to it. The bite was deadly, and the farmer fell and knew he must die. As he drew his last breath, he said, "Learn from my fate not to take pity on a snake." The great lesson from the story is, that the snake didn't bite the farmer because he didn't like him, the snake bit the farmer because it's the snake's nature to bite. The moral is, if you get in bed with snakes, you're going to get bit.

Rafe knew he was in this predicament because of his own decisions. After all Colonel Gattis had warned him in no uncertain terms. He had said, "Fail to turn your bushel of corn into $50 a bushel corn, and you'll get fucked." Well, he didn't listen to the Colonel's advice, and it only took three days to get fucked. Another awful thought drifted through his alcohol-infused mind, that being, when you put a person up on a pedestal there is only one thing they can do from up there, shit on you!"

When this thought hit Rafe, who was now pretty well hammered; he thought it was outrageously funny and he slid down off his perch on the wall and sat on the ground laughing uncontrollably, like the drunk, that he now was. So, he sat on the ground and smoked and drank and ranted and raved. He realized that among the stupid, he was the King. A really stupid idiot if ever there was one. That was the last thing he remembered, as he soon passed out.

Sometime in the middle of the night, he awoke to loud voices angrily yelling. He couldn't figure out where he was and what was going on and slipped back into unconsciousness. He woke early the next morning. He was in Ella's bed. How he got there he had no idea. He felt sick as a dog. Experiencing his first hangover. No sign of Ella, thank God. He realized Ella's mother and sisters must have carried him in from the yard and laid him out on her bed. He knew he had to get out of there. If the Chinese believed in the idea of loss of face, Rafe realized he had no face left, he had been totally humiliated. He got up, threw up, took a shower, shaved, and got dressed. Since he had never really gotten unpacked, he put a few things into his duffel bag and prepared to depart. Next came the difficult part. Lined up in the living room were the girls he loved like sisters, one sweeter than the next. He gave a hug and a kiss to Emily, Delores, Mary Ann, and Evelyn in that order. He told them he would miss them, but he had to go. Finally, he gave them a last word of advice. "Do well in school. Get an education. You've come a long way, and education will carry you the rest of the way."

Rafe turned and walked into the kitchen to say goodbye to the woman he loved like his own grandmother. When he was just thinking to himself, he referred to her as Old Mother. The years had taken their toll on her physically. She looked much older than her 45 years. Rafe said, "Well old mother I have to go."

She was crying softly and looked at Rafe and said, "I know. This should not have happened to you. I raised her better than this. She'll live to regret it." Rafe wanted to comfort her and answered, "It's not your fault. Don't blame yourself. I'll be all right it will just take some time. Like getting over a death in the family."

Ella's mother nodded knowing there wasn't much else to say. She said, softly, "Vaya Con Dios, my son."

Rafe walked down the driveway for the last time. Set his duffel bag down on the sidewalk and waited for the cab he had called. When the yellow cab pulled up Rafe dumped his bag in the trunk and climbed into the back seat. The driver said, "Where to bud?" "Rafe answered, "do you know the Land of

Enchantment Motel next to the Inferno? That's where I want to go." He hardly paid attention during the short ride up Central Avenue. When they arrived at the land of Enchantment Rafe climbed out, paid the driver and went into the motel office, and registered for a room. His room was on the upper floor with a good view of Sandia Crest which somehow pleased him. He dropped his bag in a corner and lay down on the bed to try to get some sleep. He knew as soon as the Inferno opened, he'd be down there drinking away his sorrows.

Later as he entered the Inferno, he looked again at the sign over the door which was a quote from Dante, **Abandon, all hope, ye who enter here!** Rafe didn't have to worry about that since he had no hope left. He had given everything he had, been totally committed, and still lost. He was running on empty,, and he had no idea on what to do next. He walked up to the bar, took a seat, and ordered a double shot of bourbon. Before the bartender could pour the shot, he decided to order two more. Might as well since he intended to drink himself under the table. Once he had his drinks he retreated to a table in the corner and watched the artificial flames lick up the walls. He had to admit that the place did look like hell which he considered completely appropriate. His world had turned to shit and he didn't have any idea what to do about it. You can't just throw a switch and stop loving the person you had been madly in love with, or can you? That was the question he had to resolve. Everyone knows the expression "Get busy livin'," or get busy dyin'", well now he had to resolve this problem or be destroyed. He didn't bother to go through the stage of denial. Ella hadn't pulled any punches and had basically told him to go fuck himself. So, the natural progression was to move to one of anger. In other words, how could she do such an outrageous thing? However, there were no answers so he simply drank his bourbon and watched the flames lick up the walls. After three days of drinking, Rafe decided this couldn't go on forever so he did what he'd always done in a crisis situation, He prayed to God. When Brinkman had gone after him when he was seven years old, he prayed. When she killed Max, he prayed. Now that the situation was again hopeless, he prayed. It was a simple prayer. "Dear Lord, here I am again in hopeless circumstances. I don't have an answer and I could use your help if you see fit to bail me out again. I know I don't deserve it, but I need help. I leave my fate in your hands, Amen.

The answer came in seconds. "Stay the course. I will lead the way. You are my drawn sword." If Rafe had been a different person, he might have thought he was talking to himself, but not after hearing the same voice in the chapel the night Max was killed. God was going to chart his course so he had no further worries. In a flash, just as all fear had left him that night in the chapel, so did the overwhelming feeling of grief leave his consciousness. Now he was on the path to redemption. Just as Ella had played him, he had likewise played the Army. Good men had believed in him and had given him great opportunities even though he was pulling a master con job on their good intentions.

Rafe had enlisted in the Army to gain worldly experience and you could say he accomplished that goal even if it came in the form of a kick in the ass. Now that the grief had subsided, he sat in his room looking out at Sandia Crest and evaluated how he had come to fall into delusional thinking. When he looked at it rationally it was fairly simple, he fell for Ella because of her beauty. He had told her the first night, that among his buddies she would be described as being "built like a brick shithouse. Definitely crude! But. It gets the point across.

She definitely had a world-class body. Her face couldn't compare to Jill's, but on the other hand, Jill's body couldn't compare to Ella's. So, where guilt was compared, Rafe wasn't exactly innocent. Where Delusional thinking was concerned Rafe built up Ella in his mind to goddess-like proportions because he wanted to possess her incredible beauty. If she hadn't been as beautiful as she was this seemingly great romance would have never seen liftoff. Because he had wanted her so much, he, operating under the guise of true love, had lied and conned his way into OCS. The men he was lying to were men he respected and were of the highest character. In effect, Rafe had acted in a dishonorable way. Now the only remedy was to try to seek redemption and give the Army whatever it demanded. Now that he was over his delusional thinking, he had no doubt the Army would be seeking its pound of flesh and would quickly enact its, order of all orders, that being "for the good of the service." Whatever the Army would demand of him Rafe would be perfectly willing to comply.

As Rafe sat staring at the Sandia Mountains contemplating his fate he was thinking about the whole disastrous affair. The thoughts he was thinking would come out in the form of a county and western song years later. It was The Dance by Garth Brooks. It goes like this.

Looking back on the memory of the dance we shared neath the stars above.
For the moment all the world was right.
How could I have ever known that you would ever say goodbye?
And now I'm glad I didn't know,
The way it all would end the way it all would go.
Our lives are better left to chance
I could have missed the pain.
But I'd have had to miss the dance.
Holding you I held everything.
For the moment wasn't I the king?
But if I'd only known how the king would fall,
Hey, who's to say I might have changed it all?
And now I'm glad I didn't know.
The way it all would end, the way it all would go.
Our lives are better left to chance, I could have missed
The pain. But I'd have had to miss the dance.

The dance was wonderful. Rafe remembered kissing Ella on Central Avenue as they were walking home that night. He had indeed felt like a King. Was it worth the pain? He had to admit it was so glorious, while it lasted, that it made the saying "better to have loved and lost, than never to loved, at all" completely accurate.

Rafe knew he wasn't over it, but he now knew he could carry on. Like with death, there is only one thing to do, walk away from it. Did God have a destiny planned for him? Rafe was now sure that he did. Whatever that might entail Rafe was ready and willing to keep the faith. Suddenly he knew that when he went out to the Army Personnel office at Sandia Base the next day that his orders would be waiting. Where they would guide him, he knew not, but he knew he would willingly follow any directive the Army ordered, and in the process hopefully achieve a modicum of redemption. He put the drinking aside, no need for that anymore. He would just have to deal with his grief until time washed its pain away. One thing had changed though; no more mister nice guy. He remembered the immortal words of the Brooklyn

Dodger manager Leo Durocher, "Nice guys don't win ball games." From that point on Rafe was all about seeking redemption and restoring his honor.

The following morning, he took the bus up Central Avenue, down Wyoming Blvd. into Sandia Base. He identified himself to the clerks at the Personnel Office and asked if they had orders for Sergeant Rafael M. Hawkins. He had been promoted to Sergeant E5 upon completion of his first eight weeks at OCS. He was thinking, "The army probably regrets that, but they're probably going to seek their pound of flesh by using their order of all orders. Rafe could have cared less since he was now seeking redemption for his less-than-honorable behavior in conning his way into OCS. Now the cat was out of the bag, and the Army was aware that he had been trying to pull a fast one.

The Clerk handed the orders to Rafe and he saw he was to report to Brigadier General Charles T. Leicester, 1st Cavalry Division Airmobile at Fort Benning, Georgia. Rafe was thinking, "Oh yeah, Chargin' Charlie Leicester; The Medal of Honor winner from Triangle Hill in Korea. He's a real bulldog and I'm in deep shit."

Rafe walked out of Sandia Base instead of taking the bus. He was trying to conjure up something positive out of this disaster. It was only about 15 blocks down Wyoming Blvd. before reaching Central Avenue. Rafe walked along thinking about how he managed to get himself into such a fucked-up mess. He finally admitted to himself it was lust. Yep, when Ella had asked him how she compared to Jill he at first tried to skirt the issue. Finally, he admitted, she was built like a Brick Shithouse. Definitely crude and course, but it painted the picture. Ella was hotter than hot. On the other hand, Jill was classically beautiful; her eyes were hypnotic, and she was a vision of loveliness. When that idea popped into his head Rafe began to think about his ridiculous Prophecy. As he walked along Wyoming Blvd. Rafe was thinking about the lovely young girl with extraordinary blue eyes who had never said an unkind word to him. Too bad she's so far out of reach.

Although far from his consciousness, floating along above him was the Lord God Almighty, and he was thinking, "You forget one thing young man, and it came from your own mouth, "What God hath joined together, let no man put asunder!"

The Leper Colony

For the second time in 18 months, Rafe walked across the tarmac of the Albuquerque Airport heading for a TWA 707 airliner. He could have thought back to the day over eighteen months ago when he took the same walk, with Ella and her family waving goodbye. However, this time his mind was somewhere else; he was thinking about religion and more specifically 1st Corinthians 13 which he had long ago committed to memory. It went like this; "If I speak in the tongues of men or angels, but do not have love, I am only a resounding gong or a clanging cymbal. If I have the gift of prophecy and can fathom all the mysteries and all knowledge, and if I have a faith that can move mountains, but do not have love, I am nothing. If I give all I possess to the poor and give over my body to hardship that I may boast, but do not have love, I gain nothing. Love is patient, love is kind. It does not envy, it does not boast, it is not proud. It does not dishonor others, it is not self-seeking, it is not easily angered, and it keeps no records of wrongs. Love does not delight in evil but rejoices with the truth. It always protects, always trusts, always hopes, and always preserves. Love never fails. But where there are prophecies, they will cease; where there are tongues, they will be stilled; where there is knowledge, it will pass away. For we know in part and we will prophesy in part, but when completeness comes, what is in part disappears. When I was a child, I talked like a child, I thought like a child, and I reasoned like a child. When I became a man, I put the ways of childhood behind me. For now, we see only a reflection in a mirror; then we shall see face to face. Now I know in part; then I shall know fully, even as I am fully known. And now these three remain; Faith, Hope, and Love. But the greatest of these is Love."Rafe was thinking God shows himself in the world through love. God is Love. Rafe hoped that somewhere in the future he would experience love again, but until then, in his heart and in his mind, he was focused on redemption.

This time when the mighty engines roared pushing the jetliner down the Albuquerque Airport runway, Rafe's mind was far away. When the 707 lifted off and roared over Ella's place on Broadway, Rafe didn't even look down. He looked at the beautiful vista of Sandia Crest towering above the city and turned his mind toward his upcoming meeting with Brigadier General Leicester. Rafe was well aware of General Leicester's reputation. His sobriquet was Chargin' Charlie earned when he was a Battalion Commander with the Seventh Division at a place called Triangle Hill in Korea. Rafe knew all about Triangle Hill as his Platoon Sergeant in basic training Francisco Matta-Rosa talked about little else. Triangle Hill made such an indelible impression on Sergeant Matta-Rosa that he took the lessons learned in that battle, and impressed them on his young recruits. Matta-Rosa had his 3rd platoon run everywhere they went. He was a fanatic about fitness and it wasn't long before his platoon began to complain that they ran everywhere while the other platoons marched. At first, Matta-Rosa ignored his pathetic group of recruits until he thought telling them the truth might be a powerful learning experience. It was at this point that he related the story of Triangle Hill. The gist of the story was that his battalion assaulted Triangle Hill four times and was driven back three times. The casualties were excessive to the point that Matta-Rosa became obsessed with the events of the battle. After a month of jogging around Fort Dix, rather than, marching or moving at route step, Matta-Rosa's 3rd platoon was near mutiny. Why did they have to double-time wherever they went while the other platoons walked? At this point, Matta-Rosa thought it was the right time to explain the method to his madness. At a remote area out in Fort Dix's pine barrens, he gathered the 3rd platoon around him.

He put it to them in no uncertain terms. "This is just training; The real thing, Combat, is a horse of another color. I was at a place in Korea called Triangle Hill. None of you have ever heard of it. To put it simply Triangle Hill was a real meat grinder. The casualties were off the charts. My Battalion was led by the incredible Army leader Chargin' Charlie Leicester. He would lead us up that damn hill four times and every time when we got to the summit, it was always the same group that survived the assault. What did we survivors have in common? All of us were trained by Chargin' Charlie at Fort Carson, Colorado in the Rocky Mountains. It was at Fort Carson that Lt. Colonel Leicester ran his battalion up and down the Rocky Mountain foothills until we were more like mountain goats than regular GIs. Why was this conditioning so important? This is the reason why I run you to death. When you get to advanced infantry training, you'll find out that the American method of infantry assault depends on unit discipline and firepower. You advance on the enemy putting down on his position such overwhelming firepower that he can't pop out of his foxhole and gun you down. You then simply walk up to him and shoot him in his hole. At Triangle Hill, we had a distinct problem. We were attacking up a steep uphill grade. Many in the assault companies were becoming exhausted, and when that happened those that were exhausted put down their head, bent over at the waist, and gasped for air. While they were doing that they were mowed down. Those of us, that could run, climb, and fight lived. Now that's why I'm going to run your asses off, and if you live long enough, you'll thank me for the lesson."

The 3rd platoon took the lesson to heart, shut up, and ran as men possessed now that they understood their lives could depend on it. If Matta-Rosa was a hard-ass one would do well to remember that he was one of Chargin' Charlie's disciples. However, to Rafe, it mattered not at all. He didn't fear General Leicester or anything else. Whatever lay ahead he could handle, it made little difference to him as to what that might be. It was with this attitude that Sergeant Rafe Hawkins flew into Columbus, Georgia, and Fort Benning.

When he located the Headquarters of the First Cavalry Division he walked in and found an orderly and asked where could he find the assistant division commander Brigadier General Leicester. The orderly led him into another wing of the building and turned him over to Sergeant-Major Fitzgerald. The Sergeant-Major looked at his orders and then gave Rafe a knowing look that alluded to the fact that his arrival had been expected. Then Sergeant Fitzgerald said, "Take a seat here Hawkins, I'll tell the General you're here and I'll let you know when he's ready to see you." Rafe took a seat and prepared himself for the upcoming confrontation.

About thirty minutes later Sergeant Fitzgerald came back and told Rafe to follow him. When they arrived at the General's office the Sergeant-Major told Rafe to Knock, enter, and report to the General. After knocking, Rafe entered, walked to a position in front of the General's desk, snapped to attention, and saluted. When General Leicester returned his salute Rafe remained at attention with his eyes fixed on the photo of a helicopter on the wall behind the General's head.

General Leicester gave Rafe the once over and thought to himself, "He doesn't look as formidable as he's cranked up to be, but looks can be deceiving." He finally said, "Stand at ease, Hawkins." It was at this point Rafe got his first good look at the famous warrior. He was fit and trim, but it was his eyes that revealed his strength of character. They were hard and very direct. Rafe knew he wasn't going to be fooling around or playing games with this character. He was tough, and not unlike Rafe, he had the stare of a predator. The General was tapping a pencil he held between the fingers of his right hand and his desk. This went on for what seemed an eternity as the General decided what he was going to say. Finally, he said, "Do you know who I am?"

Rafe answered in the affirmative saying, "Yes Sir, You're General Chargin' Charlie Leicester."

In reply, General Leicester asked, "Do you know where and under what circumstances I earned that nickname?"

Rafe answered, "Yes sir, it was earned at Triangle Hill in Korea where you led your battalion up that hill four times, and where you were outnumbered about 10 to 1."

Chargin' Charlie was taking another long hard look at Rafe and was thinking, "They said he was as sharp as a tack, but how in the hell does he know what happened at Triangle Hill." He then asked, "Hawkins, how in the hell do you know what happened at Triangle Hill as it's not exactly the most famous battle fought in Korea?"

Rafe quickly answered, "My platoon sergeant in basic training, Francisco Matta-Rosa, served with you at Triangle Hill."

The General came back with, "You were trained by Matta-Rosa?"

"Yes sir, and he related the whole story of Triangle Hill while he was in the process of running us to death."

This brought a wry smile to the General's lips. The General then asked, "Did he say why he was running you to death."

Rafe answered with, "Yes Sir, he related the story of Triangle Hill as well as the training he received under your command at Fort Carson, Colorado. He said that if you hadn't been as tough as you were, none of them would have survived Triangle Hill. He told us that physical fitness and toughness lead to survival in combat."

"Did he tell you that he was awarded the Silver Star for valor in that battle?"

"No Sir, we were informed about that by the platoon sergeant of the 1st Platoon who told us that Matta-Rosa was not only a war hero but was among the toughest of the tough. Of course, he didn't have to tell us that, as we already knew firsthand."

General Leicester took a closer look at the young man standing in front of him and said, "Looks like wherever you go you come in contact with someone from the Seventh Division. First, Matta-Rosa who was a rifleman, then General Lemnitzer, the Division Commander, then Colonel Gattis from Division Artillery, and now finally me. There must be some hidden meaning in all of these coincidences, but for the life of me I can't see what that might be." The General went on to ask, "Do you know why you're here?"

Rafe stated, "I have an idea, but I'm not exactly sure."

The general countered with, "Hawkins if you're going to get along with me when I ask a question, I want a direct answer. Do you understand?"

Rafe thought to himself, "The General wants the truth, well I'll give him the truth." He looked the general straight in the eye and said, "General the reason I'm here is that I tried to pull a fast one on the army, and they figured out what I was doing. I could have gotten away with it, but my ego got the best of me. If I had stayed number 41 in my class at OCS, when I asked to resign, they would have been glad to see me go. In all likelihood, I'd have been reassigned to Sandia Base and my mission would have been accomplished. Where I screwed up was, that I let the evaluations written about me by my classmates piss me off. I decided to put them in their place or in other words, show them up. In effect, I ran by them like they were tied to a tree and simply left them in the dust. Then when I tried to resign Colonel Gattis wasn't hearing it. He spoke to me like a Dutch Uncle. He told me I was making the biggest mistake of my life and the only thing that could make me do such a thing was a woman. Unfortunately, I didn't listen. I tried to play hardball with the Colonel and threatened him with the Inspector General. That's why I'm here General."

General Leicester simply nodded in agreement. Then said, "Yes, that's about it. So at least you know what got you here, but what you can't possibly know is why you're standing where you are. Have you ever heard the expression, Duty, Honor, Country?"

Rafe quickly answered, "Yes Sir."

The General went on, "Well it seems you've forgotten about that statement in favor of your own selfish agenda. I'll ask you another question, do you know what Section 892, article 92 of the Uniform of Military Justice entails?"

"Yes, sir."

"And what might that be?"

Rafe knew where this was going as he answered, "It deals with dereliction of duty."

"Are you aware of what dereliction of duty entails?"

"Yes Sir, I'm aware of the definition."

The General then said, "Good! Because that's why you're here. You not only threatened Colonel Gattis with the Inspector General when he was only trying to help you, but you were derelict in your duties. Dereliction of Duty is a court-martial offense. We could lock you up or kick you out of the army with a dishonorable discharge, or both. Do you understand what I'm saying?"

Rafe was thinking to himself, "So this is where you're going with all of this. Unfortunately, you can't court-martial me for Dereliction of duty. For one, you never gave me my rights under Article 31 of the Uniform Code of Military Justice. Therefore, anything I may have said about my departure from OCS can't be used against me in court. Secondly, and more important, Military Regulations state that I can resign from OCS after eight weeks for whatever reason I wish. You'll never bring any charges against me because the only way to make them stick is in a Kangaroo Court. That would mean Colonel Gattis would need to perjure himself, and I doubt he'd do that." Rafe kept thinking to himself, "The General is just trying to intimidate me to get me to do whatever he has in mind. That's all right with me because I've already decided to do whatever he commands."

Rafe then answered the General saying, "Yes Sir, I understand exactly the implications of your statement. I'm aware of what you could do if you so desired."

"Good, seeing that you understand your predicament let me explain how you can redeem yourself if redemption is what you have in mind. Then the General went on to ask, "Have you seen the motion picture Twelve O'clock High?"

Rafe quickly answered, "Yes Sir, I've seen it a few times and it's my favorite movie.

The General responded with, "Good that makes things a lot easier since you'll know right from the beginning what I'm driving at. What is the plot of the film as you remember it?'

Rafe explained, "Gregory Peck's character is a Brigadier General Savage who is ordered to take over command of the 918th Bomb Group which is suffering inordinately high losses. Savage determines that the group suffers from a lack of discipline where they fail to fly tight formations which invites enemy fighters to zero in on their group. Savage cracks down on the bomb wing and has them practice formation flying over and over until they're ready to revolt. In fact, the entire bomb wing puts in for a transfer which the Adjutant Major Stovall sits on, to buy Savage some time. While in the process of restoring discipline, Savage relieves the Air Exec. Lt. Colonel Gately demotes him to an aircraft commander because he suspects him of cowardice.

He then assigns all of the worst personnel in the wing to Gately's crew. He tells Gately to either straighten out his crew of misfits or expect to be shot down in short order."

Genera' Leicester nodded his head in agreement and said, "Well you have the plot down pat. So, you must remember the name given to Gately's plane full of misfits?"

Rafe nodded, and replied, "It was called the Leper Colony."

"Good you're aware, so now we can get down to the nitty-gritty. Every military command has a number of misfits not unlike those General Savage found in the 918th Bomb Group. We have around sixteen thousand enlisted men in the First Cavalry Division of which maybe, one in one thousand, is the sort we'd assign to the Leper Colony if we had one. However, this isn't a Bomb Group and we don't have aircraft. Therefore, I'm creating a new group to be called the Leper Colony. It will be a small platoon led by you, and answerable to me. It's going to be up to you, Sergeant Hawkins, to transform these misfits into a first-class fighting outfit and you'll do it within six months. If you succeed then we'll put aside any charges we may be considering regarding dereliction of duty. On the other hand, if you fail, you may find yourself being cashiered from the Army with a less-than-honorable discharge. And the same will hold true for your contingent of misfits. Do I make myself clear?"

"Rafe answered, "I think you made it quite clear. However, I have a question." The General responded, "Go ahead, what do you want to know?"

"Just this General, I have to do it my way and I'll need you to support me logistically as we train."

The General said, 'Ok you'll have my support, now do you have any other questions?"

Rafe replied, "Just one. Is there anything I can't do?"

This brought the hint of a smile to the General's lips as he answered, "Well, you can't kill them!"

Rafe had a feeling that he and Chargin' Charlie, were on the same page. The General went on to say, "The lepers are down the street in the barracks of a platoon that's in the field. The Sergeant Major will give you directions. I want you to go down there and tell them, Where the bear shit in the buckwheat! Do you get my drift.? Let them know exactly where they stand, and what it's going to take to extricate themselves. Have I made myself clear?"

"Yes, Sir, Extremely, clear."

"Good, then report back to me tomorrow at 0800. Let me know how things went, and your plan to whip them into shape."

"Yes, Sir. Will that be all Sir?"

Yes, that's all. You're dismissed."

Rafe saluted, did an about-face, and left the General's office.

The Sergeant Major told Rafe where he could find the 16 misfits now sporting the sobriquet The Leper Colony. Rafe walked down the company street knowing that he had a rendezvous with destiny. He was thinking, "Not to worry, my footsteps are being directed by the Lord God himself, which means I can't fail. I just have to feel a little sorry for the lepers. They're in for a rude shock as they have no idea as to what's about to descend on them."

With that in mind, he entered the designated barracks and walked toward the squad bay. He heard the lepers before they came into view so he dropped his duffel bag and walked confidently up to the relaxed group which was sprawled out on cots, playing cards and shooting the breeze. They looked at him like "Who the hell is this." Then it started! Rafe said, with a Command Voice, which had been drummed into him at OCS, and that definitely commanded attention. "Listen up! I'm Sergeant Hawkins and I'm your new platoon leader."

It only took a second for one of the troopers to show why they were classified as Lepers. The loudmouth answered, "You're no platoon leader. Platoon leaders are officers and you're nothing but a buck sergeant." The wise guy was sitting on a foot-locker at the rear of the group and he got to his feet as he made his assertion. Rafe quickly figured out why he thought he should speak for the group. He was about 6'5" and weighed in the neighborhood of 240 to 250. He was, from Rafe's point of view, a Big Black Bull as he was a very dark-skinned, negro. He was sporting an aggressive look which suited Rafe just fine. He needed to make an example of someone and this one was made to order.

"Well things have just changed, I'm the platoon leader and you will address me as sir, just as if I am an officer, or else!"

The Big Black Bull advanced from the back of the group which parted to let him through. He was sort of chuckling to himself as he said, "Or else what? What's a little pipsqueak like you going to do to us?"

Rafe came right back with, "Tear you a new asshole!"

Now the Black Bull was laughing out loud as he said, "You and what army? What makes you think someone your size can tear me a new asshole?"

"Because it's obvious to me that you lack character. It wouldn't be surprising if your father was a shit-eating dog, and your mother a stupid bitch."

With that, the Black Bull charged just as Rafe was expecting. He came running like a fullback trying to break through the line. Rafe waited until the charging trooper was almost making contact before he suddenly dropped to his hands and knees causing his adversary to trip as if he'd just hit a fallen tree and go sliding across the barracks floor, head first. His momentum carried him forward until he ran into one of the support posts holding up the ceiling. He hit the post hard enough to knock down a butt can, filled with foul-smelling liquid, that splattered all over his face. Before he could recover Rafe moved with lightning speed, grabbed his left wrist, levered up his arm, and gave him a swift powerful kick in the armpit. Rafe was trying to restrain himself remembering General Leicester's admonition that he could do everything he wanted, except kill them. When the stunned trooper began to rise Rafe hit him with a right uppercut that sent him sprawling right flat on his back. If the trooper had been angry before now, he was now in a fit of rage. He was thinking, "How can this little piece of shit be manhandling me." As those overtaken by rage often do, he forgot what he was doing and made the big mistake of reaching into his pocket and pulling out a switchblade knife. When he pressed the button and the blade popped out Rafe again moved with blinding speed and kicked the knife out of his hand where it went tumbling through the air to stick into the same post the butt can had been hanging on just seconds before. Fortunately, it didn't end up sticking in the body of one of the other nearby Lepers. Rafe's antagonist began to rise to his feet when Rafe turned and ran back about 20 feet then turned and ran at full speed right at the unsteady big black bear. Just before he reached him Rafe leaped up and hit him with a flying drop kick driving him backward. Unfortunately, there was a cot behind the bear, and he was knocked backward over it doing a somersault while landing face up. In a flash, Rafe plucked the knife from the post and leaped on the black bear straddling his chest. When the Bear came to his senses, he was looking into the eyes of what appeared to be a fearsome bird of prey, and to make matters worse he had the knife to his throat. His only thought was, "Oh Shit!"

A sinister smile crossed Rafe's lips as he said, "I'm only going to ask you one question, and you better get it right." Then Rafe asked, "Who's the boss?"

The pinned trooper knew he was screwed so he did the only thing he could, he nodded and answered, "You are!"

Having received the right answer Rafe stood up, retracted the blade of the knife, and offered it to his beaten adversary. He then asked the Big Black Bear, "What's your name?"

"Tim Spencer, Sir."

Rafe offered Tim his hand and pulled him to his feet. He told Tim to take a seat on one of the cots and told the others to gather around.

He ran his predatory gaze from one end of the semi-circle of troopers to the other. He met the gaze of each and every man. Then he began. "I suppose you're asking yourself what just happened here, and beyond that, what does all this mean? Well, now I'm going to give you an explanation. Where life is concerned, you're standing at a fork in the road. Your choice is to go down one path that will lead to everlasting glory or to take the other which will be the path you're already on. In case you're not aware of the path you're on now, and how you're perceived by the Army, let me explain that in a short and simple manner. In case you're not aware of it, the Army thinks you're lower than Whale Shit at the bottom of the ocean. In other words, you're next to worthless. And, don't think I'm not included in that estimation. In fact, the Army has given this little group, of which we are now all part, a name. Since you'll never guess what it is, I'll just tell you; We are now known as the Leper Colony. That should tell you all you need to know. Now, If, they think you're bad, they think I'm even worse, that's why I'm the chief leper or the leper in charge. Gentleman, We're on the road to Hell."

"We all know by now some of the key axioms of Army jargon things like, the right way or the Army Way, Never Volunteer, or how about this one which pertains to us; Shape Up, or Ship Out! So, let me put it to you bluntly, the Army has given us 100 days to shape up or to be discharged with a less than honorable discharge."

At this point, one of the lepers raised his hand to ask a question. Rafe nodded and said, "Stand up and state your name, rank, and where you're from. The young trooper stood up and said, "Private First Class, Sam Radle, Laredo, Texas." Rafe asked, "Do you have a question?" Radle answered, "Yes, Sir, why should we be concerned about being discharged when all of us are less than a year from being discharged?"

Rafe nodded his head and said, "You hit the nail right on the head Sam. What the hell difference does it make if they throw us out now? If you want to know the truth? It can be shown in one word, Status!"

"Now listen up and listen very carefully because your future may hang in the balance. I'm going to ask you a question and I want an honest answer. I don't expect you'll give me the obvious answer immediately because in all likelihood it's not in your conscious train of thought, rather it's subconscious. However, whether or not it's conscious or subconscious, it's a very powerful motivator. Here's the question, in your free time, if you could do anything, what would that be?"

Of course, Rafe didn't get the answer he wanted, in fact, he didn't get any answer because the newly dubbed Lepers thought it was some sort of trick question. Rafe waited a minute and then said, "It's getting laid!" This of course brought out a chorus of guffaws and snickering as the men knew this was right on.

Rafe continued, "Ok, so can we all agree that our number one goal in life after eating and breathing is getting laid?" To a man, they all nodded in agreement. "This is a good starting point for our discussion. We all agree that our primary motivation is sex. The question is how did we get into this situation? It's not intellectual. If you remember back to being ten years old, you'll recall you had no interest in girls. Then around the age of twelve or thirteen, they suddenly began to look good, and not just a little good, but really good. Then the next thing you know you've become obsessed with them. Now believe me when I say, you didn't think this up, it was the power of nature driving you in the direction it wants you to go. Nature has one goal, and that is to produce the next generation. In order for that to happen mating has to occur. To get this accomplished nature made your body produce male hormones, like testosterone, and once this was pumped into your cells you became very interested in the opposite sex. Now, I'm going to tell you something else that's very important. If you were to pursue any goal in life with the same energy and intensity that you pursue getting laid, you'd succeed in almost any endeavor. Since we all agree that getting laid is at the top of our list of priorities the question arises what is the best way to accomplish this? Does anyone have any idea?"

The answers were varied and most carried a kernel of truth. One was money, another was power, then came charm, and even good looks. Rafe listened and then nodded his head in agreement. He then continued. "All of your answers are correct, but one word sums it all up, Status. If you have status, you'll get laid, if you don't, it's damn hard. Now, since we all want to get laid, then it's in our best interest to acquire status. Do you all agree?" To a man, the lepers all nodded in the affirmative.

"Let me ask you this, where do you think we stand, right now, at this moment where status is concerned?" No answer, just a bunch of blank stares was their response. Since you don't know or if it's slipped your mind, the Army considers us to be Whale Shit at the bottom of the ocean. And the sobriquet of the Leper Colony is further evidence of our collective lack of status. Now if you think this is bad, believe me when I say it could get much worse. The Army has it in its mind to give us all a General Discharge. What does that mean in the real world? It's as if the Army is going to place a monkey on your back which you'll carry for the rest of your life. Imagine going into a place like TWA World Airlines once you're discharged, and applying for a job. Once they see you've been in the Army, they'll ask what sort of discharge you were given. If it's Honorable, you're in like Flynn, but a General, or Dishonorable, and you're fucked. That's what lack of status will do for you, get you fucked, and I don't mean in the way you want to get fucked.

So, why am I standing up here feeding you this line of shit? Because as bad as the Army thinks you are, they think I'm a lot worse. What did I do that has them so pissed off? I fucked with their rules. I used their own regulations against them. What does that mean to them? It's a direct threat to what they call, "Good order and discipline, and that is the one thing that has to be maintained at all costs. Why does that affect you? I'll tell you why, it's because you're all just like me. You can think for yourself, and therein lies the problem. They don't care if you can think for yourself, just don't have the temerity to act on it.

Now I'm going to tell you a story. It happened about 66 years ago and I'm sure none of you have ever heard about it although it bares great significance to our current situation. How many of you have ever heard of Chilkoot Pass?" There weren't any hands raised, just some vacant stares. Rafe began, "When Gold was discovered in Yukon Territories in 1897 it precipitated the usual Gold Rush. Everyone who was within traveling distance of Dawson rushed in. Then winter set in; the Yukon River froze into a block of ice and supplies could not be moved till spring. The vastly increased population of Dawson almost starved to death. The Canadian Government knew that when spring arrived a huge migration of gold seekers would head to the Yukon from all over the world, thereby making what happened the previous winter that much worse. The solution was simple; each miner had to carry 2,000 pounds of supplies into the Yukon, most of which had to be food. It was a simple solution, except it wasn't that simple for the miners. There was essentially only one way into the Yukon; Take a streamer from Seattle or Vancouver to Skagway, Alaska. From there you would make your way up Chilkoot Pass which was 25 miles long and about 4,000 feet high. The last 1,500 feet was called the Golden Staircase. It was an ice staircase rising at about a forty-five-degree angle, with a rope alongside, so the miners could pull themselves upward. Keep in mind each miner had to carry 2,000 pounds of supplies to the summit. That would require each person to carry 40 pounds per trip to move 2,000 pounds in 50 trips. However, there was another problem; the line at the bottom of the Golden Staircase was so long that a person could only make two trips up, per day. So, it took at least 25 days to get your supplies to the summit, where it was weighed by the Canadian Mounties. That is 25 days to move your supplies to the summit, but keep in mind, it was 25 miles from Skagway to the Golden Staircase.

"Once over the summit. it was another 500 miles to Dawson and the diggings. The truth is very few miners that arrived during the second year found gold. The early arrivals got the choice claims. So, most experienced a grueling ordeal, packing a ton of supplies to Dawson for nothing. If that's the case, what's the point of the story, and how does it relate to our situation? It's the rest of the story that counts. This is the rest of the story. If you're the sort of person that can climb the Golden Staircase with 40 pounds each trip, and do it 50 times; then you've proved yourself to be a hell of a person where fortitude and grit are concerned. That sort may fail to find gold in the Yukon but would succeed later in life because they had proven themselves, to themselves. We find ourselves in a similar situation. The Army thinks we're Whale Shit, but does that matter to us? Hardly! Frankly, I don't care much about what the Army thinks of me. They have their way of doing things and have the power to make men adhere to their will. We're here because we have a rebellious attitude toward their dictates. What we're about to embark on is not about winning the approval of the United States Army, it's about our own self-image. Essentially, we are going over Chilkoot Pass. When we're finished, we'll have status in our own eyes and in the eyes of our fellow Lepers. Here's one final thought. Before we're finished The Leper Colony will not be an object of derision, in fact, it will be the elite strike force for this Division. You might say we'll be the Tip of the Spear. Getting to that point, from where we are now, will be a challenge. You'll be facing the hardest one hundred days of your life, and then it will continue from there onward. Only one thing is certain; by the time we're finished, The Leper Colony will be a force to be reckoned with. We'll take a lot of shit at first, but in the end, hundreds will be begging to join us. When you leave the Army, you'll have status, primarily in your own eyes, and keep in mind, this one salient point; Everyone wants to be part of something great because greatness stays with a man. If you want to stay a member of the Leper Colony and earn the highest form of status, you don't have to do anything. If you want out, see me sometime during the night and you'll be out of the Army by the end of the week. One last warning; the next six months will be hell!"

    Rafe turned and walked to the end of the barracks and into the platoon sergeant's room. He sat on his cot for a few minutes before getting up and walking back into the squad bay. As he approached the lepers stopped talking and turned to face him. He stopped and said, "Spencer, follow me." With that, he turned and walked back to his room. When Tim Spencer walked in

Rafe pointed to the cot opposite his and said, "Sit!" Tim Spencer sat opposite Rafe wearing a rather sheepish look. Rafe got right to the point. "Do you know what went on in the Squad Bay in the last 20 minutes?" Tim just nodded in the negative. "Well let me set you straight on that. I was just getting your attention. Not just yours, but the whole group. That went well because there's no doubt, I have your attention."

Tim was looking straight into Rafe's eyes when he said, "Can I ask you a question, Sir?"

Rafe came back with, "Sure, Shoot."

Tim asked, "Sir, how does someone your size have so much strength? I've been in a lot of scrapes in my life, but I've never been up against someone with such power. It's not just that you have the power, it's the relation of the power to your size."

Rafe thought about it for a minute. It was a simple question, but it needed to be answered in exactly the correct manner. Finally, Rafe Said, "Do you believe in God, Tim?"

Tim only took a second to answer, "Yes, I believe in the Lord with all my heart."

"Good", Rafe answered, "otherwise you'd never be able to accept what I'm about to tell you. About eight years ago I suffered a very traumatic event in my life, I was crushed and left in despair. I went to the chapel and prayed to God. He answered me, and at that point, you might say I had what can be called an epiphany. Do you understand what that is?" Tim Spencer just nodded his head, no. Rafe continued, "An epiphany is a sudden revelation or insight. Did I understand what was happening? No. I only knew that from that point on I was being directed by the hand of the almighty. I grew from 5' tall to 6' tall in fourteen months and gained seventy-five pounds. I developed incredible speed and power which was basically hidden from view. In other words, I don't look as fast and powerful as I am, but it is hidden below the surface. I don't exactly understand what it means, but it's brought me to this place and time and into this group called The Leper Colony. God has his hand in this; Why it's happening isn't exactly clear, but I'm sure over a period of time, it will be. I also don't think it's an accident that you and I are sitting across from each other having this conversation. From my perspective, it's directed by the will of God. Carrying this a little further; as I mentioned earlier, from the Army's point of view we are Whale Shit at the bottom of the Ocean, but it's a known fact that everyone wants to be part of something great. That's what is about to happen, the Leper Colony is going to become the "Best of the Best. Do you want to be part of it?"

Tim nodded his head in the affirmative and replied, "I'm In."

Rafe then said, "Good, because I need your help. The Leper Colony is not yet an organized group. There is no rank, I'm a buck sergeant and the rest of you are PFC's. The chain of command is very simple. General Leicester, then to me, then to you. You're going to be my First Sergeant, but by that, I mean First Sergeant in name only, otherwise, you'd outrank me. I hope you see what I'm driving at. We'll organize the Leper Colony to function the way we want it to, not the way the Army wants it to be. In fact, for practical purposes, they'll never know precisely what we're doing. Only General Leicester will know. I'm going to need you to carry out the day-to-day, operations of the group. Are you up to it?"

Tim nodded and said, "Yes Sir, I'm up to it, in fact, I think I like the idea of the Leper Colony, so I'm fully on board."

"Good, then this is what I want you to do. Tell the Lepers that it will be lights out at 2200 and reveille at 0600. Get the men up. March to the Mess Hall for breakfast then back to the barracks. Have the men pack their gear in preparation to move to the field, and then clean the barracks. I'll be meeting with General Leicester and when I return, we'll go to Supply to pick up equipment. I'll be gone until about 1000 hours after which the fun will begin. That's it. Carry on." That's how it started, but only Rafe knew where it was headed.

The following morning at precisely 0800 Rafe reported to General Leicester. He entered the General's office came to attention in front of his desk, saluted, and said, "Sergeant Hawkin's reporting as ordered." The General returned his salute and told him to stand at ease. General Leicester was somewhat amused by Sergeant Hawkins. He could usually size people up very quickly, but Hawkins was different. The General just hadn't been able to figure him out. The General said, "Have a seat, Hawkins. Something tells me this is going to take some time." Rafe took a seat in a chair to the right side of the General's desk, Once seated the General got right to the point. "How did your meeting with the Lepers go?"

Rafe looked over at Chargin' Charlie and said, "I would say it went very well, better than I expected."

That got the General's attention and he responded with, "What did you do?"

Rafe thought about it for a minute then said, "I walked in and told them I was Sgt. Rafe Hawkins, their new Platoon Leader. The immediate response was you're not a Platoon Leader because Platoon Leaders are officers. I then told them that I was the new Platoon leader whether they thought so, or not and that they would address me as sir, or else! With that one of their members got up and challenged me saying, "Or else what? What's a little pipsqueak like you going to do?" The trooper was a big black dude about 6'5" and maybe 250. So, he outweighed me by about 70 pounds. I simply told them, "I'm going to tear you a new asshole!" I then antagonized him into attacking me by saying some very uncomplimentary things about his family. He obliged and unfortunately for him, he lasted about 45 seconds. I did this to get their absolute attention and this served its purpose. Once I had their attention, I did what you told me to do."

General Leicester was beginning to enjoy the story and asked, "Exactly what did I tell you to tell them?"

Rafe answered, "With all due respect sir, you told me to tell them where the bear shit in the buckwheat."

General Leicester chuckled to himself and with a smile on his face said, "All right Hawkins, exactly what did you tell them?"

Rafe decided that his report was going well so he

continued, "I told them that they were now part of a group called the Leper Colony. That name was a reflection of their perceived status in the 1st Cavalry Division which was the equivalent of being lower than Whale Shit at the bottom of the ocean. I could tell from the expressions on their faces that, that didn't go over too well. I went on to say that a very bad situation can lead to opportunity because it was obvious that we couldn't sink any lower. The best course of action was to become like a Polaris Missile rocketing from the depths into the stratosphere. Amazingly, they all signed on.

The final thought I put to them was that everyone wants to be part of something great because greatness stays with a man. This was a chance to turn our lives around and become part of something great. In the end, the Leper Colony will be something you will be proud to be a part of."

General Leicester sat behind his desk smiling to himself. He didn't let it show on his face because he didn't want Rafe to know he was that approving of what he had accomplished. The General was well aware that before anything could happen where the development of the Leper Colony was concerned, then men had to be willing. The fact that Hawkins has got them all on board in less than 24 hours was very positive. Another thought entered the General's mind, "Colonel Gattis was right, Hawkins is a born leader, in fact, he reminds me of myself when I was the same age."

After thinking for a minute General Leicester said, "That was good work getting the men on the same page, but that was the easy part. What is your plan to whip them into a fighting unit? I suppose you have one?"

"Yes Sir, indeed I do. First, I'm going to run them into condition. We'll start with at least 10 miles a day, of course, it's a distinct possibility that they won't be able to do it from day one, but they'll work their way up to it. This is where I'll need your support. If you can arrange it, we'll need a place to set up camp somewhere out in the boondocks about ten miles from the Judo Pits. We'll live in the field six days a week, and every morning we'll make the ten-mile run from the camp to the Judo Pits for an hour of hand-to-hand combat training. I don't expect they'll be in any condition to put up much of a fight for the first weeks as they'll be exhausted from the run. If they can't fight, we'll just do some lite training such as how to break a fall when being thrown, and watching the instructors, demonstrating throws and holds. Over a period of weeks, they'll build up their stamina to where we can break up the sixteen lepers into eight pairs. Then they'll begin to really fight. Since I'll be the seventeenth and the odd man out, I'll match up with one of the instructors."

General Leicester looked at Rafe with a skeptical expression and asked, "You sure you want to tangle with those Judo instructors? They outweigh you by seventy or eighty pounds." Rafe looked straight at the General and said, "Yes Sir, I'm going to have to fight, as the Lepers will expect it, but don't worry; I won't hurt them."

"The third part of the Leper's training will be stealth. I'm going to train them to sneak into an enemy stronghold, wipe it out, and get away unseen. We'll start this training in the afternoons when we return from the Judo Training, the men will be completely exhausted from the twenty-mile round trip, however, the stealth training will initially be done at what could be called a very leisurely pace. Crawling around on one's belly does not require much energy. Finally, when we've achieved the required fitness, we'll take up weapons.

General Leicester shook his head and smiled and said, "Well all right, do it your way. Is there anything else you need?"

"I just need logistical support in moving the equipment and setting up the camp. I want the Lepers living in the field six days a week only coming in on Sunday. We'll live on C and K Rations most of the time, except I want the troops served two hot meals a week from a mobile field kitchen. I think that's about it for now. Once the camp is organized, I'm sure there will be other contingencies that will need to be addressed. This is something I've never been involved with before and setting up the base camp will be the most difficult so I'd rather have others who specialize in such things pitch the tents. The Leper Colony will be involved in more important things."

"That makes sense Sgt. Hawkins," General Leicester interjected. "We'll provide all the logistical support you need to get set up. From there we'll play it by ear until you're up and running. Get out there and continue what you're doing; during the next few days we'll set up a means of communication so you can report your progress."

Rafe asked, "Will that be all Sir?" The General rose from his chair behind his desk and said, "Yes, that will be all for now, Carry on."

Rafe got up came to attention, saluted, and said, Thank You, Sir"

Then it began. Slowly at first since the lepers were far from ready for the arduous training they would be subjected to. Rafe returned to the barracks and called out the Leper Colony. "OK, it begins now. We're moving out to the field. Pack the stuff you'll need for a week in the field and leave the rest in your duffle bags to be stored. You're going to get the luxury of riding out to our base camp in trucks so we can check out the route, but starting tomorrow you'll be either marching or running the ten miles from our camp to the judo pits every day of the week except Sunday, the Sabbath. You'll come back into these barracks one day a week. This isn't going to be fun and it isn't going to be easy, and you're going to hate my guts before this is over. However, in the end, the Leper Colony will be a force to be reckoned with. So, get ready to move out. You have an hour and a half till we move." Rafe wasn't going to waste time having the men set up a base camp, no matter how small, since the object was to turn them into a peerless strike force. First, they'd get fit, then they'd learn to fight like demons before they were taught to sneak up on their enemies and cut their throats, even if the enemy knew they were coming. Finally, they'd become proficient in the use of every conceivable weapon. Then we'll give them a final test.

The accommodations at the camp were livable since the focus was not on subjecting the lepers to the most spartan conditions, but on building up their physical stamina. They lived in eight-man tents and slept on portable army folding cots. Not the greatest, but a lot better than sleeping on the ground especially when it rained.

The first morning the Lepers were up at 0600 and by 0700 they had eaten a breakfast of Army Rations and were dressed for their first run to the Judo Pits about ten miles away. The uniform for the run was combat boots, red army shorts, tee-shirts, an Ammo belt with a canteen filled with salt water, a helmet liner with a steel pot, and each leper would be carrying an M1 Grand Rifle. The process was simple; run them to death. Of course, a caveat has to be added. The idea was not to run the lepers to death literally but to push them to their limits so as to make them feel they were a group of bad assed warriors. Once they accepted the idea that they were bad assed they would push themselves to the limit. That first day Rafe formed the lepers in a column of twos and set off on the ten-mile trek to the Judo Pits. First, they marched for 500 yards with rifles on their shoulders. Then they were ordered to port arms and they double-timed with their rifles across their chests for another 500 yards. Rafe had learned this method at OCS, doing dozens of Jark Marches. Eventually, the lepers would run ten miles and then fight for ten minutes, but the fight for ten minutes meant fighting like demons for ten minutes. They would fight with each other just like Rafe had fought with Captain Haldane.

As the lepers jogged along, they chanted various Candance songs like,
Got a letter in the mail Go to war or go to jail
Sat me in the barber's chair, spun me around I had no hair
Used to drive a Cadillac, now I pack it on my back
Used to drive a limousine, Now I'm wearing Army green
Dress it right and cover down
Forty inches all around
Nine to the front and six to the rear
That's the way we do it here
Used to date a beauty queen
Now I date my M-16
Ain't no use in looking down
Ain't no discharge on the ground
Ain't no use in going back
Jody's got your Cadillac
Ain't no use in going home
Jody's got your girl and gone
Ain't no use in feeling blue
Jody's got your sister too
Took away my faded jeans
Now I'm wearing Army greens
Took away my gin and rum
Now I'm up before the sun
Mama Mama can't you see
What the army's done for me
Mama Mama can't you see
This army life is killing me.

The Leper Colony was formed into three distinctive five-man squads. This was done at the order of their leader who was now operating under the nickname Crazy Horse which had been quickly bestowed on him by the lepers. The first squad was called the Cowboys and its five members were Sam Radle from Laredo, Texas, he was also known as Laredo for short. Next came Radle's counterpart Jackson Slade from Waco, Texas, known as Waco.

These two were your typical wild west cowboys of the Bronco, and bull-riding rodeo types. Generally, they acted like wild men in any endeavor. The third cowboy was Frank Holman from Mustang, Oklahoma. He was just as much a cowboy as the Texans he just wasn't as wild. You could say he contributed as moderating influence to his freewheeling Texas buddies. Naturally, his nickname was Oakie and because of his friendly nature was one of the most popular lepers. The fourth of this dynamic squad was Ken Settle from Purcellville, Virginia. He was from Virginia but not far from the border of West Virginia. His nickname was Country Boy and every inch of his six-foot-five-inch frame was a poster for the country way of living. However, Ken was a person of high intelligence and great common sense. He was the natural leader of the Cowboys. Last but not least was Robert Stewart from Lexington. Kentucky. Rob Stewart was the smallest of the lepers but arguably the best-looking. He was about 5'7" tall and bore an uncanny resemblance to the movie star James Dean. One might assume that his small stature and striking good looks might foster some bullying on the part of his counterparts however, this wasn't the case. If fact, he was treated more like a younger brother by his older and larger teammates. His nickname was Mouse.

The second squad quickly became known as "The Birdmen". The reason for this was that not unlike the Cowboys, three members of the squad were fanatic hunters of Geese and Ducks, or for that matter, anything else that moved. The three hunters were John H. Magruder, from Lentner, Missouri, Jerry Johnson from Bassett, Nebraska, and Robert I. Haglund of Bismarck, North Dakota. Those three were the core of the Birdmen to which could be added another fellow traveler in Bruce A. Smith of Fairbanks, Alaska. Bruce loved to hunt although he liked quarry, other than Canadian Geese. So, the Birdmen were all into hunting except the fifth member Kenneth Lingenfelter of East Freedom, Pennsylvania. It was puzzling as to how Lingenfelter got into the lepers, to begin with as he was a medic. You wouldn't think that a medic would have a rebellious nature, but Ken Lingenfelter was the exception. Like County Boy from the Cowboys, he had exceptionally good judgment and common sense. He quickly assumed the mantle of leadership. Lingenfelter being a medic was nicknamed Doc.And because of his good judgment was named squad leader.

The sobriquet of the third squad was The Falcons. Why the Falcons? Because Falcons are the swiftest of the birds of prey. You could easily cast the lepers into that mode, as Birds of Prey. Rafe assigned the leadership position to Tom Mulcahy of Brooklyn, New York. The reason was his intelligence and his ability to size up situations instantaneously; not unlike Rafe himself had been during the leadership course at OCS. Mulcahy was a street kid with enough ambition to attend CCNY (City College of New York) at night. Mulcahy was quickly saddled with the moniker, Hit Man. Where that tag originated is anybody's guess. A strong backup to Mulcahy was Richard B. Elliott of Chicago, Illinois. Elliott had been a student in Physics at the University of Chicago before dropping out for some unknown reason. Of course, he was called The Professor. He was joined by Frank Muscato from Niagara Falls, Ontario. A Canadian citizen serving in the U.S. Army to gain citizenship. His nickname was Canuck and was bilingual in English and French. Another French speaker was Henri Desormeaux from Thibodaux. Louisiana. His nickname was Gator. The fifth member of the third squad was John Clemmons of Los Angeles, California. John was probably the most unusual member of the leper colony in that he was a trust fund baby from an extremely wealthy family. He was drafted which didn't seem to bother him one bit. It could be that he was actually the perfect candidate for the lepers in that he definitely had something to prove. John felt that he was more than just another rich kid. The idea of proving himself in an elite unit was right up his alley. Clemmons nickname was McDuck, after the comic book character Scrooge McDuck.

The organization of the Leper Colony was simple. A leader (Rafe Hawkins) a second in command (Tim Spencer) and three squads of five men each. The first step was fitness and unit cohesion. Everything else would follow in good order. Rafe made it crystal clear that there would be no fighting between members of the leper colony. If you want to fight, you do it in the judo pits. Pair off and settle your differences. Fight outside the pits and you'd find yourself matched up against Crazy Horse and the outcome would not be good.

That's how it started. Jogging in a column of twos, ten miles up and ten miles back. In between an hour of hand-to-hand fighting in the Judo Pits.

There was no way they were going to make the ten miles non-stop, so every two miles Crazy Horse would call a halt and call out, "Take ten, smoke 'em if you got 'em" The lepers would sprawl out and have a smoke. Ten minutes later they'd be on the road again. At first, when they reached the Judo Pits, they'd be so exhausted they could hardly do anything except fall against each other. There would be no hand-to-hand fighting for the first few weeks.

The forming of the Leper Colony began in the middle of June. At that time the weather in Columbus, Georgia was hot and humid. It was not unusual for the temperature to be in the 90s, with humidity so high you could cut the air with a knife. Rafe had been through Military Police School at Fort Gordon, Georgia during the month of June two years previously, and was well aware of the debilitating effect of the hot humid heat.

Since the Lepers would be marching ten miles and then fighting for ten minutes, he decided to leave their base camp just after sunrise so the downward run to the Judo Pits would be done before the humid heat began to rise to unbearable levels. He also arranged for an army water truck to be stationed at the base camp so the lepers could be hosed off after their return runs from the Judo Pits. After running 20 miles in high heat and humidity the lepers would strip naked on returning to their base and be hosed down. The truck held 1500 gallons and soon became even more popular than the trucks that brought hot chow a couple of times a week. There's nothing like having your body covered with itchy sawdust from the Judo Pits for days at a time. Anyone experiencing 90-degree heat, high humidity, and a coating of sawdust would soon come to love the water truck. Rafe could have let the lepers suffer the effects of the conditions as the Army would take the attitude that it was "Good Training", however, Rafe wanted them focused on their training rather than discomfort. It was slow steady progress knowing that the lepers would need a certain degree of fitness before performing in hand-to-hand combat.

It took about four weeks before the lepers could run ten miles and fight for 10 minutes, but the intensity of the fighting increased as their level of fitness increased. The intensity of the fighting brought about the first crack in unit cohesion. One evening before they hit the sack Robert Stewart the smallest of the lepers and the one with the nickname Mouse asked to speak to

Rafe who was now called Crazy Horse by the lepers. Once he was seated on a footlocker in Rafe's tent Rafe asked him, "What's up Mouse?" The answer was swift and to the point. "Sir, what you just said is a big part of the problem."

"What exactly do you mean?'

"It's the nickname Mouse. It's sort of derogatory not like some of the other nicknames like Hit Man, Gator, Professor, or even your own, Crazy Horse. To me, it's like a putdown and I think the others like to beat up on me in the Judo Pits because of my size. It's a sort of bullying."

Rafe looked at a Mouse for a minute and then asked, "Do you like being a part of the Leper Colony?"

"I love being part of the Leper Colony. It's the most exciting thing I've ever been part of."

Rafe went on to say, "If you want to remain in the Leper Colony, I can tell you a few stories that may prove helpful. First, do you know where I came from to lead the lepers?"

Mouse shook his head in the negative and said, "Nope I haven't the foggiest."

"I came from Artillery OCS at Fort Sill, Oklahoma. When I resigned guess where I ranked among the cadets in my barracks a when I resigned?"

Mouse replied, "Knowing you, you were number one."

"Actually, I was, but when I started, I was number 41, and was considered to be Whale Shit by the other candidates. In the end, I ran by them like they were tied to a tree. I ended up being number one because they pissed me off. Anger made me number one."

Mouse just nodded as Rafe continued, "When I was growing up, I attended a private boarding school in the Hudson Valley of New York State. I was a rebellious student and that led to an incident. By misbehaving I got my 2nd-grade class kept after school for about 45 minutes on a beautiful Indian summer day. When I came out of the schoolhouse my classmates were waiting for me and roughed me up pretty well. After they left me in the dirt, I got up, dusted myself off, and made my way to the woods around the back of the dormitory. I found a big stick, filled my pockets with rocks, and then came out of the woods to re-engage my foolish classmates. When they saw me coming, showing no fear, they came running over to put the fear of God into me. To put it crudely I had to tear them a new asshole. In seconds they went screaming in terror. That night I was severely paddled on my bare ass with a ping pong paddle. However, during my next nine years at that school, I never had another fight. Other students wouldn't take the chance that I might get a baseball bat and do them serious injury. When I left the school at sixteen years of age, I was 5' tall and weighed 100 pounds, yet no one dared fight me."

Mouse had a small smile on his face as Rafe continued. "When I arrived at Supreme Headquarters in Paris, France I needed two recommendations to get into OCS, my boss the Supreme Allied Commander, and my Company Commander. My Company Commander, Captain Haldane was a sixth-degree blackbelt holder and was an aficionado in the arena of martial arts. He was greatly pleased when I volunteered to become his sparring partner, In the course of events, I was taking a tremendous beating from the captain who not only had the expertise but outweighed me by about 60 pounds. The captain admired my fortitude but wondered how much punishment I could take. From that perspective, he offered me some advice, "Hawkins if you want to hold me at bay, attack me as if your life depends on it."

"I followed his advice and as it turned out I was faster and in better shape than the captain, and when I threw everything into the fight, I could hold my own."

"There's one other point I'd like to put forth. I'm sure you're aware that in the wild, predators always attack the young and the weak. Why do you suppose they do that?"

Mouse thought about it for a minute and then said, "Because they're easy pickings?"

Crazy Horse answered, "Partly, but more specifically it has more to do with self-preservation. Any mature healthy animal might get in a lucky kick or a quick stab with a horn. Remember out on the veldt there are no veterinarians. If a predator can't run or hunt it dies, especially if it is a lone hunter. Why take the chance when you can attack the weak? It's not just wild animals that adopt these methods, human predators use them also. Muggers attack those who are not aware of their surroundings, those who travel alone, or those who walk in darkened areas. So, Mouse, if you want to be known as Mighty Mouse, become a wildcat in a fight. Even if you're pretending. Most can't tell the real thing from a put-on. Basically, the predator always looks for easy prey. Make sure you look and act like their worst nightmare. Do you think you can do that?"

Mouse answered, "I'm not sure, but I'll give it a try. Being called Mighty Mouse is a hell of a lot better than just Mouse."

Rafe said, "Ok Mighty Mouse make your plan operational the next time you hit the Judo Pits."

Mouse got up and as he left the tent said, Thank you, sir! I think I'll do a lot better now."

It didn't take long for Mouse's new attitude to reveal itself. The following day in the Judo Pits, Mouse was matched up with Laredo, one of his squad mates. Right from the beginning Mouse tore into Laredo as if he wanted to tear his head off. Rafe was nearby watching and after two minutes into the ten-minute skirmish he heard Laredo mutter, "What the fuck!!" A few minutes later Laredo exclaimed, "Jesus, Mouse, what's gotten into you?"

Mouse never answered, he just kept attacking like a demon. For the rest of the week, no matter whom Mouse was matched up with the result was the same. His fellow lepers were taken aback. Where did this new mouse come from? Early the next week while talking with Triple B, also known as the Big Black Bull, Rafe suggested, "The next time you have the lepers in a group call out to Stewart, but instead of calling him by his nickname Mouse call him Mighty Mouse. In fact, do it a few times the same day."

Triple B asked, "What's the purpose of that?"

Rafe answered, "Just say it's a little experiment in unit cohesion."

Triple B did as asked and by the end of the following week, the entire Leper Colony was calling Mouse by his new nickname, Mighty Mouse. And they really meant it as they now saw Robert Stewart as Mighty Mouse. Little by little the Leper Colony was achieving a very high level of fitness. The fitter they became the higher their Esprit de Corp. They were beginning to believe they were badass mothers, and they were beginning to act like it.

Mornings were reserved for running the ten miles and fighting for ten minutes in the Judo Pits. Not just fighting, but fighting like demons. Following the ten-minute fight, the instructors would demonstrate new holds and throws. By noon the lepers were back at the base camp being hosed down before chow. Afternoons were spent primarily creeping around in the bush learning to move like serpents, silent but deadly. After weeks of practice and instruction, the lepers could sneak up on anyone and cut their throats.

When not practicing the art of deception the lepers were down at the rifle range becoming experts in all matters of weapons. Two weapons Crazy Horse insisted that the lepers become proficient in their use, were Claymore Mines and the Laws Rocket. Why he wanted this done was a mystery to everyone including General Leicester. However, the General had promised Crazy Horse logistical support and since the Leper Colony was performing at such a high level the general let him have his way.

After about ninety days of intense training. during which they were pushed to their limits, the Lepers were ready for a final test. General Leicester called Crazy Horse into his office and briefed him as to how the Lepers would be put to the test. General Leicester said, "We're going to have a series of maneuvers in which each regiment of the division will track down and corner a group of insurgents and wipe them out. Your Lepers will be the adversaries to each of the three regiments and I expect you to lead them on a merry chase. All of this will take place in an area of ten square miles which will be large enough, but not too large to contain the exercise. The exercise will be monitored by observers acting in the dual capacity as umpires to ensure all participants follow the rules. Do you have any questions about how this will be carried out?"

Crazy Horse responded immediately with, "I have quite a few questions, but foremost is can I take an airborne tour by chopper of the ten square mile area in which the exercise will be conducted? To sort of get the lay of the land?"

General Leicester tapped his pencil on his desk, scratched his chin, and then responded, "Why do you think it's necessary to take an airborne tour of the area? What is your intention?"

"General, I look at it like this. If this were Viet Nam, we as the insurgents would have the advantage of knowing the lay of the land. That would be our advantage. The invading force, in this case, the First Cavalry, would be at a disadvantage. I just think we should make the exercise as realistic as possible.

The General responded with, "Ok that's reasonable enough. Get yourself down to Lawson Field by 0800 tomorrow morning and I'll have Huey waiting to give you the tour. It shouldn't take too long. Then the next day we'll send two duce and a half's down to pick up the Leper Colony and take you to the area to be contested. You can take them on a day-long patrol to survey the scene, so to speak"

"That's just the sort of thing I had in mind, that should do the trick."

At 0800 the next morning Crazy Horse and the three squad leaders Country Boy Settle, Doc Linginfelter, and Hit Man Mulcahy boarded a Huey and took a forty-five-minute tour of the five-square mile area soon to be contested. That evening just after dark the Leper Colony held a meeting around the campfire to be briefed on the up-and-coming maneuvers.

Crazy Horse had everyone's attention when he told them, "Gentlemen, and I use that term loosely, we've come a long way in the last 100 days. Now that we're well trained and fit, it's time to show our detractors where the bear shit in the buckwheat!" That brought out some friendly pushing and shoving with some laughter and guffaws. Gator yelled out, "How are we going to do that Sir?"

"It won't be as hard as you may think if we perform the way we have been trained to perform. If you think back to how the Leper Colony came into being, you'll remember we're here because we can think for ourselves, or put another way, we can think outside the box. The Army is organized to operate within certain parameters. This exercise is organized to be conducted as a search and destroy mission. The Regiments will conduct the mission exactly like we would expect them to. However, we won't follow their lead. We'll operate outside the box and deliver a nasty surprise.

John Magruder, nicknamed Goose, piped up with "What can 17 of us do against a regimental force of 2,500 men?" It was a good question and Crazy Horse had the logical answer. He replied, "We're going to ambush them by using the Cowboys to lure them into a wild goose chase while the rest of us are dug into spider holes around the perimeter of the landing zone which will contain their regimental headquarters. Then at a time of our choosing, we'll emerge and wipe out their command post. All hell will be raised because the regimental commanders are going to lose face, big time.

They'll accuse us of cheating and disobeying the rules of engagement. However, the key to our attack will not be to win the approval of anyone other than our own chain of command and that is General Leicester. We are bound to receive a lot of criticism because the leaders of the 1st regiment are going to lose face. Hopefully, they'll learn from their mistakes and when they get into the real thing, they'll pay more attention to security.

"With this in mind, tomorrow we'll move out to the selected landing zone and prepare our spider holes. We've received hours of training over the last three months from the Army's top experts in cover and camouflage and now we'll put it to the test. Make no mistake, our reputation will be at stake. When we succeed, General Leicester will begin to see us as a force to be reckoned with. Everything else we'll just have to put up with. It's not going to matter what the rest of the command structure of the 1st Cavalry Division thinks of us as long as General Leicester holds us in high regard."

The following morning the Leper Colony was out early, at the landing zone Crazy Horse had selected as the one most likely for the 1st Regiment to assault. Before they ventured out to the landing zone Crazy Horse had asked General Leicester to provide the Lepers with camouflage netting. Exactly what he intended to do with it was questionable. Chargin' Charlie asked, "What do you need the camouflage netting for? I thought you were going to be footloose and speedy leading the 1st regiment on a wild chase. I wouldn't expect you to be carrying something as heavy and bulky as camouflage netting." Chargin' Charlie noticed the slight smile on Crazy Horse's face before he answered, "Well maybe we won't be carrying it that far."

"Ok, I'll have it delivered to the largest of the two landing zones by truck by midday tomorrow." After Crazy Horse left the General was sitting at his desk thinking, "I have a sneaking suspicion that Crazy Horse is planning an ambush of the 1st Regiment. I think he has it in his mind to cut off the head of the snake. What audacity! This is turning out better than I thought. They actually are turning out to be an elite strike force as I first envisioned." Chargin' Charlie began to laugh. "This is developing into something I have to observe. I'm going to land with the first elements of the 1st Regiment and see for myself how this plays out."

Early the following morning the Leper Colony was out at the landing zone surveying the scene. Crazy Horse had the lepers form a circle close to the tree line on the North West side of the Landing area. He stood in the center of the circle and addressed the group. "Listen Up men this is important. We've been training together now for over three months. We've made great progress, and now comes the final test. This is the straight poop on what's going to take place over the next six days. The First Cavalry Division has three infantry regiments, each of these regiments will land on this landing zone and pursue a group of insurgents with the intent of surrounding them and wiping them off planet Earth. Each regiment will have 48 hours to accomplish this mission. We, lepers, will act as the insurgents." That brought about a murmur of approval from the troops. Crazy Horse went on, "The object of these maneuvers is to give the three infantry regiments some, what we could call, on-the-job training in tracking and eliminating an insurgent force. With that in mind when the 1st of the three regiments lands the Cowboys will reveal their presence and then proceed to lead them on a merry chase into the boondocks. My guess is that our adversaries will pursue the Cowboys with a certain reckless abandon. It won't be any concern for us as long as the enemy is led away from the landing zone. Their overconfident pursuit will prove to be their undoing. At this point, Hit Man from the Falcons asked, "Sir how can the 17 of us make a dent when opposing 2,500 men?"

"That's a good question Hit Man, and the answer is simple. If the Cowboys can lead the regiment on a wild goose chase, the rest of us will conceal ourselves right on the periphery of the landing zone under camouflage netting and natural foliage; then at the optimum time, we'll emerge and wipe out their headquarters. That's right, we'll be concealed right at the edge of the landing zone where they least expect us, then we'll use stealth and cunning to wipe them out. Not only that, but we'll do it in front of General Leicester and then make our escape into the forest. How does that sound."

Canuck from the Birds of Prey chimed in with, "Fuckin' A. We'll nail them to the wall." The rest of the Lepers roared their approval.

Crazy Horse went on, "We're going to use their unimaginative approach against them. They have no idea who we are. They don't know that we're a bunch of rebels drafted into the Leper Colony because we think outside the box, so to their everlasting regret, we're going to give them an object lesson they won't soon forget.

After Doc Lingenfelter added his, "Right On!" Crazy Horse continued, "Triple B and I will remain together digging a shallow trench to conceal ourselves, and covering it with camouflage netting, leaves, pine needles, etc. The Falcons and the Birdmen will do the same, digging a slight depression for a group of five, only about two feet deep. The two squads will dig in, in close proximity to each other, while Triple B and myself will be some distance away. After dark Triple B and I will emerge from hiding and reconnoiter the area checking for posted sentries and the location of the command tent. Then the fun begins! We'll come and alert you that it's time to attack. Once you emerge from your camouflage, we'll approach the command center knowing in advance if they have sentries posted nearby, or not. The Falcons will circle the tent to the left and the Birdmen from the right. All of this has to be predetermined as we can't gather around for a briefing once we come out of cover. If there is a sentry at the front of the command tent the Birdmen circling from the right will expose themselves getting the sentry or sentries to turn in their direction while the Falcons circling around the tent from the left side take them from behind. Then Triple B and I will each take one of the tent flaps and pull them back allowing the two squads to enter with silenced pistols drawn. When entering, the Falcons will continue to the left while the Birdmen move to the right. You're going to have to know which direction to take in order not to run into each other. Surprise is of the essence. Five seconds after entering the tent I will give the order to open fire. Each of you will fire your first eight-round clip. With twelve of us present that will give us a total of 96 rounds to take out whoever is present. Since this is only a simulation each of us will say in a normal tone of voice, Bang, Bang, Bang, eight times as if we're playing a game of guns as we did as kids. Following this, I'll say, "You're all dead."

"At this point, you'll all file back out and create a low profile up against the side of the tent until you regain your night vision. I'll remain inside for a minute and have a very short conversation with General Leicester following which I'll come out and lead you into the forest where we'll disappear.

"We've trained for 100 days and we are a unit that can be called Silent but Deadly. Those attributes are the same which will prove to General Leicester that we are indeed a force to be reckoned with. We're going to step on some toes. Not everyone is going to view our actions in a positive light. In fact, some are going to lose face, big time. However, we work for General Leicester and only care about how he evaluates our actions.

That was a plan which depended on the leaders of the 1st Regiment to view the exercise as one of strict training and nothing like real combat. They would therefore be unlikely to provide serious security for their headquarters. If Crazy Horse was right, they'd end up screwed. It would also prove to be a good object lesson.

The remainder of the day was spent preparing their camouflaged hideouts. They were so good that a person could walk right up on them and not see a thing. The Cowboys scouted the trails they would use to lead the infantry away from the landing zone. Once the preparations were complete the Lepers returned to their barracks on base to await the big events.

The following day the Leper Colony was in place at the landing zone at 0400 awaiting the air assault. Shortly after 0800, the thumping rhythm of helicopter engines could be heard and the first wave of the airborne assault began. The Hunters and the Birds of Prey went to ground and so did Crazy Horse and Triple B. Crazy Horse had a small periscope made that allowed him to watch the deployment of the regiment while being completely concealed. Even if it was right at your feet, it would be almost impossible to see the periscope sticking up. The Cowboys remained in the open actually demonstrating to attract the attention of the first units to land. Once they were certain they had been seen, they disappeared by hightailing it down a preselected trail into the forest.

The Leper Colony had trained for months to freeze in place for hours and to move silently as predators on the prowl. They had developed into a force both silent and deadly. Now they were ready to prove it.

It was fall, and it was dark by 1800. Shortly after 1900 Crazy Horse and Triple B arrived to rouse the lepers from their concealment. Crazy Horse had already scouted the area around the Command Tent and to his surprise detected no sentries anywhere close by. He advised the squad leaders Hit Man and Doc Lingenfelter that they would not, go creeping across the 150 yards between their places of concealment and their objective, but form into a column of twos and march right up to the command tent. In the dark, any observer wouldn't be able to distinguish them from regular troopers from the 1st Regiment. However, if they were observed crawling through the grass there would be no doubt as to their intent.

When approaching their objective, the falcons circled around the tent from the left while the birdmen circled to the right.Crazy Horse and Triple B pulled back the tent flap and the lepers marched in with their silenced pistols drawn within seconds, while the assembled staff gawked in shock, they simulated opening fire with each leper saying bang, bang, bang, eight times. In all 96 rounds would have been fired from silenced weapons killing all of the occupants of the headquarters tent. Only one exclamation was heard, a very loud, "What the fuck is this?" coming from Colonel Stevens the Regimental Commander.

Rafe answered, "This is an ambush by the insurgent force and you're all dead." The shock effect was incredible with no one knowing how to react. Of course, there was an empire on hand, and so was General Leicester. Colonel Stevens started to argue that this was outside the rules of engagement, but he was quickly overruled by General Leicester. Everyone then started yelling and while this was going on Crazy Horse made his way over to General Leicester and whispered to him, "This was for you General. To show what we're capable of delivering under simulated combat conditions. We'll make our way out of here now, and disappear into the forest as if we had really attacked and wiped out the regimental headquarters and got away unscathed, Tomorrow we'll come in and surrender and give the regiment the real training this is all about. Do I have your permission to carry on?"

General Leicester nodded and said, "Carry on Hawkins."

Crazy Horse left the tent formed the lepers into a column of twos and marched them across the landing zone about 100 yards into the forest. Anyone seeing this movement in the dark, unlit confines of the open area, would just assume they were a unit being marched to their rendezvous point and not a group of insurgents that had just wiped out, regimental headquarters. Upon reaching the tree line they disappeared into the forest and weren't seen again until the next day. The annihilation of regimental headquarters had taken less than fifteen minutes and had been completely successful.

Inside the headquarters tent, the regimental commander was raising hell about the events that had just transpired. His basic complaint was that the lepers were operating outside the rules of engagement and the whole operation was bogus. The Colonel continued with his harangue until interrupted by General Leicester who said, "Calm down Colonel. Let's put everything into perspective. In case you're not aware of it the assault on regimental headquarters was not done to make anyone look bad. In fact, it was done for my benefit. As you may well know the Leper Colony is my creation and they answer directly to me. The little performance they put on tonight was strictly for my benefit. They are striving to convince me that they are developing into a force to be reckoned with, and tonight they went a long way towards convincing me that is indeed the case. My advice is to take this ambush as a learning experience so that when you get into the real thing you won't get wiped out."

The Lepers made a rendezvous at a preselected location the following morning. Once together they began an unconcealed march back to the landing zone. Along the way, they were ambushed and wiped out by one of the first regiment's battalions. Of course, being wiped out was strictly in a figurative sense. Crazy Horse was allowing the Leper Colony to be ambushed to provide the rest of the Division a chance to save face and to allow the maneuvers to provide the training they needed in counter-insurgency. If he had wanted the Leper Colony to move through the 1st Regiments lines that could have been accomplished with relative ease.Crazy Horse wasn't that concerned about how things looked in the field knowing that when the maneuvers concluded he would report to General Leicester and give him a clear view of what the Leper Colony was out to accomplish.

In the end, there was just one problem, and Rafe had to admit that it was one of his own makings. In fact, it was typical of Rafe's line of thought. As far as he was concerned the Leper Colony was exactly where he wanted it to be. He had no doubt that General Leicester would agree, but there was one more test to pass. In life, there's a lot to be said about having the right attitude. Rafe had learned from Captain Haldane the importance of fighting like your life depends on it. He had passed this on to Robert Stewart, at the time saddled with the moniker of Mouse, but soon to be reclassified as Mighty Mouse. He thought back to being a six-year-old at Greer School when the other 2nd graders had jumped him after school. He straightened them out by attacking the group with unparalleled ferocity. After that, while he remained at Greer School, he never had to fight again. The final test for the Lepers was to develop a group identity where confidence was concerned.

It wasn't going to be too difficult to accomplish since they were trained to run ten miles and fight for ten minutes. It wasn't just to fight for ten minutes but to fight like demons for ten minutes. To test the Lepers the only thing required was a target. That wasn't particularly hard to locate as the Recon Company had a favorite hangout in Columbus called the Hanger Club. They were a little touchy about outside groups invading their territory, especially other military outfits.

The mission was simple. Take the Leper Colony on an outing to the Hanger Club and when the Recon Outfit challenged them, show them where the bear shit in the buckwheat. Or, put in more polite terminology, kick their butts.

That Friday when the maneuvers ended the Lepers returned to their barracks. No more living in the field. Once settled into the barracks Crazy Horse arrived to have a talk with the assembled group. He was direct as usual. He said, "Men, you've come a long way in the last three months. I'm very proud of you. However, although we are almost there, we still have one last step before we emerge as a force to be reckoned with. Before we get there, I think we should celebrate our return from the boondocks by heading down to Columbus tomorrow for a night of celebration. Sort of let off a little steam; What do you think?"

The Lepers looking for a little entertainment after 100 days in the field murmured their approval. Hitman piped up with a question, "Where are we going to have some fun?"

Crazy Horse answered, "I heard the Hanger Club might be the right place."

Hitman answered, "Isn't that where the Recon Company hangs out? Rumor has it they don't like other outfits encroaching on their territory."

"Well gents I have only one thing to say about that; if they try to kick us out, they'd be barking up the wrong tree!" "Am I right?"

The Lepers enthusiastically roared, "Hell Yes!"

Crazy Horse then said, "OK it's settled then, tomorrow we head down to the Hanger Club. Meet me here at 1800 hours and the uniform is civies.If anyone raises an objection to our entry into the Hanger Club, in the words of Chargin' Charlie, we'll show them where the bear shit in the buckwheat" Another shouted approval settled the issue.

The following evening at 1800 the Leper Colony gathered in the barracks ready to go downtown and blow off a little steam. They hadn't been off base for almost three months and were ready for a little diversion. They took a bus into town and then six cabs to the Hanger Club. They met in the parking lot where Crazy Horse had a few final words before the fun began. "Listen up! We're going to go in there and see what happens. If the Recon boys want to be friendly, we'll be buddy-buddy, but if on the other hand, they want to dispute our right to be there then all hell will break loose.Keep your eyes on me because if trouble starts, I'll be the one to initialize it. Then join in, and fight like your life depends on it. Just one thing, don't kill anyone." The don't kill anyone comment, brought about a series of guffaws from the Lepers.

With that said, Crazy Horse told the Lepers to give him a minute and walked over to Mighty Mouse and said, "Wait at the door and when the fighting starts call this number and tell the Desk Sergeant at the base Military Police Station you are the manager of the Hanger Club and that a riot involving about 50 troopers had broken out, and to respond in force before they destroy your establishment. Then hang up and join in the mayhem."

The Lepers filed into the Hanger Club as if they owned the place. Standing at the bar was Master Sergeant Sapp, who as far as Rafe was concerned, was appropriately named. The Lepers filed in and spread out so that when they attacked it wouldn't come in a single file, but more like a human tsunami.Rafe greeted Sergeant Sapp with, "Evening Master Sergeant, how's it going?" Sergeant Sapp rudely replied, "What are you doing here?"

"Well, we've been restricted to the base for three months and we thought we'd go out and be a little sociable."

"I'm afraid you've picked the wrong venue for sociability. In fact, you picked the wrong place in all of Columbus for socializing," said Sapp.

Rafe asked, "Why would that be Master Sergeant?

"Because we consider the Hanger Club to be our private hangout and outsiders like you are not welcome."

"That's interesting Sergeant Sapp, have you ever heard of the Bill of Rights? I hate to say it, but assholes like you don't tell the Leper Colony where it can go unless, of course, you're able to throw us out." At this point, the leader of the Recon outfit got up on his high horse and countered with, "From the look of you that wouldn't be too much of a problem. Rafe was almost laughing when he replied, "I hate to tell you this Sapp, but one of the first things they teach you in grade school is Never Judge a Book by Its Cover! However, some people never learn it primarily because they suffer from a malady called, Shit for Brains."

Sapp snapped, "Are you suggesting I have shit for brains?"

"More than that, I'm saying your parents are shit-eating dogs." Rafe was expecting Sapp to respond by throwing a right cross to his jaw, and he was right, it was forthcoming immediately. Rafe easily slipped the punch and countered with a short straight right to the tip of Sapp's Jaw knocking the tall NCO flat on his back. The old adage should have rung true, in his mind, if he was capable of thinking clearly, "Never Judge a Book by its Cover!" Rafe Hawkins looked like a middleweight, but he punched like a heavyweight, and, Sergeant Sapp found himself sitting on his ass while his brain was in LaLa land. He wasn't out cold, but he wasn't far from it.

When the Lepers saw Rafe throw the punch they erupted toward the Recon Troopers. Trained to run ten miles and fight for ten minutes, like demons, the Lepers tore into the Recon Company like a force-five tornado. Mayhem ensued! The Lepers were ready to fight from the moment they walked into the Hanger Club while the Recon Company was totally unaware, and they never had a chance. It was a colossal brawl. Rafe had a chair broken over his back which knocked him to his knees. While attempting to get up he was hit in the eye from the left side, a blow sure to cause a black eye. Unfortunately for the Recon troopers, they weren't as highly trained as the Lepers, and only the timely arrival of dozens of MPs saved them from total annihilation.

That's the way Rafe had it planned. Let the fight last five minutes then have the military police intervene before anyone got severely injured. It worked perfectly with the MP's arresting and transporting those of the Recon Company, unfortunate enough to be present, to the Fort Benning Stockade. Of Course, the entire Leper Colony was also arrested and was sent along with them to be placed in a separate holding area.

Rafe knew that the following morning there would be a reckoning with the General and that there was no avoiding it. He hoped that he could convince the General as to the necessity of this act against what the military would call Good Order and Discipline.

Sure enough, at about 0830 the following morning, the Officer in charge of the stockade had a pair of MPs bring Rafe to his Office. The conversation was short and sweet. "General Leicester has ordered you brought to his office immediately, and from his tone of voice, he's far from pleased. If I was you, I'd be prepared for a real ass-kicking." Rafe had been expecting this, the only question was how would the meeting go. Since the whole exercise was carefully planned Rafe had an explanation already planned.

He walked in and reported, standing at attention in front of the General's desk. One look at Chargin' Charlie told Rafe the general was not in any mood for bullshit. The General stared at him for about 30 seconds to ensure Rafe was well aware of the gravity of the situation. Finally, the General spoke. "All right Hawkins. What in the Hell is going on?"

"Well sir, to start I want to apologize for the course of action I ordered!"

"That's what I thought. This whole shitstorm was organized. Why in hell after your great showing during the exercises, did you have to order this clusterfuck? What was the purpose?"

"In order to make my point I have to tell you a story. Have you ever heard of the story called, The 51st Dragon?"

General shook his head in the negative and answered, "Can't say I've ever heard of it."

Rafe began like this, "In medieval Britain during the age of dragons there existed a school for knights. In this particular year, a young knight named Gwaine Le Coeur-Hardy was entered into the school for dragon slayers. Unfortunately, he lacked spirit. Although he possessed enormous strength, speed, and grace he was basically a coward. As the months went by it was determined that the best course of action was to expel the young man. However, the headmaster had a solution. He called the young knight into his office and told him that there was a secret to dragon slaying. The secret was a magic word that once spoken before combat make the knight invulnerable to the dragon's fire. The magic word was RUMPLESNITZ.

The knight graduated and went out into the field to slay dragons. Much to everyone's surprise, he became the greatest dragon slayer of all time. Everything was fine until he faced his 50th dragon. He encountered this 50th dragon after a late night of drinking but approached it with his usual detachment. He just had one big problem. His alcohol-addled brain couldn't recall the magic word. Sir Gwaine and the Dragon engaged in a conversation during which the dragon tried to lure the knight into a false sense of security. Suddenly the dragon charged and as he was nearly onto the terrified knight when Sir Gwaine remembered the magic word. However, he didn't have time to say it. In desperation, he swung his battle ax and with one mighty blow decapitated the dragon.

Sir Gwaine despite being the slayer of a world record fifty dragons was unsettled by the loss of the magic word. He traveled back to the school for knights and found the headmaster and asked him why he was able to slay the dragon number 50 without the use of the magic word. The headmaster explained that the magic word was not magic at all and he had just given it to Sir Gwaine to instill confidence. He went on to explain that he didn't need a magic word to kill dragons. This explanation didn't really satisfy the young knight, but what could he do? After a short leave, he headed back to the field to continue his mission to slay dragons. The following day a dragon was reported on the far side of the ridgeline making a nuisance by eating the livestock. Sir Gwaine was dispatched to take care of the rampaging dragon and was never seen again. They found his shield and battle ax, but not much else. Apparently, Sir Gwaine had been eaten by the 51st Dragon."

Rafe looked over at the General and said, "You might ask what's the moral of the story, and different people might come to different conclusions, However, I believe the moral is that you're only as bad as you think you are. Yesterday in the Hanger Club the lepers showed who they are. Not to you and I General, but to themselves. They think they're a force to be reckoned with, and if anyone wants to throw them out of a place they had better be prepared to fight."

The General didn't answer at first, he just sat contemplating what Rafe had just said. He finally said, "Is that all?" Rafe replied, "Just one more thing. You tasked me with producing a first-class fighting unit and I think I've achieved that end!"

General Leicester sat contemplating what he'd just been shown. Finally, a slight smile began to appear on his lips. He was thinking to himself, "We should never have let him resign from OCS. Like Colonel Gattis told me, he could have been a general. In fact, I'm beginning to think he's just like me."

When General Leicester finally spoke, he said, "All right Hawkins I get your point. However, since I'm your commanding officer and since you all but destroyed all concepts of good order and discipline, there has to be a price. Do you understand what I'm saying?"

Rafe replied, "Yes Sir I understand completely"

"Good, then that makes things easier. This is what we'll do, The Leper Colony, as a group, will accept Article 15 and plead guilty, throwing themselves on the mercy of the commanding officer, which happens to be me. I'll fine each of you a month's pay and restrict you to the base for a month. After a short pause, the General added, "Don't worry too much about the restriction as we'll be moving out in less than thirty days. Keep that under your hat as it's for your ears only. I'm only telling you so that you can get the lepers ready for an overseas deployment. If you can do it in a subtle way, I want you to let your men know that I'm feeling good about the progress they've made during the last three months. With that being said, is there anything else you'd like to bring up?"

"Just one thing General. I'd like to equip each member of the Leper Colony with a Laws Rocket. I'd also like the training in the use of the Laws Rocket to be completed during the next two weeks."

The General looked at Crazy Horse as if he was actually crazy. After a minute he said, "Hawkins are you out of your mind? What in the hell do you intend to use the Laws Racket on? Do you think we'll be encountering Armor over there?"

"Sir I just have a deep feeling in my gut that we will have an important use for the rockets, so now is the time to get equipped. Not only equipped but trained."

General Leicester sat behind his desk tapping his pencil as was his unconscious habit. He was thinking, "This kid is nothing short of unbelievable so, in view of what he's accomplished in so short a period of time, I'm going to humor him and let him have the Laws Rockets. What he needs with 17 one-man bazookas is beyond me, however, I'll let that be his reward." After a minute the general finally said, "Ok Hawkins have it your way. I'll authorize the rockets and arrange for the training. Do you have anything else for me?" Rafe answered, "No Sir"

"All right, we're about done here. Go down to the stockade and pick up your men. I'll call the commander and have them released to your custody. You're dismissed."

Rafe saluted, did an about-face, and left. Rafe was elated, the general had accepted the Lepers as his own. The punishment was nothing more than a slap on the wrist. Once he had retrieved the lepers from the stockade and marched them to the barracks, they gathered in the squad bay for a briefing.

Rafe began with, "I suppose you want to know how my meeting with Chargin' Charlie went?" They responded with a murmur of assent. The truth is they were more than a little interested. "I'll give you the bad news first. We are all going to take Article 15, which by now all of you are familiar with. We submit to the General's judgment which will be forfeiture of one month's pay and restriction to the base for one month."

This brought forth cries and moans of protest. Rafe interjected, "Guys it could have been a lot worse. It's only because the General thinks we've come a long way in developing into a force to be reckoned with that we got off so lightly. We are not only becoming a force to be reckoned with, but we are his. That's the key. To be sure the General was behind us 100%, I asked him to equip each of us with an M72 Laws Rocket. Normally there's no way the army would allow that sort of expenditure, but the General did. It was our reward from the General. We'd have never gotten it if wasn't pleased with our development."

Hitman piped up with, "Sir, what in hell's name do we need with 17 Laws Rockets?" Crazy Horse responded with, "Good question Hitman, and this is the answer. I have a sneaking suspicion that we're going to need them when we get into the real deal. Secondly, I wanted to see if General Leicester would authorize their use. The only reason he agreed to issue them to the Leper Colony was as a reward for what we've accomplished. If we get into the right situation they'll come in very handy. Just one final thought before we end this meeting. Get your affairs in order. We should be shipping out soon."

Three weeks later a regiment of the 1st Cavalry Division Airmobile was leaving Fort Benning by train bound for Jacksonville, Florida to board the transport carrier U.S.S. Boxer; destination Qui Non, Republic of South Viet Nam. The Leper Colony was part of this movement. The U.S.S. Boxer was an 888-foot, Essex class carrier displacing 27,100 tons, commissioned on 16 April 1945, a little too late to see action in World War II. However, she was ideal for transporting hundreds of Helicopters and thousands of troops to Viet Nam.

While in transit, every waking hour found the Lepers training. There was PT twice a day so they didn't lose their hard-earned fitness. They trained on taking apart and reassembling their weapons blindfolded, directing and adjusting artillery fire as well as calling in gunships and airstrikes. Further training was in map reading and radio communications and the enemy and his weapons. All things considered, the twenty-three-day cruise to Viet Nam wasn't as bad as was anticipated, although their quarters were cramped with the men sleeping in hammocks, the Navy chow wasn't half bad.

On the 23rd day, the Boxer dropped anchor in Qui Nhon. They had plenty of company as the harbor was filled with every conceivable type of naval vessel. After three weeks at sea, the Leper Colony was ready to put down on dry land even if it was rumored to be inhospitable. However, sometimes you have to be careful about what you wish for. Crazy Horse always believed the Army was in the habit of choosing the most miserable places for its bases.

Into the Valley

Three Uh-1H helicopters lifted off the deck of the U.S. S. Boxer destination An Khe, Republic of Viet Nam some 41 miles distant. The choppers flew at an altitude of 2,000 feet to avoid ground fire. From that altitude, Viet Nam was a wonderful sight with gleaming rice paddies displaying every hue of green, and beautiful mountains covered with thick rain forests. It was quite an inviting vista, however, Crazy Horse, who was a student of military history, was thinking about how the Marines had first viewed the island of Guadalcanal when seeing it from offshore. From there it looked like a luxuriant tropical paradise yet when upon landing it turned out to be a malarial hellhole. The author Jack London said, "He doubted his heart was cold enough to banish his worst enemies to a place so dire, where the air is saturated with a poison that bites into every pore, and that many strong men who escape dying there, return as wrecks to their own countries." This observation was made despite the fact that Guadalcanal looked like a paradise from a few miles offshore.

Within a few minutes of landing, the Leper Colony realized Viet Nam was no paradise. In fact, the beautiful flight now seemed like a sick joke. Viet Nam, and in particular An Khe, was the hottest, ugliest, filthiest, and most unmerciful place on earth. The lepers quickly learned that An Khe was no base. Instead, it was a squalid concentration camp surrounded by guard towers and barbed wire. The base was still under construction and as each battalion arrived, they were put to work hacking down the undergrowth to enlarge the landing zone. It was hot, miserable, back-breaking work. If there was a ray of sunshine for the leper colony it came in the form of an order from General Leicester that they were not to take part in the ground clearing for the base. Instead, the leper colony was to start patrolling, immediately.

After clearing a location for their tents which only took 24 hours the lepers prepared for patrol. Crazy Horse had always been a keen observer of animals. One group he found most interesting was cats. He had observed that when you first let a cat venture out from a new home, something unusual occurs. When first allowed outdoors a cat will carefully move about ten or fifteen feet from the door. It will check out everything within that distance. It then returns to the entrance to ensure it can get back in. The next time the cat goes out it extends its circle of exploration. After several days of this exploration, the cat knows the way home and can come flying back at full speed if endangered. This is the method Crazy Horse followed when leading the Leper Colony on patrol. Venture a few hundred yards outside the base perimeter and then do a complete circle of the base. Each day the distance outside the perimeter was extended.

During their patrols, the lepers observed everything that walked, flew, or crawled. They mastered the environment, and terrain to where they could remain silently concealed for hours on end. They were being trained to move through the jungle, like serpents; silent but deadly. They learned to set up ambushes along trails, and how to avoid walking into ambushes. The worst of the training came when setting up night ambushes. The jungle was bad enough during daylight, but terrifying at night. It was the noises that got to you at night. Noises were created by things that couldn't be seen; the screeching, cackling, squealing, and unexplained night sounds. If this wasn't bad enough, then came the clouds of buzzing mosquitoes followed by the ubiquitous yet silent leeches. After two months of this torture. the Leper Colony was ready for anything. Just point them in the right direction and they would destroy anything in their path.

It was good they were ready because when November rolled around the Army was ready to put the First Cavalry Division to the test. Airmobile warfare was a new concept and the professional cadre wanted to know how well it would work in the real thing, meaning combat. On the 14th of November, the 1st battalion was airlifted into Landing Zone X-Ray. A fierce battle resulted in which the 1st battalion won despite being outnumbered at odds of 10 to 1. This battle was followed a few days later when the 2nd Battalion of the 7th Cavalry marched from Landing Zone X-Ray to Landing Zone Albany. There was just one problem for the Americans. The problem was they failed to realize the North Vietnamese leadership's ability to recognize and adjust to superior American firepower, and how quickly they could accomplish this. At X-Ray, the Americans had held the North Vietnamese at a distance where they could use artillery bombardments and airstrikes to decimate their adversaries.

On the way to Landing Zone Albany, the NVA set up an ambush and brought their attacking units in too close for the Americans to use Artillery and Air Strikes. This resulted in the Air Cavalry suffering 155 dead and 121 wounded. When Crazy Horse heard the casualty report he knew the United States was in deep trouble and was likely to lose the war.

A few days after the debacle at Albany, Rafe was ordered to report to General Leicester. On reporting, the General told Rafe to get the Leper Colony ready for action. He was to report to headquarters the next day at 0700 for a briefing and to expect a troop movement the next day.

During this brief meeting, Rafe and the General had an interesting conversation. It started when the General asked Rafe if he had heard about the casualties from the previous day's battles. Rafe told the General he was aware of what had taken place. Rafe then asked General Leicester, "Sir can I speak to you man to man, off the record?"

The General responded with, All right Sergeant Hawkins, what's on your mind?"

"Sir I hate to say this, but I think we're going to lose the war."

That got Chargin' Charlie's attention and he replied, "That's going to take some explaining so would you mind explaining yourself?

"Well Sir, it starts with this question. Are we not the most powerful country on Earth? With a huge, well-trained, and well-equipped army, backed by the best Airforce and most powerful Navy on Earth? And, are we not fighting a tiny third-world country with virtually no Navy and no Airforce? And to make matters worse isn't our population two hundred million and Viet Nam's population thirty-eight million?

The General answered in the affirmative and said, "So what are you getting at?"

Rafe went on to say, "Sir this war should have been over in two weeks, or more accurately it should never have started. If President Johnson had called Ho Chi Minh and told him to either cease and desist in his invasion of South Viet Nam, or we'd blow his county off the face of the earth, what should have happened?

General Leicester responded, "There are other parts of the equation that have to be considered."

Rafe asked, "What's that Sir?"

"Well, there is the question of China. How might they respond if we invade North Viet Nam which sits on their border?"

"Sir I've thought about that and I think I know what's going on. The Administration is afraid that if we invade the North, the Chinese will enter the war on their side. It's beyond me why we fear the Chinese considering that they just tested their first nuclear weapon last year, and to date, their stockpile consists of about 5 nuclear warheads, on the other hand, our stockpile is about 3,500 warheads, Yet, we're the ones worried as to what they might do to us if we invade the North. It seems to me that we have everything ass-backward. Shouldn't they be the ones worried about what we might do to them if they interfere? And Sir, can I go a little further? It seems to me that we're really the big behemoth that's really a pussy in disguise. And I'm not talking about the average American but about our political leaders. What's the point of having power if you're afraid to exercise it? The way I see it we'll fight a defensive battle keeping our forces in the South and fighting the Commies on their terms; Using M-16s against Ak-47s. This is the way I see it going down! We'll kill them at a rate of 20 to 1 and after about five years of fighting and the loss of 50,000 young Americans the public will get sick and tired of seeing their sons die for nothing and will demand that the government pull out. After all, do you really think Americans care about what's happening in this little 3rd world country that no one can find on a map? So, if we lose 50,000 to their one million do you think they'll give up? If they don't, we'll lose. Americans, just aren't going to stand for that sort of bloodshed over a country they don't even care about. In my opinion, this war will turn out to be a cluster fuck of monumental proportions."

General Leicester gazed at his determined-looking troop leader and just shook his head. He was somewhat taken aback because never in his long army career had he witnessed a subordinate, pontificate to a General Officer in such a manner. Then on the other hand he thought, this is not a normal person. Not only that, but he may be right. So rather than getting on his high horse, which he could easily have done, he asked Crazy Horse a question.

"All right Crazy Horse, just for the sake of argument, what would you have done the other day at Landing Zone X-Ray?"

"I would have started out the same way by airlifting a battalion into Landing Zone X-Ray the purpose of which would have been to lure the North Vietnamese out into the open. At the same time circling offshore, about 100 miles away, we'd have a wing of B-52 bombers each carrying 98 five-hundred-pound bombs and 24 one thousand-pound bombs. Once the enemy attacked in force, we'd rapidly pull out our battalion leaving behind some equipment, our opponents, the commies, are sure to view as fruits of their victory. While they were gloating over their good fortune the B-52s would show up at 40,000 feet, barely within hearing, and unload on the unsuspecting enemy 500,000 pounds of high explosives. End of game!"

The General looked at his subordinate and felt a tinge of sympathy. He was thinking. "He should have stayed in OCS. He'd have made a great officer. He'd have even made a great Chairmen of the Joint Chiefs, maybe then he'd learn how bureaucracies work.General Leicester finally said, "Look Sergeant, I know where you're coming from and maybe it's even understandable, however at this stage of the game we can't be questioning the war plans of the elected civilians running the government. Let me ask you a question. When you go into a hot landing zone in a couple of days will the Leper Colony fight?"

Rafe responded with, "Sir we'll be ready to fight the Devil himself."

"Good then let's end this discussion with a line from my favorite poem, The Charge of the Light Brigade. "Theirs not to make reply, theirs not to reason why; theirs but to do or die. Into the valley of death, rode the six hundred. Do you get my drift, Hawkins?"

"Yes Sir. We'll be ready."

"Good that's what you need to do, get the Leper Colony ready for action. Get everything squared away. You're dismissed."

Rafe saluted and left. As he disappeared from sight the general was thinking. "I just left out one small line from the Charge of the Light Brigade. It goes like this, "Into the Jaws of Death, Into the mouth of hell, rode the six hundred."

Rafe assembled the Lepers and told them to get ready for combat which was imminent. Each Leper was carrying an M16, a Laws Rocket, a silenced pistol, and a Claymore Mine. They went over these weapons with a fine-tooth comb, cleaning them and making sure they were in perfect working condition. Rafe told the lepers, "Take care of everything. Write letters home, and tomorrow after I attend the briefing, I'll brief you as to what our responsibilities will be in the assault. By the time we go into the objective, we'll be ready."

At 0600 the following morning, an hour before the briefing was to begin, Rafe showed up at the prefabricated headquarters of the 3rd Battalion of the 7th Cavalry. He sat in the briefing room which was nothing more than a large room filled with chairs and a blackboard across the front of the room. The map of the objective of the air assault was covered and Rafe made no attempt to discover which landing zone was the target. However, next to the covered map was another, showing the area of the Central Highlands bordering Cambodia. On the map, about ten kilometers inside the Cambodian Border was a photograph of a large Pagoda next to which was written 4th North Vietnamese Army Corp, and underneath that was written Red Dragon. Rafe stood looking at the photo and was thinking, "Son of a Bitch. Ten kilometers across the Viet Nam-Cambodia border is the Headquarters of the 4th North Vietnamese Army Corp led by their top expert in the insurgency, General Chu Khan Man, also known as the Red Dragon. We know it's there, and yet it stands unmolested when it should be nothing more than a giant hole in the ground. It's just like I told General Leicester yesterday, we're going to lose this war. The enemy has its headquarters right across the border, in a so-called, neutral country, with God knows how many troops hidden in the jungle, just waiting for the opportunity to sneak across the border and attack us. Then, before we can marshal our air power and wipe them off the face of the earth, they sneak back across the border to their sanctuary. We're going to lose this fucking war. What they should do is let me lead the Leper Colony across the border, sneak up on their headquarters pagoda and blow it off the face of the earth. Maybe that's why I had the premonition to arm the Lepers with Laws Rockets. Seventeen of them could turn their headquarters into a towering inferno. Kill every one of the Sons of Bitches ensuring that we got the Red Dragon. In the long run, it would save thousands of American lives. But that's not going to happen, unless, of course, God directs things otherwise!"

Rafe took out his notebook and made some notes about the exact location of the Pagoda. It was on the South side of Route 78 about ten clicks across the Cambodian border. Find route 78, which wouldn't be too hard, and you find the pagoda. Rafe filed it away for future reference.

At 0700 the officers involved in the coming Air Assault filed into the briefing room. Included in the briefing was the newly promoted Major General Leicester. The plan was relatively simple. They would assault by Huey Copters into Landing Zone Yankee which was situated at the bottom of a low mountain ridge and flanked by a small river. The river flowed in a horseshoe-shaped pattern with the open end facing the low ridge. The plan was to place the three infantry companies in line abreast across the open end of the horseshoe-shaped landing zone.

General Leicester laid out the strategy very simply, "the landing zone is bordered by the river on three sides. The only avenue of attack is off the ridge line and through the open end of the horseshoe. The North Vietnamese will be facing three companies of infantry backed by machine guns. In an assault, they'll have to cross a mostly open area extending about 200 yards across. There is some cover, but not nearly enough. In addition, our battalion will be supported by artillery and airstrikes. There is very little chance of a frontal assault being successful. However. We do have one vulnerability. If you turn your attention to the map and precisely to the area at the bottom of the horseshoe, you'll see the initials LC. That position will be held by the

Leper Colony. At exactly that position, the river shallows to a depth of about two to three feet. In other words, that area is a Ford. On the far bank across from the Ford is a grassy valley that slopes uphill towards the Northeast, leading to another hill about one mile distant. This valley could prove to be our only vulnerability. We don't have enough good intelligence as to exactly where the enemy troop concentrations are, nor for that matter, how many are in which locations, as to that we can only guess. The Leper Colony will cross the river using the Ford and take up positions in the valley to observe any approaching enemy force.If they come down the valley in overwhelming force the Lepers will alert Colonel Reynolds and the choppers will be called in to evacuate the battalion. We don't need a repeat of the Little Big Horn. If on the other hand, no overwhelming assault materializes down the valley, we'll just kick the shit out of them in the Landing Zone. I'll now turn the briefing over to Colonel Reynolds."

As General Leicester walked towards the back of the room, he motioned for Crazy Horse to follow. While everyone turned their attention to the briefing the General addressed Hawkins. In a very quiet tone, he said, "I know it appears that the Lepers are not going to play a big part in the assault on Landing Zone Yankee however, that's misleading. In my opinion, there is a very strong likelihood that there is a much larger concentration of NVA troops in that area than has been reported. If I'm right, and they're on the East side of the river, then eventually they'll be coming down that valley. You will be the eyes and ears of Colonel Reynolds. If the enemy comes down the valley in great force it will be your mission to get a handle on their strength. This information must be transmitted to the Colonel immediately. My suspicion is that there may be a whole hell of a lot of them which might require the battalion to be lifted out by our copters. As I said before, we don't need a repeat of the Little Big Horn."

"There's one other thing you need to be aware of. Yesterday you said that in your opinion we shouldn't fight the enemy on their terms, but instead just appear to be, while luring them into a trap. If the battle develops as I think it might, we're going to set up a trap for the North Vietnamese. This is how it will go down. We'll assault the Landing Zone at 1000 hours on Thursday. While this is happening, we'll have nine B-52 bombers orbiting off Qui

Nhon. These bombers can stay airborne for hours. They'll only be about 30 minutes away from the Landing Zone and will come in at something like 35,000 feet when ordered. For us to spring the trap everything will depend on the NVA actually being on the East side of the Valley. If they are, and if they come down the valley in force, they'll be playing right into our hands."

Rafe was thinking, "Well I'll be damned. If, when we make the assault, there is a large contingent of the enemy on the East side of the river it will appear to them that the battle is setting up to be a repeat of that at Landing Zone X-Ray. Except from their point of view, they'll be set up to attack the third battalion from the rear. If they're present, and if they attack down the valley they'll be in for a very unpleasant surprise."

Rafe was smiling when General Leicester inquired, "So, Sergeant, what do you think of that plan?"

"I'm all for it, Sir, you can count on the Leper Colony to do our part."

"Good, that's what I thought you'd say. So, let's go back and listen to the rest of the briefing." They returned and participated in the rest of the planning.

That afternoon Rafe returned to the Leper Colony encampment and called the men together. The lepers formed a circle around Rafe and he began with, "Here's the word. Tomorrow we will assault Landing Zone Yankee. I'm going to draw a diagram in the dirt showing the terrain around the Landing Zone." Rafe drew the river where it formed the horseshoe-shaped landing zone. Across the open end of the landing zone, he drew the positions the three infantry companies would hold, in a line abreast. He showed the Ford at the bottom of the landing zone which would be held by the leper colony. He also drew the valley leading away from the Ford stretching about three-quarters of a mile and ending in a tree line backed by some hills. "What we expect to happen is the NVA will conduct a frontal assault in great force against our line of infantry. It's not very likely to succeed."

Triple B asked, "Why are you so sure they won't succeed?"

Rafe said, "When I was at OCS, they demonstrated how much firepower an infantry company can generate when backed by heavy machine guns, as in the .50 caliber variety, with added artillery support. You can't imagine how much power that company can project. It's a firestorm of unimaginable proportions. Of course, if they come with enough manpower they might break through, but the losses would be unacceptable. Herein lies the problem; General Leicester believes there may be another enemy force of up to two regiments in strength sequestered in the hills to the East of the landing zone. This would mean the enemy in the immediate area would be a full division. There is no way under ordinary circumstances that one battalion can hold off a division, and this is where the Leper Colony comes in. If the NVA comes down the valley in force, I'll radio Colonel Reynolds so he can pull out the third battalion by helicopter. The problem for us will be that we may not be able to reach the landing zone before it becomes too hot for extraction. The difficult part of our situation is that we'll be retreating down the valley while slowing down the enemy's advance by calling in artillery and airstrikes. If we get to the landing zone too late for a lift out, we'll have to go to ground."

At this point, Hit Man piped up with, "So what the fuck do we do then when we're surrounded by up to a division of NVA?"

"We do what we've been trained to do. First, we go into the river and float about one mile downstream. Then we disappear into the jungle and head for home."

At this point Doc. Linginfelter asked, "How the hell do we float down the river with the enemy shooting at us from both sides of the river banks? We'll be sitting ducks!"

Rafe answered with, "We would be under normal circumstances, but not if the river is blanketed by smoke. That's the plan. The last thing we'll do before we hit the water is call for an extended smoke barrage from the artillery batteries. Then we'll ditch the radios in the river and enter the water. We only have to get about a mile down the river before we make our way into the jungle and disappear. Keep one thing in mind; when we retreat into the river we'll have to move at high speed. Once the Hueys are called to evacuate the battalion, the B-52s orbiting off the coast will prepare to make an Arc Light bombing run which will start at the landing zone and extend all the way up the valley. What's likely to happen is the NVA will advance on the landing zone from both the West where the original assault began, and from the East where one or two regiments will come streaming down the valley. Their intent will be to surround the 3rd battalion and wipe it off the face of the earth;

after all, we are the Seventh Cavalry, General Custer's old regiment, and they'd like nothing better than to repeat the slaughter of the Little Big Horn. Unfortunately for them, the valley they'll come charging down will suddenly become "The Valley of Death." What they'll never be able to anticipate is that while they're streaming down the valley nine B-52s will be preparing a bomb run that will annihilate their entire force. Why am I so sure they'll be annihilated? Because each of the nine bombers will be carrying 84 five-hundred-pound bombs internally, plus twenty-four 1000-pounders externally. Each bomber will carry 66,000 pounds of bombs and nine together will drop a total of 594,000 pounds of high explosives. Anything in the valley will cease to exist.So, you can see the need for us to exit the area around the valley, and the landing zone, very quickly, once the battalion is pulled out. As the French would say, we need to exit the area tout suite!"

Country Boy had to get his two cents in so he asked, "How do we get down the river with our weapons, they'll pull us under and we'll drown?"

Rafe answered, "We're going to take care of that problem right now.Remember that stand of Bamboo we pass every day on patrol, the one right outside the perimeter? We're going down there, right now, and each of us is going to cut down two tall bamboo trees. We'll haul them back here where we'll cut them into shafts, three feet long. These will be bound together to form small rafts, one for each member of the leper colony. When we hit the river, we'll place our weapons on these rafts to carry them down the river. We'll be carrying our individual rafts on the Hueys when we assault Landing Zone Yankee. If things go the way we expect the NVA will suffer a catastrophic defeat." Rafe knew there would be plenty of time for further discussion while they were assembling their rafts so he simply said, "Let's go!"

Later as the lepers were working on their rafts Rafe explained how important the rafts were involving a river escape. "Once we enter the water with our weapons on the rafts, it will be of critical importance not to do anything that will overturn your raft. Do that, and your weapons plunge to the bottom of the river, and you're in a world of hurt. We'll have a rope about forty feet long, and each of us will hold on to the rope with one hand and to their raft with the other. If everything goes as planned, we'll float down the river about three-quarters of a mile and then make our way to shore. Everything depends on us making it down the river with our weapons. A moving barrage of smoke will move down the river banks ahead of us concealing our movements so it's imperative that you hold onto the rope so you don't become separated from the group. Once ashore we'll move rapidly to the North away from the Landing Zone."

The Lepers completed building the rafts and then made a final check of their weapons. Rafe had them turn in early as the next day would be the day of days.

When dawn rose, the lepers were up and ready. They moved to the airfield when summoned; where they found three Hueys waiting. Minutes later, to the sound of the whump, whump, whump of the rotors, they lifted off and headed to Landing Zone Yankee, thirty-five minutes away. The first part of the flight was at two thousand feet which gave a panoramic view of the central highlands, then as they approached the landing zone, they dropped to fly the nape of the earth at a height of two hundred feet. Just ahead of their flight were the helicopter gunships not unlike destroyers escorting troopships. They came over the last ridge from the East and there laid out before them was Landing Zone Yankee, already surrounded by smoke and fire. The gunships made a pass down the river and laid down a wall of .50 caliber machine gun fire then turned and came back inundating the far bank with rocket fire. Anything that looked like it could conceal the enemy was hosed down by a devastating fusillade of lethal fire.

The three Hueys carrying the lepers followed the gunships along the river bank, which was concealed by a line of smoke delivered by artillery fire. When they set down on the river bank the lepers exited in seconds each carrying his makeshift raft.

Rafe called them together for a brief meeting under the cover of the smoke screen. He laid out the plan, "Country Boy you'll take the 1st squad up the left side of the valley remaining under the cover of the tree line. Remember our job is not to engage the enemy but to do a reconnaissance looking for a sizable enemy force. Doc, you and Hit Man will take the 2nd and 3rd squads up the right side of the valley remaining under the cover of the tree line. Once we reach the far end of the valley we'll spread out, hunker down and watch. Division thinks that sooner or later the enemy will come down the valley in force, with the idea of crossing the river at the Ford thereby surrounding the battalion and recreating Custer's Last Stand. Put in other words, they'll wipe out the battalion. Whenever the enemy is sighted we'll use artillery concentrations to herd them back toward the Valley. We want to know where they are, and where they're headed, we don't want them running wild, all through the jungle. Pick your positions carefully. Make sure it offers maximum visibility into the surrounding area. Is that understood?" The lepers answered in the affirmative with a resounding, "Yes, Sir!"

Once the lepers had found suitable terrain and set up their observation posts they became acutely aware of what was taking place on the other side of the river. The NVA (North Vietnamese Army) was attacking the 3rd battalion in what must have been regimental strength. Although they had a three to four times advantage in numbers, the 3rd Cavalry battalion was backed by Fifty Caliber Machine Guns and concentrations of artillery fire. It sounded like the Normandy Invasion was taking place over there, and to make matters worse from time to time three or four A1 Skyraiders would make bombing, and strafing runs on the NVA positions.

Just as the Americans had a plan so did the NVA. In fact, they were stealing an axiom from one of our most famous generals none other than George S. Patton. One of Patton's favorite strategies was "Hold them by the nose, then kick them in the ass." It was a good strategy if your opponent wasn't aware of your intentions. In this case, the leaders of the 1st Cavalry Division were well aware of what the leader of the North Vietnamese 4th Army Corp. might well be thinking. Previously at Landing Zone X-Ray, they had used a frontal assault by a numerically superior force to try to overrun a U.S. Battalion That didn't work too well. They followed this up by getting in close to another American Battalion where the U.S. Forces couldn't use artillery or air support. That was Landing Zone Albany where the U.S. took a beating.

If the NVA commander General Chu Khan Man, also known as the "Red Dragon", was a little on the arrogant side, then he might respond by attacking down the valley with the intent of trapping the U. S. Cavalry troopers before they could be evacuated by helicopter.That was the plan. Wait and see. If the NVA came down the valley they were toast. Orbiting 60 miles off the coast of South Vietnam would be nine B-52 Bombers each carrying 108 bombs. Keeping in mind that two or three 1,000-pounders can sink an aircraft carrier, then you have a good idea as to what sort of destruction one bomb load from a B-52 can cause. When you add the flight of nine flying in a formation you would have 972 heavy bombs; Even the concussion from one of these bombs landing in your vicinity can kill you. Everything was contingent on the NVA taking the bait.

The Leper Colony took up positions at the far end of the valley about 100 yards inside the tree line. From there they listened to the roar of the battle taking place about one mile down the valley where the 3rd battalion was taking on a full regiment of NVA. Throughout that first day, nothing took place in their area.

The night was relatively quiet with just sporadic artillery and small arms fire in the vicinity of the landing zone. When dawn brought its first light the lepers were on high alert. If the NVA were coming, now would be the time.

At approximately 0830 Country Boy's first squad saw them, first moving quietly along the left side of the area to the front of the valley. Just platoon strength, but the vanguard nonetheless. County Boy radioed his sightings to Crazy Horse and then to Colonel Reynolds. By 0930 the enemy presence was at company strength, all of which was reported up the chain of command. When by 1100 the enemy was showing signs of being a major concentration Crazy Horse advised Colonel Reynolds it was time to pull the plug and evacuate the battalion. The evacuation lift by the Huey's would take about 30 minutes with 5 choppers landing together on the landing zone every two to three minutes. The battalion had practiced this procedure and was well adept at carrying it out with speed and alacrity. All the troopers knew what was a stake, survival.

At 1130 the first of the fifty choppers began to land, and the troops poured out of their positions and quickly hopped aboard. As soon as a group of five Huey's lifted off another group of five landed. By 1200 the battalion was headed back to the base at Pleiku. During the half-hour interval during which the helicopters were lifting the battalion out of Landing Zone Yankee a massive concentration of artillery fire hit the open end of the horseshoe-shaped landing zone where the opposing forces had their lines. When the artillery fire let up, a squadron of F105 Thunderchiefs struck the NVA lines at the open end of the landing zone dropping 168,000 pounds of high explosives. The purpose wasn't to drive them off but to slow down their advance.

Once the last of the battalion troopers lifted off, the commander send a message which was immediately forwarded to the nine-plane flight of B-52s orbiting in a holding pattern off the coast. The B-52s were about 300 miles away and would approach at about 500 miles per hour. The B-52s continued holding for another 20 minutes before they headed inland on their bomb run, giving the Leper Colony time to escape.

When Colonel Reynolds radioed Crazy Horse that the last of the Huey's were lifting off, he ordered the Leper Colony to begin a rapid retreat down the valley only stopping periodically to call in an artillery barrage to slow down the advancing enemy. When they were less than 150 yards from the river ford, Crazy Horse called in a waiting squadron of A1 Skyraiders to make a bombing run. An A1 Skyraider is a single-engine propeller-driven aircraft, that carries a bomb load equivalent to a World War II B-17. Its usual offensive weaponry included four 20MM cannons, Rockets, Napalm Canisters, as well as Cluster Bombs.

For the most part, the eight Skyraiders dropped Napalm and Cluster Bombs. Unfortunately, because of drifting marker smoke, one of the Cluster Bombs landed too close to the Lepers and a fragment from it grazed Crazy Horse along his left temple. It was a wound that looked worse than it actually was, however, Crazy Horse slapped a dressing on the wound, and led the Lepers into the river. He tied a rope about 40 feet in length around his waist and told the Lepers to take their rafts and place their weapons carefully on board. Once this was accomplished, he led the Leper Colony out into the middle of the river under a cloud of smoke from preregistered artillery shells. The rope was used to keep the lepers from drifting apart in the smoke screen. The current was quite strong and they were swept down the river at a moderate speed. About 25 minutes later Rafe steered the lepers to shore near a long sweeping sandbar. They grabbed their weapons and also picked up their rafts which would be dismantled, and tossed, once deep in the forest. No sense in leaving an easily discernible trail. For another ten minutes, the Lepers headed North away from the landing zone at all possible speed. When they came upon a small gully about ten feet deep Crazy Horse ordered the Lepers to hunker down and prepare for the bomb run. It didn't take long and about four minutes later all hell broke loose.

When the B-52s came they arrived in three sets of three. Each set carried 324 bombs and was separated at one-minute intervals which were to prevent midair collisions. Usually, a B-52 Arc Light Raid had only two sets separated by ten minutes, but in this case, the commanders wanted all 972 bombs delivered from the three sets to arrive within three minutes, not twenty minutes which would be normal separation. Why the one-minute separation? Because if there were 4,000 to 5,000 NVA regulars in the Landing zone area you wouldn't want to give them 20 minutes to run. A person can cover a lot of ground when running for their life. The object was to achieve total surprise with little chance of escape.

The Lepers were hunkered down in the gully when the ground started to shake. Although a mile and a half away it felt like a massive earthquake had struck. Then came the thunder of the bombs which went on for three minutes. They were all aware that whoever had the bad luck to be in the landing zone and the surrounding area, had ceased to exist.

The lepers stayed frozen in place with shocked looks on their faces. Finally, Crazy Horse broke the silence. "Ok, it's time for us to make tracks and get the hell out of here!"

Before he could say anything else, Doc Linginfelter said, "You'd better let me take a look at your wound before we move out." Rafe replied, OK Doc, do what you need to." After taking a look at the wound Doc said, "I'd better stitch it up, or you'll end up with a nasty scar." Knowing Doc didn't have that much experience Rafe still said, "Ok Doc stitch away while I address the lepers."

He then continued, "Ok, listen up, and listen very carefully as this may be the most important piece of information you'll ever hear. First, you performed excellently at Yankee." This brought up the question from Oakie from the 1st squad, "Does that mean we've climbed Chilkoot Pass?"

Rafe looked at all of them and then responded, "Well almost, but not quite! We're out here to become a force to be reckoned with, to be recognized as men amongst men. More importantly, to be those things in our own eyes, rather than in the eyes of others. What we are about to do is so extraordinary and outrageous that I even considered not telling you the identity of our next assault. The reason for not giving you the identity is to provide you with what is called Plausible Deniability! In other words, if you don't know what you're attacking you can't be held responsible.

The next question came from Frank Muscato, the Canuck, "So what's the forbidden target?"

"Within 15 to 20 klicks from here is the Headquarters of the 4th North Vietnamese Army Corp. It's located inside the border of Cambodia which is supposed to be a neutral country."

With that, Bruce Smith of the 2nd squad piped in with, "So What's the big deal of us sneaking across the border and attacking their headquarters?"

Rafe responded, "The problem lies within our own government. The Johnson administration won't allow us to cross the border and attack the enemy."

At this point the Gator, Henri Desormeaux piped in with, "Sir, what kind of government wouldn't want us to track down the enemy and destroy them no matter where we found them?"

Rafe replied, "Good question Gator. I'll tell you what kind. That would be one led by pussies or what could be called Girlie Men. Let me ask you this. If General Leicester was in charge. would he let us go in and wipe out the enemy?"

Gator answered, "Of course, he would, he'd probably lead the way himself."

Rafe asked another question. "How about General LeMay, would he let SAC bomb the shit out of the commies we're about to attack if he knew their location?"

Triple B answered with, "There's no doubt that LeMay would crush them like bugs, but isn't there a question about China intervening?"

"Of course, there is", countered Rafe. "However, here's the deal. Do you know how many nuclear weapons the United States has in its arsenal?"

Triple B nodded, "Nope!"

"Would you believe 3,400 vs 5 for China? That's right 3,400 to 5 yet we Kow Tow to them, it's almost like the Elephant being afraid of the mouse. So, what it really boils down to, is that the United States is too timid to flex its power, and what that means is, that we're going to lose the war. The commies will see that even if they suffer a 10 or 20 to 1 casualty disparity they will still win. The commies could care less about how many men they lose whereas the mothers and fathers in the United States will be screaming over the waste of their sons and daughters. When that happens, the United States will capitulate.

Tim Spencer, asked, "So what's our objective?"

"We're going to do something so outrageous that it will go down in history. They might even try to suppress the fact that we've attacked the enemy in Cambodia, and keep it a deep dark secret. But you know how that goes? The secret tends to leak out."

"Before we begin, I have to ask this question. Are you all on board? Even if one of you, objects, we call off the attack and turn East and make our way back towards An Khe. Be very aware that your life and future are on the line, but that's what it takes to achieve the status we're after. Does anyone object?" There were no objections, so the attack was on. The Leper Colony was halfway up Chilkoot Pass and now they were going to scale the heights.

While Doc Linginfelter finished stitching his head Crazy Horse ordered the Lepers to check their equipment paying special attention to their silenced sidearms which would be critical in the upcoming assault. Fifteen minutes later the Leper Colony moved out in a single column into the jungle.

Crazy Horse led the column himself knowing they had to locate Highway 78 which crossed the border of Viet Nam into Cambodia. Once they found the highway finding the Pagoda would be easy. From what he had seen at Division Headquarters Crazy Horse knew the Pagoda was located on the South side of Highway 78 about 15 kilometers inside the Cambodian border. To find it was easy; the Lepers would advance down the south side of Highway 78 spread out, and seek a roadway leading off the highway which would lead to the Pagoda. Once located, they would reconnoiter the area intent on finding the sentry posts which would inevitably be surrounding it. This was the key factor. Find the sentry posts, without themselves being detected. Once located, the mission was to find a way to get in close to these posts with the object of taking them out suddenly and silently. All they had practiced in months of training would be put into action. The silencing of the sentries was critical to the following assault.

In addition to finding the sentry posts, it was essential to determine if the Red Dragon was present. The entire attack was planned with the idea of taking out the Red Dragon. Once it was determined that he was on site the plan of attack was relatively simple.

After two days of reconnaissance, everything was in place. Crazy Horse called for a meeting of Lepers which took place 500 yards East of the Pagoda deep in the jungle. He laid out the plan of attack.

"We've determined that the Red Dragon is present. I saw a picture of him when I initially discovered the Pagoda on a map at our headquarters at An Khe. Next to the photograph of the Pagoda was one of the Red Dragon. I saw his staff car arrive yesterday and saw him enter the Pagoda while I was watching their operation through binoculars. It was definitely him. We have to attack tonight at 0300 exactly."

Mighty Mouse inquired, "Why do we have to attack tonight?"

Rafe answered, "After what happened at Landing Zone Yankee the North Vietnamese were given an example of the awesome power of the B-52 Stratofortress. They're aware that if we send in six B-52s to strike the Pagoda the place will disappear in less than a minute. The only thing stopping us from blowing the Pagoda to hell is willpower. In other words, if we want to blow the Pagoda to hell nothing can stop us. If you were the Red Dragon, would you want to be sitting there trying to figure out if the Americans would want to disregard, so-called Cambodian neutrality, and blow him away? He's been there a while so he might feel comfortable in the fact that the United States hasn't got the balls to attack. At any rate, he may decide, at any time, to pull out before those in power in the United States change their mind. So, adhering to the old saying, Strike while the Iron's hot, we'll attack tomorrow night before they get a chance to change their minds.

The rest of the day was spent in further reconnaissance which discovered that the Vietnamese had a camp in a village about 4 kilometers down Highway 78. The officers stayed in the Pagoda while the enlisted troops stayed in the village. This worked out well for the Lepers as they wouldn't have to deal with the regular troops because the attack would occur, and the lepers would be gone before they could respond.

Twenty-four hours later at the same time and place, deep in the jungle, the lepers met again. Crazy Horse laid out the plan of attack. "We've discovered that the enemy has eight sentry posts surrounding the Pagoda. We've already discovered the best approaches to these posts. At exactly 0300, teams of two lepers per sentry post will attack and eliminate the sentries. Gentleman, this means you kill the sentries with headshots from your silenced pistols. You've been trained for this from the time the Leper Colony was formed. We're a stealth operation, trained to get in close and kill. You have to strike as close to 0300 as possible, as shortly thereafter Triple B and I will emerge from the motor pool area carrying jerry cans of gasoline. It wouldn't be good for us to be caught out in the open from any failure to take out the sentries. Once the sentries are neutralized, you'll advance in pairs, out of the jungle, into the clearing surrounding the Pagoda. You'll set up your Claymore Mines facing any opening from which egress is likely, and then prepare your Laws Rockets to fire. While you're doing this Triple B and I will get into their small motor pool area and pick up four of the Jerry Cans we saw sitting there, making sure each has five gallons of gasoline."

"About 0310 Triple B and I will take the Jerry Cans of gasoline, and enter the front door of the Pagoda. Triple B will be carrying two Jerry Cans, and I will carry two more. We'll place the Jerry Cans at the front entrance and take a couple of minutes to position our Claymores and Laws Rockets directly across from the front entrance. Then we'll enter the Pagoda with Triple B carrying two Jerry Cans while I provide cover with my silenced revolver. Any NVA that appears I'll take down before they can spread the alarm. Once inside the Pagoda, we go up the stairs and spill the contents of Jerry Cans all over the area at the head of the stairs. We'll quickly retreat down the staircase and bring in the second two cans of gasoline which we'll spill in the doorway at the bottom of the stairs. In less than two minutes we'll be outside ready to fire the Laws Rockets.

"I'll fire the first Rocket which will be followed seconds later by Triple B's. Once you hear our rockets detonate, you'll fire yours. They don't have to be fired simultaneously just make sure all the rockets are fired within thirty seconds of the first. Once you've fired your Laws Rockets prepare to unleash the Claymores because, within minutes of the Rockets exploding, all hell will break loose inside the Pagoda. Anyone left alive will head for an exit. When they make that attempt, they'll be met by a hail storm of ball bearings from the Claymores. At this point, pick up your M-16s and finish off any survivors. The entire assault will take about 10 minutes at the end of which we'll rendezvous at the southeast corner of the clearing where I'll take a headcount. If all are present and accounted for, we'll make tracks.

As the sun began setting and the shadows lengthened the Lepers crept into place. They had to get as close to the sentry posts as possible while there was still light. It was already determined that the guard changed at Midnight, 0800, 1600, and again at Midnight, every eight hours. The lepers would make their way to positions close to the sentry posts and lay in wait until the changing of the guard at midnight. Then while there was an increase in activity, when the new sentries rotated, the lepers would advance as close in as possible and then lay in wait until the moment of attack. This is what their training had consisted of, to lay in place for long periods of time, completely silent, then strike.

Rafe was positioned at the edge of the Jungle next to the small motor pool area. They had observed that the NVA had a small gasoline tanker truck along with a few troop carriers parked together on the North side of the Pagoda. Rafe located four Jerry Cans and placed them next to the tanker truck and waited for 0300. He filled each Jerry can with five gallons of gasoline. At the appointed hour everything was dead silent. Rafe waited for the first muffled cough of the silenced pistols. He remembered how dark and quiet the night was with a half-moon and the scent of Jazmine drifting on the air currents. That was all about to change radically. Then came the first coughing sound followed by others. Silencers are not completely silent and this worked to the leper's advantage. When the first shot took out a sentry the second sentry who'd usually be sleeping, or half asleep, would pop his head up to survey the scene. Humans don't react like other animals their safety revolves around their ability to evaluate. When a Horse hears an unusual noise, it may bolt because its safety revolves around speed. Humans have to see what's going on first and then decide how to react. When a sleeping sentry hears a sound, he has to wake up, look around and evaluate the circumstances, then decide on a course of action. In this case, when he wakes up and put his head up to see what was going on, he'd have two or three silenced rounds fired into it.

The silencing of the sentries worked to perfection primarily because of complacency.Sit in the jungle every night for a couple of months without seeing a single threat and your focus is going to decline. That's what happened, and the NVA paid the price.

When Triple B showed up at Rafe's location next to the tanker truck, they picked up the four jerry cans and headed for the front door of the pagoda about sixty yards away. The next 30 seconds would be critical as they both were carrying Jerry Cans and neither had a silenced weapon drawn and ready. If they were discovered the alarm would be sounded. The motor pool area was around the corner from the front entrance of the Pagoda. Rafe and Triple B made their way along the side of the building and then Rafe put down his two Jerry Cans. He Pulled his silenced handgun and with great caution made his way around the side of the building. Standing next to the entrance was an NVA soldier with an AK47 slung over his shoulder. He was half asleep as it was 0300 and nothing much was happening. Rafe crept in close and when about 20 yards away he stood up and approached with his pistol ready to fire. When the North Vietnamese soldier saw Rafe approaching, and when he finally realized the danger, he began to unsling his AK47 from his shoulder. He didn't get very far before Rafe put two .22 caliber rounds into his forehead. The soldier dropped in his tracks whereupon Rafe advanced to his position, grabbed him by the collar, and dragged his body around the corner of the building to where Triple B was waiting.

The two of them made their way to the entrance where Rafe placed his Jerry Cans and then advanced ahead of Triple B up the stairs into the Dragon's Lair. Rafe was aware that the next two minutes would decide the success or failure of their mission. Rafe's pistol was ready to fire and he was as good a marksman with a pistol as existed in the United States Army. If any NVA were to appear they would be dead in seconds. At the top of the stairs, the Jerry Cans were overturned and the gasoline spilled out to form a huge pool, part of which began to run down the staircase. Rafe and Triple B were down the stairs in seconds where they quickly positioned the second two Jerry Cans and spilled their contents at the base of the stairs and all around the entrance of Pagoda.

Once the gasoline was flowing down the staircase Rafe and Triple B raced to a position about thirty yards in front of the entrance where they prepared to launch their Laws Rockets. There was no point in setting up Claymores since no one was coming out the front entrance. As Rafe prepared to fire, he was aware of the calmness of the night and the scent of Jasmine wafting on the air currents. He was also aware of the violent explosion about to occur. Nevertheless, he sighted his Laws Rocket on the base of the staircase and pulled the trigger. The rocket slammed into the base of the staircase and exploded with a thunderclap. Seconds later Triple B's rocket hit the upper floor and the combination ignited the gas which started a raging fire. Once the first rockets exploded the other lepers unleashed theirs which followed every few seconds.In less than a minute the Pagoda was turned into a raging inferno. Its occupants were awoken to chaos and at first thought they were under air attack. The first thought was to get the hell out of the fire, which began the run for any close exit. Unfortunately, for the NVA any potential exit was bracketed by Claymore Mines. The panic-stricken North Vietnamese ran into a firestorm of ball bearings cutting them down like a scythe in a wheat field. Once the Claymores were released the Lepers picked up their M16s and blasted away from the cover of darkness.

The entire assault took only ten minutes at which point the lepers assembled at the Southwest corner of the clearing in which the Pagoda was now blazing away. Rafe took a headcount and asked if anyone had been wounded. When all were accounted present and none with wounds, Rafe said, "Let's get the hell out of here." With that, the Leper Colony made its way into the Jungle heading South.

A few minutes later a convoy of reinforcements from the NVA camp a few klicks down Route 78 showed up after seeing the light from the fire reflecting off the overcast. They had tried to contact the Pagoda by radio but had received no response. By the time they arrived, nothing could be done. There were no visible survivors, just a blazing inferno.

The Lepers made their way through the jungle as fast as possible with the darkness making speed almost impossible. It also made tracking them completely impossible so they weren't worried about that. After a mile, Crazy Horse stopped the column and briefed the men. "First, I want to tell you that your performance was perfect. The mission was carried out exactly as planned. From now on we can refer to our attack as **The Battle of the Dragon's Lair.** However, if you think you've just succeeded in scaling Chilkoot Pass you'd be almost right, but not quite. The only thing left to do is to escape and get back to U.S.-held territory. We could do it the easy way which is to head southeast, cross back into Viet Nam and make our way back to a U.S.-held base. That's the easy way. But, just keep in mind we're not in this to do anything the easy way. We're here to become a legendary force, a force to be reckoned with. So, instead of heading Southeast, we'll head Northwest toward the Mekong River and from there down the river to Phnom Penh."

Bruce Smith one of the more outspoken lepers asked, "Sir how are we going to get from here to Phnom Penh without being seen? It's got to be hundreds of miles through unfamiliar territory, how can we do it?"

"Actually, it isn't that hard. We'll head North to the Mekong River which is about 100 miles, then we'll follow it toward Phnom Penh. When we're close enough, we'll steal a boat and go down the rest of the way at night. Upon arriving at the waterfront at Phnom Penh it's only four blocks to the American Embassy." Rafe was also aware of something else about the American Embassy, it was closed. It had closed in May of 1964 and had only a residual force of marines left behind to guard it.

"There is one other thing of Paramount importance. I'm sure you've all heard the old-World War Two expression, Loose lips, sink ships. Well, take that to heart. We're going to get out of here and back to U. S. Territory, however, once we're back, there's going to be a political attempt to put us in Leavenworth. They'll never be able to accomplish this if we do one simple thing; that is, keep our big mouths shut. So, once we're back at our base do not discuss what happened in Cambodia under any circumstances. Do not take a polygraph and do not listen to their lies which will say some of the others in the Leper Colony have admitted to complicity in the attack on the Dragon's Lair. Also, be aware, that areas you may bivouac in could be bugged. Remember, the safety of the Leper Colony means keeping your mouth shut.

It took 10 days for the Leper Colony to make the 230-mile trip. They could have done it a lot faster if they hadn't been avoiding every small hamlet along the way. The last 50 miles were accomplished in a stolen boat down the Mekong River landing on the waterfront of Phnom Penh only four blocks from the Embassy. Getting into the Embassy was relatively easy. It was just before dawn and the Lepers were hidden across the street from the Embassy entrance. Rafe approached the entrance and identified himself to the Marine guards. He showed them his Army ID and told them he was the leader of a special strike team that was hiding across the street. It was imperative that they be admitted to the Embassy grounds and hidden there until U.S. Army Headquarters in Viet Nam could be contacted. After some hesitation, the young marines at the gate agreed to admit the Lepers who came running across the street into the Embassy. They were unarmed having dropped their weapons into the Mekong River as they approached Phnom Penh. The reason for ditching the weapons was even if the Cambodian and U. S. Governments colluded to get spent bullets from the bodies of the NVA at the Dragon's Lair there wouldn't be any way to do a forensic ballistics examination without the firearms. Crazy Horse was thinking ahead, He knew that the United States government wasn't going to give them a hero's welcome even if they had eliminated the Red Dragon, quite the contrary, they'd try to crucify them. With that in mind, he threw a roadblock in their path. It was one thing to think they knew who was behind the attack on the Dragon's Lair, and it was another thing to prove it in a court of law.

Once the Leper Colony was safely inside the Embassy, the Marines found an area where they could crash while Crazy Horse was escorted to meet Major Dundee, the marine's commanding officer. The Major was very direct in his questioning of the leader of the Army unit. "How in the hell did you get from Landing Zone Yankee to Phnom Penh which is about 250 miles without being seen? Also, why did you choose to head in this direction when Pleiku was only about 30 miles?"

"I'm afraid I can't tell you anything about our activities after Landing Zone Yankee as they are highly classified and will only be revealed to our commander General Leicester."

Major Dundee came back with, "I hope you realize that your activities have caused an international firestorm of mega proportions!"

"So, what did we do to create this, so-called, firestorm?"

"Someone surrounded and destroyed the Headquarters of the Fourth North Vietnamese Army Corp, they wiped it out, and in the process killed their top general."

"Sounds like a good thing to me. Why would anyone be upset about that unless, of course, you're a communist or a communist sympathizer?"

"The Johnson Administration are the ones raising hell about the raid across the border into neutral Cambodia violating international law."

"I don't have anything to say about the Johnson Administration. They're running the show so they'll do what they want. I just need to get on the phone with General Leicester and let him know where we are.

"All right Hawkins, why don't you go down to the mess hall and get some chow? I'll call you when we get General Leicester on the phone.

A couple of hours later, just after sunrise, Major Dundee summoned Rafe back to his office and handed him a phone. General Leicester was on the other end.

"Hawkins where in hell have you been, and more importantly what have you been up to."

"We high-tailed it out of Yankee, using the river, then used our ability to remain unseen to cross Cambodia to Phom Penh. That pretty much sums it up."

"Any casualties?"

"Only myself. I took a piece of shrapnel across my left temple. It looks worse than it is."

"Well, the top priority is to get you out of Phom Penh surreptitiously. Since you snuck in, we'd just as soon no one found out you were ever there. I hope you realize you've created an international firestorm; To put it mildly; The shit has hit the fan."

"Exactly what do you mean we created some sort of shit storm?

"Let's not go there now, we'll discuss your activities when you're back. Right now, we need to extract you from your current location with no one the wiser. Taking you down the Mekong by boat will be dangerous when you get near the border. Do you have any ideas on how we can make the extraction?"

Actually, Crazy Horse had a very good idea if the High Command would go for it. Again, it involved risk, but so would any other option. Crazy Horse laid it out for the General who was immediately receptive. From there, the Army acted with great dispatch. They wanted the Leper Colony out of Cambodia as quickly as possible.

Three days later at 0130, the Leper Colony left the Embassy compound in the back of a 2 ½-ton truck affectionately nicknamed a Douce and a half. Crazy Horse had already taken a trial run down to the Phom Penh airport to scout the departure end of the runway. Generally, the wind direction was from the Northeast and that was the forecast for the next five days. At the southwest end of the runway where the aircraft turned onto runway 50 for takeoff to the Northeast, was a small lake surrounded by rushes that would provide excellent cover for the Lepers as they awaited the C130 which would whisk them out of Cambodia.

The Plan was a simple one. A C130 would arrive in the evening bringing a replacement jeep for the Marine Detachment at the Embassy. The 130 had a cargo ramp under the tail to load cargo and troops which could be easily raised and lowered by a crewman. The aircraft would be scheduled to depart the cargo area at 0245. The Leper Colony would be undercover in the reeds surrounding the lake at the departure end of the runway. When the C130 reached the runup area 100 yards short of the runway it would drop its cargo ramp and the lepers would come running. It would only take around 30 seconds for the lepers to board, and then a quick retraction of the ramp and the aircraft would taxi the last 100 yards and turn onto the active runway for takeoff.

That evening when the Douce and a half stopped near the perimeter fence, the lepers were off in seconds. They had no weapons only their K-bar knives and a pair of wire cutters. Within a couple of minutes, they were in the marshy area next to the small lake well concealed in the rushes and silently waiting.

At 0250 they could hear the whine of the C130's four turboprop engines, and as it approached the runup area it flashed its landing lights. A couple of minutes later it stopped. The ramp came down and the lepers emerged from their concealment in full flight. One could say they came out of the rushes like bats out of hell, running for their freedom. It didn't take long, and about 45 seconds after stopping, the C130's cargo ramp was retracted and the aircraft taxied the remaining yards and tuned into position for takeoff. The captain advanced the throttles to full power and the C130 roared down the runway lifting off and beginning a gentle left-hand turn. As the aircraft lifted off the lepers let out a mighty cheer knowing that they were now heading for the sanctuary of U.S. held territory.

About 1 ½ hours later the C130 flew into Da Nang, Republic of Viet Nam, making a gentle turn from the South China Sea and landing to the Northeast. The aircraft taxied in and the Leper Colony deplaned into a waiting bus. It was only a short ride to a temporary barracks where the lepers made themselves as comfortable as possible. They were issued new uniforms since they'd been in the ones, they were wearing for over two weeks. Shortly after 1300, a Captain arrived to escort Crazy Horse to a meeting with General Leicester recently arrived from An Khe. Crazy Horse was well aware that this meeting would determine the fate of both himself and the rest of the Leper Colony. He wasn't overly concerned because deep down he knew Chargin' Charlie was if anything, a warrior. If he was right the general would have their six, if he was wrong, they were in deep shit.

Once he walked in and reported to General Leicester, the drama began. The General gave Rafe the once over, then said, "Hawkins, you look like shit."

Rafe answered, "I know Sir. The fortunes of war!"

"Have you had a doctor look at it yet?"

"Not yet Sir"

"Well, I suppose you've looked at it in a mirror. The white of your eye is blood red and you look like some sort of monster. As soon as we finish here you go right over to the hospital and get checked out."

"Yes Sir."

"Now let's get right down to the nitty-gritty. What in the hell were you doing in Cambodia?"

Rafe was very concerned about telling General Leicester anything about the assault on the Dragon's Lair. He had the other sixteen lepers to consider. If the administration was as livid as he suspected, they would be hell-bent on court martialing the Leper Colony and putting them in Leavenworth for a very long stay. His superiors had just one big problem; It was one thing to suspect that the lepers were responsible for the annihilation of the North Vietnamese Fourth Army Corps Headquarters, and it was another thing to prove it. If there was going to be a Court Martial there needed to be proof. So, admitting what happened to General Leicester was sort of akin to letting the "Cat out of the bag." The problem was that the General wanted to know the facts, and in fact, he insisted on knowing.

Facing a critical moment of truth not unlike the one he had faced at OCS; Rafe was in a quandary. He had to face it head-on since that is how the General was wired, he wanted a direct answer, not a bunch of bullshit. When he gave the General an answer, he knew the lives of the Lepers were on the line.

"Sir I'll tell you exactly what you want to know on one condition."

"And that is?"

"Whatever I tell you stays in this room."

"You don't think I'd betray you, do you."

"That's not exactly the problem Sir. As we were retreating from our assault on the Dragon's Lair, I gathered the Lepers and told them that the only thing likely to land us in prison was our own mouths. I reminded them of the old-World War II saying, "Loose Lips, Sink Ships." In other words, the only way we'd end up in Leavenworth was if we admitted what we did. Otherwise, there was no proof, we even deep-sixed our weapons in the Mekong River so it would be impossible for there to be any forensics. No matter what the politicians in Washington, may think, they have no proof. We even dumped what was left of the Laws Rockets and claymore mines in the river.

The General responded, "I understand your concern, but here's something you're not aware of. Although the administration in Washington may hate the action you've taken, that feeling is far from universal. In Fact, I'm proud of my Leper Colony. I only wish I had led you in on the raid myself. By taking out the Red Dragon you've saved countless American lives. You can be absolutely sure that I won't say a word that will endanger my men, and to carry that a little further, I'll be covering your ass."

"That's all I needed to hear General. So, this is what happened. Do you remember when we were in the headquarters at An Khe the day before the assault on Yankee?

"Yes, I remember it well."

"On the wall next to the map of Yankee was one of Southern Cambodia showing a pagoda and a photograph of a General. I asked you what that map represented and you said the pagoda was the Headquarters of the 4th North Vietnamese Army Corp the same group we were engaging in the Ia Drang Valley. I asked if we knew where they were, why we didn't obliterate them with an Arc Light raid by B52s. You said there was a problem concerning Cambodian neutrality. When I continued to stare at the map you make a final comment, "Don't even think about it!" Meaning don't get any ideas in your head of sneaking over the border and taking them out."

The General replied, "Yes, it wasn't a direct order, but a suggestion since I never thought you'd attempt it. So, the question remains; why did you do it? We both know you could have led the lepers south through the North Vietnamese Divisions back to our base at Plekiu, you didn't have to turn North and go after the Red Dragon thereby putting your men at great risk. Yet, that's exactly what happened, you succeeded, and now you and your men face a political shitstorm. So, you must have had a very good reason for doing it."

"I had a very good reason for doing it, Sir. When you commanded the forming of the Leper Colony I went down to their barracks, and after getting their attention, let them know the gravity of the situation. I then told them the story of Chilkoot Pass in the Yukon. Let me relate the story of the miners and Chilkoot Pass." Rafe then told the story of the scaling of the Chilkoot in 1898. After telling the prospective lepers the story I reiterated the moral, that a man must prove himself in life, and most important he must prove himself to himself. The object for us, the newly formed Leper Colony, was to become a force to be reckoned with, and as individuals, Men amongst Men. General, I believe we've scaled Chilkoot Pass."

General Leicester nodded his head approvingly, and Crazy Horse continued, "They say a picture is worth a thousand words so let me show you this, as I think it explains everything." Rafe reached into the breast pocket of his fatigue blouse and pulled out a folded 8x10 sheet of paper. He unfolded it and handed it across the desk to the General. The General looked at the image and a smile slowly started to grow on his usually gruff countenance. The image portrayed was a tabby cat peering into a mirror. Staring back at him is a huge black-maned Lion. The caption over the picture was "What matters most is how you see yourself."

After a moment of contemplation General Leicester said, "Ok Crazy Horse, I get the picture. Now I see what the Leper Colony was really all about."

To which Rafe replied, "We've achieved our objective. Figuratively, we've conquered Chilkoot Pass, but I haven't told the men that yet. They're all waiting for that affirmation with bated breath as they're somewhat obsessed with the idea, however, I feel that confirmation should come from you."

"I think you're right, so here's the deal; tomorrow morning at 1000 the Leper Colony will board a C130 destination Subic Bay, Philippine Islands. You'll overnight and the following day board a chartered jet to Honolulu, thence to Los Angeles, and on to El Paso, Texas. The Army is going to warehouse you at Fort Bliss until the Johnson Administration can decide your fate. Your personal gear currently at An Khe will be forwarded to Fort Bliss expeditiously, but until then you'll have to make do. Before you take off for Subic Bay, I'll have a few words with the lepers. Where you're concerned Hawkins if you were seeking redemption for that fiasco at OCS, consider the debt paid in full. I fully believe that when they write the history of the 1st Cavalry Division Airmobile the Leper Colony will be remembered as a legendary strike force, a great tribute to you and the men you led."

Rafe responded with, "Thank you, sir, that means the world to us."

"Just one more thing." The General walked around his desk and handed Rafe a business card. He went on to say, "It's my mailing address, keep me updated on what the administration is doing to railroad my Leper Colony. Remember, those of us in the field will cover your rear as best as possible."

With that General Leicester extended his hand and he and Rafe shook hands. The General then said, "Get over to the hospital and have your eye checked out before you join the fun at the barracks."

Rafe had his eye examined and found no permanent damage. The blood-red cornea was simply the seeping of blood into that area. The doctors told him that he'd make a complete recovery, but his eye would look like hell for a couple of months.

Relieved at not having to worry about his eyesight Rafe returned to the barracks to brief the lepers on their upcoming redeployment. He walked into a party going full tilt. The Lepers had gotten hold of a substantial quantity of beer and were letting off steam. Singing and yelling and generally having a good time. When Triple B greeted him, Rafe asked, "What the hell's going on here B. Where'd you get the beer?

"Compliments of General Leicester. He sent two galvanized garbage cans filled with ice and five cases of beer. I'll tell you nothing hits the spot better after being in the jungle for a month."

"Ok, this is great, it's a message to the men as to where General Leicester stands vis a vis our current situation."

Rafe called the group together and said, "Ok gentleman here's the straight poop. We've been relieved. Tomorrow, we ship out for the States, we'll fly from here to Subic Bay, thence to Honolulu, then on to Los Angeles, and from there to El Paso, Texas. We'll be based at Fort Bliss. We're all way past our normal ETS (Estimated Time in Service) we've been extended way past when we normally would have been discharged. We may be extended for another six months while the administration tries to railroad us into Leavenworth. Keep in mind we'll have the support of General Leicester and others as we go through the investigation. I have just one last thing to say about the situation in which we find ourselves. The greatest threat to ourselves is ourselves. There is no proof that we were the ones who wiped out the Dragon's Lair. The way they can convict us is if we admit our complicity. So, I have only one thing to say. Don't discuss the raid with anyone not even yourselves. The Criminal Investigative Division is going to interview each of you and they're going to try to trick you. Remember they'll lie like hell to get you to admit you took part in the raid. They'll say that one of your buddies admitted to it, and if you don't come clean your sentence will be greater; don't listen! The only thing the Leper Colony did in Cambodia was transit through it. Keep your mouths shut and I'll handle the political side. Do I make myself clear?

The answer was a resounding, "Yes Sir!"

1000 hours the following morning the Leper Colony was aboard their C130 waiting to begin their journey home. The engines had just started and were idling, waiting for the crew to begin taxing. The loading ramp was still down as if the crew was waiting for last-minute cargo. Crazy Horse was a little bit concerned as the General said he'd show up for a final farewell.

Then suddenly there he was, striding up the ramp looking more like an NFL linebacker than an Army General. Rafe saw him coming and called out, "Attention!"

The General said, "Stand Easy." He looked around the group and said, "I'll make this short and sweet. What I say, will tell you how I feel about your actions during the last 30 days. It comes from the last lines of my favorite poem.He began;

When can their glory fade?
O' the wild charge they made!
All the world wondered.
Honor the charge they made!
Honor the Light Brigade,
Noble Six Hundred!

The General saluted, and the Leper Colony returned his salute. Then the General did an about-face and strode down the cargo ramp, and across the tarmac. The Crew Chief raised the ramp and the engines began to spool up. Rafe reached into his breast pocket and pulled out the picture of the tabby cat looking into the mirror. He passed it to Triple B who looked at it and smiled. Rafe said, "Pass it around."

As the C130 began to taxi for departure the picture made the rounds from one Leper to another. When it finally made its way back to Rafe, he folded it, put it back in his pocket, and stood up. Then came what members of the Leper Colony had been waiting for; "Gentleman You've scaled Chilkoot Pass. You're a force to be reckoned with, and, you are men amongst men. I couldn't be prouder. You'remy brothers."

Their war was over; in another minute they'd be out of Viet Nam and heading for home, and they were as happy as anyone could be. As the aircraft taxied into position for takeoff Triple B, who was sitting next to Rafe asked. "What do you think?" As the aircraft roared down the runway Rafe answered with five words, "Greatness stays with a Man."

The C130 gently banked to the left and climbed out over the South China Sea. The lepers sat back with smiles on their faces. They had made it!

WHAT MATTERS MOST IS HOW YOU SEE YOURSELF.

You Know Who!

As the transport aircraft climbed on an easterly heading it began to encounter a buildup of towering cumulous clouds. The pilots, flying visual flight rules, avoided flying into the cumulous buildups which could contain violent updrafts and downdrafts. In doing this they flew down cloud canyons that towered on either side of the aircraft. It was a once-in-a-lifetime experience as usually, the aircraft would fly right through the clouds rather than skirting them. Rafe was in a state of reverie thinking back to the day he was finally freed from Greer School after almost ten years. The ride out of Viet Nam, heading for home reminded him of the ride down the Taconic State Parkway heading towards New York. They say the best journey is the one that leads to home, and this was another example.

Rafe had a feeling deep in his soul that everything he had experienced so far was leading up to something extraordinary. What that something was he had no idea, but somehow, he knew it was waiting just over the horizon. Destiny awaited and it was close at hand. "Fate is the Hunter!"

It took over 36 hours to fly from Danang to El Paso, Texas, however, it mattered little as the Lepers were feeling no pain. Despite what they might be facing politically at the hands of Lyndon Baines Johnson & Company, it was counterbalanced by how they now felt about themselves.

Upon arrival, the Leper Colony settled into concrete air-conditioned barracks on the Northern end of Fort Bliss. While Triple B handled the usual supply issues such as bedding, meal cards, and such, Crazy Horse met with the Commanding General of Fort Bliss, Major General Eli Summerville. The meeting went better than he expected. The Leper Colony hadn't landed in a hostile environment, and General Summerville made that clear from the start.

He began with, "Sergeant Hawkins you've been assigned to Fort Bliss primarily due to the auspices of General Leicester with whom I had the privilege of serving in Korea. He mentioned that you seem to have a penchant for serving under members of the Seventh Division which seems to be continuing as I served alongside Chargin' Charlie at Triangle Hill. Just to set you at ease General Leicester told me that the Leper Colony was made up of the same sort of warriors that stormed Triangle Hill. He set up this deployment so you are outside any political intrigue leading up to the investigation by the administration. You realize, of course, that the United States Army doesn't like to see troops sitting around doing nothing, and that's what led to your assignment to Fort Bliss. Unknown to practically everyone, the United States has a Top Secret, installation called Site Monitor situated up near the Southeast corner of White Sands Missile Range. It's about 30 miles from here, out in the middle of nowhere. At present, the site is patrolled by members of a CIA contractor which we call, The Range Riders. The Leper Colony's assignment will be to augment the Range Riders. An extra 17 men will prove very helpful in maintaining security. What's going on at Site Monitor no one knows, but it's very Top Secret. I'll set up a meeting between you and the leader of the Range Riders so they can coordinate some on-the-job training. Then once you get the lay of the land you can supplement their patrols."

It wasn't particularly difficult as the only things out in the area around Site Monitor were sand, sagebrush, tumbleweeds, and an assortment of Horned Toads, Rattlesnakes, and an occasional Armadillo. Whatever was in Site Monitor had to be very important since the government placed a significant level of security around what appeared to be a barren strip of nothing. Later Rafe would learn that the Nike Zeus, and Nike X, Antiballistic Missile technology was being developed there. The Leper Colony easily settled into patrolling the perimeter around Site Monitor which to them was ridiculously easy. It was a lot better than being shot at in Viet Nam.

After being at Fort Bliss for about three weeks the lepers were beginning to hear from the members of the supply company, with whom they shared a barracks, that there was a wild time to be had across the border. Prostitution was legal or at least tolerated, and the city of Juarez was filled with thousands of young women in that line of work. Having already had the conversation with the lepers that their number one priority after breathing and eating was getting laid, Rafe wasn't surprised when the rush to the border began. With their comrades from the barracks to show them the way, it wasn't long before the lepers were spending most of their off time in Mexico. Rafe wasn't one of them. His experience with members of the opposite sex had left a very bad taste in his mouth. To his everlasting regret he had assumed, as do most young inexperienced men, that if it looked good, it was good. At this stage of the game, he could almost laugh at his stupidity. So, while the lepers made the rounds of the bordellos across the border Rafe spent his off-duty hours at a horse ranch not far from Site Monitor. Since he had long been obsessed with Thoroughbred racehorses, he thought it might be a good idea to learn as much as he could about horses since he might be going into the racing industry, that is, if he could avoid Leavenworth.

First, he learned to ride, and then he helped out around the ranch learning everything he could about the care and welfare of horses. While the lepers ran wild in Mexico, Rafe contemplated the future and prepared a list of how to avoid the traps the CID (Criminal Investigation Division) would try to play on them when they inevitably arrived. While patrolling at night around Site Monitor Rafe would brief each individual leper on how the CID would try to trap them into making damming admissions. He told them the interrogators would lie about everything in an attempt, to catch them in lies. The story the lepers would stick to was a simple one. The Leper Colony left Landing Zone Yankee and transited across Cambodia keeping out of sight, after having lost their weapons in the swift river in which they made their escape.

Things at Fort Bliss were going well for the Leper Colony, but unbeknownst to Rafe, there was trouble on the horizon. In fact, what lay ahead was the most incredible event of his life. It came without warning and in a most inauspicious way. It started with a trip to the drive-in movie and then accelerated. One evening Rafe suggested the eight lepers who were off duty that evening, head down to the nearby drive-in movie, to see the new film, Zulu. On the surface, it seemed like a good idea as the movie was about the Battle of Rourke's Drift where 110 British Regulars held off over 4,000 Zulu Impis. Going to see the film Zulu seemed like a good idea, but once the film progressed into the battle scenes the lepers began to get uncomfortable. It hadn't been more than a few weeks previous that the Lepers were sneaking up on unsuspecting enemy sentries and blowing their heads off. Zulu was a film of absolute mayhem and savagery. More Victoria Crosses had been awarded in the twenty-four-hour period in which the Battle at Rourke's Drift took place than any other battle in the history of the British Empire. The film showed why. Halfway through the movie, Rafe noticed the lepers were becoming decidedly uncomfortable, and he had the solution. The lepers had arrived in two cars with four men in each. Country Boy was driving Rafe's car so he turned to him and said, "What do you say we get out of here, and go Hoopin'?" Country Boy felt like he'd been hit by an electric current. He responded immediately with, "You want to go to the Hoop?"

Rafe replied, "Yeah, maybe I need a change of scenery, check out what you boys have been doing south of the border." Country Boy rolled down the window of the car and yelled over to Hit Man who was driving the other vehicle, "Hey Guys, Crazy Horse wants to go to the Hoop (Juarez), what do you say." The answer was instantaneous, "Crazy Horse wants to go Hoopin? Hell yes, we've been waiting for this for weeks, let's cut out of here. We'll show him the Virginia Club."

With that, they replaced the speakers on their stands and rolled out of the Drive-in Theater, headed South. About forty minutes later they parked near the Virginia Club and made their way in. Rafe was surprised at the elegance of what was a high-class, den of iniquity. He walked around and took it all in. Two ballrooms, carved staircases, and crystal chandeliers, along with fringed settees and gilded mirrors. The bar in the entrance ballroom was at least one hundred feet long and had a portrait of a naked woman stretched out on a couch behind it. Of course, then there were the girls, dozens of them of all shapes and sizes, one more beautiful than the next. Rafe could understand why the lepers loved the Virginia Club.

After he had checked the place out the lepers guided him to a seat at the very end of the bar where it made a ninety-degree turn. There were two more bar stools around the corner of the bar, and then an opening where the waitresses picked up drinks. Rafe had no idea he was being set up when the lepers who were in a very ebullient mood hung around to watch what promised to be a once-in-a-lifetime event. Rafe who had become aware of the leper's unusual, effervescent attitude felt deep down that there was trouble on the horizon. But, what the hell, he was here to have a good time and ordered two double bourbons from the bartender. He had just downed the first when it happened. From around the screen that shielded the door leading to the rooms in which the girls "entertained" their clients, came the most beautiful woman Rafe would ever lay eyes on. She didn't look Hispanic, but because of the shape of her eyes, she brought to mind one of Eurasian descent. It was the combination of raven black hair, porcelain skin, and a perfect body that was enough to make your heart start pounding. Then there were her deep emerald-green eyes reminiscent of crystal clear, tropical waters. When she turned and looked at Rafe she had that haughty, heartbreaking look that drove men to distraction. Two things quickly came to mind, first was, what was she, doing in a place like this, and second, a seven-letter word; It's spelled out TROUBLE.

She only hesitated a moment before walking straight over to the bar, and taking the seat right where the bar turned, just three feet away from Rafe. It didn't take him long to figure out, "This is a setup!" Not more than fifteen feet away the lepers stood in small groups whispering with sneaky smirks on their faces. Rafe was thinking, "So, this is why they've been obsessed with trying to get me to visit the Virginia Club. What he didn't know was the lepers had been interested, for some time, in witnessing what would happen when the Irresistible Force met the Immovable Object. That clash was now a minute or two away.

After she was seated one of the bartenders placed a drink in front of her without saying a word. Rafe took a closer look at her and couldn't help but notice her deprecating if not openly hostile stare, not that he cared. To him women were trouble and this one was probably ten times worse than most.

A couple of minutes after her appearance some poor soul walked up and asked if he could buy her a drink. Obviously, he didn't know her, or anything about her character. She responded, "You think I'd drink with you, if you do, you're crazy. I'd rather drink with a pig." Under normal circumstances this could lead to violence, however, Rafe had noticed by using the full-length mirrors behind the bar, that each bartender had near his position a sawed-off shotgun and a club.People who frequented the Virginia Club knew it wasn't a place where you could manhandle the girls. Do it and you were taking your life into your hands.

A few minutes later Larado, one of the more confident lepers, tried his luck. He walked up and said, "Hi beautiful, how about I buy you a drink?" Rafe was looking at him like he was out of his mind; thinking, "Damn Larado, being from Texas you should be able to recognize a rattlesnake when you see one." Well, the die was cast, The Immovable Object was about to meet the Irresistible Force and collide they did. The beautiful woman turned her attention to Larado looking at him like he just crawled out from under a rock and said, "I wouldn't accept a drink from a filthy gringo like you, I'm surprised they allow dogs like you in here." Larado took a step back and turned his head toward Crazy Horse giving him the raised eye look meaning, so?

That's all it took. Rafe sprang into action. When the young woman turned her gaze back toward him, he asked, "How in the hell do you expect to earn a living with an attitude like that? You may be beautiful, but you speak like a drunken sailor."

That did it! She glared at him with a venomous look, and if looks could kill that would have been the end of him, then said, "Why don't you mind your own business Chicken Fucker!"

To say the least, Rafe was shocked. No woman had ever called him a name even approaching that. He wasn't about to let her get away with it and responded with, "Take a look at the calendar behind the bar!" He had noticed it when he first took his seat. It wasn't October, but someone had failed to flip the calendar to the following months leaving October's depiction of a witch riding a broomstick. He pointed to the calendar and responded to her insult with, "You may be beautiful, but you're nothing but a little witch!" The lepers who were standing nearby thought Rafe called her a little Bitch, and as far as they were concerned, the name stuck.

If the little witch was giving him a look that kills before he called her a little witch, it only intensified her fury. She retorted, "I'd slap you but that would be animal abuse."

Rafe chuckled and replied, "I was going to give you a nasty look but, I see you already have one."

She wasn't about to let him get away with that so she responded with, 'You stink like the pig you are. You're just jealous that I don't like you."

Rafe was beginning to warm up to this verbal diatribe so this prompted him to say in response, "I'm jealous of all the men who haven't met you."

She came back with, "You're so ugly you make the blind cry."

"Yeah, well someone should tear you down and replace you with a lady."

And so, it went, all evening, tearing each other apart, to the general delight of the leper colony.

Back at the base, Rafe thought about his encounter with the extraordinarily beautiful, but bitchy broad. She was definitely one of a kind. But, then on the other hand maybe she wasn't. She was just another beautiful woman using her beauty to denigrate men. Not much different from someone else he knew. So, in a perverse way, his interaction with the "Little Bitch" acted as therapy. Furthermore, he decided to go down to the Virginia Club every chance he got and continue to put her in her place.

At about this time, the Criminal Investigation Division showed up to investigate what the lepers referred to as the Battle of the Dragon's Lair. What CID ran into was a group of very confident young men that appeared to believe in the principle of, Hear no evil, See, no evil, and most importantly, Speak no evil. The lepers were no longer the inexperienced rowdies they were in 1964. The members of the Leper Colony were men amongst men, and their attitude was, "You think we did something warranting a Court Martial, prove it."

While this interrogation process continued Rafe began to spend most of his time off at the Virginia Club, in his mind, dueling with the Devil. In Rafe's mind, the "Little Bitch" was the Devil in female form, and he liked nothing better than putting her in her place.

Their verbal fights became somewhat of a spectator sport at the Virginia Club. They were so bad as to be almost comical. Generally, they ended in a tie. This went on for about three weeks before an incident took place that broke the ice between the two adversaries. During the course of the fighting, Rafe found out the little bitch's real name was Rosa Martinez.

Three weeks after their initial fight Rafe and Rosa were in their usual spot, getting their nightly fight started when it happened! From across the dance floor came a blood-chilling scream. Rafe immediately swung around on his bar stool to see what the hell was going on. Across the dance floor in a booth was a sorry-looking Mexican dressed like a down-and-out cowboy with a .45 pressed against Isadora's temple. Isadora was one of the youngest and sweetest of the Virginia Club's girls. Rafe slid off his stool and headed across the dance floor like he was taking a walk in the park. He knew instantly what he was going to do, although most bystanders would regard it as insanely dangerous.

The Mexican saw him coming out of the corner of his eye and turned the .45 in Rafe's direction. Rafe kept coming and stopped about two feet away from the seated scumbag. Most people in their right mind would never do such a thing, but what they didn't know was that Rafe believed he was protected by God! That night in the Greer School Chapel had made an indelible impression on him. The Lord God Almighty had spoken to him and said, "Fear Not I Am with You." From that moment on Rafe feared nothing.

Rafe said, "Hey Asshole, didn't your mother teach you not to pick on girls? Why not pick on someone your own size?" It was a direct challenge one that couldn't be avoided by an armed jerk in a roomful of people. The Mexican slid out of the booth keeping his .45 trained on the gringo. Unbeknownst to him, the other eight lepers had pulled the razor-sharp, K-Bar knives they kept in a sheath strapped to their ankles. Mexico was a dangerous place and the lepers never crossed the border unarmed.

The fool placed the .45 up against Rafe's forehead and began pushing. Rafe retreated back towards the bar. His plan was working, he wanted to get the Mexican away from Isadora and the other girls. Rafe stared into the

Mexican's eyes in a direct challenge. This kept the Mexican's eyes from peering past Rafe into the mirror behind the bar. If he had looked into the mirror, he probably would have seen Mighty Mouse slip up behind him with his knife drawn and ready. The mouse stayed very low being trained to use any form of camouflage, or distraction to remain unseen.

When Rafe's back hit the bar he asked, "What are you going to do shoot me?"

The Mexican said, "That's exactly what I'm going to do.

There's just one problem in doing that.

"Oh yeah, what's that? Asked the dirt bag.

"It would be mutual suicide." Rafe allowed that to sink in before continuing. In a loud voice, he said, "Boys show him what you keep under the bar!" With that, the bartenders pulled out seven sawed off shotguns. "And, it's worse than that. See my men advancing towards us with their razor-sharp, knives?" The Mexican checked them out in the mirror. Fear began to show in his eyes. "Shoot me and they'll cut your balls off, then cut open your belly and pull out your guts. You'll die, but you'll die slowly, and painfully."

The Mexican's response was, "You crazy Gringo!" Rafe's answer was, "You got that right asshole, I'm as crazy as a loon, and I'm not afraid to die. So, if you want to live, you're going to let me reach up and take the gun. Shoot me and you're dead."

With that, Rafe reached up to his forehead, took the pistol by the barrel, and pushed it up to point at the ceiling. Fortunately, it didn't go off. Rafe pulled the pistol out of the gunman's hand and in a quiet voice said, "Get the hell out of here, and if you ever come back, you're dead." The gunman bolted for the door when the lepers parted to let him flee. Unfortunately for him, one of the customers had dropped a drink near the exit when the commotion started. When he hit the wet spot, he slipped and went sliding across the floor into the wall. When he rose to his feet and started running, he looked like a cartoon character where he was slipping and sliding in place, unable to gain traction. He finally bolted out the door yelling down the street outside, "the gringo is crazy, the gringo is crazy!"

Rafe swung around and picked up his bourbon and downed it with one swallow. He looked over at Rosa who was staring at him with intense interest. After a minute she said, "Is that why they call you Caballo Loco?"

Rafe gave her a slight smile and responded with, "So how do you know my call sign?"

She came right back with, "Actually, it's quite simple. The lepers talk to the girls, and the girls tell me everything. You'd be surprised how much I know about you." With that Rosa said she had to go over and see to Isadora. She swung off her bar stool and walked over to where the girls were gathered around the terrified girl.

While Rosa was escorting Isadora upstairs the lepers gathered around Rafe who ordered drinks. Carlos the head bartender set a glass of bourbon in front of Rafe that must have contained five shots. After recovering from the shock of the incident everyone was in high spirits. The lepers were in the process of congratulating Crazy Horse on his cool demeanor in the face of extraordinary danger when Rosa reappeared. She slid back onto her barstool and placed her hand over Rafe's and rewarded him with a dazzling smile. The girl absolutely radiated beauty, and Rafe felt complemented by her change of attitude.

She took a hard look at him and then said, "Thank you for looking after Isadora, not many men would have done that." She went on to say, "You're fearless, aren't you? You do not know fear?"

Rafe looked at her for a moment then answered, "You're right Rosa I don't experience the emotion of fear."

Rosa then asked, "Do you know why?"

Rafe thought about that for a while then answered, "I'm protected by the hand of God!"

Rosa now, very interested, asked, "How do you know?"

Rafe smiled and answered, "Because he told me."

"You mean you can talk to God?"

"I did a couple of times."

"Do you know what that means?"

"No! Why don't you tell me!"

"Either you can actually talk to God, or you're delusional, or one might say, Loco, Crazy."

Rafe answered, "I know what you're saying as I've considered that myself. At a moment of extreme stress, how do you know if it's the voice of God, or if you are talking to yourself? It could be either one, however, I believe it was God, and I act as if it was. So far, no matter what the situation, and how dangerous, I come out unscathed."

The incident with Isadora broke the ice between Rafe and Rosa. When he left to return to Fort Bliss, he could actually talk to her in a respectful manner.

In the interim between the Isadora incident and the leper colony's return to the Virginia Club, another visit from the Criminal Investigation Division took place.Despite telling more lies, than a military version of Pinocchio the CID investigators didn't get very far in their interrogation of the lepers. They all told the same story. Nothing happened in Cambodia, they just transited through Cambodia and were airlifted out. Along the way, they lost their weapons in the river when their small rafts proved inadequate to withstand the current. The undercurrent of their response to all the lies the CID interrogators were putting forth was, "If you don't believe us, prove it." Of course, nothing could be proven with no surviving witnesses and no forensic evidence.

Having no success with the members of one of the Army's elite strike groups the CID mistakenly turned their attention to the leader Raphael Hawkins. Want to talk about a big mistake? They were like babes in the woods. Rafe's intellect dwarfed his adversaries, and he had thought out all of the administration's possible options.

His primary inquisitor was a full Colonel by the name of Warren Burr. He started the interrogation in the usual way asking the same questions over and over in hopes of tripping up the young sergeant. Finally, after a couple of hours of that stupidity Rafe finally said, "Look Colonel, I'm not going to answer any more of your questions. You've given me my rights under Article 31 of the Uniform Code of Military Justice and I don't have to answer any questions. If the Johnson Administration wants to Court Martial the members of the Leper Colony the only way they can succeed, without any corroborating evidence, is to convene a Kangaroo Court."

Colonel Burr somewhat taken aback by the young sergeant's confidence said, "I think you underestimate the ability of the administration in putting together any kind of court it desires. Meaning they could easily find ambitious officers that would love to have the opportunity to prove their loyalty."

Rafe took a hard look at the Colonel and told him that it was going to be difficult to convict the lepers considering their role in the Battle of Landing Zone Yankee. He wasn't particularly surprised when the Colonel added, "You may be surprised that the actions of the Leper Colony at Landing Zone Yankee may be suppressed, due to it being immaterial to any actions taken later in Cambodia."

Rade was looking at the Colonel as if he was out of his mind before answering with, "I hate to tell you this, but if you use that tactical maneuver, we'll have no choice but, to go to the press."

"I don't think you have the connections to make much of a splash in the Media, so that's somewhat of a hollow threat."

Rafe laughed and said, "Actually, I have virtually zero recognition with the Media, but my surrogate Father does. I don't have a father, but the man who thinks of me as his son has all the connections needed. If push comes to shove, you'll be in for a very unpleasant surprise."

In reality, Everett had never adopted Rafe, but he did think of him as his son. Everett was a naval war hero from Guadalcanal, he was a friend of J. Edgar Hoover, knew the Mayor of New York, was an honorary member of the International Association of Chiefs of Police, and more importantly, he was a Knight of St. Gregory in the Catholic Church and a good friend of Cardinal Spellman, the Catholic Cardinal of New York. The fact was, if Everett wanted to get the Leper Colony's story into the press it wouldn't be too hard.

When the CID Colonel realized he had run into a dead end he ended the questioning and said, "Good Luck Hawkins, because you're going to need it."

Rafe's answer was "Thank you sir, but we're not the ones who need it. It's President Johnson and his administration who'll need good luck because if they come after the Leper Colony, they're going to unleash a shitstorm of unimaginable proportions."

A few days later the Lepers were headed for their favorite place for rest and recuperation, The Virginia Club. Ever since his heroics regarding Isadora,

Rosa had changed her behavior regarding Rafe. If one didn't know her better, she appeared to be almost friendly. This wasn't going to last for long primarily because of the frat-boy antics of the lepers. They were about the same age as frat boys and exhibited some of the same stupid attitudes. The Virginia Club like many other establishments in Mexico tried to help the other Mexicans who were struggling to survive. The Club allowed various vendors to come in, to market their wares. One of the leper's favorites was the Mariachi Bands that would come in and play for a few dollars. There were also those selling flowers and candy which the lepers regularly bought for the girls.

One evening an artist came in doing caricatures, and immediately the lepers decided they had to have one done of their leader Crazy Horse. Finally, after some coaxing Rafe agreed. As it turned out he and Rosa sat next to each other on a divan with the artist sitting on a chair across from them. The members of the Leper Colony gathered around to watch the proceedings. Rafe and Rosa were pretty much hammered which in itself was quite unusual, and they were actually having a good time. At least they were having a good time until the artist finished the portrait, at which point, as usual, all hell broke loose. It was Waco, from the cowboys, that slapped a pair of handcuffs on what seemed to be friendly enemies. With that, hell broke loose. Rosa jumped to her feet screaming, "What do you filthy pigs think you're doing." The lepers were heading for the exit at high speed not wanting to face the ire of either Crazy Horse or worse, You Know Who.

Rafe just sat there and shook his head not believing his men could be so profoundly stupid. His problem was he was handcuffed to a seething spitfire. It only took a few seconds for her to turn to him and say, "You're behind this! This is your idea." Rafe responded, "Now wait a minute Rosa, this has nothing to do with me. They're just young and stupid and this is their idea of a big joke." Rosa was furious and went on to berate him by saying, "This is your idea to get me into bed. All of you stupid men are alike. I know you're behind this."

Rafe was getting a little upset himself and replied, "You think this is my idea? That I somehow planned this. I'd rather be handcuffed to a rattlesnake."

Rosa said, 'You miserable Cabron, I know you're behind this." But the truth was they were trapped and until the lepers came back and freed them, they were stuck.

Rafe finally said, "Look Rosa we're trapped, and there's not much we can do about it. Let's make the best of a bad situation."

"Exactly what do you mean by that?"

"Let's just say we got off on the wrong foot. Why not just sit here, and have a good time until they come back and set us free? They think this is a big joke, but they know better than to carry it too far. If they do, they'll have to answer to me, and then you, and the thing is, they fear you, more than me. They usually refer to you as You Know Who. They're too intimidated to use your real name."

Rosa thought about it for a few minutes and then said, "I have an idea that will drive them wild. Let's go over to the bar and get a drink and then go to one of the rooms in the back."

Rafe couldn't figure out where this was leading so, he asked, "You mean go back to where the girls entertain their clients?" She answered, "That's exactly what I mean!"

They found an empty room and Rafe was impressed with its décor. It had an ambiance that fits well with the rest of the Virginia Club which was very high-class. Being handcuffed together created a problem since it prevented them from getting into a comfortable position for any length of time. In the end, they decided to lie on the bed side by side while they talked. Once they were comfortably situated Rosa asked, "I have to ask you a question."

"Ok, you might as well as you have my complete attention."

Rosa asked, "Why do you hate women?"

"What makes you think I hate women? Does it have anything to do with the way I interact with you?"

"You know it does. For one thing, no man treats me the way you do."

"Is that because you radiate beauty?"

"Yes, I believe that's the case. It either intimidates men or they covet it. But, let's not talk about how beautiful I am, tell me about your problem with women."

"Well since we have nothing better to do, this is how it began," Rafe told her the story of his chance meeting with the Ice Princess. When he finished Rosa admitted, "Well that's pretty bad, and it only goes to show that the world is full of snakes and sharks" She went on to ask if that was his only experience with the elixir of life known as love.

Rafe explained that his only other experience was his relationship with Jill who was his high school sweetheart, and that had its problems also. Rosa asked, "What kind of problems did you have with your first love?"

Rafe answered, "She was a movie star."

Rosa giggled and said, "You're kidding me, right."

"No, I'm not kidding you!"

"How did you get a starlet as your first girlfriend?"

"I was her tutor in high school."

"Wow, that must have been an exciting experience for you."

"I thought she was a miracle, brought into my life by God himself."

"So, what happened"

"I didn't have any status, and she went to Hollywood to continue her career."

Rafe went on to tell Rosa about his prophecy concerning their being reunited in the future. He also explained he had just told Jill the prophecy so she wouldn't head to Hollywood in low spirits seeing she was just beginning her career and was only sixteen years old.

Rosa looked at Rafe for a minute and then said, "Have you given up on getting her back?"

"Pretty much. I still don't have any status, while her last film was with John Wayne and Kirk Douglas."

"I think you're selling yourself short. My intuition tells me you will be reunited."

Rafe just shook his head and said, "Fat chance."

The two of them sat up on the bed, picked up their drinks, and toasted each other's good health, then started laughing at their ridiculous predicament. The only positive development was that against the odds Rafe and Rosa were becoming friendly.

After putting their drinks on the nightstand, they lay back down on the bed as there was no telling how long they would be there. Rafe then asked

Rosa, "Well we now know about my hostility towards women, so how about your hatred of men? There must be quite a story there.

Rosa turned her head towards Rafe with a very serious look and said, "You think your experience with the *Ice Princess* was bad?"

"It was as bad as anything I could imagine!"

"Well, what happened to me was worse. This is how it happened. I was born in the city of Chihuahua. My father died in an accident when I was young. My mother raised me as best she could but in difficult circumstances. We moved to Juarez when I was 18 and I was able to get a job in a bank as a teller. That only happened because I was so beautiful.

"I'm going to make this story short as it is so painful for me to tell, and the less I dwell on it the better. To make a long story short I met a handsome gringo Army Lieutenant who had come into the bank. We went out together and he seduced me. He was my first sexual experience. I fell in love and thought I had found true happiness. Things were going along wonderfully. He said we would get married and my mother and I would move to the United States and we'd live happily ever after. My dreams were coming true. Then I got pregnant. I was afraid he might not like the idea of having a child, and I was terrified of telling him, but When I told him, I realized my fears were unfounded, and he seemed overjoyed. For about two months things seemed wonderful. We would get married and life would be good. Then it happened! He stopped coming across the border to see me. I couldn't cross the border so I had a friend who had a green card go to his unit at Fort Bliss and ask about him. I was convinced that something had happened to him, like an illness or accident. The news I received destroyed my life. He had been transferred to Germany along with his wife. He was married and had been using me. I wanted to die. I think you know the feeling. My first love had broken my heart."

Rafe was stunned, He was filled with genuine sympathy when he said, "I'm so sorry Rosa. I can't believe any man could do such a thing to a woman as beautiful as you. That's unbelievable!"

Rosa turned and looked at him her eyes brimming with tears and answered, "It goes to show that there are some real monsters in this world; Disciples of the Devil, and we just happened to run into one. Now I have a four-year-old daughter with no father, now do you understand what I'm doing in this sex business? One other thing you might as well know; I own the controlling interest in the Virginia Club."

"So, what you're saying is that you can have the lepers thrown out of here anytime you want?"

"That's exactly what I'm saying. However, they have one saving grace."

"May I ask what that is?'

"It's you, my dear, Caballo Loco."

"And why am I the saving grace?"

"Because you can speak to God!"

"What if I'm delusional?"

"I don't think you are."

"Why not?"

"Because I can speak to him also."

"Maybe we're both crazy."

"Well let me ask you this. What did you think when you saw me walk up to you when first we met?"

"Truthfully, my first thought was, what is she doing here!"

"Let me ask you another very serious question. You say you've talked to God, but do you believe he's guiding your destiny?"

It was quite a question and Rafe thought back to the second time he heard the voice of God saying, "Stay the course. I will lead the way. He answered Rosa by saying, "Actually, I do believe he is, but for the life of me I can't understand what my mission is."

Rosa then said, "I have a mission too, that's why I'm in this place. I'm waiting for someone to whom I have a message of world-changing gravity. I'm beginning to think that person is you!"

"Whatever gave you that idea?"

"Maybe it has to do with the way we met, but I have a very strong feeling about you, and I believe you're the one I've been waiting for."

"Can you tell me what that message might be?"

"No, not unless I determine you're the right one."

"How will you know?"

"God will let me know!"

"So, what do we do in the meantime?"

"I have an idea for now. Let's rattle the cage of your men, the lepers."

"How do we do that?"

"Let's play with them the way they've been playing with us."

"I'm listening! What's your idea?"

Rosa was smiling now, for the first time since they'd met. When She was happy and smiling, she was dazzlingly beautiful. "When they come back to free us, we won't be where they expect to find us. We'll stay here until one of the girls comes for us, and then we'll reappear and act like we've been back here, doing, you know, what the girls do back here with men."

"You mean act like we've been back here Makin' Whoopee?"

"That's exactly what I mean." Rosa was laughing now. "We'll make them think they drove us into each other's arms. "They think by handcuffing us together they've instigated a catfight, and we'll make them think quite to the contrary.Instead of fighting, we'll make them think we've spent the evening in a back room, Makin' Whoopee, as you call it! That will drive them crazy.

It was Rafe's turn to laugh. Her idea was just too funny. His response was, "You know Rosa you're not only incredibly beautiful, but you're as smart as you are good-looking."

"That's not what you said when we first met, do you remember? You said I should be torn down and replaced with a lady."

"I don't think that's as bad as being called a Chicken fucker," Rafe responded.

Rosa was smiling and giggling as she said, "I guess our interaction when we first met was something less than ideal.'

"That's a major understatement."

"Rosa snuggled up close to him and placed her head on his shoulder, and said, "Maybe we should turn over a new leaf?

"Exactly what do you mean by that?"

"Well, for one thing, we need to learn to be friendly. No?"

"I'm not sure I follow you!"

"When the lepers come back, and we go out there, we have to look like we've been, how do you say, Makin' Whoopee. In order to accomplish that, we need to practice, like we're rehearsing for a play. We have to get our part down pat."

"How do we do that?'

"You can start by kissing me. You know practice a little!"

Rosa brought her lips close to his and since she was this incredibly beautiful woman, he kissed her, and it was very, very good. It was like she said, practice makes perfect so he kissed her again. Things were getting a little heated when Rosa said, "This is better than cussin' each other out, no?

Rafe said, "I'll say. We keep this up and it might lead to the start of a beautiful friendship"

They didn't carry it any further than just making out, but as the minutes passed, they were beginning to like each other. Rafe suddenly felt that this was the start of something big. Not just big, but something of, what did she say, something of incredible gravity.

They lay on the bed, handcuffed together, and dozed off. After a couple of hours one of the girls knocked on the door and said, "Senora Rosa, they're back!"

Rosa and Rafe got up and walked down a corridor, around the screen, and into the ballroom. There, gathered at the end of the bar were the 10 lepers who had instigated the plot, looking very sheepish. As if on cue Rosa and Rafe embraced and kissed each other in a most passionate way. They then turned and walked towards the lepers who were frozen in place with astounded looks on their faces.

Neither Rosa nor Rafe said a word. They just stretched out the hands that were handcuffed together and waited. Rafe gave them the don't mess with Texas look he had given them when they'd first met in the barracks at Fort Benning. It was the don't fuck with me look, or you'll live to regret it. Laredo stepped forward with the key and quickly unlocked the handcuffs, then quickly added, "We were just kidding Crazy Horse, it was just a joke."

Rafe handed the handcuffs back to Larado and said, "Follow me." Rosa followed Rafe across the room with the lepers following closely behind. He set himself down on a comfortable divan in a corner up against the far wall. No sooner had he taken a seat than Rosa slipped onto his lap and gave him a lingering passionate kiss. The lepers stood there looking like the sky had just fallen. They all had that "What the fuck" look on their faces. Their scheme had just blown up in their faces, and by this time they were all thinking, "We should have known!"

Rafe gave them his bird of prey look and then said, "You fucked up gentlemen; and I use that word, gentlemen loosely! I don't know what you were thinking, or what made you think you could pull a frat boy trick like that on us, but now you're in deep shit. For your information guess who owns the controlling interest in the Virginia Club, and guess who can ban you for life? Slowly seven pairs of eyes turned toward Rosa. "That's right, **You Know Who!**" Waco whispered, "Oh Shit, under his breath." Rosa was staring at them as if looks could kill.

"Honestly, if you men want to be able to continue to come in here and see your favorite girls, you'd better all apologize to, You Know Who, and hope she's in a forgiving mood."

Mighty Mouse being one of the smartest and by far the most social of the lepers came forward and said as sincerely as he could manage, "Miss Rosa, I'm very sorry for handcuffing you and Crazy Horse together. It was just meant to be a joke, but it was a terrible idea. Please accept my humble apology." Rosa just nodded and then Hit Man stepped forward and apologized. When all of the lepers had sincerely apologized Rosa said, "All right since you've shown contrition, you're forgiven. Now go over to the bar, and have a final drink before leaving. And, don't linger because I may change my mind.

On the ride back to Fort Bliss, Doc. Lingenfelter who was driving the car Rafe was in, asked, "That had to be the most incredible turn of events we've ever witnessed. We leave you handcuffed to a rattlesnake and when we come back three hours later, we find the rattlesnake eating from the palm of your hand. Would you mind explaining how you managed that?"

"Well for one thing, as much as I've taught you boys, you still have a lot to learn. First, never underestimate the opposition. In conjunction with that, <u>You Know Who</u> is one hell of a smart broad whom you underestimate at your own peril. Secondly, and more important, is a famous old saying, <u>Never Shit In Your Playpen.</u> You can play grab-ass and all your silly games in the barracks or out in the field, but once you get into polite society, you need to conduct yourself with a little bit of decorum."

Hit Man interjected, "Are you trying to tell us that a House of ill Repute is polite society?"

"Let's put it this way Rafe added, wherever you don't know the people and their intentions, that's polite society. Have you ever considered what could have happened?

"What could have happened, asked Waco?"

Rafe was getting a little annoyed with his men and said, "What could have happened? Are you kidding? Don't you realize that the eight bartenders each have a sawed-off shotgun under the bar at their positions, as well as a club? If Rosa had begun screaming when you handcuffed us, all hell could have broken loose. You're just very lucky you handcuffed the rattlesnake to a snake charmer, or your joke could have turned into a catastrophe. We'll have a meeting tomorrow and get this shit straightened out."

The following morning the leper colony assembled in the squad bay. Rafe began with, "Listen up! By now you all know what transpired last night at the Virginia Club. That was a boneheaded idea because of the assumption that you knew how *Rosa Martinez* would react. If you had guessed wrong a lot of people would have been hurt. Do you remember what happened at Landing Zone Yankee when the North Vietnamese assumed what the U.S. Forces were doing? When their assumptions proved, incorrect, thousands died. You're combat veterans, not Frat Boys, so conduct yourselves accordingly."

Rafe went on to another subject, "I believe the Johnson Administration's investigation into what happened in Cambodia is coming to an end. We've all been interrogated by the CID, and it is now time for them to either shit or get off the pot. We've all had our ETS's (Expiration of term of Service) extended way beyond what should have happened so, I believe they'll either court-martial us or give us a discharge. Within a couple of months, we should be discharged, so if you're going to have fun down at the Virginia Club, you'd better make hay while the sun shines."

The following week was Rafe's 23rd birthday and the lepers decided to celebrate his birthday at the Virginia Club. Most of the lepers were down at the end of the bar toasting their leader's longevity when Rosa made her appearance. As she approached the group County Boy, not having witnessed the handcuffing exhibition, said to her as she passed by, "Don't give Crazy Horse a hard time tonight, it's his birthday."

Rosa stopped and turned toward County Boy and said, "Did you say it's his birthday?"

"It sure is, so let him have a good time."

Rosa smiled and said, "Ok if you insist." She made her way through the crowd of lepers and slid into her usual seat at the bar. Rafe was in what was now his usual seat also. Rosa gave him a sultry look and said, Happy Birthday Caballo Loco! It was the look that gave her away. It was the same look Jill had given him moments before she said, "I think you should take me out!" Rafe knew something was coming he just had no idea what. Rosa quickly asked, "What year were you born?"

Rafe answered, "1941."

After his answer Rosa's eyes took on the most intense look Rafe had ever seen, it was almost unnerving. He was thinking to himself, "What the hell's up."

Rosa leaned towards Rafe and when their lips were inches apart whispered, "Kiss Me!" Rafe kissed her and complete silence fell over the gathered Leper Colony. Frank Holman, nicknamed Oakie who hadn't witnessed the handcuffing episode, muttered, "Are you kidding me!"

The kiss was long and passionate and when it ended Rosa said, "We were born on the same day. I was born today in 1941 also." Rafe stared at her in disbelief. Then Rosa said, "Where were you born, and do you know the time of day?"

Rafe answered, Brooklyn, New York at 5:30 in the afternoon.

Rosa said, "Almost, but not quite. I was born in the city of Chihuahua, Mexico at 3:30 in the afternoon on the same day. We were almost born at exactly the same time."

Rafe stared at her as the realization began to penetrate his consciousness, then he said, "Rosa we were born at the same time, Chihuahua is in the Mountain Time Zone which is two hours behind the Eastern Time Zone. In Brooklyn, 5:30 P.M. is 3:30 P.M. in Chihuahua."

Rosa didn't say a word, the only effect of the impact of Rafe's words was reflected in her eyes. The pupils dilated to let in more light as when you look at a person you find highly attractive. Rosa began to think, "It's him. This is the one I've been waiting for all this time. The only question now is how to deliver a message that is so extraordinary it will be hard to believe. But, not to worry, since delivering the message is my sole reason for existence, I'll find the way."

The party continued late into the night, and for the rest of the evening, Rosa made it quite clear that she was very interested in the leader of the lepers. For their part, the lepers couldn't believe what they were witnessing. None of them could fathom how Crazy Horse had tamed the Bitch from Hell. In the end, it didn't matter much, as it was a hell of a lot better to have this extremely beautiful, and now friendly woman circulating among them, treating them like brothers, rather than acting like a mean-spirited bitch. As Rafe was kissing Rosa goodnight at the entrance to the Virginia Club she whispered, "Come back soon, we need to talk."

A couple of days after his birthday, Rafe headed back to the Virginia Club. This time he was traveling alone which was rare since Juarez could be a dangerous place.

He took public transportation to the border, and then once across the border a cab to the Virginia Club. When he entered there was no sign of Rosa so he walked down the length of the bar and took his regular seat. Rosa showed up a few minutes later once the girls advised her of his arrival. The transformation that had taken place between Rafe and Rosa was truly amazing. Rafe didn't understand it at all. It stemmed from Rosa's belief that Rafe was the person for whom she had been waiting for years. Up to this point in his life, his relationship with women had been problematic. From his perspective, Jill had been a gift from God, yet he knew right from the beginning that he would lose her to Hollywood. Rafe, on the rebound from Jill, had fallen hard for Ella who could be described as extremely sexual. The difference between the two would be the difference between Audrey Hepburn and Marilyn Monroe. Which one was the more desirable? That depends, as beauty is in the eye of the beholder.

Where Rosa was concerned, she was in a class by herself. Rafe thought she was the most beautiful woman he had ever seen. She was perfect, but he didn't understand why he felt that way. She was just extraordinarily beautiful.

They spent the evening drinking and playing, basically getting to know one another. Rafe was having a great time, but drinking way too much. Finally, he decided he'd had enough and decided to say goodnight and head back to Fort Bliss. At this point, Rosa placed a small object in his hand. As he was pretty much hammered, he couldn't figure out what she was up to. It was a piece of paper wrapped around something. He unwrapped it and found a key. Rosa pressed up against him in the booth, and whispered to him, "It's the key to my house, the address is written on the paper. It's two blocks down the street and to the right. It's a big white Moorish-looking building, you can't miss it. Let yourself in, take a shower, and take a short nap in the master suite, I'll be down in a couple of hours, then we'll have a serious talk."

An hour later Rafe was naked in her bed covered only by a sheet. While waiting he drifted off to sleep and was awoken when he heard her walk into the room. She went into the bathroom and came out a few minutes later carrying a large manila envelope. She left the bathroom door open with the light on behind her so he could see her in silhouette. She walked over to the bed and handed Rafe the envelope and said, "Look at this."

Inside the envelope was a framed photograph of Rosa taken two days before on their birthday. She was wearing a silver sequin dress that looked like it was spray-painted on her perfect body. Rafe had never seen anything more beautiful. Rosa said, "What do you think." Rafe looked over at her silhouetted figure and said, "It's the most beautiful thing I've ever seen." Then he added, "Can I have it?" Rosa gave a little giggle and responded, "No, it's just a prop. You think it's the most beautiful thing you've ever seen because you've never seen the real thing." She then walked across the room and placed the framed picture on the nightstand near the bed.

She turned and walked back to where she was silhouetted by the light from the bathroom and began to unbutton her blouse. When finished, she slipped out of it and placed it over the back of a chair. Next, she reached behind her back and undid her bra. It slid down her arms and followed the blouse onto the chair. Rafe stared at Rosa as if in a hypnotic trance. "My God! She's the most beautiful thing on earth." Rosa smiled at Rafe and continued with her tantalizing strip tease. Down slid the zipper on her skirt; It slid off and dropped to her feet. As she bent over and picked it up her large, perfectly formed breasts swung back and forth. As she stood up, she smiled at Rafe and hooked her thumbs in the elastic of her panties. Rosa slowly turned away from Rafe as she bent over and slid the panties down her legs revealing what could only be called an ass of unbelievable symmetry and perfection. She pirouetted in silhouette and stopped looking into his eyes and asked, "You like?"

"Rafe answered with, "Are you kidding, you're the most perfectly made woman ever created." She stood there smiling wearing nothing but heels and thigh-high stockings knowing what was going through his mind. After a momentary silence, Rafe finally said, "Come here."

Rosa simply shook her head and replied, "Not until we talk. Remember I have a message for you." She went on to say, "Look at the picture on the nightstand." As he was looking at the picture she added, "Now look to its right, what do you see?"

He answered, "A clock."

"What time is on the clock?" He answered, "02:05"

She went on to say, "Remember the time. Now, look back at the picture. This will be something akin to a Rorschach Test. When you look at the picture what is the first word that enters your mind?"

Rafe answered immediately, "Angelic!"

Rosa smiled and said, "Good choice of words, my Lord Raphael"

"What's this all about Rosa? Why are you suddenly referring to me as My Lord?"

"Do you remember a few days ago when we were handcuffed together, and the conversation we had?"

"Yes."

"I asked if you thought God was guiding your destiny. You said you believed he was, but you didn't understand how or what that destiny is. Remember that?"

"Yes, I remember it very clearly."

"Good, now I'm going to tell you something that's very hard to believe, but before this conversation is done you will believe me."

"What do you have to tell me that is so unbelievable?"

"My Lord, the reason the picture brings to mind the word angelic is that I am an Angel. I'm a messenger of the Lord God Almighty."

Rafe stared at her as if she were out of her mind. After considering what she had just said, Rafe said, "You know that sounds more than a little bit crazy!"

"I know it's hard to believe, but I've been directed by the Lord God to give you this message, and to let you know what you really are, and why you're here."

"Why do you have to tell me? Why don't I already know?"

"Because the Lord works in mysterious ways and there is no way to know why he does things as he does."

"Can you understand why I may be very skeptical about what you're saying?"

"I completely understand the doubts you have, however before I finish, you'll be a believer."

"How can you be so sure?"

"First, because I'm an Angel. Second, I'm going to give you a brief history of your life telling you things that only you know. I'll reveal that I have knowledge of your most intimate thoughts."

Rafe looked a Rosa while thinking, "This is insane, but I might as well hear her out. If she's making this up, I'll just walk away." After lying on the bed for a minute Rafe said, "Ok Rosa, the ball is in your court, let's hear what you have to say about my past."

Rosa started with "Good, now that I've got your complete attention, let's start with the first day of your life you can remember completely. Your mother takes you to a place called Greer School and leaves you without even saying goodbye. This leads to your developing a rebellious attitude and being classified as a resistive personality. Am I right so far?" Rosa is smiling at him, and Rafe lay there, kind of dumbfounded.

Rosa continues, "You try to adjust, but the following June you run into the person known to you as **The Devil's Handmaiden.** She attempts to kill you three times, but in truth, she's wasting her time. You're protected by the greatest power in the Universe. Life gets better when your nemesis leaves the school, and you are given the greatest gift of a lifetime, your beloved pet, Max."

"Life is all right for about five years until the monster returns. You lead a resistance movement against her which leads to Max being killed. You decide to kill her, but at the last minute are restrained by the hand of God. You switch tactics to one of counter-terrorism, and just when you think the showdown is at hand your mother pulls you out of the school."

Rosa stops and looks at Rafe. "How am I doing?"

Rafe just stares at her and nods. Then he says, "You're right on!"

Rosa continues, "You finally make it home after nine years, eight months, and twenty-six days. Then comes a life-changing event, a person who in heavenly terms we call a guardian, not a guardian angel, but a human guardian arrives on the scene. Whom am I referring to?"

There was no question in Rafe's mind who that might be so he quickly answered, "Henry Everett Massoletti."

Rosa continued, "From that point on life takes a new and positive direction. Everett, or Pop as you call him, sends you to Rhodes School on the agreement that you will become the top student. Not wanting to disappoint your benefactor you excel and become an excellent student, and then the first miracle happens. Into your life drops a beautiful young starlet, who you secretly refer to as your Golden Daffodil."

At this point, Rafe just smiled remembering the day he met Jill. When Rosa continued, she said, "Just to prove a point I'll tell you what you were thinking as you rode the subway home, from Manhattan to Queens!"

"Ok, make your point. What was I thinking?"

"You were thinking, "God Loves Me!"

Rafe chuckled at that because that was exactly what he was thinking. There was no way something so extraordinary could have happened without the intercession of God.

Rosa went on to review the second miracle which was their wonderful first date and the romance that followed. After talking about Jill, and Rafe's first taste of love she stopped, and asked, "Now you know that I am aware of everything that has ever happened to you. I'll just add one more incident. Do you remember sitting in Central Park with Jill when the three thugs approached?" Rafe answered, "Yes, I remembered it clearly. Then Rosa said,

"The Hound from Hell appears from seemingly out of nowhere, and attacks! Take a guess about where the Hound came from?"

Rafe in response just shook his head and said, "Truthfully I have no idea." Rosa smiled and answered, "My Lord Raphael it originated in your own head and materialized in an instant." Remember its attack? How the hound almost seemed to be following your directions. How it kept looking over to you for guidance. And finally, when it left, do you remember how it was running over the hill, but it never quite got there, it simply disappeared?" Rafe thought for a minute then answered, "Both Jill and I thought about what had happened, but it was so unbelievable that we decided, to talk about it was a waste of time." Rosa smiled and nodded then said, "It could have been a lot worse for the thugs for you have the power to rearrange their atoms so they would simply disappear from the face of the earth."

I could go on to The Ice Princess and even Cambodia, but only to prove the point that I am an angel and the messenger of the Lord God Almighty. Now I'll make one final point before we proceed. Remember when we started this conversation?I said, look at the clock! You did, and the time was 02:05 A.M. How long have we been talking?"

Rafe thought about it and said, "About fifteen minutes."

Rosa said, "Look at the clock."

When Rafe turned his head and looked at the clock he was stunned. It still said 02:05. He couldn't believe his eyes. He was thinking, "What the hell is going on."

Rosa then told him, "I hope you realize what you're looking at. The Lord God has interceded and froze the Universe until this conversation is concluded."

This exercise was a little too much for Rafe to absorb. He was thinking, "This is all crazy. In fact, it's more than crazy." But there were the facts staring him in the face. The clock stopped. Finally, Rafe looked at Rosa and asked, "This is some sort of setup, isn't it? If you weren't the most beautiful woman I've ever seen, and if you weren't standing there naked to get my undivided attention, I'd never believe a word of this!"

"My Lord Raphael, you will believe what I have to say. What you have just witnessed is that Lord God Almighty has interceded, and put the Universe into a state of immobility. In a word, God froze the Universe, and time has stopped until we finish this conversation." Caballo Loco, you're in another dimension."

"All right Rosa, what's this all about? You've shown me that you know everything I've ever thought or done. Now you've stopped time, and now I have only one question, "Why?"

"Good, we've finally gotten to the focal point of our discussion. I was sent with a message from the Lord God to inform you that you are not really human, and you are on earth to carry out a very specific mission."

Rafe was thinking, "This is too much, my head is spinning, not really human!" Rafe went on to say, Ok, Rosa if I'm not human, what am I?"

"Let's journey back in time to the night Max was killed and you went to the Chapel of the Child. You prayed to God because you were beaten, you didn't want to go on another step, then you heard the voice of God. He said "Fear Not", and since that time you've been completely fearless. The next thing the Lord said was far more powerful. He said, "You are my Drawn Sword!"

"Rafe just stood there dumbfounded then asked, "What does that mean exactly, The Drawn Sword of the Lord?"

Rosa responded. "You my Lord Raphael are an Angel disguised in human form. You are an instrument of Almighty God!" Rosa continued, "I know this is hard to believe but let's go back to your childhood and to the very same chapel. Remember Hymn number 551 in the hymnal?" Rafe just nodded as he well remembered one of his favorite hymns written by none other than Martin Luther.

Rosa said, "Would you mind reciting it?"

Rafe thought about it and then began,

A mighty fortress is our God,
A bulwark never failing;
Our helper he amid the flood
Of mortal ills prevailing;
For still our ancient foe
Doth seek to work us woe;
His craft and power are great,
And armed with cruel hate,

On earth is not his equal.

After reciting verse one Rosa said, "Now recite verse three which you also know by heart,"

Rafe continued.

And though this world, with devils filled,
Should threaten to undo us;
We will not fear for God hath willed
His truth to triumph through us:
The Prince of Darkness grim,
We tremble not for him;
His rage we can endure,
For lo! His doom is sure.
One little word can fell him.

After Rafe concluded Rosa said, "Very good, you remember it word for word."

Rafe laughed and said, "I should, I recited it hundreds of times while growing up."

Rosa continued, "This is what I came to tell you, at the end of verse one, it says, on earth is not his equal. That was true, but not anymore! You my lord Raphael are more than his equal, and here you are, on earth."

"This is the craziest thing I've ever heard. You don't really expect me to believe this?" Rosa answered, "I do, and before I allow the hands of time to move, you'll believe in who and what you are."

Rafe looked at her and shook his head then said, "Is there anything else you have to add that will convince me." Rosa nodded her head in a positive manner and then said, "Listen to this passage from Revelations chapter 20 verse 1 where John says, **And I saw an angel come down from heaven, having the key to the bottomless pit and a great chain in his hand. And he laid hold on the dragon, that old serpent, which is the Devil, and Satan, and bound him for a thousand years, and cast him into the bottomless pit, and shut him up, and set a seal upon him, that he should deceive the nations no more, till the thousand years should be fulfilled.** That is your mission, sanctioned by the Lord God of Hosts. You will seize Satan and throw him into the bottomless pit.

Rafe quickly thought back to Liz's painting in Paris showing him with the key and the great chain in his hand. That couldn't be discounted. Liz was psychic.

Again, Rafe just stared at her. What she was saying was the most incredible thing he had ever heard. Seize Satan! Rafe shook his head and said, "Look Rosa what you're telling me is just too much. You're saying that I've been an Angel living in human form for twenty-three years without having any knowledge of, or being aware of, the deception."

"My Lord Raphael, you have been an Angel "in training" for the last twenty- three years."

"Exactly what do you mean by that?"

"It's somewhat complex, but it starts with God himself, and why Satan exists. To begin, God is all that is! Two of his salient traits are Love and Creativity. God's greatest act of creativity is Man. God then creates a perfect environment in which man resides. In the Garden of Eden all is good, evil does not exist, and the lion lies down with the lamb. Animals, including man, do not need to eat. One would think God would be satisfied with what he had created, however, this was not true. As God pondered his creation, he realized that man was not quite like him, in that man had no choice, but to be good. God could do whatever he chose whereas man was a slave to goodness. God considered this and this led to his most monumental thought; He would let man have free choice. In order for man to have a free choice between good and evil, evil would have to exist, and therefore God would have to create it. That's where Satan comes in."

Rosa continued, "Satan's decline from Archangel to the Prince of Darkness is the forerunner of man's own dilemma, and it all revolves around hubris. Hubris is a Greek word describing extreme pride, especially pride, and ambition so great that it offends God, and leads to one's downfall. A saying that sums up hubris is "**Pride Goeth Before a Fall.**"

Rafe stood there pondering what he had just heard. It was more than a little too much. If he were to believe what Rosa had just said, then all of the extraordinary events of his life were essentially directed by God. If that were true, and if God was Love then why had he inflicted on not only himself but also on Rosa and Jill such heartbreaking encounters with the opposite sex?

As he thought about all of these incredible revelations, he couldn't help but think, "Why did I get involved with the Ice Princess? What was to be learned from that?" So, he asked Rosa, "Why did God make us go through the terrible experiences we had concerning Love? If we're angels we didn't have a free choice we had to be directed by God himself, so why would he want to do that to us?"

Rosa answered, "That's a good question, and in a roundabout way it gets to the heart of the matter!"

Rafe asked, "And what might that be?"

Rosa went on with her explanation. "God wanted us to know about the perfidy of man. To understand the full consequences of such betrayal he had us live it. Think of this My Lord Raphael, the Lord God created man and even gave him free choice, but some humans are so corrupt and arrogant that they abandon God. Imagine that! They turn their back on the very power which created them. How does that compare to what happened to us? What happened to us was bad, but not as bad as man's sin against his creator. Now having lived it; We understand it. No experience can be considered a complete failure; It can always serve as a bad example. Cats. Dogs, horses, and others, considered lesser animals, do not bite the hand that feeds them, and unlike man, they wouldn't stab their benefactor in the back, even if they could."

Rosa went on, "While we're on the subject there's something else I need to enlighten you about. What happened to us, also happened to Jill, your first love, and the reason is, like us, she is an Angel. In fact, right after God created you, he created her to give you someone to love and to be loved by. What I'm telling you my Lord is that you and Jill were made for each other. You already know that she has suffered the same rejection that you did while she was in Hollywood, but you don't know where she is at the present moment. Would you like to know?"

By this time Rafe was completely overwhelmed, but he nodded in the affirmative.

She continued, "Jill is in New York where she just landed the leading role as Sally Bowles in the new musical Cabaret. It will prove to be a smash hit, but more importantly, it will set in motion your Prophecy which will bring about the two of you being reunited. Jill is completely unaware of her heavenly status and went to New York with the intention of winning the starring role in a musical to set in motion the prophecy. Under normal circumstances her chance of winning the starring role would have been astronomical, however, she is unaware of God's intervention. Actually, my Lord Raphael, you were also unaware of God's intention when you made the prophecy. It just popped into your head like magic. You only proposed it to Jill to keep her in high spirits as she headed for Hollywood. Both of you knew it would take a third miracle for your fledgling romance to have a chance of survival, and guess what? That's exactly what the Lord God had in mind. The Lord has a deep interest in the love you and Jill have for each other, and the Lord takes care of his own, although he sometimes does it in mysterious ways

"Everything changes from this moment on. Up until now, your life was one of training and more specifically giving you human experience so that when you meet Satan, he'll never be able to recognize you as anything else but a mere mortal. That's when you lower the boom! Once I set time back into motion, you will be what God created you to be, in other words, an angel." You might even say an undercover Angel. But when you think about it, all of we Angel's are undercover."

"In that regard, tomorrow you will be ordered to report to the Commanding General of Fort Bliss. He will inform you that the day after tomorrow you will take a flight to Washington, D.C., and report to the President of the United States at the White House. Don't concern yourself with meeting the President, as although he thinks he's going to take you to task over what happened in Cambodia, you're going to have him set up the plan you're creating to capture Satan, and the truth is the President won't even be aware what you've commanded him to do. You'll simply freeze time, give him his orders, and when you set time back in motion, he'll think everything you told him was his own idea."

Rafe was smiling now thinking about the possibilities then, he finally said, "I think I'm going to like being an Angel. The Johnson Administration is in for a rude shock."

Rosa only laughed and responded, "Actually not! They're going to think everything that transpires is their own idea. Beyond that, you will now be aware of the great power you wield and know for certain that whatever you want to happen, will happen." Rosa went on to say, "My Lord Raphael, have I made my point? Are you convinced?"

Rafe smiled at her and said, "Yes, I believe you. You're very persuasive!"

"Good" Rosa said, "Then we're ready to set the Universe back in motion." With that, she snapped her fingers and said, "Voila!"

"What happens now?", asked Rafe.

Rosa beaming with delight said, "Now I get my reward"

"And what might that be?" asked Rafe.

Rosa began walking towards the bed as she answered, "You! My Lord"

"Me! What do you mean?"

"You know I've had to travel through hell just to get to you in order to deliver the Lord's message, and he said I could have anything I wanted as a reward, So, I asked for you. More specifically, for you to make love to me! After all, God created this lovemaking thing for humans, and since we're still in human form, you're what I want.

Rafe was thinking, "This is way beyond my ability to comprehend. I love Jill yet here is the most beautiful woman on earth ready to jump in bed with me." He asked Rosa, "Are you sure this is the way the Lord wants things to go down?"

"Of course, I'm sure, and the Lord agrees that it's the perfect way to wash away bad memories, and that goes for both of us. Rosa slowly continued to approach the bed with a radiant smile on her face. She said, "You find me irresistible, don't you, my lord?" Rafe just nodded in the affirmative as Rosa lifted the edge of the sheet and slid across the bed until her body was pressed full length against Rafe's. "Now show me how an Angel can make me forget the past."

Rafe was thinking, "If it's God's will, I have no choice, so with my newly infused power I'm going to give this beautiful angel an experience she'll remember forever." And that's the way it went; torrid, intense, and what could only be described as heavenly lovemaking. The Angels fell asleep wrapped in each, others, arms, as exhausted as Angels, could ever be.

When morning broke Rafe and Rosa got up showered together and said goodbye. Rosa said, "I'm being recalled to heaven so within a few days, I'll be gone. You'll never see me on earth again, but We'll meet again in Heaven."

"What happens to your daughter and mother? Don't they have to die to leave Earth for heaven?"

"Not if it's God's will. Everything is possible with him."

The two kissed goodbye in the doorway of Rosa's house, and Rafe said, "I don't know how to thank you, Rosa, I won't forget you," She just stood there smiling, knowing that was true.

The President of the United States

Rafe walked across the border and took the bus back to Fort Bliss. Now he was living in a different world one which he controlled. The only limit to what he could or couldn't do depended on the will of God. If this had been a week earlier and he learned he was being summoned to the White House it would have caused him great concern, but now it was just opportunity. He didn't have to worry about any action Lyndon B. Johnson might have in mind as he now knew The President was going to do whatever he wanted him to.

Just as predicted Rafe was ordered to report to the Commanding General the following morning. General Summerville came right to the point after Rafe reported, "Push has come to shove, and you've been ordered to report to the President tomorrow at the White House. Rafe didn't answer so the General continued, "How do you feel about that?"

"I'm not particularly concerned. I suppose he wants to read me the Riot Act. Rain executive hell down on the little Sergeant E5 by the most powerful man in the world. However, that's not going to work."

"May I ask why not? Keep in mind he may intend to Court Martial you and the lepers."

"If he were going to Court Martial us, he wouldn't have me fly to Washington. He'd just let the administrative system do its thing. Carrying that a little bit further Court Martialing the lepers would be a potential political catastrophe."

"Why do you think that's the case?"

"Just consider what went down at Landing Zone Yankee. Who was the rear guard that held the line and slowed down the NVA advance giving the battalion time to be lifted out? Then we had to find a way to extricate ourselves. If in the course of making our escape, we find a way to cross the border into Cambodia and wipe out the headquarters of the North Vietnamese Fourth Army Corp killing the Red Dragon in the process, who's going to court-martial us for that."

"Well, that's fairly easy to predict, it would be the Johnson Administration," Rafe retorted, "Only if they're crazy,"

"Why do you say that.?"

"Look at it this way General, the political left is already against the war. Court Martial the Leper Colony after what they accomplished at Landing Zone Yankee and you could turn the political right against the war also. It's now a no-win situation for the Administration."

General Summerville asked, "What makes you think a court-martial will garner enough attention nationwide to make a difference?"

"Because I have friends in high places that will ensure that the press gets involved. Think of what the press already thinks of the war. Give them a juicy story and they'll run with it."

"Well, I hope you're right because the Administration has it in for you, and would like nothing better than to nail you to the wall."

"Good luck to them on that. It's one thing to accuse us of wrongdoing and another to prove it in a court of law. They should have figured out by now that there is simply no evidence. It now looks like if we somehow got into the Dragon's Lair and slew the dragon, we're going to get away with it!"

General Summerville looked at Rafe and thought to himself, "Kid has big cojones! Going up against the President of the United States like he's taking a walk in the park. He's not being naïve either. He's completely aware of what he's up against yet he has complete confidence. I have to agree with General Leicester, Hawkins would have made a great officer. On the other hand, he's already a great officer. What the Leper Colony did at the Dragon's

Lair is an example of superlative military skill. Seventeen men cross the Cambodian border, locate the Dragon's Lair, reconnoiter it, then attack it, wiping it off the face of the earth, then disappear like the Will O' The Wisp! That attack will become legendary in the annuls of the First Cavalry Division."

After completing his thought, the General said, "Ok Hawkins go over to personnel and pick up your ticket on American Airlines, you leave at 0630 tomorrow morning. You'll arrive at National Airport in Washington, D.C. at 1430 and meet with the President at 1630 at the White House. You'll be met in Washington by Major General Dempsey who will escort you."

General Summerville looked at Rafe and then added, "Just a final piece of advice; Don't get too far over your skies! You'll be dealing with some very powerful people!"

Rafe thanked the General, and then walked over to personnel to pick up his airline ticket. Later that evening Rafe assembled the Lepers out at Site Monitor and gave them a briefing on what would take place during the next seven days. Their group had seen their tour in the Army extended way past their ETS (Estimated Time in Service), and they all were aware of the reason. The Army wanted to maintain jurisdiction in case punitive action was warrened. Rafe advised them what was going to happen. It wasn't as if Rafe thought he knew the outcome because he did. Ever since achieving his heavenly status Rafe realized he could predict future events primarily because he had the power to make things happen. Whereas a couple of days before the idea of meeting with the President of the United States would have been overwhelming, now it was an opportunity to set in motion his long-term goals.

Rafe began, "Gentlemen, tomorrow I'll fly to Washington, D.C. to meet with President Johnson at the White House."

Hit Man responded to that with, "Oh No! The shit's about to hit the fan."

Rafe only laughed and continued, "It may appear to be that way on the surface, but don't worry. I'll make sure the President sees things our way."

Oakie, then had to put his two cents in and said, "How can you be so sure? We're nobodies and the President has all the power, and we all know he wants to crucify us."

Rafe looked over the group and replied, "You're forgetting something Oakie, we're a force to be reconned with. We used to be nobodies, but now we're the Leper Colony. Believe me when I say I'll get the President to see things our way."

With that said, Country Boy added, Yeah! But if you're wrong, we're all fucked!" Rafe looked directly at Country Boy and asked, "Have I ever been wrong?" Have a little faith, I'll tell you this, when I come back from Washington, I'll have the greatest news you've ever heard, and you'll be out of the Army within a month. I've only called this meeting to let you know where I'm going and why and to advise you to keep a very low profile and your big mouths shut. Keep this very important point in mind, "More men have been hung by their tongues than by a rope."

At 0600 the following morning Triple B drove Rafe to the airport to catch the early flight to Washington. On the way, he reiterated what he had said the day before. "Keep the lepers in line. No crossing the border, no Virginia Club. If they want to drink do it at the beer hall on the post or some local bar. The next seven days will decide our fate. We don't need any complications. Triple B responded, "Don't worry Crazy Horse, I'll keep a tight rein on them till you return."

What Rafe didn't know, although he could have if he directed his mind in that direction, was that his beloved starlet, Jill had made a call to Everett Massoletti and had arranged to have lunch with him at his restaurant the day before Rafe was to meet with the President. Jill was completely unaware of their heavenly status, not much different than Rafe had been before Rosa gave him her briefing.

When Jill arrived at Massoletti's, Everett was waiting for her at the Maitre d' stand as he wanted to be sure to greet her when she arrived. Everett saw her come in through the 70 Pine Street entrance and immediately walked over to greet her. They kissed each other on the cheek and Everett said, "My, My, Jill you've developed into a very beautiful young woman." Jill gave him a dazzling smile and replied, "Thank you, kind sir, it's so good to see you again."

Everett took her by the arm and said, "Let's go over to my special table where I entertain my most important guests." They walked over to a small table next to a column in the center of the huge restaurant. Once seated, Everett asked his beautiful visitor, "To what do I owe the honor of your visit? Although in truth, I have a good idea."

Jill turned her incredible blue eyes on Everett and asked, "Can I call you Pop? I know Rafe does."

Everett smiled, deeply flattered, and said, "I'd be honored." Jill looked directly at Everett and said, I came to see you because I'm in love with Rafe, and I want him back. I know I've treated him badly, but going to Hollywood was something like being thrown into a pool of hungry sharks. I was only sixteen years old. Now I've alienated him and I may never see him again." With that, Jill began to cry. It wasn't just a few tears running down her cheeks, she was sobbing." Everett handed her his handkerchief and said, "There, there, Jill, things may not be as bad as you think. Let's go down to my office where we'll have some privacy."

Everett led her down to his office on the floor below the restaurant. Everett took the seat behind his desk and Jill took the chair alongside. Everett immediately said, "Things may not be as bad as you think. Although you have no way of knowing this Rafe had an experience with a girl in Albuquerque just as bad as the one you had in Hollywood.

With that piece of information, Jill stopped crying. "You mean some girl in Albuquerque dumped on Rafe?"

Everett answered, "It couldn't have been much worse."

Jill asked, "Is he all right? Is he OK?"

Everett said, "We'll get to that in a minute.

Jill started with "I think I should tell you the whole story starting at the beginning. Then you might understand why I'm here. She began with, when Rafe and I met at Rhodes School we began to think of it as, what we eventually called, the first miracle. We became great friends almost immediately. I was 15 years old and I was beginning to think it was time I had a boyfriend. All the other kids were beginning to go steady and I was thinking if I was to have a boyfriend, I already had the perfect candidate, and it was Rafe. When I finally said to Rafe, "I think you should take me out", he tried to back out of it. I was surprised because I was aware of how Rafe felt about me, so I sort of pushed the envelope. I said, "You're not turning me down, are you? That did the trick! How could he turn me down, after all, I was a starlet, and I knew he was secretly crazy about me. He agreed to take me out but needed to think about it over the weekend. And, then you entered the picture and set up the most wonderful date imaginable. When He kissed me goodnight, I knew I was in love. I never experienced a feeling like that in my life.

Six days later I said to Rafe, "I think we should go steady!" I thought he would readily accept, but he didn't. Rafe seemed to be backing away from the idea of us going steady and I started crying. His solution was to lift me to my feet and kiss me, and then within minutes, we were going steady. Over the next hour, Rafe explained why he had reservations about the two of us being a couple. It revolved around my being a movie starlet and in his mind, he was nothing. What he meant by that was he had no status and under those circumstances, our high school romance wouldn't be acceptable. In other words, it wouldn't be acceptable to those who wielded power. After discussing this at length we decided to carry on our romance in secret. So, no one knew what we were doing, not our mothers or our family members or for that matter even you, who was instrumental in starting our romance to begin with. But Rafe had the solution! The following six months were the happiest days of my life, I wish I could explain it, but it's not possible.

When June finally arrived, I was scheduled to go to Hollywood to start my next picture. I had a contract to make four more films after Exodus. I was devastated! I didn't want to leave Rafe for anything, which just goes to show why our romance would have been frowned upon. Many would look at our romance as a threat to my career, and that would never be allowed to happen.

Please bear with me Pop, because something happened when Rafe and I were parting in June of 1961, and what Rafe told me then, is what brought me to see you today. You know how Rafe is. He didn't want me heading to Hollywood feeling down and out, so he came up with what he called a prophecy. I was beginning to cry so he said, "Do you want me to make a prophecy about our future." Of course, I did, so he began. Rafe said that our relationship was a miracle created by God. That our romance was so improbable that God's hand must be involved. A second miracle came with our date and our getting together for six months. He went on to say that the only way we'll overcome the odds against us is through the will of God. If he wanted us together no force on earth could deter his will. Rafe said that I would go to Hollywood and fulfill my contract to make four more motion pictures, and then I would return to New York and win the starring role in a smash Broadway musical. My winning the starring role would set in motion the prophecy that would lead to Rafe returning to me. He even told me how the prophecy would play out. One day, just before the show began, I would receive an envelope from someone in the audience. In the envelope would be a card with a seat number, and it would be signed by Heathcliff. That would signify Rafe had returned and was in the audience."

"My landing the role of Sally Bowles in Cabaret had to be an act of God. I had never once sung on stage professionally and was up against two hundred of the most talented actresses in America. It's a miracle I got the part. I think I got the role of Sally because I worked for it as if my life depended on it. That's why I came to see you Pop. I haven't heard from Rafe in almost five years. I don't even know if he's aware that I have the leading role in a Broadway musical. I also came to ask, how is he? Is he OK?

Everett looked at the beautiful young woman who was obviously distraught. It wasn't an act either, she was overcome with despair. "Look, my dear, what I'm going to tell you is strictly confidential. It is strictly between you and me, and Rafe's future could well hang in the balance."

Jill looked at Everett with shock showing in her incredible eyes. "What's going on?" she asked.

Everett quickly decided to tell her the truth. "Rafe managed to get himself involved in a situation that has completely outraged the Johnson Administration, including President Johnson. To tell the whole story would take too long so I'll give you the condensed version. From New Mexico, Rafe was transferred to Paris, France where he was the Bodyguard of the Supreme Allied Commander. From there he was admitted to Artillery Officer Candidate School at Fort Sill, Oklahoma. When his course started Rafe was at the bottom of the class rated number 41 of 41 in his barracks. Twenty-one weeks later Rafe was number one by far, having run by his classmates like they were tied to a tree. The Army was thinking Rafe might have been the best officer candidate seen since the program started. Then the trouble began; Rafe decided to resign from OCS with only three weeks remaining before graduation. I won't go into his reason for resigning, but the Army wouldn't accept his resignation. The Army was trying to look out for Rafe as they had seen he was a leader of extraordinary talent. The Army thought Rafe was making the mistake of a lifetime. When the Commandant of OCS refused to let Rafe resign, Rafe threatened him with the Inspector General. Then the shit hit the fan. The Army was furious and threatened to Court Martial Rafe for Dereliction of Duty. After finally being allowed to resign, Rafe was transferred to Fort Benning, Georgia to join the First Cavalry Division. Rafe was under the command of General Chargin' Charlie Leicester a Medal of Honor recipient and considered to be one of the top combat leaders in the United States Army. General Leicester told Rafe that he was going to be given command of 16 misfits who seemed to have a problem following orders. Rafe was to turn these misfits into a first-class fighting unit within 100 days or the whole group would be Court Martialed and given a dishonorable discharge."

By now Jill had a very troubled expression and was near tears. She asked, "What happened?"

Everett continued, "As one might expect if you knew Rafe, he amazed General Leicester by carrying out his mandate to the letter. Rafe was making a comeback in the eyes of the Army. Then, the 1st Cavalry Division was shipped to Viet Nam. Everett stopped his narrative for a moment and asked Jill, "Do you remember when I gave you a subscription to Time Magazine back in 1960?

"Yes, it was very sweet because Rafe had told you I had a very keen interest in current events."

"Do you still read Time?"

"Yes, I kept renewing my subscription."

"Do you remember last year, reading about the exploits of the First Cavalry when it first arrived in Viet Nam?

"Do mean the campaign in the Ia Drang Valley?"

"Yes, that's exactly what I'm referring to. What do you remember about the initial deployment of the First Cavalry Division?"

Jill smiled thinking it was unusual for her to be discussing the military with a man who had been awarded the Navy Cross, but due to her interest, she felt up to it. Jill started with, "I believe that when the First Cavalry was introduced to Viet Nam the Army wanted to see how their new concept of Air Mobile Infantry would work during actual combat. The campaign started with a battle at Landing Zone X-Ray when a battalion of the Seventh Cavalry was airlifted into a landing zone where the surrounding area was thought to have concentrations of North Vietnamese Army Regulars. That assumption proved correct when thousands of North Vietnamese attacked the four-hundred-man American Battalion. The U.S. prevailed by supporting the infantry with air strikes and concentrated artillery fire. The day after the battle ended the 2nd Battalion of the 7th Cavalry marched from Landing Zone X-Ray through the jungle to Landing Zone Albany. Along the way, they were ambushed by a large number of North Vietnamese regulars. The North Vietnamese had learned from their experience at Landing Zone X-Ray and quickly got their force in so close that the American advantage of Airpower and Artillery couldn't be used because of the likelihood of hitting our forces. You could say that the North Vietnamese prevailed at Albany because the United States suffered such high casualties.

About a week later came Landing Zone Yankee which in reality was the American adjustment to X-Ray and Albany. Landing Zone Yankee was a trap set up to lure large numbers of North Vietnamese out into the open where they would be bombed by B52s. The 3rd battalion was also that of the 7th Cavalry, General George Armstrong Custer's old command. Everyone knew what happened to Custer's men at the Battle of the Little Big Horn. The North Vietnamese knew that a repeat of the Little Big Horn massacre would bring them great credibility on the international stage and shock the American electorate. The American plan was dependent on large Vietnamese Regiments, actually being in the area, and that they would take the bait.

When the battle started the third battalion was inserted by helicopter into an easily defended clearing where a river made a U-turn. The battalion was protected on three sides by the river with the only obvious point of attack being the open area at the top of the U. Only the top brass were aware that Landing Zone Yankee had another vulnerability which was a ford that existed at the place where the river made a turn and then swung back forming the U-turn. At the Ford, the water was only up to three feet deep. A large force of infantry could easily wade through the shallow water and attack the American battalion from the rear. Stretching in a northerly direction leading away from the Ford was a grassy valley that extended about three-quarters of a mile into the jungle. That would be the avenue a large force of Infantry would logically use to approach the Landing Zone from the rear.Screening any attempt to advance down the valley the U.S. placed a group called the Leper Colony who were highly skilled in reconnaissance and stealth. When, and if, the NVA showed up in the jungle at the head of the valley, the Lepers would radio the landing zone and advise the battalion commander to begin evacuation. At the same time, the B52s which would be flying a holding pattern off the coast would turn inland and begin their bombing run.The B52 flight was carrying almost one thousand bombs, enough to destroy everything in the landing zone and the adjacent valley. The Leper Colony was the key! They had to slow the NVA advance down the valley in order for the 3rd battalion to escape, and yet have the enemy exposed, in the open, when the B52s arrived.

The plan put the Leper Colony in grave danger because as they retreated down the valley, they had to keep a very superior enemy force at bay using Artillery and Air strikes. However, when they got to the Landing Zone, in all likelihood, it would be too hot for extraction. The plan was if this eventuality occurred, the Lepers would take to the river under the cover of an artillery smoke barrage. The Lepers had to get far enough down the river before the B52s arrived as anything in the vicinity of the landing zone and the adjacent valley would be consumed in an exploding inferno. The poor NVA wouldn't have a chance as the B52s would bomb from such an altitude that they couldn't be heard. The first indication of disaster would be the cascade of bombs exploding in the Landing Zone, and with lightning-like speed moving up the valley.

The plan worked to perfection and the NVA suffered thousands of men killed. The lepers escaped down the river and disappeared." Jill smiled and asked, "How was that for a summation?"

Everett was amazed at Jill's memory of the events and her understanding of military tactics. Everett responded, "That was great Jill, like Rafe, you should have joined the military. It's beginning to look like you two, think alike!" Jill smiled and added, "You don't know how right you are Pop; Rafe and I are very much alike."

Everett continued, "Now we get to the heart of the matter. Do you remember what happened a few days after the battle at Landing Zone Yankee that caused an international furor?" Jill thought for a minute and finally said, "Do you mean the assault on the headquarters of the Fourth North Vietnamese Army Corp?" Everett nodded, and continued, that the military has begun to call it the Battle of the Dragon's Lair primarily because it was the headquarters of the General responsible for the campaign in the Ia Drang Valley. The General in question Chu Khan Man was killed in the Dragon's Lair attack. General Man was the North's leading expert on insurgency warfare. He was staging his forces in neutral Cambodia, then having them cross the border to attack our forces before fleeing back to the neutral sanctuary. When he was killed it was a catastrophic loss to the North Vietnamese and that's why there is such an international outcry. Now here's the question! Who do you think made the assault on the Dragon's Lair?"

Jill had no idea and just shrugged her shoulders and then said, "I have no idea."

Everett answered, "Who went missing after disappearing into the river?"

Jill gave Everett a quizzical look and then said, "Was it the Leper Colony?"

"Indeed, it was. They could have turned southeast and crept through the North Vietnamese troops between them and their base at Pleiku, but instead, they turned Northwest and crossed into Cambodia. Their intention was to find, and wipe out the Dragon's Lair, and kill the Red Dragon!

Jill couldn't believe what she was hearing so she asked, "Why would they take a risk like that, crossing into Cambodia instead of turning toward home?"

Everett wasn't sure how Jill would handle what he was about to tell her, but the die was cast. He went on, "They did it because they have an extraordinary leader whom they call Crazy Horse. He led them into Cambodia knowing that if they succeeded in killing the Red Dragon countless American lives would be saved during the course of the war."

Jill asked, "And he did it, knowing the risks?"

"Like I said he's an extraordinary leader, and you should know that because you know him!"

Jill stared at Everett for a minute and then the pupils of her blue eyes started to expand until they were huge. Everett could tell what thought was sinking home. Finally, her hand came up and covered her mouth and she said, "Oh my God! You don't mean it's, Rafe?

"That's exactly what I'm telling you, my dear! Rafe trained the Leper Colony, and led them either to glory, or disgrace."

"What's going to happen to them?"

"Well, it's not as dire as it looks, the administration, who are politicians, would like to hang the lepers, however, the commanders who lead the troops in combat are of a different persuasion. An even more important consideration is if the administration wants to lock up the Lepers they'd have to Court Martial them. This is where their problem lies. There is no evidence to be presented in a court of law. Rafe made sure the lepers were aware, that the only thing that could land them behind bars was their own mouths. The plan they followed was to say nothing happened in Cambodia. In fact, they told the interrogators that they had just transited through Cambodia keeping a low profile, and hadn't engaged in any form of combat. Near the end of their transit, the lepers dumped their weapons in the Mekong River where they'd never be found. There are no eyewitnesses and no forensic evidence so it becomes problematic for the Army to convene a Court Martial."

"Jill was shocked. She had no idea that Rafe had even been in Viet Nam. She asked, "Do you have any idea how long before this is resolved?"

"Truthfully, I think it's coming to a head. I believe it will soon be over; primarily because the lepers have already been extended way past their ETS which stands for estimated time in service. They can't keep the lepers in the Army forever just to keep them under the administration's jurisdiction. Whatever they intend to do they'll have to do it soon."

"Oh Pop, I'm so afraid for Rafe. Isn't there anything I can do?"

"My dear, would you like some advice?"

"Yes, that's exactly why I came to see you. Now I need your advice more than ever!"

Everett reached across his desk and took one of his cards from a cardholder. He scribbled something on the back of the card and then handed it to Jill. "Here my dear, on the back of the card is Rafe's address at Fort Bliss. Write him a short letter telling him that you talked with me and know what's happening regarding Cambodia. Then tell him you landed the leading role in the new Broadway Musical, Cabaret, and that means the prophecy has been set in motion. Close with some terms of endearment, and that you pray every day for his return. If he loves you and knows you want him back, he'll return. Just be patient. Just one last thing. Make it a short sweet letter putting the ball in his court. If he loves you, he'll come back to you."

With that, Jill smiled. She said, "Thank you so much Pop. At least now I have hope. I'll write to him and tell him I love him, and that I pray for the prophecy to come true."

Everett and Jill went back up to the restaurant and had lunch. Everett insisted Jill try his famous Lobster Bisque Soup. Things went along fine and about forty-five minutes later Everett saw Jill into a cab right outside the 70 Pine Street entrance. Everett waved goodbye as the cab pulled away and headed uptown. For her part Jill was happy and excited as now she would be able to recontact Rafe, and she was sure she could overcome any problems that stood in the way of their being reunited. Hope springs eternal, and now she had hope. She'd just have to be patient.

A few days after Jill met with Everett Massoletti in New York, Rafe boarded an American Airlines jet in El Paso on his way to Washington, D.C. The flight was uneventful with a stop at Love Field in Dallas and a change of planes to a new 727 which would land at Washington, National Airport. Rafe had been briefed that he would be met by Major General Dempsey who would escort him to the White House.

As confident a person as Rafe was, if this meeting had taken place before his conversation with Rosa Martinez, Rafe might have been feeling a bit of trepidation. However, under the new set of circumstances, Rafe was looking forward to his upcoming confrontation with President Johnson. Talk about being overmatched! The President thinks of himself as the most powerful man in the world, but he was up against an entity more powerful than anything Lyndon Johnson could even imagine. Rafe was sitting in his coach seat deciding how he was going to program the President into doing exactly what he wanted him to do. Actually. It was quite simple. The President would do exactly what Rafe programmed him to do, and he would think the ideas he came up with were his own.

As he walked out of the Jet Bridge into the National Airport terminal Rafe quickly spotted the uniformed Major General waiting in the departure lounge. Rafe walked over and reported to the General giving his name and rank. General Dempsey gave Rafe the once-over thinking like most seeing him for the first time, "He's not that tough-looking, certainly not the person you'd think could lead 16 men into Cambodia and wipe out the Red Dragon's Headquarters. I guess looks can be deceiving! However, he'd better be prepared as the President would like nothing better than to have his head on a silver platter."

Once they were seated in the staff car and headed onto the George Washington Memorial Parkway towards Memorial Bridge, General Dempsey asked, "Well how do you feel about your upcoming confrontation with the Commander-in-Chief?"

"Well, I wish it wasn't a confrontation, but it is what it is. I think by the time my meeting with the President is over I'll have convinced him to see things my way."

"I'm glad you're confident, however, I think your chances of convincing the President of seeing things your way has the same chance as a snowball has in hell!"

"We have something else going for us, that isn't quantitative or even visible," Rafe added.

General Dempsey raised an eyebrow, looked over at Rafe with a quizzical look, and said, "And what might that be?"

Rafe immediately responded with, "God is on our side!"

"You actually believe that?"

"General, you will see, right after my meeting with the President concludes, that what I'm telling you is the absolute truth."

After that, the two remained silent for the remainder of the short trip up the parkway, over Memorial Bridge, and then up to 15th Street to The White House.

One hour after landing at National Airport. Sergeant Raphael M. Hawkins was sitting in a corridor outside the Oval Office waiting to report to the President. For the half-hour, as he was waiting Rafe was thinking, "This is going to be interesting. The Commander in Chief squares off against a Sergeant, with the President having no chance of prevailing, even if he's completely convinced otherwise." After what seemed an intolerably long time which was only about forty-five minutes a member of the President's Staff came down the corridor and said to Rafe, "The President will see you now."

Rafe followed the aide into the Oval Office walked up and stood in front of the President's desk and said, "Sergeant Raphael M. Hawkins reporting to the Commander in Chief, as Ordered." Rafe kept his eyes on the American Flag behind the President's desk, not even glancing at the President. He knew the President was giving him the once over, sizing him up. Finally, President Johnson said, "So, you're the one who single-handedly screwed up my entire foreign policy!" Rafe thought he'd better respond and get the conversation started so he said, "Sir, do you want me to respond, or just stand here and keep my mouth shut?"

"All Right Hawkins. You and I are going to have it out, right here and now. You can stand at ease, and answer any question I have to ask." Rafe was thinking to himself, "Good now let's get down to the nitty-gritty, and it's not what you think Mr. President. In fact, where this confrontation is concerned, everything is ass-backward! I'm not the little piss ant sergeant you think I am. In fact, you will end up doing exactly what I say even if you don't know I've ordered you to do it."

"Hawkins, I want to know why you took your band of ne'er do wells across the border, into Cambodia, where you proceeded to attack and wipe out, to the last man, the headquarters of the 4th North Vietnamese Army Corp. Carrying that a little further you totally screwed up my foreign policy. You did this knowing Cambodia is a neutral country?"

"Sir, before I tell you what really happened in Cambodia, I need you to give me your word that nothing will happen to the men of the Leper Colony, except me. They were simply following orders, and they were only aware of what I decided to let them know. They weren't even aware that they were in Cambodia." Of Course, this was a complete lie on Rafe's part as before the attack on the Dragon's Lair the implications were discussed in detail and then voted upon. None of this mattered, as in the end, the President was going to do exactly what he was told to do. Rafe was just starting a conversation that would lead where ever Rafe decided to take it.

"All right! I'll give you, my word. You tell me what I want to know and your men are out of harm's way. Rafe looked at the President and could tell from the way he was glaring at him that this was going to be an unpleasant interrogation. With that in mind, Rafe asked the President, "What would you like to know, Sir?"

The President almost growled his question showing his anger, "Why did you lead your men across the border, into a neutral country, and attack the Dragon's Lair?"

"The basic reason is that Cambodia is not a neutral country. In fact, it's the exact opposite."

The president became even angrier and snapped back, "So, now you're an expert in what constitutes a neutral country, amongst your other accomplishments? So, sergeant what in your opinion constitutes a neutral country?"

Mr. President, I'll tell you what the dictionary definition of a neutral country is, it goes like this. "All military forces are similarly bound by the rules of war with regard to neutral countries. By definition, a neutral country is not a party to a military conflict between belligerent states. Unless bound by a treaty, governments are not required to remain neutral in a war, but they are presumed to be neutral unless they manifest adherence to one side or the other by word or act. Neutral countries must neither help nor harm a belligerent state nor allow a belligerent to make use of their territory or resources for military purposes. Instead, neutral states must assume a position of strict impartiality."

President Johnson was staring at Rafe thinking, "Son of a Bitch! They warned me he was smart. But they apparently forgot to tell me he's a walking, talking encyclopedia." The President thought for a while then said, "All Right, Sergeant, tell me how that statement authorizes your entry into Cambodia and the subsequent assault on the Dragon's Lair."

"Sir, It's relatively simple. The dictionary definition states that a neutral country neither helps nor harms a belligerent state nor allows a belligerent to make use of its territory or resources for military purposes. The Cambodians did allow the North Vietnamese to establish a base and headquarters on their territory, and then use it as a staging area to attack our forces. After attacking our units, they would retreat back across the Cambodian border where they were granted sanctuary. Therefore, they are not a neutral country by definition, and if your administration declares it so, that doesn't make it neutral. That's one reason we attacked."

By this time Lyndon Johnson was highly pissed off. He was seething with anger as he asked, "Ok Smart Ass, what's the other reason?"

Rafe looked at the President while thinking, "Well, ok, you asked for it!" Then he began to tell the President of the United States something he definitely didn't want to hear. "The second reason we went into Cambodia was to show the North Vietnamese what we could do to them if we so choose. In other words, we could tear them a new asshole! Why did we feel we needed to send them that message? I hate to say this to you, Mr. President, but the way you're fighting the war, we're going to lose!"

With that explanation President Lyndon Johnson was fit to be tied so, he said, "Now I've heard it all! So, a little 23-year-old Sergeant thinks he has more knowledge than all the experts in my administration. I can't think of anything more outrageous! So why are we going to lose the war?"

"Actually, it's more simple than outrageous! We're going to lose the war because you don't have the will to win it. Simply put, you're not fighting to win."

If the President wasn't outraged before, he certainly was now. He practically yelled at Rafe, "You'd better explain yourself, and fast, or you'll find yourself on the fast track to Leavenworth!"

"My point of view is not one of a politician or someone involved in governance, it's from that of an average citizen. First, our population is five times as great as that of both North and South Vietnam combined. We have the strongest military on earth and also have the strongest industrial base. To put it mildly, we are the elephant and they are the mouse. If we wanted to, we could wipe them off the face of the earth in a week. I hate to say this Sir, but this is a test of wills. The North Vietnamese know they have no chance to defeat us militarily, but they've already proven victory can be accomplished in another way. Now you might ask yourself which way is that?

"That's exactly what I'd like to know, which way is that?"

"Mr. President you've already shown them that you don't want to use our overwhelming might to just crush them, and that means you're going to fight them on their own terms. The rules of engagement will be a fight in the South with us on the defensive, and they will be the aggressors holding the initiative. Or put another way, it will be our troopers with M16s versus their guerrilla types with AK47s. They'll only attack when it suits their purpose and after attacking, they'll run for a sanctuary, just like they did in the Ia Drang Valley. In spite of them holding the initiative, we'll kill them at a rate of twenty of their men for every one of ours."

President Johnson was paying closer attention now because he had never heard someone presenting such an idea, in such a way. After thinking about what Rafe had just said the President asked, "Then how do we lose if we kill them at the rate of 20-1.

Rafe continued, "Sir, I don't mean to be impertinent but, it comes down to a matter of will. Ask yourself this; will the United States fight a war in Vietnam if it takes twenty years? I think the answer is clearly, no. Then the question becomes what if the Communists decide to hold out that long; what will we do? Let's say the war is still going on five years from now, and the North has lost two million men. During the same time period, at the rate of loss differential of 20 to 1, we will have lost 50,000 dead. How do you think the average American is going to take the loss of 50,000 young Americans fighting a war for a country they could care less about? If you listen to anyone else, you'll be fed a pile of bullshit without even being aware of it.

"How the hell can someone like you have the audacity to say something like that to the President of the United States?"

"If you want to know the truth, Mr. President, it's because I'm one of the people who would vote you out of office. I'm one of the enlisted men who feels like he's being used as cannon fodder. If you want to win the war blow North Vietnam off the face of the earth, and if you don't have the balls to do it, pull us the hell out of this stupid war."

"That does it, Hawkins, if it's the last thing I do, you'll end up in Leavenworth. What do you think of that?"

"Look Mr. President, I'm sorry to make you this angry, however, you wanted to know why I led the Leper Colony into Cambodia and wiped out the Dragon's Lair. If I haven't made myself clear; It's to make a statement. The statement to the North Vietnamese is, we can kick the shit out of you whenever we choose, so rein in your aggression! If you choose Mr. President, you can carry that attitude on, and make it policy, or you can try to court-martial me."

Lyndon Johnson sat and stared at what he considered to be, a little, low ranking, upstart of a sergeant, and wondered how he had the balls to talk to, arguably the most powerful man in the world, in such a disrespectful way. Finally, he said, "What do you mean to try to court-martial you? If I want to do it, then I will."

Rafe almost wanted to laugh, but he restrained himself. Instead, he put himself in the shoes of the President. He's faced with a young punk sergeant who thinks he can talk to the President of the United States as an equal. Too bad the President doesn't know he's faced with an emissary of the Lord God of Hosts. An entity, more powerful than anything he can possibly imagine.

Finally, Rafe said, "Mr. President, I think the idea of a court-martial is, to say the least, counter-productive; or you could say it's inadvisable, and carrying this a little bit further, it's not cost-effective."

"This time the President started laughing. Actually, he was laughing pretty hard. When he finally caught his breath, he said. "Hawkins you are something else. What in the hell do you mean it's counter-productive? Would you mind explaining yourself?"

Rafe started with, "Well Sir when you got us involved in a war with the little third-world country of Viet Nam you alienated the political left. That leaves you with only the right backing. If you were to take the heroes of Landing Zone Yankee and the Dragon's Lair and court-martial them, for doing what any red-blooded American warrior would do, you alienate the political right. So, where does that leave you? Sir, there are a couple of Army expressions for that. The first is, "Caught between a rock and a hard place," but the more appropriate one is, "Up Shit's Creek, without a paddle."

President Johnson couldn't help himself and began laughing even harder. Secretly he was beginning to like this outspoken young man, and this was primarily because no one ever spoke to him this directly. He was thinking to himself, "This is what I really need to hear. Someone who actually says what he thinks instead of serving me up a load of bullshit."

The Commander in Chief sat quietly for a minute, which seemed like an eternity to Rafe, all the time looking intently at the young enlisted man before finally saying, "Ok what's the solution?"

That's when Rafe froze time. The truth was Lyndon Johnson was far out of his depth. He was so far out of his depth that he couldn't even imagine what was happening. In effect, Rafe transported the Oval Office to another dimension. During the short period of time that Rafe and the President were in this new environment, Rafe would program the President to do exactly what he wanted. President Johnson was completely unaware that he was anywhere but, in the Oval Office talking to this unusual upstart of a sergeant whom he was beginning to find rather amusing.

Everything on planet Earth stopped, except what was taking place in the Oval Office where Rafe and the President were conversing. Rafe finally said, "The solution Mr. President is not to waste an asset such as the Leper Colony. You know what we are, and you've seen what we can do; I would argue that dismantling the Leper Colony would be a colossal waste of a proven asset. Imagine if you were to discharge the Lepers, have them form a company, and then have the CIA contract with them to be a Top Secret, Strike Force answerable only to yourself, the President of the United States. The fact that this contract group even existed would only be privy to yourself and those you considered completely trustworthy. We could serve as your own secret weapon!

"We could be a Black Operations Unit of the Central Intelligence Agency although almost no one in the agency would be aware of our existence." Rafe wasn't really carrying on a conversation with the President; he was actually programming him to do exactly what he wanted to be done. When Rafe set the world back into its usual paradigm, Lyndon Johnson would believe that every idea Rafe had programmed into his consciousness was his own. Among the ideas placed in the Presidents, consciousness was that Sergeant Raphael Hawkins was to be given a battlefield commission to Captain. The United States Government would purchase Hope Farm, the property which had previously been Greer School, as a base of operations for the Leper Colony. The Leper Colony would have the option of purchasing Hope Farm from the U.S. Government after five years for a set price. Finally, each member of the

Leper Colony would be compensated at the sum of $100,000 per year, a staggering price in 1966.

Rafe didn't have any great desire to be a commissioned officer since he'd only be in the Army another four or five weeks, however on the way back to Texas he would be traveling through New York where he would see Everett and his mother. Since his mother saw Rafe as the Black Sheep of the family, Rafe thought it would give his mother the greatest satisfaction to see him in an officer's uniform. After discovering his universal and extraordinary power, Rafe thought, "Why not, if it makes Mom happy, I'll do it."

Since events were going to happen at an accelerated pace, Rafe told the President to have a special representative of the CIA on board the 20th Century Limited when it departed New York for Chicago the day after tomorrow. Rafe and the CIA man would discuss anything required to set up Hope Farm as the Leper Colony's base of operations.

Once Rafe had programmed the President, he snapped his fingers and the earth returned to normal. President Johnson was sitting behind his desk staring at Rafe as he had been doing when Rafe froze time. It was almost like nothing had transpired, and to a certain degree that was true. No time had passed, and The President sat across the desk from Rafe apparently thinking about what he was about to say. He finally said, "I've been thinking about a solution, and I don't mind saying I think it's a brilliant idea." Rafe almost smiled, but he restrained himself. He simply asked, "What solution have you arrived at?"

"I think you're right in saying that pursuing charges against you and the lepers wouldn't be cost-effective and a complete waste of a valuable asset, so instead I'm going to have the CIA hire the Leper Colony as extremely classified contractors, answerable only to the President of the United States. In effect, I'll have my own Top Secret and highly skilled strike force."

Rafe stared at the President and sort of laughed to himself and thought, 'I think I'm going to like this Archangel business. Here I am directing the most powerful man in the world, and he's not even aware of what's happening."

"The President continued with his plans for the Leper Colony by saying, "Since I'm no longer pursuing the idea of a court-martial, I'm going to give you a battlefield commission to Captain effective immediately. What do you think of that as a turn of fortune?" Rafe answered, "Sir you don't have to do that, after all, I'll be out of the service in four or five weeks."

"Nonetheless in view of your accomplishments, I think it's appropriate. After all, neither you nor your men will be getting any decorations for valor. I do feel, however, that the extraordinary salaries we'll be paying you as contractors will more than makeup for lack of recognition."

Things were going along just great, so Rafe asked, "Sir if I may ask, what about the international brouhaha over the Dragon's Lair?"

"Well, to put it in simplistic terms I'm going to tell the commies to go suck an egg!"

"What about the United Nations and the rest of the global diplomatic community," Rafe Asked.

Looking very serious President Johnson said, "I'm going to tell them to go fuck themselves! Well maybe not in those exact words, but they'll get the message. If the commies can use Cambodia as a sanctuary, then it's not neutral. What do you think of that response, Hawkins?"

"Mr. President, that sounds like the response from a President from Texas, one in the mold of none other than Sam Houston." The President was very pleased with Rafe's assessment, and said, 'I'm a little pressed for time so I'll have to conclude our meeting, but I'll turn you over to the care of General Dempsey who will make sure you get fitted for an appropriate uniform and get a new Id Card. I'll also make sure an operative of the CIA is on the 20th Century Limited day after tomorrow to get Hope Farm up and running. We're also going to set up communications between you and me, just in case I have need of your services.

"Rafe answered with, "Will that be all sir?"

President Johnson walked around his desk, put out his right hand, and he and Rafe shook hands. The president then said, "Good luck Captain Hawkins, I'm glad we had this meeting. I'll be in touch, once you get Hope Farm up and running."

Rafe left the Oval Office and walked over to General Dempsey. The General stood up and asked, "How did it go?" Rafe said, "Much better than I hoped for"

383

With that said, the President's chief of staff opened the door leading into the Oval Office and said, to General Dempsey, "General, the President would like to see you."

While Rafe sat and waited for General Dempsey, he reviewed his meeting with President Johnson and was satisfied that everything was on the right track. Ten minutes later the General came out of the Oval Office, walked over to Rafe and said, "Son of a Bitch! I've never seen anything like this in my life. You go in, ready to be crucified, and come out a Captain. Not only that, but the president is of the opinion that you're the greatest fighting man in the Army! How in the hell did you pull that off?"

"Rafe tried to keep a straight face as he said, "General I guess I convinced President Johnson to see things my way."

"You must be very persuasive because you just talked yourself right out of hell and straight into heaven!"

Rafe laughed and responded with, "I think you may be even more correct than you realize General." Rafe was dropped off at a clothier where he was fitted for a new uniform and then reported to General Dempsey at the Pentagon where he was issued a new ID Card. Taking a day to have his new uniforms tailored, Rafe took in sights like the Smithsonian Institute and the Washington Monument. There wasn't any point in visiting the White House, he'd already seen that close-up, and personal.

The following day, wearing his new uniform, Rafe boarded the train for New York scheduled to arrive at Penn Station at 3:00 o'clock in the afternoon. Rafe called Everett and told him the arrival time so he and Rafe's mom could meet him for dinner before he boarded the 20th Century Limited for Chicago. Rafe was only taking the 20th Century Limited because a meeting had been set up between himself and a member of the CIA. A discussion would take place detailing the foundation of Hope Farm which would appear to be a Thoroughbred Horse Farm, but in actuality would be the training base for the Leper Colony. Once things were set in motion where the CIA was concerned Rafe would get off the train in Chicago and take an American Airlines flight to El Paso. Rafe was smiling and thinking to himself what a surprise his walking off the flight in El Paso would have on the waiting lepers. Seeing him in a Captain's uniform would tell them all they needed to know about how his meeting with LBJ had gone. However, once he related the rest of the story, they'd all think they had landed in seventh heaven. Rafe sat by the window watching the scenery fly by, sort of lost in a reverie, thinking of how quickly things had changed for the better.

Rafe walked down the platform at Penn Station feeling he had the world by the tail. He was very happy to see his mother and Everett standing just inside the gate to the terminal as it had been over two years since he was home. After his mother gave him a big hug and kiss, she said, "My son, the captain!" Rafe laughed to himself thinking, "I knew she'd react that way. She's thinking, "The black sheep makes good!" The trio made their way out to Eighth Avenue and caught a cab to the Waldorf Astoria which was the site of one of Rafe and Everett's favorite restaurants, The Bull and the Bear. His mother was in exceptionally good spirits seeing that Rafe seemed to be turning a corner and was beginning to build a reputable persona. Over dinner, Rafe's mom wanted to know how he had managed his seemingly impossible rapid promotion, and Rafe told her as much as he could. She couldn't believe that two days before he had been in the White House meeting with the President of the United States.

After a very pleasant dinner, Rafe and Everett went to the men's room where they had an interesting conversation. While they were washing their hands Everett said, "I had a visit from a friend of yours at the restaurant a few days ago." Rafe answered with, "A friend of mine, from where?" "This friend is an acquaintance of yours from Rhodes School." Rafe laughed and replied, "That could only be one person since I only had one friend at Rhodes. Is she five foot two, with eyes of blue, and possibly the cutest girl on planet Earth?" Everett laughed and replied, "You're right about that. Jill came downtown inquiring about you. Do you know what she's been up to of late?" Rafe replied, "Nope, but I'm sure you're about to tell me." Everett chuckled and said, "Your little dancer has landed the leading role in the smash Broadway Musical, Cabaret. It was in the news, so I already knew that, but then she went on to tell me about the prophecy you made when you two last saw each other. Do you remember that?" Rafe was smiling at that revelation and responded with, "How could I forget? I told her if she won the leading role in a major Broadway Show it would set in motion the prophecy which predicted we would get back together." Everett nodded and continued, "She went on to tell me about your secret high school romance which no one but the two of you was privy to. Now that she has somehow won the leading role, she expects you to come back to her. The girl is in love with you Rafe, and she is a very lovely young woman. What do you plan to do about it?"

"What can I do Pop? I'm still in love with her, but back when we were teenagers, I thought I didn't have the status to be pursuing a starlet. Since then, things have changed for the better."

"Have things changed that much? Son? I know you're wearing a Captain's uniform, but it wasn't very long ago that you were on the President's shit list."

"They've changed dramatically, but let's keep what I'm about to tell you just between the two of us. Let's keep Mom in the dark until I'm ready to let her see more of the big picture. You know, that if she gets it into her mind, she can prove to be a very disruptive influence. I'll tell her what's going on when the time is right, and even that will not be the complete truth."

"Ok, so what's going on?"

"The government of the United States is going to purchase Greer School, Hope Farm, and lease it to the Leper Colony, at a very reasonable price, with an option to buy. At present, Hope Farm is 1,500 acres which is going to be expanded to about 4,500 acres. The Leper Colony will remain intact and be contracted to one of the federal agencies for a specific task, which will remain Top Secret. That's all I can tell you Pop! It's a very secret operation, and the less anyone knows the better. Also, as a cover for our mission, on the surface, Hope Farm will be a thoroughbred nursery. We'll be breeding and racing Thoroughbred horses as a cover."

"So, when do you intend to reestablish your relationship with Jill?"

"Just as soon as I get Hope Farm up and running, and I have refurbished Main House with a suite of rooms fitting the lifestyle she's accustomed to. Two maybe three months should do it. Then I'm coming down to New York and fulfilling the prophecy exactly as written."

"Just don't wait too long. She's as lovely a young lady as I've ever met."

"Don't worry Pop, I'm not going to let her get away.!"

When Everett and Rafe returned to their table, they found Rafe's mom in an ebullient mood. Actually, Rafe had never seen his mother in such high spirits. He figured she just liked seeing her wayward son doing well. Being a Captain in the Army, especially one who had received a battlefield commission from the President of the United States, had his mother thinking "Maybe he's not as bad as I think!"

Since Grand Central Station was only seven blocks down Lexington Avenue from the Waldorf, they decided to walk rather than take a cab. Since it was early March, they endured the blustery North wind which was blowing down Lexington Avenue between the towering buildings which lined the street. Rafe was beginning to like his role as a heaven-sent, instrument. For the first time in his life, he was in total control. He only answered to one entity, the Lord Himself. This meant he could be creative and disguise the ground which would prove to be the ultimate trap for the serpent of old. Within the next few hours, that plan would begin to take shape. He remembered the day his mother had taken him to Greer School, and how she explained that the train with the red runner running down its platform was the 20th Century Limited. Now about eighteen years later he was going to ride the 20th Century to Chicago during the course of which, Hope Farm would come back into existence.

After saying goodbye to his parents in the huge main concourse with its famous Zodiac Ceiling, Rafe walked down the red carpet and boarded the 20th Century Limited. He was traveling in a first-class compartment as the CIA wanted the meeting between Rafe and its representative to be out of public view or hearing. After settling in, Rafe left his compartment and made his way to the Club Car which was the last car on the train. He ordered a Hennessy Cognac and Coke a taste he developed while working with the Surete in Paris. Most would consider mixing Hennessy with coke a travesty, but Rafe had developed a taste for it. Thinking back to his past Rafe realized that taking this route on the 20th Century Limited was only the second time he had taken the train to Poughkeepsie. The first time had been on August $15^{th,}$ 1948 when he made that fateful trip to Greer School, and now this was the second time he was taking the Grand Central Railroad on a route that led through Poughkeepsie. It was while the train was stopped at Poughkeepsie that a tall, grey-haired, and portly man approached him. The man said, "Do you mind if I join you?"

Rafe answered, "Not at all, pull up a chair."

Before the man seated himself, he thrust out his left hand and said, "the name is Abraham Hewitt." Rafe shook hands and responded with, I'm Rafe Hawkins." As Rafe took a closer look at Mr. Hewitt, he realized he looked like a man of stature. It was probably the direct look in his eyes, but while Rafe was taking a few seconds for a closer look at this imposing stranger he realized the man had the look of a Roman Patrician or maybe an English Lord. After ordering a drink Mr. Hewitt asked, "Is your military call sign, Crazy Horse?" Rafe smiled and answered, "I think you know it is."

"Actually, I know all about you Captain Hawkins, however, there is one question that remains a mystery."

"Well go ahead and ask your question, and I'll answer it as best I can."

"Before I ask the question may I suggest we retire to your compartment as some of the topics in our conversation are going to prove to be highly classified." Rafe agreed and the two men made their way up toward the front of the train until they reached Rafe's compartment. Once they were comfortably seated at a small table by the window Rafe asked, "What is the question that remains a mystery?"

Mr. Hewitt took a hard look at Rafe and then said, "Once President Johnson got involved, we had the FBI do a much more thorough background investigation, and what they found would have disqualified you from being awarded a Top Secret Security Clearance if the information had been discovered earlier. As it turned out the FBI only checked you out as far back as Rhodes School since it's such an outstanding institution. If they had gone back a little further to Greer School you would have been perceived in a different light."

"You must be talking about the second great American Revolution!"

"Well, that's one thing, but another discovery brings me to the question I have for you."

"What's that?"

"Do you remember a young woman named Ruth Vance?"

"Sure, she was the young lady from Vassar College doing her thesis on Intelligence testing."

"Did anyone ever tell you what she discovered when testing you?"

"No, actually, they never revealed anything to me."

"She found something quite extraordinary. Do you know what a savant is?"

"Vaguely, I've heard of the savant syndrome, but don't know the exact definition."

"Well let me explain what Ruth Vance discovered when testing you. She concluded that you have what she refers to as directed intelligence. Rather than just being a savant, you can direct your mind into any area of endeavor and test at the very highest level, while a savant is a person who is highly knowledgeable about one subject but knows little about anything else. Usually, a savant has only one exceptional skill. So, let's put this in another context. When we investigated your record at Greer School, we discovered you are a very intelligent person, one usually described as a genius. Now with that being said, here is the question that your high intelligence brought to mind. Why did you do it?"

"Do it? What exactly do you mean by that?"

Mr. Hewitt smiled and continued, "Why did you attack the Dragon's Lair? As intelligent as you are, you knew what an international firestorm that would cause. Considering your ability, you could have led the Leper Colony back through the NVA lines to Pleiku, without too much risk. But instead, you turned in the opposite direction and crossed into Cambodia to assault the Dragon's Lair. I'm curious, why?"

It was a very serious question from a very serious person. Rafe knew that all the major consequences of that action in Cambodia had now been settled, so he decided to give Mr. Hewitt a truthful answer. "It all started when I reported to General Leicester at Fort Benning. It didn't take him long to tell me that I would be in command of a group of misfits that he was labeling The Leper Colony. He then went on to say that the Army considered the members of the Leper Colony to be lower than whale shit at the bottom of the ocean. I knew why they felt that way about me, however, I couldn't speak for the other sixteen, and frankly, it pissed me off. Let me ask you a question, Mr. Hewitt. Have you ever heard of the quote, "Life is a struggle to achieve Self Worth?"

Mr. Hewitt shook his head and answered, "Can't say that I have."

"To put it succinctly those eight words, explain my decision. You could say the Leper Colony had something to prove."

"Are you saying that you invaded a neutral country to win the approval of General Leicester?"

"Let me set the record straight on one point; Cambodia is not a neutral country. It allowed the North Vietnamese to set up their headquarters in their country and provided them with a sanctuary from which to attack the forces of the United States and the Republic of Vietnam. Even in view of the non-neutrality of Cambodia, that is not why we attacked the Dragon's Lair; we did it to achieve self-worth!"

"We did it to win the approval of ourselves. Let me show you something. Rafe walked over and reached into his small overnight bag and retrieved an 8x10 piece of paper. He handed the sheet of paper to Mr. Hewitt and resumed his seat across from him. Mr. Hewitt took the picture and took a long look, and as he did so a smile appeared on his lips. Rafe then added, "The caption says it all. What matters most is how you see yourself. A year ago, we lepers were considered whale shit at the bottom of the ocean, now we're a force to be reconned with, and we're earning $100,000 a year each. Try to imagine how we see ourselves now. That's what makes your life! When you achieve Self Worth."

Mr. Hewitt smiled and nodded in agreement and said, "Indeed that's truly the case. I just had to ask; I knew there was something more to your assault on the Dragon's Lair than meets the eye."

"It was all about achieving self-worth, and now that we've accomplished that, we can move on to bigger and better things. We wouldn't be here talking about establishing Hope Farm if the attack on the Dragon's Lair hadn't taken place."

Mr. Hewitt nodded in agreement and then said, "Ok, let's get to the business of establishing your base of Hope Farm."

For the next three hours, Rafe and Mr. Hewitt went over how Hope Farm would come into being. First, the government would purchase the old

4,500 acres that had once been Greer School. The Leper Colony would establish a corporation that would be contracted to the United States Government. Included in the contract would be a clause allowing the Leper Colony to have the option to purchase the Hope Farm property at any time for up to ten years allowing the government to recoup the expenditure they put out for the original purchase. The rest of the time was spent discussing how the CIA and other branches of the U.S. Government would support the training the Lepers would constantly undergo.

An example would be Airborne training at Fort Benning, Georgia. Since the Leper Colony would all but cease to exist as a function of the U.S. Government the means for them to be trained in secret would be handled by the CIA. Rafe explained to Mr. Hewitt that Hope Farm would operate as a Thoroughbred Horse Nursery on the surface, giving it cover for the continuous training the Leper Colony would undergo. Most of their conversation concerned logistics and communications since the very existence of the newly organized Leper Colony would be Top Secret. The meeting served to establish a starting point that would become more involved once the Lepers were discharged from the Army and began to develop their base of operations. Mr. Hewitt would serve as the Liaison between Rafe and the President of the United States. It was determined that Mr. Hewitt would visit Hope Farm once it was up and running which was fine with Rafe as he was beginning to see Mr. Hewitt as a man of great character. After a three-hour conversation, Mr. Hewitt left the train and flew back to Washington, D.C.

Rafe continued on to Chicago and upon arrival in the Windy City took a cab to Midway Airport and caught an American Airlines Flight back to El Paso. As the flight landed in El Paso Rafe was thinking about how his arrival wearing the uniform of a Captain was going to affect the lepers. As he walked into the terminal, he was greeted by eight members of the Leper Colony all wearing big grins. Then the realization hit them that Rafe was wearing the uniform of an officer. With smiles on their faces, they came to attention and saluted, which Rafe returned.

Then Frank Holman (Oakie) blurted out, "What the hell happened in Washington? You're a Captain."

Rafe grinned at his men and replied, "A lot happened in Washington, and as you can see it was all positive for us. The President gave me a battlefield commission to Captain, against all probability, and I can only say this; We are no longer viewed as whale shit at the bottom of the ocean, quite the contrary in fact; we're now seen as we see ourselves, as a force to be reconned with."

Later that night, after Rafe reported to General Summerville, who like the lepers couldn't believe his eyes, Rafe held a meeting of the Leper Colony out at Site Monitor where a number of the lepers were on duty, and where it was easy to walk to a remote location out of sight or hearing. They gathered some sagebrush and tumbleweeds and lit a fire. Once the lepers were assembled Rafe began, "Gentleman, my being promoted to Captain is just the tip of the iceberg. My meeting with President Johnson can only be described as extraordinary in more ways than one. First, within the next four to six weeks all of us will be discharged from the Army with an Honorable Discharge. We are no longer looked upon as whale shit, but are now held in the highest esteem by the Johnson Administration."

The lepers all nodded and smiled at that revelation. Rafe continued, "Don't expect to be awarded any medals for valor, or anything else like that, however, we're getting something much better."

"Well, what are we getting?" asked Bruce Smith.

Rafe then asked, "All right gents, here it is, how many of you need a job once discharged?" All sixteen lepers raised their hands. Rafe asked, "Raise your hands if you'd take a job starting at twenty thousand a year. Sixteen hands shot up with zero dissenters. "That's what I'd thought you'd say. So, here's the straight poop. We're going to form a corporation which will be contracted to work for the Federal Government, and each of us will receive a salary of $100,000 per year." The lepers just stared at him dumbfounded. John Magruder was the first to answer, "Are you shitting us? 100 grand is a fortune. What will we be doing to earn that amount?"

"It's true. Which only goes to show what a great negotiator I am. Just believe what I'm saying. If you keep your noses clean for the next four to six weeks, you'll have it "made in the shade!" Here's the deal; I'll be running the corporation which will have the contract. Our mission will be to be a top-secret strike force answering to the President of the United States. While pursuing this goal I can hire whomever I want. I'm already well versed in your background and capabilities or put another way I know your character. So, you're all hired." This brought about a round of laughing and back-slapping. Jackson Slade, alias Waco, asked, "When do we start?"

"As soon as you make your way to Hope Farm, in Duchess County, New York. Here's what I suggest. Upon discharge go home for two or three weeks and see your families. Tell them that you have a job working for the government, but you can't tell them much about it because it's top secret. I'll give you contact information so you can let me know when you'll be heading to New York. Finding your way to Hope Farm from New York is relatively easy; simply go to Grand Central Station in midtown Manhattan and take a train to either Poughkeepsie or Dover Plains where I'll pick you up. Just a word about Hope Farm, it's one of the most beautiful places you'll ever see. It's got about 20 buildings on it which we'll be working to renovate into apartment suites where you'll be living. Keep in mind once we have these apartments ready for occupation you will have a wonderful place to live, rent-free. One other thing you'll be glad to hear. Before I'm discharged, I'll provide each of you with a cash advance, from your future salary, of $2,000 each for you to use on your return home and to fund transportation to Hope Farm." That brought about a surge of excitement among the Lepers as it took away any worries, they may have had about financing their homecoming."

Finally, Rafe raised the final point, he asked, "How many of you know about horses, and by that, I mean not just the ability to ride them, but knowledge about their handling and care?" Five of the Lepers raised their hands. Rafe then continued, "As a cover, Hope Farm will be developed as a nursery for Thoroughbred Race Horses. You will learn everything about horses from nose to tail, and to assist in that endeavor we'll hire one of the best horsemen in the country to educate us toward this goal. After a few years, we'll be turning out some of the finest horses in the world. Using the horse farm as a front, we'll continue to maintain our military skills in the event our services are required. I'll have a lot more information for all of you over the next month, but to put it succinctly, we have it made. Just don't screw it up with stupid behavior"

When Rafe finished with his short meeting, he was barraged with questions about how things had gone in his meeting with President Johnson. Overall, the Lepers were feeling no pain. They had done it.Everything that had been discussed during that fateful first day had been resolved. The Leper Colony was a force to be reconned with and now they were about to reap the rewards.

Over the next thirty days, the lepers were slowly pulled out of the rotation providing security at Site Monitor, and began the process of being discharged from the United States Army. With the threat of court-martial removed the men began to focus on returning home and the new life which lay ahead.

Time flies when you're having fun and in what seemed like a few days Rafe was ready to be discharged. Since things were taking such an unusual turn Rafe had each leper have business cards printed with their home addresses and the contact information for Hope Farm as well as the address and phone number of Rafe's Mother and the Massoletti Restaurant Corporation. Once they left for home their only real challenge was to make their way to Home Farm which was not yet operational. It had no staff, therefore no one to answer the phone and no way to give Rafe information as to when to meet the arriving lepers. Once the method of communication was set up Rafe was free to leave.

Rafe received the letter a few days after returning from Washington. He knew who it was from with a glance. He recognized Jill's handwriting. He opened the letter and found it short and sweet; it began, Dear Rafe, please forgive me for my past behavior, but I want you to know that I'm deeply in love with you, and need you to come back to me. Against all the odds I won the leading role in the Broadway musical Cabaret, which sets in motion your prophecy. I pray, every day, that the Lord God will not keep us separated much longer. I love you so much! Please come home to me. Love, from your little dancer.

Hope Farm

Rafe drove through the stone gates and made a left turn into the Gate House driveway. He pulled his Pontiac convertible off the road onto the grass and got out. He was standing in precisely the same place he had stood eight years ago when he said goodbye to his friends before heading for the greener pastures of home. Nothing was the same. Greer School had ceased to exist, and the property was now owned by the United States Government and fell under the management of none other than Raphael M. Hawkins. To Rafe, the whole scheme seemed more than a little bit ridiculous, but that was only if you were unaware of the incredible divine power driving it. Within the next three or four weeks the Lepers would begin to arrive after taking a well-earned leave.Once they were all present and accounted for, the task of renovating what had been a boarding school would begin. The property would comprise 4,500 acres which meant Hope Farm was about seven square miles in size.

Greer School comprised eight cottages named Plum, Greer, Crest, Ledge, Marcy, Daisy, Gate House, and Rapallo. Each cottage had been the home of about twenty-five children meaning the sleeping areas were dormitories separated into individual cubicles. The cottages were going to be renovated into luxury suites for the lepers, and Rafe had the workforce to accomplish this, but only one thing was missing, a construction foreman to supervise the lepers. Only a couple of the lepers had ever worked in construction, and only for a limited time. Rafe was convinced that once the lepers had the right leadership to educate them in the building trades the renovations would proceed at a rapid pace. In the interim, Rafe needed to find the caretakers that were keeping an eye on the property until new management took over.

Rafe drove around what he had known as Greer School looking for a vehicle parked in front of one of the buildings. It was March and not bitterly cold as winter was coming to an end. Greer School was a very beautiful property and had a certain beauty even in the dead of winter. Since it had been eight years since Rafe's departure, he took his time as he made his rounds. Not much had changed except the now absent children.

After leisurely driving around the campus Rafe came upon a battered pickup truck parked in front of the High School building. The school building was very impressive being three stories high and made of stone. Rafe stared at it and thought back to the almost ten years he had spent in this beautiful environment. But now he understood why he had been placed here and why he had experienced the events which had occurred. Rafe entered the building through the front door and began to holler "Hello"! It took about two minutes for a man to appear at the front entrance. Dressed in overalls and looking like a typical dairy farmer Rafe quickly recognized him as Vernon Ladue the man who had run the dairy farm at Greer School when he was a student.

Rafe walked over and said to the man, "Hello Mr. Ladue, do you remember me?"

The farmer took a closer look at Rafe and then said, "Well there is definitely, a resemblance to someone I know, but something's not right.

Rafe laughed and said, "That's because the last time you saw me, I was a foot shorter. I'm Rafe Hawkins from the class of '59, I used to wash and sterilize the milk bottles up at the farm.

Vernon Ladue took another look at Rafe and said, "Well I'll be damned. It sure as hell is you. Where have you been for the last eight years?"

"Well amongst other places New York, New Mexico, Paris, France, and Viet Nam, but now I'm back to oversee the development of the new Hope

Farm. I've been looking around hoping to find you to ask it you'd like a new job opportunity with the new Hope Farm.

Vernon Ladue smiled at that and said, "I'd be delighted to entertain your offer as I was dreading the day, I'd have to leave this beautiful place.

Rafe then asked, "How about George Van Alden, is he still here, and do you think he might be interested in staying on?"

Vernon now had a big smile on his face, and he told Rafe, "I think George and his family would be equally delighted in staying on."

"That's great news as I was hoping that would be the case. Just to give you an idea as to what Hope Farm will be all about, it's going to be a breeding farm for Thoroughbred Horses. I intend to breed the very highest-quality horses here. It's going to be a long-term undertaking so you can spend the rest of your lives here if you wish, and we'll make sure your families prosper financially also.

Vernon Ladue had a big smile on his face as Rafe continued to expand on how great a place for families Hope Farm would be. Finally, Rafe said, "I'll tell you what, Mr. Ladue, See if you can get your family along with George Van Alden's family to meet with me in the Main House dining room about 4 P.M. this afternoon. It's still furnished so we can sit down and discuss the conditions of your employment.

Later that afternoon the two families met with Rafe to discuss their employment. Rafe suggested that each family become independent contractors that would contract with Rafe's organization regarding compensation. By the time Rafe laid out his proposal the Ladue's and Van Alden's were ready and willing to sign a contract with Rafe.

While the discussion was ongoing Rafe mentioned he needed someone to answer the telephone at the Hope Farm office which would soon be set up. That's when Vernon's wife, Maddy said, "I can do that, in fact, I have a background in secretarial work, why not hire me as your secretary?"

This brought a big smile to Rafe's face as it was the perfect solution to a few pressing problems. Hire Maddy, and he had someone to answer the phones as soon as they were installed. He could even have a line run to the LaDue residence on the farm so Maddy could answer the phone from home, then a few times a day Rafe could drop by and pick up any messages. Rafe had to add one more piece of extremely important information that had to be kept secret at all costs. Hope Farm in addition to raising Thoroughbred Horses was also a Top Secret, United States Government Installation. Anything the LaDues and Van Aldens witnessed that concerned the military was to be kept in the strictest confidence; in other words, it was never to be discussed with anyone. The only thing that could jeopardize their future employment would be to allow anyone outside of Hope Farm, to hear what was really taking place concerning the military. Rafe swore them all to secrecy. When the meeting concluded Rafe said he'd have contracts drawn up contracting the La Dues and Van Aldens to work for the new Hope Farm.

The last thing Rafe asked Vernon LaDue was if he had the address and phone number of Helen and Mapledorm Fink who were originally from Duchess County and might still be living in the Area. Vernon said the Finks were retired and living in Hyde Park about 20 miles from Hope Farm. Rafe was pleased that things were moving so fast. In just a few hours Rafe had hired the people who would maintain Hope Farm until the entirety of the Leper Colony showed up and he had even found a secretary who would be living on the farm and wouldn't have to commute. His next step was to ask Mr. Fink if he knew of a retired construction Foreman who would sign on to teach the lepers how to renovate the buildings.

Rafe spent the night on a cot in Main House. The following morning, which was cold and blustery like the day before, Rafe got up and called the Finks to see if he could drop by and see them. They were overjoyed to hear from the school's bad boy and told Rafe they would be delighted to see him. It was almost like the return of the prodigal son. The first thing the Finks wanted to know was how someone, at his age, which was only 24 years old, had somehow gained financial control of a property as extensive as Hope Farm. Rafe related that the only way it could have happened was if he had the intent to make it so. Most people weren't interested in the Greer School property the way he was. In many ways, Rafe considered Hope Farm to be not unlike the Garden of Eden and carrying that a little bit further, a place for happily ever aftering. Rafe told the Fink's that Hope Farm would remain exactly like it had been when it was Greer School, the only difference being all of the Cottages would be renovated on the interior. In the back of his mind, Rafe was thinking, "Hope Farm will retain the same sleepy beauty it had when it was called Greer School.

After a long talk with the Finks Rafe finally got to the point of his visit. The buildings at Hope Farm needed to be renovated turning the cottages that had been dormitories into luxury suites that would be the living quarters for the leper colony. There was just one problem! Rafe had seventeen able-bodied men to do the labor, but none knew anything about construction work. Rafe needed a retired construction foreman to run the project. Someone who was no-nonsense and really knew what he was doing. Mr. Fink thought about it for a minute and finally said, "I think I have the perfect candidate; if he'll work for you."

"Why do you think he might not work for the new Hope Farm?"

"Well, he's quite a character, tough as nails. He's an ex-marine raider from Guadalcanal. If you two hit it off, he'll be perfect, as he's the best construction foreman I've ever seen.Mr. Fink told Rafe how to best contact Andrew Jackson Fiske who could be counted on being down at the River Run Bar every night, which was located at the junction of Duchess Ave and Albany Street, in Poughkeepsie, right under the approach to the Mid-Hudson Bridge.

Before leaving the Finks, Rafe told them that in the very near future, Daisy Cottage was being renovated into a luxury hotel for the visitors and guests of Hope Farm and that they, the Finks, were forever welcome to come and stay as long as they liked.

Upon entering the River Run Bar, Rafe asked the bartender if Mr. Fiske was in attendance and was told Mr. Fiske was the big man at the end of the bar. Rafe walked up to what could be called a big bear of a man, bearded, grizzled, and tough as nails. Rafe said, "Mr. Fiske, I'm Rafe Hawkins, I was told if I needed the best Construction Foreman in New York State to look you up. Mr. Fiske took a harder look at Rafe trying to get a handle on whom he was dealing with. It was the eyes that allowed him to realize exactly who Rafe Hawkins actually was. "This guy can look right through you; reminds me of the look Red Mike Edson had at Bloody Ridge."

"So, what sort of project do you need my help with?"

Rafe answered, "Myself and my unit have been recently discharged from the Army. We've taken control of the property which used to be Greer School a few miles from Verbank. Are you familiar with the place?"

"Actually, I am. I used to visit my friends Mapledorm and Helen Fink, so I'm familiar with the layout of Hope Farm."

"That's good Mr. Fiske. Here's what we want to do. We're going to turn Hope Farm from what used to be a boarding school into a premier Thoroughbred Horse Farm. Right now, there are about 20 buildings on the property of which 8 were cottages that served as residences for the children. Those cottages were set up to be dormitories and need to be renovated into luxury suites for my colleagues. We'd like the buildings to remain the same on the exterior but be completely changed on the interior. The biggest project will be Main House which is a very large complex with the main building and three connected wings. One of the wings housed the Infirmary, another the Central Kitchen, and Laundry, while the third is for housing and offices. Once we have Main house set up, we'll move on to the cottages. I think the project will take a couple of years.

"You talk about your colleagues from the military, which branch did you serve in?"

"United States Army, specifically the 1st Cavalry Division, 3rd of the 7th." That simple statement got Mr. Fiske's undivided attention. Unknown to Rafe Hawkins, Mr. Fiske had been involved in a terrible accident where a drunk, driving the wrong way on the Taconic State Parkway, had hit Mr. Fiske's car killing his wife and almost killing him. The injuries from that accident had put him into his semi-retired state. Since the loss of his wife, the childless ex-gunnery sergeant spent his time on two interests, one was Military History and the other was playing the ponies. When Rafe told him that Hope Farm was going to be developed into a Thoroughbred Horse Farm, Gunny Fiske was almost ready to commit himself to Rafe's project. However, what he was about to learn, would immediately place him in Rafe's corner.

Gunny Fiske asked Rafe if his unit had seen combat in the Ia Drang Valley since that was where the 1st Cavalry was first deployed. Rafe's response was very direct, "Indeed we did!"

"Then You must have landed on one of the three landing zones that were the source of contention?"

"That's true too, we were at Yankee."

"That must have been a real circus, getting the battalion airlifted out before the B52s arrived. I hope you got out early and weren't Tail End Charlie with those big bombers coming down the pike."

"Actually, it's worse than that. We didn't get out with the others. We went into the river under an artillery smoke barrage!"

Gunny Fiske stared at Rafe as if seeing him for the first time. He seemed to be in deep thought before he suddenly exclaimed. "Jesus! You're the fucking Leper Colony! Then as the realization hit him, he blurted out, if you're the leader, you're Crazy Horse! So, you have to be the ones who destroyed the Dragon's Lair in Cambodia."

Rafe simply gave the gunny an enigmatic smile and nodded in the affirmative. Rafe finally said, "Look Gunny, we need your services to facilitate what the Leper Colony is now proposing to do. If you agree to join us and become a member of the Leper Colony, I can tell you what actually went down in Cambodia."

It took only a second before Gunny Fiske thrust out his hand and said, "I'm on board, Crazy Horse!" With that, they shook on it, and that's how the gunnery sergeant became a leper. Rafe went on to say, "Look Gunny, I have to clear this with Washington so until that happens, I can't go into the details of what happened in Cambodia as it's still very highly classified, but don't worry, I'll get you cleared in rapid order."

Andrew Jackson Fiske just sat there trying to comprehend how his life had changed so dramatically in just minutes. When his wife was killed by the wrong-way driver of the Taconic State Parkway, Gunny Fiske had been seriously injured also. During his recovery, he slipped into a deep depression that eventually turned into an obsession. He came to believe that if he sat at a certain place in the River Run Bar in Poughkeepsie something good would happen. He had no idea what that something good would entail, but he did it anyway. He sat and drank for about fifteen weeks until it happened. The tall slender man with grey penetrating eyes shows up. Then, in a flash, everything changed.

Rafe told the gunny he had to return to the farm but asked if he could meet him the next day around ten in the morning. "Look for me at Main Horse, the big Victorian Complex on top of the hill. I'll be waiting for you in the dining room."

The two shook hands and Rafe headed back to Hope Farm feeling at the top of the world. His goal had been to find someone to be a caretaker of the complex until the lepers started to return from leave and to find the foreman who could lead the renovation of the buildings. That was now accomplished, and the project was well on its way. Rafe had only one task left to accomplish which was to call Mr. Hewitt about Gunny Fiske.

While Rafe had been off the farm meeting with the Finks and Gunny Fiske, Maddy Ladue had been escorting members of AT&T who were putting initial phone service in the various cottages which would house the lepers. Rafe's office at Main House now had a telephone and Rafe called Mr. Hewitt to have Gunny Fiske added to the roster of the Leper Colony. Mr. Hewitt had his objections, but the truth is, he was no equal to Rafe, and it was agreed upon that Gunny Fiske was now a member of the Lepers. Mr. Hewitt initialized a background check which would lead to Top Secret security clearance for the ex-marine raider

Right, about ten o'clock the next morning Gunny Fiske arrived at Main House where Rafe had a pot of coffee brewing. Rafe and Gunny Fiske had a lot to talk about seeing that Gunny Fiske was deeply into betting on horses, and Rafe was an expert handicapper. Then, there was the project that the leper colony was involved in concerning the President of the United States. While they had their coffee, Rafe told Gunny Fiske that he had talked to Washington and the gunny was now a member of the Leper Colony and was now making $100,000 per year. He was also to be given a house on the farm in which he would live rent-free. That was rent-free, with a catch. Half of the leper's earnings would go into a pool which would be used for the restoration and development of Hope Farm. After a few years, the lepers would purchase Hope Farm from the Federal Government as they had the option to do. Rafe had pretty well convinced Gunny Fiske that Hope Farm, once it was up and running, was destined to be a great source of revenue. In one remarkable day, Rafe had found the help he was looking for and had Hope Farm up and running. He now only needed to await the arrival of the Lepers.

Rafe and Gunny Fiske spent the next couple of weeks contacting an architect to redesign the cottages and began purchasing building materials. In between Main House and the School Building was a garage that held up to twenty cars. Since it had no purpose at the time with Hope Farm not yet up and running Rafe and Gunny bought building supplies and had them stored undercover in the Main House Garage. This way when needed a large amount of the required materials, they would already be on site.

On Sunday, April 3rd Rafe was informed by Maddy that three of the Lepers had called and said they would be arriving at the Dover Plains railroad station the following day at 1300 hours. They said to tell Rafe that it was three of the Cowboys, namely Laredo, Waco, and Oakie. Rafe laughed when learning their identities as he was thinking "Birds of a feather, flock together." In his mind, those three were like brothers. He was looking forward to meeting them the next day.

At 1310 the next afternoon the trio of Cowboys stepped off the train onto the platform at Dover Plains. There was no mistaking them, they looked like characters from a Hollywood script. No doubt about them being cowboys with their big cowboy hats, buckles, and boots. No sooner than they spotted Rafe than the yelling of greetings began, followed by the hugging and back slaps. It was all genuine as the lepers were good friends. Rafe couldn't help but think that most of the fun experienced by the lepers had a way of starting with the Cowboys, and then making its way into the other two squads. Once they had their belongings packed into the VW Van Rafe had rented for a month, to pick up the arriving lepers with all their gear, they pulled onto route 343. On the way out of Dover Plains, Rafe began to give the Cowboys a rundown on what to expect on their new home grounds.

"So, gentleman, welcome to New York State! Not a bad time to be arriving either, Winter just passing, and Spring is in the air. During the next few weeks, the countryside around here is going to become a very beautiful place to explore. This road we're on, leaving Dover Plains, is route 343; if we were to follow it for another ten miles we'd come to the town of Millbrook. Dover Plains is nine miles East of Hope Farm while Millbrook is five miles North. Just one thing to keep in mind! The nearest store is three miles away which is the General Store in the village of Verbank. However, the grocery stores are in Millbrook, Dover Plains, or Poughkeepsie. So, keep in mind the things you want to keep stored at home." Okie piped right up with, "Well we have an immediate problem right from the git-go!"

"What's that Oakie"

"Well with everything being located a considerable distance from the farm the first thing we need is wheels."

Rafe laughed and said, "Don't worry boys, tomorrow we'll go car shopping. You can buy anything you want."

Oakie asked, "Don't you think we should wait till we get our first paycheck?

Rafe responded with. "Not really! But you can if you want. Do you remember when I got back from Washington after the meeting with the President?" They all nodded yes, so Rafe continued. "We had a meeting at Site Monitor and I explained that the Leper Colony was now under contract to a U.S. Government entity. Do you remember that?" They all agreed that they remembered. "Rafe went to explain, "What I didn't tell you was that you went on the clock, so to speak, the minute I uttered those words. So, in effect, you've been earning about $8,800 per month for the last six weeks which will place about $13,000 in your Bank Account which I set up with Bessemer Trust in New York.

"Larado chimed in with, "Thirteen Grand, are you shitting us?" Rafe just laughed and said, "No it's all real, but I can see why you have a problem believing it. Remember, it was less than a year ago when we were considered by the Army to be Whale Shit at the bottom of the ocean. Now here we are making 100 thousand dollars a year and living the life of Riley. However, there's one thing I want to impress on you; with all of this privilege comes responsibility."

Here's an example. I've already bought my car. It's a Pontiac LeMans Convertible with a 317 Cubic Inch Engine. It's a fast and beautiful automobile however, I could have bought a Pontiac GTO with a 389 Cubic Inch Engine. The cars look alike, but the GTO is faster. The question is, how fast do I want to drive around the neighborhood? Do I want to drive 120 miles per hour down the Taconic State Parkway when I go to New York or just 70 miles per hour? We being new to the area, will be watched by our neighbors to get an idea of what sort of characters we are. Remember we're undercover. The one thing we don't want to do is bring attention to ourselves in a negative way. We want to blend right into our new surroundings."

It doesn't take very long to drive nine miles, and about 15 minutes after leaving the Dover Plains Railroad Station they passed a small lake off the right side of Camby Road. Rafe told the cowboys that the reservoir, as it was called, marked the Eastern boundary of Hope Farm. Rafe also told the lepers they could swim in the lake, but only if they didn't mind the blood-sucking leeches that inhabited the place. Rafe said he could tolerate them as a youngster, but those days were long gone. A couple of minutes later they pulled up to a grassy triangle in front of a stone gate. Rafe stopped the van and announced, "Gentlemen behold your new home. Pass through these gates and you'll be on Hope Farm which comprises 4,500 acres of the most beautiful meadows and forests. That big white house right across from the grassy triangle is called Gate House; I used to live in it eight years ago. You could even say that my familiarity with this terrain is the reason I picked Hope Farm as a base of operations."

Waco asked, "Are you going to give us a guided tour?"

Rafe replied, "Actually that's not a bad idea." He slipped the van into gear and slowly entered through the stone pillars. He gave them a slow five-mile-an-hour tour of the developed part of the farm. While they were slowly making a circuit of the farm Rafe decided to add some more good news so he said, "Oh another thing I forgot to mention we'll be billeting you, gents, in Crest Cottage temporarily, but your meals will be served in the big dining room of Main House. I've hired a very good cook who will be preparing three meals a day for you. Crest Cottage is only about 250 yards from Main House where the central dining room is located. You'll have the option of walking over for your meals, or after tomorrow you can drive. However, there is an apparent downside to this that we'll have to discuss once all of the lepers arrive. That being, one-half of your $8,800 per month salary is going into an account to run and develop the farm." Waco complained, "Oh man, $4,400 a month is a lot."

Rafe smiled and looked at Waco and replied, "Technically you're right, but only partially. Here's what I mean. Consider this. How much were you making three months ago?" Waco answered immediately, about $165 per month. "OK so now you're making $4,400 a month, but you have no real expenses. Your car will be paid for, you'll be living rent-free, and your food will be paid for out of the $4,400 per month Hope Farm will retain. So, in reality, you'll now have about $4,400 per month left to pursue your favorite pastimes, that is drinking beer, and chasing tail. If you could do the same thing on $165 per month you sure as hell can do it on $4,400."

The Cowboys readily agreed. But Laredo asked, "We might have plenty of money, but where do we find women? This place isn't exactly a target-rich environment."

Rafe laughed and said, "Well I think you may be wrong about that."

Laredo asked, "I'd like to know where they could possibly be when the nearest town only has a population of around 2,500.

Then Rafe dropped the bombshell, "Oh, I forgot to tell you, Millbrook has in its environs a school called Bennett Junior College. The thing you're going to love about Bennett Junior College is it's a college for girls. So, about 5 miles away is a place with 200 young women all eighteen to twenty-one. Now if you want to talk about a target-rich environment! Oakie practically freaked out. "Crazy Horse you are a magician! Two hundred girls all the right age not more than five miles away."

"Yep! So, to put things in perspective, you have 200 young ladies not five miles away, many of whom are away from home for the first time, and probably lonely. Think of this, what would they have to do on weekends in the middle of nowhere? Then out of nowhere comes the sixteen new guys in town, lean, fit, driving fancy new cars, and developing a 4,500-acre Thoroughbred horse farm not far outside town. Then if you played your cards right and began to go to church in Millbrook on Sunday, soon you would be the hottest commodity on the social scene. All three lepers laughed over that basically because they thought it was true. Rafe added, "Oh one more piece of strategic information. Located not seventeen miles away in Poughkeepsie, is Vassar College, one of the top universities for women. When they pulled into the driveway of Crest Cottage Rafe pointed to a big red brick Victorian building about 200 yards away and said, "That big red building is called Main House. Among the other facilities located in Main House is our central dining room in which you'll be eating your meals. Breakfast will be at 0730, Lunch at noon, and dinner at 1800. Be sure to show up for dinner tonight because I'll be introducing you to other members of the Hope Farm community."

After Rafe showed the lepers around Crest Cottage, he left them to find Gunny Fiske to make sure he was at dinner that evening to meet the new arrivals. Rafe was pleased, things were developing in a very positive way. As each group of lepers or those arriving by themselves showed up, Rafe would give them the same sort of briefing and tour he had just given the cowboys. After about a week they'd be settled in and the unit cohesion so strong in combat would begin to re-establish itself. In his own mind, Rafe was focused on one thing, that being renovating Main House to where its accommodations would be suitable for the lovely Jill. Rafe, being what he was, knew the agony Jill was living through. The two hadn't seen each other for over five years, and much had transpired in that time. Both of them had found other lovers, although in truth they were unaware of the Lord God's intercession in that. The Lord wanted his angelic creations to be aware of the pain of rejection just as God himself was rejected by his own creation, Man. Rafe was lucky, he had been informed by Rosa as to what was really taking place, whereas Jill was still in the dark. Rafe knew Jill was suffering and he, having experienced it himself, wanted her back in his arms. He knew how to fix what was ailing her!

As the weeks progressed Rafe pushed the renovation of Main House and the lepers responded with increased enthusiasm. They were aware that for some reason getting Main House renovated, was very important. Finally, in early June Rafe's suite in Main House was ready and he decided it was time to set the Prophecy in motion. Monday was the dark day for Broadway shows so Rafe knew he had to attend on a Sunday when Jill would not be performing the following day. He also knew he had to get her to take Tuesday off so he would have two days to accomplish his mission. In his mind, he was thinking, "Well that's what they have understudies for. With everything taken into consideration, he decided June 13th had to be the day. He wasn't going to give the lepers any heads up about the big surprise he was about to spring on them, he was just going to show up with Jill. The great adventure was swinging into high gear.

The Third Miracle

June 13th dawned sunny and beautiful. Rafe couldn't have asked for a lovelier day. He only needed to accomplish one more goal which he did right after breakfast in front of Main House. He walked up to Mighty Mouse and said, "Hey mouser, can I borrow your Mercedes-Benz for a few days? We can trade cars and you can drive my Le-Mans."

Mighty Mouse looked at Rafe in a curious manner and said, "Sure Crazy, but what do you need my car for?"

"I'm going to drive down to New York and pick up my girlfriend and bring her up for a few days; that's why I was in such a big hurry to get Main House renovated. I wanted to have a place fit for the style she's accustomed to.

Is that why you want my Mercedes? A fancier car for your girl? Do you want to impress her?"

"Nope that's not it, Mighty, I don't need to impress her. But there is another much more pressing issue."

"What is it?"

"Well, simply put, my Le Mans has two bucket seats separated by a console. Therefore, if my girl is riding back from New York in one of the front seats she'll be at least two feet away from me for the whole ride, however, in the Mercedes, she'll be pressed right up against me."

"Damn Crazy Horse, you thought this whole thing out right down to the last fraction of an inch!"

"Indeed, I did Mighty, and that just shows how important all of this is. Also, make sure everyone knows, not to be around when I show up at 0100 in the morning. It's all part of a plan."

Mighty Mouse flipped his car keys over to Rafe who plucked them out of midair and tossed his keys over to his waiting friend. "Well good luck Crazy, the truth is I can't wait to see your girl. If **You Know Who** is an example of the type of woman you attract, this one should be really something."

"You're right about that Mouse, she may not compare to You Know Who, in sheer beauty, but I think she's the cutest girl on earth But, you'll have to make up your own mind about that."

Around noon, Rafe pulled the Mercedes-Benz out of the circular driveway at Main House, heading down Main Road for the gate. Fifteen minutes later as he made a left turn at Hopewell Junction onto the Taconic State Parkway. Rafe was thinking, "I can't wait to see her again, and even more than that I can't wait to hold her in my arms again. Then another thought entered his mind, "God Is Great! The third miracle is happening."

Arriving in Manhattan around 1500 Rafe proceeded to Sutton Place where Jill and her mother had an apartment and parked his car in a garage a block away. He'd just take a cab down to Everett's restaurant, and then take a cab to the theater, and then later, another back to Sutton Place. Rafe hailed a cab and told the cabbie to take him to 70 Pine Street near Wall Street. As the cab turned south down 2nd Avenue Rafe couldn't help smiling to himself, and thinking, "Later tonight when I leave Sutton Place with Jill, I'll be bound for the Promised Land."

Rafe was greeted by Everett as he walked into Massoletti's and was escorted to Everett's special table. Once seated Everett said, "Well son, today's the day!"

"You're absolutely right Pop. It's been six years in coming and to tell the truth, I never thought I'd see the day."

"Why do you say that? Jill told me about your prophecy."

"Well Pop, when I made the prophecy, it was just to ease the pain of our impending separation. Deep in my heart, I felt it would take a 3rd miracle for us ever to get back together."

"A third miracle? What were the first two?"

"Miracle number one was our meeting, and my becoming her tutor. Miracle number two was our date, which you were instrumental in arranging. Then tonight, God willing, we'll see miracle number three."

"You seem very confident of the outcome."

"That's right Pop. It will happen because God loves us, and besides that, I believe it was he who set the whole thing in motion."

"What gives you that idea?"

"It's because the events that led to today are too extraordinary to have happened by chance. After all, take yourself Pop. Because of your interest in my future, you sent me to Rhodes School. Without your intercession, none of this would be happening. One could say you acted like a guardian angel preparing the way for everything that would follow. For instance, take our date, that was a work of genius on your part. After that, our romance was in full bloom. The truth is Pop, I'm not worried at all, I know how this will go down."

"Well with the Jill issue settled in your mind, how is everything else going on at Hope Farm?"

"Couldn't be any better Pop! We're getting the cottages renovated and once that's completed, we'll start building barns and fencing for the horses. In regards to the horses, I'm going to seek out and hire the best trainer in the United States."

"Now that sounds a little ambitious! How do you propose to accomplish that?

"It's not as difficult as it sounds. First, and most important, is knowing who the best trainers are. I'm looking for a trainer that can consistently have his runners win the first time out. Very few trainers know when a first-time starter is dead fit and ready to win the first time out, so what they do is enter the horse in a race to use the first start as a tightener to move the horse forward and increase its level of fitness for the next start. If that doesn't work, they give the horse another start to gain an additional degree of fitness. When the horse gains enough fitness, from its previous starts, it finally wins. However, a few trainers can gauge a horse's level of fitness to the minute and routinely have their horses win the first time out. I'm after one of those people and I think I'm zeroed in on the right person."

"May I ask who that might be?", asked Everett

"Not at all. He goes by the name Archer Madden, however, his nickname is "Speed Kills. There is just one problem regarding Mr. Madden, He was ruled off for five years after being accused of using drugs."

"Well, doesn't that disqualify him right from the start?"

"Under normal circumstances that might be the case, however, I believe Mr. Madden is innocent of the charges. He was railroaded because he was simply too good. So, I'm going to take my shot with him, if I'm wrong, I'll suffer the consequences, if right we're headed to everlasting glory."

Everett then asked, "What do you mean by that?"

"Pop, I'm going to breed the fastest racehorse ever, and Archer Madden is going to become legendary as, her trainer. In effect, by doing so, he's going to knock his detractors on their asses. That's how I'm going to pitch it to him. I have no doubt that he'll join us."

Everett smiled then said, "Well you certainly have an ambitious program, you even have the sex of the horse picked out, but I don't see how you can manage that."

"Well don't worry about what's going to take place, just come along for the ride. We're even building a suite for you in Main House, so you can come up and spend time with us and watch the scenario unfold. If nothing else it's going to be fun."

Time flew by as Rafe was having such a good time, but soon it was time to head uptown to the Broadhurst Theater on 44th Street. Rafe wanted to be there early since the delivery of the note was the whole shootin' match.

After standing outside the theater for about half an hour, Rafe entered, picked up his ticket from the box office then made his way to one of the three entrance corridors. As he entered, he was greeted by an attractive raven-haired, young woman, who took his ticket and began to take him to the proper row. When they arrived at row 14 the young lady told Rafe that he had the aisle seat. That's when Rafe asked the big question. "Miss, could I ask a big favor of you?" She had that look on her face, "Oh no, what's this all about." Rafe took the envelope out of his jacket pocket and handed it to her along with a one-hundred-dollar bill. He went on to say, "This is the most important message I'll ever send! It's for the leading lady, Jill Haworth."

The young girl who was now becoming more intrigued responded with, "I'll deliver it and be right back.

While this was taking place Jill was in her dressing room applying what could only be described as a prodigious amount of makeup. While doing this she was thinking, "I can't take much more of this; he's got to come back soon. Jill was struggling through a wave of depression. She thought Rafe would have come back to her by now. He said he would, and her belief in him was absolute. Surely it will be soon.But slowly she began to think, what if Rafe was like the rest, what if he's playing me too? Yet, somehow deep in her soul, down where she really existed, she knew, the only man on earth who would never hurt her was Rafe. Her train of thought switched to the Bible and the beatitudes, one of which states, Blessed, are the pure in heart for they shall see God. From Jill's perspective Rafe was pure in heart and if he said he'd come for her, he would, so she just needed to be patient for a little while longer and pray.

With that in mind, she began her prayer. "Dear Heavenly Father, it's your faithful servant Jill again. I need your help because I'm really getting down. With me, it's, no Rafe, no happiness, and I don't seem able to control my emotions. If he doesn't come back to me, I think I'll die of a broken heart.I know you're aware of our plight so, please have him come back soon. If you do, I guarantee I'll make him the happiest man that ever walked the earth. I ask it in the name of your Son, the Lord Jesus. Amen.

The Amen had barely cleared her consciousness when the tap came. A slight tap, tap, tap on the dressing room door. Jill raised her head and said, "Yes, come in."

Lilly half opened the door, stuck her head in, and said, "Miss Jill, something unusual just came up!A young man in the audience just handed me a note to bring to you."

Jill felt like she had been struck by a bolt of lightning! She jumped to her feet and yelled, "Oh my God! He's come back. Oh my God!"

Lilly, somewhat taken aback by Jill's reaction asked, "Who's back." "Who is he."

Since Jill was having a hard time speaking, she just reached out, and Lilly placed the envelope in her hand. It was unsealed, so Jill simply pulled out the card and stared at the content. It was simple. **Row 14 Seat A...Heathcliff.**

"Oh, My God! I can't believe it. It's the Third Miracle. He's back."

Lilly not having a clue about what was going on said, "Who's back Miss Jill?"

"Rafe, my high school sweetheart!"

"How long since you last saw him?"

"About six years,"

"And he still brings out that passionate response?"

"You have no idea, Lilly. I think I'm going to cry, from sheer happiness. Then on the other hand I can't cry, my makeup will run and it's too close to curtain call. I'm so happy, but I don't know what I'm going to do."

"Where has he been for the last six years?"

"He's been all over, but he recently came back from Viet Nam."

"Would you like some advice, Miss Jill? It will keep you from crying!"

"Of Course, what advice do you have."

It's simple Miss Jill, go out on stage and put on the performance of a lifetime. Sing and dance your heart out, and welcome your man home. Cry when you're safely in his arms!"

"Gosh, That's the perfect solution, Lilly!"

Jill rushed over and gave Lilly a Hug and a kiss. Then as Lilly was leaving, she said, "Oh Miss Jill, your young man, asked if there was a reply to the message, to bring it to him. What should I tell him?

"Tell him to wait in his seat after the performance, and you'll come for him when I get cleaned up. Can you help me with this Lilly? It will only take about 25 minutes."

"I'd be glad to help. After all, you said a miracle is taking place. I'll see you after the show."

The show began and Rafe watched with rapt attention. As thrilled as he was seeing Jill for the first time in six years it didn't take him long to realize that she was aware of where he was seated and was performing for him. That put a big smile on his face and only made him wish the show would soon end. As much as he enjoyed seeing Jill on stage for the first time, the thought of what was going to happen afterward had his heart racing.

It couldn't happen too soon from Rafe's perspective, but the final curtain fell, and the audience began to make their way to the exits. Rafe just got out of their way and then returned to Row 14 Seat A. About five minutes later Lilly reappeared and said to Rafe, "I'm Lilly, Rafe. Jill told me your name but we've never been properly introduced. I'm Lilly Mendoza.

Rafe extended his hand and took hers saying, "I'm Rafe Hawkins, and it's a pleasure to make your acquaintance. Thanks for delivering the note. I can't even express to you, how important that note was."

Lilly laughed and responded, "You don't have to explain anything to me, I saw Miss Jill's reaction. When I said I had a note from a young man in the audience she jumped to her feet and began to say over and over, with great passion, Oh My God! Oh, My God! It's Him. He's come back. She then said it was the third miracle. So, Mr. Rafe, is she right? Is it the third miracle?"

"Well, Miss Lily you are looking at a man who is about 15 or 20 minutes from the greatest moment of his life; and yes, it's a miracle."

"Since I'm involved in the miracle, could you tell me how it all came about?"

Rafe gave her a short version of how he and Jill met in High School, their amazing secret romance, followed by the prophecy and then her departure to Hollywood. The prophecy wasn't supposed to come true. Rafe only made it up to keep Jill in good spirits as she left for Hollywood. Yet here they were six years later and the prophecy was about to reach its climactic conclusion.

Lilly thought it was a miracle too and was thrilled to be involved. After about fifteen minutes Lilly headed back to Jill's dressing room to see how the makeup removal was progressing. Left alone, Rafe thought about what was happening from the perspective of an Angel. He knew he didn't think up the idea of a Prophecy, it just popped into his head one day, before it finally broke through into his consciousness; This was the work of the Lord God, no doubt about it! There is a saying that anticipation is nine-tenths of the fun, and Rafe was definitely enjoying the nine-tenths, just sitting with a smile on his face.

A few minutes later Lilly came walking up the aisle from the stage. She had a big smile on her face as she approached Rafe. She walked up and said, "Are you ready?" He was thinking, "You have to be kidding? Am I ready?"

Lily led the way down the aisle toward the stage with Rafe close behind. One minute later they were standing in front of Jill's dressing room door. Lilly just nodded her head towards the door and Rafe reached out with his right hand and knocked twice. Jill's voice answered with, "Come In."

Rafe stepped into the room and saw Jill standing across the room next to her dressing table. Her face lit up with the most radiant smile he would ever see. Before he could say a word, she shot across the room, like an angel in flight, right into his arms. Rafe just wrapped his beloved girl in his arms, and thought, "Thank God! It's happening!"

Jill had her arms around him and was squeezing him so tight he could barely breathe. While doing this she was whispering, "You came back. You said you would come back, and you did! It's a miracle, the third miracle." Rafe just stood there holding his beloved girl tightly in his arms. When she looked up at him, with the tears welling up, he leaned down and kissed her. Then it happened, the same overwhelmingly beautiful feeling they had in their first kiss. There was nothing comparable on the face of the earth. Rafe felt it was the presence of God. After all, God is Love, and this was the most perfect feeling he had ever felt. When they broke the kiss, they were staring into each other's eyes, and Rafe felt like he was in heaven. He whispered, "I love you Jill!" She responded with, "I love you too, Sir Knight!" They really didn't have to say anything. Rafe now knew that Jill loved him and Jill Knew Rafe belonged to her.

Jill still tightly held in Rafe's arms said, "I think I'm going to cry."

Rafe laughed and said, "Don't you dare! I have some important questions to ask you."

Jill held back her tears and looked up into Rafe's eyes. He asked, "Do you still have that secret sympathy for me?"

Jill nodded, yes, and whispered, "More than ever!"

Rafe then asked, "Do you have a boyfriend?"

Jill shook her head back and forth and whispered, "No"

Then she asked, "Do you have a girlfriend?"

He shook his head, no.

The two of them were staring into each other's eyes. The moment of truth, so to speak, had just arrived. Rafe whispered, "I only have one more question." Jill still looking into his eyes nodded yes. Rafe said, "Do you want to go steady?"

Jill laughed and Rafe leaned down and kissed her again. This time their kiss seemed to last an eternity, and when they finally came back to reality, the miracle had happened and they were back together.

Jill was smiling radiantly at Rafe when she asked, "What happens now?"

In reply, Rafe asked, "Can you get Tuesday off? I want to take you somewhere which will take two days.

Jill answered, yes. "But where are you taking me?"

Rafe looked at her thoughtfully, then answered, "Do you remember why we were secretly dating back in 1961?

Jill thought about it for a minute before saying, "You thought you didn't have enough status to be dating me, and if it were to be known, I'd be in California in two days."

Rafe nodded and said, "Exactly! Since then, I've gained some status, and It's increasing rapidly. I want to show you what I'm working on, and how I'm going to achieve an incredible rise in status."

"I knew you'd have a plan. You can take me anywhere Sir Knight! I am so happy."

"Ok, this is what I have planned. Let's start by stopping by Trader Vic's to celebrate our good fortune. Then from there to your place where you can pick up some clothing and things for two days. I'll also be seeing your mother for the first time in six years. I'm looking forward to that."

"Rafe there is something you should know about my mother."

"Ok, what should I know?"

"She knows about us. I told her everything."

"So, she knows about our secret romance!"

"Everything; I told her the whole story, and I had a very good reason. I fell into a deep depression after the awful betrayal in Hollywood. I felt I had betrayed you only to have my world come crashing down to a terrible end. Where you were concerned, I was down to one last hope; the prophecy. I remembered you said, that what God had joined together let no man put asunder and that if he loved us, he could create a miracle to bring us back together. Because of my depression my mother, becoming worried about my state of mind decided to have a mother-to-daughter talk. It was then that I told Mother the whole story, which ends in the prophecy. I told my mother I wanted to leave Hollywood, return to New York, and audition for every major musical coming into production.I knew the odds of becoming a leading lady on Broadway were incalculable since I had never sung on stage, but if I couldn't win you back, I'd die."

Mother asked, "So you want my advice on what you should do?"

"That's It, Mother, this may be the most important decision I'll ever make."

Mother remained silent for about a minute and then answered, "Go for it!"

I said, "Do you mean to go to New York and win the lead role in a Broadway Musical?"

"That's exactly what I mean. The truth is, true love is God's grace, the most valuable thing on earth. I think you've found it, and it's worth fighting to keep, even against insurmountable odds, I think you'll succeed."

"I jumped up and ran over to Mother, and gave her a great big hug." It was then that I realized I had a chance. The third miracle was possible. So, we moved to New York, and the rest is history!"

Jill picked up the telephone and began to dial. Rafe asked, "Are you calling your mother?"

Jill nodded in the affirmative as the phone rang. When her mother answered, Jill, said, "Mother, He's here, it has happened!"

Her mother asked, "What has happened?

"What we've been waiting for all this time!"

There was silence for a minute and then her mother responded with, "You don't mean the prophecy?"

"Yes mother, Rafe came back to me. He's standing here next to me holding my hand."

After a brief pause, Mrs. Hayworth exclaimed in a very loud voice, "Oh my God. It's a miracle. Thank the Lord! She went on to say to Jill, "This is the most incredible turn of events I've ever witnessed this is so wonderful."

"Mother we'll talk to you about all of this when we get home. Right now, Rafe and I are going to stop by Trader Vic's to have a drink to celebrate, and then we'll come right home. Do you remember when I told you that when Rafe and I were getting romantically involved he was concerned about his lack of status, and his reasoning was that society wasn't going to tolerate a nobody like him dating a starlet?" "Yes, I remember quite clearly."

Rafe says he's gained in status and is working on the rest. Since what he's working on is not far away, he and I are going to make the next two days a big adventure, and he's going to show me his place. How does that sound?"

"Darling girl, I'm just so happy for you. Hurry home I can't wait to see Rafe!"

After hanging up the phone Jill turned to Rafe and said, "Are you ready? Let's get out of here and head for Trader Vic's!"

Upon arriving at the Plaza Hotel, they made their way down a few corridors to the stairs that led downstairs to Trader Vic's which was located in the basement. As they approached the stairs Jill looked up at Rafe and said, "Giacomo (the maître d') is going to go crazy when he sees us!"

"Why is that?" Rafe responded.

Jill smiled and said, "Whenever I've come in here over the past five years Giacomo has always managed to whisper in my ear, "Someday you and Mr. Rafe will come in here together again." When I asked how he knew that, he'd say he just had a strong feeling that it was, as he called it, "God's Will!"

When they reached the bottom of the staircase and entered the foyer Giacomo, who was standing at the maître d' stand looked up and saw them. At first, there was a look of confusion on his countenance, then the realization hit him, and his face lit up as he loudly said, Oh my God! It has finally happened. He rushed over to the smiling couple and seized Rafe by the shoulders and kissed him on both cheeks then proceeded to do the same to Jill before putting an arm around each and hugging both at the same time. He kept repeating, "I knew it would happen! I knew it would happen!"

Jill who was smiling at him said, "You're absolutely right Giacomo, you always said it would happen, and now it has."

Rafe then asked, "How did you know Jill and I would get back together?"

"I can't tell you how I knew, I just knew, I had a very strong feeling that you two were made for each other and that sooner or later there would be a reunion. No matter where that insight came from it appears to be right." Giacomo led Rafe and Jill to the same table they had shared on the evening of their first date. Both Rafe and Jill were delighted to relive that first romantic evening. They didn't stay too long because after visiting with Jill's Mother they had a 2 ½-hour drive. As they were leaving Trader Vic's Rafe assured Giacomo that he would be seeing a lot more of them as he was now living in the New York area.

It was a short ride from Trader Vic's to Jill's apartment on Sutton Place. Jill knocked on the door before turning the key allowing her mother to know they had arrived. She was waiting for the happy pair as they stepped through the doorway. Jill's mother took Rafe by the shoulders and kissed him on both cheeks and said, Rafe Hawkins, you're a sight for sore eyes, how good to see you again."

"I feel the same way Mrs. Haworth, I'm so happy to see you. Jill announced she was going to her room to put together whatever she needed for the two-day trip leaving Rafe and Mrs. Haworth to chat.

They sat across from each other in the living room and Mrs. Haworth began with, "So, Rafe, what have you been up to for the last six years, where have you been." Rafe gave her a condensed version ending with his meeting with President Johnson. Jill's mother, somewhat taken aback by the revelation of Rafe's meeting with the president asked, "What was the outcome of your meeting?"

Rafe smiled and said, "He promoted me to Captain and set in motion the course of events the Leper Colony is now pursuing.

Jill's mother nodded and asked, "What course is the Leper Colony now on?"

Rafe thought for a minute then answered, "I've acquired a seven square mile piece of land 85 miles north of here. It's in Duchess County, about 17 miles East of Poughkeepsie. Right in the middle of the county.

Mrs. Hayworth's eyebrows went up and she asked, "How did you manage that?"

"It came out of my meeting with President Johnson, but it's so Top Secret I can't discuss it with you. At least not at this time. However, that is just half of the equation. Our place is called Hope Farm, and it comprises 4,500 acres. On 1,500 acres of the property, we're going to establish a Thorough-

419

bred horse breeding farm. We'll breed both to race and for the sales market. On the remainder of the acreage, we'll perform the duties our government contract requires. In the contract, we have the option to purchase the 4,500 acres after five years, and for a set price."

Mrs. Haworth was impressed she said, "You seem to have it all thought out, and you do know that Jill loves horses.

Rafe replied, "Yes, I'm aware of Jill's love for horses, and that brings me to what we, meaning the Leper Colony, are really building at Hope Farm. The thought begins when on Jill and I's first date when we went to see Camelot. At the very end just before the final curtain falls King Arthur sings, "Don't let it be forgot; that once there was a spot; for happily-ever-aftering. You could say that the real mission of the Leper Colony is to build a place for happily-ever-aftering. That's the sort of place I want for your daughter. I want Jill to be happy because I love her more than words can express, and I have loved her since we first met.

Mrs. Haworth smiled as she thought, "This is so wonderful, Imagine, Jill attracted a young man like this when she was only 15 years old. It must be divine providence, and if that's the case, they'll be together forever.

About this time Jill walked into the living room carrying a small suitcase. She gave Rafe a dazzling smile and announced, "I'm ready!" They kissed Jill's mother goodbye and headed for the elevator. As it descended Jill looked up at Rafe and said, "We did it! We made it, despite the odds. We're together again!"

Rafe smiled at her and said, "You're absolutely right, we beat the odds which had to be in the millions to one."

Once outside they walked down the street to the parking garage where Rafe had left the car. Once in the car, Jill exclaimed, "Nice car Rafe."

Rafe laughed and said, "It is, but, it's not mine. I only borrowed it for two days."

Jill asked, "Don't you have your own car?"

"Sure, I do, but mine is a Pontiac Lemans Convertible which is a very nice car, but it has one deficiency!

Jill asked, "What's that?"

"My car has two bucket seats with a console in between, so if we were in my car, you'd be sitting two feet away, instead of being right up against me like you are now. Jill smiled and said, "You planned this all down to the last inch, didn't you?" Rafe laughed and said, "Indeed I did. It may seem like a little thing, but after six years of not seeing or, touching you, having you where you are now, became a very big deal."

As they pulled out of the parking garage Jill said, "Let the big adventure begin!"

Rafe headed crosstown on 59th street to pick up the West Side Highway. Before they had traveled very far Jill asked, "Where are you taking me, Sir Knight?" Rafe gave her a hug and said, "To a very special place about 85 miles north of here." Jill asked,"

"What makes it so special?"

Rafe answered, "You'll see!"

They followed the Saw Mill River Parkway to Hawthorne Circle an intersection where several parkways meet. From there they branched off onto the Taconic State Parkway which they would follow to the Hopewell Junction exit which was 15 miles from the farm. Jill was snuggled up against Rafe and was beginning to get into a playful mood. A few minutes after turning onto the Taconic State Parkway, Jill said to Rafe, "Tell me how much you love me!"

Rafe thought about it for a minute then responded with, "I can't do it, It's impossible."

Jill was somewhat taken aback because deep in her heart she knew Rafe was madly in love with her, so she said, "Why Not." In a way, the question was light-hearted, but it was serious too.

Rafe thought about it for a minute then answered, "Because my darling, my love for you can't be described in words. The English language, or for that matter, any language, would be totally inadequate. Jill replied, "Knowing you, I think you'll find a way".

Rafe sat behind the wheel thinking, "What is she up to?" Finally, the realization hit him; she's playing with me." His next thought was, "Well if we're in love with each other we can certainly play with each other just as we did six years ago." Rafe finally said, "You want to talk of love don't you my darling girl."

Jill answered, "Can you think of a better subject?"

Rafe then asked Jill, "Do you know that I love you?" Jill replied, "Yes, I have no doubts."

Then Jill asked Rafe the same question "Do you know that I love you?"

He responded the same way, "Yes, Jill I know that you love me, and how do you think I know that?"

Jill answered, "I'm not sure!"

In answering Rafe took a slightly different tack he said, "When did you realize you were in love with me?"

Jill knew the answer immediately, and responded with, "The first time you kissed me!"

"So, then let me ask you this my darling, how did the kiss convince you that you were in love?"

Jill thought for a minute before replying, "It was the most beautiful feeling I've ever experienced."

Rafe then said, "Describe it."

Jill sat there thoughtfully and then said, "It's too beautiful. It's beyond description!"

Rafe countered, "That's what I meant a few minutes ago when I told you I couldn't tell you how much I loved you because it's beyond description. I can tell you non-verbally with a kiss, but words are inadequate."

Jill was pleased with that, and then said, "I have another question, an important one.

Rafc was having fun and said, "Go ahead, shoot!"

Jill dropped the bombshell, "Are we going to sleep together tonight?"

Rafe didn't laugh he just smiled, before saying, "You know little dancer, since I can't tell you how much I love you in words, because they're inadequate, then the only other way is through non-verbal means like kissing. When we kiss, we have no doubt about how much we love each other, however, there are other means of non-verbal communication that can be used to express our love, and if we sleep together, we'll get a chance to practice them."

Jill was absolutely beaming when she replied, "It's going to take a lot of practice to get it right."

Rafe countered with, "Probably more than we think."

Jill then said, "You know what they say?"

Rafe took the bait and asked, "What do they say?"

Jill giggled and replied, "Practice makes perfect!"

Rafe was grinning as he added, "With that in mind we have little choice but to sleep together since we have so much catching up to do. So, what do you think?"

Jill had a beautiful smile on her face when she responded, "My darling Rafe, this is the best drive I've ever been on, and that's considering I don't even know where we're going."

Rafe laughed at that, and asked, "Do you want to know where we're going?"

Jill just said, "Of course I do."

Rafe then said, "This is what I told your mother about where I was taking you. Do you remember when at the end of Camelot King Arthur sings the refrain that goes, "Don't let it be forgot that once there was a spot, for happily-ever-aftering?"

Jill remembering Camelot said, "How could I ever forget."

Rafe went on to say, "That's where I'm taking you. I've found the spot for happily-ever-aftering."

Jill hugged Rafe tighter and responded with, "Take me anywhere Rafe, as long as we're together, I'm in heaven!"

As they drove through the night Jill drifted off with her head on Rafe's shoulder. Thirty minutes later Rafe nudged Jill and brought her out of her sleepy state. She shook her head and looked at Rafe as if to say, "Yes!" Rafe simply pointed over the hood of the Mercedes. There, about 50 feet ahead were two old stone pillars that in previous years had been the entry gate. In front of the stone pillars was a grassy triangle measuring 60 feet per side and out in the center of the triangle was a sign that said, Hope Farm.

Rafe said, "This is your new home, this is the spot."

Jill looked at Rafe with a slight smile on her face and asked him, "What is Hope Farm? What does it do?"

Rafe answered, right now it doesn't do anything, but very shortly it will be transformed into a Thoroughbred Nursery. We're going to breed the fastest horses in the world." Jill clapped her hands together and exclaimed, "Horses! Rafe, you know how much I love horses."

Rafe answered, "Indeed I do, and it's a passion we both share. Remember, this is the place for happily-ever-aftering. Jill, there will be a lot of people that will find happiness in this place, us included."

Jill smiled as she said, "My darling, it seems that since you've gotten back, every hour that goes by, I become happier than in the one that preceded it."

Rafe put the car in gear and crept through the gate at about 2 miles per hour. He stopped the car about 100 yards inside the gate and turned to Jill and said, "In the happiness department, how do you think you'll be feeling at the end of another hour?"

Jill's eyes were shining, and she looked as beautiful as he had ever seen her, she looked at Rafe and said, "Do you mean after we've made love? " He just nodded, and she just smiled back. They both knew it wouldn't be long now! Six years of pent-up emotions were about to be released. Rafe drove up the main road about half a mile to where a circular driveway branched off to the right. He followed the drive and pulled up to a huge redbrick Victorian structure called Main House. He parked in a spot near the entrance and helped Jill out of the car. Carrying her overnight bag, the two entered Main House.

Off to the right of the entrance foyer was a wide staircase. Rafe led Jill over to the staircase, placed her bag at the bottom, and swept her up into his arms. Once he had her firmly in his arms, he carried her up the stairs and into their just completed suite. He didn't stop to show her around, he just walked straight into the bedroom and set Jill down lovingly on the bed. Jill gave him a loving look and said, "You need to get my bag. There is something in it I need to put on!"

Rafe headed for the staircase and was back in a minute. When he returned Jill jumped up took the bag and disappeared into the bathroom. As she closed the door she said, "I'll be out in a few minutes." It was more than a few minutes, but when Jill emerged, she was a vision of loveliness. Wearing a black teddy that hid her curves to a degree but left enough visible to set the imagination running wild. Jill stopped near the end of the bed and posed as if to say, "Here I Am!" Before Rafe could say a word or move, Jill reached down took a hem of the teddy in each hand, lifted it off her body, and tossed it aside. There she stood in all her magnificence. Rafe was stunned. The first thought that entered his mind was perfection. "She's absolutely perfect." A second thought flashed through his mind that the reason he thought she was perfect was that God had created her to appear that way in his eyes. Rosa Martinez had said that Rafe and Jill were made for each other by the hand of God. There was no doubt that Rafe would see Jill as being perfect. That's the only thought that went through Rafe's mind when he first saw Jill naked, but that one thought galvanized him into action and he jumped from the bed and made his way around it to sweep Jill into his arms. He kissed her and it lasted for what seemed an eternity. They were drunk with desire, and driven by six years of pent-up, passion.

He carried her to the bed, gently stretched her out on it, and then stripped off his clothes in record time. He stretched out and pulled her close, and in an instant, their bodies were intertwined. To the happy couple just holding each other, in this erotic embrace was holding the world. True to his word Rafe began to communicate his love for Jill by nonverbal means. It didn't take very long until they were swept away by the throes of passion. After that, things got a little wild, but who cared, they had six lost years to make up for. A few hours later they drifted off to sleep utterly exhausted.

The sun, shining into the bedroom from the East, wakened Rafe. He found himself lying in the spoon position pressed up against Jill's back. His arms were around her, and his face pressed against the back of her neck. He pulled his head back to look at her as he became aware of her soft breathing. He couldn't get over how beautiful she looked even as she slept, because he was well aware, that she was ten times more attractive with her eyes open. Rafe thought Jill had the most beautiful eyes he had ever seen. Rafe closed his eyes for a moment and when he opened them, he was staring into Jill's shining blue eyes. Jill said, "Good morning, Sir Knight?"

Rafe whispered, "Good Morning, Little Dancer." Rafe asked her, "Where do you stand where happiness is concerned?" Jill smiled and said, "Rafe, now I know what happiness means. "What about you? How do you feel."

Rafe smiled and said, "I feel like I'm in heaven."

Jill snuggled up against Rafe and said, "I don't want to move. I want to stay here in your arms, forever!"

Rafe laughed and responded with, "Sorry, my love, but the Leper Colony awaits, they're probably already down in the dining room, waiting with bated breath. But I'll tell you what, I'll find some excuse for us to go to bed early tonight. Remember, we have a lot of practicing to do before I figure out how to convince you that I love you without using a backward medium like language."

"Do you promise? Early to bed tonight," Jill Asked.

"Yes, I promise we'll be in bed early."

With that settled Jill slipped out of bed and headed for the bathroom. Of course, she was naked as the day she was born, and Rafe's eyes were riveted to her perfection. Halfway across the room Jill turned her head toward Rafe and giving him a saucy smile said, "Want to take a shower with me?" In a flash, Rafe was across the room and right behind her into the bathroom.

About 45 minutes later Rafe and Jill, hand in hand, walked down the staircase toward the dining room. Jill was wearing a blue dress and was the epitome of loveliness. When they appeared at the French Doors, leading from the corridor into the dining room, the raucous chatter from within abruptly stopped. The only sound was the silver utensils hitting plates. Jill had a lovely way of moving having been trained as a ballerina in England, and she had the undivided attention of 17 pairs of eyes. They stopped near the table and Rafe said, "Gentlemen, and I use that word loosely, I'd like to present to you my girl Jill." In unison, they all said hello or good morning. Rafe continued, "Since there are so many of us, and since we can't all talk at once, I'm going to go around the table and introduce each of you to Jill in order. I'll give her your name and the call sign you go by since she'll eventually be calling you by either one or the other.

So, first on the list, on the far left is Frank Holman, known as Oakie. He followed this up with Sam Radle, Laredo. Then Tom Mulcahy, Hitman. John Clemons, McDuck, and then he got to Mighty Mouse. Rafe went on and said, "Next is Robert Stewart, also known as Mighty Mouse.

Each Leper in turn had been greeting Jill with a hello, or so nice to meet you, but Mighty Mouse just stared at Jill like he'd seen a ghost. After maybe ten seconds Mighty Mouse exclaimed, "She's a Movie Star."

Everyone began to stare at him in disbelief; "What are you talking about", asked Jerry Johnson, known by the code sign Elvis.

Mighty Mouse continued with, "She's also a star on Broadway. Remember when we first got here? The first thing I did was go down to New York to see the new musical Cabaret. Guess who the star of Cabaret is? "It's Jill. She plays Sally Bowls the lead character."

Hitman chimed in. "This is all crazy, how could she be a movie star when Rafe hasn't been out of the army long enough to find one, he's been up here most of the time."

Confusion reigned when suddenly, a deep voice sounded from the end of the table, it was Gunny Fiske. He loudly proclaimed, "She's a movie star. I've seen her in two movies; one was Exodus, and the other was In Harm's Way, with John Wayne and Kirk Douglas.

Mighty Mouse then asked Jill, "You're Jill Haworth, a movie star, am I right?"

Jill smiled beautifully and said, "Yes, I've made three movies, and I am the leading lady in Cabaret, and I'm Rafe's girl."

The remainder of breakfast was fun for all after the Lepers realized that they actually had a movie star in their midst. As breakfast was breaking up and everyone was heading for their work areas Jill asked Rafe, "Do you think they like me?"

Rafe smiled at his girl and said, "Does a cat like catnip? Of course, they love you! You are part and parcel of what has been taking place ever since the leper colony was formed, and that is, their perception of themselves has been growing by leaps and bounds. They're thinking if I can have a movie star as a girlfriend, what's next? They're thinking, it's going to be something very good."

Rafe and Jill returned to their suite and Jill changed into jeans and a blouse and a pair of sneakers, Rafe was going to give her a guided tour of Hope Farm which included hiking through the forest and meadows with some briars and brambles thrown in. Once Jill was changed, he walked over and kissed her gently and asked, "What do you think of the Leper Colony?"

Jill smiled and said, "I think they're adorable. I'm so happy you brought me here, and I'll tell you a secret, I can't wait to go for a walk with you. It's going to be like our days in high school when we'd be walking all around New York hiding our secret romance."

Rafe looked into her beautiful blue eyes and couldn't get over how lucky he was, then he said, "Since we arrived at night when you couldn't see anything, let's take a walk from Main House to the Chapel which is only about 250 yards, and along the way is a beautiful vista where you can see from the ridgeline Hope Farm is built on all the way across Clove Valley to Clove Mountain which is about five miles away."

Off they went hand in hand and happier than any couple had the right to be. As they walked along Chapel Road Jill was taken by the vista off to their left which was a meadow about 40 acres in size with a road along its perimeter, lined with huge maple trees. Since Chapel Road flanked the meadow, it was also lined by maple trees. The big leaved maples formed a tunnel, at the end of which was The Chapel. Jill was seemingly beckoned by the front of the stone chapel that commanded the end of the tunnel. Her pace quickened as she walked towards the bell tower standing stately above the door. Rafe smiled to himself thinking, "She's still an angel in training and has no idea as to what is leading her on. Jill seemed to be in a hurry to get to the chapel so Rafe just let her pull him along. When they got to the 8-foot-tall wooden doors Rafe opened one allowing Jill to step in. She had only taken a few steps into the interior when she suddenly stopped and slowly looked around. She felt an unusual aura of calm and serenity surrounding her and it was from the atmosphere inside the chapel. She slowly walked along the back rows until she came to the center aisle between the rows of maybe 20 pews. She began walking up the aisle towards the stained-glass window behind the altar when she suddenly stopped. She stopped at exactly the pew Rafe had been sitting in when he'd first heard the voice of God that terrible night. Since Rafe knew where she was going to stop, he simply walked up and said, "Why don't you slip into this pew and I'll take a seat next to you."

Rafe settled in next to Jill and then said, "This place is very important to me, and it's interesting that you chose this particular place to pause as you walked down the aisle." Jill looked at Rafe and replied, "Is this where you heard the voice of God, the night you lost Max?"

Rafe answered, "Yes this is the exact place, except it was at night with the only light coming through the stained-glass window."

Jill was a little skeptical and asked are you sure it was the voice of God?" Rafe looked over at Jill and then answered, "At first, I had my doubts, after all, who hears the voice of God? It could have been me having a delusionary episode, like listening to my own thoughts and thinking it was God. Since then, I've changed my mind."

"What made you change your mind?" Rafe looked at Jill again, and then said, "Someone told me the truth." For Jill, this was getting more mysterious by the minute.

She responded by asking, "May I ask who?" Rafe told her "I can't tell you who the messenger was, at least not at this time, but in the not-too-far distant future, I'll tell you everything. Will you trust me?"

"Rafe, after last night I'm so in love with you I'll trust you with anything."

Rafe laughed and said, "How about I tell you what I can, and brief you on the rest at a later time?" Jill just nodded in the affirmative."Rafe began, "First what is happening here at Hope Farm is very important. I'll tell you as much as I can about the first part of what we're doing. First, the leper colony although discharged from the army is still operational. Although not in the U.S. Military we are now contracted to work directly for the President of the United States. I don't even know how that was set up; I only know I answer directly to the President."

"This is where a problem arises. The operational status of the Leper Colony is considered extremely Top Secret. Very few people in the United States are aware of its existence nor are they aware of its basic mission. So, Hope Farm, on the surface will be a Thoroughbred Horse Breeding operation, while in reality, the horse breeding will be a cover for a Top-Secret military mission. This is the way we should handle the problem. You, your mother, my mom, and Everett will all be spending a considerable amount of time at the farm. While you're here you will, just by chance, see us involved in military activities. The way to handle this is to simply ignore what you observe. Don't discuss it with anyone, and don't ask any of the lepers what they're up to. Basically, just ignore anything you see concerning military activity. Remember, the old-World War II slogan, Loose lips sink ships!"

After saying a prayer at the altar, Rafe and Jill walked back to Main House and jumped into the Mercedes for a quick tour of the Farm. Jill asked, "Where does the tour start?"

"How about right where we entered the farm last night?" They drove down the Main Road to the gate, made a turn around the grassy triangle in front of it, and reentered the farm property. Rafe told Jill, "This house on the left, just inside the gate, is called Gate House. I was living here when the great revolution started." They continued up Main Road about 150 yards where they came upon a road crossing Main Road. Rafe pointed out the cottage about 100 yards to the Right of the intersection that was called Marcy Cottage. It had been the domain of Nellie Morton, affectionately known to the boys as Mom Morton. Rafe exclaimed to Jill that he considered Mom to be as close to being a saint as anyone he had ever encountered and that she had more impact on the development of his character than anyone he'd ever known. If one were to take a left at the same intersection the road led to what had been another of the boy's dormitories named Daisy Cottage. It had been a cottage for boys 10-12 years of age. During Rafe's stay at Greer School, Daisy was under the supervision of Joe and Beatrice Fischer. Hundreds of boys who were raised at Greer School used Joe Fischer as a role model. In stature, he was a six-foot-four-inch former marine and was as straight a shooter as ever existed. From Daisy Cottage the boys moved on to Gate House or Rapello Cottage once they reached thirteen. Once past the Marcy, Daisy intersection Main Road bore left and began its uphill rise to Main House and the rest of the campus.

About one hundred yards up Main Road another road bore off to the left that led to Rapello Cottage. Off to the right of Rapello was a large meadow comprising about 30 acres. Along the top of the ridgeline at the far end of the meadow were the Chapel and Main House. Rafe was taking this route in the tour as he wanted to swing by Plum Cottage which was being renovated to accommodate the new trainer of thoroughbred horses Rafe was about to hire, and also a rider. The beautiful accommodations would make Rafe's offer of employment too good to pass up. Because they wanted this project completed quickly about eight of the lepers were working together at Plum Cottage as they drove up.

When Rafe pulled up and the lepers saw who it was the word spread rapidly. Needless to say, the lepers were very interested in this beautiful movie star. After everyone was present and accounted for, and Rafe, had reintroduced them, the fun began. First, the lepers rained down every conceivable question about Hollywood and movie stars, and then finally got around to Jill working with John Wayne and Kirk Douglas. After about fifteen minutes of nonstop chatter, Doc Linginfelter stepped up with the big question. He asked Jill how was it possible for her and Rafe to end up as a couple.

Jill looked at the assembled lepers and noticed she had their undivided attention. This is what they really wanted to know, so she began. "I came to the United States from Great Britain after my debut in the Film, Exodus. The studio didn't want me in Hollywood until the next film was ready for production because they felt Hollywood would be a bad environment for a fifteen-year-old. Jill was thinking, "No one knows what a jungle it is unless you're an insider, and Otto Preminger who signed me to my contract, was an insider." Jill continued to address the lepers saying, "I ended up being warehoused in New York. While In New York I attended the Rhodes School one of the top private schools in Manhattan. It was there that I met Rafe. We were introduced in the principal's office at Rafe's request. Apparently, he wanted to check me out." Hit Man shouted out, "Wanted to check you out! Was he crazy!" Jill smiled at him and continued, "I think you misunderstand, Rafe wanted to see if he and I were compatible, if we weren't, he wouldn't have become my tutor. We stood on the stairs leading from 54th Street into the school building and talked for about 25 minutes, by the end of which we had started what turned out to be a very strong friendship. By being together after school five days a week, and with our friendship growing by the day it didn't take long for me to begin thinking, Rafe needs to be my boyfriend. I just needed to figure out a way to make it happen. It didn't take long to develop a plan; I'd get him to take me out. That would be a good start. So, a week later while we were studying in the library, I said, "Rafe, I think you should take me out!" One of the lepers shouted, "You mean you asked him out?" Jill looked over at Rafe who was sitting with a smile on his face and said, "Can you imagine that, I'm a movie starlet and I had to ask him out! But seriously, he had good reasons why he wouldn't ask me out. Regardless of what was in his mind, he wasn't going to get away easily, so finally, in frustration, I said, "You're not turning me down, are you?" That did the trick and he then agreed to take me out. I knew he wanted to, all along anyway." Jill explained that Rafe had never been out on a date because a year earlier he'd been 5' tall. Now he was 6' tall, but she would still be his first date, and She was a movie star."

After Rafe finally agreed to take her out, she agreed that he needed the weekend to come up with an idea for their date. Rafe went home and told his mother he needed advice on a big problem that had just arisen. She was completely shocked that Rafe had run into a problem he couldn't handle for in her estimation Rafe could handle anything.

When Rafe went upstairs to study, she called Everett and told him "Your son has a big problem."

Everett thinking Rafe had got himself into some serious trouble asked, "What sort of big problem?"

Rafe's mom responded with, "His starlet has asked him out."

Everett responded, "What's wrong with that, It's the greatest thing I've ever heard of."

Rafe's mom didn't think of the situation in the same light. She said, "Everett, Rafe's never been on a date. Remember a year ago he was 5' tall, then add to that, she's a movie starlet, and this is New York."

Everett thought about it for a moment then added, "Don't worry El, I'm going to fix the whole thing, those two are going to have the greatest date, ever."

Rafe's mom asked, "How do you intend to arrange that?"

"Don't worry, I've got the solution, you'll see!"

Doc Linginfelter asked, "What happened, what was the big date?"

Jill looked around at the gathered lepers and could see she had their rapt attention. She told them, "The date was to go to Trader Vic's for dinner, and then to attend the opening night of Camelot with Julie Andrews and Richard Burton. Mr. Massoletti (Everett) knew Julie Andrews was my idol since Rafe was constantly talking about me. When Rafe told me what our date would be I was thrilled beyond belief. By the time Rafe kissed me goodnight we were madly in love. But, then up came another problem. Six days later I got Rafe to take me on a walk up to Central Park where I said, "I think we should go steady!" After all, we were in love. But, to my shock and surprise, he started to back out again. I knew he loved me, so how could he not jump at the chance." Jill went on to say, "Then he told me the reason. Regardless of how we felt about each other society would not accept a rising starlet dating someone from nowhere. If they even suspected such a relationship, they would ship me to Hollywood in a heartbeat. We would probably never see each other again. My reaction was to start crying. Rafe who knew what I was feeling lifted me to my feet and kissed me. That took care of that problem instantaneously, but I asked him, "What's going to happen to us? I can't lose you, Rafe, I'll just die! Rafe suggested we walk over to the Plaza Hotel where we could sit and talk out of the cold. After a long talk, Rafe said, "The only way we can keep our love, is in secret. No one, not even our mothers can know. Think of it this way, no one can break up what they don't know exists." So, that's the way it went. On a Saturday or Sunday when we weren't in school, we'd say we were going to the Metropolitan Museum of Art to look at the masters when in reality were having the time of our lives. We were running free and madly in love."

    Those six months were the happiest of our lives, but then it happened. That which Rafe had always feared. We ran out of time. The school year ended and I was headed for Hollywood. On an early June afternoon, we said goodbye in the lobby of the Gotham Hotel. I was distraught, like at the end of the world type of distraught. Rafe did the only thing he could do to give me hope. He said our meeting and subsequent secret romance were God's will. He then reminded me of the line from marriage vows, "What God has joined together, let no man put asunder." But, being Rafe, he didn't stop there. He said, "Do you want me to make a prophecy about our future? Of course, I wanted him to, desperately, so this is what he told me. "We are separating in a few moments, and our separation could last years". The prophecy said I would go to Hollywood and make four more motion pictures completing my contract. After completing my contract, I would return to New York and audition for a new Broadway Play. Against the odds, I would get the leading role in what would turn out to be a smash hit Broadway Musical. This would set in motion the Prophecy which says once I got the lead role, Rafe would come back to me and we'd live happily ever after. However, Rafe didn't leave things at that, he said specifically that the prophecy would come about like this. One night just before the start of the performance I would receive a note from a member of the audience. It would be in a white unsealed envelope containing a card that would simply say Row 14 Seat A, signed, Heathcliff. If my love for him was still the same, I could send him a message and we'd be back together. When I was awarded the lead role of Sally Bowles in Cabaret the prophecy was set in motion. I had only one remaining problem, and that was to make sure Rafe knew I had the lead role in Cabaret. I wanted to be sure he knew, and was aware of what was taking place. Luckily, I had a surefire way of getting the news to Rafe, it was through Pop, otherwise known as Henry Everett Massoletti. He'd be sure to know the whereabouts of Rafe and how to deliver the news."

"I made an appointment to visit Massolett's to have lunch with Mr. Massoletti. I was received like visiting royalty and I soon told Pop the whole story right from the beginning. I told him about our secret romance after our date. Finally, I told him about the prophecy. We discussed my concern that Rafe, wherever he was, may never hear that I had the leading role in Cabaret, and therefore wouldn't come back to me. Pop quickly dispelled any fears I had concerning that, and went on to say where Rafe was, and all about the Leper Colony and the difficulties you found yourselves in. Pop gave me Rafe's address at Fort Bliss and advised me to write a letter to Rafe that was short and sweet, telling him about landing the leading role in Cabaret. If he loved me, he'd come back.

Last night just before the show opened, Lilly, one of the ushers came to my dressing room and said, "Miss Jill, something a little unusual has come up." She went on to say, "A young man in the audience asked me to bring you a note!" Nothing more needed to be said. I felt like I had been struck by lightning. This came seconds after saying amen in my prayer. I knew what it was! The Third Miracle. Rafe had come back for me. The lepers were all smiling now. Jill was smiling also thinking "Well I definitely won them over." She continued with, "That was less than 24 hours ago, just last evening, and

I can assure you that you're looking at the happiest girl in the world. You'll be seeing a lot of me from now on since Rafe and I are back together. I'll be coming up from the city as often as I can and I'm excited about meeting Rafe's elite companions known as the Leper Colony.

After leaving Plum Cottage, Rafe and Jill visited every work site where any of the lepers could be found. By noon all of the Lepers had been introduced and had spent time getting acquainted with Jill. It was a toss-up as to whether the Lepers liked Jill more, or she was more taken by her new friends. Rafe had arranged for a basket lunch to be prepared and Rafe and Jill risked driving down the rutted and winding dirt road to the camp. The camp was situated on the Northeast side of the property, in a valley. The camp itself consisted of redwood cabins resting at the edge of a tree line that surrounded an open meadow. Jill and Rafe sat on the stairs leading to the Recreation Hall called the Rec Hall, which was shaded by towering Oaks, and had lunch in that serenely beautiful place. As they were putting things back in the picnic basket Rafe asked Jill, "How are you doing in the happiness department?"

Jill looked at him with her eyes shining like never before and replied, "It hasn't even been twenty-four hours yet and I feel like I've found myself in this beautiful dream, from which I'll eventually wake up. But it doesn't end, and it just keeps getting better and better as time goes on." With that, Jill walked over and slid into Rafe's lap, put her arms around his neck, and kissed him. It was a long passionate kiss and when it finally ended both Jill and Rafe were breathless, and madly in love.

Jill smiled at Rafe and said, "Remember when we talked about what you would have to do to convince me that you loved me?" Rafe just nodded, yes!" Jill gave Rafe one of her come hither looks with her eyes firmly fixed on his and said, "Well? Remember, practice makes perfect came up as well, and that was only last night. We have a lot of making up for lost time to do, don't you think?"

Rafe was thinking, "How could I not remember while I'm holding the cutest girl in the world in my lap." Rafe thought a minute then said, "I know what you mean. I know I'm in need of a lot of practice where communicating how much I love you is concerned; however, this is not the place for it."

With that, Jill gave Rafe a hurt, crestfallen look, to which he responded, "I know a better place for practicing. I was going to take you there next anyway, so come on, let's go."

She jumped out of his lap and they headed for the car. Since last night everything was now an adventure, even the twisting, rutted, dirt road leading back to Chapel Hill. On the way to their destination, Rafe made a stop at Main House and picked up a blanket. The spot, he had in mind was only about half a mile further down the county road, that ran right through the center of Hope Farm. He was looking for a little tractor trail used to haul the hay wagons from the meadows behind the wood line. Rafe pulled his convertible a few feet into the tractor tail and the two love birds alighted. Rafe said to Jill, "This is a very special trail which we students called Lover's Lane."

Jill found that piece of information intriguing and asked, "Why is it called Lover's Lane?

"Well at Greer School there was no way for the high school students to go out on a date, mainly because there wasn't any place nearby to go to. However, the school set up something for them. On weekends when school was out on Saturday and Sunday afternoons you could sign up for different activities. One could be Ice Skating on Rapello Pond, or you could sign up for the Gym and play basketball. The library was another option. You might just want to stay out of the cold and read. One of the activities was called Walking which the High School students could sign up for. It simply consisted in taking your girlfriend for a walk. The grounds were simply magnificent and ideal for a nice walk, and it just so happen that the favorite destination for a walk was down this tractor trail which soon picked up the name, Lover's Lane."

Jill smiled and asked, "How many girls did you walk down Lover's Lane with?" Rafer quickly answered, "None!" Jill was very surprised at that and said, "None, are you kidding me?" Rafe shrugged and said, "Remember, back then I was 5' tall and weighed 100 pounds, girls weren't interested in me. So here I am about to take a walk down Lover's Lane and who do I have to accompany me? My first love! There's also a surprise waiting for you at the other end of the trail."

Jill was beaming as she said, "You've thought this all out in advance, haven't you?"

Rafe laughed and said, "You know I have, and let's just say there are some very interesting things to be experienced down that trail." Jill took Rafe's hand and they began their walk down Lover's Lane. The trail had a loveliness of its own with the surrounding forest creating a canopy of branches that shaded the trail from the hot afternoon sun. The only obstacles were occasional puddles left by recent rain. Upon emerging from the trail, they found themselves in a meadow covered with grass already about two feet tall. Not thirty yards away stood a small herd of deer, about ten in number, all gazing at the young couple. They knew no fear having grown up in this protected habitat. When Rafe and Jill moved forward, the deer began to run across the meadow. It was quite a sight with two bucks five does and three fawns. Reaching the far end of the meadow the deer disappeared into the wood line. Rafe looked over at Jill and she was wearing a smile you could see from a mile, and he knew she was very happy. They continued down the gently sloping back side of the ridge which Hope Farm encompassed, passing through two more meadows before coming to a partially flooded forest.

Jill looked up at Rafe and asked, "What happened here?"

Rafe gave Jill a quick grin and said, "That's what we're here to see. There is something special hidden here." They walked about 50 yards when they came upon a carefully crafted blind where they could remain out of sight while watching the flooded forest. They laid the blanket out and sat on it with a sense of anticipation.

Jill looked at Rafe and asked, "What are we waiting for?" Rafe glanced back at her and said, "Just be patient, with luck, they'll be along shortly." Rafe put his arm around Jill, and held her close as the minutes ticked by.

Suddenly, Jill exclaimed, "I see something, over there to the right!" Rafe looked and sure enough, there were the little heads followed by the small wakes as they swam along. Jill whispered, "What are they Rafe? Are they muskrats?" As they continued to watch the little heads grow closer Jill said, "What are they Rafe, give me a hint?"

Rafe whispered in her ear. "Well, they used to make hats out of their fur!"

Jill looked at him in astonishment and then excitedly exclaimed, "You don't mean they're Beavers?"

Rafe smiled and said, "Yep, they're Beavers, and they've been here about ten years. To be exact, I watched them build their Beaver Dam."

Jill perked up and said, "This is so exciting. Can we come down here and watch them whenever we want?"

Rafe nodded and said, "Yeah, after a while they'll get used to us watching and they won't pay us any mind."

After watching the Beavers for about half an hour Rafe finally told Jill, "I think we'd better go as I have one more mission to accomplish before we finish our walk down Lover's Lane."

"And what may that be if I may ask?", countered Jill.

Rafe responded with, "You'll find out in a few minutes if you'll follow me." He took her hand and they headed up the gentle sloping ridge line back towards Lover's Lane. When they reached the shaded tractor trail Rafe Said, "Before we head down Lover's Lane there's something I have to ask you."

Jill just nodded, so Rafe asked, "Do you remember a spring afternoon when we were walking through Central Park, and I asked you if you'd like to sing a duet?"

This brought a big smile from Jill who said, "God, Rafe how could I ever forget? We sang People Will Say We're in Love. It was so beautiful"

Then Rafe added, "Well if you liked that, I have another one!"

He was rewarded with a big smile before Jill said, "This is so exciting! What song is it." Rafe reached into his pocket and pulled out a sheet of paper with the Title and Lyrics of the song. Jill looked down and saw the title and beamed with happiness. She said to Rafe, "This is perfect, how did you think this up."

Rafe simply smiled and said, "It's just one of the things I like to do. Rafe suggested, "Start singing after you refresh your memory regarding the lyrics. Start when you're ready." Beaming with delight Jill looked over the words of the song and a minute later said to Rafe;

"OK I'm ready."

Rafe looked at Jill and said, "Ok you start. Your line leads off." This is how it went.

Jill Sings
They say we're young and we don't know we won't find out until we grow

Rafe Sings
Well, I don't know if all that's true
Cause you got me, and baby I got you

Rafe Sings
Babe

Jill and Rafe Sing
I got you babe, I got you babe

Jill Sings
They say our love won't pay the rent
Before it's earned, our money's all been spent

Rafe Sings
I guess that's so, we don't have a lot
But at least I'm sure of all the things we got

Rafe Sings
Babe

Jill and Rafe Sing
I got you babe, I got you babe

Rafe Sings
I got flowers in the spring
I got you to wear my ring

Jill Sings
And when I'm sad you're a clown
And if I get scared, you're always around
So let them say your hair's too long
Cause I don't care, with you I can't go wrong

Rafe Sings
Then put your little hand in mine
There ain't no hill or mountain we can't climb
BABE!
I got you babe. I got you babe

Rafe Sings
I got you hold my hand

Jill Sings
I got you to understand

Rafe Sings
I got you to walk with me I got you to talk with me
I got you to kiss goodnight

Jill Sings
I got you to hold me tight
I got you; I won't let go
I got you to love me so

Rafe and Jill Sing
I GOT YOU BABE
I GOT YOU BABE
I GOT YOU BABE
I GOT YOU BABE

When the song ended Rafe took Jill into his arms and kissed her passionately in such a way that lifted their spirits to the heavens. It was now a done deal. They were in love and back together, and Rafe knew nothing would ever break them apart again. He'd see to that. When the kiss ended Rafe's thought was, "God takes care of his own."

The following afternoon as Rafe guided Mighty Mouse's Mercedes down the Taconic State Parkway towards Manhattan, he was thinking. "Well, I've got Jill back, something I used to envision as being impossible, and now comes the glory. Wait till they see what I have planned.

Speed Kills

The following afternoon found Rafe and Jill cruising down the Taconic State Parkway towards Manhattan in Mighty Mouse's Mercedes. Just as he planned Jill was pressed tightly against him and enjoying the ride. Now that he and his beautiful girl were back together, his mind was turning towards hiring a trainer for the farm. As they cruised along the beautiful parkway Rafe mentioned that he was going to hire the best trainer in the world to work for Hope Farm. That brought a raised eyebrow from Jill, followed by the question, "How are you going to do that? If we're a new farm without the reputation for breeding good horses, why would a top trainer leave a lucrative position to come to work for us?"

Rafe just laughed and replied, "Because I'm going to make him an offer he can't refuse!"

Jill responded, "Really, how do you plan to do that?" Rafe explained that when he had first arrived home from Greer School he was tutored in handicapping by Burly Parke and Lucien Lauren, two top trainers. They taught him how racing was actually organized. He was taught how the races were written by the Racing Secretaries and another key fact that most didn't know; How the races were written, determined who was eligible to get in the race, and then, because of how the races were written, there were usually only three real contenders in any given race. The trick was to pinpoint those three. It took Rafe about nine months to master the Condition Book and be consistently able to determine the contenders.

It was then that his mentors told him, "Now that you've mastered the Condition Book and learned how to zero in on the contenders, you have just one big problem!"

"What's that," asked Rafe.

Lucien Lauren answered, "Because if there are three contenders and you pick one, the odds are two to one against you. And if you play those odds, over the long run, you'll lose."

Rafe looked over at the future trainer of the great Secretariat and asked, "So what's the solution? Or is there a solution?"

Lucien said, "Play an exacta box where you play all combinations of the three contenders finishing one, two. This means if one of the contenders wins and another runs second you win. But, like everything in life, it depends on how good you are at what you do."

Rafe continued to study and now turned his directed intelligence towards horse racing. He began reading the Racing Form every day which had the past performances of all the entries. After several months Rafe noticed that one particular trainer's runners almost always finished 1st or 2nd. The other trainers would have a horse win, and in its next start run last, then come back and run fourth, then finally win again. The name of the trainer that caught Rafe's attention was Archer Madden. On one of his visits to the track, Rafe asked Burley and Lucien if they knew Archer Madden.

"Do you mean SK Madden?" Burley asked.

Rafe answered, "I don't know! What does SK stand for?"

Lucien spoke up and said, "Speed Kills!" Burley added, "That's Madden's nickname when they're not simply calling him Old Man. The reason for the nickname, Speed Kills is that all of his horses have speed although no one else can figure out why. So, he has these cheap horses that outperform their pedigrees, and although not having as many starters he is near the head of the trainer's list. But remember one thing, all his runners have speed. Hence the nickname Speed Kills."

After that pronouncement, Rafe was sure SK Madden was a great trainer.Later, Lucien and Burley were talking while Rafe was watching a race, after the race, the pair came over and asked Rafe, "How'd you like to meet SK Madden?"

Rafe stared at them in astonishment and said, "You mean right now?"

Burley responded with, "Yep, we mean right now, come on, follow us. Off he went following the trainers down the line of Box Seats. When they came to the right row they led Rafe to a box seat, occupied by a medium-sized, grey-haired, man, dressed in a dark suit.

The trio walked up and Burley said, "Hey SK we have a youngster here that thinks you're the greatest in the world so we thought we'd introduce you two.

After a proper introduction, Burly and Lucien left to place some bets leaving Rafe alone with SK; The first thing SK said to Rafe was, "Well how did a young Whippersnapper like you figure I'm a great trainer."

Rafe thought he'd give him a dose of his own medicine, and said, "Well, Old Man, the numbers tell the story."

SK asked, "What do you mean by that?"

Rafe went on, "Well Mr. Madden just a small percentage of horses win their first time out, yet your runners win first time out at an extraordinary percentage rate. The question is why?"

SK took a close look at Rafe and was thinking, "Damn, this Whippersnapper is smarter than hell. That's a great question from a novice, and since he wants to learn, I'll give him a little tidbit of knowledge."

When Mr. Madden answered he said, "The reason my horses win first time out at such an extraordinary percentage rate is that I don't run them until they tell me they're ready."

Rafe thought, "This is a little bit crazy how can a horse tell you he's ready when horses don't talk?

Well, he knew who had the answer, so he asked SK, "Mr. Madden how can a horse tell you he's ready if he can't talk?"

SK laughed to himself and asked Rafe, "You don't have much experience around horses, do you?"

Rafe answered honestly, "I really don't know anything about them, except statistically."

"Ok, Whippersnapper, your education begins right now. I'm going to tell you why my horses almost always come in, 1st, 2nd, or 3rd. That's the object of a race right; to get the money?" Actually, what I'm about to tell you is too valuable to tell anyone, however, I have a peculiar feeling that you and I may eventually do something together. So, here's the deal! I start training my horses when they reach the end of their yearling year or, early in their two-year-old year. The process takes months, but eventually, the young horses achieve a level of fitness where they can begin to develop speed. As the horse develops speed his persona changes. Even a horse with a mild disposition will begin to become aggressive. By aggressive I mean they'll begin to bite and kick even if that's not their usual temperament. When they finally start kicking the stall walls that's a sure sign, they're ready. Once we're convinced, they're ready to run, we find a race. A good way to explain it is the horse is like a spring, and we keep winding it tighter and tighter. When it's fully tightened, we let it go. The spring unwinds, driving the horse to win. Once the spring is unwound the horse is depleted of energy and we begin the whole process over, which means essentially, winding the spring again. One thing that has to be considered is that all horses take a different amount of work to get wound tight enough to win again. Some take a week or two, some take a month, and some even take three months however, no matter how much time a horse needs to recover, we see that he gets it. That's why my horses always run 1st or 2nd. We never run them until they're ready."

Rafe was impressed with Old Man Madden's approach to training, so much so that he asked Mr. Madden, "Sir when I get out of school, in a couple of years, can I get an apprenticeship with you so I can learn to train horses. I could work for you for five or ten years until you say I'm ready, then, go out on my own."

Old Madden liked the idea as it was easy to see that the kid was some sort of genius. So, he responded with, "That may prove to be a brilliant idea, so, I'll tell you what, when you're ready, you come and see me, and we'll see about getting you started."

Rafe was very excited, in his mind, he was thinking, "This could be the start of something big!" When Burley and Lucien returned Rafe bid Mr. Madden goodbye and went off feeling higher than a kite. Of course, what he had been hoping for never happened. A few years later disaster struck the Old Man. That's what happens when you're too good, for your own good. A few years later one of Mr. Madden's horses came up positive for a banned substance. The end result of the doping scandal was that Archer Madden was ruled off for five years and had his reputation ruined.

When Rafe finished telling his story, Jill asked, "Are you sure you want this man as Hope Farm's first trainer?"

Rafe looked over at Jill and said, "Absolutely, and I'm beginning to think this might be representative of a little divine providence. If Mr. Madden hadn't been ruled off for five years, we wouldn't have had a chance of getting him as our trainer. I'm going to use all of my persuasive power to get him to join us as the trainer of Hope Farm."

Jill was beaming as she said, "Rafe this is all so wonderful, it's like stepping into a beautiful dream.

Two weeks later found Rafe at Belmont Park looking for Old Man Madden. He inquired at the stable gate as to where he might locate the stable area of the Old Man. Ten minutes after arriving at Belmont Park, Rafe was walking down a shed row towards the tach room at the far end. As he approached, he saw SK sitting on a director's chair in front of the tach room. Rafe was laughing to himself thinking that Fate was approaching, and Old Man Madden was completely unaware of its presence. Rafe walked up to the old man and said, "Mr. Archer Madden?"

The old man gave Rafe the once over then responded with a gruff, "You found me! So, what can I do for you?"

Rafe smiled at the old man who obviously didn't remember him, and said, "Actually, it's what we can do for each other. I'm looking for a trainer."

SK just laughed and said, "You look a little young to be looking for a trainer. You one of those Trust Fund kids?"

SK was sort of chuckling to himself when Rafe responded with, "You don't remember me, but we met eight years ago when I was a foot shorter. I called you a great trainer and you called me a Whippersnapper!

SP took a closer look at Rafe before the recognition showed in his eyes, he then exclaimed, "Well I'll be a Son of a Bitch! You're that kid Hawkins that wanted to be my apprentice. Where have you been for the last eight years?

Rafe let the old man know where he'd been after which the old man said, "Well you can see I'm in no position to take you on as an apprentice, in fact, I'm down to one horse, Old Roman. If it wasn't for him, I'd starve."

Rafe then said, "All that's over now. I've just acquired a seven-square-mile horse farm up in Duchess County, and, on it, we're going to breed the fastest horse in the world. And, if I can convince you to train for Hope Farm, we'll knock the industry on its butt. That's why I'm here, to convince you to join us. With you, we'll be unbeatable."

SK was grinning as he replied, So, what you're proposing is, instead of you working for me, I'll work for you."

Rafe's answer was simple, "As ridiculous as that may seem that's exactly what I'm proposing; you have the knowledge, and I have the means. Together we can accomplish something truly great.On the other side of how this plays out, I know what they did to you, and how despicable that was, however, join us, and you'll run by them like they're tied to a tree, or as we use to say in the Army, we'll show them where the bear shit in the buckwheat!"

With that Old Man started laughing and then finally said, "You know we haven't even got started yet, and I'm ready to sign on. So, what are you proposing Whippersnapper? What do you want to do?"

"Well to start, can you get the next 24 hours off? Get someone to watch Old Roman while I give you a tour of Hope Farm. If we leave soon, I can have you back by this time tomorrow." Old Man nodded and said, give me an hour and I should be ready. Need to find someone reliable to watch my old warrior."

Rafe said, "OK, I'll just walk around and check the scene."

Rafe hadn't gone too far when rounding the end of a shed row, he came upon a young lady sitting on a bale of straw, crying her eyes out. Rafe thought, "This is not good, I guess I should see if she needs help."

He sat down on a bale across from the young lady and asked, "Are you all, right? Maybe I can be of some help?" The girl looked up and Rafe couldn't help noticing she was a pretty redhead. She shook her head no.

"What happened," Rafe asked while handing her a handkerchief. She dried her eyes and said, 'I was fired from my job as an exercise rider, now I have no money, no place to live, and I'm in a foreign country." Rafe had noticed her Irish accent so he knew where she came from.

Rafe asked the inevitable question, "Why'd you get fired?" The young lady gave him a defiant look and said, "Because I wouldn't grant him sexual favors."

Rafe sat there thinking, "Well, we're going to need an exercise rider, and we have the accommodations, in fact, she can share Plum Cottage with Old Man Madden where he can have the downstairs, and she can have the upper suite." "What's your name miss? I'm Rafe Hawkins."

She tried to smile and said, "I'm Brenda Kay Ryan."

Rafe smiled at her and said, "Brenda Kay, have you ever heard the expression it's darkest just before dawn?" Brenda nodded and said, "I've heard it, I just don't know if I believe it or not."

Rafe laughed and said, "Well, I take it you're in the market for a job?"

Brenda nodded and answered, "I guess you could say that, do you know where I can find one?"

Rafe nodded, yes, and then went on to say, "I came to Belmont today to hire Old Man Madden to train for my new farm which is located in Duchess County, 87 miles north of here. It just so happens we could use an exercise rider also. I'll tell you what!Old Man Madden is looking for someone to babysit his horse Old Roman, overnight. If you could do that, you could sleep on the cot in his tach room tonight. That way you have a place to sleep tonight, then when I bring the old man back tomorrow, I'll take you to the farm, and if you like it, we'll hire you too."

Brenda looked at Rafe and thought to herself, "Darkest before dawn, he just mentioned that and here comes the dawn. How long did that take, about a minute? Brenda gave Rafe his first slight smile and said, "Yes, I can watch Old Roman, after all, I often exercise him. Then she said, "Lead the way, you've got me interested."

When they approached Old Man Madden's tach room, he was standing out front. He asked Brenda, "Where you been girl? I've been looking for you."

Brenda smiled, as she liked the old man, and said, "You mean about watching Old Roman?

"Yeah, how did you know?

She responded, "I got fired and was crying my eyes out when Mr. Rafe walked up."

SK asked, "So, what happened?" "The bottom line is, he told me if I watched Old Roman tonight, he'd hire me too."

Old Man Madden simply shook his head and said, "Then we had better get him out of here before he hires the entire Belmont backstretch." They had a good laugh over that before the old man briefed Brenda on everything she needed to know, and then he and Rafe jumped into Rafe's Pontiac and headed for the Whitestone Bridge and then the Saw Mill River Parkway. Along the route, Rafe and the old man chatted about the past eight years, which included two traumatic events, the first of which was The Old Man's railroading for the drugging offense, and Rafe's trials at Landing Zone Yankee, and the Dragon's Lair. Rafe impressed upon Speed Kills that his group from the Army, the Leper Colony, was contracted to the Government and that the work was very top secret. He also advised the trainer that the Leper Colony, which consisted of 18 men ages 20 to 25, was the major part of the Hope Farm workforce. He advised SK that any military-type activities on the Farm were strictly confidential and should never be discussed except with Rafe.

Upon arrival, Rafe showed him Plum Cottage and then led SK up a dirt road which led up a slight rise to a crest. From there they were looking down at a huge meadow that covered the flat area below the rise. Rafe looked over at Old Man and said, "Good place for a training track?"

The old man simply nodded with a smile on his face and said, "Looks perfect from here."

"Well, Mr. Madden this is where it all starts. We build the track. We breed the horses, and then we take a slightly different tack. We sell the horses we don't believe are the best of the crop as yearlings. The horses we retain are those we figure to be the best bred, best conformed, and the smartest. That's your area of expertise. Those we keep are put in training on the farm. Then in the spring, we enter them in some of those early two-year-old races. When they win, first time out we sell them for ten times what they would have gone for as yearlings. When we have a young horse, you believe to be exceptional, we simply never offer it for sale. When we sell one of the horses that win 1ˢᵗ time out, you'll get 10% of the sales price. So, a horse that might have sold for $10,000 as a yearling will sell for $100,000 after winning 1ˢᵗ time out. At first, the pickings will be slim, but we'll produce more and more thoroughbreds every year so your commissions will increase. And if you want to, you can be our agent when we sell yearlings in Kentucky also. You'll also be paid $2,000 monthly which will increase as we get profitable. Also don't forget, you get 10% of the earnings of the horses we retain for our Hope Farm racing stable."

Rafe went on to say, "Old man I have no doubt in my mind, whatsoever, that we'll make a load of money here at Hope Farm, however, that's not the real objective. I want to establish the premier horse farm in the world. I also want to breed the fastest racehorse to ever live. Making money is relatively easy, whereas creating something great is a real challenge. It's the struggle to achieve something great that makes a man great himself. I told my girl that we're going to make Hope Farm a place for happily ever aftering, and that's the real goal. I know with you by our side we can accomplish just that. It's now up to you."

SK answered, "Whippersnapper, I'll tell you right now, I'm taken by your vision. I'd like to do something great, and I think joining your organization puts us on the right track to achieve just that. So, draw up a contract, and I'll sign on

.The Old man offered Rafe his hand, and as they shook hands as Rafe breathed a sigh of relief. At that moment he knew the deal was done, nothing could stop them now. Rafe looked at SK and said, "Well now that you've joined the party, let's go over and take a look at your new cottage. They walked back over the rise and down the road to Plum Cottage. Rafe gave him the tour and the Old Man thought his suite was perfect.

Once back outside, the Old Man asked Rafe, "What now?" Rafe answered, "Dinner."

As they walked down the path towards Main House, Rafe explained to Old Man Madden that Hope Farm had a central Kitchen, which was left over from the days when Hope Farm was a boarding school, and Breakfast, Lunch, and Dinner was served in the Main House Dining Room. He then brought up a more sensitive issue regarding Brenda Kay. "Old Man, I'm going to hire Brenda Kay as an exercise rider and she'll be living in the suite above yours at Plum Cottage. My first impression of her is that she is a lovely girl, however, I'd really appreciate it if you'd look after her like a surrogate Father." Old Man Madden was somewhat caught off guard by Rafe's turning the conversation to Brenda Kay.

SK looked over at Rafe and asked, "Why do you think she needs a surrogate Father?"

Rafe only smiled and added, "You're going to find out about the potential problem in a few minutes. Remember when I told you that an important part of the workforce at Hope Farm is made up of my unit from the Army? We were called the Leper Colony, but the important fact to consider is that all sixteen men are between 20 to 25 years old. Just the right age for Brenda Kay. Of course, nothing may happen, but the one thing I can't allow to happen is the diminution of Unit Cohesion. Right now, everything is perfect, but we both know how sexual desire can be overwhelming. I can't allow the Lepers to become obsessed with Brenda Kay to the point that jealousy breaks down unit cohesion. It's the one thing that could ruin everything."

The old man looked at Rafe in a serious way and said, "I see what you're driving at. Brenda Kay is a beautiful girl and a little wet behind the ears. Don't worry I'll play the father role, and that should go a long way towards keeping the wolves at bay."

Rafe grinned at the Old Man and said, "I'm really glad you're on board with that. So, let's say we go over and meet the wolf pack."

An uproarious welcome greeted the pair as they entered the dining room. Rafe had promised the lepers that he would return from New York with Hope Farm's new trainer, and as usual, he delivered. The lepers were well aware that once they had their trainer, the development of Hope Farm would swing into high gear. During dinner, SK was introduced to Gunny Fiske and the two got along famously. Rafe was pleased that the two older men got along so well seeing that the young men of the Leper Colony could use steady leadership, as the one thing the group lacked was experience. With these two old salts on board, Rafe knew they would have just the right steadying influence.

As they were walking down the path leading from Main House to Plum Cottage the Old Man said to Rafe, "I think you're off to a good start with the farm. I'm sure when you bring Brenda Kay up here, she's going to be delighted. Don't underestimate her either, as she's a hell of a talented rider, and might even make a great jockey in the future." Rafe agreed that things were moving along perfectly. He told the Old Man that he'd pick him up at 0800 for breakfast after which he'd take him on a tour of Hope Farm and the surrounding environs, places like Millbrook, Verbank, and maybe even Poughkeepsie, then they'd head down the Taconic to New York.

The following day around 2 P.M. they arrived back at Belmont Park where they were greeted by a very excited Brenda Kay. After greeting them the first thing she asked was, "What is it like?"

The Old Man looked at her and whispered in her ear, "Take any position he offers you. The place is incredible. It's much more than I thought it could be, and I've already agreed to sign on.After that business was concluded Rafe asked Brenda Kay if she was ready to go. She was ready, all she needs to do was collect her meager possessions from the tack room and they were ready to go. The Old Man bid Brenda goodbye and said, "I'll see you in less than a week." Then they were off, on what would prove to be Brenda Kay's life-changing adventure.

They pulled out of the stable gate onto Hempstead Turnpike heading for the George Washington Bridge. Near the bridge, they branched off onto the Saw Mill River Parkway. Once they were headed North, Rafe said to Brenda, "Now the great adventure begins. Are you excited?"

Brenda looked over at Rafe and responded, "I'm so excited I really don't know what to do. Just 24 hours ago I was down in the dumps, my life in ruins and now here I am headed for this place that Old Man Madden thinks is terrific. If that cynical old man thinks it's great, it must be."

Rafe glanced over at Brenda and replied, "Do you like the old man?"

She quickly replied, "Yes, very much! Of all the people I've worked with since arriving in the United States, he's been the nicest person I've met, but I think what happened over the drugging scandal has hurt him deeply."

Rafe said, "I think you're right, but things have a way of changing very rapidly."

Brenda smiled at him and replied, "Don't I know it? This time yesterday I was down in the dumps thinking my life was ruined and you show up. Then you tell me it's darkest just before dawn, and here I am headed for a new life. I find it hard to believe this is actually happening."

Rafe laughed and said, "Well you can believe it, but there are a couple of things we need to discuss before we arrive at the farm?"

Brenda smiled and said, "Ok go ahead, I'm ready."

Rafe began, "Ok, there is more to the Hope Farm operation than meets the eye. Also, keep in mind everything we're about to discuss is Top Secret. Don't discuss this with anyone but me. First, along with me, my unit from the Army, known as the Leper Colony, is in residence at Hope Farm. There are 17 of them and they'll serve as the workforce for the farm. You will be meeting them at dinner tonight. Here's the problem. While you're living on Hope Farm you will probably, inadvertently, come across some of us lepers performing military types of activities. The best thing I can tell you is, to ignore what you see, and don't talk to anyone else about what you see. It's that important. Do you think you can do that?" Brenda nodded yes, and said, "I can do that."

Rafe went on to say, "The second issue is equally important. Have you ever heard of the term Unit Cohesion?" Brenda shook her head, no. Rafe went on to say, "It's a little complex so let me give you a reasonable explanation. It deals with the nature of bonds between team members of a military organization, particularly concerning performance, combat motivation, and social support. Strong bonds can help military service members cope better with stressful events, particularly in combat. Do you see where I'm going with this?" Brenda shook her head in the negative, and said, "Can't say that I do."

Rafe went on, "I really didn't think you would understand what I'm aiming at, so I'll explain. You could say the problem stems from the fact that you are a very beautiful young woman."

This resulted in Brenda giving Rafe a big Smile, and she said, "Do you think so?"

He responded with, "Yup, there's no doubt about it, you are a gorgeous young thing. To explain things let me make a slight deviation. All of us in the Leper Colony usually go by our call sign. For instance, my call sign is Crazy Horse, and some of the other call signs are Waco, Oakie, County Boy, Hit Man, Gator, and Mc Duck. While we're on the subject I'm about to confer upon you your very own call sign. After all, you have to fit in with the rest of your new colleagues, so you will now be referred to as Goldilocks."

Brenda responded with, "Gosh, I like that call sign." Rafe continued, "Remember the fairy tale Goldilocks and the three bears?" Brenda nodded yes, and then Rafe added, "Well your story could be called Goldilocks and the sixteen bears. Do you know where I'm taking this?" Again, Brenda nodded no. Rafe then said, "This is the deal; once the lepers see you, they're almost sure to want to pursue you in a romantic way. Maybe not all of them, but enough to cause real trouble, trouble that can cause a sharp decline in Unit Cohesion. This can never be allowed to happen as that can lead to a loss of life if we go into a combat situation. So, what I'm asking you not to do, is to flit from one leper to another. Just to make sure you understand what I mean, let me make it crystal clear. If you develop a strong feeling for one of the lepers or fall in love, that's perfectly all right, as long as you don't go from one to another. The result of that will be jealousy, and that emotion can tear apart any semblance of Unit Cohesion, that could lead to disaster in combat. Rafe looked at Brenda and asked, "Can you handle that?"

Brenda looked directly into his eyes and answered, "Yes I can."

Rafe smiled at her and said, "That does it then, you are now one of us. You, and old man Madden."

Brenda was thinking, "You don't have to worry about me hooking up with one of the lepers because the one I want is you." With that in mind, she asked, "Do you have a girlfriend?"

She got an immediate response when he said, "Yes I Do."

He could read the disappointment on her face before she said, "Is she very beautiful?

Rafe looked over at her and said, "She's very beautiful, in fact, she's a movie star."

Brenda looked at Rafe as if he were crazy, then said, "You can't be serious.

Rafe replied, "Yes, I'm serious, not only is she a movie star, but she's also the leading lady in the top musical on Broadway!"

Brenda looked across at Rafe and said, 'I've seen the top musical; you're talking about Cabaret, right?"

Rafe nodded and said, "You got it."

At first, Brenda didn't say anything, for a minute, then asked, "Is your girlfriend, Jill Haworth?"

With a big smile on his face, Rafe answered, "She is indeed." Brenda was speechless. She was thinking, "This is the craziest thing I've ever gotten involved in. At every turn, things get better and more exciting, I can't even imagine what comes next."

After thinking about it for a minute, Brenda asked, "Mr. Rafe, how did you get a movie star as your girlfriend?"

Rafe smiled at Brenda and said, "Do you really want to know?"

Brenda exclaimed, "Oh Yes, I'd really like to hear the story." Rafe said, "Ok, we have another hour and a half to the farm, so this is how it all came about." Rafe began with how he became the tutor to the starlet.

When he finished Brenda just shook her head in amazement and said, "That's the most incredible story. How could such a thing happen?"

Rafe smiled at her and answered. "It's not too difficult when God is on your side."

Brenda responded, "Is that what happened? Is God on your side?"

Rafe quickly answered, "When I made the prophecy, I told Jill if God wants us together nothing can stand in our way." Then he added, "I guess God Loves us."

When they reached the farm Rafe took the same route he took when he was driving Old Man Madden and after driving past the beautiful stone chapel, and the Victorian colossus of Main House, he pulled into the driveway of Plum Cottage. He said to Brenda, "This is your new home otherwise known as Plum Cottage."

They entered Plum and Rafe led her to the upper floor which was where she would be living. When she saw the three-bedroom suite she almost fell over. Not only did it have three bedrooms, but two bathrooms, a kitchen a living room, and a study, as well as a beautiful deck. Brenda was stunned. She walked over to the dining room table and sat down with her hands over her eyes.

It looked like she was about to start crying. Rafe asked, "Are you all right? Don't you like it?"

Brenda was beginning to cry and she answered, "Don't like it! It's unbelievably perfect!

Rafe asked, "Then why the tears?

Still crying, Brenda answered, "There's something I haven't told you about."

Rafe then said, "Well now's as good a time as any. What haven't you told me?"

"Five years ago, my parents were killed in an automobile accident. My brother and sister are in an orphanage in Ireland. I came to the United States to try to earn enough money to bring them over to live with me, but it's complicated."

Rafe asked, "How so?"

Brenda went on to say, "I have to convince the Catholic hierarchy that I have the wherewithal to support them, and I need to get them Green Cards. That's why getting fired was such a setback, even though I hadn't been making much headway on their behalf."

Rafe shook his head and laughed a little, before he said, "I think this is your lucky day." He went on to say, "Do you know what a Knight of Saint Gregory is?"

Brenda nodded yes and said, "Do you mean in the Catholic Church?"

Rafe nodded and went on, "That's exactly what I mean. It just so happens that my surrogate father is a Knight of Saint Gregory, and as such, he became a good friend of Cardinal Spellman, the Catholic Cardinal of New York. I'm sure that between Everett and the Cardinal, they can get any problems involving your siblings cleared up. With that kind of power backing you, the problem can easily be solved. I'll even sponsor them myself."

Brenda jumped up, ran over to Rafe, threw her arms around him, and kissed him on the cheek. After thanking him profusely she looked up at him and asked, "Are you, my guardian Angel?"

Rafe laughed and said, "Well you know if I was, I'd never admit it." They both laughed and Rafe said, "Come on Brenda Kay, let's go get your belongings out of my car, and then go over to Main House for dinner."

Later after dinner, which included a very warm welcome, Rafe dragged her away from the wolf pack back to her apartment suite. As he walked back down the path to Main House he was thinking, "Guardian Angel, not bad huh! Never thought of it like that, but I guess in actuality, that's what I am. After all, I'm going to make her into a legendary race rider, so she must be right." Then he laughed to himself. He was thinking, "This angel stuff isn't half bad."

Tar Baby

By the middle of August, things were humming at Hope Farm. What used to be dormitories had been renovated into luxury suites for the Leper Colony and other members of the growing cast of characters that inhabited the farms rolling hills, forests, and meadows. One evening in late August, Rafe walked down the gravel pathway connecting Main House to Plum Cottage. As he approached Plum, he saw Old Man Madden and Goldilocks sitting on the patio outside the old man's suite enjoying the warm summer evening. They waved as he approached and, invited him to join them. Once seated Rafe began with, "Good evening Old Man."

To which he responded with, "Evening Whippersnapper." Rafe just laughed and smiled at Goldilocks.

The Old Man then asked, "What brings you by this evening? If I may ask?"

Rafe joined the banter by saying. "Well, everything is coming along just great. The cottages are being renovated, We're, starting to lay out the training track, and a couple of horse barns are under construction. So, I think it's time for me to go to Kentucky and purchase Hope Farm's foundation mare."

Old Man Madden just laughed and said, "How do you plan to do that? If she's that good she'll cost a fortune."

Rafe responded, "Not necessarily. There have been some of the greatest broodmares that sold for next to nothing."

Goldilocks chimed in with, "That sounds kind of hard to believe."

Rafe looked at her and said, "Would you like to hear the story of one of them?"

Goldi said, "I sure would. I love a good story."

Rafe smiled at Goldi and said, "Ok here's the story, and pay close attention because I'm about to show you how to breed a foundation mare. To do this we have to travel way back in the history of the breed to 1769, and the foaling of a mare to be named Atalanta. Most people investigating the pedigree of a thoroughbred would only go back 100 years, however, the story of Atalanta begins about 200 years ago, so where she's concerned, they would completely miss the boat."

Rafe continued. "If you were to trace Atalanta's female line, from her, back ten generations to the foundation mare of the number 2 female family, you would not find one classic winner. It's important to note that all thoroughbred horses trace down their female line to one of 50 foundation mares. There were more originally, but their lines have disappeared. The only positive thing in Atalanta's pedigree was that she was sired by Matchem a great and influential stallion. However, this didn't make her a valuable horse as she was once used as a cart horse, and sold for seven shillings and sixpence (equivalent to $2), a wheelbarrow, and a service to a boar hog. If one were to look at her from a market perspective, she was almost worthless. Then everything changed. When Atalanta was 20 years old, she foaled a daughter named Flora by King Fergus. Not unlike her dam, Atalanta, Flora is sired by another leading sire, King Fergus, however, this is not the catalyst that turned loose the genetic power in this family. Flora was then bred to an obscure stallion named Hyacinthus and produced a daughter to be named Mare by Hyacinthus. The question is what did the lowly stallion Hyacinthus contribute to this soon-to-be great family? The answer is he is a grandson of Atalanta. Now, we can see that Mare by Hyacinthus is inbred to Atalanta 3x2. This means that Atalanta appears in both the 2nd and 3rd generation. Still, this was not enough to turn loose the genetic tsunami soon to appear. So, what was it, that opened the door to a flood of classic winners? It begins when Mare by Hyacinthus is bred to another grandson of Atalanta, named Camillus. The result of this mating was a mare named Treasure, who was inbred 3x3x4 to Atalanta. How good a broodmare was Treasure? Well, she is the ancestress of 22 winners of 26 classic races within six generations. Not only that, but two of those classic winners were amongst the greatest of the breed."

Old Man Madden looked at Rafe and said, "That's very interesting. But how does that affect the fortunes of Hope Farm?"

Rafe came right back with, "Well Old Man, it just so happens that I know the whereabouts of a mare bred just like Treasure, and I'm going to Kentucky with the intent of basically, stealing the mare for a price way below her potential value. In other words, I'm going to purchase a mare for around $1,000, when her value is more like ten million."

Old Man Madden laughed and said, "Well good luck on that. I've never heard a more outrageous idea, however, if you can pull it off more power to you!"

Two weeks later Rafe left for Kentucky in a pickup truck pulling a two-horse trailer. Rafe drove the pickup accompanied by Triple B and followed by a chase car occupied by Waco, Laredo, and Oakie. Being who and what, he was, Rafe knew the outcome in advance, and also knew that it would take five of them to safely transport what would prove to be the equine version of "The Bitch from Hell." Rafe also knew that the farm's first purchase was going to prove to be worth tens of millions of dollars, but then again, only time would prove it to the others.

Five days later the small convoy returned and pulled up to the newly created eight-stall horse barn which was situated near the uncompleted training track. Some of the lepers were nearby working on the track, but the word quickly spread that Crazy Horse had returned with a horse. Twelve of the lepers gathered, and they were anxiously awaiting the unveiling of the farm's first thoroughbred. Before they dropped the ramp on the horse trailer Rafe said to the gathered lepers, "Ok listen up. This is important. When you see Tar Baby, that's her name, you're going to be very disappointed, and I mean very disappointed. However, you can put that initial reaction aside because it's this mare who will make our fortunes. Trust me on that." Rafe looked around at the assembled lepers and continued, "Where Tar Baby is concerned there's something else you need to be aware of! I'll put it, in simple terms, something, that you'll all understand immediately; Then when I finish what

I have to say, you'll get the message. Do you remember *You Know Who?*" The lepers just stared at Rafe and nodded yes. They were all thinking the same thing, "How could you forget someone like *You Know Who*." It was then that Rafe said something else, that brought immediate understanding. "Tar Baby is the horse version of *You Know Who*. You know one, you know the other. That means if you want to get along with her, treat her with respect; or pay the consequences." The lepers were grinning as they all again nodded. After all, they were all very experienced in dealing with the absolutely stunning madame." After this short awareness speech, Rafe asked Waco and Oakie to let down the ramp so he could back Tar Baby out. Rafe entered the trailer through the side door, gave Tar Baby a mint, put a lead shank on her halter, and backed her out.

To say the lepers had looks of astonishment on their faces would be an understatement. Their expressions were along the line of, "What! Are you kidding us? This is the farm's foundation mare?" A good word that covers their astonishment is consternation. Richard Elliott aka The Professor. Yelled out, "Come on Crazy Horse, this can't be our foundation mare!"

As he led Tar Baby in a circle around the gathered lepers he responded with, "Professor, one of the first things you learned in school was, never to judge a book by its cover! Then once you learn that, you go out into the world and judge everything on its looks. Tar Baby may be small and ugly, and she's also as mean as a snake, but she's a genetic powerhouse, so cut her a little slack."

After dinner, Rafe walked Old Man Madden and Goldilocks down to the barn to view Tar Baby. Neither had seen her when she arrived and were keen to check her out. When seeing her for the first time. they were even more appalled than the lepers had been since they were horsemen and knew more about how a horse should be made. Old Man Madden simply shook his head before saying, "Whippersnapper, are you sure you know what you're doing? She's a sorry specimen if I ever saw one. What on earth do you like about her?

Rafe took a minute to answer then said, "Old Man, this farm, above all else, is a place to find happiness and a place for dreams to come true. It's that, above all else, that makes Hope Farm special. The Old Man with a very serious expression on his face asked, "Is that all?"

It was now Rafe's turn to put on a serious expression as he answered, "No that's not all. This place is the Kingdom of Heaven, or I should say a small piece of it; What's about to happen here is beyond your imagination, but as you will see, this mare, will be the catalyst that will propel both you and Goldi to legendary status in the sport. I'd just like to ask both of you to cut me some slack on this purchase and let me do my thing. First, I will gentle her down to where she's tractable. It may take a year or two, but by the time I'm finished we'll be able to handle her, and she'll prove to be a great mother. In the future I will consult with both of you on all horses purchased for the farm, however, this is a special case because I have a sneaking suspicion, that she's a genetic powerhouse, and I couldn't pass up the opportunity. So, do you think you can live with Tar Baby?"

Both Old Man and Goldi smiled, and Old Man said, "For you, we'll make an exception, seeing that so far, you've been right about everything. How about we head over to Plum, where we can sit on my patio, have a cocktail, and shoot the shit?" They put Tar Baby back in her new stall and headed for Plum

The only one with any complaint about how things were going on the farm, was his darling Jill who couldn't stand being away from Rafe. She was working six days a week which kept her away from visits to the farm. She could visit the farm, but usually only for a day. Rafe reminded her that there was no longer a threat to their long-term happiness. In another year and a half, her contract to play Sally Bowles in Cabaret would expire, then she could move to Hope Farm permanently. Jill accepted Rafe's view of their current predicament because in her mind a year and a half was a lot shorter than the five years they'd been separated previously.

The separation from Rafe grated on Jill even though she knew their future together was assured. She wanted to do something for Rafe that would bring him happiness until she could join him. It didn't come to her right away, it took days before she had a flash of insight and knew the answer. She had thought back to her first meeting with Rafe at Rhodes School. She was taken by the tall slender young man with eyes that were a combination of gentleness, and strength. She thought back to their first walks to Central Park and sitting on a park bench as they exchanged their short biographies. That's where the flash of insight came from, Rafe's short bio! The worst thing that had happened to Rafe while growing up at Greer School, was the killing of Max. It was then that Jill knew the perfect gift, A dog. She was smiling as she was thinking, "They don't call them man's best friend for nothing. I'm going to find him a doggie friend."

Since all of this was divinely ordained right from the beginning, the search for the perfect dog was already planned out. Jill simply went to the pound in Poughkeepsie, walked down a long corridor to its end, and looked down. It was as if she knew where she was going all along. There lying in the corner of his little holding cell was a medium-sized black and white dog. He was colored like an English Shepard but with something else thrown in. He was making some sort of strange noise and when she listened closely it appeared that the dog was howling, softly. When the dog made eye contact with her, he jumped to his feet, his tail wagging in circles, and then it began! The howling. Yep, no doubt about it, this dog liked to howl. The attendant who was showing her the dogs said, "It's his third time here, No one can keep him because of the noise." Jill said, "Let him out for a minute." Once outside the cage, the dog ran around Jill in circles before putting his paws on her shoulders and licking her face, He then sat at her feet, and silent as a lamb stared up into her eyes. Jill asked the attendant, "What's his name?" The answer came right back, "Bogart!" Jill smiled, and said, "I'll take him."

That's how Bogart became part of the Hope Farm menagerie. Jill walked into their suite in Main House with Bogart on a leash. Rafe was out on their balcony when Jill turned Bogart loose. Bogart ran up to Rafe ran a few tight circles around him, then jumped up, put his paws on Rafe's chest, and tried to lick his face. When the dog jumped down Rafe laughed and asked Jill, "What's this?"

"Jill was giggling as she said, "Sir Knight, meet your new pet, Bogart."

Rafe looked at Jill with a quizzical expression and said, "My pet?"

Jill was smiling at him, obviously very satisfied with herself, and answered, "I thought you'd need someone to love you while I'm away. From what I've seen so far, he's very loveable." Then she added, "If he's with you almost all of the time, he will always remind you of me, and how much I love you, even if I'm out of sight."

Rafe walked across the room took Jill in his arms and gave her a long passionate kiss. When the kiss ended, he said, "Thank you so much for the wonderful gift, if you wanted to let me know how much you love me, you found the perfect way." Rafe went on to say, "Now I suppose when we go for our walks down Lover's Lane, they'll be three of us going along instead of two?" Jill just smiled and nodded.

To say Bogart was a welcome addition to the Hope Farm scene was a massive understatement. Although she had no way of knowing it, in her current angel-human state, Jill had been divinely directed to one lonesome dog in the kennel. Bogart was a dog filled with love. It seemed he loved everyone, and everyone loved him. Now he had a home, in what could only be described as a canine paradise. He just had one last test to pass; Tar Baby!

Rafe waited till the late afternoon before he introduced Bogart to Tar Baby. Rafe was laughing to himself as he walked with Jill and Bogart down the road to the barn near the Training Track. As they approached, Tar Baby and Old Roman were grazing together in the middle of the five-acre paddock. Bogart, full of the exuberance of youth, went charging down the paddock fence intending to run to where the paddock ended at the tree line. Tar Baby caught sight of the rapidly moving body encroaching on her domain. She quickly determined that the running animal was a dog and she decided to trot over to the fence to check it out. Bogart met up with Tar Baby at the end of the paddock fence near the tree line. It was there that Bogart turned and decided to run back down the long fence, to Rafe and Jill. As he began retracing his steps from his run down the fence line, Tar Baby followed. Bogart thought he'd have some fun and sped up until he was running at full speed. If he was thinking he could outrun Tar Baby, he was mistaken, after all, she was a thoroughbred, and just because she was ugly and small didn't mean she couldn't run. Rafe and Jill watched the pair come charging towards them separated by only the paddock fence. When they were only about 30 yards away Bogart suddenly pulled up with Tar Baby coming to a screeching halt right across the fence. Tar Baby put her chest up against the fence and stretched her neck over the fence to get a better look. The mare and the dog looked each other in the eye, and then Bogart put his paws on the nearest fence rail, stretched up, and licked Tar Baby on the nose. She squealed, reared back and up, then nickered to Bogart. Rafe thought Bogart was going to take off and run down the fence line again, however, he had other ideas and slipped between the two lower fence planks and entered the paddock. Once in, he took off running with Tar Baby in hot pursuit. This time Bogart's tactics were different; he ran out to the center of the paddock and then began running a figure-eight pattern with the mare in hot pursuit. When he began to tire Bogart came tearing across the paddock, and slipped between two bottom planks. Tar Baby came up, stuck her head over the fence, and nickered to her new friend. Bogart responded by putting his paws on the fence, then reaching up and licking her nose. Her reaction was to squeal."

As they walked back to Main House Rafe expressed his feeling that what they had witnessed was of extreme importance. Jill, not knowing where he was coming from asked, "How so, what do you mean?"

"Well before Bogart showed up Tar Baby hated everyone. Now we see that she can love something."

Then Jill said, "Yes, but that could be a rare, one-in-a-million thing, between two creatures."

Rafe then continued, "Beyond the relationship, she's developing with Bogart, the fact that she loves him shows that she has love in her, to give. So, if Tar Baby has love to give, and I'm convinced she does, it will be my job to coax it out of her. It might take a year or two, but now I know it will happen."

Jill loved to talk of love, so while they were on the subject, Jill asked Rafe, "Can I ask you something?" Rafe answered, "Sure!" Then Jill asked the big question, "I've wanted to know for years, when did you start falling in love with me? Do you remember?"

Rafe just smiled at his lovely girlfriend and answered, "It was the moment we were introduced in Dr. Moskowitz's office!" Jill was watching Rafe intently as she said, "What happened?"

Rafe remembered very well so he said, "It began when we first met. You looked at me, and I felt I was gazing into the most beautiful eyes in the world, certainly the most beautiful eyes I had ever seen. My initial thought was,

God Loves me! I never imagined what was going to happen between us, even, could happen, but somehow it did."

Jill smiled at Rafe and added, "Did you know I cried all the way to Chicago when Mom and I left for Hollywood on the 20th Century Limited? The only thing I had left to cling to was your prophecy that God would bring us back together. So, here we are, and everything worked out perfectly. Well not exactly perfect yet, because I'm 85 miles away in New York while you're up here on the farm, but before too long I'll be up here too." The two of them continued up the path towards Main House, hand in hand, with Bogart running loose ahead of them, about as much in love as two souls ever were. Unbeknownst to them, God was smiling from above, proud of his handiwork.

By the end of the year, 1966 things were developing by leaps and bounds at Hope Farm. The cottages had been renovated along with the Main House complex. The training track was well on the way to completion, and the lepers had finally gotten around to the renovation of Daisy Cottage which when completed would serve as the Hotel for Hope Farm. A place for future clients to stay as well as a place for family members when they came to spend time with their sons. For the leper's younger brothers and sisters, Hope Farm was a paradise with its thousands of wooded acres and the summer camp nestled down in the valley behind the training track.

Rafe was pleased with how everything was going. He now had the foundation mare for the farm and only Rafe knew the astounding events which lay ahead. First, he needed to get Tar Baby bred. He knew which stallion to breed her to, and he knew what the result of that mating would be. The stallion selected as Reviewer, a son of the leading sire, Bold Ruler. Both Reviewer and his sire Bold Ruler, were standing at the most prestigious farm in North America, Claiborne Farm. If Reviewer had a problem, it was that he was considered a soft-boned horse, and this was because he suffered three leg fractures in training and a fourth in a paddock accident which led to his being euthanized. If it wasn't for this weakness Rafe probably wouldn't have been able to obtain a breeding to him for Tar Baby.

As it was, in February, Tar Baby made the trip back to Kentucky to be bred. To accompany the equine, "Bitch from Hell," were Old Man Madden, Goldilocks, and Mighty Mouse. In view of what would happen, it was a good thing he sent his most experienced horse people. They got her to Kentucky and to the farm at which to board her fairly easily, but what came next was totally unexpected; she returned from being reasonably tractable to her previous Bitch from Hell behavior. They were at a loss as to why the sudden turnaround. If they could read horse thoughts this is what they would have found Tar Baby thinking, "He got rid of me. He's sending me back to the hell hole I was foaled in. He almost had me thinking humans aren't all shits, and now this. I thought I had gone from hell to heaven. I thought he believed in me, thought I was special, after all, he rescued me and gave me mints. I never even believed such things existed till he gave me my first one. Now I'm addicted, and I've seen my last mint. To make matters worse he's taken my dog friend away, and he was my only friend. So, just when I begin to adjust my attitude, they screw me, just like they always do. Tar Baby reverted to her old self, meaning, she hated the world and everything in it.

They were still able to get her teased to determine when she was in heat and ready to be bred, but she was becoming completely unmanageable, and vicious. Two days before she was to be bred Old Man Madden called Rafe at the farm. The conversation went like this, "Hey Whippersnapper, this is the Old Man. We need to talk about Tar Baby! Rafe answered, "OK what's going on?"

The Old Man said, "She reverted back to her vicious behavior, and if she keeps acting as she is, they'll probably decline to breed her. I know how important this breeding is in your plans, but we have a problem."

Rafe asked, "What's the solution?"

The Old Man quickly said, "Charter a plane and get down here to hold her when she's bred. That's the only thing that has a chance of working."

Rafe thought about it for a minute then answered, "Ok I'll do just that. After I arrange a charter, I'll call and give you the time and place of arrival."

The next morning Rafe arrived in Lexington and was picked up by Old Man and Goldilocks. They drove to Paris, Kentucky, the location of Claiborne Farm, and the farm at which Tar Baby was boarding. They showed him to her stall and he walked up and slid the stall door open. Tar Baby in her dark mood was facing the back of the stall. She heard the stall door open and turned to face the intruder. At first, she didn't know what to think only,

"It's him, the quiet one!" Rafe walked up to her and laid his hand on her neck. He ran it down to her shoulder and gently patted her. One thing Rafe was very good at, and that was, transmitting love, by touch. He then slipped her a mint. Finally, he whispered, "Whose girl, are you?" She seemed to understand and nickered. That began the transformation of Tar Baby; In her mind, all the good things she'd known in life emanated from the quiet one. He rescued her from the hell hole she was foaled in. He introduced her to Mints, He brought her to a paradise to live and, he even found her a friend. But, now, most of all, she knew he loved her and believed in her, and that she was not forsaken. She now knew she'd be going home. It was at this point that Tar Baby thought, "If he can love me, I'm going to love him back." And so began a beautiful friendship.

Rafe held Tar Baby's lead shank while she was bred, and she conducted herself with as much dignity as could be expected. The result was she was in-foal on one cover and the little entourage headed back to New York State. They were taking a big chance as to whether or not she was pregnant because it would take up to 40 days to be sure, however, Rafe, being what he was, knew the answer. The foal would be due in either late February or early March of 1968. When Rafe returned from Kentucky with Tar Baby in tow, no one noticed the difference in the mare faster than Jill. They came walking over from Main House one evening to allow Tar Baby and Bogart to frolic in her paddock. When Tar Baby came charging over to see her canine friend she went through her usual nickering and snorting to greet him. Then after greeting Bogart, she ran over and started going through the same ritual with Rafe. Jill was absolutely astounded. Witnessing the incredible turn of events Jill yelled over at Rafe, "My God! What has happened?" Rafe smiled back and yelled, "Love Conquers All, my daring!" It was obvious that it did too. There just was no other logical explanation. Tar Baby had crossed the line and was well on her way to being a loving member of the Hope Farm community. Not many were first aware of it because she continued with her obnoxious behavior, which had always worked for her in the past. However, Rafe and Jill knew the truth, and both realized where Tar Baby was concerned, the battle was won.

Everything went along perfectly until the 2nd of October, 1967. At about 1000 hours Maddy LaDue called Rafe and told him he had received an urgent call from Mr. Abraham Hewitt, and he had left a number to call back. The number he called was picked up on the first ring and the person answering was Mr. Hewitt. After he identified himself, Mr. Hewitt said, "You're operational Crazy Horse. Are all of your men present and accounted for? Rafe answered Yes, Sir. They're all here." Hewitt went on to say, "Three helicopters will arrive at the designated place at 1600. Have the Leper Colony armed, and ready to be lifted out. You'll be headed for Florida and then further South, you will be briefed on the mission upon arrival in Florida." Rafe simply answered, Wilco, we'll be ready."

Precisely at 1600 three helicopters came in from the west skimming over Fairy Land stream before alighting on what had been the boy's athletic field. The lepers boarded the choppers in three six-man teams, armed to the teeth. Once all were aboard the choppers lifted off heading West. Their immediate destination was Stewart Air Base in Newburg, New York, 30 minutes away. From there it was a C-130 headed for Homestead Airforce base just south of Miami. At Homestead, they received an extensive briefing from Mr. Hewitt and two other CIA operatives, then reboarded the C-130 for the next leg which was about 3,000 miles. Where they were going and what they were about to do was extremely Top Secret. In fact, no one but a select few ever found out about it. The lepers never talked about it and, neither did their CIA briefers. The only indication that something unusual had transpired was that on November 14th, Raphael M. Hawkins met with Lyndon B. Johnson, in the oval office.

This time the visit was not adversarial, in fact, it was congratulatory. President Johnson couldn't say enough good things about the Leper Colony. Probably the most amusing thing that transpired during their short meeting happened when President Johnson said to Rafe, "Captain Hawkins, I have to admit that when I decided to turn the Leper Colony into a Top-Secret strike team, it was a stroke of genius on my part." Rafe smiled and laughed knowing the recent deployment to South America had paid dividends. The World would learn about the events that took place in South America, however, hardly any knew of the Leper Colonies' involvement.

1967 was ending, and Jill had only four months left on her contract to play Sally Bowles in Cabaret. More than anything Jill wanted to leave Broadway and live at Hope Farm with Rafe. She also wanted to be present at the foaling since she knew it was Rafe's dream. Somehow, she had her way, and the actress who would be playing the part of Sally Bowles when she departed, agreed to start four months early, and December 15th was Jill's last performance. Of course, Rafe was in attendance, and afterward took her, her mom, Everett, and his own mother to Trader Vic's for dinner. During dinner, Jill was snuggled up against Rafe as the seats along the back of the table were more like couches. She wanted to play with him, as she was a very playful girl. She whispered in his ear, "Are you going to take me home with you tonight?"

Rafe whispered back, "You better believe it!"

Then she whispered, "Are you going to tell me how much you love me, I mean non-verbally?"

Rafe smiled realizing his girl was playing with him. He answered, "I'll do my best!"

Her blue eyes were on him when she said, "You're going to need a lot of practice, to get it right!"

Rafe laughed and said, "Don't worry, I'll keep trying."

Jill was having fun, so she playfully asked, "Sir Knight, why do you love me so much?"

It didn't take Rafe very long to come back with the answer, "Because I think you're a Goddess, and I just can't help myself!"

Jill's nonverbal reply was to squeeze his biceps tightly and smile into his eyes. Jill was thinking, "I'm so happy! This is what I've been waiting for. I don't think there's any level of happiness above where I am right now. Then on second thought, what's going to happen when I get him home tonight." Jill just sat next to Rafe with the most beautiful smile on her face, the same kind Angels wear.

The Foaling

Late Christmas Eve, 1967, Found Rafe and Jill in bed, wrapped around each other watching the fire burn down to embers, They, were naked after Rafe had just given Jill another series of nonverbal communications, meant to prove his undying love. He had succeeded, and Jill was in a state of reverie, thinking, "My dream has finally come true. Even though the fulfillment of the prophecy was an amazing and incredible event, it still didn't bring what I was longing for. I just wanted Rafe back, I wanted to be with him, I didn't want to leave him after a day or two, and return to New York, but now, I have it all."

Rafe noticed, the look on her face and whispered, "What are you thinking?" Jill rolled out of the spoon position and faced him with a most beautiful look in her very incredible eyes. She whispered back, "I'm so happy, this is my dream come true. I just want to know what's next?"

Rafe answered. "It's interesting that you should ask that question. You're right about one thing, the prophecy has been completely fulfilled, meaning we'll never part again. Maybe for short periods of time, but nothing very long. Since we've found such happiness, it's time we turn our attention to bringing the same sort of happiness to the rest of our family on the farm. That's what this place is, a big family. So, the first step will be the foaling of Tar Baby."

Jill asked, "Why is the foaling of Tar Baby so important?"

Rafe looked into Jill's eyes and said, "Tar Baby is going to foal the fastest racehorse that ever lived!" A big smile appeared on Jill's face, then she began laughing.

Finally, she stopped and exclaimed, "Oh my God! Is this another one of your prophecies?"

He looked at her and said, "Yes, my darling it is." Rafe asked Jill, "Remember when we were saying goodbye as you were leaving for Hollywood?" She nodded, yes. He went on, "It was pretty awful, we both sort of felt, that was it for us. The odds were that we would never see each other again. My heart was breaking, I loved you so much. The only good thing about it was you weren't telling me you didn't want to know me anymore; you didn't tell me to get lost. It wasn't our feelings for each other that put us in that predicament, it was fate. I didn't want to see you leaving for the huge challenges of Hollywood feeling down, so I told you that if God loved us, he'd find a way to bring us back together. Then, I made the prophecy, although I didn't really believe it. It was just to make you feel better. But God did find a way, in fact, he created the way. He made the impossible happen. I believe it's because he loves us. Now that we've been blessed by God, I think we should get busy turning this place into what I originally told you it was."

He had Jill's undivided attention when she asked, "What did you originally tell me it was?"

Rafe whispered in her ear. "Don't you remember we were driving down 59th Street on your first trip to the farm and you asked, "Where are you taking me?"

Rafe could tell from her expression that she didn't remember, so he added, "I told you that Hope Farm was a "place for happily ever aftering!"

That brought a big smile to her face as she responded with, "Oh! I remember now."

Rafe continued with, "Well that's what we should be doing now. Through the Grace of God, we found happiness, now I believe he wants us to provide his love to others. Jill nodded and Rafe continued, "It's already started although you and I haven't discussed it. You're aware of Goldi's situation involving her brother and sister being in an orphanage in Ireland, right?" Rafe was aware that just as he had predicted, Jill and Goldi were becoming good friends and confidants. Jill admitted knowing about Goldi's siblings. Rafe continued, "What you don't know is that Pop went to his friend Cardinal Spellman and asked if he could intervene on behalf of Goldi's brother, Aiden, and his sister, Erin. The Cardinal agreed and soon, the two will be given Green Cards and legal immigration status. It was just a matter of going through bureaucratic hurdles. It's going to work, because Everett Massoletti, a Knight of St. Gregory, in the Catholic Church, has agreed to sponsor them, and Hope Farm has agreed to join Pop in the sponsorship.

Jill just snuggled back against Rafe and whispered, "That's wonderful!"

Rafe answered, "It's better than you think, as Pop told me earlier today that Aiden and Erin had been issued Green Cards, and would be flown to the United States at the end of March. Rafe continued, "If you think that's beautiful, how about at the end of March when we trick Goldilocks into going down to New York, with the agreement that we're going to give her a ride back to the farm? On the ride back we have to make a little detour to JFK Airport to pick up a visitor to the farm. The visitors, as they come through the exit from customs will be her brother and sister! Do you want to talk about happiness?" But the truth is my darling, that's just the beginning. How about Old Man Madden? They destroyed his career with a phony drug charge, and all but ruined his life. What if we give him the fastest horse in the world to work with? Not only that, did you ever hear of a betting Coup, my darling."

Jill stared at Rafe and giggled, then teasingly said, "You're bad!"

Rafe also began to laugh and replied, "No I'm not. Actually, I'm the reverse.Did you think I was bad when we first met?"

They kissed and Rafe added, "Let's just try to make Hope Farm, a place for happily ever aftering."

Jill answered, "Good Idea." Five minutes later Rafe made another attempt to convince his starlet that he was madly in love with her, and he succeeded.

The rest of December, January, and early February were spent getting ready for the big event, which was Tar Baby's foaling. Rafe had never seen a mare foal, the only ones in their entourage who had, were Old Man Madden and Goldilocks. Since it was so important, Rafe asked their new veterinarian, Dr. Cavey, to give the Hope Farm residents a lesson in foaling. He complied and gave them a great dissertation. Some of what they learned were;

The mare should be in good condition

It is wise to vaccinate the mare against influenza and tetanus one month prior.

A large clean stall with high-quality straw.

Well Lit

Clean warm water

First Aid Kit with Scissors, Disinfectant, String, Wound Powder, and Towels.

Oxygen Cylinder, in case foal needs resuscitation.

Frozen Equine Colostrum.

11 months gestation. Average 340 days.

They learned about the mare bagging up days before foaling

They learned about the mare waxing up showing foaling was imminent

During the first stage of labor the foal gets itself into the final birth position in the birth canal and the mare's cervix relaxes. The mare will look restless and get up And down several times.

By the time the vet was finished, they had a pretty good idea of what to expect. Dr. Cavey said he'd be right over if things weren't going right. He was aware this was the farm's first foal and he was only 20 minutes away.

The big event happened on March 4th. That's the day Tar Baby started getting restless in her stall, she had already bagged up and waxed up, so everyone was getting ready for the imminent foaling. Once she went down and broke her water she began to push. There was just one problem. Tar Baby was small, and the foal was big. Maybe 30 minutes after she began her foaling, Rafe asked Goldilocks to call the vet. When the foal first appears the first thing you see is the forelegs emerging with the head positioned between them. That's the easy part. The problem is the shoulders. Once the shoulders are out, the rest of the foal's body tends to slip right out. After about 35 minutes of Labor, Rafe received a message from on high. It wasn't in the form of a voice talking to him, it was the certain knowledge of the correct action to take. In putting this knowledge to use, Rafe knelt down behind Tar Baby and took a firm hold of the foal's forelegs, and gently pulled whenever the mare pushed. The result wasn't immediate, but it worked. After 50 minutes of her pushing, and Rafe gently pulling, the foal slipped out. This was just about the time the Veterinarian arrived, which was a good thing. He entered the foaling stall and administered to the newborn. While the Vet was looking after the foal, Rafe moved up near Tar Baby's head, and positioned himself, sitting with his back against the stall wall. He repositioned himself with Tar Baby's head in his lap. While this was taking place the Vet ordered the mare to be milked to be sure the foal received the early milk called colostrum.

If you were aware of Tar Baby's nasty disposition you would have thought Rafe was putting himself in a very dangerous situation. In reality, he couldn't have been in a better place. Over the last few months, Rafe had made a breakthrough and instead of a hostile attitude, Tar Baby had developed a very strong positive feeling toward The Quiet One. She wasn't stupid. She knew who supplied her mints. She was now exhausted and loved having him stroke her jowls and ears while gently whispering nice things to her. Although she couldn't understand the words, she knew their meaning from his tone of voice, and she could feel the love he transmitted through his touch. So, when Rafe whispered, "Whose Girl are you?" She knew what he meant.

At this point, Bogart slipped into the stall with Jill. Bogart seeing his friend lying in the straw ran over and threw himself down on her neck, with his nose up near an ear. He howled softly to her, and then she nickered back. Rafe was lying with his eyes closed petting the exhausted mare. Jill Slipped into the stall with her Polaroid camera and took a picture of Tar Baby, Bogart, and Rafe. The picture came out perfect, and Jill knew exactly what she intended to do with it. Then Jill went back and took a couple of the foal, just a few minutes after she first stood up.

On Rafe's part, he sat staring across at the magnificent foal, who was standing on the other side of the stall. It had only taken her about three minutes to get to her feet, and she didn't stagger around and fall down like most newborn foals. She practically bounded to her feet on her powerful baseball bat-like legs. Her legs weren't weak, in fact, they were the exact opposite, strong and powerful. The Vet, who had seen hundreds of newborn foals, simply exclaimed, "My God! What a foal." Everyone was taken by her strength and symmetry. She was coal black with the only white appearing as a perfectly shaped white heart on her forehead. But, of all those present, the one most impressed was Old Man Madden. He looked over at Rafe, still cradling Tar Baby's head in his lap, and thought, "He knew this would happen all along, but how could that ugly critter, foal such a magnificent animal." Old Man tore his gaze from the foal and looked over at Rafe. Rafe was smiling at him and simply nodded, Old Man Madden knew what he meant, so he nodded back. The old man knew deep in his heart, that the horse he had waited for, all his life, was here!"

Jill and Rafe stayed with Tar Baby and the foal for a couple of hours while everyone on the farm crept up to peek at the new foal. They didn't want to disturb the new mother as there is no way to know how they'll take to motherhood. Sometimes it's a very aggressive posture, and everyone was aware that Tar Baby, was Tar Baby by this time. So, instead of coming up in a group, they came up quietly two at a time to peek around the corner at the new foal. Just after midnight, Rafe asked Old Man Madden and Goldilocks to stay with the mare and foal, and Rafe and Jill would be back at 0600 to take over the watch.

As they walked back to Main House Jill Asked Rafe, "Are you happy?" He nodded, "yes."

Jill said again, "I mean really happy,"

Rafe laughed and said, "Yes, I'm very, very Happy!"

Then Jill continued with, "Well, you should be! What just happened is so beautiful."

Rafe played stupid to see what she would say, so, he said, "How So?"

She said, "It's the whole story of Tar Baby! She's ugly, mean, and small. Everyone, but you, thought she was ridiculous. You kept saying, "Cut her some slack. Only you and Bogart loved her, and look what she did."

All of this was amusing to Rafe so he added, "I think I have an understanding of where she's coming from."

Jill wanted to know what that meant so she asked, "Do you mean you and Tar Baby are alike?"

He said, "No that's not what I mean. What I mean is she and I have had a similar background, so I tend to understand her more than anyone else."

Jill asked, "How was your background similar?" Rafe answered, "When Hope Farm was Greer School I was in a bad situation. If my mother hadn't had the good sense to pull me out when she did all hell would have broken loose. I mean like someone getting killed. I was 5' tall and weighed 100 pounds when 16 years old. Mom took me home, and Pop said he'd send me to Rhodes School if I promised to be the number one student. So, I became number one and grew one foot in a year. Then what happens? The most beautiful girl in the world drops into my lap. So, you may ask how does Tar Baby's story interconnect with mine?" Jill nodded yes, she wanted to know, so Rafe continued. "I found Tar Baby in a hell hole, just before I handed over the purchase price, the owner smacked her in the head. I advised him if he did that again I'd stick my boot up his ass. But, in the end, he just wanted to get rid of her. So, in her mind, I'm the one who took her from that hell hole to the lush pastures of Hope Farm. I was the one who brought Bogart to her, and up till that point, he was the only thing she'd ever loved. And besides that, I delivered an unlimited supply of mints, and if there's one thing Tar Baby loves its mints. Finally, over the last year and a half, I ingratiated myself with her, till she believed I was the only one who believed in her. Then, as a result, she rewards me with her super great foal. It's not unlike when I came out of Greer School in disgrace, yet Pop believed in me and had faith in me. Without Pop's faith, we would never have met. Rafe went on to say, "You do know Tar Baby thinks she's the Queen of the May, and now that she has produced her masterpiece, everyone else is going to think so too. Just wait till tomorrow when we turn them out."

Jill was so in love with her high school sweetheart that she said, "When I get you home, I'm going to show you how much I love you without saying a word." Rafe smiled and said, "Do you think you can do that." Jill gave him the same look he'd first seen just before she had said. "I think you should take me out." She had those irresistible eyes, this time smoldering with passion, then she said, 'You just wait and see!" They continued walking down the pathway towards Main House, with Bogart trotting on ahead. Things were getting very exciting at Hope Farm!

Bright and early the next morning Jill and Rafe were down at the barn where Tar Baby had given birth to what could only be described as a magnificent creature. It was good fortune that March 5th was turning out to be sunny and warm, as, In New York State, the weather in March can be anything but pleasant. It's often cold and blustery, and Rafe wanted it to be warm on the day the foal would experience the outdoors for the first time. If the weather had been inclement, they would have postponed the foal's first outing. He had it all set up in his mind. When they led Tar Baby out with her foal, Rafe would lead the mare while Goldi would lead the foal. He had a very specific reason for Goldi to be leading the foal, and that came from his ability to know the future. This filly, to be ridden by Goldilocks, was headed for equine immortality, along with her trainer, Archer Madden. This brought to mind the Legendary racehorse, Seabiscuit who during the Depression was the most beloved and popular thing in the United States. He was even more popular than President Roosevelt. His trainer was a virtual nobody in racing, his rider a journeyman jockey headed nowhere, and Seabiscuit himself was a castoff from one of the nation's top racing stables.

Rafe knew the outcome before the process even started, He knew in his mind that the actual process had started last night with the foaling of Archangel. Yes, he had already selected a name although, historically, Archangel's are male. He told Old Man and Goldi that the foal would be named Archangel. He then explained that he wanted Goldi to lead Archangel out as a means to bring about bonding. He then exclaimed that he wanted the two to bond together so they would know each and every move the other would make, and vice versa. The process would take a long time, but it was vital.

When all was ready Rafe attached a lead shank to Tar Baby's halter and led her out of the stall and down the aisle. The paddock gate was open with Old Man Madden standing by to close it once the mare and foal were safely inside. As they exited the barn, Rafe had Tar Baby by the lead shank and Goldi was following right off Tar Baby's flank with Archangel. There were no problems as Archangel followed right along beside her mother with Goldi's right arm under her neck and the left arm back behind her hind quarters. Once inside the paddock fence, Rafe released Tar Baby, and she began to trot over towards her buddy, Old Roman who was grazing about 100 yards away; She wasn't in any hurry knowing that she had her foal to consider. The two pasture mates sniffed noses and made some nickering noises as Old Roman checked out the new addition to the paddock. A minute later who should come running up, none other, than Tar Baby's dog friend, Bogart. The same ritual of greeting took place with Bogart sniffing and licking the noses of his equine friends including the new arrival. Rafe went back to Main House and returned with two lawn chairs so He and Jill could sit near the paddock and keep an eye on Tar Baby and Archangel. At about 11:00 Doc Linginfelter dove up and yelled to Rafe from his pickup, "Hey Rafe, Maddy Ladue got a message from your Pop. He wants you to call him as soon as possible." Rafe answered, "Thanks Doc, I'll call him from the tach room!"

Rafe dialed Everett Massoletti at his restaurant downtown, and he answered the phone in his office on the first ring.

Rafe said, "Hi Pop, it's Rafe,"

Everett said, "Hey Rafe, how's it going, has the mare foaled yet? "Actually, it happened last night."

Everett was excited and asked, "Well what sort of foal did that bitchy little mare produce."

Rafe quickly added, "Well Pop, she outdid all expectations. The vet says she's the most beautiful foal he's ever seen. It's a filly, and I've decided to name her Archangel if the Jockey Club approves it."

Everett responded with, "That's great news Rafe, that has to be the biggest hurdle to date."

Rafe said, "It sure is Pop, everything is looking great, but why did you want me to call?"

Everett came back with, Son, I have the greatest news, it's going to make someone on Hope Farm the happiest person on earth!"

Rafe came back with, "Well who is the person, and what is the good news?

Everett then told Rafe, "The person is Goldilocks, and the news is Her brother and sister have received their Green Cards, and we're arranging to have them flown to the United States on Thursday, March 30th.

Rafe took a minute to answer then said, "Pop, that's the greatest news, but here's the deal, we're going to make this the biggest surprise of Goldi's life. In pursuit of that end, I'm going to get together with you to plan the whole thing out. As it turned out it wasn't that difficult, they only had to enlist one other person in their scheme, and that was Jill. Once she found out what was going on she definitely wanted to play a role. This is how it went down; on the 28th, two days before the big day, Jill asked Goldi if she would accompany her to New York to do some shopping at Macy's, and then have lunch with Everett Massoletti at his restaurant. The whole idea appealed to Goldi as she was becoming good friends with Jill, and she thought Everett Massoletti might have the latest information on how things were progressing in getting Aiden and Erin entry into the United States.

On the 30th, Jill and Goldi took the train From Poughkeepsie to Grand Central, from there to Macy's on 34th Street, and then down to Pine Street and Massoletti's. They were having a wonderful lunch when Goldi asked about Aiden and Erin. Everett simply smiled and said, "Good news, my dear, it's only going to be a couple of more months. They're just going through the bureaucracy. Don't worry they'll be here to spend the summer with you, maybe even sooner." Jill and Pop smiled at each other knowing the "Maybe sooner", meant about two or three hours.

As planned, Rafe picked up the ladies outside the Pine Street exit from Massoletti's, and headed towards the Brooklyn Battery tunnel. The idea was to pick up the Belt Parkway to JFK Airport after exiting the tunnel. Goldi's brother and sister were arriving at 1500, at the International Arrivals Building. Rafe simply explained to Jill and Goldi that he had to pick up a visitor to the farm on the way home, and that explained the detour to the airport.

They pulled up in front of the International arrivals building and Rafe told the girls to wait inside while he parked the car in the lot across from the terminal. Ten minutes later he met them near the exit from customs that led into the baggage claim. Everyone taking the exit from customs had to pass by the anxious trio. For Aiden and Erin, it would be virtually impossible to walk out of customs into the baggage claim without being seen. Nevertheless, it almost happened as Jill and Rafe had never seen Goldi's siblings in real life, only photos from when they were about three years younger. As it turned out, Goldi was looking in the other direction when the pair walked out of customs, but Rafe thought he recognized Aiden and waved to him. When Aiden detected the movement off to his left, he swung his head in that direction, and sure enough, next to the man who was waving at him, was his red-headed sister. Aiden yelled, "Brenda Kay."

Goldi turned, saw Adin and Erin, and took off running right into their waiting arms. A lot of hugging and kissing and exclamations of joy were witnessed by Jill and Rafe who were standing by the exit.

Rafe said to Jill, "Let's go over and join them."

The trio of celebrating siblings had their arms around each other's shoulders with their heads looking down, not unlike football players in a huddle. Rafe and Jill walked over and joined the huddle. When Rafe and Jill appeared in their small huddle, Goldi immediately introduced them to her brother and sister saying, "Kids, these are my friends, Rafe Hawkins, and Jill Haworth, from Hope Farm."

Erin immediately said, "Oh my God! You're the movie star!" Jill just smiled and nodded."

Aiden added, "This has got to be the greatest day ever! It just seems to get better and better."

Rafe added, "If that's what you're thinking, consider this, the day's not over yet."

"What's next?" asked Aiden

"First, we pick up your baggage from the baggage claim, and while you're doing that, I'll go pick up the car, and meet you curbside. Once we're all aboard we head for the farm.

"Where is it?" asked Erin.

"It's about a 2 ½ hour drive North of the city."

"What's it like?" Asked Aiden.

Rafe said, "Would you like to know how I described it to Jill the first time I took her there?"

"Oh yes! I have to know what you told her." Said, Erin.

Jill turned in her seat, and facing the two teens in the back said, "On our first date Rafe took me to the opening night of Camelot, with Julie Andrews and Richard Burton. At the end of the play, when King Arthur is singing the reprise, he says, "Don't let it be forgot, that once there was a spot, for happily ever aftering, that is known as Camelot."

Rafe joined in and said, "That's where we're taking you kids; to that spot. It's the perfect place to find happiness, and that's not all, you're about to embark on a great adventure."

Aiden responded with, "I can't believe where we are today, compared to where we were yesterday, to tell the truth, it's already a great adventure."

Rafe then said, "Let me tell you how we're going to get to the farm since it's eight- five miles North of New York City. The road we are heading down is called the Van Wyck Expressway. Normally, we'd take a different route, but since you've never seen the city, we'll take the Van Wyck since it parallels Manhattan. That way you'll get a good first look at midtown as we pass by." Erin and Aiden were so excited about being reunited with their sister that the trip hardly seemed like 2 ½ hours.

Before long they passed through the stone gate and headed up Main Road towards Plum Cottage. Upon arrival, Goldi led her brother and sister upstairs to their apartment suite where they couldn't believe their good fortune.

Erin asked, "Do you mean this place was waiting for us, all this time?"

"Yes, it was," said Rafe. "The only problem was getting you legally into the United States, and now that's a done deal!" Rafe went on to say, "Now that you've had a glimpse of your new home, we have to go over to Main House where we are going to throw a big dinner party to welcome you."

After breakfast the following morning, Rafe took Goldi and her siblings on a tour of the farm, following which he took them to Poughkeepsie where he bought both of them a bicycle of their choice. He explained, "You've seen how big the farm is, and since you're too young to get a driver's license, a bicycle is the next best option. Just a piece of advice though, don't ride it down the hill to the camp. It would be a fun ride downhill, but then you'd have to push it back up that steep, twisting road. It would be fun riding down, but hell coming back." Both teens laughed because they were feeling no pain. Like everyone else at Hope Farm, they had found the spot.

The Foaling

Rafe walked down the path between Main House and Plum Cottage thinking about the proposal he was about to present to Old Man Madden. Four years had passed since Rafe had acquired Hope Farm. Since that acquisition, everything had gone exactly as planned, but now it was time to put it all together. As he approached Plum, he saw the Old Man sitting on his patio enjoying his usual Dewar's and water. He walked up and greeted his friend, "How goes it, Old Man?"

"Can't complain, Whippersnapper, how goes it with you?"

"Not bad at all, but I need to have a sit down with you, it's really important."

"Ok, but what would you like to drink?"

"Rum and Coke would be good."

Old Man Madden fixed Rafe a tall Rum and Coke then sat down across from him and said, "What's on your mind?"

Rafe started with, "Do you remember meeting me eight years ago?"

"Indeed, I do. You were with my friends Burley Parke and Lucien Lauren at Belmont Park."

"Do you remember why I was so interested in meeting you?"

"Yes, I remember. It was because I had the highest percentage of runners to win the first time out."

"Do you remember telling me how you would wind up a horse like a spring? A tight spring!"

"Yes, I remember our conversation, and I remember telling you about my training methods."

"Well Old Man, that was a fateful meeting, because it was then that I decided if I ever needed a trainer, and could someday afford one, it would be you. That's why I showed up at Belmont Park looking for you when I did. Hiring you is part of a master plan that you need to know about, that's why I'm here tonight."

The old man chuckled and said, "I can't wait to hear this, because after witnessing the rise of Tar Baby, who if I remember, I thought was an absolute disaster, I'll believe anything."

"OK Old Man, I'm going to lay out the plan from start to finish. It all started four years ago with the acquisition of Hope Farm. For this to work, I needed a farm. So, under the guise of a base for the Leper Colony's covert operations, I acquired Hope Farm. Then I needed a Trainer, so I got you, and almost at the same time, I got my rider, Goldilocks. Then I suppose you remember when I told you we needed a foundation mare?" Old Man just nodded. Rafe continued, "Then came Tar Baby, followed by her daughter, Archangel. But you have to understand, that was just the beginning of the story, now we get to what is called the nitty gritty. This is why I needed to see you tonight. You could say I did my part, and that was to breed the horse. Next, you train her, and finally, Goldi rides her, all to achieve a certain end."

The old man asked, "To what might that end be?"

Rafe smiled at him and said, "The biggest betting Coup in history!"

Old Man just stared at Rafe. He had heard what he said, but it was just a little difficult for his mind to process it. At first, as things began to come together in his mind, he remained silent. Finally, Old Man said, "Damn it, Whippersnapper, "Have you been planning this for four years?"

"You're exactly right there. I started the planning once I had Hope Farm and convinced you to join us as our trainer. Once I had you and Goldi, I just needed the horse. That led to Tar Baby. Here's the question, can you wind up Archangel, and have her ready by July 22nd?"

"Old Man looked at Rafe and said, "There is no such thing as a sure thing, but in view of where she is right now, I could have her, sitting on ready, by that date. The question is why that date."

Rafe looked directly into Speed Kill's eyes and said, "Because, July 22nd is opening day at Saratoga and the running of the Schuylerville Stakes."

Old Man just stared at Rafe. The big picture was beginning to form in his mind. A smile crept onto his weathered face, and He said, "I'll be damned! Tell me more."

"We're going to bet $600,000 to win on Archangel. But, let me explain the setup. Hope Farm has never bred a winner, less a stakes winner. Our trainer is in disrepute, our jockey, never having won a race, is a novice, and the horse herself, has never started; based on that, what sort of odds are we looking at?"

"Well, just based on those facts she should be eighty or ninety to one however, once you bet the $600,000 grand the odds will drop like a rock. Remember the track uses peri-mutual betting where the odds fluctuate depending on how much money is bet on each horse. The odds at the track are a ratio between the amount bet on each horse and the total amount bet on the race, and it's updated every thirty seconds."

"I've taken that into consideration. That's where having the Leper Colony involved changes the picture."

"How so, what can they do?" Asked Old Man Madden.

"We're not going to bet at the tracks. We're going to send six, two-man teams of lepers, to the six biggest casinos in the world, and bet the money on the odds their Handicappers post. We're also going to place the bets at exactly the same time based on Greenwich Mean Time. We're not going to give the casino time to lower the betting odds on Archangel before we can place all our bets. By the time they realize what's taking place, it will be too late. You do realize of course, that without all of the pieces of the plan coming together, it would never work. For instance, without trusted people to handle the money overseas, this wouldn't have a chance. So, my question to you Old Man is what sort of odds are the casinos likely to place on Archangel given her lack of form?"

Old Man Madden, now had a huge smile on his face as he answered, "As I said, I'd guess eighty or ninety to one, maybe even one hundred to one."

"So, the way I see it, you get the Archangel ready, we keep her out of sight so no one has an idea of what we're sitting on. We don't work her in public. When she requires serious work over the Saratoga Racetrack, we van her in and work her before dawn. Absolutely no one will witness these works. When the big day arrives, no one will have any inkling as to the devastating speed Archangel possesses, and we all know, Speed Kills!"

Old Man Madden couldn't help himself as he exclaimed with great emotion, "Son of a Bitch, damn if you're not right. Normally, this plan could never work, but with the training track on the farm where we can hide what we're doing, and the leper colony to place the bets, we can pull it off. I have a question though; How do the lepers feel about it?"

"To tell you the truth I haven't told them yet."

"Why not?" Asked the old man.

"I have a good reason that comes from my experience at Supreme Headquarters. As bodyguard to the Supreme Allied Commander, I would often, overhear very sensitive and highly classified material. I had a Cosmic Top Secret Security Clearance, but in addition to that, I was required to have the need to know. The only problem with that was I really didn't have the need to know anything. However, not having the need to know didn't stop me from hearing it. To give you an example, when they had Top Secret conferences, they would have one guard inside the room and one outside. It didn't make much sense to me, but that was the setup. Being on the inside I heard every word spoken. I didn't have the, need to know, but I heard it all. As an example, I listened to the Supreme Allied Commander's Nuclear Strike Plan. I had the clearance to hear it, but I lacked the need to know. You might ask yourself where the problem lies. This is the problem, If I didn't take my job very seriously, I might talk about what I knew to another of my colleagues, who also had a top-secret Clearance, the question is, who might be listening without our being aware? That's the problem. So, if I keep the Betting Coup secret for another six weeks, by the time the lepers learn about it, we'll only have two weeks left until the Race."

Old Man said, 'Well it seems to me like you've thought of everything."

Rafe laughed and came back with, "Well I should have, considering that I've had four years to think about it. Actually, when I think about it, four years isn't too long when forty or fifty million is at stake. Plus, there's something else to consider, that I know must have crossed your mind."

The old man asked, "What's that?"

"On Wednesday, July 22nd, you're going to have the opportunity to serve up to the assholes that tried to destroy your career, a giant shit sandwich; Or put another way, a great big kick in the ass!"

SK broke out laughing. Then said, "I never thought I'd have so much fun in my life, this is beyond good."

Rafe responded, "Glad you're enjoying life. Think of it, in six weeks we're going to Saratoga, to put Hope Farm on the map."

The following morning Rafe changed his schedule. He was up at 0530 and out at the training track by 0600. It wasn't very hard to find Old Man Madden as he was standing by the rail, shrouded by the early morning mist, waiting for Goldilocks to show up riding Archangel.

When Rafe walked up to Old Man Madden, he greeted him with. "Morning Old Man."

The response was "Morning, Whippersnapper!" "What are you doing out here so early? Keeping tabs on me?"

"Wouldn't think of it. After all, how would I know what you're doing? You're the best, and I haven't a clue as to how to train a racehorse, except in the most rudimentary way. That's not why I'm here."

"Ok, what are you doing?"

"I came to watch history being made."

"Old Man looked over at Rafe and said, "How do you mean?"

Rafe replied, "Imagine this is some fifty years ago. Let's just say Archangel is Man O' War and it's he, that's is getting ready to make his first start, and like we are with Archangel, his connections know he's faster than hell. Let's say they know he's a great champion, even though he hasn't started yet. My question is this; wouldn't his connections want to come out every morning and watch his progress?" Think about it. This is what it's all about. Once the whole world is aware of the Archangel's ability the game is virtually over."

Old Man said, "Yeah, I was just joking, the truth is I'll be glad having you out here with me in the morning."

"I'm glad to hear that because for the next two months, we have to react quickly to anything that arises that threatens our plan. For Instance, after I talked to you last night about not informing the lepers about the actual plan until two weeks before the race, I suddenly had a change of heart. I'm going to brief the Leper Colony tonight after dinner."

"Why the sudden change?"

"Remember during our talk last night, when I brought up my security concerns involving keeping the betting coup secret?"

"I do remember; Is there some additional question concerning security?"

"I realized I'm going to have to tell the Lepers about the plan immediately instead of waiting."

"Why would you do that?"

"I forgot about Visas. The twelve lepers who will travel overseas to place the wagers will need visas to enter the countries that the casinos call home. Visas take a certain amount of time to be issued, so we need to start the process now. With that in mind, I'll address the Leper Colony after dinner and brief them as to what is really taking place. I have to admit, they've been through very similar circumstances while in the Army, so what I have to tell them will be familiar to a great degree. It all revolves around the old, World War II expression, "Loose Lips, Sink Ships." They'll get the message."

Every morning around 0600, Rafe and Jill were out at the training track, alongside Old Man Madden, watching Archangel train. They could never figure out exactly what the Old Man was up to, but they were fascinated nonetheless. On some days she took long slow gallops, on others she sprinted short distances, but at a much higher rate of speed. When she galloped fast, she was nothing short of poetry in motion. It seemed, the faster she galloped, the more fluid her action became, and not only that but to Rafe and Jill, she was the most beautiful horse they had ever seen.

On the 29th of June, Old Man Madden told Rafe, "She ready for her final major workout, and for that, we're going to take her up to Saratoga and work her five furlongs (5/8 of a mile) over the main track tomorrow night. After that, she should be ready, except I want to put a final ½ mile work into her seven days before the race. The fractional times and the ease with which she works will tell me if she's sittin' on ready!"

The following night at midnight the small caravan left Hope Farm. It consisted of three vehicles. First, was a pickup pulling the horse trailer occupied by Archangel. The pickup was driven by Old Man Madden, with Goldilocks as a passenger. Rafe rode in the horse trailer with Archangel. The second vehicle was Mighty Mouse in his Mercedes Benz with Jill as a passenger. Finally, came the remainder of the Texans including, Waco, Laredo, and Oakie in Waco's, Camaro. Around 0230 they pulled into the stable gate at Saratoga and were passed through without incident. Just after 0300, they were ready for the workout. Archangel and Goldilocks were ready, and Old Man Madden was giving Goldi her final instructions. The only complication to the workout was the track was pitch black. Old Man told Goldi not to worry about the dark as Archangel wouldn't have any problem with it. However, to make Goldi feel more comfortable he was going to place the lepers with flashlights at key locations.

The workout would start halfway down the backstretch. From that point to the beginning of the far turn was 1/8 of a mile. Horse and rider would hit the turn and run through it to the head of the stretch. The distance around the turn was ¼ mile. As they came off the turn into the stretch, they would be ¼ mile from home. Goldi was very uneasy about working Archangel. After all, if she couldn't see, how could Archangel? To alleviate her fears Rafe placed Waco at the place where Archangel broke off to start the workout. When Archangel broke away, Waco would push a button on a flashlight sending a flash of light that would prompt Old Man Madden, who was standing 5/8 away at the finish, to start his stopwatch. As the horse and rider approached the beginning of the far turn, only 1/8 of a mile from the starting point, Laredo would be positioned with another lit flashlight allowing Goldi to see the beginning of the turn. As she and Archangel approached the end of the turn and the top of the home stretch, Oakie would be positioned with a light to allow Goldi to know her exact position. Finally, Rafe would be standing next to Old Man Madden at the finish with another flashlight. All of this was done to allow Goldi to ride with complete confidence, this workout was of vital importance.

In reality, it went off without a hitch. When Archangel flashed past the finish in full flight both Old Man Madden and Rafe stopped their watches with the same result. Archangel had worked 5/8 of a mile in 57 seconds flat.Old Man Madden was the first to speak, he just flashed Rafe a grin and said Perfect!" He went on to say, "With all your attention to statistics, when was the last time you saw a two-year-old filly win in 57 seconds for 5 furlongs?" Rafe laughed and said, "The only one that I can remember was a couple of years ago when a filly at Louisiana Downs won in 57 1/5 for five furlongs, and in the process won by 17 lengths and broke a sixteen-year-old track record."

Old Man Madden with a big smile on his face added, "Not much more to say is there. Archangel's ready. We'll return in a couple of weeks, just one week before the race, and repeat the exact same process, except this time we'll just blow her out four furlongs; Then we go for the money."

One hour later, after Archangel was cooled out and ready to travel, they headed back to Hope Farm. Early on the morning of Friday, July 17th, the same group returned to Saratoga for the final workout. They had already done it once and simply repeated the process.After Archangel flew past the finish, both Old Man Madden and Rafe glanced at their stopwatches, only to look up and shake their heads in awe. She's worked a ½ mile in 45 seconds flat. As they walked back to where the horse trailer was parked, Rafe asked Old Man Madden, "What do you think?"

"Frankly, I've never seen anything like her, She's in a class by herself. I would go so far as to say, that she'll develop into the greatest of all time!"

Rafe said in response, "I guess you could say that I've done my thing. You've done your thing, and now it's up to Goldilocks to bring her home."

"You got that right Whippersnapper, we're just about there. To tell the truth, this is the most exciting adventure in my life, and there's a good reason for that.

"What's the good reason?"

Old Man looked over at Rafe and said, "It's the place! Hope Farm. It's a very special place.

"Why do you say that Old Man?"

"It's special because when Archangel wins the Schuylerville everyone on the farm will win with her. A lot of dreams will come true on Wednesday. It won't be just a few people that will have their dreams come true, it will be everyone. Therein lies the beauty in it. It's not a select few winning, it's all of us. This is a life-changing event, one that stays with you, etched in your memory forever. So, I'm excited for myself, but for twenty-five others also."

On Sunday the twelve lepers tasked with placing the bets flew out of JFK to six different locations. They had specific instructions from Rafe which were simple but to the point. "Get to the location. Find the Bank to which the funds for betting have been transferred. Make a trial run by going to the bank, withdrawing a small amount, going to the casino and placing a bet, then returning to the bank and depositing the winnings. Even if you lose, go back to the bank as a trial run. Carry about $500 dollars to deposit just so you see everything is in order. By in order, I mean that you have no problem making a deposit. Remember, most of you will be in foreign countries where they may do things differently. A dry run will put you ahead of the game, and believe me when you're dealing with forty or fifty million dollars, that's where you want to be."

Only one item remained on Rafe's prerace checklist and that concerned Goldilocks. Because of what he really was, and not what he appeared to be, he was literally aware of everything, or more precisely he was aware of anything he wanted to be. Since he was aware that Goldi wanted to speak to him. he mentioned to her that he'd be grooming Tar Baby after dinner. Sure enough, he was sitting on a bale of straw outside Tar Baby's stall at about 7 P.M. when Goldi showed up.

He greeted her, and she immediately said, "Can I talk to you Mr. Rafe?" Rafe who thought it was sweet that Goldi had always called him Mr. Rafe, "Said, sure Goldi, pull up a bale of straw to sit on." Once she pulled over a bale of straw from the front of Tar Baby's stall. Rafe asked, "What's on your mind?"

He knew what was coming, but he let her tell him. She began, "It's the race!"

Rafe asked, "What about the race, Goldi?"

She replied, "I'm afraid!"

Rafe said, "No need to be afraid, It's, going to be a walk in the park."

Goldi shook her head and answered, "But what if I screw it up?"

Rafe simply shook his head and said, "You won't"

Goldi looked at him and said, "How can you be so sure?"

Rafe chuckled and said, "Because I can predict the future!"

Goldi stared at Rafe, her green eyes shining, and said, "Don't I know it! Minutes after meeting you, you told me that it was darkest just before dawn. Then, a couple of minutes later, dawn arrived. I want you to tell me how the race will be run! If you tell me, I'll believe what you say."

Rafe looked at her seriously, knowing that she thought of him as some sort of guardian angel, which in reality, he actually was, and said, "Goldi, as I said, the race is going to be a walk in the park. What I mean by that is, this race is all about the start."

Goldilocks stared at Rafe and asked, "How do you mean?"

"Do you remember last year when I purchased a starting gate for the farm so we could familiarize the yearlings and two-year-olds with it?" Goldi nodded yes, so Rafe continued, "How many times have you taken Archangel into the starting gate?"

Goldi answered, "Hundreds!"

Rafe then said, "You do realize that was all by design. It was done so Archangel would be so familiar with a starting gate that she wouldn't be dancing around in it, or rearing up in it. She would simply stand there as cool as could be until the starter pushes the start button and the gate springs open. Goldi, that moment when the gate springs open, is the race. If Archangel comes out of the gate with you on her back, it's game over."

Goldi looked at him intently, then said, "How could you possibly know that?"

Rafe smiled at her and said, "I'm glad you came to talk with me this evening because the reason you're worried about the outcome is you aren't privy to the whole picture. So, in order to set your mind at ease, I have to allow you to see the big picture. It isn't that we were trying to keep anything from you, we just didn't think of telling you. So, my dear, here it is. Do you remember the first-midnight workout at Saratoga?"

Goldilocks answered, "How could I ever forget that; I was scared to death."

Rafe responded to that with, "This is what you don't know. When you and Archangel flashed by us at the finish, both Old Man Madden and I both stopped our watches at the same time. You had worked five furlongs in 57 seconds flat. Do you have any idea how fast that work was?" Goldi just shook her head, no. Rafe continued Do you know what the Track Record for five furlongs is, at Saratoga?"

Goldi said, "I have no idea."

Rafe looked at her intently and then said, "It is 57 4/5; meaning Archangel broke the track record by 4/5 of a second in a workout. Now, here's the clincher! This track record was set in 1918; fifty-two years ago!"

Goldi was beginning to perk up when suddenly a big smile began to appear on her face. She said, "My God! Am I riding a super horse?"

Rafe came back with, "That's right Goldi, you are riding a super horse. Now we can carry this a little bit further. Do you know how fast a thoroughbred can consistently run 1/8 of a mile or ¼ of a mile? Generally, thoroughbreds can reel off 12-second eighths of a mile for as far as a mile. Almost all thoroughbreds breaking out of the gate can reel off eighths of a mile in twelve seconds. On a chart, it would look like this 1/8, in 12 seconds, 1/4, in 24 seconds, 3/8, in 36 seconds, 1/2, in 48 seconds, 5/8, in 1 minute, 6/8 in 1:12, 7/8, in 1:24, and 1 mile in 1:36. After running a mile the average thoroughbred begins to slow down. Only the best horses can run 1 1/8 miles in 1:48 and only one horse has won the Kentucky Derby run at 1 ¼ miles in 2:00. which is the equivalent of running 1 ¼ miles at a pace of 12-second eighths of a mile, and just for your information, up till this time, no horse has won the Belmont Stakes at 1 ½ miles in 2:24 which would be sustaining the 12 seconds eighths the entire distance. Now, my dear Goldilocks here's the clincher. The piece of information that will relieve your anxiety about the race."

Goldi said, "Oh yes, Mr. Rafe, tell me."

"Ok, this is what you need to know. When you rode Archangel in her 5/8th mile workout on June 29[th,] her time was 57 seconds for five furlongs. Add 12 seconds to her 5/8th time to get her to 6/8th of a mile, the distance of the Schuylerville Stakes, and you come up with a time of 1:09. Here's the question. What do you think the track record for six furlongs is at Saratoga?"

Goldi just shook her head before saying, "I have no idea!"

Goldilocks it's 1:09 3/5; Therefore, Archangel in her first workout over the Saratoga oval broke the 5/8th track record by 4/5th of a second and showed she can break the six-furlong track record, just as easily. That's why if you don't fall off, you'll win."

Goldilocks perked right up and exclaimed, "You mean I'm riding a superhorse?"

"You are, and as I told you previously, you're headed for legendary status."

"So, what you're saying is I don't have any problems."

"That's exactly right Goldilocks. You don't fall off the horse, you win!"

The Schuylerville

There aren't many times in your life when you're sitting on something truly fantastic, but on Wednesday, July 22nd the leper colony and their expanding family from Hope Farm were in exactly that place. They had arrived at Saratoga from Hope Farm the previous afternoon along with their Coal Black Secret Weapon. The farm itself was practically deserted with only the Ladue's and Van Alden's present to maintain security. Maddy Ladue was manning the phones to coordinate between Rafe and the lepers who were placing some huge bets at the mostly overseas casinos. By the time the track opened, Maddy reported that all of the bets were down, and surprisingly, they had been given odds of 90 to 1. Apparently, the casino's handicappers saw no merit in the unraced filly with the disgraced trainer and novice rider. Once Rafe had confirmation that the bets were down, he was free to enjoy the race.

Part of the Hope Farm contingent was seated in a box seat in the track clubhouse, while the rest were keeping a close watch on Archangel at the track receiving barn. About an hour before the race, Rafe took Jill, along with Aiden, and Erin down to the receiving barn to watch Archangel being saddled. When they arrived Old Man Madden was sitting on a bale of straw in front of Archangel's stall wearing a suit and tie, which normally you would never see him wearing. Rafe asked him, "Hey old man, looks like you're ready to get your picture taken in the winner's circle." He just smiled and nodded in the affirmative.

The old man was smiling so Rafe asked him, "How you feeling," Old Man?"

He just looked up at Rafe and said, "Well I can tell you this, I'm feeling no pain. In fact, I'll go a little further and say, I'm way up there somewhere. I think it's called Cloud Nine. This is the greatest. Something I dreamed of as a boy. Here I am, at the big race, with the horse nobody knows is fast as greased lightning, surrounded by friends, and to top it off she's 90 to 1. What could be better than that? Well, I'll tell you what could be better, Nothing! This is it."

Rafe left Aiden and Erin with the old man and walked over to Archangel's stall with Jill. Archangel was standing with her head stuck out of her stall, just taking in the scene. On either side of the stall door was a leper. Those assigned as guards were Henri Desormeaux, aka Gator, along with John Clemmons also known as McDuck. Rafe greeted the lepers and said, "How's it going, guys? Has she had any visitors?"

Gator laughed and said, "She doesn't have visitors Crazy Horse unless, of course, they're accompanied by the old man. He's not going to let anyone near that horse that might have it in their mind to stick her with a needle and inject her with some substance that will lead to her disqualification."

Rafe nodded and asked, "You guys armed?"

McDuck, chimed in with, "You know we are. We're licensed to carry in New York State which ensures no one is getting near Archangel."

Gator then said to Crazy Horse, "You know it's too bad the guys overseas won't get to see the race. I mean, after all, it could be the greatest event in our lives."

Jill looked at Gator and told him, "They'll get to see the race."

Gator asked, "How could that be?"

Jill gave Gator and Mc Duck one of her lovely smiles and said, "I was thinking the same thing myself. That it would be so unfair to the unlucky ones who had to place the bets, at the cost of missing out on Archangel's triumph. So, I hired a camera crew to make a film of the race, and not only the race but what happens before and after the race. It will be the next thing to being here."

Gator said, "You would do that?"

Still smiling, Jill added, "It's going on as we speak." She pointed to a man standing about twenty feet behind Old Man. See that fellow with the movie camera? He's one of our photographers! You're on camera right now. Wave to the camera."

Both Mc Duck and Gator smiled and waved at the cameraman." Rafe then told them. "You'll be glad to learn that your fellow lepers have placed all bets, and we now have $600,000 down at the average odds of 90 to 1. If you quickly do the math, it looks like we'll have 54 million dollars less than an hour from now."

The two lepers just smiled and shook their heads. Mc Duck said, "This is too much, can this really be happening."

After chatting for a few minutes Rafe and Jill excused themselves and headed to the box seats to pick up their mothers and Everett Massoletti. When they arrived, Everett asked, "How's the secret weapon doing."

Rafe answer was short and sweet. "She's ready to roll, Pop, it's time we get down to the walking ring and join the party." Archangel had quite the entourage in the paddock numbering fourteen in all. They were only there a few minutes when Triple B came in leading her. She was wearing a lightweight blanket and she had it on only to heighten the suspense. When she was in front of her supporters, Triple B stopped and Old Man Madden pulled the blanket from her back. It was only seconds later that the murmur from the crowd reached them. In truth, no one had ever seen such a magnificent thoroughbred. The connections of the seven horse, right next to them, were heard to exclaim, "Jesus, what the hell is this? Did you ever see a filly like that?"

His companion chimed in with, "That can't be a two-year-old filly, she looks like a four-year-old colt; No, I take that back. She looks like the second coming of Man O' War!" He was looking at his program when he realized Archangel was trained by none other than Speed Kills Madden. He turned to his friend and said, "I have a bad feeling about this. This could be a setup. Think of it, a filly that's never started, looking like a superhorse, with a jockey that's never won a race, and from a farm, we've never heard of."

His friend reminded the owner, "There are too many issues to overcome. Some of the greatest of all time didn't win first time out. That filly has just too much to overcome. That's why experience counts."

It didn't take long for many racing fans to begin to leave the area around the walking ring and head for the grandstand and the betting windows. Not all racing fans are good handicappers. But almost all of them know a super-looking horse when they see it. In the case of Archangel, they'd never seen her like before.

Goldilocks came out from the Jockey's room dressed in the Royal Blue with White Fleur de Lis, the racing colors of Hope Farm. In her own way, she was as beautiful as Archangel, and together they were a sight to behold. Goldi stood chatting with her Hope Farm family while the horses continued to walk around the oval walking ring. About 5 minutes later a voice called out, "Riders Up."

Triple B was holding Archangel when Rafe and Goldi walked up. She greeted him, and Rafe bent over put, his hands together, and Goldilocks put her boot in his hands and he lifted her onto the saddle. She sat in the saddle looking down at Rafe and asked him, "Any last minute, advice?"

Rafe looked up and smiled and then said, "God's Speed!"

Goldi urged Archangel forward and she followed the other horses around the walking ring. When all was ready the horses left the walking ring and walked onto the track for the parade to the post. Those seated in the box seats had returned to the clubhouse, while the lepers and Old Man Madden had found a spot near the winner's circle to watch the race. The level of anticipation was off the charts. It was about to happen, and all of the Hope Farm entourage were true believers.

Once back in their box seats, Rafe sprang a surprise on Aiden and Erin. He took a couple of exacta tickets out of his pocket and presented them to the youngsters. Aiden wanted to know, "What are these?"

Rafe laughed and said, "They're what are called exacta tickets."

Erin asked, "What's an exacta?"

Rafe told the teens, "An exacta is a bet where you have to pick the first two finishers to cross the finish line in the correct order. So, for you, I bet Archangel to finish first, and Lovely Honey to finish second. If they finish in that order, you're going to win a lot of money. However, If Lovely Honey wins and Archangel runs second, you lose. It's called the exacta because the finish has to be in the exact order."

Aiden asked, "Can we make a lot of money?"

Rafe gave them a big grin and said, "You better believe it. So put the tickets in a safe place."

Goldilocks was in her glory jogging her baby up the track. She had been a constant companion to Archangel since the moment of her birth, she had led her outdoors for the first time the following morning and was instrumental in breaking her and teaching her to run. It all came down to this! According to the clairvoyant, Rafe, she was on the edge of legendary status. As Archangel warmed up, Goldi was thinking about how God had placed her on that bale of straw on the fateful day when Mr. Rafe had shown up. He not only hired her but brought her brother and sister over from Ireland. It was payback time, and since her talk with him the other night, she knew no fear.

Goldi allowed Archangel to circle behind the starting gate as the inside horses were loaded first. Just before they loaded, the Jockey of the Sorority Stakes winner Grab It, the betting favorite, yelled over at Goldi, "Hey girlie, you think a novice like you can beat stakes winners with an unraced nag like that? I'm going to leave you so far up the track you'll never ride again, what do you think of that?"

"Goldilocks looked over at the little creep and simply said, "Famous Last Words!" Grab It was led into the starting gate, and one of the gate crew began to lead Archangel in. Goldi had everything set. The last thing she did as the gate crew closed the doors behind her was to grab a handful of Archangel's Mane. She didn't want to be left suspended in midair when the Angel broke. Like Rafe had predicted she was only in the gate about four or five seconds when the gate sprung open.

In his booth high above the grandstand, the track announcer spoke into his microphone, "They're all in;" quickly followed by, "And they're off!"

When the gate opened Archangel took off like she was jet-assisted. She broke perfectly and after 100 yards Goldi took her in hand and began to move towards the rail.

The track announcer after saying, "They're off," said, "It looks like a false start by Archangel, on the outside. He quickly corrected that with, "No, it's not a false start, she's just that fast. Archangel has broken with lightning-like speed, and she's opening a three-length lead after 200 yards. What speed."

Archangel reached the rail where Goldi hand rode her, allowing her to gallop along at her very high cruising speed. She had caught the opposition flat-footed putting them in the unenviable position of trying to make up ground on a very fast opponent.

The announcer continued his call saying, "Archangel leads as they approach the far turn. The first ¼ has been run in 21 4/5. Wow! Have you ever seen a two-year-old run that fast?"

Going into the far turn Goldi took a peak back, under her arm, and saw the other horses were going into a drive, with their jockeys going to the whip. They knew they couldn't let Archangel open up on her commanding six-length lead. On her part, Goldi was sitting quiet as a statue. Archangel was running easily while continuing to expand her lead. As they turned into the stretch, they had a ten-length lead and Archangel was still in hand. At this point Goldi got her to change leads, and she accelerated again.

The track announcer was on the verge of losing it! His call continued with, "Archangel is into the homestretch with a ten-length lead, and she still hasn't been asked to run; she just ran the half in 44 4/5 seconds flat, and she's not slowing down."

Goldi was having the time of her life while thinking, "The last time we did this it was pitch dark, now like Rafe said, "It's a walk in the park." She just hand-rode her home, enjoying the screaming crowd, and her first victory.

The roar from the stands was deafening for never had the fans seen a horse move with more grace and beauty, not to mention incredible speed. The victory was a universal celebration and for good reason, although Archangel ran the 3rd quarter in a pedestrian 24 ¼ she still won by 21 lengths and broke the twenty-four-year-old track record, by 3/5 of a second. The celebratory scene at the winner's circle was a sight to behold. Rafe, Jill, Aiden, Erin, and Rafe's Mom, Jill's Mom, as well as Everett Massoletti, practically had to fight their way through the crowd to get into the winner's circle. They got in just in time to see the outrider guide Archangel into the winner's circle. Old Man Madden put a lead shank on Archangel's halter and led her over to have her picture taken. He handed the lead shank to Jill who would be holding her in the picture. Standing alongside Jill was Old Man Madden, then Rafe, and the rest of the Hope Farm entourage. While the track photographer took the winning photo, not too far away, was one of the contracted moviemakers shooting the film.

After the photo, there was a lot of hugging and kissing going on in the winner's circle. When Archangel was led away, Goldilocks headed for the Jockey's room to change into civilian clothes when she was stopped by Rafe. He asked her, "How long will it take to get changed?"

Goldi, not yet over the thrill of victory beamed at Rafe then said, "Fifteen minutes if I hurry. Why!"

Rafe whispered the answer to her, and she indicated she be changed in fifteen minutes if not sooner. While the rest of the Hope Farm people followed Archangel to the receiving barn with a stop for her blood to be drawn for post-race drug testing, Jill, Rafe, Aiden, and Erin, waited for Goldilocks to return. It was at this point that Aiden looked over at the infield Tote Board and saw that the 3 horse, Lovely Honey had finished 2nd.

Aiden already excited by the victory began jumping up and down and yelling to Erin; We won, we won!

Erin completely baffled by Aiden's behavior asked, "What are you so excited about, I know she won."

Aiden, hardly able to control his excitement said, "I don't mean Archangel, I mean the exacta; The three-horse finished 2nd, so we won the exacta."

Erin excitedly asked Rafe, "How much did we win Mr. Rafe?"

Rafe smiled at the excited pair and said, "The exacta paid $376. Are you satisfied?"

Aiden couldn't believe their good luck and said, "$376, we're rich.

Rafe, Jill, and Goldi, just smiled because in 1970 $376 was a lot of money for a teenager. Rafe was enjoying this because he hadn't bought them $2 exacta tickets, but $200 exactas. Rafe just played the situation for all it was worth and decided not to tell them, but let them see the actual amount when they collected the cash.

They made their way to the betting windows to collect their winnings with the teens in a state of euphoria, but Rafe, Goldi, and Jill were thinking, if they're excited now, wait till they find out the actual amount.

When they arrived at the windows which weren't as crowded due to the approaching ninth race, Rafe handed the two winning tickets to the teller. He looked at them and said, "Wow! Just a minute."

He walked to the rear and came back in a couple of minutes with a manager who asked Rafe's party to follow him to a room behind the betting windows. Rafe was carrying a TWA flight bag, the kind they gave you as a gift when you fly first class. Aiden noticed the flight bag and asked Rafe, "Hey Mr. Rafe, what's the flight bag for?"

Rafe grinned and replied, "To put all the money in!"

Aiden not realizing what was taking place asked, "Can't I just put it in my pocket?" Rafe didn't reply, He just smiled.

Once they were seated at a table the manager and a couple of tellers wheeled in what looked like a four-wheeled serving cart stacked high with packets of one-hundred-dollar bills. Aiden and Erin just stared at the man wondering what was going on until finally, Aiden asked, "That isn't all for us, is it?"

The manager replied to Aiden's query with, "Maybe not all of it, but you two youngsters just won $37,600 each which comes out to 752 one-hundred-dollar bills, so, we'll be lucky if we can stuff them all into this flight bag."

That's the way the celebration started. The five of them walked back to the receiving barn where the rest of the Hope Farm party was gathered, and the celebration was already underway. Rafe, being the sort that planned everything in advance, had ordered ten cases of Champagne and 100 champagne flutes, which arrived just as the shadows were lengthening and the denizens, of the backstretch, were ready to party, even though the grooms, exercise riders and hot walkers usually weren't invited to the big celebratory bashes, this time was different," The party rolled on until the early morning hours, and there wasn't a person, who was lucky enough to attend, that didn't have a wonderful time.

By the next evening, July 23rd everyone was back at home, feeling better than they ever had in life. Archangel was in her stall across from her home paddock being groomed by Goldilocks. Another big party was planned when the lepers who were overseas returned, Rafe had told the photographers that each would be paid $25,000 if they could splice together the separate segments of the race into one complete motion picture. He explained it was for the rest of the Hope Farm residents who had missed the race. Back in 1970 $25,000 could purchase a very nice home. Since they were being so well compensated for one day's work, they guaranteed the film would be ready by Saturday morning. The photographers didn't know that Hope Farm had just won 54 million dollars, so the amount paid to the makers of the film was a drop in the bucket compared to the net winnings.

Evening found Rafe and his darling Jill lying in their bed, side by side, facing each other. Bogart was lying in his doggie bed over by the fireplace looking at them with begging eyes, saying he wanted to be called over. Rafe had something else in mind first. Jill's eyes were shining and he had never seen her look more beautiful. He said, "I have a question to ask you."

She, nodded, "Yes!"

Do you think I added to my status with Archangel's win yesterday?"

She looked at him and said, "My God yes! In one fell swoop you put Hope Farm on the map, insured the financial future of everyone on the farm, and at the same time you unveiled a future champion. I would say you definitely added to your stature. Why do you ask?"

"Because I wouldn't ask you this if I didn't have enough status. He kissed her lightly then whispered, "I love you as much as it's possible to love another person." My life changed the moment you walked into it, that day at Rhodes School. He then said, "Reach under your pillow, there's something there."

Jill reached under the pillow, and felt around, till suddenly the pupils of her blue eyes got incredibly large. Her hand came out holding a little jewelry box. Before she could open it, Rafe said, "Will you marry me?"

Jill put her hand over her mouth before exclaiming, "Oh yes! Yes, I'll marry you." They kissed and were rewarded with that same beautiful feeling that always accompanied their kisses. When they finally broke the kiss, she opened the box and saw the most perfect, beautiful, dazzling diamond, she had ever seen. She put it on and admired it on her finger. She looked at him, and he said, "The diamond has a perfect beauty, but it still can't compare to your blue eyes."

A minute later Jill looked over to Bogart who was waiting with bated breath, and called, "Boogie!" Bogart who didn't want to be left out on whatever was taking place, charged across the room and leaped up on the end of the bed. He then crawled up between Rafe and Jill and proceeded to lick their faces while they hugged and petted him.

"Before I begin to show you how much I adore you, we have one more thing we need to discuss," Rafe said.

Jill who was still admiring her diamond asked, "Ok, I'm ready for anything,"

"My darling girl, you only think you're ready for anything. Do you remember that when we first got back together, I told you that there was much more to our relationship than meets the eye, but it wasn't the right time to reveal the mystery to you?"

Jill nodded, and said, "Yes."

"Well, the time is finally here, or I should say, it's almost here! I'm going to take you to a very beautiful place on our honeymoon, and it's there that I'll tell you what's really happening."

"Why can't you just tell me now?"

"You know how I plan everything out. Well, I've got this all planned out because when I tell you the truth, you're going to find it impossible to believe; I'll have to convince you."

"What if you can't convince me?"

"That's part of the mystery, but believe me, I'll convince you."

"Where are we going on our honeymoon?"

Rafe smiled and said, "How about the South Pacific, and more specifically, Tahiti, Moorea, and Bora Bora!"

"Oh, my goodness, I've always wanted to go there. When are we going to get married?"

How about in about six weeks? If all goes according to plan, Archangel will run in the Spinaway Stakes, just before Labor Day, and after that, we can fly away for a few weeks, and be back before her next start. If it's all right with you, I'd like to have the ceremony here on Hope Farm, in the chapel."

"I would love that, but now I have to go down to New York tomorrow to tell Mother." Jill took a long look at her beloved, and said, "Rafe, how come with you, things seem to keep getting better and better? Yesterday Archangel wins 54 million dollars and today we get engaged. How do you make these things happen?"

"That's what I have to talk to you about. When we get to Tahiti, I'll let you in on the whole story. Even if at first you don't believe it, you'll find it fascinating." And while we're at it, I'll drive you down to New York tomorrow to see your mom. We'll take our passports with us and visit the French Embassy to see about getting visas for French Polynesia."

The following morning at breakfast the secret got out when Goldilocks who was sitting next to Jill noticed the diamond ring. If you want to talk about a joyous revelation, this was it. Jill and Rafe were truly loved by the residents of the Farm and everyone had been anticipating their union for a very long time.

Jill revealed that the wedding was planned for the Saturday after Labor Day since Archangel was scheduled to run in the Spinaway Stakes at Saratoga on Labor Day weekend. Although the Spinaway was a major step in winning the champion two-year-old filly title, it wouldn't have the same significance as the Schuylerville, since Archangel's first start made them all rich. Although none of the Hope Farm group was aware of it, Old Man Madden had his sights, not on the Champion Two-Year-Old filly title, but Horse-of-the-year! The only one who could understand his ambitious goal was Rafe who was an expert in thoroughbred performance. If she ran as fast in the Spinaway Stakes as she had in the Schuylerville, then her path to a championship would be through the Futurity, Champagne, and Garden State Stakes. All of these races would be against colts, and winning them all, would in all likelihood, bring her the Horse-of-the-year title.

In many ways, the Spinaway was a rerun of the Schuylerville, except this time Archangel broke from the number 2 post position. With her lightning-like speed, she jetted away from the field and won by 15 lengths in New Track Record time, covering the 7 furlongs in 1:20 4/5. The racing world was now paying close attention to the rising superstar. Two starts, two track records, while winning with commensurate ease. The question in the racing world was, "Where will she appear next." That was the question, and the only one who knew the answer was one Archer Madden."

The week after the running of the Spinaway Stakes, Jill and Rafe walked down the aisle of the Chapel of the Child and were bound together in Holy Matrimony. It was hard to tell which one of the young couple was happier, and not only were the two of them in seventh heaven but so were all of their friends and family from Hope Farm. At Hope Farm, love was the universal store of value, and it was probably the nicest place ever to find oneself.

Early the morning after the wedding a limo took the happy couple to JFK airport for an American Airlines Flight to Los Angeles. From there they transferred to a Pan American Airlines flight to Papeete, Tahiti. And then connecting to an Air Tahiti flight to Bora Bora. You could say that once they reached Bora Bora the adventure began. Why was it such an adventure? You should have been with them; First, the flight to Bora Bora was primarily not a passenger flight but instead was full of cargo. Altogether there were only seven passengers on the plane, of which five were residents of Bora Bora. The real trick was getting off the plane.

Usually, when deplaning, a set of mobile stairs would be positioned at the door, and the passengers would simply walk down the stairs. This was not the case on Bora Bora where they positioned at the exit door, the type of ladder that mechanics use when repairing planes. This egress consisted of a little platform at the top, with a ladder going straight down to the ground. One might wonder how handicapped persons would deplane. Another surprise greeted Rafe and Jill when they were off the aircraft. They were standing on the runway, but there was no terminal, just a little thatched hut to protect passengers in case of a rain squall. Since they had sent a cable to the Hotel Bora Bora indicating their flight and arrival time, they were expecting someone to meet them. It was fortunate that Rafe could communicate in French due to his service at Supreme Headquarters in Paris. The Polynesian men who were unloading the cargo told him that there was some sort of screw-up and that there was a boat waiting to take them to the Hotel Bora Bora. He also told Rafe that the person handling the boat should have told them to pick up the hotel's guests and take them to the boat which was not far away.

Once the aircraft was unloaded, it started up, taxied to the end of the runway, and took off. Once the aircraft was off, the Polynesian men servicing the aircraft, put the newly-weds baggage on the trucks, and drove them through the palm groves to a stone jetty on which was docked a boat with a sign on the back that said, "Hotel Bora Bora." Rafe thanked the natives for the ride and tipped all three of them $100 each in French francs to which they were wildly enthusiastic. They had no way of knowing that the young couple had just won $54 million dollars a few weeks before.

Once the boat was underway Rafe and Jill could hardly believe the sheer beauty of the water. It had a light luminescent green color and neither of the pair had ever seen anything like it. As the boat made its way into the channel and away from the islet on which the airstrip was built, they realized that they were not the main island of Bora Bora. The airstrip was on the barrier reef that surrounded the main island. They were not able to see the magnificent Mt. Pahia due to an incoming storm which reduced the ceiling to about 200 feet. Nevertheless, the water was so beautiful that it had their undivided attention. It took about thirty minutes before they pulled up to a wooden jetty on which was standing a lovely Polynesian girl dressed in the native style. Once on the dock, they discovered the girl was actually an American from Hawaii, working in French Polynesia. After they were checked in the girl took them to their thatched overwater bungalow which to their delight had a living room floor that was part glass, giving them a window from which to watch the fish on the reef underneath. Attached underneath their bungalow were floodlights to allow them to watch the reef fish at night.

It wasn't an accident that Rafe had decided to take Jill to the Hotel Bora Bora. While in Army Rafe had read James A. Michener's book Return to Paradise, in his book Michener had related that right off the point of land on which the Hotel and been built were the most beautiful coral gardens in the world, lying in crystal, clear water. In the morning Rafe and Jill were going to make a beeline to the lagoon to explore this exciting phenomenon.

After breakfast Rafe and Jill carrying their masks, snorkels, and flippers headed for the lagoon. It didn't take them long to discover that running parallel to the point of land on which the hotel was built was a fairly strong current that flowed over the coral gardens which were only three feet underwater. The current then continued around the point before taking them right into the wooden stairs leading to their bungalow's back porch. Once having made this discovery the honeymooners simply walked across the point of land, swam out about forty yards into the lagoon, and let the current take them on a very lovely tour. When not in the azure waters of the lagoon the happy couple was riding bicycles around the island taking pictures of its infinite beauty. Mt. Pahia, which had been obscured by the low overcast when they arrived, was truly fantastic. In fact, Bora Bora was so beautiful that it was hard to take a bad picture, and they took dozens to show the Hope Farm family when they returned. After five days in this paradise, they left for another incredible island, Moorea.

To get to Moorea they took Air Tahiti back to Tahiti and then a twin otter, aircraft to the very short landing strip on Moorea. Rafe had called the Hotel and they arranged for a jeep to pick them up when they landed. It was only a couple of miles from the landing strip to the hotel, but they were in for a surprise when they arrived. They were to discover that where the Hotel Bora Bora was luxurious, the Hotel Bali Hai was fun.

The Bali Hai had an interesting story. It was developed by three young Americans, that had been involved in a yacht race from San Diego to Papeete some years before. When they arrived in Tahiti they fell in love with the place and its people and decided to immigrate. However, the French are very restrictive where newcomers are concerned. Since French Polynesia was so beautiful and its climate so mild, they didn't want the place invaded by a bunch of beach bums. In order to prevent this, newcomers had to start a business and keep a certain amount deposited in a French bank in order to get a six-month visa. When the visa expired, they had to return to their country of origin and renew their visa. If they were good citizens for five years or married a citizen. they could acquire a permanent visa.

The three friends serious about making a new life in the tropical paradise purchased a vanilla bean plantation on the island of Moorea twenty miles across the channel from Papeete. Unfortunately, they quickly realized they'd starve to death as vanilla bean framers and decided to turn their farm, which had a quarter of a mile of beachfront property into a resort. That's how the Hotel Bali Hai came into existence. Of the three friends the one nicknamed

Muck was the one who would manage the day-to-day operations of the hotel. When you got to know him, you'd find out that Muck was a very playful guy, as Rafe and Jill were about to find out.

When the jeep pulled up to the entrance to the hotel, Muck was out front with his entire staff of young Polynesian girls. He had them lined up by order of height with the tallest standing next to him and each succeeding girl from right to left in order of height. As Jill and Rafe alighted from the jeep, Muck introduced himself and then took Rafe down the line of young ladies introducing each in turn, with Jill following right behind Rafe. Rafe and Jill thought this welcome was very sweet, and it was, yet they were unaware that it was a setup. Rafe discovered this when he shook hands with the shortest girl at the end of the line. When Rafe shook hands with her, Splat! The girl had a handful of canned butter in her hand, and when their hands met, Splat. The girls broke out in uproarious laughter, and Rafe and Jill couldn't help but join in. When things started to quiet down, Rafe looked at Muck and he realized he had seen him somewhere before. He said to Muck, "I know you!" And then it hit him, this guy is the Camel guy. In 1969 Camel Cigarettes had a television ad, showing a man walking down a jungle trail until he comes to a small trading post; He goes in and buys a pack of Camel's and sits on the porch, and after lighting a cigarette, puts his feet up on the table and takes a drag on the cigarette. From where the camera is positioned you can see a hole in the sole of his shoe. He then looks into the camera and says, "I'd walk a mile for a Camel."

When Rafe, related this to Muck, he just nodded and said, "Yup, that's me." While they were discussing how Muck had gotten into a television advertisement Muck took a closer look at Jill and said, "I've seen you before too, I just can't remember where." After a minute it hit him and he blurted out. "Now I remember, You're Ensign Dorn from In Harm's Way with John Wayne and Kirk Douglas. You're a movie star."

It was Jill's turn to nod her head and say, "Yes, that's me!" When Muck related this to the girls, in French, they went a little crazy. They mobbed Jill hugging and kissing her, expressing their complete adoration. Of course, for Jill, it was an overwhelming experience, talk about being treated like a celebrity. The Tahitian girls were acting like a blonde, blue-eyed, goddess had just dropped into their midst from heaven itself.

Muck and his girls led Jill and Rafe to the front desk where they registered for a ten-day stay, and then led them through the hotel grounds, down a wooden walkway to their overwater bungalow. After the crowd of well-wishers left them alone, the newlyweds checked out their accommodations. Actually, it was a very neat setup. When the fast boat from Papeete passed through Moorea's barrier reef, it proceeded straight towards the island until it was close inshore; at that point, there was a deep channel that ran towards Cook's Bay which was about two miles to the west. The channel ran parallel to the island staying about 100 feet offshore. What the three American partners in the Hotel Bali Hai had done was build wooden walkways out about 100 feet from shore where the shallow water dropped into the channel. Along the edge of the channel, the water was 80 feet deep. It was along the edge of the channel that the Hotel's over-water bungalows were built. It was a perfect setup where the guests could dive right off their back deck into the deep water of the channel and then walk up a set of wooden stairs to return.

Rafe and Jill changed into their bathing suits and dove off their deck into the channel. It soon became clear that the coral wall that dropped off into the channel was a wonderland of tropical fish, Morey Eels, and even an occasional Octopus. Jill who had never experienced snorkeling in tropical waters was completely mesmerized.

They swam until they were exhausted then climbed onto their deck and lay down on a lawn chair, stretched out side by side. It wasn't long before Rafe realized that the sun was too strong for Jill's very fair skin so he went into their bungalow and brought out some suntan lotion to protect Jill from the tropical sun. He was smiling as he rubbed the oil all over her body, realizing he was actually, feeling her up. It was very erotic!He knew Jill was enjoying his ministrations by the smile on her face. She finally said, "I think you need to tell me how much you love me."

Rafe laughed and replied, "I thought I just did."

Jill rolled over onto her back, looked into his eyes, and playfully said, "You know what they say?"

He knew what she was about to say as they had had this conversation many times before, so he said, "Ok, I'll bite, what do they say?"

"Practice makes perfect!"

Rafe chuckled and said, "Ok Little Dancer, follow me." She offered her hand, and he led her inside to their bed. After almost an hour of expressing their undying love for each other, they fell asleep completely exhausted.

After a nap of about two hours, they awoke, showered, and dressed for dinner. Jill was dressed in a black tropical dress with Birds of Paradise, in yellow, red, and orange colors. Rafe had to admit she was looking like a movie star, in fact, he would have described her as a vision of loveliness. What was so unusual to Rafe was that so far, it was the Moorean women that found Jill so attractive, of course, that might have been because hardly any of the Polynesian men had yet to see her.

After dinner when they left the thatched dining room things changed fast. As they walked across a veranda, which was about 100 feet across, to another little thatched building that served as a bar, Rafe realized the word had gotten out. Muck walked over and bought them Mai Tai's, and began to explain that his girls had gotten the word out that a beautiful blonde movie star had just checked in and everyone should come over and entertain her with a night of dancing and partying. One has to realize that once the sun goes down there isn't that much to do out in the jungle. However, dancing wasn't one of them. If Tahitians like anything it's dancing, and their dance, the 'Oro Tahiti is something that will get anyone's blood up, that is, if they have a pulse. It makes the Hawaiian Hula look tame. It's the dance where the girls shake their hips in the most erotic ways. While the men leap and shout. It's been said that the dance was created to challenge an enemy, charm a lover, or to even worship God.

Within an hour after dinner, there were at least 100 Mooreans forming on the veranda setting up drums, and even a hollowed log that made a clickily clack noise to accompany the drums. Then the dancing started; First, the women danced, then the men, and then finally the men were joined by the women. After half an hour Rafe knew what all of this was leading up to; The Polynesian men wanted to dance with the Tamahine Nehenehe, or in English, The beautiful woman. What no one was aware of, except Rafe, was that Jill had been trained from an early age to be a ballerina like her mother. She was the epitome of grace and beauty and as she learned the dance, she began to dance more and more like a Tahitian to the amazement of the mostly Polynesian crowd. When the women dragged Rafe out on the veranda to dance, he called upon his angelic powers in order not to make a complete fool of himself, however as the night wore on, he realized the girls didn't care too much about how well he danced, as long as he danced. In the middle of all this dancing and partying Muck sat down next to Rafe to watch Jill dance, and asked, "Damn, Rafe, how did you ever hook up with a goddess like her?" Rafe chuckled and said, "I was her tutor in high school. She had come to New York after making the film Exodus and had missed a year and a half of school. The principal asked me if I would tutor her and I said, yes!"

Muck looked at him and said, "Rafe, you're a damn lucky man!"

Rafe laughed and said, "Tell me about it. When I was first introduced to her, and looked into those blue eyes, my first thought was, God Loves me."

Muck laughed too, and said, "He Must!"

The dance lasted till the wee hours of the morning before Rafe and Jill somehow navigated to their thatched hut and collapsed into bed. It didn't take any more than that; From that day forward, Jill was famous on the island of Moorea.

The honeymooners slept in the following morning until about 11:00 A.M. when they received a knock on the door. When Rafe opened the door, he was greeted by the young girl who had been the trickster with the handful of butter the previous afternoon. Rafe said, Bonjour! The girl had downcast eyes because of yesterday's trick. Rafe then asked, "Do you speak English?" She nodded, yes! Rafe then said, "Don't worry about yesterday, it was all in fun. What's your name?"

The pretty young lady looked up at Rafe, Smiled, then said, "Marahi!"

Rafe stood aside and said, "Come in Marahi."

She did, crossed the living room, and placed the tray with a carafe of coffee on a table. She looked at Rafe, smiled, and said, "Your wife is good dancer, make everyone happy."

Rafe's answer was, "She should be a good dancer. She attended Sadler's Wells the school for the performing arts in London to become a ballet dancer, and her mother is a ballerina."

Marahi looked at Rafe and said, "She very good, not too many people can dance the 'Oro Tahiti so quickly, it takes years, but she learns in thirty minutes."

Rafe laughed and said, "Marahi, where we live, everyone has a nickname, do you want to know what we call Jill?"

Marahi, nodded yes, then said, "Oh yes."

Rafe smiled at her and said, "We call her Little Dancer!"

She answered with, "Little dancer, that's her nickname? Is she a professional dancer?"

Rafe said, "No, she's a movie star and a star in Broadway musicals!"

Marahi stared at Rafe for a few seconds and then said, "Oh my God, you're not serious?"

Rafe said, "I'm very serious, although she's now semi-retired. She's just hanging out on the farm with me."

Just then Jill came out from the bedroom wearing a silk robe. Jill looked at Marahi and said, "Hi, aren't you butterfingers?"

Marahi started to giggle and Rafe said, "Little Dancer, this is our new friend Marahi, who was nice enough to bring us some coffee. He went on to say, Marahi, this is my wife, Jill."

After the two young women had greeted each other, Rafe said, "Jill I was thinking; Marahi needs a nickname and I think I have one!"

Jill asked, "What's that?"

"How about Bloody Mary?"

Jill wrinkled up her nose and shook her head.

Rafe smiled at them and said, "Don't you remember this, "Bloody Mary is the girl I love, Bloody Mary is the girl I love, Bloody Mary is the girl I love. Now, ain't that too damn bad!" From South Pacific!"

Marahi smiled and said, "I like it, but you can call me Mary, no one else will know it means, Bloody Mary."

Rafe added, "Ok I now dub you Mary!"

-Mary then said, "I have to get back."

Before she left Rafe asked, "Can you do us a favor?"

Mary said, "Of course,"

Rafe said, "Could you stop by the kitchen and ask if they could fix us a box lunch? We're going to ride around the Island on bicycles and won't be back for lunch."

"Ok, I'm sure they'll do it, and I'll bring it back in a little while."

Rafe then asked, "Do you know where Jill could buy some Polynesian attire because if you're going to have another dance party she'll want to be dressed appropriately."

Mary smiled and responded, "Yes, there is a very nice place called Ma Robe a Moi, about 3 kilometers to the left of the Hotel entrance. It's easy to find."

With that, their new friend Mary headed back to her duties, and Rafe and Jill dressed for another adventure. About an hour later Mary returned with a small basket with lunch, that contained a bottle of wine with a couple of wine glasses. She also had something else that delighted both Jill and Rafe. Her surprise was flowered headdresses, that definitely made them look like natives of Moorea. Just before they climbed aboard their bicycle, they had one of the staff take a photo of them standing with Mary in between them. It was really very sweet as Mary looked like she had just won the greatest prize on earth.

Unless you've been to Moorea, you'd never realize how a bicycle ride could be a great adventure. The truth is Moorea is a tropical paradise. After riding down the perimeter road that encircled the island, they reached the road next to Cook's Bay. At the end of the bay was a towering exotic peak called Mount Mouaroa. What few knew, when discovering this peak, is that it was the one used in the motion picture South Pacific, as Bali Hai, hence the name of the Bali Hai Hotel. Of course, Jill and Rafe used up a whole roll of film taking pictures of themselves and the beautiful scenery.

After about an hour they had transited both Cook's Bay and Opunohu Bay, and came upon the entrance to the Club Med Moorea. This was the spot Rafe was looking for. The happy pair rode through the Club, parked their bikes near the beach, and walked through the shallow water to a small island just offshore. When they were finally on the side of the island facing seaward, towards the barrier reef, Rafe said, "This is the spot."

Jill was wondering to herself, "The Spot for what? Although she didn't say anything to Rafe, she knew him well enough to know that this was no coincidence. Then it started!

The Revelation

Rafe had no doubt in his mind that Jill loved him as much as a human could love another. They were virtually Soulmates created by God the Father, for their pleasure, as well as his own. What was about to happen was not Rafe's plan, but God's plan.

He looked into Jill's eyes and said, "My darling, we're about as intimate as two humans could possibly be, however. there is something about me that you're not aware of."

Jill looked at Rafe, and she became somewhat alarmed; She asked Rafe, "What do you mean, you're scaring me!"

Rafe took her hand in his and said, "Don't be alarmed, this is not going to turn out badly, it's just what I'm going to tell you will seem to be unbelievable. However, when I'm finished, you'll believe."

Jill looked at Rafe with some trepidation in her eyes then said, "Ok, you know I'd trust you with my life, Go ahead!"

"My darling Jill, I'll just tell you the truth. I won't beat around the bush. You and I are not completely human! We are only half-human and that is the way God created us. He has his reasons for doing so, and I'll soon explain all of that.

Jill looked at Rafe and he had the feeling she was about to cry. He knew what was going through her mind as he had been in the same position himself when Rosa had told him the same thing. To a human what he was saying wasn't possible. Then, if it was impossible, was Rafe losing his mind? It had to be one or the other. Jill stared at him for a long time before asking, "If we're only half-human, what's the other half."

Rafe said, "We're Angels!"

Jill put her hand up to her mouth and said, "Oh my!"

Rafe continued, "Let me carry on my darling. When God created me, he created you simultaneously, and he created us to love one another; In each other's eyes, we're perfect. Humans would refer to us as soulmates but, we're much more than that. At this point in time, I'm the most powerful force on earth. I can, if ordered, destroy the earth and everything on it, but only if ordered. When Max was murdered, I went to the Chapel on Hope Farm, which was then Greer School. I was crushed, so I prayed to God. He answered, and a very clear voice came through the stained-glass window. He said, "Fear not, I am with you." Followed by, "You are my drawn Sword." I wasn't sure whether or not I was hallucinating, but I accepted it. In fact, I never felt the emotion of fear again. Usually, God doesn't speak to me directly, it comes to me as a feeling, but I should say it's a very definite feeling. One of these definite feelings that suddenly popped into my mind, was the prophecy. I didn't think that up, it somehow arrived in my consciousness fully formed, and I passed it on to you. I had my doubts about it. I thought I was going to lose you forever. At that point, I was unaware of our angelic status.

Jill had gotten serious, and when Rafe talked about definiteness she said, "It's true about you, you are the most definite person I've ever met. Not only that, but everything you say comes true."

"That's exactly right. And the reason it comes true is, that I make it happen. I know I can make things happen because I do it all the time. I could do it even before I knew I had angelic powers. Even you Jill, had these powers, before today."

By now Rafe had Jill's rapt attention. She asked, "Can you give me an example of when I used these powers, I didn't know I possessed?

Rafe smiled and said, "Sure that's easy! Remember when you decided you needed to win the role as a leading lady in a major Broadway Musical in order to set the prophecy in motion?"

Jill looked at him and said, "Yes, how could I ever forget that!"

"You didn't have much of a chance either, considering you had never sung on stage, and you were up against two hundred of the top actresses in the world. Yet, you won the part as Sally Bowles. That's an example of your angelic powers being exercised. However, as a human, you could never imagine that you had the power to make it happen."

Jill sat thinking about it for a while, and then asked, "If we're Angels why did God put us through the awful experience of betrayal, when in fact, we do live to serve him, and he loves us?"

Rafe said, "That's a good question, and this is my interpretation. God is the creator. Man owes everything to God including his very existence. Yet, despite this blessing, many men betray their creator in the worst possible way. That betrayal comes in the form of man's denial of the very existence of God. What we experienced was bad, but no one denied our existence, and consider this, we weren't the creator of those that betrayed us, they for their own reasons rejected us.

Jill said, "I've never thought about it that way before."

Rafe continued, "Carrying this a little further, God wanted to humanize us, to disguise our angelic qualities, and he has a good reason for doing that. We are not here to live a life like most humans. We are here to carry out a vital mission, and we are being directed by the Lord God, himself! As soon as I convince you of your angelic status, I'll tell you what we're here for."

Jill was smiling now, and asked, "How are you going to convince me?"

"It won't take more than an hour, but before we start let me ask you a question."

Jill said, "OK, ask away."

He said, "Do you think angels can fly?"

Jill asked, "What are you driving at? I guess they can fly because they're always depicted by artists as having wings."

Rafe asked, "If I can get you to fly, would you believe you're an angel?"

She answered, "Of course. I'll have no choice!"

Rafe just grinned and said, "Follow me." He led her over to where they had deposited their lunch basket and camera on the beach. At this point Rafe said, Take off your bikini!"

Jill was startled but began to take off her bikini. Rafe followed suit and soon they were completely naked. Rafe led Jill back to where the water was about three feet deep. Facing her he took both of her hands in his, and said, "To start, we're going to fly about fifty feet straight up, at which point we'll stop and hover, just like we're helicopters."

Jill couldn't believe what was happening, but she just nodded. Once Jill accepted, they began their ascent. They left the water and rose straight up as if in an elevator. When they reached the height of fifty feet they stopped in midair. Jill was blown away by the experience; She was flying. They just hovered at fifty feet, facing each other. Rafe laughed and asked, "Are you getting the feel for flying?"

Jill didn't know what to do. This was utterly fantastic. She said, "I don't know, this is too much for me."

"Rafe then told her, "I think you need a little more practice, so with that in mind let's fly out towards the barrier reef, and once there, we'll turn towards the Hotel Bali Hai and land on our Bungalow's rear deck. Rafe started towards the barrier reef, leveled off, and ascended to 100 feet with Jill in close pursuit. The amazing part of the flying lesson was Jill knew in advance when Rafe was about to speed up, slow down, or turn. There wasn't any chance of their colliding in midair because she could anticipate his every move. Jill was beginning to become a believer as it was nothing short of a miracle. Not only was it the miracle of flying, but she was overcome by the sheer beauty of it. The water in the lagoon was crystal clear, and she was able to see everything from the coral formations to the larger fish swimming about. When they were directly off the Hotel Bali Hai, they turned inland and slowed down their approach to make a perfect landing, feet first, on their deck.

Once down, Jill with a big grin on her face, Said, "This is fantastic, but we're naked! Someone is sure to see us!"

Rafe laughed and countered with, "No they won't, you're not yet aware of how we angels can operate. Before we took off for the Club Med. I made us invisible. We could walk right through the hotel, and not a person will see us. Now I want you to follow me, as I want to conclude your flight training."

Jill who by now was extremely excited walked over, gave Rafe a kiss, and said, "Lead on, I'll follow you anywhere."

With that said they took off again climbing as they crossed the lagoon and heading toward the reef. Once they hit the reef they continued in a climbing turn towards Cook's Bay. If someone could have observed them, they'd have been amazed how the two could fly in such a tight formation like a pair of fighter jets. But, then again, they were angels, which can do anything in pursuit of the Lord's goals.

Jill was loving this, and she had already accepted Rafe's assertion that she was an Angel. However, at this point, she just wanted to fly. They flew down Cook's Bay and climbed until they were even with the summit of Mt. Mouaroa, also known as Bali Hai Peak. The pair then made a slow approach and alighted on the very highest rock at the summit, and then just stood there surveying the scene which was nothing short of spectacular. Rafe looked over at Jill, who was standing with a big grin on her face, and said, "What do you think."

Jill looked back at Rafe and said, "I think I'm going to like this Angel thing. Actually, in the last thirty minutes, things are beginning to make a lot more sense. Now I understand why things happened the way they did."

Rafe looked over at Jill and responded, "The difference between being human and being an Angel, is in certainty. Most humans have no idea what life is all about, but not so with us. We know exactly why we're here and what the purpose of our being is! You, my Little Dancer, still don't know why you're here, just as I didn't know until I was told. However, within the hour you'll know; because I'm the one who is going to tell you.

"Rafe, "I accept what you've told me, but before we proceed further with this, I have one request."

Rafe answered, "Your wish is my command.

"Before you tell me what this is all about, can we fly around the entire island? I want to see it from the air."

"Ok let's go, You, lead the way. "With that, Jill dove head first off the summit of Bali Hai Peak, with Rafe close behind. They dove about 500 feet straight down before leveling off and gliding over Cook's Bay on the way to the barrier reef. From there they took a fifteen-minute tour of the island staying over the reef, which was about half a mile offshore. Rafe was laughing to himself thinking, "She sure is an adventurous girl, and no one on this planet is as lucky as me." When they had completed their circle of the island, they came in for a perfect landing, not very far out from where they had left their lunch basket.

The girls in the kitchen had fixed them a nice lunch with a bottle of Chateau Neuf du Pape to top it off. After lunch, as they were sipping their wine, under a beautiful palm tree, Jill asked, "All right, Sir Knight, I've been waiting long enough. Tell me what sort of trouble you've gotten me into?"

Rafe smiled at Jill, realizing she was playing with him, then he began; He said, "Are you familiar with the chapter of Revelation in the Bible?"

Jill answered, "Only slightly."

He said, "Let me recite Revelation Chapter 20 verse 1. It goes like this."

"And I saw an angel come down from heaven,

having the key to the bottomless pit and a great chain in his hand.

And he laid hold on the dragon, that old serpent. Which is the Devil and Satan, and bound him for a thousand years, and cast him into the bottomless pit, and shut him up, and set a seal upon him,

that he should deceive the nations no more, till the thousand years should be fulfilled."

Jill just stared at Rafe. She was incredulous!"Oh my God, she thought! This is serious, in fact, it's more than serious; How can we capture Satan?"

Rafe knew what she was thinking and said, "Quite the challenge isn't it?"

She was looking straight into his eyes and he could read her confusion.She exclaimed, "Rafe, something like that is impossible."

He said, "I can see why you might believe that. It's something, someone who just discovered they were an angel would believe. You're forgetting one thing, we're angels, but you can't yet realize what that means. I know what you're thinking; Because I thought the same thing until the messenger angel told me the truth. My dear, your problem is you are unaware of the power we possess, and because of that, you're reverting back to human thinking. One of your human ideas is, for instance, how could we possibly defeat Satan? Yes, it would be impossible for a human, but not for another Archangel.

Jill shook her head and said, "This is so overwhelming. When I try to process this; An hour ago I was a human, or should I say, half-human, and then suddenly I discover I'm an angel."

Rafe smiled at Jill, and said, "I know, it's overwhelming so let's go back in the past and look at things with a new perspective. In the beginning, there was God and he was creative. Everything that exists, is created by him. When he created man, his greatest creation, there was a problem. A man was a slave to goodness; because evil didn't exist, so God created the dark side to test man's loyalty. Being what he is, man strayed. Some just strayed a little, then when realizing their error, they asked for forgiveness; and redemption. The Christian religion is based on that; Man is flawed and strays but can seek redemption. The problem lies in Hubris! What is that? It's overwhelming pride or arrogance. That is man's greatest flaw; because it leads to every other despicable sin. Carrying this a little further; Man in order to do anything he damn well pleases, has to commit the ultimate sin, and that is to deny the very existence of the creator. Put another way, if God doesn't exist, you can do anything, without fear of punishment."

Rafe looked over at his beloved companion and said, "Are you following me so far?" When Jill just nodded in the affirmative. Rafe continued, "Now we get to the crux of the matter, and that is Lucifer! Remember, Lucifer was an Archangel who, when given free choice, didn't deny the existence of God, which was impossible, since he had an intimate relationship with The Almighty, but through hubris, thought he was superior to his own creator. This is the very height of delusional thinking, and it's the reason God sent us down to earth. To put it in the simplest terms, God sent us to earth to kick Satan's ass. We are to capture him, humiliate the evil bastard, and then throw him into the bottomless pit, and lock it and seal it for a thousand years!"

Jill just stared at Rafe unable to speak. It was just too much to absorb. After a minute she responded with, "Capture Satan!

How do we accomplish that?"

"It's not as difficult as you might think. First, there are a few things you are completely unaware of. For instance, I had a very specific reason for wanting to gain control of Hope Farm."

Jill, now intensely interested asked, "Why did you want to gain control of Hope Farm?"

"I'm glad you asked, "I needed control of Hope Farm because that's where the Bottomless Pit is located."

"Oh, My God! Where is it, do you know the exact spot?"

"Yes, it's on the hill behind the White House at the camp."

"Are you talking about the place where you encountered the one you refer to as The Devil's Handmaiden?"

"Yes, that's the place, and believe me I find it a perfectly appropriate place to give Satan, the deep six!"

Jill was beginning to smile as she asked, "Ok, one last question. How are we going to track down and capture Satan?"

"That's a good question, and the answer is quite simple. We won't have to track him down, he'll come to us,"

Jill looked at Rafe and then asked, "How do you plan to accomplish that?"

"Well, first you have to remember who is directing this operation. Satan has no chance, but what will lead to his demise is his penchant for seduction. Satan likes nothing more than to lure a good person over to the dark side. What we're going to do is set a trap. A trap that will lead him to Hope Farm with the intention of seducing me. When he comes to Hope Farm, he'll never leave. Or, should I say, he won't leave for a thousand years."

Jill asked, "Sir Knight, can you handle Satan?"

"My darling there is no doubt of that, whatsoever. The first time the Lord spoke to me he said, I was his drawn sword. You and I are his chess pieces, we're his instruments, backed by the power of the universe. Personally, I think God wants to humiliate Lucifer, and we're the ones he'll use for that purpose. He's using his angels because he doesn't want to dirty his hands."

Jill asked, "Will I be like you, able to see into the future, and therefore be able to know what's about to happen in advance?"

"Yes, you will, you're going to be just like me. You're going to be surprised, as to what you've suddenly become capable of."

"Is that it? Am I fully briefed on angelic protocol?"

"Almost, but I have one more question for you."

"Ok, I'm ready."

Rafe looked at his lovely angelic wife and said, "You may not realize it just yet, but you just lost the right to free choice. Humans have it, but we angels don't, except in a very limited capacity. And, because the Lord God, deprived us of this freedom, he, in all his glory, decided to compensate us, to make up for what we lost. The question is; if you had one wish, certain to be granted by God, what would you ask for?"

"Jill fixed Rafe with her extraordinary blue eyes, and thought for a minute, before replying, "What if I already have it?" She had the same look in her eyes she had when she had first asked him to take her out, almost nine years ago.

He asked, "What is it?"

"True Love!"

"Do I have anything to do with that?"

"You have everything to do with it."

Rafe then said, "My darling, I feel exactly the same as you, but what is so miraculous is that we didn't have to ask God for anything, he knew our deepest desire, and he granted it before it entered our consciousness."

"Dear Rafe, true love is God's grace, and I think that's why we can't describe it with words. The first time we kissed at the end of our date, we knew without a doubt we were in love. Is that not the truth?"

"There's no doubt about that. I never knew such beauty existed. I wouldn't even attempt to describe the feeling."

"Now I know what you mean Rafe. The greatest feeling ever, came when you walked through the door of my dressing room, and I flew into your arms. It was at that point I knew all of my dreams had come true."

"Just further proof the Lord takes good care of his angels!" As they stood on the small, palm tree-shaded beach, facing each other, holding hands, Rafe asked, "Now that our little angelic powwow is complete, what should we do now?"

Jill pulled him towards the luminescent water and with a lovely smile on her face said, "I think we should do what all honeymooners do."

"What's that?" Asked Rafe

Jill gave him a mischievous look and replied, "I think you should tell me how much you love me. You know how!" So, the two angels swam out to frolic in the crystal clear, tropical waters.

Later as they were attaching their picnic basket to one of the bicycles Jill asked, "Where to now?"

"How about we head over to that little Boutique Mary told us about, the one on the road near the Bali Hai Hotel? You're going to need some Tahitian garb for what's coming up."

"By that, do you mean for the big party tomorrow night?"

Rafe laughed and said, "Well I can see you're quickly developing the angelic quality of looking into the future. So, you know the party tomorrow night will be the party to end all parties! I suppose you know why also."

Jill said, "I'm a little embarrassed to say, but I think it's about me."

As they began to pedal their bikes down the road that circled the Island Rafe said, "It is all about you! To the Mooreans, you're the Blue-Eyed Goddess." They rarely see someone like you. In case you're too modest to notice, you happen to have the most beautiful eyes on earth. They're Angel Eyes. I should have known that when I met you. Do you remember when I said you had the most beautiful eyes I'd ever seen, and that the eyes mirror the soul? Well, the Tahitian men are seeing the same thing I saw, and are completely mesmerized. After that, they were shocked by how well you could dance. Well, I have news for them; Yesterday, you didn't know you're an angel, and when you dance tomorrow, they are going to think you're a goddess!"

They stopped at the little boutique named Ma Robe a Moi, run by a friendly French couple, and spent at least an hour and a half shopping. Jill must have tried on twenty dresses and Pareos until she settled on seven. Since they were riding bicycles, the proprietors said they'd deliver the Pareos and Sarongs to the hotel. For the rest of the afternoon. the honeymooners snorkeled up and down the coral reef upon which their bungalow was sitting.

After breakfast the following morning Rafe and Jill took advantage of a unique amenity of the Hotel Bali Hai called the Liki Tiki, a motorized raft about thirty feet long and twelve feet wide used to take the guests on excursions to explore the coral gardens in the lagoon.

Jill loved the Liki Tiki and loved snorkeling in the warm tropical waters. During their first Liki Tiki cruise, they encountered all sorts of multicolored tropical fish among which could be counted, Yellow-tailed Snappers, Sea Bass. Amberjacks, Crevalle, Blue Tangs, Striped Damselfish, Lionfish, Triggerfish, Sting Rays, Morey Eels, and even an occasional Octopus.

After a couple of hours of snorkeling off the Liki Tiki, Rafe asked Jill, "Well how do you like cruising in the lagoon."

"Rafe this is so much fun. Bora Bora is beautiful, but Moorea is fun. We've got to come back here in the future."

Rafe laughed and added, "It is fun, but I can't wait to see how you'll feel after tonight."

Jill laughed too and added, "Can't wait!"

After dinner, Rafe and Jill returned to their bungalow and Jill changed into her dance attire. She was wearing a beautiful pareo with a lovely Orchid design which consisted of a very short skirt and top. Mary brought her another flowered headdress which when placed on her head completed the picture of an incredibly beautiful young woman.

Mary led them down the wooden walkway from their bungalow to the large veranda between the bar and restaurant. Even before the musicians were set up, over 200 natives had gathered and were ready for the festivities. Even Muck and his American partners were present. There was an air of excitement spreading throughout the crowd. The word had spread that they had a beautiful blonde movie star at the Hotel who could dance up a storm, and everyone was coming to check her out.

Once the musicians were ready, a tall handsome Moorean man walked over to where Rafe and Jill were sipping Mai Tai's and asked Jill to dance. By this time the crowd of revelers had swelled to nearly 400 and every eye was on the blue-eyed beauty. For good reason, the Mooreans couldn't believe that any Westerner could possibly dance the 'Oro Tahiti without years of practice. Of course, there was no way they could possibly know what Jill actually was. If this had taken place a couple of days before the result would not have been that spectacular. However, the day before the big event Jill had been briefed by Rafe as to her heavenly status. If you were to think about it objectively, If, an angel wanted to dance the 'Oro Tahiti better than anyone else on earth, could she, do it? Of course, nothing could stop her once she set her mind to it.

It all started with the first male dancer, then when the Mooreans realized how well Jill could dance the 'Oro Tahiti, they began to join in. First, the dancing couple was surrounded by a circle of about 10 men, following which about 30 women dancers formed a circle around the inner circle of men. Soon there were about 40 dancers participating at the same time. It wasn't long before half the crowd was dancing and even Rafe was dragged out onto the veranda to dance with Mary. In Rafe's mind, this became the party to end all parties. All through the night and into the wee hours of the morning the dancing and singing continued, until Rafe walked out on the veranda, swept Jill into his arms, and carried her down the walkway to their overwater bungalow, to the cheers of the native population.

Once inside Rafe lay Jill down on their bed and stretched out alongside and drew her into his arms and said, "How do you feel, Little Dancer?"

She looked at him and answered, "I'm exhausted!"

Rafe said, "Well Little Dancer, you should be exhausted since you all but danced yourself to death!" They curled up together and Rafe held Jill in her arms until she quickly slipped into a dreamless sleep.

Midmorning a knock on the door awaken them. Rafe slipped on a pair of shorts and opened the door. There to greet him, with a tray carrying coffee and croissants, was none other than Marahi, aka Bloody Mary, or just plain Mary. She walked in, set her tray down on the dining room table, and greeted Rafe with, Bon Jour, Mr. Rafe.

Rafe responded, "How are you this morning Marahi? Did you have a good time at the dance last night?"

"She answered, "Oh, Mr. Rafe, that was the most wonderful dance we've had on Moorea since I can remember."

Mary didn't see Jill walk into the room, and continued with, "Your wife is a wonderful dancer, we've never seen anyone, not even a Polynesian dance the 'Oro Tahiti like Miss Jill. She couldn't dance like that the day you arrived, but yesterday she danced it like she had been doing it all her life. No, I take that back; yesterday she danced like the greatest dancer we've ever seen. I've never seen anything like it. It made everyone very happy. Miss Jill is now famous on Moorea."

Jill now standing behind Mary said, "Wow, I think that's the nicest compliment I've ever received!"

Mary turned around and beaming at Jill said, "It's true Miss Jill last night was very special. Are you sure you're not half-Moorean?"

Jill answered, "No I'm not, but if I say here much longer, I'm going to wish I was."

Mary then, using hand gestures beckoned Jill and Rafe over, and whispering said, "Later, after lunch, we girls on the hotel staff are going to take you to see the underwater Tiki Gods! It is a very special thing. Hardly anyone other than native Mooreans has ever seen them. They are sacred to us, but after last night we feel you are one of us, so we would like to honor you with a special visit! Would you like to come?"

Rafe knew where this was going, and watched as Jill reached over to Marahi, took her in her arms, hugged her, and said, "We'd love to come and see the Tiki Gods. Where should we meet you?

Mary said, "Wait here until we're ready and we'll come and get you around 2:00 P.M."

Just before 2:00 P.M. Mary showed up and led Jill and Rafe down to the dock where the Liki Tiki was moored with Muck about to navigate the craft through the coral heads of the lagoon. It only took about twenty-five minutes to reach the spot which was right off the point of land separating Cook's Bay from Opunohu Bay. Muck knew the exact spot and dropped anchor in about twelve feet of water. With Mary leading the way about twelve Moorean girls leaped over the side followed by Jill and Rafe. About twenty yards away they came upon the six Tiki Gods, positioned in a semi-circle facing inward. Rafe watched the Polynesian girls cavort among their gods in the same playful way they interacted with each other. He wished he had an underwater camera to record this rare opportunity, but on the other hand, it would have been inappropriate considering the Mooreans had obviously placed the Tiki Gods underwater to keep them hidden. As much as Rafe enjoyed swimming among the Tiki Gods, it was Jill that had the most fun. After all, once she danced the 'Oro Tahiti the way she did in front of half the population of Moorea, she achieved a mystical status to the young people of Moorea as she seemed to communicate with the infinite reality. It was this feeling they had for her, that led to the happy honeymooners being invited to visit the sanctuary of their Gods. Little did they know, but Jill actually could communicate with the intimate reality. In effect, the natives saw Jill as she really was, and they adored her.

When you're vacationing on the Island of Moorea you'll soon find that there isn't that much to do, other than eat, drink, swim, and make love! If you love the beauty of nature, and a friendly, and beautiful native population, it's the place for you. However, it's not for everyone.

One afternoon, after lunch, Rafe and Muck were sitting in director's chairs, under the overhang extending from the thatched roof of the dining room. They were sipping Rum Punch and just shooting the bull. Muck asked, "Where's your lovely wife?"

To which Rafe responded, "She's out in the lagoon snorkeling with Marahi and her friends. Which brings to mind a subject I'd like to talk to you about."

Muck replied, "Sure go ahead, shoot!"

"Something very extraordinary just happened to Jill and me, and our friends in the States. We have a thoroughbred horse farm about 85 miles North of New York City, and our first runner started in August at Saratoga. To make a long story short, she won at odds of 90 to 1, and we had a $600,000 bet on her to win. Consequently, we won 54 million dollars!"

Muck stared at Rafe for a moment then responded with, "54 million, are you kidding?"

Rafe simply answered, "I kid you not! So, this is what I'd like to talk to you about. Jill and Marahi have formed an attachment where Marahi looks upon Jill as some sort of visiting Goddess! What I'd like to know is does Marahi have a few close friends she hangs with, like her best friends?"

Muck said, "Interesting that you should ask because Marahi does have two very close friends who, along with her, we call the trio. The other two are Nohealani, and Kaleah. Usually, where you find one, you find the other two. Why do you ask?"

"Well Muck, you've heard the expression, what goes around, comes around."

Muck answered, "I sure have, but what are you driving at?

"Jill and I have been talking, and since Marahi has made our stay on Moorea so unforgettable, we'd like to do the same thing for her. This is what we came up with. We'd like to invite Marahi and her friends to visit our farm in New York. We need your assistance at this end to help them get passports and visas for the trip. We're thinking we'd have them come next June as our filly Archangel, in all likelihood, will be running in a classic race in June and I'm sure the girls would love to see that. We'll also show them the sights of New York, and maybe even take them to see Washington, D.C."

Muck was smiling when he said, "You'd do that for my girls?"

"Of course, they made our honeymoon such a great adventure, it's the least we can do. So, just as Jill and I will never forget Moorea, Marahi and her friends will never forget New York. Let's just say it's a little bit of reciprocity between Hope Farm and the Bali Hai Hotel.

"Rafe that's the most wonderful idea. To the girls, it will be the adventure of a lifetime, one they'll never forget."

"You may not realize it, but Hope Farm and the Bali Hai are very similar in one particular way. They are both the sort of places where dreams come true, and one can find true happiness. I like this place so much that I'll be encouraging my friends from Hope Farm to come down here and stay in this magical place. Taking this a step further, you're welcome to stay with us at Hope Farm whenever you like and stay as long as you like. I know you're not married, but bring a girlfriend with you. We'll have a wonderful time. I'd just like to ask one thing!"

Muck said, "Ok, whatever you want."

Rafe answered, "Don't tell the girls about our big plans. We'll tell them when we board the boat to leave. It will give them something to look forward to."

Muck answered, "Ok I've got it. You'll surprise them as you're leaving. I won't let them know!"

When the day of departure from the Bali Hai Hotel arrived, there were at least 300 Mooreans gathered at the dock to see them off. Jill told Marahi about the planned trip to New York the following spring. Marahi was overjoyed as a trip to the United States was beyond anything she ever dreamed of. After hugging and kissing their newfound friends goodbye Rafe and Jill boarded the passenger ferry and watched the gangway be pulled. The engines gurgled to life, and the boat cast off. At that point, as the cutter drifted away from the dock the Mooreans began to sing. Whatever they were singing it was extraordinarily beautiful. Rafe suspected it was a hymn sung in Polynesian. As the boat drifted away from the dock the crowd kept singing and it reminded Rafe of a movie, he had seen filmed in the 1940s. Finally, the engine was put in gear and the boat slowly made its way into the channel that would lead to the break in the barrier reef. Jill was teary-eyed as the Bali Hai faded out of sight. Rafe whispered in her ear, "Don't worry, we'll be back,"

The following day the newlyweds were on a Pan Am flight to Los Angles, connecting to American Airlines to New York. When they finally arrived at JFK airport in New York, Mighty Mouse was waiting to greet them along with Goldilocks. It was a very happy reunion and everyone had a lot of questions to ask about what had transpired in the last two weeks. The first topic of conversation was Archangel. This came up first because Goldilocks needed to be dropped off at Belmont Park as Archangel was no longer being trained at the farm, but was now training at Belmont in preparation for the upcoming Champagne Stakes about a month away. Goldi explained that Old Man Madden had decided it would be more advantageous to train her over the track on which the Champagne would be run. His thinking was they no longer had to hide her blazing speed since there was no longer any point in betting on her. They were all rich, besides, when she ran in future races, she'd be 1 to 10, and you're not going to make money at those odds.

Just before leaving, Rafe and Jill told Goldi that they would act as surrogate parents to Aiden and Erin until she returned. In all likelihood, Archangel would be on the Kentucky Derby trail and Goldi could be away for an extended period. It all depended on whether or not Old Man Madden decided to take the New York route to the Derby, or the Florida, or possibly even the West Coast route.

During the 2 ½ hour drive to the farm, Mighty Mouse asked them a thousand questions about their trip to the South Pacific. Jill as much as told him that when he got married or met that special girl, the place he should take her is the Bali Hai Hotel on Moorea. On the way, Jill asked Mighty Mouse, who had Bogart? The Mouse told them that their pet spent the night with Aiden and Erin, and during the day had been hanging out wherever he could find Tar Baby, sometimes in her paddock, or in her barn."

The first thing they did was go over to Plum Cottage to pick up Bogart. He must have heard them coming as they didn't even get up the stairs before he began howling. It wasn't a little bit of howling either, it sounded more like a pack of wolves than one dog. When they entered Goldi's suite, Bogart went a little crazy. Jumping up on them, running in circles, and howling like a wolf. It took quite a while to quiet him down, while at the same time, they were trying to greet Aiden and Erin with hugs and kisses. Finally, they headed over to Main House to have dinner with the rest of their friends. It was quite a reception because the residents of Hope Farm sincerely loved one another, and as it turned out Rafe and Jill had quite a few tales to tell of their great adventure in the South Pacific.

After dinner, the happy couple took a short walk to the barn next to the training track. They had only just arrived when they heard a whinny and the thunder of hoofs as Tar Baby came running over to greet her mint supplier, as well as Jill, and Bogart. Once they'd given her the treat, and her buddy Bogart had rubbed noses, she headed out to the middle of her paddock. Rafe and Jill headed up the road to Main House with Bogart in tow. They were home and all was right at Hope Farm.

It was at that time that Rafe received the message. It was a message from on high. It came directly from *All That Is*, and when you receive such a message there's no doubt about its origin. It said, "Look for him in London. He directs a secret group called the Mithra Society!"

The Mithra Society

Rafe and Jill lay in their bed with their beloved pet Bogart, pretty much exhausted from their long trip home. Rafe was pondering the thoughts which had just entered his consciousness, allowing him to know his heavenly mission was about to swing into high gear. Jill was next to him with her head on his shoulder. As he reached down to caress Bogart's head which rested on his abdomen, Jill noticed the very serious look on his face and asked, "You're looking so serious, Sir Knight, is everything all right?"

"In a way it is, and the reason I'm looking so serious is that I've just been divinely informed that our reason for being here is about to commence.

"What have you learned?"

"I just received a message telling me where Satan is located!"

Jill asked, "Where did the message come from, and how was it delivered?"

Rafe looked straight into her eyes, and said, "It came from *All that is,* and it was delivered directly into my consciousness, not unlike the prophecy. Remember that?"

Jill answered, "I do remember the prophecy, but at first you didn't know if it was real or imagined."

"Yes, but that was before I knew what I was. Everything is different now. When I get a message from God, now I know what it is. I used to be an angel in training, but now I know what the Lord has planned."

"All right my darling," Jill Said, "Tell me what the Lord God placed in your consciousness?"

"Rafe looked at her and said, "He told me that Satan was living in London and his name is Constantine Galerius!"

"Is that all he told you?"

"No, but let me ask you a question before we proceed further. What was the prior religion of Rome before Christianity?"

Jill Said, "I have no idea."

"That's what I thought you'd say. But, don't feel bad because if I asked the entire population the same question less than a small fraction of 1% would know the answer, just as about 1% would know why Brutus and the senators murdered Caesar in the Senate. They know he was murdered, but have no idea why. So, my dear, let me tell you about the prior religion in Rome. First. It's called Mithra or Mithraism. It was the approved state religion of Rome for more than 300 years until totally suppressed in the 4th Century by Emperor Constantine and replaced by Christianity. One of the Western World's most powerful shared cultural roots is the Roman Empire. What I'm about to tell you is how Rome adopted Christianity to mold existing traditions and rituals to solidify its domination over politics, money, and world thinking."

"Where the Romans at first despised the Christian Religion as a threat, to the point, they beheaded the Apostle Paul in 67 AD, and crucified Saint Peter, upside down in 64 A D, they eventually began to realize that Christianity was slowly becoming the majority religion and had to be reckoned with. Many believe that when Emperor Constantine converted to the Christian religion, his objective was to gain unanimous approval, and submission to his authority from all classes. Emperor Constantine's conversion was most likely a political act rather than a spiritual one."

"What Constantine actually did was merge the two religions together since many of their doctrines were identical, or nearly so. Some of the similarities were, that Mithra was born of a virgin who was given the name

"Mother of God". This god remained celibate throughout his life, and valued self-control, renunciation, and resistance to sensuality among his worshippers. Mithras represented a system of ethics in which brotherhood was encouraged in order to unify against the forces of evil. Another similarity was the worshippers of Mithra held strong beliefs in a celestial heaven and an infernal hell. They also believed the benevolent powers of God would sympathize with their suffering and grant them the final justice of immortality and eternal salvation in the world to come. They looked forward to the final day of judgment in which the dead would resurrect and a final conflict would destroy the existing order of all things to bring about the triumph of light over darkness. Carrying this a little bit further, they believed purification, through a ritualistic baptism, was required of the faithful, who also took part in a ceremony in which they drank wine and ate bread to symbolize the body and blood of the god.Sundays were held sacred and the birth of God was celebrated on December 25th. After the earthly mission of this god had been accomplished, he took part in the last supper with his companions before ascending into heaven, to forever protect the faithful from above."

Jill finally said, "My God!That sounds almost like the Christian religion."

Rafe answered Jill, "It does indeed sound like Christianity, so would you like to know how this came about?"

Jill said, "Yes please tell me!"

Rafe went on to say, "Constantine had a political problem in that the established religion of Rome, Mithraism was in decline while the new religion of Christianity was ascendant. What did he do? He convened the Council of Nicaea in 325 A.D., which was an ecumenical council to determine the orthodoxy of the Catholic Church. It was here that the blending of Mithraism with Christianity took place. However, there were some serious disagreements as to whether Jesus, the son, was the equal of God the Father, and a major conflict emerged over the subject of the Trinity."

Jill asked, "How did it all work out?"

Rafe explained, "It's a good thing Constantine had the foresight to arrange for the council. Because of it, the Roman Empire never fell. It was transformed into the Roman Catholic Church, and The Vatican became fabulously wealthy, guiding our lives, our money, and our reality for the next 1,700 years."

"What Emperor Constantine sought was to unite his empire by merging the Christian faction of his empire, with local pagan worship and Mitharic secret societies. Pagans could keep their traditional celebration dates while the Christians got to keep their traditions and idols. So, paganism and Mithraism got dressed up in Christian clothing. It was a compromise by all the parties that allowed Constantine to expand his empire and secure his throne, with him as the undisputed, sacred dynastic ruler. That's why they named Constantinople after him."

Jill asked, "Rafe why are you giving me this ancient history lesson?"

Rafe smiled and said, "Because after all these years Mithraism exists only as an obscure secret religion, and guess who uses it for his own purposes?" Jill only shrugged so Rafe continued with, "None other than Constantine Galerius, aka Satan!

Jill answered, "Are you kidding?"

Rafe answered her with, "And guess what his group is called?" Before Jill could answer he went on to say, "The Mithra Society."

Jill, not knowing where all this was leading asked, "Why are you bringing up all of this Mithra business? Why did Satan choose that name for his organization?"

Rafe laughed and answered, "It's because Satan is delusional, and thinks he's a lot smarter than he really is. Satan, without his knowledge, is a foil to God. His problem is that he thinks he's God's equal when in reality he is only what God allows him to be. So, while Satan only exists to give mankind a choice between good and evil, he thinks he is on the level of The Lord God. I think he chose the name Mithra, for his organization, because that religion allows its members to work their way up to becoming a Divine Being."

"So, my darling Sir Knight, do you have the plan to capture and bring the Prince of Darkness to justice?"

"Yes Jill, I know how to bring him down, and it all revolves around luring him into a trap, and that trap will be here at Hope Farm. When I originally took control of Hope Farm, I thought it was for different reasons, however, I now know why. The Bottomless Pit, where I will deposit Satan for a thousand years, is right here."

"Do you know where on Hope Farm it's located?" Jill Asked.

To which Rafe replied, "It's down at the camp!"

Jill asked, "Do you know its exact location."

Rafe said, "Yes! It's on the hill behind the White House where I first encountered the Devil's Handmaiden when I was seven years old. I'm going to throw him into the bottomless pit in exactly the same place where I met one of his degenerate followers. How appropriate is that?"

"Do you now have it all in your head as to how you're going to capture Satan?"

"I do Jill, and it's relatively easy, or I should say, it's easy for an Angel."

Jill asked, "Tell me how you're going to do it?"

Rafe started with, "It's a little complex, but let me begin with our bodies. Do you know approximately, how many atoms are in our bodies?"

Jill just shook her head since she hadn't the foggiest idea."

Rafe gave her the answer, "Would you believe 7 Octillion. That is a seven with 27 zeros behind it! It's almost unimaginable. Here is what I'm trying to tell you. An atom has the basic shape of our solar system with a nucleus, which is energy, with electrons, or you could say planets, in orbit around the nucleus. So, Little Dancer, this is what I'd like you to be aware of; The nearest star to our own is Proxima Centauri which is 4.2 light-years away, which is 4.2 years, traveling at the speed of light. Therefore, in our universe, as well as in our own bodies, there is an infinite amount of space between either the atoms in our bodies or the stars in the galaxy. In reality, we are more space than substance. Keeping this in mind; This is how I'm going to defeat Satan."

Jill said, "Go on, I can't wait to hear your plan."

Rafe looked at her seriously and then said, "The Lord God has given me the power to rearrange a subject's atoms so they lose all substance and simply disappear. It will be through this mechanism that I will lead Satan into the trap. This is how it will go down. A fact, unknown to practically everybody, is that Satan's Mithra Society is a secret consortium of the world's Central Bankers. Satan, using his talent to seduce, or one could say bribe, essentially bought the loyalty of the bankers by offering them anything they desired.

Once they were in the fold it became impossible to leave because of the threat of blackmail. If you want to know why he formed this particular organization, the answer, is simple and it comes from the Bible, specifically 1ˢᵗ Timothy, Chapter 6, verse 10 It says, "The love of money, is the root of all evil." The Mithra Society is actually a cabal created to control the money supply, and in so doing control the world."

Jill couldn't believe what she was hearing, so she exclaimed, "My God! Rafe this is unbelievable. So, is this why we're here?"

"Pretty much. This first step for Satan is the bottomless pit for 1,000 years, and then after that, Armageddon, which will lead to his final destruction."

"Jill asked, "How are you going to lure him to Hope Farm."

"It's actually quite simple. I'm going to make three of his Central Bankers disappear. I'm going to do this myself, but I'm going to take the Leper Colony along with me to establish the fact that they were in the cities when our targets disappear. Eventually, Satan, using his unlimited resources, will discover that the Leper Colony exists and that it is an ultra, top-secret strike force. When he checks further, again using his unlimited resources, he will find that the Leper Colony was in all three cities where his bankers disappeared, and were there, at the time in question. With this now in his mind, the Leper Colony will have to be eliminated. He'll contract to have a force of highly trained military operatives attack Hope Farm and eliminate from the face of the earth the threat to his plans for world domination.

Jill shook her head in disbelief and asked, "How do you plan to stop them?"

"It would be impossible for a human, but child'"s play for an Archangel. I'll simply draw a circle of demarcation extending out a mile and a half from Main House. All of the developed parts of Hope Farm will be inside this circle. Unknown to our adversaries that line represents a circle of death. Anyone crossing it with evil intent towards any resident of Hope Farm, upon touching that line, will cease to exist!"

Jill looked a Rafe a little wide-eyed and said, "Wow! You don't fool around, do you?"

"If you think about it another way, you'll realize we don't really have a choice. You and I are instruments of the Lord God. It is he who calls the shots. God is playing chess with Satan and we are his chess pieces which he moves as he pleases. I suspect that Satan, after seeing his contracted strike force disappear, will fall back on his usual method of accumulating power, that being seduction. Keep in mind Satan won't know what happened to his contracted killers, they'll simply disappear. When he realizes that the Leper Colony is his adversary, and the use of force isn't going to work, he will then come to Hope Farm to make an offer we can't refuse.He'll literally offer us anything we want as long as he succeeds in bringing us into his cabal. What he'll never realize is, that when he comes to Hope Farm to carry out his nefarious plan, he won't be leaving for 1,000 years. We're going to throw him into the bottomless pit.

Jill then asked, "How will we know when it's time to take action?"

"It will be quite simple. When it's time for action, the Lord will notify us and we'll take the appropriate action. Until then we have an undefeated filly to manage and a group of broodmares to purchase to supplement Tar Baby's incredible genetic heritage. While we wait for heavenly orders, we'll revert back to our human identities, and build a secure future for our friends and family."

Three weeks later Rafe and Jill along with Aiden and Erin were driving to New York in Rafe's convertible. This was the day of the Champagne Stakes in which Archangel would take on the boys in a race that could lead to Horse-of-the-year honors. It's only under very rare circumstances that a filly would take on the colts as a two-year-old, however, when the filly has devastated her opposition, winning both of her previous starts in track record time, there's a very good chance she could be one of the greatest of all time. This was an exceptional opportunity considering that Archangel was Hope Farms' first starter, and the entire racing world was anxious to see how good she was.

As they cruised along the Taconic State Parkway on the way to the running of the Champagne Stakes at Belmont Park, Aiden who still hadn't gotten over Rafe having won $37,600 each, for both he and his sister, on one bet, asked, Rafe, "Can you teach me to handicap like you?"

Rafe simply asked Aiden, "Why do you want to know?"

Aiden came back with, "Because I want to learn to bet on horses like you."

Rafe answered, "If I were you, I'd be very careful of that."

Aiden asked, "Why?Is there some hidden danger that I'm not aware of?"

"Yes, Aiden, there is a great hidden danger. It revolves around man's desire to be omnipotent, or you could say the ability to know all and see all. The truth is most gamblers eventually become addicted, and in that regard lose control."

Aiden responded, "But, you did it when you won $75,200 for Erin and me with one bet."

"That's true Aiden, but that was under very unusual circumstances where I knew in advance Archangel would win, therefore I only had to handicap who would run second in the exacta. I already knew about Archangel's incredible speed before she made her first start. If I hadn't been an insider, I would not have had that advantage. I know what you're thinking. You think you've discovered a simple way to make big money with very little work, right?"

Aiden was smiling when he answered, "Well, sort of!"

Rafe went on to say, "Well since you're asking my advice, I'll tell you the course to take, that will bring you great wealth and success in life, and even more importantly, a feeling of self-worth. Is that what you're looking for?"

"You're a mind reader Rafe, that's exactly what I'm hoping to find."

"This is what I would suggest. If you're going to gambol on horses, do it in a way that you control. With that in mind during the next hour, as we drive to the track, I'm going to tell you how to make a fortune in a way that you control. To begin, will you admit that the purchase of Tar Baby wasn't a huge gamble considering that I bought her for $1,000?"

Aiden answered, "I'll say, no one can figure out why you bought her."

"I bought her for a very specific reason, and I can show you what that is, which will give you a huge advantage in the thoroughbred industry. But, before we get started in unraveling the mysteries of thoroughbred breeding, this is the path I suggest you follow. You're a good student, so upon graduation apply to a top veterinary school. Graduate with a degree in veterinary medicine which will teach you everything you need to know about the care of horses under your control. After veterinary school, I would suggest you serve an apprenticeship to Old Man Madden and learn to train exactly like him. Finally, return to Hope Farm where I will teach you the mysteries of thoroughbred breeding, and genetics. What I'm trying to tell you is that by the time you've finished your apprenticeship to Old Man Madden, you will have become an excellent handicapper, but you'll have no reason to gamble because you'll be making too much money breeding, racing, and selling horses."

Aiden looked at Rafe and said, "Do you think I can do that?"

"Of course, you can, but it's up to you. That's what life is all about. You set your mind on something, and then find a way to get it done."

Aiden responded, "Mr. Rafe, Hope Farm has some sort of magical quality. When Erin and I got here it was like landing in paradise. We couldn't believe how great it was, and every day it keeps getting better. But here's a question for you, will Archangel beat the boys in the Champagne Stakes today?"

"Simply put Aiden, she'll beat the boys easily, and in the process set a new track record, eclipsing the old one that was set 28 years ago by Triple-Crown winner, Count Fleet when he was a two-year-old. His track record was 1:34 4/5 for a mile. I believe Archangel will run the mile in 1:34 2/5, but she'll do it easily."

Erin asked, "Is Archangel some sort of superhorse?"

Rafe answered, "That's exactly what she is. Usually, only one such horse appears every 25 to 50 years. The last was Citation about 25 years ago. The difference between Citation and Archangel is that he started 20 times as a three-year-old, and won 19, which is an extraordinary record. Archangel will probably never start more than 10 times in one year."

Erin asked, "Why not? If she's that good why not run her as many times as we want, and win everything in sight?"

Rafe said, "Inadvertently you've asked the right question. It gets right down to what Hope Farm is all about. So, let me give you a lesson in Thoroughbred history; Seabiscuit, a great horse from the 1930s started 58 times as a two, and, three-year-old. He was then sold and fell into the hands of Silent Tom Smith who is very similar, in approach to training as our own, Old Man Madden. After changing owners, as a four-year-old Seabiscuit started 15 times with 11 wins. And then as a five-year-old, he started 11 times. Here's the difference; in his first two years of racing his 58 starts garnered earnings of $41,505. In the next two years, he started 26 starts and earned $298,975. You might ask yourself why the big difference. It was simply how he was treated. Silent Tom Smith took this beaten-down, over-raced colt and treated him like a champion, and voila, he became one. Let me give you an example of how I evaluate a horses' performance. I have a list of the average purse offered for racing in North America, by year, and last year it was $3,224. If Archangel wins today, and her next start, which is scheduled to be the Garden State Stakes in November, her total earnings for 1970 will be around $431,402. Divide her total earnings by her number of starts and you get $107,850 which is her average earnings per start. We then do a ratio between her average earnings per start and the average purse for the year to get her racing index. Her racing index, if she wins her next two starts will be 3293 which will be the highest of all time. To put this in perspective the great Native Dancer who won 21 of 22 starts with his only loss coming in the Kentucky Derby, which he lost by a head, had a racing index of 1282. Here's the deal, we aren't going to run Archangel specifically to earn money, because we don't have to. She made us 54 million dollars in her first start, we'll only run her when she tells us she's ready, and because of that she'll probably retire with the highest racing index of all time."

Erin responded, "Wow! That's amazing."

"Kids it's even more amazing than you think. If we were to travel back in time, to the first day that I can remember, do you know where I ended up at day's end?"

They both shook their heads, and Rafe went on to say, "I ended up at Greer School, Hope Farm, which back then was a school for disadvantaged children, I spent my first night on a cot in a dormitory at Plum Cottage in a corner of the dorm which is now your room, Aiden."

"Holy Moley! Are you kidding?"

"No Aiden, I'm not kidding, and you have no idea how I hated being there. My mother never told me she was leaving me. I felt as though she had dumped me, and I would never see home again. I think you can understand the feeling, although, how we arrived in those circumstances was different. The circumstances of my arrival set in motion a series of events that led to real trouble, and when I finally got out of the school almost ten years later my mother thought I was bad. It didn't matter that how she decided to place me in Greer School, led to a very bad outcome. But, to make a long story short when I returned home to New York my mother thought of me as a delinquent. Then who arrived in my life, but my guardian angel? You know that person, but you have no idea how he has served as your guardian angel also. That person is Mr. Massoletti, who is one of the greatest men I have ever known. There are a few reasons he's a great person in my eyes. When I first arrived home, you could say it was under a dark cloud, except Everett Massoletti thought I was a great kid. I never knew why he thought that way about me, but he did, He said he would send me to the top private school in the city if I promised to be the number one student. I agreed, and a year later, I was number one, and guess what that got me?"

Aiden answered, "I can't even imagine."

Rafe didn't say anything, but Jill tuned in her seat and looking back at Aiden and Erin, Said, "Me!"

Erin sat straight upright and exclaimed, "Oh my God! Is that true?"

Jill answered, "It's completely true, and without Pop, we would probably never have met, and certainly, never married." She then went on to tell them how their story began. She included in her story the three miracles, and how Everett played an important part in each."

Erin said, "Wow! What a great man."

Rafe then said, "He's greater than you think. Now that you know how he affected the lives of the two of us in the front seats of the car, would you like to know how he affected you two in the back seat?"

Aiden said, "Did he affect us too?"

Rafe answered, "Big time! Would you like to know how?"

Erin said, "Of course, tell us."

"When I went to Belmont Park to hire Old Man Madden, I met your sister who had just been fired by her first employer in the United States. To say she was upset is an understatement. I then hired her along with Old Man Madden. When I brought her to Hope Farm and showed her what would be her living quarters at Plum Cottage she was overwhelmed because it had three bedrooms. It was then that she told me about your circumstances in Ireland and the difficulty she was having getting you two to join her here. I told her that I thought I had the answer and that I would speak to Everett about it. What you don't know is that Everett Massoletti is a Knight of St. Gregory in the Catholic Church, and is a good friend of Cardinal Spellman in New York. When I told Everett of your plight he went to the Cardinal and it was arranged for the two of you to be issued Green Cards enabling you to become legal residents in the United States. After that, it was just a matter of going through the bureaucracy and its paperwork."

Aiden asked Rafe, "So, you're saying that Everett Massoletti, had a major impact on our lives just as he had on the lives of yourself and Jill?"

"That's exactly right Aiden, Everett has been like a surrogate father to me, and the lifeline he threw to you is just another example of the type of person he is. I consider him to be one of the greatest men I've known."

Aiden replied, "Wow! So, we're lucky to have him hang out with us at Hope Farm. Maybe, Erin and I should thank him for everything he's done to get us here?"

"Actually, I would take a different tack. If you're not aware of it, Everett likes to come up on weekends and his favorite activity is to sit on the lawn between Main House and the old school building on nice evenings, and simply socialize with whoever is around. Usually, that's Jill and me, our mothers, and often Old Man Madden, as well as Gunny Fiske. It's usually the older residents. If you two want to please Everett, stop by, on some of those evenings, and hang out. He'd like to know how you're doing and what you're interested in. Just think of him as the grandfather you never had, just as he's the father I never had. If you do that, you'll make him very happy."

"That would be pretty easy to do," Erin replied, "sort of like a big family."

Rafe went on to say, "That's exactly what it would be like, a big family, and while we're on the subject, there's something else we need to discuss. Brenda Kay is likely to be away from the farm for quite a while as Archangel moves around the country preparing for her classic engagements in the spring. Those races will most likely include the Kentucky Derby. Her prep races will probably be in Florida. So, seeing she'll be away from home for an extended period, Jill and I will act as surrogate parents while she's gone. This means you can sleep at Main House at night, or we'll have someone sleep in Old Man Madden's suite downstairs from you. Later when you're 16 we'll train you on the use of firearms to a point where you'll be able to defend yourselves. How does that sound?"

Erin asked, "Are we really in any danger at Plum Cottage?"

Rafe responded, "Actually it's very safe, but as we were taught as Boy Scouts, be prepared!"

They continued down the parkway heading for Belmont Park where Aiden and Erin, and the rest of the Hope Farm contingent, watched as Brenda Kay guided Archangel as she cruised to an eight-length victory, covering the one-mile distance in 1:34 1/5 breaking Triple Crown winner, Count Fleet's track record by 3/5 of a second. Since the previous record was 28 years old, the acclaim following the race was unparalleled. With three wins in three starts where she broke the track record in each race while winning in hand; the racing world had a new heroine.

The next race on the agenda was the Garden State Stakes which had become the richest race for two-year-olds in the nation with a winner's share of about $210,000. In contrast, the Champagne Stakes which was first run in 1867, and historically had much greater prestige, had a winner's share of about $145,000. If Archangel won the Garden State Stakes and broke another track record, she would undoubtedly be the next Horse-of-the-Year.

Everything went according to plan. The Hope Farm family showed up at Garden State Park three weeks after Archangel's victory in the Champagne Stakes where she made short work of the boys again and covered the 1 1/16 miles of the Garden State Stakes in 1:40 3/5 breaking the track record by 3/5 of a second. There no longer remained any doubt that Archangel was a superhorse, and the racing world's only question was, how good is she? After the race, Old Man Madden and Rafe discussed the path she would take, in preparation for the following year's Kentucky Derby. It was decided to give the filly a short vacation, which meant vanning her home for six weeks. Fortunately. Hope Farm had its own training track which could be used to keep the filly in light training. If all went according to plan Old Man Madden and Goldilocks would be home for the holidays and leave for Florida after New Year's.

The six-week vacation from the track with everyone getting together over the holidays was exactly what was needed. They all had a wonderful time over that holiday season. What a year! If any group ever had a reason to celebrate it was the group from Hope Farm.

After a six-week rest at the farm Archangel was set to begin her three-year-old campaign in Florida.If they took the southern route to the Kentucky

Derby the races would most likely include the Bahamas Stakes, Flamingo Stakes, and the Florida Derby. There was also a possibility that the Florida Derby could be substituted with either the Wood Memorial in New York or the Bluegrass Stakes in Kentucky. However, to Rafe, the great undefeated Archangel was not the focus of his attention; Satan was!

With that in mind, he walked over to Plum Cottage one evening to have a sit down with Old Man Madden. Of course, Old Man Madden was pleased to see his young friend and greeted him in his usual way with, "Hey there Whippersnapper, to what do I owe this unexpected pleasure?"

Rafe smiled at his trainer and said, "We need to talk about something concerning Archangel."

The Old Man answered, "Nothing serious I hope?"

Rafe said, "Actually, it's about as serious as any discussion could be, however, it's not anything that will upset Archangel's career unless she can't run on grass. That's what I came here to discuss with you."

"Exactly what is it you want to know?" answered Old Man Madden.

"It's fairly simple. I need to know if Archangel is just as good on grass as she is on dirt, if she's faster on grass than dirt, or if she's not as good on grass. It's vital that we know this sometime during her three-year-old season. There isn't any rush but the information is of vital importance."

Old Man Madden then asked, "May I ask why this is so important?"

"Rafe answered, "Not at all; here's the deal! You're aware that the Leper Colony spends a great deal of time on the back 3,000 acres training to maintain a very high level of proficiency in what we do best, that being stealth, and then where necessary, assault. The real purpose of Hope Farm is not the breeding and racing of Thoroughbred horses, but rather what we are contracted to do for the government of the United States. What we do is so top secret that it can't even be discussed. In fact, even the existence of the Leper Colony as a strike force is known only to the number of people that you could count on the fingers of one hand."

Old Man Madden asked, "I know you lepers are up to something important out there in the forest, but how does Archangel fit into the picture?"

Rafe answered, "Well you hit right on the subject of our discussion. I can't tell you what we're up to, but it's something of vital importance. What

I'd like to do is take Archangel to Europe and Australia either as a four-year-old, or five-year-old with the intent of winning the Ascot Gold Cup, the Eclipse Stakes in Great Britain, the Grand Prix de Paris, and the Prix de l'Arc de Triomphe in France, and finally the Melbourne Cup in Australia."

"May I ask why those particular races?"

"The truth is it's not so much those particular races we're interested in winning, but those races are the ones that a horse of Archangel's quality would run in. What's really going on is a huge but subtle subterfuge where it's not Archangel's presence in those countries that is of primary importance, but the presence of the Leper Colony in those countries as her owners. We're going to trick an adversary of great guile and cunning into making a fatal mistake. I can only say this; it's of critical importance that we succeed. If you determine that Archangel isn't as good on turf as she is on dirt, we'll scrap the plan and devise another. Just give me your best analysis."

"Can't you tell me what's actually going on?"

"I'll tell you what. After all is said and done, I'll let you in on the secret, that is if you can believe it. How does that sound?"

"Couldn't ask for anything more, I'll just keep my mind on Archangel's undefeated status. And you just point me in the right direction."

Rafe answered, "Great, that's all I needed to know."

What Old Man Madden couldn't possibly know was that Rafe already knew the outcome, and he was just getting everyone on board as if it were their own decision.

Right after the holiday, Archangel was vanned to Stewart Airforce Base in Newburgh, New York where she was flown out to Miami, Florida, and Hialeah Park. Her first start was scheduled to be the Bahamas Stakes run at Seven furlongs as a prep for the much more important 1 1/8 mile Flamingo Stakes. The Bahamas Stakes was of special interest to Rafe as he became aware of the race in 1957 when he was still five feet tall and weighed one hundred pounds, those were the days when he saw himself as a future jockey winning the Kentucky Derby and all of the other classic races. The year 1957 was the year in which a great crop of three-year-old colts was emerging which included Bold Ruler, Gen. Duke, Round Table, Iron Liege, and Clem. Now he was an owner, planning the path his undefeated filly would follow to the Triple Crown races, the first of which would be the Kentucky Derby run on the first Saturday in May.

Needless to say, the entire Leper Colony and their associates made the trip to Miami to watch the race which was not televised. They weren't disappointed either as Archangel resumed her winning ways by speeding away from the gate to open a six-length lead in the first quarter of a mile to win in hand, equaling Bold Ruler's track record. The time of 1:22 flat was impressive as in 1957 Bold Ruler had won the Bahamas Stakes in that same time beating, Calumet's Gen. Duke with the very fast colt Impressive third.

The next step on the Kentucky Derby trail, was the Flamingo Stakes run at 1 1/8 miles. The racing public knew Archangel was very fast, and the only question left was could she carry her blazing speed over the Derby distance of 1 ¼ miles, and later the 1 ½ miles of the Belmont Stakes? Rafe knew the answer however, he was the only one with that certain knowledge. As Rafe expected, Archangel under the patient ride of Mary Beth cantered home by nine lengths barely working up a sweat. The entire entourage from Hope Farm didn't attend the Flamingo since they were still under contract with the President and had to be available for any unexpected contingency. At this point, Old Man Madden decided to take the route to the Derby through New York and began to prepare Archangel for the Wood Memorial to be run two weeks before the Kentucky Derby.

Shortly before the Wood Memorial, Rafe had a talk with Jill as they were sitting by the Beaver Dam watching the beavers cavort in their pond, He started with, "There's something we need to talk about my darling."

Jill turned her gorgeous eyes on him and asked, "And what might that be, Sir Knight?"

"It's only about five months until the Belmont Stakes in New York. I think it would be the perfect time to bring Marahi and her friends to New York to see Archangel win the Triple Crown and at the same time see the sights of the city."

"I think I have an idea to add to that!"

"Rafe asked, "What do you have in mind?'

Jill answered, "Have them come three weeks earlier for the Preakness which is run only forty miles from Washington, D.C. and we can show them Washington as well."

"That's a wonderful Idea," Rafe said, "In fact, I have something else to add to it. What if we hire the same crew that made the film of Archangel's debut in the Schuylerville Stakes and have them make a movie of Archangel's Belmont Stakes, as well as the girl's entire visit to the States? That way when they return to Moorea everyone can come down to that little Quonset Hut they use as a theater, and watch their entire trip."

Jill sat there smiling then leaned over and gave Rafe a kiss on the cheek before whispering, "I was thinking the same thing myself; I think it's amazing how much we think alike."

"Rafe laughed and said, "My darling, we think alike because we were created that way. Remember, we were made for each other."

Jill simply looked over at Rafe and replied, "I know what you mean. I sometimes revert back to human thinking and tend to forget what we're really here for."

"Speaking of that, I have something to tell concerning how we're going to lure Satan to Hope Farm and deposit him in the Bottomless Pit."

Jill asked, "And pray, tell, what do you have in mind?"

Rafe gave Jill a serious look and began, "We're going to run Archangel in Europe as a four-year-old. This means she'll be running on grass instead of dirt, but it won't make a difference since she'll be faster on grass. The point of running Archangel in Europe is not to enhance her status by having her win a championship across the Atlantic but to give an excuse for the Leper Colony to be in town when she runs. This little piece of information is only for you and me because when Archangel runs in a race like the Ascot Gold Cup, the head of the Bank of England will disappear. The same will take place in France when she runs in the Grand Prix de Paris or the Prix de l'Arc de Triomphe, in which case the Central Banker of France will also disappear. Finally, we'll run her in Australia where their Central Banker will also disappear."

Jill simply asked, "How do you plan to make them disappear?"

Rafe answered, "I'm going to rearrange their molecules so they no longer have form. The bankers will simply disappear, never to be seen again."

Jill said. "Are you sure you can do that?"

Rafe smiled and said, "Remember, we're instruments of the Lord God. If he wants it done, he gives us the power, so yes, I'll make it happen.

"I guess you've already thought of how these bankers are going to disappear?"

Rafe answered, "It's going to be very simple. We'll have the lepers make an appearance in the nearby environs from which the Central Banker will disappear. During the party, or whatever else we may set up, I'll disappear and make my way to the banker's residence and redeploy his atoms. It will be very simple, I'll simply make myself invisible, and fly there and back. There isn't any level of security capable of stopping me. I'll walk in, freeze the culprit in place, read the indictment against him, and then snap my fingers. He'll be rearranged, and I'll leave. What you need to keep in mind is that when the Central Bankers who are members of the Mithra Society begin to disappear, Satan will have no way of knowing what's going on. After the first three disappear we'll have concocted a very subtle plan to lead Satan to his inevitable imprisonment."

Jill asked, "How is all of this to work out?"

Since you'll be so deeply involved, this is how we'll capture Satan. When Archangel wins the very prestigious races in England, France, and Australia, Satan will never connect these races with the disappearance of his bankers. Having the lepers present when she wins her races won't in itself arouse the suspicions of Satan. Therefore, we'll have to plant that seed in the fertile ground, or put another way, we'll have to leak the suggestion that the lepers were within range when the bankers went missing. Once Satan gets the idea planted, it will grow like a weed, leading him to make the mistake of a lifetime."

Jill said, "How will he react when he learns that the lepers could be involved?"

"If he comes to the conclusion that we really were responsible, he'll send a strike force of 25-30 contractors to wipe the Hope Farm contingent off the face of the earth. "I'll make sure that doesn't work because I will personally wipe his strike force off the face of the earth, with no trace left behind."

Jill asked, "What then?"

"If he can't wipe us out with his contractor's men, he'll fall back on his usual method of corruption, that being seduction. What I mean by that is Satan will come to Hope Farm to make us an offer we can't refuse. That shouldn't be too hard for him since he does control most of the Earth's money supply. When he comes to Hope Farm to make his offer, that's the end of the game. He'll come in expecting a victory, and he'll end up in the Bottomless Pit. It's almost too easy considering what's at stake."

Jill said, 'Do you think it will go off without a hitch?

"I have no doubt, answered Rafe, remember whom we're working for!"

With that issue settled Jill and Rafe turned their attention to the upcoming Triple Crown and to the visit of Marahi and her friends. They decided that Jill would handle the arrangements for Marahi, Nohealani, and Kaleah's trip to attend the Preakness Stakes and the Belmont Stakes. She immediately contacted Muck at the Bali Hai in Moorea to get him involved in obtaining Passports and visas for the girls.

Rafe concentrated on Archangel's Triple Crown campaign which was moving ahead right on schedule. The majestic black filly, as could be expected, won the Bahamas Stakes in a canter crossing the finish line five lengths ahead of her nearest rival winning in 1:22 flat equaling the track record. Her time equaled that of Bold Ruler in his first start against Calumet's Gen. Duke who may have been the better horse.

Next came the Flamingo Stakes also run at Hialeah Park at a distance of 1 1/8. The outcome of the Flamingo was different from the Bahamas in that in the Flamingo Goldilocks was teaching Archangel to rate and not to run out of the gate at high speed. As a result, the Flamingo was run in 1:47 2/5 just 2/5 off Bold Ruler's track record of 1:47 flat.

Next on Archangel's schedule was the mile and an eighth Florida Derby run at Gulfstream Park at the end of March. Like she did in the Flamingo Stakes she just cruised to a five-length victory in 1:47 1/5 just 2/5 of a second off Gen. Duke's track record of 1:46 4/5. It was at this point that Old Man Madden made the critical decision on where to have Archangel make her final start before the Kentucky Derby. He decided to take the route through New York, in the Wood Memorial which was run two weeks before the Derby.

Archangel's Wood Memorial victory was only by two lengths which was the smallest margin of victory of her career due to Old Man Madden's plan "not to squeeze too much juice from the lemon" just before the Kentucky Derby. In the Old Man's mind, Archangel was sitting on ready and was as tight as a spring. After the Wood victory, she'd have only one more workout prior to the Derby.

While Rafe kept his mind on the Run for the Roses, Jill was making sure that everything was ready regarding passports and visas for travel from French Polynesia to New York. Both Jill and Rafe wanted the girls from Moorea to have a once-in-a-lifetime trip to America. That was only fair seeing that the girls played a major role in making their honeymoon trip truly unforgettable.

The Kentucky Derby is a big deal to anyone involved in horse racing, however, in this case, the Derby couldn't compare to the Schuylerville. After all the Schuylerville had made them all rich. The Hope Farm contingent showed up at Churchill Downs on the first Saturday in May to watch the 95th running of America's number one classic race. There was a very large gathering in the paddock for the saddling after which the very excited group returned to their box seats to watch the race.

The race itself was somewhat anticlimactic where Archangel won as she pleased by five lengths and she could have won by fifteen if Goldilocks had asked her. The plan was to conserve her energy for the final two races of the Triple Crown, the Preakness Stakes in two weeks, and then the Belmont in five weeks. The reason the Triple Crown is so difficult is it encompasses three races in five weeks with the mile-and-one-half Belmont Stakes being the longest. Expend too much energy in the first two races and there's a good chance you'll come up empty in the Belmont.

Goldilocks knew exactly how to ride the Derby; Break alertly from the number seven post position, then on the long run into the first turn guide Archangel to the outside going into the Clubhouse turn, then break from her usual style of building up and unsurmountable lead down the backstretch, to one of sitting, in a stalking position one length off the leaders. Then from the head of the stretch to the finish, let her run a little; End of story!

That's exactly how the race was run with Archangel winning the Kentucky Derby by five lengths, 1/5 off Northern Dancer's Derby, and track record. The important thing was it didn't take too much out of her. There remained two more races in the next five weeks which would decide the Triple Crown.

Needless to say, the celebration in the winner's circle was one for the record books. Nothing like having a Broadway star holding the horse's bridle in the winner's circle. It wasn't just a few people that experienced the thrill of a lifetime, but the whole Hope Farm entourage. They'd be sharing the memory for years to come.

The next big event on the Hope Farm calendar was the arrival of the Marahi and her friends for their six-week adventure in the United States. Jill arranged for a large contingent of the leper colony to be present to greet the girls when they arrived on a Pan American 747. The girls were beaming when they saw the group of young men accompanying Jill and Rafe to welcome them to New York. After greeting the girls and collecting their luggage the happy group headed for Hope Farm taking the round-about scenic route. There were four cars in their little convoy with Rafe's leading the way. Rafe and Jill were in the front seat while Marahi, Nohealani, and Kaleah were in the back seat. They entered the Belt Parkway and headed toward Coney Island and the Brooklyn Battery Tunnel. Once through the tunnel, they headed uptown on the East River Drive which skirted the East side of Manhattan Island giving the girls a close-up view of the skyline and the bridges between Manhattan, Queens, and Brooklyn. There were a lot of exclamations of excitement as the girls had only seen New York in movies.

Jill wanted to stop in Manhattan but, on second thought, the girls were tired, as it's a long way from Moorea to New York; they'd go shopping tomorrow after the girls had a good night's sleep. They could return to the city and spend the next day shopping and sightseeing at the Empire State Building, and the Statue of Liberty. The ride up to the farm was a beautiful one with the girls getting their first glimpse at what is referred to as an Eastern Deciduous Forest. An Eastern Deciduous Forest is one in which the trees produce large leaves that they lose seasonally. The trip was delightful as the girl's wonder and excitement were contagiously allowing Rafe and Jill to share in their excitement. Rafe and Jill grinned at each other enjoying the ride almost as much as the girls. This is what they had hoped would happen, and Rafe already knew it was going to get better and better. There's an old saying, "What goes around comes around."

The girls were greeted at the farm like visiting royalty, after all, they were lovely young ladies and the lepers took to them like bees to honey. After a quick tour of the farm, dinner was served and the girls retired early with a big day on tap.

After breakfast, the following morning Rafe, Jill, and Mighty Mouse picked up the girls at Daisy Cottage and headed for New York. Jill led the girls on a shopping spree making sure they were well-attired for the upcoming festivities that would accompany the Preakness and Belmont Stakes. The shopping started with Bonwit Teller located at Fifth Avenue and 56th Street, and thence to many of the other stores throughout midtown Manhattan. Trailing along and recording the girl's big adventure was the team of moviemakers hired to record the event.

A few days later the girls and most of the Leper Colony left for Washington D.C. for more sightseeing and to witness the running of the second leg of the Triple Crown, the Preakness Stakes run in nearby Baltimore on May 16th two weeks after the Kentucky Derby. The lovely Moorean girls were having the time of their lives, but little did they know what Rafe had in store for them on Preakness Day. They left for Washington D.C. on May 15th the day before the race, and before they left Rafe whispered to Jill as they lay in bed about his plan to drive the girl's visit to another level. When he whispered to Jill that he had a plan for Preakness Day that would lift the girl's spirits to the stratosphere, she just smiled and said, "What do you have in mind?"

Rafe asked, "Do you remember what we did for Aiden and Erin on Schuylerville Day?"

A big smile broke out on Jill's face and she responded with, "Do you mean winning the exacta?"

Rafe nodded and said, "That's exactly what I have in mind, make them a small fortune with a well-placed bet. I think it's a good outcome; the girls leave on vacation and return relatively rich."

Jill laughed and replied, "I think it's a great idea, let's do it."

And so, they did! The girl's betting coup was almost more fun than seeing Archangel canter to victory in the 2nd jewel of racing Triple Crown. It happened before the 4th race when Rafe walked up to the box seat in which Jill and the girls were seated and presented each with a $200 exacta ticket with number 4 to win and number 1 to run second. Rafe explained to the girls that the Four horse had to win, and the one horse had to run second in order for them to win. The race itself was a sight to behold. The one horse led throughout and looked a sure winner at the head of the stretch, but with a 1/8 of a mile to run the four horse came charging. Although it looked impossible, she caught the one horse a few yards from the finish and won by a head. Needless to say, the girls went crazy when they realized they had won, and quickly asked Rafe how much they had won. After the race was declared official the exacta price went up on the tote board showing the 4-1 exacta had paid $299. Rafe and Jill looked at each other and Rafe winked at Jill, who smiled in return; they knew that the $200 dollar exacta paid 100 times more than the $299 showing on the tote board, which was for a $2 dollar exacta payoff.

Rafe turned back to the girls and said, "No my beautiful friends, your $200 dollar exacta pays $29,900.

Nohealani stared at Rafe and then said, "Do you mean $29,900 each?"

Rafe looked at the girls nodded and said, "Yes, you won $29,900 each,"

Well, that set them off! When they processed what had been said, they started jumping up and down, screaming and yelling, having just lost it. Everyone was so happy for them, and as for the girls, they felt they'd just been touched by the hand of God. You could say it was the defining moment of their trip.

With that task accomplished they moved on to the running of the Preakness Stakes which was somewhat anticlimactic after winning the big bet. The Preakness Stakes is run at 1 3/16 miles which is 1/16 of a mile shorter than the Kentucky Derby. Old Man Madden was thinking he didn't want Archangel running too fast in the 2nd jewel of the Triple Crown as he wanted to save something for the Belmont Stakes to be run three weeks after the Preakness. He'd seen too many horses win the first two legs of the Triple Crown only to have their exertions in the first two cause them to lose in the Belmont. Goldilocks was instructed to go for the lead out of the gate, not to ask Archangel for too much speed, but to just gallop the Colts into submission. If she was challenged, Goldilocks would let out a little to keep Archangel running easily on the lead.

That's the way the race was run. Archangel cruised to an easy three-length victory and headed for New York and the final leg of the Triple Crown now only three weeks away. After a huge victory celebration in Baltimore, the Hope Farm entourage headed back to the farm while Old Man Madden, Goldilocks, and Archangel took up residence at Belmont Park to prepare for the Belmont Stakes.

The Hope Farm community was very tight-knit. On summer evenings most of the residents would meet on the lawn behind Main House for what was simply a gathering. It had started a few years ago when Rafe and Jill and their mothers, along with Everett Massoletti began to sit on the lawn just to enjoy each other's company. Then it began to expand. First Gunny Fisk started dropping by followed by the Leper Colony, and then everyone else. The three Moorean Princesses took to the evening meetings like ducks to water. After all, they were exotic beauties surrounded by sixteen attractive young men.

Just before the girls arrived from Moorea, Rafe had a talk with the lepers about how he expected them to act toward their visitors from the Islands.Simply put, there would be no sexual interaction with the girls while they were visitors to Hope Farm. At a meeting, held in early April, outside the broodmare barn, Rafe briefed the lepers. He was direct and right to the point as he said, "Gentleman, this is serious, so listen up. Jill and I had the best time of our life on Moorea at the Bali Hai Hotel. Our visitors are the same girls who were instrumental in making our stay so memorable, and that's why we invited them, to provide them with an equally memorable trip. Here's the problem; the girls are both beautiful as well as real sweethearts, a devastating combination! Or I could put it another way, they're pretty much irresistible. So, the inevitable will take place, meaning you'll be attracted to them like bees to honey. To simplify things so I don't have to give an hour-long dissertation, here is what I want you lepers to do, and it's very simple; Treat our three lovely visitors like they're my sisters!"

That being said, the lepers gave each other a knowing glance, and that potential problem was settled.Just when it appeared that all was said and done Rafe Said, "By the way gentlemen, there is another side of this you probably haven't thought about. Remember I told you we were going to make a film of the girl's visit which will include the Preakness and Belmont Stakes. In fact, we will film their entire vacation. This you already know, however, what you haven't considered since you've never been to Moorea is the big impact the film of the girl's vacation will have on the natives of Moorea. Considering everything you've been exposed to, Moorea, for all its limitless beauty, is still a remote place. One of their most popular pastimes is going to the movies. The theater is a big Quonset Hut which is regularly filled with the native population anxious to see images of what's taking place in the rest of the world. When the girls return to Moorea with their homemade motion picture it's going to be the most popular film ever shown on Moorea. Now if you look at things from the right perspective you might come to the conclusion, that you'll find yourselves sitting in a very enviable position. What do I mean by that?By playing the role of escorts for the visiting Polynesian ladies you will be in many of the scenes in the movie. Before you ever set foot on Moorea the ladies of that enchanting place will know who you are. Not only that, but you will be friends with the three girls that made the trip. You have enough money from the betting coup on the Schuylerville to fly down there whenever you like. Just remember the old saying, what goes around, comes around! Remember it, because it's true."

After Rafe's short talk with the lepers, things moved along as smooth as silk. As usual, the lepers followed their leader's advice since it was their experience that he was always right. In fact, they liked the idea since from their perspective it opened the door to future adventures, and the next one would be in the tropical paradise of Moorea.

Rafe turned his attention back to Archangel who was on the verge of becoming thoroughbred racings' first filly Triple Crown winner. Rafe met with Old Man Madden and Goldilocks in the tach room near Archangel's barn at Belmont Park three weeks before the race.Both Old Man and Goldilocks were in the tach room when Rafe walked into a very warm welcome.

Old Man quickly jumped to the point, "So what brings you by this fine afternoon, my young friend?"

Rafe answered, "I just wanted to see how you were taking the expected arrival of what is probably going to be the greatest day of your life."

Old Man laughed and responded, "Although you may not realize it that day may have already occurred. It could have been the day you showed up at Belmont Park and hired Brenda Kay and me. In fact, the entire Hope Farm experience has been one amazing experience after another. First, you hire us, then you show up with the equine Bitch from Hell, Tar Baby. I'll tell you Rafe when you brought Tar Baby back from Kentucky, I thought you'd lost your mind. I had never seen a more pitiful-looking broodmare in my life. Then low and behold she produces Archangel. Not stopping there, you bring Aiden and Erin over from Ireland, just before Archangel wins the Schuylerville Stakes, making us all rich. It's as if everything at Hope Farm has a magical quality. Even bringing the girls from Moorea to experience the Triple Crown fits right into what Hope Farm is all about. It's all very special."

"Glad you feel that way Old Man", replied, Rafe. "To tell the truth it started the night Jill and I were reunited. As we drove out of the city Jill asked, "Where are you taking me?"

I responded with, "To a place for happily ever aftering! That's what I told her, and that's what we're building at Hope Farm, and so far, it seems to be working."

Goldilocks added, "From my perspective, it's working unbelievably well. Aiden and Erin are here, and are so happy. Just having them here with me makes me happy beyond belief. Everything at Hope Farm is wonderful so Old Man is right, we'll most likely win the Triple Crown, but it will be just another extraordinary event in a series of them. Even having the girls from Moorea here to witness the big race is wonderful, but I hope you know because as lovely as they are, we'll be soon seeing a massive exodus of lepers leaving for Moorea as soon as the right conditions present themselves."

"So, Old Man, am I right to assume that Archangel is ready to make racing history by becoming the first filly Triple Crown winner?"

Old Man smiled at Rafe and said, she's sittin' on ready Whippersnapper. The only way she'll lose is if Goldilocks, here, falls off. I would say the only question left concerning Archangel is will she retire undefeated."

Rafe said, "Good that's all I wanted to hear. I'll just go back to the farm and show our Moorean lovely's the time of their lives." That's what happened. Actually, only Rafe and Jill knew what was taking place. It wasn't anything that Rafe did that thrilled the young Moorean girls, it was Jill. The girls had no way of knowing that Jill was an angel. When she had danced that night on Moorea the natives had never seen anything like it. Here's the thing; humans aren't aware when angels are in their midst. Sure, Jill was beautiful and could dance like a goddess, but they didn't know she could fly! Therefore, since they couldn't perceive her being an angel, they couldn't understand that as an angel she could outdance everyone on the planet. That's what they had witnessed, an angel dancing. Since the girls saw Jill as a dancing goddess, they saw themselves as visiting royalty. Another factor playing out was that wherever the girls, along with Jill and an entourage of escorting lepers went, the film crew followed making a film to show the folks back home. All of it came to a climatic end with the running of the Belmont Stakes.

This time it wasn't going to be like the Schuylerville Stakes where a third of the Leper Colony was spread halfway around the world placing bets. This time all would be present and accounted for, to witness the big event. When Rafe said, "all" he meant all. He hired a security firm to watch the farm so the LaDues and the Van Aldens could share this event with everyone. It was like a big family gathering for an event that would be shared and relived for generations.

Rafe was pleased with the harmony shown by the residents of Hope Farm. Secretly he knew he was creating a little piece of heaven for Jill and Himself here at Hope Farm as well as for anyone else that wanted in. Seemed to him that everyone had decided to join as they now had something much more like a family.

Rafe wasn't worried about the outcome of the race, after all, he already knew the outcome. Rafe knew that Archangel could gallop along at 24-second-quarters of a mile. This is true of most thoroughbreds, however, what is not well known is that most thoroughbreds can maintain that speed for only

¾ of a mile, but after that, they begin to slow down. Where the Classic Thoroughbred is concerned it is at one mile in 1:36 that time begins to separate the "men from the boys." Most thoroughbreds can get six eights of a mile in 1:12 but only a minority can get one mile in 1:36. When you move another ¼ of a mile by adding 24 seconds to 1:36 you get 2:00. In the history of the Kentucky Derby only one horse (Northern Dancer in 1964 ran the 1 ¼ miles distance in 2:00), and up until that time no horse had ever won the Belmont Stakes in 2:24. In 1973 Secretariat would win the Belmont in 2:23 4/5, and he was a superhorse.

The truth was Archangel simply had to run quarters of a mile in 24 seconds for six quarters and she would cruise home by a substantial margin, she was capable of running, at least, 2 ½ miles at that pace. There would be a lot of drama leading up to the big race and this included everyone from the Hope Farm family.

Rafe and Jill worked on the logistics of having the families of all the current Hope Farm residents visit to participate in the incredible victory celebration. To accomplish this Rafe enlisted the assistance of Maddy LaDue who would coordinate the arrival of the guests and transportation to either the Plaza Hotel or Daisy Cottage on Hope Farm. Maddy handled having the arriving visitors meet at either one of the three New York City airports which took quite a bit of effort since there were at least 100 arriving visitors and family members. The newly created Daisy Cottage only had 25 rooms so the overflow had to stay at the Plaza Hotel which was the home of Trader Vic's, Rafe, and Everett Massoletti's favorite restaurant, and the place where the Triple Crown victory celebration would take place. The whole operation was strictly a matter of coordination. It was simple, but it had to be done right.

Thanks to Maddy's hard work and attention to detail the logistics of the arriving family members went very well. The day before the Belmont Stakes was to be run the families met at Massoletti's restaurant at 70 Pine Street for a pre-race celebration and dinner. What was actually taking place was the unification of the Hope Farm Family. The members of the Leper Colony knew a whole lot about the families of their buddies, however, they had never met them. The running of the Belmont Stakes would present the opportunity for all the members of the extended Hope Farm Family to get to know one another, and then celebrate a great victory together. Rafe made it clear to the attending family members that they were welcome to stay at the Farm for a few weeks if they so desired rather than a few days.

As race day approached Rafe knew he had only one duty left to perform, he needed to have a final talk with Goldilocks, knowing she was anticipating it. There was a lot riding on her, and when it came right down to it when Archangel took to the track on Saturday it would be only her and Goldilocks out there to bring home the Triple Crown. Rafe knew his words would only serve as reinforcement as by now Goldilocks had growing confidence in her ability to ride with anyone. A week before the big race Rafe showed up at Belmont early one morning and encountered Goldilocks outside Old Man Madden's tack room. Goldi smiled as Rafe approached and she said, "I knew you'd come."

He answered, "What made you so sure?"

"Because you're my guardian angel."

"What makes you think so?"

"Remember when you showed up and sat down on that bale of straw when I was sitting there crying my eyes out? You asked if I had ever heard the expression, It's darkest just before dawn?"

"Yes, I remember asking you that."

Goldi answered, "I think I said, I've heard the expression, I just don't know if I believe it or not." Then, within a couple of minutes, dawn rises. Just like that, my life changed from one of desperation to one of hope. From there it only got better when Aiden and Erin arrived, and we make the big betting coup. I have to admit that being involved in the Hope Farm Renaissance is sort of like living on a little piece of heaven. And it is not just me, as it seems everyone involved feels the same. If you were to ask Old Man Madden how he feels about how things have evolved I'm sure you'd get the same response. So, Mr. Guardian Angel, how will the race play out?"

"Well, my dear, it couldn't be easier, Archangel will simply gallop the others into submission. The other horses in the Belmont Stakes can run 24-second quarters of a mile, but only for a mile, after which they'll slow down dramatically. Only one horse has run the 1 ¼ miles of the Kentucky Derby in 2 minutes flat and that was Northern Dancer in 1964. Up until this time, no horse has won the Belmont Stakes in 2 minutes and 24 seconds which would be six 24-second quarters of a mile. Archangel will be the first, and she'll do it in under 2:24. Your only challenge is to get her to the outside where she has a clear run, and let her gallop away from the opposition."

Goldi answered, "That doesn't seem too difficult. Take her to the outside where she has a clear run, and let her roll."

"That's it in a nutshell, Goldi, you keep her in the clear and she'll run away from the others."

After their short chat, Rafe and Goldi went and found Old Man Madden, and sat around anticipating what lay ahead. Old Man Madden was happier than Rafe had ever seen him. After all, why not! The racing authorities had banned him for five years, but now he was back with an undefeated filly who might be the best of all time. The racing world was alive with excitement, but the most excited people on the planet were those connected with Hope Farm. Having the girls from Moorea on hand just added to the festiveness of the occasion. Everyone was to be on hand to witness the big event. Rafe arranged for a security firm to watch the farm for a couple of days so that the Ladeau's and the Van Anden's could be on hand for the race and the celebration afterward. Hope Farm was not unlike a family, and everyone had been on hand right from the beginning when Rafe had brought in what he referred to as the "Farm's Foundation Mare". From there, the magic began. The ugly Tar Baby, who was also as mean as a snake, proceeds to produce the magnificent Archangel, the polar opposite of her homely mom.

If that were not enough, Archangel makes them all rich in her first start and follows that up by being named Horse-of-the-Year. To a very great extent, it was like being caught up in a fantasy that seemed to be getting better and better. In the end, the race itself was somewhat anticlimactic, as Archangel simply galloped the opposition into submission. She could run the 1 ½ mile distance of the Belmont Stakes in 24 second quarters of a mile. The others could too, up to a mile, at which point they begin to slow, Not the Archangel though. She just keeps galloping along at the 24-second quarters of a mile rate, being 10 lengths in front at 1 ¼ miles and winning off by herself by 25 lengths completing the mile and a half in 2:23 4/5 a new world record on dirt.

The biggest problem facing the Hope Farm contingent was finding a way to get everyone into the winning photograph. This was mediated by having the Preakness and Belmont Stakes filmed by a professional film company insuring, the girls from Moorea would have a record of their great adventure to show their people back home.

Following the celebration at the track, the Hope Farm entourage boarded busses that transported them to the Plaza Hotel in midtown Manhattan where many of the group were staying, and also the home of Trader Vic's where the victory celebration continued. Giacomo had arranged for the whole of Trader Vic's to be closed for this special victory celebration.

Jill was going from table to table to have her picture taken with the families since everyone wanted to be photographed with the star of Cabaret. Next most popular in the picture-taking were the three lovely ladies from Moorea, along with Goldilocks and Old Man Madden. One has to remember also that the motion picture crew was filming the whole evening.

Later when Rafe and Jill were lying together in her bed in her mother's apartment on Sutton Place, Jill asked Rafe, "Well now that we've created a sensation by winning the Triple Crown with a filly, what's next?" Rafe looked at her seriously and said, "Now the real work begins.

Jill was being playful and she snuggled up against him and asked, "What does that Mean?"

The Bottomless Pit

After finishing her three-year-old campaign undefeated and receivingher second consecutive Horse-of-the-Year title, Archangel returned to the farm for a little R&R before beginning her overseas tour. After careful evaluation of the time separating each major race, it was decided to have her contest four overseas races. These races would be the Ascot Gold Cup over 2 ½ miles in June, King George VI and Queen Elizabeth Stakes in July, both run in England, followed by the Prix De l'Arc De Triomphe in Paris, to be run in October. The Arc would be followed by a return to the United States where she would begin her five-year-old campaign which would culminate in contesting the Melbourne Cup in Australia that fall.

Old Man Madden wasn't kidding when he said Archangel was even faster on grass than dirt. In March Old Man Madden, Goldi, and an escort of six lepers made the trip to England to begin preparations for the Ascot Gold Cup. It quickly became clear that as fast as she was on dirt, Archangel was considerably faster on grass, if that could be believed. In the race itself, Archangel cantered hope, in hand, by an incredible 35 lengths. Considering that St. Simon had won the Ascot Gold Cup by twenty lengths made Archangel's performance nothing short of astounding!

The victory celebration was held in Windsor only six miles from Ascot and it was a huge party attended by the entire Leper Colony, making sure their presence was noted by the press. There were at least 300 people attending the celebration from which Rafe slipped away and flew to London. He alighted in front of the residence of the head of the Bank of England. There were a couple of armed guards next to the front door, but they were hardly a match for something like himself who simply made himself invisible, walked past the guards, and right through the door into the residence. Once inside he didn't waste any time, he simply walked to the banker's study, walked through its closed door, and stopped in front of the man's desk. Rafe, who was still invisible, knew he was about to give the man a great shock, but on the other hand; The Wages of Sin!

Rafe materialized and when the banker saw him, he almost jumped out of his skin. The shock was extraordinary. Where did this apparition come from? Rafe just stared at him and made a mental note to mute him before he could cry out. Rafe didn't want to waste time dealing with people he considered to be degenerate so he made it short and direct. He said, "I'm the Archangel Raphael, sent by the Lord God Almighty to administer justice. You have been tried by the Lord, for Crimes against humanity, have been found guilty, and sentenced to be, how should I put it, eliminated. That's why I'm here. I just wanted you to know why your existence is at an end. With that said Rafe snapped his fingers and the unfortunate con man ceased to exist.

That mission accomplished Rafe walked through the study door, out the front door, and returned to the venue hosting the victory celebration. There would be no evidence left at the scene from either the banker's body or his clothing or anything he was carrying. It was all simply gone.

Rafe alighted outside the Men's room and simply reappeared and returned to the Hotel Ballroom as if he's just visited the Men's room. No one was any the wiser as he was only gone ten minutes. As Rafe contemplated what was taking place he began thinking, "This Angel stuff is wild! I can't believe I have this sort of power. I can actually make anything happen just as long as it meets with God's approval. Instead of flying to the banker's residence If I chose, I could freeze time, then eliminate the subject, before setting time in motion. Maybe I'll try that on the Central Banker of France after the Arc."

Rafe couldn't stand Satan and decided to eliminate his henchmen as efficiently as possible. Archangel won the King George VI and Queen Elizabeth Stakes by 12 lengths with commensurate ease and was beginning to build a huge international following, and the talk was that she might be the greatest thoroughbred of all time. Of course, there wasn't any Central Banker to eliminate after her victory since he had already been put in his place after the running of the Ascot Gold Cup.

The Prix De l'Arc De Triomphe run in October presented the opportunity to take down the head of the Central Bank of France. Rafe only flew to his residence to do the deed because he wanted to see the look on his face when he read the indictment. As it turned out the look on the banker's face was one of confusion, and he never could figure out what was going on before he was history.

The Arc was a tour de force that left no doubt that Archangel was one of a kind. Against the best male grass horses in the world, she simply galloped away from them winning by 20 lengths with commensurate ease. Everyone knew she could have won by 50 lengths if asked!

After a short period of rest, Archangel was flown to Santa Anita Racetrack, in Los Angeles. Her primary objective would be the Santa Anita Handicap for which she would be carrying 135 pounds, a staggering impost for a filly running against males. Of course, if she won, she would be elevated to the pantheon of stars. More amazing was that Old Man Madden trained her up to The Big Cap without a prep race.

The race was a triumph for Archangel, and everyone connected to her, for she went straight to the lead and galloped her male rivals into submission. It was considered to be a remarkable performance as the previous high-weighted winner, Round Table in 1958 had only carried 130 pounds. Archangel carried 5 pounds more to victory than any previous male high-weighted winner. She was beginning to attract a huge following once the press began to report her incredible achievements. The press was beginning to talk of her as the best of all time, and this was before her running in the Metropolitan Mile Handicap.

In the Met Mile, Archangel was assigned 136 pounds by the Racing Secretary, a staggering impost under the scale of weights. It didn't make any difference, she being a divinely directed horse. A week before the running of the Met. Mile Rafe met with Old Man Madden and Goldilocks to discuss strategy. Rafe spoke first beginning with, "She's down to her last two races and they'll determine her bid for thoroughbred immortality. You could almost say now she's the people's horse and they'll be hanging on her every move. No one has seen anything like her before, but what they don't know is they haven't yet seen her true capabilities. I think we should let her show them what real speed is. Like letting her break the world's record for a mile with 136 pounds up?"

At first, the Old Man just stared at Rafe before a smile slowly began to creep onto his face. He said, "I think you're right. Her fans have the right to see just how much we've been holding back where her speed is concerned. Since it's her 2nd to the last start Let's turn her loose."

Goldi shook her head, yes, and smiled before saying, "I'd like to see how fast she really is. I've been sitting on this rocket for three years wondering what would happen if I turned her loose. We want to know, and so does the racing world. I say we let her do it!" So, it was decided Archangel was going to show the world who she really was, and there couldn't be anything more exciting than that.

The Metropolitan Mile is the Memorial Day feature at Belmont Park. What makes the race unusual is that it is a one-turn mile. If you're looking to put on a display of speed the Met. Mile is the place to do it. On race day the crowd was enormous and the race was televised. By this time the world wanted to know if she was one of the ones. The race left no doubt.

Archangel came out of the gate like a rocket, building a five-length lead in the first 1/8 mile. She ran the first quarter in 21 seconds flat and passed the 3/8 pole in 33 1/5. At this point, Goldi let out a notch and she sped past the half-mile pole in 43 3/5 seconds. By this time, she had widened her lead to eight lengths and was well within herself. She came out of the backstretch straightaway and cruised around the far turn at her very high cruising speed getting five furlongs in 56 2/5 seconds and approached the head of the stretch where Goldilocks would ask her to run. Archangel turned into the stretch where Goldi got her to change leads and then let her go, the response was instantaneous.From those watching her accelerate at the head of the stretch, the vision was breathtaking. She leveled out and left the competition in the dust. Seeing her in full flight was simply amazing. Archangel moved away from her competition so rapidly that it made them look like they were slowing to a stop. That combined with her beautiful flowing stride brought out the spirit of the crowd as they roared their approval to the magnificent mare.

Goldilocks was scrubbing on her neck with the reins but never went to the whip as she charged to victory by 28 lengths while lowering the world's record for a mile to 1:32 3/5. To say the crowd went wild is a massive understatement as they knew they had just witnessed the crowning of a new champion, maybe the best of all time.

After the race, Old Man Madden decided to rest Archangel at Hope Farm for a month before beginning the journey to Australia which was going to be long and tiring. Both Rafe and Old Man Madden knew that the Melbourne Cup would be the true test of greatness. The selection of the Melbourne Cup as Archangel's last start wasn't an accident. It was in this same race in 1890 that Carbine, the most popular horse ever to race below the equator, won the race carrying the staggering impost of 145 pounds over the distance of two miles. The acclaim that greeted Carbine's victory was incredible. The crowd went crazy hugging and kissing each other while men threw their hats in the air by the hundreds. Rafe knew that the Australians would set this up to be a race to be remembered. By now Archangel had a huge international following now all dying to know if she was indeed the greatest of the great. There was no doubt that the Australians would assign Archangel a staggering impost likely to be in the area of the 145 pounds Carbine had carried.

It turned out Archangel was assigned 150 pounds which was the exact limit her connections would allow her to carry. Had she been assigned 151 she would not have started.

As for the race itself, you could say it was a display of, "The Power and the Glory!" After all, she was special to the Lord God Himself. There was a 27-horse field in which Archangel laid eighth or ninth for the first mile and a half, at which point she began to move. It's said that a great racehorse feels like a heavy luxury automobile where you hardly feel a bump. They say greats are as smooth as silk; but how many have ever ridden one? One person who had, was Goldilocks who was having the time of her life feeling the surge of power as Archangel was allowed to get into full stride. Turning for home, at the head of the stretch, Goldi let her have her head and the result was electrifying. Archangel surged away from the field with her rhythmically flowing stride, leaving the competition struggling in her wake. It was a sight to behold as she flew past the finish line 30 lengths ahead of her nearest competitor which was carrying only 99 pounds. The crowd started roaring as she took the lead at the top of the straight and only got louder as she drew away. At the finish, you couldn't hear anything as the crowd roared its approval.

That's how Archangel ended her career, in a blaze of glory, just as she had started it! There was a tremendous celebration after the race with the same camera crew that had captured her first start and the Triple Crown series was on hand trying to capture the tumultuous celebration. They captured much of the crowd's response but still missed even more. Archangel's victory threw the spectators into a riot of excitement and jubilation, many people became hysterical with delight; women shrieked and some wept; old men shook hands with all around them and threw their hats into the air. That evening as the celebration continued Rafe slipped away and paid a visit to the residence of the Head of the Central Bank of Australia. It didn't take him long as he knew exactly what he wanted to do. The next day would find the banker missing, without a trace. With that done. The trap was baited! The only thing left to do was to expose Satan to the trail that would lead him to Hope Farm.

Most of the Hope Farm entourage left for home a few days after the race whereas a small contingent remained behind in Australia for a couple of weeks until Archangel was well-rested and ready for her charter flight home. One evening as Rafe and Jill sat on a bale of straw outside Archangel's stall Rafe glanced over at Jill and asked. "Hey Little Dancer, I have an idea I'd like to run by you."

Jill smiled at him and responded with, "Ok what's on your mind, Sir Knight."

"I suppose you're aware that enroute to the States, we have to fly past Tahiti?"

Giving him a very cute look Jill said, "Yes I was aware of that, in fact, I've been thinking about it."

"Well, this is what I was thinking darling. How would you describe our honeymoon on Moorea?"

Jill smiled and replied, "It was like spending ten days in heaven!"

Rafe continued, "This is what I've been thinking. On the way back to the States we make a short stop on Moorea, but we'll bring Goldi and Mighty Mouse along. Then after a week, we'll leave, and the two of them can stay as long as they like. How does that sound?"

Jill had a big grin on her face as she responded, "Rafe I think you've got a little bit of the Devil in you! You know that if we leave them in Moorea for a few weeks by themselves, we'll soon be having another wedding in the Chapel.

Rafe laughed and said, "That's what I had in mind. If they're on the brink of deciding on a future together, Moorea will push them over the edge. But, On the other hand, maybe your presence and what will accompany it, will ruin the ambiance of the Bali Hai. You know what I'm talking about, those sleepy tropical nights?

Jill smiled at Rafe and then said, "I think you may be right Rafe, I think we should allow them to discover Moorea on their own. A few months from now we can rent the entire Bali Hai and bring everyone to the South Pacific for a vacation to be remembered forever."

Two men stood in the predawn darkness on what had been the towpath of the Chesapeake and Ohio Canal, just outside Georgetown in Washington D.C. Unusual place to meet? Very! The reason for the location? No one was to know the meeting ever took place. The only others to know were, the four heavily armed security agents, two 20 yards ahead, and two 20 yards behind. One of the two men standing almost invisible in the fog was Satan, and next to him was Victor Trombley, Satan's mole in the CIA. Satan was very concerned about the disappearance of three key Central Bankers, critical in his master plan to control the world's money supply. He was paying Trombley $500,000 a year for inside information and now he had great need of it. Trombley had contacted Satan and said he had important info concerning the bankers but it could only be delivered face to face.

Standing on the foggy canal Satan finally said, "All right Trombley, tell me what I'm paying $500,000 a year for!"

Trombley answered, "I think I have a pretty good idea as to who is responsible for your bankers disappearing!"

"All Right, what do you know?"

Trombley began with, "Have you ever heard of an elite strike group called The Leper Colony?"

Satan simply said, "No."

Trombley took another tack and asked, "Ever heard of the Battle of the Dragon's Lair?"

Satan looked a little puzzled then answered, "Is that the one that created an international outcry over infringing on Cambodian neutrality?"

Trombley replied, "Indeed it was, but where you're concerned what matters most is, who was responsible.

Satan asked, "What do you mean by that?"

Trombley explained, "It all starts with the Leper Colony. The Lepers were the rear guard at Landing Zone Yankee where they couldn't be airlifted out in time, and escaped down the river. Then, instead of turning towards the base at Pleiku, they crossed into Cambodia located the headquarters of the Fourth North Vietnamese Army Corp, surrounded them, and with a night attack, wiped them off the face of the earth. Killed every one of them and then slipped away into the jungle to somehow show up in Phnom Penh. The attack caused an international outcry since among those killed was the North's leader in Insurgency, General Chu Khan Man. The leader of the Lepers, Raphael Hawkins, was summoned to meet with President Lyndon Johnson where he went into the meeting as a Sergeant and came out a Captain! The rumor that's been circulating is that the Leper Colony has been a top-secret strike force answering only to the President of the United States. It's also been rumored that the Leper Colony is now an independent force somehow in league with the Government of the United States, although no one seems to know the exact extent of the relationship.

Satan gave Trombley his usual deprecating look before saying, "Well for once you're beginning to earn the Millions, I've been paying you."

Trombley quickly responded, "You haven't heard the most important part. The Leper Colony once discharged from the Army, started Hope Farm, a thoroughbred breeding farm in New York State. The first foal bred by Hope Farm is the undefeated superstar Archangel who just completed her racing career with an astounding victory in Australia's Melbourne Cup. However, there is a hidden nugget of vital intelligence attached to Archangel's foreign invasion.

Satan answered, "And what might that be?"

Trombley stared back and Satan, not a bit afraid, although he should have been, said, "Whenever one of your Central Bankers has disappeared, Hope Farm's Archangel has won a major race the same day as the disappearance, in a nearby city. The entire Leper Colony was placed within striking distance when and where, if they were needed, could act. On the days of the running of the Ascot Gold Cup, Prix de l'Arc de Triomphe, and Melbourne Cup the entire Leper Colony was in the area. In view of their expertise as a stealth strike force, I would say all fingers point to them.?"

A grim smile crept onto Satan's lips as he said, "Well I'll be damned Trombley, now that's what I call valuable information. It seems as if you've finally begun to earn the hefty payments that have been flowing your way these past years. However, deeper down in his consciousness, he was thinking, "Too bad you never realized whom you're working with, as now that you've pinpointed my adversary you yourself have just become a liability. There's no way I'm going to leave a trail connecting me to the Leper Colony. Since you're the one who pointed us in the right direction, you'll have to go. With the same sardonic smile on his face, Satan thought, "You can be replaced, Trombley, in fact, I think I'll arrange for you to have a meeting with a hit-and-run vehicle in the next few days which will take care of having to worry about you betraying us."

The following day Satan took a private jet from Dulles Airport to London and on the way decided on a course of action. His original Idea was to hit Hope Farm with a special operations force, not unlike the Leper Colony, and simply wipe them off the face of the earth. In Satan's mind, it was poetic justice. The Leper Colony had wiped the Red Dragon and his headquarters off the face of the earth, and now it could be the Leper Colonies' turn. There was just one problem. It was too messy, too many people involved, and it would be in the United States. There would be too many bodies making the scene one of a massacre. The media would have a field day. If it was in some third-world country rather than the United States it was feasible, but not in the good old USA.

If he couldn't use force there was only one other approach; Bribery! Being the Prince of Darkness one of his most efficient tools was bribery or seduction. He decided to visit Hope Farm and make Raphael Hawkins an offer he couldn't refuse. After all, if he had the Leper Colony working for him, he would acquire a proven strike force capable of taking out almost any adversary, but more importantly, they wouldn't be going after members of his own organization. Satan just suffered from one shortcoming, that being, he was overmatched. He thought he was equal or superior to the Lord God when actually he suffered from what could be called the Shit for Brains syndrome. Where Satan was concerned, he thought showing up at Hope Farm and incorporating the Leper Colony into the Mithra Society would enhance his ability to enslave mankind. What he never realized was he was being directed by the Lord God and he was going to show up at Hope Farm whether he wanted to or not, and he was going to think it was his idea, to begin with. The joke was, Satan was in over his head, and didn't even realize his peril. His fate now hung on one simple little decision which revolved around bringing Rafe Hawkins and the Leper Colony to accept his offer and become members of the Mithra Society. He only needed to call Hope Farm and make an appointment to see Rafe Hawkins. Satan was thinking, "I just need to lead Rafe Hawkins down the Primrose Path along with his entourage, and I'll have the world at my command. Several months later Satan called Hope Farm and made an appointment with Maddy LaDue to see Rafe. Satan was thinking, I'll just visit New York, call Hawkins, make an appointment, and offer him a private contract he can't refuse. I wonder how he'll act to a 500-million-dollar offer?

The trap had been baited, and it was now only a matter of time.

One evening at about 6 P.M. the long black limo pulled onto the circular drive leading up to Main House. Rafe was standing near the entrance waiting for his fateful meeting with the Prince of Darkness. From his perspective, the limo radiated an evil countenance even though that was virtually impossible, after all, one black limo is the same as another. It could be his perspective came from his knowledge of what the limo was carrying, that being, the epitome of evil.

Rafe was standing by the entrance thinking, "Well, the game is over. He's here and doesn't have a clue that he's not leaving for 1,000 years. I'm sure he's thinking I'm some sort of human who has absolutely no knowledge of the big picture; In other words, easy prey."

The limo pulled up and stopped. Two big security guard types jumped out and gazed around looking for threats. When the driver emerged, he was the same type as the other two, meaning he was a security guard who doubled as a driver. It was clear from the bulges under their jackets they were all armed, and it was nothing more than Rafe expected. The driver walked around to the passenger side and opened the door for the central character, none other than Satan himself. Rafe was curious as to what style Satan would choose for his material representation. Rafe watched as Satan walked around the rear of the limo issuing orders to his security staff as he walked toward Rafe. He was about six feet tall and weighed about 170 or 175, and carried himself well. As he approached, Rafe saw that he could almost be considered handsome, except for his eyes, which were as black and emotionless, as the hole he'd soon be introduced to. They say the eyes mirror the soul, and that explained why Rafe thought Jill's reminded him of paradise. Satan looked good from a distance, but when close, and you got a good look at his eyes, you were not inclined to view him in a positive light. After all, he was the most profoundly bestial creature ever to walk the earth. From Rafe's perspective, this was all a big joke. Here was Satan, who was under the impression that he ruled the earth, while God ruled in heaven. It was his eyes that gave him away. The only emotions expressed in his eyes were hauteur, arrogance, and grandiosity, meaning Satan thought he was more than he actually was!

As Satan approached, Rafe put out his right hand and shook hands. He said, "Mr. Galerius I presume? I'm Rafe Hawkins, manager of Hope Farm!"

Satan answered, "Glad to make your acquaintance Mr. Hawkins, I've some interesting things I'd like to discuss with you."

"Why not come into my office where we can chat? If you want there's a room down the hall where your people can relax."

"I require that they remain right outside your office while we meet!"

"That's fine with me, whatever makes you comfortable."

Once in Rafe's office, Rafe took the seat behind his desk with Mr. Galerius seated across from him. Rafe began the conversation with, "Well you've come a long way to have this conversation. So, what's on your mind?"

Satan answered, "It could be that I'm interested in investing in your fledgling horse enterprise!"

It was at this point Rafe decided to cut to the chase and avoid what would be a long song and dance leading up to Satan making what he perceived to be an offer that couldn't be refused. To Rafe, the issue was settled. Satan was on Hope Farm and was never leaving; The only thing left to do was to inform Lucifer that he wasn't leaving and that his near-term future, was a pitch-black, bottomless pit. No point in letting Lucifer make his pitiful bribe offer as it would just be a waste of time. No offer had a solitary chance of being accepted. With that in mind, Rafe said, "Mr, Galerius, we both know that you aren't here to make an offer that has anything to do with Thoroughbred horses. The fact is, you're here because you're interested in the other activity secretly pursued by the residents of Hope Farm. I'm talking about the Leper Colony and the top-secret work we are contracted to do for the President of the United States. Is my assumption correct?"

"Since you're somehow aware of my intentions, maybe I'll just get up and leave."

"Good luck with that. You're not going anywhere for a very long time."

Rafe watched Satan try to struggle up from his chair, and that his attempt wasn't going anywhere." Satan then called out, "Carlo!" Must have been one of his security people. The result was no answer. He called the other two, with the same result.

That's when Rafe told him the truth about his predicament. "Look! I hate to tell you this, but you're fucked. Don't waste your time trying to escape, or yelling for your goons, because they're gone." With that, Rafe walked over to the office door, opened it, then turned back to Lucifer, and motioned as if to say, they're gone! Sure enough, they were gone.

Lucifer asked. "What happened to my men?"

Rafe answered, "I rearranged their molecules!"

"What in hell are you talking about?"

Rafe laughed and said, "It gets back to an old religious saying, what the lord giveth, the lord can take away. In their case, the lord took them away, and in that regard, he simply made them cease to exist. He could do the same for you, but he has other plans. "Are you following me?"

"Hardly, I need a clearer explanation than that."

"Ok, here's the deal. You're not here by accident. Hope Farm is a trap created just for you. We've been spending the last three years planning the moves that would eventually bring you to Hope Farm. That included running Archangel in The Ascot Gold Cup, Prix de l'Arc de Triomphe, and Melbourne Cup so as to have the Leper Colony in the specific countries where their central banker would disappear. Slowly, and inauspiciously we'd leave a trail that led to Hope Farm. We even planted some information sure to keep you on the trail. It worked as planned, for here you are. However, there's a lot more to this than meets the eye. To begin, I know you're Satan or Lucifer, or whatever else you may call yourself, Constantine Galerius is an alias. So, I know who you are, but your problem is, you don't know who I am. Do you?"

Lucifer answered; I haven't a clue!"

"That's what I thought you'd say. Let me ask you a question. Are you familiar with the Bible? I'm sure you have to be at least some way familiar with it; since so much of it is about you."

Lucifer was glaring at Rafe as he said. "I'm familiar with it."

"Good, then let me direct you to Revelation chapter 20, verse 1. It says; Then I saw an angel coming down from heaven, having the key to the Bottomless pit and a great chain in his hand. He laid hold of the dragon, that serpent of old, who is the Devil and Satan, and bound him for a thousand years; And cast him into the bottomless pit, and shut him up, and set a seal on him so that he should deceive the nations no more till the thousand years were finished. But after these things, he must be released for a little while.

"Lucifer, old boy, I hate to tell you this, but I'm that angel with the key and the chain, and I'm the one who is going to cast you into the bottomless pit. My mission was to lure you to Hope Farm where the bottomless pit awaits. I guess my mission is accomplished; just one last thing to do!"

Satan snarled as he replied, which was, "You're just another lap dog to Jehovah, you sorry son of a bitch!"

"Well, you know what Satan? There is an old saying, we learned as kids, that goes like this, sticks and stones may break my bones, but words will never hurt me. Call me anything you like, but the jokes are on you. I'm not the one going into the bottomless pit."

Satan yelled, "Just wait, you scumbag. I'll get even; If it takes me more than 1,000 years!"

"You're a sorry case Lucifer, you're as delusional as the day is long. That's why you're here. Somehow you got it into your mind that you were the equal of the Almighty. Who knows what would have happened, if when given free choice, you had decided to follow God? But, off you went, doing whatever you wanted. The truth is, you're a legend in your own mind, and believe me that's a very dangerous position to find yourself.For now, you get one thousand years in the bottomless pit, however when you get out, something much worse will be awaiting; On the other hand, look at me. I have everything I've ever wanted!"

Lucifer came right back with, Yeah, what have you got that's so great?"

Rafe looked over at Lucifer and said, "I have everything, or put in other words, I have the Grace of God!"

Lucifer scowled at Rafe and answered with, "And what pray tell do you call the Grace of God?"

"Before I answer you, I need to call someone. Rafe walked over to the door and shouted, Jill, hon! Can you come down here, and bring the thing you've been holding for me, with you?"

Thirty seconds later Jill walked into the office holding something in her right hand. Rafe said, "Jill this is the notorious Lucifer." Before, another word could be said Rafe turned towards Lucifer and said, "And don't get any ideas in your head about bringing harm to Jill because, like me, she's an angel, and way beyond your reach." Rafe then continued, "You want to know what the grace of God is? It can be expressed in one word, Love! From my perspective love is completely out of your train of thought; That in itself; is a good explanation as to why you're where you are, and the circumstances that brought you here.

Lucifer responded, "It doesn't look like you have that much, I have one thousand times more."

"That may be so, but who loves you? I would guess no one loves you. I would go so far as to say you probably don't even have a pet. After all dogs and cats are the perfect purveyors of love. Have a kitty, or a dog and you'll be loved. I would suspect if you had a dog, it would run away, and the truth is, one has to be a complete asshole to have your dog run away. So even with all of your power, wealth, and position, you're still nothing. Then there's the problem of loyalty, or should I say disloyalty?

Lucifer simply shrugged and replied, "Who needs love or loyalty?"

"Well Lucifer, you do! However, you're too stupid to know it. It wasn't by accident that the Lord God picked you, to be what you are."

"And what am I?" Lucifer asked,

Rafe looked right into his hate-filled eyes and said, You're nothing but a choice!"

"What do you mean by that?"

"When the Lord God Almighty created man, he created him to be good. Everything was perfect. Man lived in the Garden of Eden. His life couldn't be better. But God realized all was not perfect because mankind was a slave to goodness. Men were created to be the children of God, and being godlike, men were creative, but unlike God, Man was not in possession of free will. In other words, he couldn't do whatever he wanted, just what God allowed. It was then that God made the decision to change the destiny of mankind; He did this by creating evil. Therefore, God the Father, in all his majesty, allowed man to experience the alternative to good, that is evil. That's where you enter the picture, Satan, you represent the choice. You're the first to cross over, you're the first to betray God for self-glorification. Therein lies the sin! The choice is between God's Grace (Love), and self-glorification (Evil)."

Satan stared at Rafe and Jill with all the hatred he could muster, and said, "So what!"

Rafe looked at Satan with pity and said, "So What? Well up until now there haven't been any consequences, but now they're here. It may be wonderful to have free will, but with it comes answering for your choices; everything is a matter of choice. God wanted us to choose what is right, but you might say Man had a propensity for doing otherwise."

"What's all this bull shit about?"

"Since you're delusional I'm simply trying to talk some sense into your head. Think of it! You, who probably made the biggest mistake, since the beginning of time, when you began to think you're the equal of God.

Satan snapped, "What's the big mistake?"

"I'm surprised you haven't figured that out yet. The big mistake was when you betrayed the creator. In my mind, I can't think of anything worse. Then, you somehow got it into your dimwitted brain that you were actually smart. If you had been, you'd still be a mighty Archangel, like me, instead of as a synonym for revolting behavior."

"So, you think you're high and mighty? Doesn't that fly in the face of what you're trying to tell me?" Satan added.

Rafe asked Jill to place the collar she had in her hand around Lucifer's neck and fasten it. While she was doing that Rafe addressed Satan. "Actually, talking to you is a waste of time, what you can never understand is that I am high and mighty, as you call it; because I'm beloved by the Lord God Almighty. I'm a recipient of God's Grace. And I'm not talking about a little bit of it either, we're talking about a whole lot of it. And, if I am High and Mighty, it's because he made me so. I don't require any more than that, I'm complete.So, Mr. Dark Angel, I'm now going to take you on a walk down to the camp, which is the location of the Bottomless Pit. In order to make our walk more pleasant for Jill and me, God himself is going to make you buoyant so you float through the air, then I'm going to attach a lead shank to your collar and lead you down to the camp as if you're a balloon filled with hot air. And come to think of it, that's exactly what you are. It's a lovely walk, and you better enjoy it because it's the last thing you'll see, for what will seem an eternity."

Five minutes later Rafe, Jill, Bogart, and Satan left the front of Main House heading for Chapel Road.It would have been a sight to behold if anyone could have seen it. Rafe had staged a party in the school auditorium to keep the Hope Farm people away from what was really going down. To make certain no one would see Satan floating through the air, Rafe made the entire captive Satan procession, invisible.

It should have been a pleasant walk from the front of Main House to the Camp, however, it didn't start out that way. To Rafe, Satan was a dark cloud hovering above him every step of the way. Actually, he was a lot worse than a dark cloud. Rafe's feeling was one of revulsion; he couldn't stand the presence of this creature. He radiated hatred, and evil, a truly malignant presence.

Rafe was thinking, "I'm glad I silenced him before we started, he'll be able to think anything he wants, he just won't be allowed to verbalize it. I don't need to listen to some foul diatribe about how he'll get us in the end. This guy really gets my blood up. Makes me want to fight. I guess I'll just walk along and flirt with Jill who's not more than six feet away. Once we jettison this sorry sack of solidified nitrogenous waste into the Bottomless Pit, we'll have a very nice walk home. For Jill and I, this is beyond weird. Here we are walking Satan down to the Bottomless Pit, where an event that was prophesied 2,000 years ago, is about to take place, and no one is aware of it happening. In the end, no one will ever know, except us!"

They had just walked up to the front of the chapel when they heard the voice, loud and crystal clear, say, **"I'm Here!" I'm Here and Watching!"**

Rafe looked over at Jill and saw the look of wonder expressed by her smile. He whispered to her, "The Lord God Almighty!"

Jill simply nodded and looked upward. Rafe thought how unusual it was that two of the occasions where God had talked directly to him took place in the Chapel or right next to it. The voice came again reminding him that God knew every thought he had. It said, **"I speak to you from this chapel because it sits on sacred ground. It is one of the places I choose to spend time. I wanted you to know that from here, to the bottomless Pit at the camp, I will accompany you. I know how you feel about being around Satan, so I'll just trail along until we drop him into the void. I have one last thing to say before returning to the ether, you Raphael, and you Valerie Jill, are beloved of me. You represent God's Grace, or Love, which are interchangeable. I created the two of you to love one another. I arranged your romance. Now watching the two of you, together, warms my heart. My desire is for you to continue to the bottomless pit, and give Satan a push so he'll float out over** the void. Then when I'm ready, I'll reduce the buoyancy and he'll sink out of sight into the gloom.

Continue down to the Pit and let the Prince of Darkness, discover his own private hell."

Jill looked over at Rafe and said, "My God! He just spoke to us!"

Rafe smiled and said, "Not only that, but we're walking with him! He's right here beside us; and will stay with us until we complete our mission, not that we don't have the power to make it happen, but it sure is depressing. Now I feel a lot better in God's presence."

Jill answered, "So do I. Satan gives me the creepiest feeling I've ever had. What an awful creature."

That's why I sealed his mouth. I don't even want to hear his last words, it's nothing but a bunch of BS; No point in listening to that." Suddenly, what had been a grim, unpleasant walk, turned into one with a cheerful atmosphere. "Let's just take another of our beautiful walks, with Bogart running down the road ahead of us, even if we do have to haul this pile of waste down to the bottomless pit, once we're rid of him, we'll be fine."

Once that was settled, they continued past the chapel and the training track, to the dirt road that twisted its way through the forest canopy to a wooden bridge across a small stream. Once across the bridge the road leveled off and continued another ¼ mile into an open area in which the camp was situated. The camp was lovely because of its location in the forest. It had a quiet peaceful atmosphere because of the way it was nestled in a small valley with a forest stream on either side. Normally, Rafe and Jill would stop and sit on the stairs to the Rec. Hall and just sit and talk for a while, but today they were in a hurry.

Rafe led the way through the center of the camp slowly bearing into the woods on the east of the White House. He was taking the same route he'd taken the day of his first encounter with the Devil's Handmaiden; when he had felt an irresistible force pulling up the hill towards his rendezvous with destiny. Now he knew from where the irresistible force originated! It was the hand of God.

They found what was left of the old trail which was rapidly becoming overgrown, and followed it about 200 feet to where the clearing used to be.

Since Rafe was ten inches taller than Jill, he saw it first. What used to be the clearing, was a black hole. There it was, right where it was supposed to be, the Bottomless Pit. A gapping black hole. Rafe called Bogart to his side where he attached a leash to his collar. He gave the leash to Jill and Said, "Keep Bogart with you. I'm going to walk right up to the edge and give Satan a little push so his buoyant self will float out over the maw. When he drifts far enough out, God will eliminate the buoyancy, and Satan will rapidly disappear into the darkness. Rafe led Satan to the edge of the pit. The place gave him the creeps. Even though he could fly, the pit still gave him an awful feeling. When the message arrived telepathically it said, "**Push him out!**"

Rafe put one hand on Satan's left knee and the other on his left foot, then pulled him back before thrusting him forward, watching him float out over the Bottomless Pit. Rafe just watched him float out to the middle before God pulled the plug, and Satan sank into a thousand years of darkness, or if you had a mind too, you could say, he sank into Hell. As Rafe walked away from the pit, he couldn't help but think that Satan's punishment was very creative on God's part. Want to talk about Hell? How do 365,000 days of absolute darkness grab you? No stimulation of any kind. Only your own thoughts. It would take less than 1 week to drive you stark raving mad.

Rafe took Jill's hand and they walked down the trail through the forest, back to the camp, with Bogart bounding along ahead. As they walked along, they could hear the land at the top of the hill being rearranged by the hand of God. Within minutes there would be no sign that anything out of the ordinary had taken place there in recent memory. It was when they reached the center of the camp that they heard the voice. "**Raphael, Valerie Jill. My Angels!**"

Rafe and Jill looked up toward the darkening heavens and said in unison, "Yes, my lord!"

The voice was loud and clear it simply said, "My children, we must talk."

Rafe and Jill just looked skyward and said again, "We're listening my lord."

They heard the voice of the Lord God Almighty say, "Listen to what I say! What you have just witnessed started before I even thought of using my own chosen angels in establishing order among the Heavenly Hosts, and before I created you. Long ago I determined Satan's betrayal was so great an offense that it must be punished in the most punitive manner, hence the Bottomless Pit. You Rafael Hawkins and Valerie Jill Haworth are mine. I created you for a specific purpose that you just completed. It may seem like a small task that I imposed on you, but to me it was critical. I could have done it myself, but I chose to have my angels deliver Satan to his solitary hell."

"In order to carry out your assignment, you would need preparation to learn how the world works whenever the forces of evil are present. Some of the methods I used to steer you in the right direction were subtle to the point you were unaware of my intentions. For instance, Rafe, do you remember going to the Greer School Library in 1955 and checking out the book Paradise Lost by John Milton?"

"Rafe replied, "Yes, My Lord, I remember doing that."

"Did you memorize it, word for word?"

"Rafe answered, "Only a few passages."

"Does one begin, So spake the Seraph Abdial, Faithful found?"

"Yes my Lord there is such a passage."

"Repeat it for me, word for word."

Rafe began:

"So spake the Seraph Abdial, faithful found;
Among the faithless faithful only he;
Among innumerable false unmoved,
Unshaken, unseduced, unterrified,
His loyalty he kept, his love, his zeal;
Nor number nor example with him wrought
To swerve from truth, or change his constant mind
Though single.
From amidst them forth he passed,
Long way through hostile scorn, which he sustained
Superior, nor of violence feared aught;
And with retorted scorn his back he turned
On those proud towers, to swift destruction doomed."

God asked, "And what did that passage mean to you?"

"It was like walking from darkness into light. I knew I was on the right path, and nothing could deter me. I felt although everyone else looked at me with derision and scorn, God loved me. In other words, I was in the hands of God, safe from all earthly threats."

God continued, "When you left Greer School you followed the path of Seraphin Abdial where it says, from amidst them forth he passed, long way through hostile scorn, which he sustained. That was all part of my plan to bring you to this place and time. You and Valerie Jill are my special Angels and from the time of your creation, you were destined to bring the Prince of Darkness to the first of his humiliating defeats. What I'm telling you now is that your lives have been directed by me right from the start. I created you to be the representatives of what I am, and that is Love! That's why you get that special feeling when you kiss.

God went on to say, "I'm sure you wonder why I caused the two of you to separate coming out of Rhodes School. Well, there is a very good reason for that, and it all has to do with the greatest sin. If you're not aware of what I consider to be the greatest sin, it's betrayal. Because of the direction, I had you take, both of you are now aware of the despicable effects of betrayal. The fact is, betrayal is worse than murder. If you think about it seriously, once you're dead you feel no pain, however when betrayed by someone you love, that pain is eternal, and it stays with you forever.

You, Rafe, are aware of its force, as betrayal brought you to your knees and almost ended your life. Valerie Jill, the betrayal you experienced in Hollywood was just as bad or worse than that inflicted on Rafe. This explains why I found it necessary to separate you when you left Rhodes School. If you were to be tasked with throwing Satan into the Bottomless Pit you needed to have first-hand knowledge of his offense.

God went on to say "Where sin is concerned, Satan's was the greatest of all. I am his creator. Without my creativity, he would be nothing, wouldn't even exist. I created Satan, yet he betrayed his creator, is there anything worse?"

Jill and Rafe both agreed, that betraying the creator was, by far, the greatest sin. They looked up. They couldn't see God, only feel his presence. They heard his voice say, **"It was with a heavy heart that I set up the relationships that led the both of you to experience betrayal. Now you both have firsthand knowledge of its effects. Because you're beloved of me I set the** prophecy in motion that brought about your reunion. I choreographed the whole thing. You followed my orders and in doing so, suffered great pain. I then alleviated that pain by allowing you to experience the greatest of human emotions, True Love.

"This is where it all stands. You have accomplished the mission I set aside only for you. It seemed to be a ridiculously simple task, but as I said, this was an expression of my will. I could have done it myself, however, I chose to use the antidote for evil, to settle the score. That antidote is love. One might say I was rubbing salt in his wounds by allowing him to see, in the two of you, where he might have ended, instead of the Bottomless Pit. If Lucifer was as smart as he thinks he is, he'd be in the arms of a lovely angel, instead of sinking into Hell."

Rafe and Jill hand in hand began to walk down the dirt road leading, through the forest, back up the hill to the Training Track. Jill asked, "What now?"

"I think it might be a good idea to walk back up to the farm and make it our mission to make our friends as happy as we are."

Jill replied. "You're right. Let's do it!"

Rafe smiled and answered, "Well, we've completed our mission in life and have been rewarded with the gift of true love, so I guess there is only one thing to do!"

It was very dark, but Jill was flashing a devastating smile as she knew where this was leading, she said, "And what do you have in mind, Sir Knight?"

"We walk up to Tar Baby's paddock. Give her a mint, let her lick noses with Bogart, then we head home. When we get there, we'll have to practice the art of true love. And, you know what they say?"

Jill was laughing when she replied, "Yes, I do know what they say!"

"What do they say," asked Rafe"

While giving him her patented come-hither look Jill said, "Practice makes perfect."

They continued up the road, hand in hand, happier than any two souls had the right to be.

And, the reason for that, being?

They were in Heaven! One created by God for themselves, and their friends.

They walked up the hill and past the chapel on the road leading to Tar Baby's paddock. As they passed the chapel The Lord God who was in temporary residence in one of his favorite places was thinking "My angels have discovered the most important truth of existence, that being, "**Where love is, there God is Also!**"